Teachers Discovering Computers

Integrating Technology and Digital Media in the Classroom

Fourth Edition

Gary B. Shelly
Thomas J. Cashman
Glenda A. Gunter
Randolph E. Gunter

THOMSON
COURSE TECHNOLOGY

THOMSON COURSE TECHNOLOGY
25 THOMSON PLACE
BOSTON MA 02210

SHELLY
CASHMAN
SERIES.

Australia • Canada • Denmark • Japan • Mexico • New Zealand • Philippines • Puerto Rico • Singapore • South Africa
Spain • United Kingdom • United States

THOMSON

★

COURSE TECHNOLOGY ™

Teachers Discovering Computers
Integrating Technology and Digital Media in the Classroom
Fourth Edition

Gary B. Shelly
Thomas J. Cashman
Glenda A. Gunter
Randolph E. Gunter

Managing Editor:
Alexandra Arnold

Developmental Editor:
Pam Conrad

Senior Product Manager:
Karen Stevens

Product Manager:
Reed Cotter

Associate Product Manager:
Selena Coppock

Editorial Assistant:
Patrick Frank

Production Editor:
Danielle Slade

Proofreader:
Karen Annett

Indexer:
Elizabeth Cunningham

Manufacturing:
Justin Palmeiro

Cover Artist:
John Still

Composition House:
GEX Publishing Services

CONTENTS

Teachers Discovering Computers
Integrating Technology and Digital Media in the Classroom
Fourth Edition

**Hardware
for Educators**

Chapter
4

Special Feature

Special Feature

Evaluating Educational Technology and Integration Strategies Chapter **7**

Special Feature

Security Issues, Ethics, and Emerging Technologies in Education

Chapter 8

Special Feature

Preface

The Shelly Cashman Series® offers the finest textbooks in computer education. We are proud of the fact that our previous *Teachers Discovering Computers* books have been so well received by instructors and students. This latest edition continues with the innovation, quality, and reliability you have come to expect from this series. The previous edition's popularity was due to (1) the integration of the World Wide Web; (2) the currency of the materials; (3) readability; (4) extensive exercises; (5) supplements; and (6) the ancillaries that allow an instructor to teach the way he or she wants to teach.

We are pleased to announce the publication of *Teachers Discovering Computers: Integrating Technology and Digital Media in the Classroom, Fourth Edition*. In addition to the standard technological updates and appropriate content changes, the fourth edition of *Teachers Discovering Computers* includes these enhancements:

- Increased emphasis on technology integration
- A new companion Web site
- New emphasis on digital media and both teaching and reaching today's digital generation
- New end-of-chapter section, Digital Media Corner, offers information to help teachers integrate digital media, supplemented with digital video clips
- New end-of-chapter section, Assistive Technologies Corner, which contains information that all teachers need to know
- New step-by-step project that covers how to incorporate various digital media components in a PowerPoint presentation

The content of the textbook and the companion Web site also have been enhanced to allow for curriculum-specific learning by all K-12 educators. That is, students using the *Teachers Discovering Computers* textbook will be able to learn both how to use, and more importantly, how to integrate technology into their current or future classroom curriculum. In addition, this fourth edition of *Teachers Discovering Computers* has been updated to address the changing learning needs of the digital generation and to provide instructional strategies that will equip students with techniques to address these needs.

Objectives of This Textbook

Teachers Discovering Computers: Integrating Technology and Digital Media in the Classroom, Fourth Edition is intended for use in a one-quarter or one-semester undergraduate or graduate-level introductory computer course for educators. Students will finish the course with a solid understanding of educational technology, including how to use computers, how to access and evaluate information on the World Wide Web, and how to integrate computers and educational technology into classroom curriculum. This book also can be used for in-service training workshops that train teachers, administrators, and counselors how to use and effectively integrate educational technology.

The objectives of this textbook are to:

- Present practical, efficient ways to integrate technology resources and technology-based methods into everyday curriculum-specific practices

- Provide students with an understanding of the concepts and skills outlined in the National Educational Technology Standards for Teachers (NETS-T) and the Technology Standards for School Administrators (TSSA)
- Present the fundamentals of computers and educational technology in an easy-to-understand format
- Make use of the World Wide Web as a repository of the latest information and as an educational resource and learning tool for K-12 education
- Provide information about both Macintosh computers and PCs
- Give students an in-depth understanding of why computers are essential components in society, the business world, and K-12 education
- Provide students with the knowledge of how to use educational technology with diverse K–12 student populations
- Offer numerous examples of how to use educational technology in various subject areas and with K–12 students who have special needs
- Provide students with knowledge of responsible, ethical, and legal uses of technology, information, and software resources
- Provide students with knowledge of technology to enhance their personal and professional productivity

Distinguishing Features

Teachers Discovering Computers: Integrating Technology and Digital Media in the Classroom, Fourth Edition includes the following distinguishing features.

The Proven Shelly Cashman Series Pedagogy

More than five million students have learned about computers using the Shelly Cashman Series computer concepts textbooks. With World Wide Web integration and interactivity, streaming audio and animations, extraordinary visual drawings and photographs, unprecedented currency, and the Shelly Cashman Series approach, this book will make your introductory educational technology course for educators exciting and dynamic — an experience your students will remember as a highlight of their educational careers. Students and course instructors will find this to be the finest textbook they have ever used.

World Wide Web

Teachers Discovering Computers continues the Shelly Cashman Series tradition of innovation with its extensive integration of the World Wide Web. The purpose of integrating the World Wide Web into the book is to (1) offer students additional information and currency on topics of importance; (2) make available alternative learning techniques with Web-based curriculum-specific content, learning games, practice tests, and new interactive Student Edition Labs; (3) underscore the relevance of the World Wide Web as a basic information tool that can be used in all facets of K-12 education and society; and (4) offer instructors the opportunity to organize and administer their campus-based or distance education-based courses on the Web. The

Teachers Discovering Computers Web site (*www.scsite.com/tdc4*) works hand-in-hand with the text in three central ways:

- End-of-chapter assignments, many of the Special Features, and two of the appendices in the book have Web components. While working on an end-of-chapter assignment, students can go to the Teachers Discovering Computers Web site to look up key terms, explore the vast resources the Web has for education, or get an alternative point of view. The Teachers Discovering Computers Web site provides students with thousands of links to additional sources of information on a chapter-by-chapter basis. These sources have been evaluated for appropriateness and are maintained by a team of educators.

- *Teachers Discovering Computers* Web site provides a rich multimedia learning experience. Students can listen to an audio version of the end-of-chapter In Brief sections, reinforce their learning by playing interactive games, watch video clips to learn about new technologies, and explore concepts through 25 new interactive Student Edition Labs.

- Throughout the text, marginal annotations titled Web Info provide suggestions on how to obtain additional information via the World Wide Web about an important topic covered on the page. The Teachers Discovering Computers Web site (*www.scsite.com/tdc4*) provides links to these additional sources of information.

This textbook, however, does not depend on Web access to be used successfully. The Web access adds to the already complete treatment of topics within the book.

A Visually Appealing Book that Maintains Student Interest

The latest technology, pictures, drawings, and text have been artfully combined to produce a visually appealing and easy-to-understand book. Many of the figures show a step-by-step pedagogy, which simplifies the more complex computer and educational technology concepts. Pictures and drawings reflect the latest trends in computer and educational technology. Finally, the text was set in two columns, which research shows is easier for students to read. This combination of pictures, step-by-step drawings, and tested text layout sets a new standard for education textbook design.

Latest Educational Technology and Computer Trends

The terms and examples of educational technology described in this book are the same ones your students will encounter when using computers in the school setting and at home. The latest educational software packages and programs are shown throughout this book.

Macintosh Computers and PCs

Unlike many businesses, both Macintosh computers and PCs are used in the K-12 school environment. This textbook addresses both computer platforms and describes the appropriateness and use of educational software for both Macintosh computers and PCs.

Student Edition Labs

Twenty-five unique, hands-on exercises allow students to use the computer to learn about computer technology. These online labs utilize Macromedia Flash® to provide an interactive learning experience.

WEB INFO

For more information and ideas about classroom teachers integrating technology, visit the Teachers Discovering Computers Web site (*scseries.com/tdc4*), click Chapter 1, click Web Info, and then click Integration Ideas.

End-of-Chapter Activities

Unlike other books on educational technology fundamentals, a major effort was undertaken in *Teachers Discovering Computers* to offer exciting, rich, and thorough end-of-chapter materials to reinforce the chapter objectives and assist you in making your course the finest ever offered. As indicated earlier, each and every one of the end-of-chapter pages is stored as a Web page on the World Wide Web to provide your students in-depth information and alternative methods of preparing for examinations. Each chapter ends with the following activities:

■ **In Brief** This section summarizes the chapter material for the purpose of reviewing and preparing for examinations. Links on the Web pages provide additional current information. With a single click on the Web page, the student can listen to an audio version of this section.

■ **Key Terms** This list of the key terms with page references will aid students in mastering the chapter material. A complete summary of all key terms in the book, together with their definitions, appears in the index at the end of the book.

■ **Checkpoint** Matching and short-answer questions, together with a figure from the chapter that can be labeled, are used to reinforce the material presented within the chapter.

■ **Teaching Today** This section is designed to help students gain an appreciation of the value that technology and the World Wide Web have for K-12 education by visiting exciting educational Web pages and completing suggested curriculum integration tasks. The Web pages provide links to challenge students further on a vast array of interesting teacher-related topics.

■ **Education Issues** The use of computers and other technologies in education are not without controversy. At the end of each chapter, several scenarios are presented that challenge students to examine critically their perspective of the use of technology in K-12 education and society in general. Other nontechnology related scenarios allow students to explore many current controversial issues in education, such as school violence. The Web pages provide links to challenge students further.

■ **Integration Corner** This innovative section provides students with extensive ideas and resources for integrating technology into their classroom-specific curriculum. Each chapter provides information on and links to approximately 100 outstanding educational Web sites organized in 12 Corners: Early Childhood, Elementary, Middle School, Secondary, Reading/Language Arts, Social Studies/History, Math, Science, Special Education, Post Secondary, Administrator, and Research.

■ **Digital Media Corner** Today's K-12 digital students need their learning to be meaningful and relevant to their lives. Digital Media Corner provides links to videos, ideas, and examples of how students can use digital media to enhance their teaching as well as the learning of their K–12 students. The Web pages provide links to challenge students further.

■ **Assistive Technologies Corner** This new section provides information on current hardware, software, and peripherals that will assist students using this text in delivering instruction to their K-12 students with physical, cognitive, or sensory challenges. The Web pages provide extensive additional information and links to dozens of current and emerging assistive technologies.

- Software Corner Today's educators can choose from a variety of high-quality and often inexpensive educational software. Students learn about popular software programs by researching them on the Web and, in many cases, even downloading or ordering a free evaluation copy so they can evaluate a program before buying it.

- In the Lab These exercises are divided into two areas: productivity and integration. Students can use the productivity exercises to improve their software-specific skills in using word processing, spreadsheets, database, desktop publishing, curriculum and Web page development, and other productivity software programs. They can use the integration ideas for incorporating these programs into their classroom-specific curriculum. The Web pages provide links to tutorials, productivity ideas, integration examples and ideas, and more.

- Learn It Online These exercises allow students to improve their computer and integration skills by learning exciting new skills online. This section includes video clips, Student Edition Lab exercises, practice tests, learning games, and much more.

Timeline: Milestones in Computer History

A colorful, highly informative, 18-page timeline following Chapter 1 steps students through the major computer technology developments of the past 70 years, including the most recent advances.

Guide to World Wide Web Sites and Searching Techniques

More than 150 popular Web sites are listed and described in a general guide to Web sites that follows Chapter 2. These Web sites are organized into general categories, such as Entertainment, Health and Medicine, Government and Politics, Shopping, and more. This guide also introduces students to searching techniques and provides links to numerous popular education search tools.

Creating a Teacher's Web Page Using Microsoft Word

Following Chapter 3, a 17-page project provides students with instructions on how to create a basic teacher's Web page using Microsoft Word. By completing this step-by-step project, students will acquire many of the basic skills needed to create educational Web pages.

Buyer's Guide

A 15-page guide following Chapter 4 introduces students to purchasing a personal computer, desktop computer, notebook computer, Tablet PC, and Personal Mobile Device.

Digital Imaging and Video Technology

This special feature following Chapter 5 introduces students to using a personal computer, digital camera, and video camera to manipulate photographs and video.

Learning Theories and Educational Research

The special feature following Chapter 6 provides information about educational learning theories and research. This feature introduces students to educational terms, learning theories and theorists, educational research, and learning strategies.

Creating a Curriculum Page Using Microsoft Word

This special feature following Chapter 7 teaches students how to create a curriculum page using Microsoft Word. By completing this step-by-step project, students will acquire many of the skills needed to create educational Web sites and curriculum pages.

A World Without Wires

This special feature following Chapter 8 presents an overview of the Wi-Fi revolution. It describes the growth of wireless technology and presents the latest in hardware and applications.

Guide to Professional Educational Organizations

More than 30 popular, professional educational organizations are listed and described in Appendix A. Updated links to the most current URLs for these professional organizations are located at the textbook Web site.

Guide to State and Federal Government Educational Web Sites

The federal government, state governments, and state institutions and organizations are providing a multitude of Web resources for K-12 teachers and students. Educational resources provided by 30 federal government agencies and all 50 states and the District of Columbia are listed and described in Appendix B. Updated links to the most current URLs for these state and government organizations are located at the textbook Web site.

References

Appendix C lists the various books, articles, and other sources of information used in developing *Teachers Discovering Computers*.

Shelly Cashman Series Instructor Resources

The two categories of ancillary materials that accompany this textbook are Instructor Resources (ISBN 1-4188-5963-X) and Online Content. These ancillaries are available to adopters through your Thomson Course Technology representative or by calling one of the following telephone numbers: Colleges and Universities, 1-800-648-7450; High Schools, 1-800-824-5179; Private Career Colleges, 1-800-648-7450;

Canada, 1-800-268-2222; Corporations with IT Training Centers, 1-800-648-7450; and Government Agencies, Health-Care Organizations, and Correctional Facilities, 1-800-477-3692.

Instructor Resources CD-ROM

The Instructor Resources for this textbook include both teaching and testing aids. The contents of the Instructor Resources CD-ROM are listed below.

- **Instructor's Manual** The Instructor's Manual is made up of Microsoft Word files. The Instructor's Manual includes detailed lesson plans with page number references, lecture notes, teaching tips, classroom activities, discussion topics, projects to assign, and figure references. The figures are available through the Figure Files described below.

- **Syllabus** Any instructor who has been assigned a course at the last minute knows how difficult it is to come up with a course syllabus. For this reason, sample syllabi are included that can be customized easily to a course.

- **Figure Files** Illustrations for every figure in the textbook are available in electronic form. Use this ancillary to present a slide show in lecture or to print transparencies for use in lecture with an overhead projector.

- **Solutions to Exercises** Solutions for the Checkpoint exercises and In the Lab are available.

- **Test Bank & Test Engine** The test bank includes 110 questions for every chapter (25 multiple-choice, 50 true/false, and 35 fill-in-the-blank) with page number references, and when appropriate, figure references. A version of the test bank you can print also is included. The test bank comes with a copy of the test engine, ExamView. ExamView is a state-of-the-art test builder that is easy to use. ExamView enables you quickly to create printed tests, Internet tests, and computer (LAN-based) tests. You can enter your own test questions or use the test bank that accompanies ExamView.

- **Data Files for Students** The author-supplied files for the projects created in this book are included.

- **PowerPoint Presentation** PowerPoint Presentation is a multimedia lecture presentation system that provides PowerPoint slides for each chapter. Presentations are based on the chapters' objectives. Use this presentation system to present well-organized lectures that are both interesting and knowledge based. PowerPoint Presentation provides consistent coverage at schools that use multiple lecturers in their courses.

Thomson Course Technology provides the following Online Content options so you can customize your classes using the latest course management tools.

MyCourse 2.0 - Course Management Made Easy

MyCourse 2.0 is a flexible, easy-to-use course management tool that gives you true customization over the online components of your course. MyCourse 2.0 allows you to personalize your course home page, schedule your course activities and assignments, post messages, administer tests, and file the results in a grade book. You also can use text-specific preloaded content for this book, add your own content, select from a pool of test bank questions, or create questions yourself. MyCourse 2.0 is hosted by Thomson Learning, allowing you hassle-free maintenance and student access at all times. For more information, visit course.com/onlinecontent.

Blackboard and WebCT Online Content

Course Technology offers you options for online content. For those who want online testing, we provide a Blackboard test bank and a WebCT test bank, available for download in the Instructor Resources section on course.com. For those who desire more content, we offer course management and access to a Web site that is fully populated with content for this book. Also see Blackboard and WebCT Online Content in the Supplements section. For more information, visit course.com/onlinecontent.

Acknowledgements

For this fourth edition, the authors would like to thank Vicki Rath, Robert Kenny, Dorothy Hesson, Brandi Evans, Katie Kaag, Rachael Joyce, and Joel Hartman for assisting in the development of the end-of-chapter materials and features.

Gary B. Shelly
Thomas J. Cashman
Glenda A. Gunter
Randolph E. Gunter

Integrating Educational Technology into the Curriculum

1

Objectives

After completing this chapter, you will be able to:

[ISTE NETS-T Standards I A-B, II A, III A-D, V A-C, VI B,E]

- Explain the difference between computer, information, and integration literacy

- Explain the necessity of moving instructional strategies from traditional to new learning environments

- Describe the evolution of computers and digital media

- Describe the characteristics of today's digital students

- Explain how speed, reliability, accuracy, storage, and communications enable computers to be powerful tools

- Differentiate among the various categories of software

- Explain the purpose of a network

- Discuss the uses of the Internet and the World Wide Web

- Explain why computer technology is important for education

- Describe the National Educational Technology Standards for Teachers (NETS-T)

- Provide examples of how computers are changing the way people teach and learn

Computer technology and digital media play an essential role in how individuals work, live, and learn. Organizations of all sizes — even the smallest schools and businesses — rely on computers to help them operate more efficiently and effectively. At home, work, and school, computers help people do work faster, more accurately, and, in some cases, in ways that previously were not possible. People use computers at home for education, entertainment, information management, and business purposes. They also use computers as tools to access information and to communicate with others around the world. In the classroom, computers and computer-related technologies are having a profound influence on the way teachers instruct and students learn. Even the activities that are part of your daily routine — typing a report, driving a car, paying for goods and services with a credit card, or using an ATM — involve the use of computer technology.

WEB INFO

For more information and ideas about classroom teachers integrating technology, visit the Teachers Discovering Computers Web site (*scsite.com/tdc4*), click Chapter 1, click Web Info, and then click Integration Ideas.

As they have for a number of years, computers and related technologies continue to influence the lives of most individuals. Today, teachers in K-12 schools are educating students who will spend all of their adult lives in a technology-rich society. To help schools better educate students, the federal government, state governments, and school districts are spearheading massive funding efforts to equip classrooms with computers, with connectivity to networks, and with access to the Internet and the World Wide Web. Teachers in these classrooms must be prepared to utilize both current and emerging computer technologies.

The purpose of this book is to provide you with the knowledge to begin to use and integrate technology into your specific classroom curriculum. Chapter 1 introduces you to basic computer concepts and digital media as well as how teachers and administrators integrate computer technology and digital media into K-12 education. As you read, you also will begin to understand the vocabulary used to describe computer technology and digital media and educational technology. While you are reading, remember that this chapter is an overview and that many of the terms and concepts that are introduced are presented in detail in later chapters.

Curriculum-Specific Learning

As you review the materials and concepts presented in this textbook and the accompanying Web site, continuously ask yourself how you can use and integrate the knowledge you are gaining into your specific curriculum interests. Reflect on three ways you can use your newly acquired knowledge: (1) for your own professional development; (2) using technology as a productivity tool in your classroom; and, most importantly, (3) extensively integrating technology and digital media in your instructional strategies, lessons, student-based projects, and student assessments to improve student learning; in other words, throughout the curriculum. By doing this, you will be involved in **curriculum-specific learning** or **discipline-specific learning**, which is when you are learning how to apply teaching principles, knowledge, and ideas to authentic and practical classroom lessons and projects that can benefit your students.

Traditional twentieth-century educational practices will no longer provide you with the necessary skills you need to teach your students effectively how to become productive citizens in today's high-tech, global workplace. Figure 1-1 lists characteristics representing traditional approaches to learning and corresponding strategies associated with new learning environments for K-12 students. As you continue to use and integrate educational technology and digital media, you will find yourself transitioning from using traditional teaching and learning strategies to using many new and exciting technology-enriched teaching and learning strategies. Refer to this chart often as you learn how to integrate technology and digital media

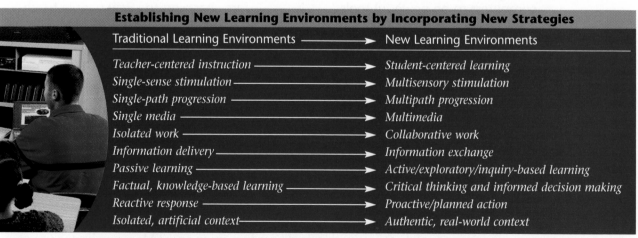

Establishing New Learning Environments by Incorporating New Strategies

Traditional Learning Environments	⟶	New Learning Environments
Teacher-centered instruction	⟶	Student-centered learning
Single-sense stimulation	⟶	Multisensory stimulation
Single-path progression	⟶	Multipath progression
Single media	⟶	Multimedia
Isolated work	⟶	Collaborative work
Information delivery	⟶	Information exchange
Passive learning	⟶	Active/exploratory/inquiry-based learning
Factual, knowledge-based learning	⟶	Critical thinking and informed decision making
Reactive response	⟶	Proactive/planned action
Isolated, artificial context	⟶	Authentic, real-world context

Source: International Society for Technology in Education (ISTE)

Figure 1-1 This chart shows the characteristics that represent traditional approaches to learning and corresponding strategies often associated with new learning environments for K-12 students.

into your classroom curriculum and practice using these new teaching strategies.

Another important issue is that teachers no longer have the time to create their various lesson plans and other documents from scratch, or in other words, constantly reinvent the wheel. The primary reason for extensively Web-enhancing this textbook is to provide you with hundreds of outstanding curriculum-specific sources of information and integration ideas that you can modify for use in your classroom curriculum. These resources are organized so you can choose the best curriculum-specific content to improve your students' learning. We encourage you to interact with the curriculum-specific content that works for you and then adopt and modify the content and other information, integrating it into your classroom curriculum.

Computer, Information, and Integration Literacy

Today, the vocabulary of computing is all around you. Before the advent of computers, memory was an individual's mental ability to recall previous experiences; storage was a place for out-of-season clothing; and communication was the act of exchanging opinions and information through writing,

speaking, or sign language. In today's world, these words and countless others have taken on new meanings as part of the vocabulary used to describe computers and their uses.

When you hear the word "computer", initially you may think of computers used in schools to perform activities such as creating flyers, memos, and letters; managing student rosters and calculating grades; or tracking library books. In the course of a day or week, however, you encounter many other computers. Your home, for instance, can contain a myriad of electronic devices, such as cordless telephones, VCRs, DVD players, handheld video games, digital cameras, and stereo systems including small computers.

Computers help you with your banking when you use automatic teller machines (ATMs) to deposit or withdraw funds. When you buy groceries, a computer tracks your purchases and calculates the amount of money you owe; it may even generate custom coupons based on your buying patterns. Even your car is equipped with computers that run the electrical system, control the temperature, and run sophisticated antitheft devices.

Experts anticipate that by the year 2010, all occupations will involve the use of computers on a daily basis (Figure 1-2). As the world of computers advances, it is essential that you gain some level of

Figure 1-2
Computer technology and digital media are present in every aspect of daily living — in the workplace, at home, in the classroom, and for entertainment.

FAQ

What is media literacy?

Media literacy, similar to information literacy, is when a person understands, analyzes, evaluates, and can communicate in a variety of forms.

computer literacy; that is, you must have a knowledge and understanding of computers and their uses.

Information literacy means knowing how to find, analyze, and use information. Information literacy is the ability to gather information from multiple sources, select relevant material, and organize it into a form that will allow the user to make decisions or take specific actions.

Students must learn to make informed decisions based on information obtained in all areas of their lives. For example, suppose you decide to move to a new city and need a place to live. You could find a home by driving around the city looking for a house or apartment within your price range that is close to school or work. As an information literate person, however, you might search for a home using the Internet, which is a global network of computers that contains information on a multitude of subjects. Using Internet resources to locate potential homes before you leave will make your drive through the city more efficient and focused.

How does computer technology relate to information literacy? They relate because, increasingly, information on housing, cars, and other products, as well as information on finances, school systems, travel, and weather, is accessible by computers. For example, with communications equipment, you can use a computer to connect to the Internet to access information on countless topics. After you have accessed the desired information, computers can help you analyze and use that information.

Although computer and information literacy are very important for educators, today's teachers also must use computers as a tool to facilitate learning. Teachers must be able to assess technology resources and plan classroom activities using available technologies. These skills are part of **integration literacy**, which is the ability to use computers and other technologies combined with a variety of teaching and learning strategies to enhance students' learning. Integration literacy means that teachers understand how to match appropriate technology to learning objectives, goals, and outcomes. A solid foundation

of computer and information literacy is essential to understanding how to integrate technology into classroom curriculum successfully.

As an educator, computers will affect your work and your life every day — and will continue to do so in the future. Today, school administrators use computers to access and manage information, and teachers use computers to enhance teaching and learning. The computer industry continually is developing new and different uses for computers and digital media, and making improvements to existing technologies. Learning about computers, digital media, and other technologies will help you function effectively in society and become a better facilitator of learning.

What Is a Computer and What Does It Do?

In basic or traditional terms, a **computer** is an electronic device, operating under the control of instructions stored in its memory, that can accept data, process the data according to specified rules, produce results, and store the results for future use. In other words, a computer is a computational device.

Data is a collection of unorganized facts. Computers manipulate and process data to create information. **Information** is data that is organized, has meaning, and is useful. Examples are reports, newsletters, receipts, pictures, invoices, or checks. As shown in Figure 1-3, for example, computers process several data items to print information in the form of a check.

Data entered into a computer is called **input**. The processed results are called **output**. Thus, a computer processes input to create output. A computer can hold data for future use in an area called **storage**. This cycle of input, process, output, and storage is called the **information processing cycle**.

The electronic and mechanical equipment that makes up a computer is called **hardware**. These components are covered in Chapter 4. **Software** is the series of instructions that tell the hardware how to perform tasks. Software is covered in

FAQ

Is data singular or plural?

With respect to computers, it is accepted and common practice to use the word data in both singular and plural context.

Figure 1-3 Data is processed into information. In this example, the company name, the date, the number of cameras, and the cost per camera each represent data. These items are processed into information, which, in this case, is a check.

Chapters 3 and 5. Without software, hardware is useless; hardware needs the instructions provided by software to process data into information.

The Evolution of Computers and Digital Media

The evolution of modern technologies started over 100 years ago, first with the telegraph, then telephones, radios, television, early computers, large and bulky mainframe computers, and, finally, the development of the personal computer in the early 1980s. The enormous popularity of the Internet, in particular the World Wide Web, has resulted in a computer that is more than a simple computational device. In fact, the computer has morphed into a device used for communication, media creation, learning, and so much more.

Recent advancements in personal computers merge the various forms of communications (the telephone, television, and computers) into effective, interactive, digital media systems. Even though the merging of these forms into personal computers is still evolving, the first decade of the twenty-first century is already being known as the **age of convergence**. This merging of technologies is possible because significantly faster processors and high-speed networks have been able to capitalize on the advancements made in the areas of digital graphics, video, animation, and audio. Today's personal computer architectures take advantage of a computer's individual power, digital media capabilities, and the ability to be interconnected with others in networked environments. As a result, multimedia technology systems have become increasingly more powerful and better able to handle information rich in visual and aural content.

The goal of multimedia computing and communications is to assist individuals in organizing and managing vast amounts of information in various types of media. Figure 1-4 on the next page shows the components of a typical digital media computer system that allows the average person to use multiple senses when working

digital photo printer

PC video camera

CD/DVD drive

monitor

hard disk drive

digital video camera

3.5-inch disk drive

speaker

microphone

digital camera

keyboard

mouse

system unit

card reader/writer

scanner

modem

USB flash drive

Figure 1-4 Common computer hardware components associated with a digital media center computer.

and communicating. To see just how far personal computer technology has come in a relatively short period of time, compare this figure to the pictures of the original personal computers developed by IBM and Apple in the early 1980s shown later in this chapter on page 10.

WHAT IS DIGITAL MEDIA?

Digital media is defined in a variety of ways; however, for the purposes of this book, **digital media** is defined as those technologies that allow users to create new forms of interaction, expression, communication, and entertainment in a digital format. The term digital media has been coined to reflect the evolution of multimedia computing into multisensory communications. The goal of multimedia and now

digital media is to reproduce as closely as possible the reliability and effectiveness found in face-to-face communications and then emulate that in telecommunications and computer systems.

Computing in the Digital Age

Digital technology allows greater participation in the creative process, turning viewers into producers. Individuals can customize formats, outcomes, and usage of the information presented to them. Today, individuals use digital technology to input, edit, manage, publish, and share all kinds of information that was previously either impossible or too expensive for the average person to create and share. This digital revolution has accomplished in only 50 years that which took hundreds of years to accomplish beginning with the invention of Gutenberg's printing press in the late sixteenth century — that is, the democratization of information flow, the flow of the production process down to the masses.

DIGITAL STUDENTS: WHO ARE THEY AND HOW DO THEY LEARN?

The digital revolution has resulted in one unintended consequence. Today's youth are much more media-centric than previous generations. In fact, many people believe that the brains of today's youths have actually become rewired to accommodate the thousands of hours they spend in front of computer screens watching and creating video, listening to music, and playing computer games. It also has been said that today's youth actually speak digitally.

Today's students play on electronic playgrounds with a variety of powerful media functioning as their recreational equipment. Watch how they read e-mails, send instant messages and text messages over handheld devices, and speak to one another in short sound bites; also notice how visually oriented these students are. You will soon see that something is different about today's youth. Many have called this new generation the **digital generation**.

The world in which today's students live is significantly different from the past. Today's students use different technologies to communicate and to access information from multiple resources. They use computers, smart phones, pagers, instant messaging, personal digital assistants (PDAs) and other handheld devices, Tablet PCs, and laptops to connect to teachers, friends, family, and others in their community and all over the world. Digital students now have a virtual world at their fingertips — with all its pitfalls and promises. Apple Computer defines these **digital students** or **digital kids** as kids who are (1) hypercommunicators who use multiple tools to communicate, (2) multitaskers who do several things at once with ease, and (3) goal oriented as they pursue multiple goals at the same time. Today's digital generation is profoundly different from previous generations and these differences need to be understood by teachers if they are to facilitate effective learning for today's digital students. The stark contrasts and differences between generations become more apparent when they are viewed in graphical form (Figure 1-5).

Today's students are essentially different from previous generations in the way they think, in the way they access, absorb, interpret, process, and apply information and, above all, in the way they view, interact, and communicate in this technology-rich world. Today's digital kids like watching TV, listening to music on their iPods, checking out school pictures on their iPod photos, listening to their favorite shows via podcasts, talking on their cell phones, instant messaging their friends, and blogging. Perhaps the most amazing

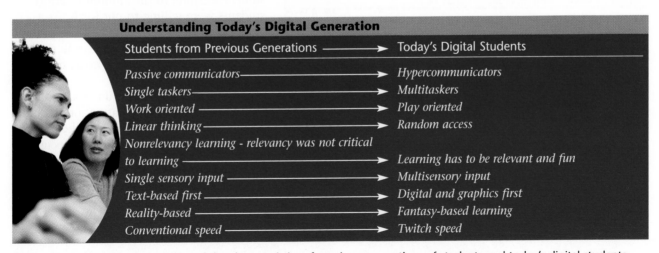

Understanding Today's Digital Generation

Students from Previous Generations ——→	Today's Digital Students
Passive communicators ——→	Hypercommunicators
Single taskers ——→	Multitaskers
Work oriented ——→	Play oriented
Linear thinking ——→	Random access
Nonrelevancy learning - relevancy was not critical to learning ——→	Learning has to be relevant and fun
Single sensory input ——→	Multisensory input
Text-based first ——→	Digital and graphics first
Reality-based ——→	Fantasy-based learning
Conventional speed ——→	Twitch speed

Figure 1-5 This table shows some of the characteristics of previous generations of students and today's digital students.

aspect of this scenario is that they are doing all of these activities while completing their math homework assignment.

Understanding today's digital kids and how they learn has profound implications not only for how teachers teach these digital students, but also, and perhaps more importantly, for how teachers reach them. Educational technology and digital media can be valuable tools when they are integrated into the curriculum appropriately to achieve learning gains, particularly when they are combined with a twenty-first-century curriculum.

Teachers have to decide whether to try to pull digital students away from their native digital world or to motivate digital students by tapping into their digital world and using their natural inclination and inquisitiveness about all that is digital. A quick look at the school system today, which has been so slow to change, makes it easy to see the disconnect between how teachers teach and how students learn. Most of the schools today were designed for the Industrial Age and yet, the students attending schools today are living in the digital age. The world in which digital students live has changed drastically and it continues to change in a techno fast-paced manner. Unfortunately, many school environments have not kept up with that change. Marc Prensky stated in 2001 that

digital kids are the digital natives and teachers are the digital immigrants. Today's students speak digitally; they are all native speakers of the digital language. Review carefully the information shown in Figure 1-6 as it provides insight into the profound differences between how digital kids learn and how digital immigrant teachers teach.

Digital media allows teachers to use a combination of technology tools to appeal to an array of learning styles digitally. If integrated properly, digital media also has the capability to stimulate imagination and develop critical thinking skills all while allowing students to take an active role in their own learning. The ARCS Motivational Model, which is discussed next, can help you reflect on ways to modify your teaching techniques and strategies to find innovative ways to motivate today's digital students to learn.

ARCS MOTIVATIONAL MODEL

The **ARCS Motivational Model** was developed by John M. Keller in 1983 and is applicable to learning in the digital age. Keller stressed that even the best designed instructional strategy will fail if students are not motivated to learn. Many students are only performing to pass the test. Without a desire to learn, retention is unlikely. Thus, teachers should strive to create a deeper motivation in learners to learn new skills.

Frustrated that so much of the interest in psychology was concentrated on differences in learner ability, Keller developed a model that would attribute differences in student learning to the amount of effort students were willing to put forth. As a result, he cataloged four specific areas that could account for the differences in student effort. A discussion of these areas follows.

ATTENTION Effective learning techniques seek to capture students' attention to eliminate boredom and arouse natural curiosity. Lessons should increase students' focus by using novel, surprising, out of the ordinary, and uncertain events. Effective techniques should stimulate the sense of wonder and

Apple - Digital tools for digital kids - The Disconnect - Microsoft Internet Explorer

File Edit View Favorites Tools Help

Address http://www.apple.com/education/digitalkids/disconnect/landscape.html

The differences between digital native learners and digital immigrant teachers.

Digital Native Learners	Digital Immigrant Teachers
Prefer receiving information quickly from multiple multimedia sources.	Prefer slow and controlled release of information from limited sources.
Prefer parallel processing and multitasking.	Prefer singular processing and single or limited tasking.
Prefer processing pictures, sounds, and video before text.	Prefer to provide text before pictures, sounds, and video.
Prefer random access to hyperlinked multimedia information.	Prefer to provide information linearly, logically, and sequentially.
Prefer to interact/network simultaneously with many others.	Prefer students to work independently rather than network and interact.
Prefer to learn "just-in-time."	Prefer to teach "just-in-case" (it's on the exam).
Prefer instant gratification and instant rewards.	Prefer deferred gratification and deferred rewards.
Prefer learning that is relevant, instantly useful, and fun.	Prefer to teach to the curriculum guide and standardized tests.

*Ian Jukes and Anita Dosaj, The InfoSavvy Group, February 2003

Science Teacher
Mansfield Middl
Storrs, CT

More resources

"Growing U
Kids" by Do
Tapscott

"How Peopl
Brain, Mind
Experience
School" - Jo
Bransford,
Brown, and
R. Cocking

"High Score
Education:
Not School,
Teaching K
Think" by J
Paul Gee

"Child Powe
New Learnir
Digital Cen
Irrelevancy
School" by
Papert

Figure 1-6 Differences between digital native learners and digital immigrant teachers.

maintain interest. Most students are not only auditory or visual learners, but also multisensory learners. Digital media has the ability to capture the attention of the learner because it addresses a variety of learning styles. Today's students expect to use digital media devices in their daily lives, so these devices, or similar media technology, should be woven seamlessly into their classroom experiences.

RELEVANCE When students feel that learning is relevant or important to their lives, they will become motivated to learn. By using digital media to develop lesson concepts, teachers bring familiar technology into the classroom. Concepts developed with digital media utilize technologies that students value.

CHALLENGE/CONFIDENCE Students who believe they can achieve often do. Lessons created with digital media allow students to develop confidence by enabling them to succeed. Lessons created with digital media present a degree of challenge that allows for meaningful success through both learning and performance conditions. Lesson content created with digital media can be leveled to challenge multiple skill levels, to generate positive expectations, to provide feedback, and to support internal attributions for success — all of which means students are working at a level at which they can achieve success and gain

confidence. Assignments completed using digital media allow students to see just how far their imagination can take them. Using digital media will be natural for some but a struggle for others because not all students will be at the same skill level when it comes to using digital media. It is important to develop lessons that have several achievement levels so students can progress at a pace that meets their needs, that is, that challenges them while building their confidence.

SATISFACTION/SUCCESS Feeling good about one's self is a natural motivator. Digital media provides opportunities for students to use newly acquired knowledge or skills in simulated settings successfully. Lessons developed using digital media can be designed to provide feedback that will sustain the desired behavior. Using digital media, students can showcase their achievements, allowing them to share their successes with others, which increases their desire for positive peer evaluation.

Figure 1-7 summarizes the key concepts of Keller's ARCS Motivational Model. As you continue to explore the concepts and resources provided in this textbook, use the information to help you transition from being a digital immigrant teacher to one that facilitates students' learning in the digital age. The next few sections briefly cover the various types of computers, some of the reasons computers

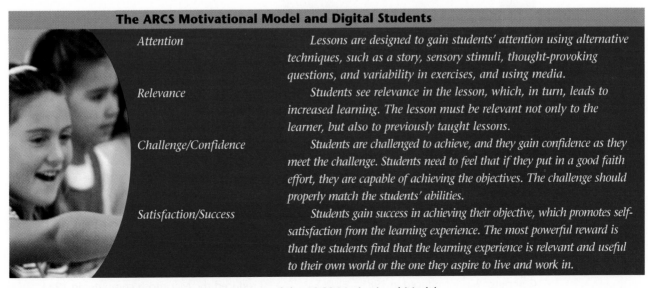

The ARCS Motivational Model and Digital Students

Attention	*Lessons are designed to gain students' attention using alternative techniques, such as a story, sensory stimuli, thought-provoking questions, and variability in exercises, and using media.*
Relevance	*Students see relevance in the lesson, which, in turn, leads to increased learning. The lesson must be relevant not only to the learner, but also to previously taught lessons.*
Challenge/Confidence	*Students are challenged to achieve, and they gain confidence as they meet the challenge. Students need to feel that if they put in a good faith effort, they are capable of achieving the objectives. The challenge should properly match the students' abilities.*
Satisfaction/Success	*Students gain success in achieving their objective, which promotes self-satisfaction from the learning experience. The most powerful reward is that the students find that the learning experience is relevant and useful to their own world or the one they aspire to live and work in.*

Figure 1-7 This figure highlights the components of the ARCS Motivational Model.

are so powerful, computer software, networks, and the Internet.

Categories of Computers

Computers can be organized in three general categories: personal computers; mobile computers and mobile devices; and servers, supercomputers, and embedded computers. All of these types of computers are discussed in detail in later chapters and special features. The next few sections briefly cover personal computers; mobile computers and mobile devices; as well as servers, supercomputers, and embedded computers.

Personal Computers

A **personal computer**, or **PC**, is a computer that performs all of its input, processing, output, and storage activities by itself. A personal computer contains a processor, memory, and one or more input, output, and storage devices.

Many people associate the term personal computer, or PC, with computers that use Microsoft Windows, which is a popular operating system used on many of today's computers. All personal computers, however, do not use Windows. For example, Apple Macintosh computers use a different operating system, Mac OS, but still are a

WEB INFO

For more information about Macintosh computers, visit the Teachers Discovering Computers Web site (*scsite.com/tdc4*), click Chapter 1, click Web Info, and then click Macintosh.

type of personal computer. Why the confusion?

In 1981, IBM Corporation released its first personal computer, the IBM Personal Computer (Figure 1-8). The IBM Personal Computer was an instant business success and quickly became known by its nickname — the PC. For marketing reasons, IBM allowed other companies to copy its computer design; therefore, many companies started making IBM-compatible computers. These computers were called IBM-compatible because they used software that was the same as or similar to the IBM PC software. All subsequent IBM computers and IBM-compatibles were called PCs.

Three years after the introduction of the first IBM PC, the Apple Computer Company introduced the **Macintosh computer** (Figure 1-9). Macintosh computers could accomplish many of the same tasks as IBM PCs, but they were very different from each other. In addition to the Macintosh computer, Apple also introduced a pointing device called a mouse. Macintosh computers were incompatible with the IBM PC because they used different operating system software than the IBM and IBM-compatible computers. As a result, a distinction developed between the terms Macintosh and PC, even though Macintosh computers are personal computers. This distinction and confusion between the two types of computers continues today. To avoid confusion, users often refer to these two types of

Figure 1-8 The original IBM Personal Computer was introduced in 1981.

Figure 1-9 Apple Computer Company produced the Macintosh computer in 1984.

personal computers as Windows environment or Mac environment.

Today, businesses, homes, and K-12 schools use dozens of different models of Apple and IBM-compatible personal computers. To avoid confusion in this textbook, personal computers that use Microsoft Windows are referred to as PCs and all Macintosh personal computers are referred to as Macintosh computers (Figure 1-10). When this textbook refers to the terms personal computer, desktop computer, or computer, the subject matter being discussed is applicable to Apple, IBM, and IBM-compatible computers. Most of the concepts and terms covered in this textbook are applicable to all types of personal computers.

Personal computers shown in Figure 1-10a and Figure 1-10b also are called **desktop computers** because they are designed so the system unit, input devices, output devices, and any other devices fit entirely on a desk.

Mobile Computers and Mobile Devices

A **mobile computer** is a personal computer that you can carry from place to place. The most popular type of mobile computer is the notebook computer. A **mobile device** is a computing device small enough to hold in your hand and usually does not have disk drives. Popular mobile devices include handheld computers, PDAs, and smart phones.

MOBILE COMPUTERS

A **notebook computer**, also called a laptop computer, is a portable, personal computer small enough to fit on your lap. Today's notebook computers are thin and lightweight, yet they can be as powerful as the average desktop computer (Figure 1-11). Notebook computers normally are more expensive than desktop computers with equal capabilities.

[a] IBM computer (PC)

[b] Apple Macintosh (Mac)

Figure 1-10 Figure 1-10a shows a typical PC and Figure 1-10b shows a typical iMac computer.

Figure 1-11 Notebook computers are available in Windows and Mac environments. Shown is an Apple PowerBook G4.

FAQ

How long have schools used Tablet PCs?

In December 2002, Ocoee Middle School in Orlando, Florida, was the first public school to provide students with this new technology.

TABLET PC

Resembling a letter-sized slate, the **Tablet PC** is a special type of notebook computer that allows you to write on the screen using a digital pen (Figure 1-12). Users also can use an attached keyboard (not shown). Tablet PCs are covered in later chapters and the special feature that follows Chapter 8.

MOBILE DEVICES

Some mobile devices are **Internet-enabled,** meaning they can connect to the Internet wirelessly. Mobile devices usually do not have disk drives. Instead, these devices store programs and data permanently in memory chips inside the system unit or in small storage media such as memory cards. Four popular mobile devices are handheld computers, PDAs, smart phones, and smart watches. Some combination mobile devices also are available, for example, a PDA/ smart phone.

HANDHELD COMPUTER A handheld computer is a computer small enough to fit in one hand while you operate it with the other hand. Because of their reduced size, the screens on handheld computers are quite small. The primary input device on a handheld computer is a small keyboard.

PDA A **personal digital assistant,** or PDA, provides personal organizer functions, such as a calendar, appointment book, address book, calculator, and notepad (Figure 1-13). The PDA is one of the more popular lightweight mobile devices in use today. Most PDAs also offer a variety of other application software, such as word processing, spreadsheets, and games. In addition, a large array of educational software is available for use on PDAs, including concept mapping tools, periodic tables, graphic

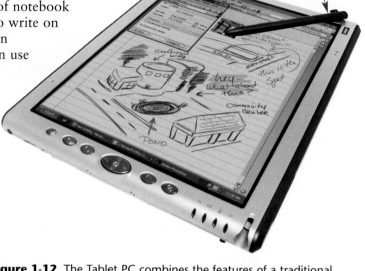

digital pen

Figure 1-12 The Tablet PC combines the features of a traditional notebook computer with the simplicity of pencil and paper.

calculators, and much more. Many PDAs are Internet-enabled so users can check e-mail and access the Internet.

SMART PHONES Offering the convenience of one-handed operation, a **smart phone** is an Internet-enabled telephone. In addition to basic telephone capabilities, smart phones allow you to send and receive e-mail and access the Internet. Some models have color screens, play music, and allow you to take and send digital photos and short video clips.

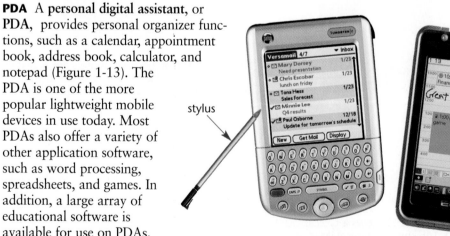

stylus

Figure 1-13 PDAs are widely used in both business and education; many include Internet access and telephone capabilities. Shown here are two different styles of PDAs.

FAQ

Why are they called smart phones?

They can be a PDA, a telephone, and/or a camera, and provide music, news, sports, and more in one device. The manufacturers for these phones also call them intelligent phones because of the many different things they can do.

SMART WATCH A **smart watch** is an Internet-enabled watch. In addition to basic timekeeping capabilities, a smart watch automatically adjusts to time zone changes, stores personal messages, reminds you of appointments, and wirelessly accesses news, weather, sports, and more (Figure 1-14). One day soon, you may very well wear your telephone on your wrist.

Figure 1-14 A smart watch.

Servers, Supercomputers, and Embedded Computers

A **server** manages the resources on a network and provides a centralized storage area for software programs and data. You will learn more about servers and how they are used in education in Chapter 2. A **supercomputer** is the fastest, most powerful computer — and the most expensive. The fastest supercomputers are capable of processing more than 100 trillion instructions in a single second. Supercomputers are used for tasks such as analyzing weather patterns, tracking hurricanes, and identifying safety issues regarding the space shuttle. Although schools do not have supercomputers, teachers do use the output from supercomputers in their lessons.

An **embedded computer** is a special-purpose computer that functions as one component in a larger product. Embedded computers are everywhere — at home, in your car, at work, and at school. These computers perform various functions, depending on the requirements of the product in which they reside. Figure 1-15 shows some of the many embedded computers in cars.

Advanced airbag systems have crash-severity sensors that determine the appropriate level to inflate the airbag, reducing the chance of airbag injury in low-speed accidents.

Adaptive cruise control systems detect if cars in front of you are too close and, if necessary, adjust the vehicle's throttle, may apply brakes, and/or sound an alarm.

Tire pressure monitoring systems send warning signals if tire pressure is insufficient.

Cars equipped with wireless communications capabilities, called *telematics*, include such features as navigation systems and Internet access.

Drive-by-wire systems sense pressure on the gas pedal and communicate electronically to the engine how much and how fast to accelerate.

Figure 1-15 Some of the embedded computers designed to improve safety, security, and performance in today's automobiles.

Why Is a Computer So Powerful?

A computer derives its power from its capability of performing the information processing cycle (input, process, output, and storage) with speed, reliability, and accuracy; its capacity to store large amounts of data and information; and its capability of communicating with other computers.

SPEED

Inside the system unit, operations occur through electronic circuits. When data and information flow along these circuits, they travel at close to the speed of light. As a result, computers process billions of operations in a single second.

RELIABILITY

The electronic components in modern computers are dependable because they have a low failure rate. The high reliability of the electronic components enables computers to produce consistent results.

ACCURACY

Computers can process large amounts of data and generate error-free results, provided the user enters the data correctly. If a user enters inaccurate data, the resulting output will be incorrect. This computing principle, called garbage in, garbage out (GIGO), points out that the accuracy of a computer's output depends on the accuracy of the input. In fact, human mistakes cause most instances of computer errors.

STORAGE

Many computers can store enormous amounts of data and make this data available for processing when needed. Using current storage methods, a computer can transfer data from storage to memory quickly, process the data, and then store the processed data for future use.

COMMUNICATIONS

Most computers today can communicate with other computers. Computers with this capability can share any of the four information processing cycle operations — input, process, output, and storage — with another computer. For example, two computers connected by a communications device such as a modem can share stored data, instructions, and information. A **network** consists of two or more computers connected together via communications media and devices. The most widely known network is the Internet, linking together millions of businesses, government installations, educational institutions, and individuals.

Today, hundreds of millions of people routinely send and receive messages using **electronic mail (e-mail)**, which is the electronic exchange of messages to and from other computer users. The Internet also allows individuals to access a global network of computers to gather information on practically any subject, send e-mail and other types of messages, and obtain products and services (Figure 1-16).

Figure 1-16 The Internet is a worldwide collection of networks that links together millions of businesses, the government, educational institutions, and individuals.

Computer Software

Software, also called a **computer program** or simply a **program,** is a series of instructions that tells the hardware of a computer what to do and how to do it. For example, some instructions direct the computer to accept your keyboard input and other instructions direct the computer to store this input in memory. Other instructions cause data stored in memory to be used in calculations, such as adding a series of numbers to obtain a total. Some instructions compare two values stored in memory and direct the computer to perform alternative operations based on the results of the comparison; and some instructions direct the computer to print a report, display information on the monitor, draw a color graph on the monitor, or store information on a disk.

Before a computer can perform, or **execute,** a program, the instructions in the program must be placed, or loaded, into the memory of the computer. Usually, they are loaded into memory from storage. For example, a program might be loaded from the hard disk of a computer into memory for execution.

When you purchase a program, you will receive one or more CD-ROMs, or a single DVD-ROM, on which the software is stored (Figure 1-17). To use this software, you often must **install** the software on the computer's hard disk. Today, many programs can be purchased and downloaded from the Internet.

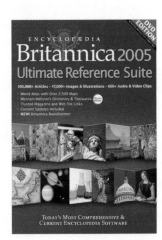

Figure 1-17 When you buy software, you receive media, such as a CD-ROM or a DVD-ROM, which contains the software program.

Sometimes, a program can be loaded in memory directly from a CD-ROM or DVD-ROM so you do not have to install it on a hard disk first.

When you buy a computer, it usually has some software already installed on its hard disk. Thus, you can use the computer as soon as you receive it.

Figure 1-18 on the next page illustrates the steps required when a user installs and runs a greeting card program.

Software is the key to the productive use of computers. With the correct software, a computer is an invaluable tool.

Software can be categorized into two types: system software and application software. The following sections describe these categories of software.

SYSTEM SOFTWARE

System software consists of programs that control the operations of a computer and its devices. System software also serves as the liaison between a user and the computer's hardware. Two types of system software are the operating system and utility programs.

OPERATING SYSTEM One of the more important programs on a computer, the **operating system** contains instructions that coordinate all of the activities of the hardware devices. The operating system also contains instructions that allow you to run application software.

When you start a computer, the computer loads, or copies, the operating system into memory from the hard disk. The operating system remains in memory while the computer runs and allows you to communicate with the computer and other software. Many Macintosh computers use a unique operating system called the Macintosh operating system, or **Mac OS;** many of today's PCs use a popular operating system called **Microsoft Windows.**

USER INTERFACE All software has a **user interface,** which is the part of the software with which the user interacts. The user interface controls how you enter data and instructions. The user interface also controls how the computer presents information on

Step 1: INSTALL
When you insert a greeting card program disc in the CD drive for the first time, the computer begins the procedure of installing the greeting card program on the hard disk.

CD-ROM

Step 2: RUN
After it's installed, you can instruct the computer to run the greeting card program. The computer transfers instructions from the hard disk to memory.

instructions transfer to memory

Step 3: USE
The greeting card program executes. Using this program, you can create custom greeting cards.

Figure 1-18 This figure shows the steps involved in installing and running a computer program.

the screen. Many of today's software programs use a **graphical user interface**, or **GUI** (pronounced *gooey*), which allows you to interact with the software using visual items such as icons. An **icon** is a small image that represents a program, an instruction, or some other object. Figure 1-19a shows the Windows graphical user interface and Figure 1-19b shows the Mac OS graphical user interface. The Mac OS desktop also shows the new wide-screen display that is becoming more popular.

UTILITY PROGRAMS A **utility program** is a type of system software that performs a specific task, usually related to managing a computer, its devices, or its programs. An example of a utility program is an uninstaller, which removes a program previously installed on a computer. Most operating systems include several utility programs for managing disk drives, printers, and other devices. You also can buy stand-alone utility programs to perform additional computer management functions.

APPLICATION SOFTWARE

Application software consists of programs designed to perform specific tasks for users. When you think of the different ways people use computers in their careers or personal lives, you are thinking of examples of application software. Educational, business, and scientific computer programs are all examples of application software.

Popular application software includes word processing, spreadsheet, database, and presentation graphics. Word processing software allows you to create documents, such as letters and reports. Spreadsheet software allows you to calculate numbers arranged in rows and columns and create charts and graphs. Teachers and schools use spreadsheet software for gradebooks, lesson plans, and other school-related tasks. Database software allows you to store data in an organized fashion, as well as to retrieve, manipulate, and display that data in a meaningful form. With presentation

icons

[a] Windows graphical user interface.

Figure 1-19 Graphical user interfaces, such as Microsoft Windows (Figure 1-19a) or Apple's Mac OS (Figure 1-19b), make computers easier to use. The small pictures, or symbols, on the screen are called icons. The icons represent programs, folders, files, or documents. The icons are selected by using a mouse or other pointing device.

[b] Macintosh graphical user interface.

graphics software, you can create electronic slides for use when giving classroom presentations. Computer software manufacturers frequently package these four applications together as a single unit, called a software suite. A **software suite** contains individual software applications sold in the same box for a price that is significantly less than buying the applications separately (Figure 1-20).

Many other types of application software exist that enable users to perform a variety of tasks. Some widely used software applications include the following: reference, education, and entertainment; desktop publishing; photo and video editing; multimedia authoring; network, communications, electronic mail, and Web browsers; accounting; school and student record keeping; and

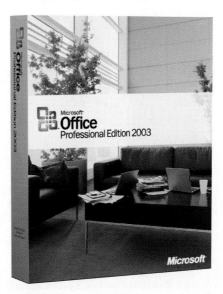

Figure 1-20 Microsoft Office is a popular software suite used by teachers and students — on both PCs and Macintosh computers.

WEB INFO

For more information about application software packages, visit the Teachers Discovering Computers Web site (*scsite.com/tdc4*), click Chapter 1, click Web Info, and then click Application Software.

WEB INFO

For more information about shareware, freeware, and evaluation software, visit the Teachers Discovering Computers Web site (*scsite.com/tdc4*), click Chapter 1, click Web Info, and then click Shareware.

personal information management. Each of these applications is discussed in future chapters.

The number and quality of software applications designed specifically for the K-12 learning environment have increased dramatically in the past few years. Education software and the use of productivity software in education are discussed extensively in Chapters 3 and 5. In addition, you can learn about dozens of education software programs by reviewing the Software Corner at the end of each chapter.

PACKAGED SOFTWARE Packaged software is designed to meet the needs of a variety of users, not just a single user, school, or business. Programs required for common educational, business, and personal applications are available for purchase off the shelf from software vendors or stores that sell computer products (Figure 1-21). You also can purchase packaged software on the Internet.

CUSTOM SOFTWARE Sometimes, a user or organization with unique software requirements cannot find packaged software that meets all of its needs. In this case, the user or organization can use **custom software**, which is a program developed at a user's request to perform specific functions. For example, a state Department of Education may design a custom gradebook and attendance program for use by its school districts.

OPEN SOURCE SOFTWARE Open source software is software provided for use, modification, and redistribution. This software has no restrictions from the copyright holder regarding modification of the software's internal instructions and redistribution of the software. Open source software usually can be downloaded from the Web at no cost.

SHAREWARE, FREEWARE, AND PUBLIC-DOMAIN SOFTWARE **Shareware** is software distributed to a user free for a trial period. If you want to use a shareware program beyond the trial period, the person or company that developed the program expects you to send a small fee. When you send this small fee, the developer registers you to receive service assistance and updates. **Freeware** is software provided at no cost to a user by an individual or company. Thousands of inexpensive shareware and freeware programs are available for download from the Internet. **Public-domain software** also is free software, but has been donated for public use and has no copyright restrictions.

SOFTWARE DEVELOPMENT

People who write software programs are called **computer programmers** or **programmers**. Programmers write the instructions necessary to direct the computer to process data into information. Programmers must place the correct instructions in the right sequence so the program performs the desired actions.

Complex programs can require hundreds of thousands of program instructions. Programmers use a programming language to write computer programs.

When writing complex programs for large businesses, programmers often follow a plan developed by a systems analyst. A **systems analyst** manages the development of a program, working with both the user and the programmer to design the program.

Figure 1-21 You can buy packaged software programs from computer stores, office equipment suppliers, retailers, and the Internet.

Networks and the Internet

A network is a collection of computers and devices connected together via communications media and devices such as cables, telephone lines, modems, or other means. When you connect your computer to a network, you are online with the network.

Businesses and schools continue to network their computers so users can share **resources**, such as hardware devices, software programs, data, and information. Sharing resources saves time and money. For example, instead of purchasing one printer for every Macintosh and PC in a computer lab, schools can connect a single printer and all the computers using a local area network, or LAN. The network enables all of the computers within a lab to access the same printer.

These networks can be relatively small or quite extensive and they can be wireless or wired. A **local area network (LAN)** is a network that connects computers in a limited geographic area, such as a school computer laboratory, business office, or group of adjacent buildings (Figure 1-22). A **wide area network (WAN)** is a network that covers a large geographical area, such as one that connects the district offices of a statewide school system or the offices of

a national corporation (Figure 1-23 on the next page).

The world's largest network is the **Internet**, which is a worldwide collection of networks, that links together millions of businesses, governments, educational institutions, and individuals using modems, telephone lines, and other communications devices and media. More than one billion people around the world access the Internet for a variety of reasons (Figure 1-24 on the next page). For teachers, the Internet opens doors to a myriad of educational activities, including the following:

- Sending messages to other connected users, including teachers and students

- Accessing a wealth of information, including curriculum and lesson plans, activities, and teacher's guides

- Joining an educational community to collaborate with teachers and students around the world

- Accessing sources of educational content, such as encyclopedias, online museums, magazines, and other project collections

- Taking an online class or enrolling in an online master's degree program

Figure 1-22 A server manages the resources on a network. In this example of a local area network (LAN), three separate computers access the resources of one server (one wirelessly), which allows all three computers to share one printer.

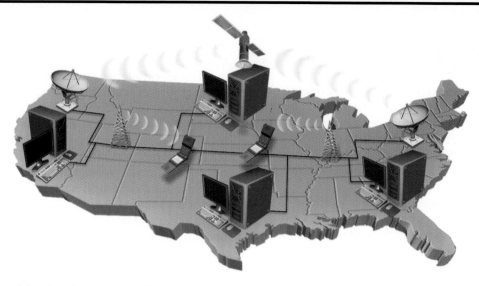

Figure 1-23 A wide area network (WAN) can be quite large and complex, connecting users in offices around the country.

One of the more popular parts of the Internet is the **World Wide Web**, also called the **Web**. The Web portion of the Internet consists of computer sites that contain billions of electronic documents called Web pages. A Web page is an electronic document that contains text, graphics, sound, animation, or video, and has built-in connections, or links, to other documents. Web pages are stored on computers throughout the world. A Web site is a collection of related Web pages that you can access electronically for information on thousands of topics. You access and view Web pages using a software program called a Web browser. The most popular Web browsers are Microsoft Internet Explorer, Netscape, and Mozilla Firefox.

[a] send a message

[b] access information

[e] entertainment

[d] meet people

[c] shop

Figure 1-24 Users access the Internet for a variety of reasons: to send messages to other connected users, to access a wealth of information, to shop for goods and services, to meet and converse with people around the world, and for entertainment.

Why Use Computer Technology in Education?

In any society, educators have the ability to make an enormous positive contribution. Making such a contribution is a challenge and teachers must willingly embrace new teaching and learning opportunities. Educators are beginning to recognize that they must teach students, the future leaders and citizens of society, using current technologies so that these students will be comfortable using future technologies.

Technology and digital media are everywhere and integrated into every aspect of individuals' lives. Today's educators must provide students with the skills they will need to excel in a technology-rich society. Parents no longer are urging schools to incorporate technology into the classroom; they are insisting on it. When used appropriately, technology has the potential to enhance students' achievement and assist them in meeting learning objectives.

An extensive body of education research is showing that technology can support learning in many ways. Using technology in the classroom, for example, can be motivational. Teachers have found that using modern computers, digital media, and other computer-related technologies can capture and hold students' attention. Computers also can provide many unique, effective, and powerful opportunities for teaching and learning. These opportunities include skill-building practice, real-world problem solving, interactive learning, discovery learning, and linking learners to a multitude of instructional resources.

Computers also support communications beyond classroom walls, thus enabling schools and communities to provide an environment for cooperative learning, for development of high-order thinking skills, and for solving complex problems. As demonstrated by these examples, technology, when placed in the hands of teachers and students, can provide unique, effective, and powerful opportunities for many different types of instruction and learning.

Several national and international organizations support education and

educators in the use of technology. The leading organization is the **International Society for Technology in Education (ISTE)**, which is a nonprofit group that promotes the use of technology to support and improve teaching and learning. ISTE supports all areas of K-12 education, community colleges and universities, administration of K-12 education, and teacher education organizations.

ISTE has been instrumental in developing the National Educational Technology Standards (NETS) for the **National Council for Accreditation for Teacher Education (NCATE)**. NCATE is the official body for accrediting teacher education programs. To date, ISTE has developed standards for K-12 teachers, students, and school administrators. As you work through this textbook and its related Web site, you will gain an understanding of the concepts and skills outlined in the **National Educational Technology Standards for Teachers (NETS-T)**, which define the fundamental concepts, knowledge, skills, and attitudes for applying technology in K-12 educational settings (Figure 1-25 on the next page).

STANDARDS FOR STUDENTS ISTE also provides National Educational Technology Standards for Students. These standards are organized in six broad categories: Basic Operations and Concepts; Social, Ethical, and Human Issues; Technology Productivity Tools; Technology Communications Tools; Technology Research Tools; and Technology Problem-Solving and Decision-Making Tools. They also include grade-specific performance indicators for Pre K–2, 3–5, 6–8, and grades 9–12. For information about how to access these standards, see the Web Info on this page.

STANDARDS FOR SCHOOL ADMINISTRATORS ISTE's standards for school administrators also are organized in six broad categories: Leadership and Vision; Learning and Teaching; Productivity and Professional Practice; Support, Management, and Operations; Assessment and Evaluation; and Social, Legal, and Ethical Issues. For information about how to access these standards, see the Web Info on this page.

WEB INFO

For more information about the International Society for Technology in Education (ISTE), visit the Teachers Discovering Computers Web site (*scsite.com/tdc4*), click Chapter 1, click Web Info, and then click ISTE.

WEB INFO

For more information about ISTE's standards for students, teachers, and administrators, visit the Teachers Discovering Computers Web site (*scsite.com/tdc4*), click Chapter 1, click Web Info, and then click Students, Teachers, or Administrators.

ISTE NATIONAL EDUCATIONAL TECHNOLOGY STANDARDS AND PERFORMANCE INDICATORS FOR TEACHERS

All classroom teachers should be prepared to meet the following standards and performance indicators.

I. TECHNOLOGY OPERATIONS AND CONCEPTS
Teachers demonstrate a sound understanding of technology operations and concepts. Teachers:

A. demonstrate introductory knowledge, skills, and understanding of concepts related to technology (as described in the ISTE *National Educational Technology Standards for Students*).

B. demonstrate continual growth in technology knowledge and skills to stay abreast of current and emerging technologies.

II. PLANNING AND DESIGNING LEARNING ENVIRONMENTS AND EXPERIENCES
Teachers plan and design effective learning environments and experiences supported by technology. Teachers:

A. design developmentally appropriate learning opportunities that apply technology-enhanced instructional strategies to support the diverse needs of learners.

B. apply current research on teaching and learning with technology when planning learning environments and experiences.

C. identify and locate technology resources and evaluate them for accuracy and suitability.

D. plan for the management of technology resources within the context of learning activities.

E. plan strategies to manage student learning in a technology-enhanced environment.

III. TEACHING, LEARNING, AND THE CURRICULUM
Teachers implement curriculum plans that include methods and strategies for applying technology to maximize student learning. Teachers:

A. facilitate technology-enhanced experiences that address content standards and student technology standards.

B. use technology to support learner-centered strategies that address the diverse needs of students.

C. apply technology to develop students' higher-order skills and creativity.

D. manage student learning activities in a technology-enhanced environment.

IV. ASSESSMENT AND EVALUATION
Teachers apply technology to facilitate a variety of effective assessment and evaluation strategies. Teachers:

A. apply technology in assessing student learning of subject matter using a variety of assessment techniques.

B. use technology resources to collect and analyze data, interpret results, and communicate findings to improve instructional practice and maximize student learning.

C. apply multiple methods of evaluation to determine students' appropriate use of technology resources for learning, communication, and productivity.

V. PRODUCTIVITY AND PROFESSIONAL PRACTICE
Teachers use technology to enhance their productivity and professional practice. Teachers:

A. use technology resources to engage in ongoing professional development and lifelong learning.

B. continually evaluate and reflect on professional practice to make informed decisions regarding the use of technology in support of student learning.

C. apply technology to increase productivity.

D. use technology to communicate and collaborate with peers, parents, and the larger community in order to nurture student learning.

VI. SOCIAL, ETHICAL, LEGAL, AND HUMAN ISSUES
Teachers understand the social, ethical, legal, and human issues surrounding the use of technology in PK–12 schools and apply that understanding in practice. Teachers:

A. model and teach legal and ethical practice related to technology use.

B. apply technology resources to enable and empower learners with diverse backgrounds, characteristics, and abilities.

C. identify and use technology resources that affirm diversity.

D. promote safe and healthy use of technology resources.

E. facilitate equitable access to technology resources for all students.

Source: International Society for Technology in Education (ISTE)

Figure 1-25 The ISTE technology standards and performance indicators provide a framework for implementing technology in teaching and learning.

An Example of How One School Uses Computers

To illustrate how a typical school might use computers and other computer-based technologies, this section takes you on a visual and narrative tour of a typical day at Ridgedale High School, home of the Fighting Tigers. Ridgedale High School is taking advantage of the Federal Communications Commission's **Education Rate**, or **E-Rate**, program, which is a government initiative designed to provide discounts to schools and libraries on all communications services, including network installation and Internet access.

All of the computers at Ridgedale High School are part of a local area network that allows teachers and students to share information with one another and with others around the world. First, Ridgedale networked the computers in all three of its computer labs. Two of these labs contain 30 PCs and the third lab contains 30 Macintosh computers. The school then installed at least five computers connected with hi-speed access to the Internet in each classroom. Ridgedale High School also maintains a Web site to provide up-to-date information for students, teachers, and parents (Figure 1-26).

As the day starts, students are hurrying down the halls toward their classrooms, trying to reach them before the first period bell rings. For these students, the day is just beginning. For the administrators, teachers, and staff of Ridgedale High School, their day started much earlier.

SUPERINTENDENT

Early this morning, Dr. Helen Hartley, superintendent of Washington County Public School District, reviewed the final touches on the district's Three-Year Technology Plan (Figure 1-27). Dr. Hartley is very interested in the progress of the district's Technology Committee, whose members include administrators, teachers, parents, media specialists, technology coordinators, university professors, and business partners from the community.

Although pleased with the work the committee has accomplished thus far, the superintendent has found that, as more

technology initiatives are launched, the committee's planning meetings are becoming too long (and are hard to fit into the extremely busy schedules of the members). To help with this problem, Dr. Hartley asked the district Webmaster and network specialist, Bob Still, to develop an interactive template for the committee's Web page. Now, all the committee members can access the page with their password and work on their sections of the report.

WEB INFO

For more information about the FCC's E-Rate Universal Service Program for Schools & Libraries, visit the Teachers Discovering Computers Web site (*scsite.com/tdc4*), click Chapter 1, click Web Info, and then click E-Rate.

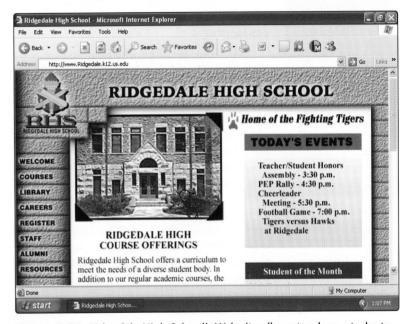

Figure 1-26 Ridgedale High School's Web site allows teachers, students, and parents to have direct access to extensive and up-to-date school-related information.

Figure 1-27 The superintendent discusses with her staff the final touches of the school district's Three-Year Technology Plan. She will use charts and graphs to present the plan at the next school board meeting.

WEB INFO

For more information about national Technology Standards for School Administrators (TSSA), visit the Teachers Discovering Computers Web site (*scsite.com/tdc4*), click Chapter 1, click Web Info, and then click TSSA.

Dr. Hartley has several other items to attend to and people to visit before heading to Ridgedale High School for the 3:30 p.m. Teacher/Student Honors Assembly. Dr. Hartley knows that Ridgedale's new multimedia presentation system, which was purchased with money donated by a local business, should be up and running for the assembly. She is looking forward to seeing it used during the presentation. She plans to arrive early to review the national Technology Standards for School Administrators (TSSA) with the principal of Ridgedale High School.

PRINCIPAL

Mr. Tony Hidalgo, the principal at Ridgedale High School, starts his day by completing several administrative tasks, which he accomplishes by sending various e-mail messages to teachers and staff. He sends an e-mail message to Ms. Jenny Marcus, Ridgedale's technology coordinator, to remind her to test the new presentation system before the Teacher/Student Honors Assembly. Mr. Hidalgo also sends an e-mail message to Dr. Hartley requesting an update on his latest budgeting request for new educational software for the math and science teachers and for new computer software to run the school's security system (Figure 1-28).

He also is interested in the new cross-curriculum digital storytelling writing project that some of his teachers have integrated into their curriculum. He has been doing some research on digital storytelling and so far he is intrigued by, but not convinced of, the significance of the project. However,

his research does say that if students start writing more and enjoy the learning process, then scores will go up. He decides to find out a lot more about digital storytelling.

Before the students arrive, Mr. Hidalgo sends an e-mail message to all teachers and staff reminding them that the Teacher/Student Honors Assembly begins promptly at 3:30 p.m. He also sends a message to Mrs. Acosta requesting more information about her digital storytelling projects. Mr. Hidalgo finishes his early morning administrative tasks in time to walk the halls and greet students arriving for school.

SCHOOL SECRETARY

When she first started at Ridgedale High School, Ms. Clara Rich, the school secretary, spent much of her day answering and routing incoming telephone calls. Several years ago, however, the school board approved the installation of a computerized telephone system that routes calls directly to the appropriate person. Ms. Rich's day now starts in a different manner, as she checks her e-mail and voice mail messages to determine if any teachers are going to be late or absent. If necessary, Ms. Rich accesses the school's teacher database to identify potential substitute teachers.

Next, Ms. Rich uses her PDA to connect to the school's inventory database to check the quantities of certain supplies and confirm delivery of recent purchases (Figure 1-29). Ms. Rich reviews the customized certificates she has created for the Honors Assembly. She is sure the certificates, which she created using her desktop publishing program and the school's color printer, will impress students, teachers, and parents.

Figure 1-28 Mr. Hidalgo is pondering the wording of his important e-mail message to the superintendent.

Figure 1-29 By using various databases, the school secretary can locate potential substitute teachers and manage equipment purchases, inventory, and supplies easily.

TECHNOLOGY COORDINATOR

Ms. Jenny Marcus, technology coordinator, arrives early to attend to several items and browse the Web to locate information on installing new software and testing the new presentation system. Ms. Marcus has several questions about the presentation system that she is unable to find answers for on the company's Web site. By accessing its technical assistance chat room, she is able to talk directly with a technician. The technician promptly answers most of her questions, but several deal with individual decisions that the principal needs to approve before the installation can be completed. Ms. Marcus calls and leaves a message on Mr. Hidalgo's voice mail asking if they can meet in her office at 10:00 a.m. to resolve these details (Figure 1-30).

Figure 1-30 The technology coordinator leaves a voice message for the principal after she has gathered technical information on the new presentation system from the Web.

TEACHERS

Mrs. Acosta understood from the first day she entered her classroom that she had to start incorporating new strategies for her teaching of history — she knew that her digital students were different and that they learn differently than she had learned in school. She decided to start looking into the principles of **community digital storytelling**, which combines basic educational pedagogy with creative writing, oral history, movies, filmmaking, and digital media. Because it is a community-based project, she plans to involve top local citizens in her classroom as guest speakers. She also hopes her students, as they work on their assignments, will add value to other community-based projects. Her

students will be learning about the art of the **transmedia story** — the art of telling stories using various forms of media.

Mrs. Acosta knows that when students find the assignment fun they also are motivated to learn. She also knows that students become active learners when they use digital media (Figure 1-31). Mrs. Acosta plans to start class by showing a video that Mr. Finley obtained through the state's interlibrary loan program. The video shows how history students across the country are telling stories using various forms of digital media.

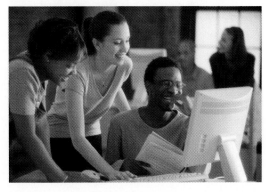

Figure 1-31 Students actively engage in their own learning when teachers integrate digital media and other technologies.

Mr. Dourden Boone is in his classroom preparing for his advanced placement biology class. He is having his students work on their class projects in groups of three. The class is using 10 wireless notebook computers that are part of a 10-station wireless mobile lab that the students call the 10 pack. Each wireless notebook computer is connected without wires to the school's network, providing students with instant and wireless access to the Internet and dozens of educational and productivity software programs.

Mr. Boone has found the new wireless mobile lab easy to use and extremely beneficial both for his instruction and for student learning. Before the wireless lab became available, he had to take his students to a traditional computer lab that was located in a different building on the other side of campus. Now, he simply rolls the lab to his students for use in his classroom, saving valuable instructional and on-task time. The students' first assignment is to visit numerous biology Web sites that Mr. Boone has evaluated for

WEB INFO

For more information and ideas on integrating digital media into your lessons and to learn more about digital storytelling, visit the Teachers Discovering Computer Web site (*scsite.com/tdc4*), click Chapter 1, click Web Info, and then click Digital Storytelling appropriateness and instructional value. Then, each group uses the wireless notebook computers to run experiments, log their research findings, type their findings into a report, and create digital presentations for the class (Figure 1-32). Mr. Boone plans to shares his wireless mobile lab experiences with four other science teachers over lunch. He is confident they will benefit from using the lab as well.

Figure 1-32 Students create projects, experiments, research reports, and papers using a wireless notebook computer.

At the other end of the school, two of the physical education instructors, Mrs. Rita Simpson and Mr. Gary Roberts, are installing and testing video equipment so they can video tape gymnastics routines for personal and class evaluation of performance and techniques. Mr. Roberts, who also is the girls' soccer coach, taped last week's soccer game. He wants to show the soccer team how they can improve for the state finals competition next week.

The school recently received 30 handheld devices and software as the result of a physical education improvement grant (Figure 1-33). A new software program was purchased with money from the grant, too. The software program helps students evaluate their running techniques, cardiovascular activities, and nutritional needs. The software interfaces with their handheld devices so they can enter data in the handheld device regardless of where they are and what activity they are doing. When students are back at their classroom computer, they connect the handheld device and download all the pertinent data to their password-secure folders on the school's network. This way, they can keep track of and analyze the data.

Figure 1-33 Physical education students are downloading personal information into a software program that will monitor and chart their personal fitness.

MEDIA SPECIALIST

Mr. Chris Finley, the media specialist, arrives at school very early because many students need access to media center resources before first period classes begin, for example, some students need resources for their digital storytelling projects. While the students are searching the online catalog for materials, both in their own media center and other centers in the district, Mr. Finley completes his final preparations for Mrs. Acosta's tenth-grade history class.

Mr. Finley and Mrs. Acosta work together to create activities that help students not only learn history and their community, but also sharpen their research skills as they experience learning in a very different way. After confirming that all of the center's computers are up and running, Mr. Finley starts gathering resources for Mrs. Acosta's students, including books, CDs, DVDs, videos, graphics, and other digital media. He also assists students with their research projects. (Figure 1-34).

Figure 1-34 After locating electronic resources, textbooks, and other materials in the school media center, the media specialist works with students on their research projects.

STUDENTS

The biggest excitement every morning is the live broadcast of the *Ridgedale News Show* in the TV Production Lab. Students gain experience in TV production and communications as well as learn what it is like to work in front of and behind the camera. Students form the complete production team, from the camera operator to reporters. Crew members rotate on a weekly basis through each of the broadcast production jobs. This project provides the opportunity for students to learn how to use video outside the studio and bring it into the classroom for each one to share his or her story (Figure 1-35).

Figure 1-35 Prior to doing the live broadcast, students often practice their broadcasting skills using a PC video camera and digital media computer.

Students also are beginning to talk and instant message each other about the new digital storytelling projects that Mrs. Acosta is adding to her history curriculum. Many students are not sure how they feel about the new projects and what all is involved. Fulton Gaffney, the head of the student government, plans to talk to Mrs. Acosta so he can learn more about what media tools he will need for his project. He has lived in Ridgedale all his life. His grandfather often tells stories about the town. Fulton has gathered pictures, audio clips, and video clips of his grandfather's stories. Fulton is glad he is going to use technology to complete his project. He plans to compile his grandfather's stories on CD and he knows his grandfather will certainly be surprised when Fulton presents him with the CD.

Addison Kenny is excited to learn more about digital storytelling and oral histories. Her family has only recently moved to Ridgedale and she wants to learn more about her new town. She is going to have to find materials for her video from the media center and, perhaps, the central library, which has an extensive collection of newspaper clippings. Unlike Fulton's story, hers is not going to be a personal history, so she is going to have to find a new angle.

Becky Tillery has already begun working on her project on her native ancestry. Her ancestors include a line of Native Americans and her story will take on a different perspective, for sure.

PARENT

Using her home computer, Catherine Rosa accesses Ridgedale's Web site to check the time of the Teacher/Student Honors Assembly (Figure 1-36). While she was looking up the time, Catherine notices a new graphic that reads, We Need Your Support! Curious, she clicks the graphic and links to a Web page requesting parent volunteers to chaperone the girls' soccer team on its trip to the state finals. Catherine sends an e-mail message to Mr. Roberts, stating that she gladly will chaperone the trip. Catherine then quickly browses through the state Department of Education Web site to read the latest information released on Ridgedale High School before heading to the school for the assembly. Then, she clicks on the link about the digital storytelling project. Wow, that looks interesting!

Figure 1-36 A parent of a Ridgedale High School student logs on to the school's Web site to find out the start time for a special event.

COMMUNITY

Kevin Lee, a 72-year-old, retired construction worker, starts his day by reading e-mail messages from 16-year-old Brian Johnson, a student at Ridgedale High School (Figure 1-37). Kevin and Brian communicate online regularly as part of a program called Seniors Online. Seniors Online is a school program designed to match students with special needs with senior citizens, who serve as mentors. Each week Kevin, along with 13 other senior citizens, visits the school to work with a student, one on one.

Figure 1-37 A successful program at Ridgedale High School matches senior citizens with students with special needs. In this photo, a retired construction worker is checking his e-mail for a message from his new friend.

The students teach the senior citizens how to use a computer, send and receive e-mail messages, and browse the Web. Their mentors, in turn, help the students understand the challenges and opportunities they likely are going to experience after they graduate from high school. The interaction between the seniors and students with special needs is a remarkable success story. Brian has decided his digital story will be about Mr. Lee's family history. Brian knows Mr. Lee has lived in the community for 72 years and his family for 150 years. Mr. Lee is thrilled to be able to

tell his family's story and so happy to work with Brian!

The students send e-mail messages to their mentors to seek advice or just to share everyday news. For senior citizens such as Kevin, learning to use a computer is a great experience, but working directly with the students is the most rewarding experience of all. Kevin is looking forward to telling the history of his family as a story. He feels this is a great opportunity to pass on his family's history to the next generation. He also knows it will strengthen his connection with Brian.

Using the Textbook Web Site

Each chapter in this textbook contains 11 end-of-chapter sections, all of which are stored either completely or partially as Web pages on the World Wide Web. In addition, the textbook includes eight special features (one follows each chapter) and three appendices; many of these also are located on the textbook Web site. To enhance your learning experience, be sure to view the end-of-chapter materials, special features, and Appendices A and B on the Web, where you will find curriculum-specific information, integration ideas, interactive exercises, and links to thousands of popular educational sites.

In all eight chapters, annotations in the margins, called Web Info, (for example, see page 10), sends you to the textbook Web site, where you will find links to current and additional information about Web Info topics. Also located in the margins are FAQ boxes that consist of frequently asked questions and their answers.

To access the textbook Web site, start your browser and enter the following Web address, *scsite.com/tdc4* (Figure 1-38). To display an end-of-chapter section, click the desired chapter number at the top and then click any of the end-of-chapter sections displayed on the left sidebar; for example, click Chapter 1 and then click Teaching Today (Figure 1-39). The special features located below the end-of-chapter sections may be accessed at anytime. Use the scroll bar to view information on the Web page that is not in the current window (Figure 1-39).

INTERACTING WITH END-OF-CHAPTER MATERIALS

The following sections explain how you can interact in a curriculum-specific way with the resources available in the various end-of-chapter materials. This will help you transition to using the new learning environments described in Figure 1-1 on page 2.

IN BRIEF This section summarizes the chapter materials; you can use these short summaries to prepare for examinations. Click the Audio button at the top and the summaries will be read to you in streaming audio.

KEY TERMS Click any term to see and hear a term definition. Click the Web link to visit a Web page for supplemental information on the term.

CHECKPOINT Use these interactive questions and answers to check your knowledge level of the chapter and to prepare for quizzes and examinations.

TEACHING TODAY This section provides you with an appreciation of the value that technology and the Web have for K-12 education. Each segment contains one or more links that reinforce the information presented in the segment.

EDUCATION ISSUES Education Issues contains several scenarios that allow you to explore controversial and current issues in education; for example, school violence. Click the links for additional information on the issue.

INTEGRATION CORNER This innovative section provides you with extensive ideas and resources for integrating technology into your classroom-specific curriculum. Each chapter provides information on and

chapter links

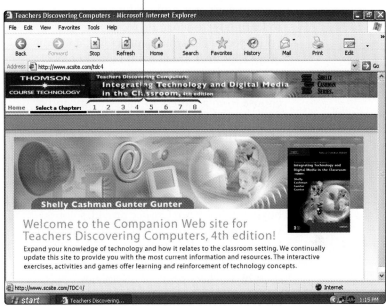

Figure 1-38 The home page of the Teachers Discovering Computers Web site (*scsite.com/tdc4*).

Chapter 1 selected   Teaching Today section displays   scroll bar

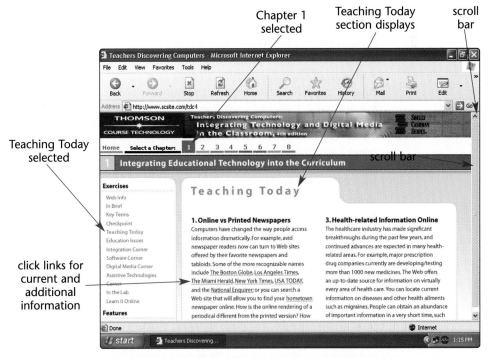

Teaching Today selected

click links for current and additional information

Figure 1-39 Teaching Today end-of-chapter section for Chapter 1 displayed at the textbook Web site. Use the scroll bar to see the additional Teaching Today segments.

links to approximately 100 outstanding educational Web sites organized in the following 12 corners: Early Childhood, Elementary, Middle School, Secondary, Reading/Language Arts, Social Studies/ History, Math, Science, Special Education, Post Secondary, Administrator, and Research. Choose your area and explore the resources to learn how to integrate technology into your specific classroom curriculum and how other educators are integrating technology.

SOFTWARE CORNER Today's educators can choose from a variety of high-quality and often inexpensive educational software programs. You can learn about popular software programs by researching them on the Web and in many cases even download or order a free evaluation copy so you can evaluate a program prior to you or your school buying it. Software Corner provides you with information on and links to additional information and download instructions for dozens of educational software programs used by teachers from all disciplines.

DIGITAL MEDIA CORNER A recurring theme throughout this book emphasizes that today's teachers need to make learning meaningful and relevant to the lives of today's K-12 digital students. This section provides you with videos of selected chapter topics that can be used to supplement your digital lessons. This section also provides you with ideas and examples of how you can use digital media to enhance your teaching and your students' learning.

ASSISTIVE TECHNOLOGIES CORNER This section provides important information on current hardware, software, and peripherals that will assist you in delivering instruction to students with physical, cognitive, or sensory disabilities. Links and extensive additional information, strategies, ideas, and more are available at the textbook Web site.

IN THE LAB These exercises are divided into two areas: productivity and integration. Use the productivity exercises to improve your software-specific skills in using word processing, spreadsheet, database, desktop publishing, curriculum and Web page development, as well as other productivity software programs. Use the integration ideas for incorporating these programs into your

specific classroom curriculum. Click the links for tutorials, productivity ideas, integration examples and ideas, and more.

LEARN IT ONLINE These exercises allow you to improve your computer and integration skills by learning exciting new skills online. This section includes interactive lab exercises, software tutorials, scavenger hunts, practice tests, learning games, and much more.

Timeline — Milestones in Computer History

At the end of Chapter 1 is an interactive, colorful, and highly informative multipage timeline of the history of computers from 1937 to the present. This entire special feature also is stored as Web pages at the textbook Web site. The timeline contains dozens of links to extensive supplemental information, including historical audio segments from National Public Radio, animations, videos, and much more.

To display this interactive special feature, click Timeline on the left sidebar at the textbook Web site (Figure 1-38). All of the graphics and pictures contain links to the Web. Explore the special feature with your mouse; to access the interactive links, click when your mouse pointer changes to a hand.

Summary of Introduction to Integrating Technology in Education

This chapter presented a broad introduction to concepts and terminology related to computers and computers in education. You now have a basic understanding of what a computer is and how it processes data into information. You were introduced to digital media and how today's digital students learn. You also have seen some examples of how computers are being used in K-12 schools and integrated into classroom settings. You should be starting to formulate your own strategies to teach your digital students. Reading and learning the concepts in this chapter will help you understand these topics as they are presented in more detail in future chapters.

In Brief

INSTRUCTIONS: In Brief summarizes the concepts presented in this chapter. To listen to the audio version of this In Brief, visit scsite.com/tdc4. Click Chapter 1 at the top of the Web page and then click In Brief on the left sidebar.

1. Personal Computers

A **personal computer**, or **PC**, is a computer designed for use by one person at a time. Macintosh computers and PCs are the two primary types of personal computers used in schools, businesses, and homes. Apple Computer manufactures Macintosh computers; several companies manufacture PCs.

2. Computer, Information, and Integration Literacy

As the world of computers advances, it is essential that you gain some level of **computer literacy**; that is, you should have a knowledge and understanding of computers and their uses. Information literacy means knowing how to find, analyze, and use information. In addition, teachers must know how to integrate technology into K-12 curriculum, or integration literacy. Integration literacy is the ability to use computers and other technologies combined with a variety of teaching and learning strategies to enhance students' learning of required basic skills.

3. Computers, Data, Information, and Processing

A **computer** is an electronic machine, operating under the control of instructions stored in its own memory, that can accept data (input), manipulate the data according to specified rules (process), produce results (output), and store the results for future use. **Data** is a collection of unorganized facts, which can include words, numbers, pictures, and sounds. **Information** is data that is organized, has meaning, and is useful, such as a report, graphic, newsletter, invoice, check, video, or photograph. **Processing** is the activity of organizing data into information. Computers perform four basic operations: input, process, output, and storage. Computer professionals often refer to these four operations as the **information processing cycle** because a computer performs these actions repeatedly while the computer is running.

4. Digital Media, Digital Students, and the ARCS Motivational Model

Digital media is defined as those technologies that allow users to create new forms of interaction, expression, communication, and entertainment in a digital format. **Digital students** are (1) hypercommunicators who use multiple tools to communicate, (2) multitaskers who do several things at once with ease, and (3) goal oriented as they pursue multiple goals at the same time. The **ARCS Motivational Model** was developed in 1983 by John Keller and is applicable to learning in the digital age. Keller stressed that even the best designed instructional strategy will fail if students are not motivated to learn.

5. Computer Power

A computer derives its power from its capability of performing the information processing cycle (input, process, output, storage) with speed, reliability, and accuracy; its capacity to store large amounts of data and information; and its capability of communicating with other computers.

6. Computer Software

Software, also called a **computer program** or simply a **program**, is a series of instructions that tells the hardware of a computer what to do. System software and application software are the two main categories of software. **System software** consists of programs that control the operations of a computer and its devices. **Application software** consists of programs designed to perform a specific task for a user.

In Brief

7. Networks

A **network** is a collection of computers and devices connected together via communications media and devices such as cables, telephone lines, modems, or other means. Businesses and schools network their computers so users can share **resources**, such as hardware devices, software programs, data, and information. Sharing resources saves time and money.

8. The Internet

The world's largest network is the **Internet**, which is a worldwide collection of networks that links together millions of businesses, the government, educational institutions, and individuals. Millions of people use the Internet to gain information, send messages, and obtain products or services. The **World Wide Web**, or **Web**, portion of the Internet consists of computer sites, called Web sites that can be accessed electronically for information on thousands of topics.

9. Computer Technology and Education

When used appropriately, technology has the potential to enhance students' achievement and assist them in meeting learning objectives. Networked computers allow communications beyond classroom walls, thus enabling schools and communities to provide an environment for cooperative learning, development of high-order thinking skills, and solving of complex problems. Computers can provide unique, effective, and powerful opportunities for many different types of instruction and learning. Several leading national and international organizations, including the **International Society for Technology in Education (ISTE)** support education and educators in the use of technology.

Key Terms

INSTRUCTIONS: Use the Key Terms to help focus your study of the terms used in this chapter. To further enhance your understanding of the Key Terms in this chapter, visit scsite.com/tdc4. Click Chapter 1 at the top of the Web page and then click Key Terms on the left sidebar. Read the definition for each term and then access current and additional information about the term from the Web.

adaptive technology [40]
age of convergence [5]
ARCS Motivational Model [8]
application software [16]
assistive technology [40]

community digital storytelling [25]
computer [4]
computer literacy [4]
computer program [15]
computer programmer [18]
curriculum-specific learning [2]
custom software [18]

data [4]
desktop computers [11]
digital generation [7]
digital kids [7]
digital media [6]
digital students [7]
discipline-specific learning [2]

Education Rate (E-Rate) [23]
electronic mail [14]
e-mail [14]
embedded computer [13]
execute [15]

freeware [18]

graphical user interface (GUI) [16]

handheld computer [12]
hardware [4]

icon [16]
information [4]
information literacy [4]
information processing cycle [4]
input [4]
install [15]
integration literacy [4]
International Society for Technology in Education (ISTE) [21]
Internet [19]
Internet-enabled [12]

local area network (LAN) [19]

Macintosh computer [10]
Mac OS [15]
Microsoft Windows [15]
mobile computer [11]
mobile device [11]

National Council for Accreditation for Teacher Education (NCATE) [21]
National Educational Technology Standards for Teachers (NETS-T) [21]
network [14]
notebook computer [11]

operating system [15]
output [4]

packaged software [18]
PDA [12]
personal computer (PC) [10]
personal digital assistant (PDA) [12]
program [15]
programmer [18]
public-domain software [18]

resources [19]

server [13]
shareware [18]
smart phone [12]
smart watch [13]
software [4]
software suite [17]
storage [4]
supercomputer [13]
system software [15]
systems analyst [18]

Tablet PC [12]
transmedia story [25]

user interface [15]
utility program [16]

Web [20]
wide area network (WAN) [19]
World Wide Web [20]

Checkpoint

INSTRUCTIONS: Use the Checkpoint excercises to check your knowledge level of the chapter. To complete the Checkpoint exercises interactively, visit scsite.com/tdc4. Click Chapter 1 at the top of the Web page and then click Checkpoint on the left sidebar.

1. Label the Figure

Instructions: Identify each element of a digital media system by placing the correct label on the numbered lines.

2. Matching

Instructions: Match each term from the column on the left with the best description from the column on the right.

____ 1. software
____ 2. digital students
____ 3. input
____ 4. digital media
____ 5. information

  a. data that is organized has meaning and is useful, such as a report, a newsletter, a receipt, a picture, an invoice, or a check
  b. data entered into a computer
  c. allows users to create new forms of interaction
  d. hypercommunicators, multitaskers, and goal oriented
  e. a series of instructions that tells the hardware how to perform tasks

3. Short Answer

Instructions: Write a brief answer to each of the following questions.

1. What is the difference between computer literacy, information literacy, and integration literacy? _____
2. Define digital students. Why are they different from previous generations of students? _____
3. What capabilities make a computer a powerful tool? Describe each. How does a computer's ability to communicate enhance a computer's power? _____
4. What is the ARCS Motivational Model? What are the four categories of the ARCS Motivational Model? _____
5. Briefly summarize why computers should be used in K-12 schools. _____

Teaching Today

INSTRUCTIONS: Teaching Today provides an appreciation of the value that technology and the Web have for K-12 education. Each numbered segment contains one or more links that reinforce the information presented in the segment. To display this page from the Web, visit scsite.com/tdc4. Click Chapter 1 at the top of the Web page and then click Teaching Today on the left sidebar.

1. Online vs Printed Newspapers

Computers have changed the way people access information dramatically. For example, avid newspaper readers now can turn to Web sites offered by their favorite newspapers and tabloids. Some of the more recognizable names include *The Boston Globe*, *Los Angeles Times*, *The Miami Herald*, *New York Times*, *USA TODAY*, and the *National Enquirer*; or you can search a Web site that will allow you to find your hometown newspaper online. How is the online rendering of a periodical different from the printed version? How are they similar? What are the advantages and disadvantages of each? Do you see a use for these online newspaper resources in your classroom? Why?

2. Online Bookstores

As the automobile led to the end of the horse and buggy, will the growth of the Internet lead to the demise of printed media? Probably not; in fact, booksellers are turning to the Internet to promote their products. Many online bookstores sell books, videos, and games. Some of these are Amazon.com, Barnes & Noble College Bookstores, and Books-A-Million, or you can visit a bookstore directory that links and describes dozens of top bookstore sites and book publishers. Visit a bookstore Web site and compare searching for a book online with finding a book in a traditional bookstore. Try looking for a particular title, a book by a certain author, and books on a specific subject. What are the advantages and disadvantages of shopping for a book online? How likely would you be to buy a book through a bookstore Web site? Why?

3. Health-related Information Online

The healthcare industry has made significant breakthroughs during the past few years, and continued advances are expected in many health-related areas. For example, major prescription drug companies currently are developing/testing more than 1000 new medicines. The Web offers an up-to-date source for information on virtually every area of health care. You can locate current information on diseases and other health ailments such as migraines. People can obtain an abundance of important information in a very short time, such as the latest treatment options. Visit the following medical site and research one specific area of health care that is of personal importance to you.

4. Instant Messaging and Class Assignments

You are a middle school teacher with numerous computers in your classroom. You keep catching your students spending class time receiving and answering instant messages (IM) instead of working on class assignments. Your students say that the IMs are a great way to keep in touch with friends and ask questions about class work. To them, instant messaging is totally cool! Should you allow your students to use instant messaging during class time? Is this a misuse of class time? If you think that it is a misuse of class time, what can you do to manage the sending and receiving of IMs in your class?

Education Issues

INSTRUCTIONS: Education Issues provides several scenarios that allow you to explore controversial and current issues in education. Each numbered segment contains one or more links that reinforce the information presented in the segment. To display this page from the Web, visit scsite.com/tdc4. Click Chapter 1 at the top of the Web page and then click Education Issues on the left sidebar.

1. School Violence

Numerous polls have shown that school safety is now the number-one concern of both parents and teachers. National leaders are calling the increase in school violence a national crisis. What are some of the causes of school violence? Do you agree that school violence should be the main concern of parents? One popular answer to the dramatic increase in the incidences of school violence is to build protective nets around the nation's schools, including fences, metal detectors, high-tech video surveillance, body searches, and armed guards. Do you agree with this solution? Other political and educational leaders stress that turning schools into armed camps is not the solution. Instead, schools and communities must address and attempt to find solutions for the causes of school violence. Do you agree with this solution? What would you suggest to reduce the incidences of school violence?

2. Possible Child Abuse

During your student internship, you notice that 9-year-old Juan Gonzales has bruises all over his arms and legs. He has been one of your more inquisitive students, but lately you have noticed that he has become moody, seems uninterested in class, and his grades are falling. The school nurse casually informs you that she has noticed that Juan has been losing weight the past couple of months. You suspect that Juan may be a victim of child abuse. You ask your supervising teacher what you should do and she says, "Oh! He is the son of a member of the school board; I am sure he is just growing and is at a clumsy age." You really like the school and would like to work there after graduation. Do you tell someone or do you ignore it? If so, who do you tell? What else could you do?

3. Reality or Fantasy

The space shuttle was first flown in July 1969 and landed on the moon that same year. An ingredient in many popular shampoos has been proven to cause cancer. It is illegal to contact space aliens. None of these statements is true, but each appeared on the Web. In today's society, some people, especially young students, think that anything in print is true, and the Web adds to that because anyone can publish anything on a Web page. Authors with a wide range of expertise, authority, and biases create Web pages. Web pages can be as accurate as the most scholarly journal or no truer than some articles in supermarket tabloids. Ultimately, who is responsible for the accuracy of information on the Web? Why? How can you verify information on the Web? How would you teach your students to make sure information is accurate?

4. Possible Cheating

Today, students come to class with cellular telephones, graphing calculators, pagers, personal digital assistants (PDAs), notebook computers, and other devices. During a test, you notice that a student is using a cell phone. As you approach the student, you realize that the student is looking at a smart phone with a picture on the screen. The student puts away the phone and apologizes, indicating that he had forgotten to turn off the phone when a call came in. After class, another student informs you that the student you caught with the phone was making calls to another student in the classroom, and they were taking pictures of the equations. This student was almost positive the two students were cheating by sending each other pictures of the answers over their smart phones. What should you do? How are you going to handle this situation? Does a way to gather proof exist? What next? Should telephones of any kind be banned in classrooms? If so, how? Explain.

Integration Corner

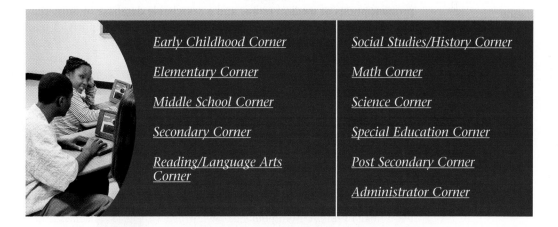

INSTRUCTIONS: Integration Corner provides extensive ideas and resources for integrating technology into your classroom-specific curriculum. To display this page from the Web and its links to approximately 100 educational Web sites, visit scsite.com/tdc4. Click Chapter 1 at the top of the Web page and then click Integration Corner on the left sidebar.

Integration Corner is designed for teachers and other educators who are looking for innovative ways to integrate technology into their content-specific curriculum. Integration Corner not only provides great Web sites with current information, but also shows what other educators are doing in the field of educational technology. Integration Corner is designed for all educators regardless of their interests. Expand your resources by reviewing information and sites outside of your teaching area because many great integration ideas in one area can be modified easily for use in other curriculum areas.

Teachers and administrators will find other colleagues in their areas with whom to connect and share the successes and hurdles of integrating technology in a classroom or an entire school system. Consider Integration Corner your one stop for integration ideas and resources. Links to educational Web sites are organized in the following 12 Corners, and different Web resources are available for each chapter. Figure 1-40 shows examples of the Web resources provided in the Chapter 1 Early Childhood Corner.

Early Childhood Corner

Elementary Corner

Middle School Corner

Secondary Corner

Reading/Language Arts Corner

Social Studies/History Corner

Math Corner

Science Corner

Special Education Corner

Post Secondary Corner

Administrator Corner

Figure 1-40 Examples of the Web resources provided in the Chapter 1 Early Childhood Corner.

Software Corner

INSTRUCTIONS: Software Corner provides information on popular software programs. Each numbered segment discusses specific software programs and contains a link to additional information about these programs. To display this page from the Web, visit scsite.com/tdc4. Click Chapter 1 at the top of the Web page and then click Software Corner on the left sidebar.

1. Kid Pix

Kid Pix is a suite of creativity programs for students from kindergarten through eighth grade. This program allows students to express themselves using electronic drawing and art tools to create pictures, illustrate their own stories, and unleash their natural creative desires. All sound effects are realistic, making this program exciting for students to use. Storybooks, projects, and movies are included with the package for use when creating multimedia projects. Two interesting features of this software are voice painting and photo editing. Kid Pix is a valuable resource for student expression through art.

2. BodyWorks

BodyWorks, from Borderbund, is a visual and textual classroom reference software of the human body. Included with BodyWorks are video lectures, high-resolution images, and thousands of audio pronunciations of medical terms, and a searchable database of more than 400,000 words with useful information for classroom lectures, presentations, and reports. A teacher's guide also is available for this intermediate and secondary science program.

3. Quarter Mile

Quarter Mile is useful in assisting students to learn math skills from basic math facts to difficult skills such as integers, converting percents and fractions, and advanced equations. Quarter Mile is a super remediation program for the exceptional student classroom as well as a great skills practice program for the regular classroom at all educational levels. What makes this program interesting for students is that they race against their own time, allowing them to see their own progress.

4. Timeliner

Timeliner allows teachers and students to create, print, and illustrate timelines using pictures or text with ease for any time period. Timeliner can be used at the elementary level by having students create timelines of their life using personal events to help them gain an understanding of the concept of time and sequence of important events. Elementary teachers can use this program to teach the concept of decade, century, millennium, and more. At the middle and high school levels, Timeliner can be used to show historical progress of specific time periods, chart world-changing occurrences and causes of important events, or even illustrate the different stages of a novel, like *The Red Badge of Courage*.

5. Making the Grade

If you need assistance with classroom record keeping and planning, then Making the Grade is for you. Making the Grade allows teachers to manage and track student grades and academic performance as well as keep attendance and plan seating charts. Teachers can drop grades, apply grading curves, customize a grading scale, and make necessary changes to student records with ease. Making the Grade provides teachers the ability to create charts, export data to word processing, database, or spreadsheet programs and print detailed reports for student and parent conferences.

Digital Media Corner

INSTRUCTIONS: Today's K-12 digital students need their learning to be meaningful and relevant to their lives. Digital Media Corner provides videos, ideas, and examples of how you can use digital media to enhance your teaching and your students' learning. To access the videos and links to additional information, visit scsite.com/tdc4. Click Chapter 1 at the top of the Web page and then click Digital Media on the left sidebar.

1. At the Movies — Walking the PC Pioneer Trail

Many of the pioneers of the technology industry in the United States established their businesses in the Silicon Valley. If you ever wondered how it got started, who created what in whose garage, and why Silicon Valley, click the G4TechTV video link and watch a fun video on Walking the PC Pioneer Trail. Locate the video and click the corresponding High-Speed or Dial-up link, depending on your Internet connection.

2. At the Movies — E-Mail Basics

Do you send and receive thousands of e-mails each year? Do you waste time because nobody ever taught you e-mail basics? To learn many techniques to help you save time while working with e-mail messages, click the G4TechTV video link. Locate the E-mail Basics video and click the corresponding High-Speed or Dial-up link, depending on your Internet connection.

3. At the Movies — Essential Dorm Room Gadgets

As a rule, most college students have little, if any, disposable income. Some great and affordable gadgets are available that can make a dorm room more functional for study and more fun too! To learn more about dorm room gadgets, click the G4TechTV video link. Locate your video and click the corresponding High-Speed or Dial-up link, depending on your Internet connection.

4. United Streaming

Video can be a key component of digital media. Video, when used appropriately in your lessons, can help students think for themselves. But before video can be viewed, it has to get to students first. Until recently, this has been a daunting task for teachers, but not anymore. United Streaming allows teachers and students to access over 40,000 educational video content clips and 4000 full video titles from The Discovery School easily. United Streaming has a huge server network that soaks up most of the work to download or stream video media. As a result, over 20,000,000 students and teachers from more than 43,000 schools can digitally enhance their lessons, group activities and projects, and much more. Click the United Streaming link to learn more.

5. Edutainment in Action in Education

A key component to the effectiveness of using digital media is the term *edutainment*, more specifically, using the attractive qualities and aesthetics of entertainment media for learning purposes. The essence of edutainment as well as entertainment and traditional literature is, was, and always will be identifying with the story. This book highlights how, why, and where implementing the benefits of digital storytelling can benefit your students' education and your lesson planning — everybody wins! If you need more information on edutainment, click the Edutainment in Action in Education link to learn more. After all, edutaining the youth of today about the invaluable information of the past by using the technologies of tomorrow and beyond is the future of education.

Assistive Technologies Corner

INSTRUCTIONS: Assistive Technologies Corner provides information on current hardware, software, and peripherals that will assist you in delivering instruction to students with physical, cognitive, or sensory challenges. To access extensive additional information, visit scsite.com/tdc4. Click Chapter 1 at the top of the Web page and then click Assistive Technologies on the left sidebar.

1. What is Assistive/Adaptive Technology?

Some people find operating a computer difficult, perhaps impossible because of some physical, cognitive, or sensory disability. Applied to computers, the term **assistive/adaptive technology** refers to any equipment, modification, or accommodation that can improve a person's capacity to learn, to communicate, to solve a problem, or to complete a task through the use of a computer.

2. Why Learn About Assistive Technologies?

The U.S. Census Bureau reports 7% of boys and 4% of girls ages 5 to 15 have some form of disability. An awareness of assistive/adaptive technology is valuable to each teacher committed to providing new learning environments in the classroom. New technologies designed for specific disabilities benefit those who need them, but anyone, at any time, may be in need of such technology as a result of injury or accident. In addition, as the population ages, more users of any technology will require some specialized accommodations in using that technology.

For a student with special needs, a learning environment without assistive/adaptive technology does not meet the requirements of the Individuals with Disabilities Education Act (IDEA). IDEA is a nondiscrimination law requiring schools to accommodate the needs of children with disabilities to provide them an equal opportunity to participate in and benefit from the general education curriculum. In the area of technology, the law specifies that computers be accessible to students who use them. In K-12 schools, students with disabilities often have an Individualized Educational Program (IEP). The program may specify that some assistive/adaptive technology be used in the student's learning environment. Teachers are often called upon for advice, or to locate, or to make recommendations for purchase of special technology. As you explore each chapter's Assistive Technologies Corner, you will gain extensive knowledge that will allow your students with disabilities to be all they can be and learn all they can.

3. Do Microsoft and Apple Operating Systems Have Built-In Accessibility Features?

In response to the many computer users who need some accommodation to use a computer, Apple and Microsoft provide accessibility features and assistance at their Web sites as well as built-in accessibility features in their operating systems. These features allow users to customize their computers to meet their needs for computer input and output.

Built-in accessibility features for Windows XP are controlled through the Accessibility Wizard. To access the Accessibility Wizard, click the Start button, point to All Programs, point to Accessories, point to Accessibility, and then click Accessibility Wizard. The Wizard will guide you through accessibility features for persons with visual difficulties, hearing problems, and special physical needs.

The Macintosh OS X System Preferences panel provides the Universal Access feature. To access this feature, click the Apple menu and then click System Preferences. When the System Preferences window displays, click the Universal Access icon. In the Universal Access panel, you will find setup instructions for zooming text, visual alerts, and keyboard and mouse modifications.

Universal Access

Follow the Web instructions at the top of this page to display additional information and this chapter's links on assistive technologies, including alternative input devices and other accessibility features.

In the Lab

INSTRUCTIONS: In the Lab provides word processing exercises that are divided into two areas, productivity and integration. To access the links to tutorials, productivity ideas, integration examples and ideas, and more, visit scsite.com/tdc4. Click Chapter 1 at the top of the Web page and then click In the Lab on the left sidebar.

PRODUCTIVITY IN THE CLASSROOM

INSTRUCTIONS: Word processing skills are essential for both teachers and students. Improving your word processing skills will save you time and energy! Many powerful word processing software applications are available today. In addition, many of the major word processing applications have online tutorials. These tutorials can provide fast and easy access to learning new skills such as setting page margins, inserting a graphic, and changing the font, font color, and font size. To learn new word processing skills or improve your current skills, click the following links: Microsoft Word, Appleworks, Microsoft Works, and Corel WordPerfect.

1. Creating and Formatting a School Activity Flyer

Problem: As the seventh-grade class trip sponsor, you need to create a flyer to notify parents and students of an upcoming informational meeting. Open your word processing software and create a new flyer as described in the following steps. Use the flyer shown in Figure 1-41 on the next page as an example. (*Hint:* if you do not have the suggested font, use any appropriate font.)

Instructions: Perform the following tasks.

1. Select a class trip destination/title for the project. Display the title in the first heading line centered in 36-point, Comic Sans MS font.
2. Select a school name and display the second heading line centered in 22-point, Arial Narrow, bold font.
3. Choose an appropriate picture, image, or clip-art graphic and insert it centered on the page.
4. Describe the field trip in three lines of text. Display the text in 14-point, Times or Times New Roman font.
5. Create a bulleted list that provides specific information about the meeting. Display the bulleted list with a one-half-inch margin in 12-point, Arial, bold font. Display a portion of each bulleted phrase in orange.
6. Provide contact information at the bottom of the flyer (your name, e-mail address, and current date). Display the information in 14-point, Times or Times New Roman, blue font.
7. Save the document to the location of your choice with a name of your choice. Print the document and then follow your instructor's directions for submitting the assignment.

2. Creating and Formatting a Band Fund-Raiser Flyer

Problem: As the band teacher, you need to create a flyer advertising the fall fund-raiser. Open your word processing software and create a new flyer as described in the following instructions. (*Hint:* if you do not have the suggested font, use any appropriate font.)

Instructions: Display the first heading line in 30-point, Lucinda Sans font. Insert an appropriate picture, image, or clip-art graphic centered on the page. Enter a second heading line below the image in 22-point, Verdana, red font. Next enter four lines of text describing the purpose of the fall fund-raiser in 16-point, Times or Times New Roman font. Create a bulleted list with a one and a half-inch margin in 14-point, Times or Times New Roman font listing the dates, items to be sold, and place of the fund-raising event. Enter a closing phrase following the bulleted list in 18-point, Verdana, blue font. Finally, enter two lines of contact information in 12-point, Times or Times New Roman font that includes the current date, your name, and e-mail address. Display the entire document in bold.

In the Lab

7th Grade Sea Camp Trip

Indian Trails Middle School

The 7th grade class at Indian Trails Middle School has the opportunity to attend Sea Camp April 21 through April 23. This is an exciting educational opportunity! Please join us at the informational meeting to learn more.

- ❖ November 19 - **Join us at 7:00 p.m. in the Media Center**
- ❖ Slide Show - **Watch an informational slide show about Sea Camp**
- ❖ Application Packet - **Packets will be available for distribution**

For more information, please contact:
Mr. Mark Allman
m_allman@ssms.k12.ca.us
November 5, 2007

Figure 1-41

In the Lab

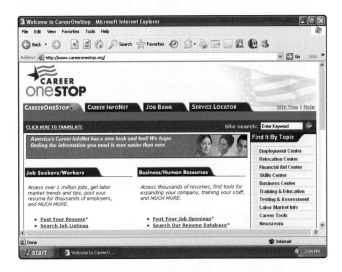

After you have typed and formatted the document, save the document to the location of your choice with a filename of your choice. Print the document and then follow your instructor's directions for submitting the assignment.

3. Creating and Formatting an Announcement Flyer

Problem: You have been asked to create a flyer announcing the upcoming school play.

Instructions: Create a document similar to the flyer illustrated in Figure 1-41. Use appropriate fonts styles, font sizes, font colors, and images. Include the current date, your name, and e-mail address on the bottom of the flyer. After you have typed and formatted the document, save the document to the location of your choice using an appropriate filename. Print the document and then follow your instructor's directions for submitting the assignment.

INTEGRATION IN THE CLASSROOM

1. Your class is studying geometric shapes in architecture. Students will locate pictures of buildings and identify at least three geometric shapes. They will create a flyer that contains the following information: a heading line, an image of the building, a few lines explaining what they found, and a bulleted list with the three different geometric shapes. Create a flyer to use as an example for your students. Include two final lines listing the current date, your name, and school name.

2. Your students are studying various careers. They conduct research on the Internet and gather information about pay scales, educational requirements, and other benefits of their chosen profession. The students then prepare a flyer to share their information with the class. Create a flyer to present as an example for your students. Use appropriate font styles, font sizes, font colors, and images. Include the current date, your name, and e-mail address on the bottom of the flyer.

3. You are teaching your elementary students about famous painters, including Vincent van Gogh, Pablo Picasso, Henri Matisse, Leonardo da Vinci, and Claude Monet. The students work in groups and select their favorite artist. They create a flyer about the life and work of their favorite artist. Create a flyer to present as an example for your students. Use appropriate font styles, sizes, colors, and images. Include the current date, your name, and e-mail address on the bottom of the flyer.

Learn It Online

INSTRUCTIONS: Use the Learn It Online exercises to reinforce your understanding of the chapter concepts and increase your computer, information, and integration literacy. To access dozens of interactive student labs, practice tests, learning games, and more, visit scsite.com/tdc4. Click Chapter 1 at the top of the Web page and then click Learn It Online on the left sidebar.

1. Student Edition Labs — Using Windows, Installing and Uninstalling Software, Managing Files and Folders, Backing Up Your Computer

For the labs to work properly, you must have your screen resolution set to 1024×768 or higher. For a short tutorial on how to change your screen resolution, click here. You also will need Flash 7.0 or higher. To download the latest version of Flash, click here. To view these interactive labs, click the Student Edition Labs link. When the Student Edition Labs menu appears, click the desired or the assigned lab to begin. A new browser window will open. Follow the on-screen instructions to complete the lab. When finished, click the Exit button. If required, submit your results to your instructor.

2. Improving Mouse Skills on a Macintosh or PC

Both Macintosh and PC operating systems include simple games, such as Jigsaw Puzzle or Solitaire, which are designed to help users learn mouse skills. Click the Improving Mouse Skills on a Macintosh or PC link and complete the exercise.

3. Introduction to Macintosh and PCs

Many software packages provide an introductory tour that offers an overview of the program. These tours usually cover any new features and provide tips on using software; many even use digital media enhancements. To learn more about taking an introductory tour of your personal computer operating system, click the Introduction to Macintosh and PCs link and complete the exercise that follows.

4. Practice Test

Click the Practice Test link. Answer each question. When completed, enter your name and click the Grade Test button to submit the quiz for grading. Make a note of any missed questions. If required, submit your score to your instructor.

5. Who Wants to Be a Computer Genius?

Click the Computer Genius link to find out if you are a computer genius. Directions about how to play the game will be displayed. When you are ready to play, click the Play button. If required, submit your score to your instructor.

6. Wheel of Terms

Click the Wheels of Terms link to reinforce important terms you learned in this chapter by playing the Shelly Cashman Series version of this popular game. Directions about how to play the game will be displayed. When you are ready to play, click the Play button. If required, submit your score to your instructor.

7. Crossword Puzzle Challenge

Click the Crossword Puzzle link. Complete the puzzle to reinforce skills you learned in this chapter. Directions about how to play the game will be displayed. When you are ready to play, click the Play button. If required, submit the completed puzzle to your instructor.

Instructions: To display this interactive special feature, click Timeline on the left sidebar on the textbook Web site. All of the graphics and pictures contain links to the World Wide Web. Explore the Milestones in Computer History with your mouse; to access the interactive links, click when your mouse pointer changes to a hand.

Milestones in Computer History

Timeline

937 (1937)

Dr. John V. Atanasoff and Clifford Berry design and build the first electronic digital computer. Their machine, the Atanasoff-Berry-Computer, or ABC, provides the foundation for advances in electronic digital computers.

1946

Dr. John W. Mauchly and J. Presper Eckert, Jr. complete work on the first large-scale electronic, general-purpose digital computer. The ENIAC (Electronic Numerical Integrator And Computer) weighs 30 tons, contains 18,000 vacuum tubes, occupies a 30-by-50-foot space, and consumes 160 kilowatts of power. The first time it is turned on, lights dim in an entire section of Philadelphia.

1943

During World War II, British scientist Alan Turing designs the Colossus, an electronic computer created for the military to break German codes. The computer's existence is kept secret until the 1970s.

1945

Dr. John von Neumann writes a brilliant paper describing the stored program concept. His breakthrough idea, in which memory holds both data and stored programs, lays the foundation for all digital computers that have since been built.

1951 The first commercially available electronic digital computer, the UNIVAC I (UNIVersal Automatic Computer), is introduced by Remington Rand. Public awareness of computers increases when the UNIVAC I, after analyzing only 5 percent of the popular vote, correctly predicts that Dwight D. Eisenhower will win the presidential election.

The IBM 305 RAMAC system is the first to use magnetic disks for external storage. The system provides storage capacity similar to magnetic tape that previously was used, but offers the advantage of semi-random access capability.

1957

1947 William Shockley, John Bardeen, and Walter Brattain invent the transfer resistance device, eventually called the transistor. The transistor would revolutionize computers, proving much more reliable than vacuum tubes.

1953 The IBM model 650 is one of the first widely used computer systems. Originally planning to produce only 50 machines, the system is so successful that eventually IBM manufactures more than 1000. With the IBM 700 series of machines, the company will dominate the mainframe market for the next decade.

FORTRAN (FORmula TRANslation), an efficient, easy-to-use programming language, is introduced by John Backus.

1952

Dr. Grace Hopper considers the concept of reusable software in her paper, "The Education of a Computer." The paper describes how to program a computer with symbolic notation instead of the detailed machine language that had been used.

Core memory, developed in the early 1950s, provides much larger storage capacity than vacuum tube memory.

Dr. John Kemeny of Dartmouth leads the development of the BASIC programming language. BASIC will be widely used on personal computers.

Computers built with transistors mark the beginning of the second generation of computer hardware.

COBOL, a high-level business application language, is developed by a committee headed by Dr. Grace Hopper. COBOL uses English-like phrases and runs on most business computers, making it one of the more widely used programming languages.

Digital Equipment Corporation (DEC) introduces the first mini-computer, the PDP-8. The machine is used extensively as an interface for time-sharing systems.

1958

1960

1965

1964

1959

1968

More than 200 programming languages have been created.

IBM introduces two smaller, desk-sized computers: the IBM 1401 for business and the IBM 1602 for scientists. The IBM 1602 initially is called the CADET, but IBM drops the name when campus wags claim it is an acronym for Can't Add, Doesn't Even Try.

The number of computers has grown to 18,000.

Third-generation computers, with their controlling circuitry stored on chips, are introduced. The IBM System/360 computer is the first family of compatible machines, merging science and business lines.

Alan Shugart at IBM demonstrates the first regular use of an 8-inch floppy (magnetic storage) disk.

In a letter to the editor titled, "GO TO Statements Considered Harmful," Dr. Edsger Dijsktra introduces the concept of structured programming, developing standards for constructing computer programs.

Computer Science Corporation becomes the first software company listed on the New York Stock Exchange.

CSC STOCK PRICE NYSE/COMPOSITE Corrected Data for Dividends			
DATE	PRICE	HIGH	LO
1/02/68	2.83	2.97	2
1/03/68	2.60	2.81	2
1/04/68	2.61	2.62	2
1/05/68			
1/08/68	2.54	2.60	
1/09/68	2.55	2.60	
1/10/68	2.46		
		.51	30,100
			13,500
		.48	23,400
		.49	7,800
		.50	18,800

IBM

Under pressure from the industry, IBM announces that some of its software will be priced separately from the computer hardware. This unbundling allows software firms to emerge in the industry.

The ARPANET network, a predecessor of the Internet, is established.

Dr. Ted Hoff of Intel Corporation develops a microprocessor, or microprogrammable computer chip, the Intel 4004.

1971

1969

1970

Fourth-generation computers, built with chips that use LSI (large-scale integration) arrive. Whereas the chips used in 1965 contained as many as 1000 circuits, the LSI chip contains as many as 15,000.

1975

MITS, Inc., advertises the first microcomputer, the Altair. Named for the destination in an episode of *Star Trek*, the Altair is sold in kits for less than $400. Although initially it has no keyboard, no monitor, no permanent memory, and no software, 4000 orders are taken within the first three months.

1976

Steve Wozniak and Steve Jobs build the first Apple computer. A subsequent version, the Apple II, is an immediate success. Adopted by elementary schools, high schools, and colleges, for many students the Apple II is their first contact with the world of computers.

Ethernet, the first local area network (LAN), is developed at Xerox PARC (Palo Alto Research Center) by Robert Metcalf. The LAN allows computers to communicate and share software, data, and peripherals. Initially designed to link minicomputers, Ethernet will be extended to personal computers.

VisiCalc, a spreadsheet program written by Bob Frankston and Dan Bricklin, is introduced. Originally written to run on Apple II computers, VisiCalc will be seen as the most important reason for the acceptance of personal computers in the business world.

The first public online information services, CompuServe and the Source, are founded.

The IBM PC is introduced, signaling IBM's entrance into the personal computer marketplace. The IBM PC quickly garners the largest share of the personal computer market and becomes the personal computer of choice in business.

Lotus Development Corpora is founded. Its spreadsheet software, Lotus 1-2-3, which combines spreadsheet, grap and database programs in or package, becomes the best-s program for IBM personal computers.

1979 1981 1983

1980 1982

Alan Shugart presents the Winchester hard drive, revolutionizing storage for personal computers.

3,275,000 personal computers are sold, almost 3,000,000 more than in 1981.

3,275,000

Instead of choosing a person for its annual award, *TIME* magazine names the computer Machine of the Year for 1982, acknowledgir the impact of computers on society.

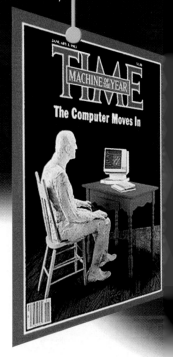

IBM offers Microsoft Corporation cofounder, Bill Gates, the opportunity to develop the operating system for the soon-to-be announced IBM personal computer. With the development of MS-DOS, Microsoft achieves tremendous growth and success.

Hayes introduces the 300-bps smart modem. The modem is an immediate success.

COMPAQ

Compaq, Inc., is founded to develop and market IBM-compatible PCs.

IBM introduces a personal computer, called the PC AT, that uses the Intel 80286 microprocessor.

Several personal computers utilizing the powerful Intel 80386 microprocessor are introduced. These machines perform processing that once only large systems could handle.

While working at CERN, Switzerland, Tim Berners-Lee invents an Internet-based hypermedia enterprise for information sharing. Berners-Lee will call this innovation the World Wide Web.

1987

1984

Hewlett-Packard announces the first LaserJet printer for personal computers.

1988

Microsoft surpasses Lotus Development Corporation to become the world's top software vendor.

Microsoft

Lotus

1989

The International Society for Technology in Education (ISTE) is formed. The mission of ISTE is to help K-12 classroom teachers and administrators share effective methods for enhancing student learning with new classroom technologies. Today, ISTE has more than 6000 members and a network of regional affiliates with a membership that exceeds 40,000.

Apple introduces the Macintosh computer, which incorporates a unique, easy-to-learn, graphical user interface.

Microsoft releases Windows 3.1, the latest version of its Windows operating system. Windows 3.1 offers improvements such as TrueType fonts, multimedia capability, and object linking and embedding (OLE). In two months, 3,000,000 copies of Windows 3.1 are sold.

Several companies introduce computers using the Pentium microprocessor from Intel. The Pentium chip is the successor to the Intel 486 processor. It contains 3.1 million transistors and is capable of performing 112,000,000 instructions per second.

Jim Clark and Marc Andreessen found Netscape and launch Netscape Navigator 1.0, a browser for the World Wide Web.

1992

1991 —————— 1993 —————— 1994 —

AskERIC (Educational Resources Information Center) starts up as a project of the ERIC Clearinghouse on Information and Technology at Syracuse University. Today, the federally funded AskERIC provides an extensive and searchable database of documents and resources; educators can send questions on any educational topic to AskERIC and receive a response within 48 hours.

The International Society for Technology in Education (ISTE) introduces the first edition of "Technology Standards for Teachers," containing 13 indicators.

The Clinton Administration creates the Telecommunications and Information Infrastructure Assistance Program (TIIAP), which supplies grants to public institutions to fund the installation of advanced communications technologies. Over the next four years, TIIAP awards 378 grants of approximately $118 million in federal grant funds, which are matched by more than $180 million in nonfederal funds.

Marc Andreessen creates a graphical Web browser called Mosaic. This success leads to the organization of Netscape Communications Corporation.

Microsoft
Windows 95
Upgrade
for users of Windows

Microsoft releases Windows 95, a major upgrade to its Windows operating system. Windows 95 consists of more than 10,000,000 lines of computer instructions developed by 300 person-years of effort. More than 50,000 individuals and companies test the software before it is released.

President Clinton launches a $2 billion, five-year, Technology Literacy Challenge — a program designed to catalyze and leverage state, local, and private sector efforts so American schools can provide students with the skills they need to succeed in the next century.

The Summer Olympics in Atlanta makes extensive use of computer technology, using an IBM network of 7000 personal computers, 2000 pagers and wireless devices, and 90 industrial-strength computers to share information with more than 150,000 athletes, coaches, journalists, and Olympics staff members, and millions of Web users.

1995

1996

Sun Microsystems launches Java, an object-oriented programming language that allows users to write one application for a variety of computer platforms. Java becomes one of the hottest Internet technologies.

U.S. Robotics introduces PalmPilot, a handheld personal organizer. The PalmPilot's user-friendliness and low price make it a standout next to more expensive personal digital assistants (PDAs).

President Clinton signs the Telecommunications Act of 1996 into law. The act's Universal Service clause requires that schools and libraries are provided affordable telecommunication services.

An innovative technology called webtv combines television and the Internet by providing viewers with tools to navigate the Web.

JAVA™

Intel introduces the Pentium II processor with 7.5 million transistors. The new processor, which incorporates MMX technology, processes video, audio, and graphics data more efficiently and supports applications such as movie-editing, gaming, and more.

The Federal Communications Commission (FCC) approves the Education Rate (E-Rate) discount program to provide K-12 schools and all public libraries with discounted telecommunications services. FCC Chairman Hundt describes the E-Rate program as, "the biggest, single national effort to change education in K-12 classrooms in the history of our country."

DVD (Digital Video Disc), the next generation of optical disc storage technology, is introduced. DVD can store computer, audio, and video data in a single format, with the capability of producing near-studio quality. By year's end, 500,000 DVD players are shipped worldwide.

Microsoft ships Windows 98, an upgrade to Windows 95. Windows 98 offers improved Internet access, better system performance, and support for a new generation of hardware and software. In six months, more than 10,000,000 copies of Windows 98 are sold worldwide.

1997

1998

Deep Blue, an IBM supercomputer, defeats world chess champion Gary Kasparov in a six-game chess competition. Millions of people follow the nine day-long rematch on IBM's Web site.

The International Society for Technology in Education (ISTE) releases the second edition of "Technology Standards for Teachers," containing 18 indicators organized into three major categories.

E-commerce, or electronic commerce — the marketing of goods and services over the Internet — booms. Companies such as Dell, E*TRADE, and Amazon.com spur online shopping, allowing buyers to obtain everything from hardware and software to financial and travel services, insurance, automobiles, books, and more.

Fifty million users are connected to the Internet and World Wide Web.

More than 10,000,000 people take up telecommuting, the capability of working at home and communicating with an office via computer. More and more firms embrace telecommuting to help increase productivity, reduce absenteeism, and provide greater job satisfaction.

iste

High school students begin taking online courses at The Florida High School Online.

Apple Computer introduces the iMac, the latest version of its popular Macintosh computer. The iMac abandons such conventional features as a 3.5-inch disk drive but wins customers with its futuristic design, see-through case, and easy setup. Consumer demand outstrips Apple's production capabilities, and some vendors are forced to begin waiting lists.

Intel releases its Pentium III processor, which provides enhanced multimedia capabilities.

Microsoft introduces Office 2000, its premier productivity suite, offering new tools for users to create content and save it directly to a Web site without any file conversion or special steps.

1998

1999

Preparing Tomorrow's Teachers to Use Technology (PT3) — The U.S. Department of Education initiates a multiyear, innovative, $125 million grant program to create technology-proficient educators at all levels: multiyear preservice teachers, in-service teachers, and faculty in higher education.

Governments and businesses frantically work to make their computers Y2K (Year 2000) compliant, spending more than $500 billion worldwide. Y2K noncompliant computers cannot distinguish if 01/01/00 refers to 1900 or 2000, and thus may operate using a wrong date. This Y2K bug can affect any application that relies on computer chips, such as ATMs, airplanes, energy companies, and the telephone system.

Intel, with support from Microsoft, launches the Intel Teach to the Future program — a worldwide initiative to help teachers effectively integrate the use of computer technology into classroom curriculum.

Shawn Fanning, 19, and his company, Napster, turn the music industry upside down by developing software that allows computer users to swap music files with one another without going through a centralized file server. The Recording Industry of America, on behalf of five media companies, sues Napster for copyright infringement.

The International Society for Technology in Education (ISTE) releases the National Educational Technology Standards (NETS) for teachers and K-12 students. The National Council for Accreditation of Teacher Education adopts the NETS for teachers (NETS-T) for accrediting teacher education programs.

According to the U.S. Commerce Department, Internet traffic is doubling every 100 days, resulting in an annual growth rate of more than 700 percent. It has taken radio and television 30 years and 15 years respectively, to reach 60 million people. The Internet has achieved the same audience base in 3 years.

2000

Intel unveils its Pentium 4 chip with clock speeds starting at 1.4 GHz. The Pentium 4 includes 42 million transistors, nearly twice as many as contained on its predecessor, the Pentium III.

E-commerce achieves mainstream acceptance. Annual e-commerce sales exceed $100 billion, and Internet advertising expenditures reach more than $5 billion.

Dot-com companies (Internet-based) go out of business at a record pace — nearly one per day — as financial investors withhold funding due to the companies' unprofitability.

Telemedicine uses satellite technology and videoconferencing to broadcast consultations and to perform distant surgeries. Robots are used for complex and precise tasks. Computer-aided surgery uses virtual reality to assist with training and planning procedures.

Microsoft releases Microsoft Office 2001 suite for the Macintosh, which includes Word, Excel, Entourage, and PowerPoint.

Apple Computers releases Mac OS X, the latest version of its popular operating system. Apple claims that Mac OS X is the most advanced and easiest-to-use operating system in history.

More than 25 million computer users subscribe to America Online and take advantage of its AOL Anywhere features, including Instant Messenger, e-mail, and customized news and information pages. AOL's merger with Time Warner combines the strengths of the Internet, entertainment, and communications industries.

2001

Microsoft releases Windows XP Professional for business and advanced home computing and Windows XP Home Edition for home use.

Microsoft introduces Office XP Standard and Professional versions, which includes voice recognition and speech capabilities. Microsoft claims that Office XP is the ultimate set of business tools and that it is a complete suite of software that is powerful enough to meet all personal and professional computing needs.

Wireless technology, especially handheld computers, achieves significant market penetration. Prices drop, usage increases, and wireless carriers scramble for new services, particularly for a mobile workforce that can access the Internet anywhere at any time.

Avid readers enjoy e-books, which are digital texts read on compact computer screens. E-books can hold the equivalent of 10 traditional books containing text and graphics. Readers can search, highlight text, and add notes.

DVD writers (DVD+RW) begin to replace CD writers (CD-RW). DVDs can store up to eight times as much data as CDs. Uses include storing home movies, music, photos, and backups. Digital cameras and video editors help the average user develop quality video to store on DVDs.

In January 2002, President Bush signs into law the No Child Left Behind Act — the most sweeping reform of federal education policy in a generation. The act creates strong standards for what every child should know and learn in reading and math in grades 3-8 and states that student progress and achievement will be measured for every child, every year.

Digital video cameras, DVD writers, easy-to-use video editing software, and improvements in storage capabilities allow the average computer user to create Hollywood-like videos with introductions, conclusions, rearranged scenes, music, and voice-over.

2002

The world of wireless communications, wireless notebook computers, and other wireless devices are breaking down traditional K-12 communication barriers worldwide and are opening new and exciting doors to a wireless world of learning.

Microsoft releases Pocket PC 2002 software that allows PDAs to interface with PCs and Microsoft software.

Handspring revolutionizes handheld devices by offering the first all-in-one device that has a built-in cell phone, Web-browsing, and e-mail features.

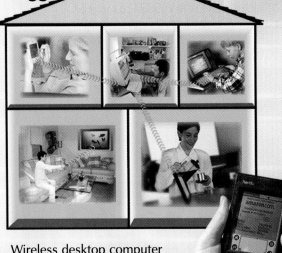

Intel releases its new Centrino mobile technology designed specifically for mobile computing with built-in wireless LAN capability, breakthrough mobile perform-ance, and Intel's first integrated computing technology designed from the ground up for wireless notebook PCs.

Wireless desktop computer components such as keyboards, mouse devices, home networks, and public Internet access points become commonplace. Latest operating systems include support for both the Wi-Fi (wireless fidelity) and Bluetooth standards. Wireless capabilities are standard on many PDAs and Tablet PCs.

Microsoft releases the Class Server Learning Management Platform that makes it easy for school districts to create, deliver, and grade standards-aligned tests and lessons over the Web — helping teachers track and improve student achievement against local curriculum standards, and meet the challenges of No Child Left Behind.

2003

The International Society for Technology in Education (ISTE) announces that by summer of 2003, 48 states will adopt, adapt, align with, or reference one set of its National Educational Technology Standards (NETS).

iste
National Educational Technology Standards (NETS)

Microsoft introduces OneNote 2003, a new program in the Office family that enables users to capture, organize, and reuse notes on notebook computers, desktop computers, or Tablet PCs — potentially changing forever the way professors, instructors, and teachers grade assignments and more.

The Tablet PC is introduced as the next-generation mobile PC. It runs Windows XP Tablet PC soft-ware and is designed like a note-book, is fully wireless, and includes note taking and other new features.

10011011000110 1110
0011001101011 10
111001010
100100
101
011

G5

Apples introduces the Power Mac G5 processor — the first 64-bit processor, which means it breaks the 4-gigabyte barrier and can use up to 8 gigabytes of main memory.

2003

Microsoft releases the latest version of its flagship Office suite in numerous versions, including a Microsoft Office Student and Teacher Edition that includes Word 2003, Excel 2003, and PowerPoint 2003.

Flat-panel LCD monitors overtake bulky CRT monitors as the popular choice of computer users. Although flat-panel LCD monitors cost more, they offer several advantages including physical size, weight, true display size, better power consumption, and no radiation emission.

Companies such as RealNetworks, Microsoft, Sony, and Wal-Mart stake out turf in the online music store business started by Apple Computer. In the previous year, Apple's iTunes Music Store Web site sold nearly 20 million songs for 99 cents each.

USB Flash Drives, which are small enough to fit on a key chain but can store up to 4 billion characters, become a cost-effective way to transport data and information from one computer to another.

2004

Apple Computer introduces the sleek iMac G5. The new computer's display device contains the system unit.

Major retailers begin requiring suppliers to include Radio Frequency Identification (RFID) tags or microchips with antennas, which can be as small as one-third of a millimeter across, in the goods they sell. When a transponder receives a certain radio query, it responds by transmitting its unique ID code. Besides carrying out the functions of the bar code, RFIDs may eventually eliminate long checkout lines.

106 million, or 53 percent, of the 200 million online population in America accesses the Internet via speedy broadband.

Spyware
Spam
Phishing
Spim   Spit

Spam, spyware, phishing, spim, and spit take center stage, along with viruses, as major nuisances to the 801 million computer users worldwide. Spam, which accounts for 45 percent of all e-mail, involves the sending of bulk e-mail that is unsolicited and masks its origin. Spyware is a program placed on the computer without the user's knowledge that secretly collects information about the user, often related to Web browsing habits. Phishing is the act of sending an e-mail to a user falsely claiming to be a legitimate enterprise in an attempt to trick the user into surrendering private information that will be used for identity theft. Spim is spam via instant messaging. Spit is spam via Internet telephony.

Microsoft
Windows^{XP}
Media Center Edition 2005

Microsoft unveils Windows XP Media Center Edition 2005. This operating system allows users to access the routine capabilities of a Windows XP-based PC while focusing on delivering media content such as music, digital photography, movies, and television.

The Mozilla Foundation, the creators of the free open source Firefox browser, predicts that by the end of 2005, it will have 10 percent of the browser market, primarily at the expense of the Microsoft Internet Explorer (IE) security-plagued browser.

2005

The smart phone overtakes the PDA as the personal mobile device of choice. A smart phone offers a cellular phone, full personal information management and e-mail functionality, a Web browser, instant message capabilities, and even the ability to listen to music, play video and games, and take pictures with its built-in camera.

SP2

To date, Microsoft has sold over 300 million copies of its Windows XP operating system. By early January, Microsoft automatically downloaded to its users' computers over 100 million copies of Service Pack 2 (SP2), its latest update to Windows XP. In addition to a new security center and firewall, SP2 adds a pop-up blocker in Internet Explorer and updated support for Wi-Fi and Bluetooth wireless technologies.

001101110
010110010
0100101
0011000

Apple introduces the Mac mini, which is basically a desktop computer in a 6.5-inch by 2-inch box. The Mac mini uses OS X and houses a G4 processor, a high-capacity hard drive, a slot-loading CD-R/DVD-ROM, 10/100 BASE-T Ethernet card, and more. Users can connect many of their existing monitors, keyboards, printers, scanners, cameras, as well as their iPods and other digital media components using the FireWire or two USB 2.0 slots.

The federal Education Rate, or E-Rate program, invests more than $18 billion, since 1998, to connect libraries and K-12 classrooms to the Internet. As a result, virtually all U.S. students now have access to the Internet from school — many have high-speed or broadband access.

2005 ———— 2006

Touted as a "supercomputer on a chip," IBM introduces the Cell chip, which is about the size of a pushpin. Experts are predicting that this new chip will revolutionize computing from smart phones to supercomputers.

By the end of 2006, experts predict that the number of e-mail messages sent daily will exceed 60 billion worldwide and slightly more than half of these messages will be person-to-person e-mails.

me@e-mail.com

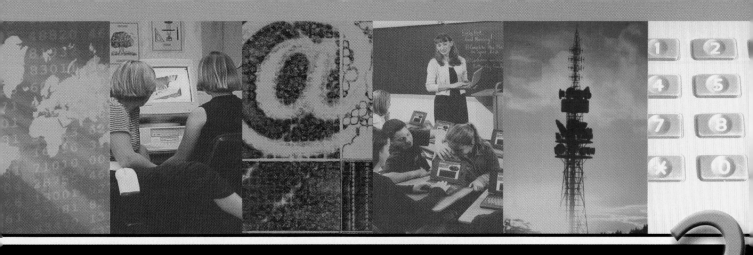

Communications, Networks, the Internet, and the World Wide Web

Objectives

After completing this chapter, you will be able to:
[ISTE NETS-T Standards I A-B, II B-E, III A-D, IV B, V A-D, VI A-E]

- Define communications

- Identify the basic components of a communications system

- Describe how and why network computers are used in schools and school districts

- Explain how the Internet works

- Describe the World Wide Web portion of the Internet

- Explain how Web documents are linked to one another

- Explain the use of Web browser software

- Explain how to use a Web search tool to find information

- Identify several types of multimedia products available on the Web

- Explain how Internet services such as e-mail, newsgroups, chat rooms, and instant messaging work

- Describe the educational implications of the Internet and the World Wide Web

- Describe different ways to connect to the Internet and the World Wide Web

Communications and networks are the fastest growing areas of computer technology and digital media. Adding tremendously to this growth is the popularity of the Internet and the World Wide Web (also called the Web), which is a service of the Internet that supports graphics and multimedia. Together, the Internet and the World Wide Web represent one of today's most exciting uses of networks. Already, these networks have changed dramatically the way people gather information, conduct research, shop, take classes, and collaborate on projects.

Businesses encourage you to browse their Web-based catalogs, send them e-mail for customer service requests, and buy their products online. The government publishes thousands of informational Web pages to provide individuals with materials such as legislative updates, tax forms, and e-mail addresses for members of Congress. Colleges give tours of their campuses on the Web, accept applications online, and offer thousands of classes on the Internet.

Today, communications media and networks are breaking down the walls of a classroom, allowing students to view the world beyond where they live and learn. The Internet is expanding student learning beyond the covers of a textbook to include interactive, up-to-date, Web-based content. Never before has any technology opened so many opportunities for learning.

The future will bring even more exciting applications of these technologies. Federal and state governments, private businesses, and organizations are investing billions of dollars in Internet-related hardware and software for K-12 schools. As a result of this substantial investment, most public schools have equipped their classrooms with multimedia computers and provided teachers and students with access to the Internet. This chapter discusses communications, networks, the Internet, and the World Wide Web; explains how they work; and reviews how teachers and administrators can use these technologies to communicate, obtain almost unlimited educational information, and enhance student learning.

What Is Communications?

Communications, sometimes called **telecommunications**, describes a process in which two or more computers or devices transfer data, instructions, and information. The ability to communicate information instantly and accurately has changed the way people conduct business and interact with each other, and the way students learn. Electronic mail (e-mail), voice mail, facsimile (fax), telecommuting, online services, videoconferencing, the Internet, and the World Wide Web are examples of applications that rely on communications technology.

Communications Networks

Computers were stand-alone devices when first introduced. As computers became more widely used, companies designed hardware and software so computers could communicate with one another. Originally, developers created communication capabilities only for large computers. Today, even the smallest computers and handheld devices can communicate with each other. Figure 2-1 shows a sample communications system, which can contain all types of devices.

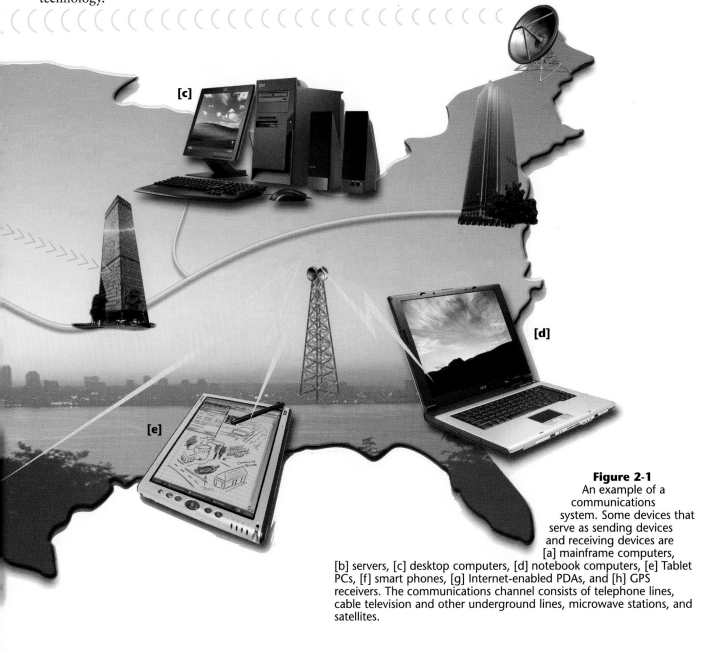

Figure 2-1
An example of a communications system. Some devices that serve as sending devices and receiving devices are [a] mainframe computers, [b] servers, [c] desktop computers, [d] notebook computers, [e] Tablet PCs, [f] smart phones, [g] Internet-enabled PDAs, and [h] GPS receivers. The communications channel consists of telephone lines, cable television and other underground lines, microwave stations, and satellites.

A communications **network** is a collection of computers and other equipment organized to share data, information, hardware, and software. A basic communications system consists of the following equipment:

- Two computers, one to send and one to receive data

- Communications devices that send and receive data

- A communications channel over which data is sent

This basic model also includes **communications software,** which are programs that manage the transmission of data between computers.

A **communications channel** is the path that data follows as the data is transmitted from the sending equipment to the receiving equipment in a communications system.

Communications channels are made up of **transmission media,** which are the physical materials or other means used to establish a communications channel. The most widely used transmission medium is twisted-pair cable. **Twisted-pair cable** consists of pairs of plastic-coated copper wires twisted together (Figure 2-2). Standard telephone lines in your home also use twisted-pair cables. Other examples of transmission media include coaxial cable, fiber-optic cable, microwave transmission, communications satellites, and wireless transmissions.

Digital signals are individual electrical pulses that a computer uses to represent data. Telephone equipment originally was designed to carry only voice transmission, which comprises a continuous electrical wave called an **analog signal.** For telephone lines to carry data, a communications device called a **modem** converts digital signals into analog signals.

twisted-pair wire

twisted-pair cable

Figure 2-2 Twisted-pair cables often are used to connect personal computers to one another or a personal computer to a regular telephone line. It is inexpensive and easily installed.

The word modem comes from a combination of the words modulate, to change a digital signal into sound or analog signal, and demodulate, to convert an analog signal into a digital signal (Figure 2-3a). Computers at both the sending and receiving ends of this communications channel must have a modem for data transmission to occur. At the sending computer, a modem converts digital signals from the computer to analog signals for transmission over regular telephone lines. At the receiving computer, a modem converts analog signals back to digital signals.

A number of different kinds of modems are in use today. Most computers purchased for home use include internal modems that can transmit data at rates up to approximately 56,000 bits per second (56K modem). An **internal modem** is built on a circuit board that is installed inside a computer and attaches to a telephone socket using a standard telephone cord. Today, many home and small business users are using cable modems and DSL modems, also called digital modems, which provide significantly higher data access rates than 56K (Figure 2-3b). Cable modems provide

FAQ

Are "digital" modems really modems?

According to the definition of a modem (analog to digital conversion and vice versa), the use of the term modem in this context is not correct. However, the industry does refer to DSL and cable modems as digital modems.

[a] digital to analog to digital communications channel

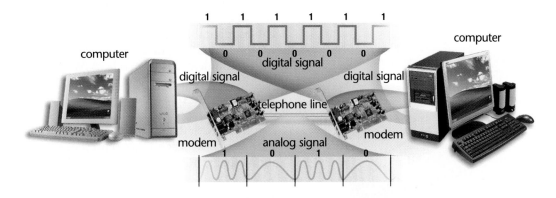

[b] all digital communications channel

Figure 2-3 A modem connects a communications channel, such as a telephone line or a cable television line, to a sending or receiving device such as a computer. Depending on the type of communications channel, a modem may need to convert digital signals to analog signals (and vice versa) before transferring data, instructions, and information to or from a sending or receiving device.

broadband access over a cable television (CATV) network and DSL modems provide broadband access over telephone lines. These newer types of modems are discussed later in this chapter. Networked computers contain a network interface card (Figure 2-4). **Network interface cards (NICs)** connect computers directly to a school or business network without using a modem. Networks are classified as either local area networks or wide area networks.

PC Card for notebook computer

network card for desktop computer

Figure 2-4 Network cards are available for both desktop and notebook computers.

LOCAL AREA NETWORKS

A **local area network (LAN)** is a communications network that covers a limited geographical area, such as a school, office, building, or group of buildings. A LAN consists of a number of computers connected to a central computer, or server. A **server** manages the resources on a network and provides a centralized storage area for software programs and data. A **wireless LAN (WLAN)** is a LAN that uses no wires. Instead of wires, a WLAN uses wireless media, such as radio waves.

WIDE AREA NETWORKS

A **wide area network (WAN)** covers a large geographical region (such as a city or school district) and uses regular telephone cables, digital lines, microwaves, wireless systems, satellites, or other combinations of communications channels. A WAN can consist of numerous local area networks organized into one larger network. For example, a large school district may establish a WAN that consists of dozens of local area networks, each LAN representing an individual school.

HOME NETWORKS

If you have multiple computers in your home or home office, you can connect all of them together with a **home network** (Figure 2-5). Some advantages to having a home network

Figure 2-5 An example of a home network.

include the following: all computers in the house can be connected to the Internet at the same time, each computer can access files and programs on the other computers, and all computers can share the same peripherals, such as a scanner, printer, or DVD drive.

Home networks can be either wired or wireless. To network computers and devices that span multiple rooms or floors in a home, it may be more convenient to use a wireless network. Local cable and other Internet service providers will help you set up a wireless home network for free or for a minimal installation charge. Monthly fees usually include the rental fee for a wireless modem. You will learn more about wireless networks in the special feature, A World Without Wires, that follows Chapter 8.

Networking the Classroom, School, and District

Due to extensive federal, state, and local funding, virtually all schools and school districts in the United States have networked their computers. Schools have installed networks for three reasons: (1) to share hardware and software resources, (2) to enable communications among schools and other organizations, and (3) to connect students and teachers to the Internet.

A school network server connects all of the computers located within a school. A server manages the resources on a network and provides a centralized storage area for software programs and data. Typically, any teachers and students who use the network can access software and data on the server, although school or network administrators can limit access to specific records and software applications.

As an example of how a school district might network its computers, consider the Washington County Public School District, which consists of one high school (Ridgedale High School), two middle schools (Dresden and Fall Hills Middle Schools), and three elementary schools (Acorn, Johnson, and Martin Luther King Elementary Schools).

Martin Luther King Elementary School is a small school with 14 classrooms. Each classroom has three modern Macintosh computers and a printer connected to the school's local area network (Figure 2-6).

WEB INFO

For more information about school networks, visit the Teachers Discovering Computers Web site (*scsite.com/tdc4*), click Chapter 2, click Web Info, and then click School Networks.

ink-jet printer

Macintosh computer

Macintosh computer

Macintosh computer

to school local area network

Figure 2-6 In each classroom, three Macintosh computers and a printer are connected to the school's local area network.

Also connected to Martin Luther King Elementary's local area network is a computer lab that contains 24 networked Macintosh computers and 4 additional computers that are used by school administrators and staff. In total, Martin Luther King Elementary's local area network consists of Macintosh computers and numerous printers all connected to a central server (Figure 2-7).

The local area network at Martin Luther King Elementary and the district's five other school LANs are connected to a large-capacity server and its associated equipment located at the Washington County Public School District's Central Office, which includes PCs. Together, these networks form a wide area network that contains more than 600 networked Macintosh computers and PCs (Figure 2-8).

Figure 2-7 The school's local area network consists of computers in 14 classrooms, in the computer lab, and four school administration computers.

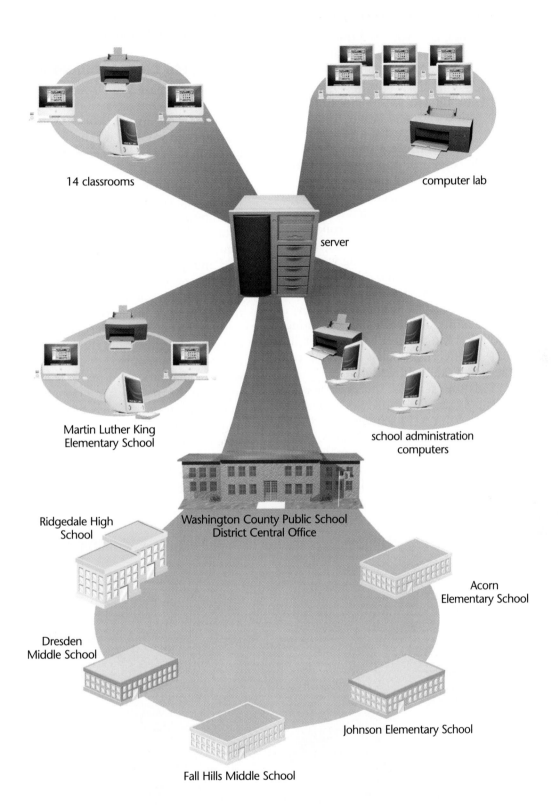

Figure 2-8 The school district's wide area network consists of the local area networks of six member schools all connected to a server located at the district's central office.

WIRELESS SCHOOLS AND CLASSROOMS

Not long ago, you used traditional telephones, connected to a telephone company by cables, to communicate with your friends, family, and fellow teachers. Today, wireless technology allows you to keep in touch with friends and family from anywhere in the world, using a variety of devices: a smart pager, a smart phone, a handheld computer, or a notebook computer with high-speed Internet access.

Teachers and students already are part of the wireless revolution that is taking place in education. Numerous colleges, universities, and K-12 schools are installing wireless networks and utilizing wireless notebook computers and other wireless devices. Many experts, including Steve Jobs, CEO of Apple Computers, believe that the future of educational computing, in both K-12 and higher education, will be wireless networks, wireless notebook computers, and other wireless devices.

Today, most major computer manufacturers provide wireless network solutions and devices for K-12 schools (Figure 2-9). Devices include wireless keyboards, wireless notebook computers, wireless mobile labs, and many other devices. The use of wireless networks and devices in K-12 schools and classrooms is discussed in future chapters

and in the special feature, A World Without Wires, which follows Chapter 8.

HIGH-SPEED OR BROADBAND ACCESS

Over the past 5 to 10 years, school districts have concentrated on installing local and wide area networks so that their teachers and students will have Internet access in their classrooms or at the point of instruction. Many school networks, however, do not provide their classroom computers with continuous high-speed access to the Internet; access speeds vary greatly. Students and teachers must be provided continuous high-speed access to allow them to find and quickly download complex, content-rich resources. The federal government recognizes this and is spearheading initiatives to provide broadband access to K-12 schools. Networks and media that use **broadband** technologies transmit signals at much faster speeds than traditional network configurations. A recent federal report to the president and Congress stated that the promise of widely available, high-quality, Web-based education is made possible by technological and communications trends that could lead to important digital media–based educational applications over the next two or three years.

FAQ

What does bandwidth have to do with Internet access?

Bandwidth is a measure of how fast data travels over transmission channels. Thus, higher-speed broadband Internet connections have a higher bandwidth than dial-up connections.

Figure 2-9 An example of a mobile wireless lab. Instead of taking your students to a school's computer lab, the lab is brought to your students.

The Benefits of Computer Networks in Education

One benefit of networking is that administrators, teachers, and students can share computer hardware, software, and data resources available throughout the school district. For example, administrators can maintain all student records and information securely at one central location. Teachers and administrative staff who have a need for access to student records can access various student information databases from just about any networked computer at any location.

By far, the most important benefit of networking school computers is that administrators, teachers, and students instantly can access the unlimited educational resources available on the Internet and communicate with other educators and students all over the world (Figure 2-10). In brief, networking provides schools with limitless possibilities for teaching and learning. Without question, the introduction of networks and the Internet into today's schools is having a dramatic impact on the current generation of teachers and students.

Figure 2-10 The Internet is useful as a tool to hold students' attention and even amaze them.

What Is the Internet?

You have learned that a network, such as the one installed at Martin Luther King Elementary School, is a collection of computers and devices connected via communications devices and media. Recall also that the world's largest network is the **Internet**, which is a worldwide collection of networks that link together millions of businesses, governments, educational institutions, and individuals using modems, telephone lines, and other communications devices and media (Figure 2-11). Each of these networks provides resources and data that add to the abundance of goods, services, and information accessible via the Internet.

Figure 2-11 The world's largest network is the Internet, which is a worldwide collection of networks that link together millions of businesses, governments, educational institutions, and individuals.

Networks that constitute the Internet, also called the **Net**, consist of federal, regional, local, and international networks. Public or private organizations own individual networks that constitute the Internet; no single organization owns or controls the Internet. Each organization on the Internet is responsible only for maintaining its own network.

Today, more than one billion users around the world connect to the Internet for a variety of reasons. Figure 2-12 on the next page illustrates sites on the Internet that represent some of the following uses:

- Access a wealth of information, news, research, and educational material.

- Conduct business or complete banking and investing transactions.

- Access sources of entertainment and leisure, such as online games, magazines, and vacation-planning guides.

- Shop for goods and services.

WEB INFO

For an overview of the Internet, visit the Teachers Discovering Computers Web site (*scsite.com/tdc4*), click Chapter 2, click Web Info, and then click Internet.

- Meet and converse with people around the world in discussion groups or chat rooms.

- Access other computers and exchange files.

- Send messages to or receive messages from other connected users.

- Download and listen to music or download and watch movies.

- Take a course or access educational materials.

To allow you to perform these and other activities, the Internet provides a variety of services, such as the World

[c] FTP File Transfer Protocol

[b] e-mail

[a] Web

Figure 2-12 A number of reasons why more than one billion users around the world connect to the Internet.

Wide Web, e-mail, File Transfer Protocol (FTP), newsgroups, message boards, blogs, mailing lists, instant messaging, chat rooms, and Internet telephony. These services along with a discussion of the history of the Internet and how the Internet works are explained in the following sections.

History of the Internet

Although the history of the Internet is relatively short, its growth has been explosive. The Internet has it roots in a networking project of the U.S. Department of Defense's **Advanced Research Projects Agency** (**ARPA**). ARPA's goal was to build

[d] newsgroup

[e] chat

[f] instant messaging

[g] Internet telephony

WEB INFO

For the history of the Internet, visit the Teachers Discovering Computers Web site (*scsite.com/tdc4*), click Chapter 2, click Web Info, and then click History.

a network that (1) would allow scientists at different locations to share information and collaborate on military and scientific projects and (2) could function even if part of the network were disabled or destroyed by a disaster such as a nuclear war. That network, called **ARPANET,** became functional in September 1969, effectively linking together scientific and academic researchers in the United States.

The original ARPANET was a wide area network consisting of four main computers, located at the University of California at Los Angeles, the Stanford Research Institute, the University of California at Santa Barbara, and the University of Utah. Each of these four computers served as the network's host. A **host** is the main computer in a network of computers connected by communications links. A host often stores and transfers data and messages on high-speed communications lines and provides network connections for additional computers.

As researchers and others realized the great benefit of using ARPANET's electronic mail to share information and notes, ARPANET underwent phenomenal growth. By 1984, ARPANET had more than 1000 individual computers linked as hosts (today, more than 200 million host computers exist on the Internet).

To take further advantage of the high-speed communications offered by ARPANET, organizations decided to connect entire networks to ARPANET. In 1986, for example, the **National Science Foundation (NSF)** connected its huge network of five supercomputer centers, called **NSFnet,** to ARPANET. This configuration of complex networks and hosts became known as the Internet (Figure 2-13).

Because of its advanced technology, NSFnet served as the major backbone network of the Internet until 1995. A **backbone** is a high-speed network that connects regional and local networks to the Internet. Other computers then connect to these regional and local networks to access the Internet. A backbone thus handles the bulk of the communications activity, or **traffic,** on the Internet.

In 1995, NSFnet terminated its backbone network on the Internet to return to its purpose as a research network. Today, a variety of corporations, commercial firms, and other companies operate the backbone networks that provide access to the Internet. These backbone networks, telephone companies, cable and satellite companies, educational institutions, and the government all contribute extensive resources to the Internet. As a result, the Internet is a truly collaborative entity.

Figure 2-13 This map was prepared by the National Science Foundation (NSF) and shows the major United States Internet connections.

Over the years, the total number of computers connected to the original network increased steadily and within the last few years, explosively. Today, experts estimate that hundreds of millions of computers distribute information over the Internet, including those at virtually all K-12 schools. More than 95 percent of K-12 classrooms in the United States are now connected to the Internet.

A new Internet, called Internet2, is an ongoing development project that went online in 1999. **Internet2 (I2)** is an extremely high-speed network that develops and tests advanced Internet technologies for research, teaching, and learning. Members of Internet2 include more than 206 universities in the United States, along with 60 companies and the United States government. Eventually it will benefit users of the Internet.

How the Internet Works

Computers connected to the Internet work together to transfer data around the world. When a computer sends data over the Internet, the computer's software divides the data into small pieces, called **packets**. The data in a packet might be part of an e-mail message, a file, a document, a graphic, or a request for a file. Each packet contains the data, as well as the recipient (destination), origin (sender), and sequence information needed to reassemble the data at the destination. Packets travel along the fastest path available to the recipient's computer via hardware devices called **routers** (Figure 2-14).

FAQ

Just how fast is Internet2?

Really fast! Recently, Internet2 researchers broke a speed record by sending data from Los Angeles to Geneva, Switzerland, at a speed that is nearly 10,000 times faster that the average home high-speed Internet connection.

sender

Step 1:
Data is divided into small pieces, called packets.

Step 2:
Packets travel over the Internet via routers.

Step 3:
At the destination, the packets are reassembled into the original message.

recipient

Figure 2-14 How data travels over the Internet.

If the most direct path to the destination is overloaded or not operating, routers send the packets along alternate paths. Although each packet may arrive out of sequence, the destination computer uses the sequence information contained in each packet to reassemble the original message, file, document, or request. **Packet switching** is the technique of breaking a message into individual packets, sending the packets along the best route available, and reassembling the data.

For a technique such as packet switching to work, all of the devices on the network must follow certain standards or protocols. A **communications protocol** specifies the rules that define how devices connect to each other and transmit data over a network. The protocol used to define packet switching on the Internet is **Transmission Control Protocol/Internet Protocol (TCP/IP)**.

Data sent over the Internet travels over networks and communications lines owned and operated by many companies. You can connect to these networks in one of several ways. Some users connect to the Internet through an Internet service provider (ISP) or an online service provider (OSP), often using a modem to establish a connection. Organizations such as schools and businesses provide Internet access for students and employees by connecting their own network to an ISP. Some school districts and states also provide Internet services for teachers and administrators so they can access the Internet from their homes.

ACCESS PROVIDERS

An **Internet service provider (ISP)** is a regional or national access provider. A **regional ISP** is a business that usually provides Internet access to a specific geographic area. A **national ISP** is a business that provides Internet access in cities and towns nationwide and broadband access in many locations. Because of their size, national ISPs offer more services and generally have a larger technical support staff than regional ISPs.

Like an ISP, an **online service provider (OSP)** also provides access to the Internet, but such online services have members-only features that offer a variety of special content and services. Typical content and services include news, weather, educational information, financial information, hardware and software guides, games, entertainment, news, and travel information. For this reason, the fees for using an online service usually are slightly higher than fees for an ISP. The most popular OSPs are America Online (AOL) and Microsoft Network (MSN).

A **wireless Internet service provider (WISP)** is a company that provides wireless Internet access to computers with wireless modems or access devices or to Internet-enabled mobile computers or devices. Internet-enabled mobile devices include PDAs, smart phones, and smart watches. An antenna on the computer or device typically sends signals through the airwaves to communicate with a wireless ISP. Some examples of wireless ISPs include AT&T Wireless, GoAmerica, T-Mobile, and Verizon Wireless.

Users and schools access the Internet through regional or national ISPs, OSPs, and WISPs using a variety of connection methods (Figure 2-15). Individual user accounts vary from about $10 to $25 per month for dial-up access to $40 to $55 per month for higher-speed access.

CONNECTING TO THE INTERNET

Teachers and students often connect to the Internet through their school network. When connecting from home or from the road while traveling, some individuals use dial-up access to connect to the Internet. With **dial-up access**, you use your computer and a modem to dial into an ISP or

WEB INFO

For a list of Internet service providers, visit the Teachers Discovering Computers Web site (*scsite.com/tdc4*), click Chapter 2, click Web Info, and then click ISP.

Figure 2-15 Common ways to access the Internet are through a regional or national Internet service provider, an online service provider, or a wireless Internet service provider.

online service over regular telephone lines. The computer at the receiving end, whether at an ISP or online service, also uses a modem. Dial-up access has traditionally been an easy way for mobile and home users to connect to the Internet to check e-mail, read the news, and access other information. Because dial-up access uses standard telephone lines, the speed of the connection is limited.

Because dial-up access is slow-speed technology, many home and business users either already have or are opting for higher-speed broadband Internet connections through DSL, cable television networks, satellite, and power lines.

With more than 100 million homes wired for cable television, it is not surprising that more and more users are getting Internet access from their cable company. Road Runner is a popular high-speed CATV online service provided by AOL Time Warner. CATV uses a high-speed **cable modem** that sends and receives data over the cable television network.

As shown in Figure 2-16 on the next page, CATV service enters your home through a single line and then is split between your television and your cable modem, which, in turn, is connected to your computer. Access speeds using CATV can be significantly faster than access speeds using dial-up, in many cases 20 to 50 times faster.

Another high-speed alternative is a **digital subscriber line (DSL)** that transmits data on existing standard telephone lines. DSL can provide Internet access from 25 to 150 times faster than Internet access using a dial-up connection. Similar to a cable or DSL modem, a **satellite modem** provides high-speed Internet connections. It communicates with a satellite via a satellite dish. Installation and monthly access fees for DSL, CATV, and satellite services vary.

All three — cable, DSL, and satellite modems — use broadband technologies. In addition to access speed, another advantage of using CATV, DSL, and satellite services is that they are dedicated or always-on connections to the Internet, unlike dial-up connection, which must be reestablished each time it is used.

Finally, a new and emerging way to connect to the Internet is based on **power line communications (PLC)** technology that allows broadband Internet connectivity from any home, school, or office using an electrical outlet.

Many hotels and airports provide dial-up or broadband Internet connections usually for a usage or per-day fee. In many public locations, people connect wirelessly to the Internet through a **public Internet access point**. Public Internet access points are appearing in airports, hotels, shopping malls, schools, and coffee shops providing Internet access either for a usage fee or for free.

THE INTERNET BACKBONE

The inner structure of the Internet works much like a transportation system. Just as highways connect major cities and carry the bulk of the automotive traffic across the country, the main communications lines that have the heaviest amount of traffic (data packets) on the Internet are collectively referred to as the **Internet backbone**. In the United States, the communications lines that make up the Internet backbone intersect at several different points. National ISPs use dedicated lines to connect directly to the Internet. Smaller, regional ISPs lease lines from local telephone companies to connect to national networks. These smaller, slower-speed networks extend from the backbone into regions and local communities

Figure 2-16 A typical cable modem installation.

like roads and streets extend to major inter-states. Figure 2-17 illustrates how all of the components of the Internet work together to transfer data over the Internet to and from your computer using a cable modem connection.

INTERNET ADDRESSES

The Internet relies on an addressing system much like that of the postal system to send data to a computer at a specific destination. Each computer's location on the Internet has a specific numeric address consisting of four groups of numbers. Because these all-numeric computer addresses are difficult to remember and use, the Internet supports the use of text-based names that represent the numeric address. The text version of a computer address is

called a **domain name**. Figure 2-18 on the next page details both the numeric address and the domain name of the Shelly Cashman Series Web site. The components of a domain name are separated by periods, each of which is referred to as a dot.

For domestic Web sites, the rightmost portion of the domain name contains a domain type abbreviation that identifies the type of organization that maintains the Web site. The rightmost portion of a university Web site, for example, is .edu, which denotes it as a site operated by an educational institution. The domain names for some K-12 school sites include the abbreviation, .k12, followed by the abbreviation for the school's state. For international Web sites, the domain name also includes a country code, such as .us

Step 1:
You initiate an action to request data from the Internet. For example, you request to display a Web page on your computer screen.

Step 2:
A cable modem transfers the computer's digital signals to the cable television line in your house.

Step 3:
Your request (digital signals) travels through cable television lines to a central cable system, which is shared by up to 500 homes in a neighborhood.

Step 4:
The central cable system sends your request over high-speed fiber-optic lines to the cable company who often also is the ISP.

Step 5:
The ISP routes your request through the Internet backbone to the destination server (In this example, the server that contains the requested Web site).

Step 6:
The server retrieves the requested Web page and sends it back through the Internet backbone to your computer.

Figure 2-17 How a home user's data might travel the Internet using a cable modem connection.

for the United States and .uk for the United Kingdom. Figure 2-19a lists common domain type abbreviations. Figure 2-19b lists several country code abbreviations.

The World Wide Web

Although many people use the terms World Wide Web and Internet interchangeably, the World Wide Web is just one of the many services available on the Internet. The World Wide Web actually is a relatively new aspect of the Internet.

Although the Internet has been in existence since the late 1960s, the World Wide Web came into existence in the early 1990s. Since then, however, it has grown phenomenally to become the most widely used service on the Internet.

The **World Wide Web**, or simply **Web**, consists of a worldwide collection of electronic documents that have built-in hyperlinks to other related documents. These **hyperlinks**, also called **links**, allow users to navigate quickly from one Web page to another, regardless of whether the Web pages are located on the same computer

Figure 2-18 The numeric address and domain name for the Shelly Cashman Series® Instructional Web site.

numeric address	198.80.146.30

domain name	www.scsite.com	identifies specific computer

identifies type of organization

[a] This table lists domain abbreviations commonly used today.

Domain Abbreviations

Domain Abbreviation	Type of Organization
com	Commercial organizations, businesses, and companies
edu	Educational institutions
gov	Government institutions
mil	Military organizations
net	Network providers
org	Nonprofit organizations
k12	K-12 schools

[b] A partial listing of country code abbreviations.

Country Code Abbreviations

Abbreviation	Country
au	Australia
ax	Antarctica
ca	Canada
de	Germany
dk	Denmark
fr	France
jp	Japan
nl	Netherlands
se	Sweden
th	Thailand
uk	United Kingdom
us	United States

Figure 2-19 Examples of domain abbreviations and country code abbreviations.

or on different computers in different countries. A **Web page** is an electronic document viewed on the Web. A Web page can contain text, graphics, sound, and video, as well as hyperlinks to other Web pages. A **Web site** is a collection of related Web pages. Most Web sites have a starting point, called a **home page**, which is similar to a book cover or table of contents for the site and provides information about the site's purpose and content.

Each Web page on a Web site has a unique address, called a **Uniform Resource Locator (URL)**. As shown in Figure 2-20, a URL consists of a protocol, domain name, and sometimes the path to a specific Web page. Most Web page URLs begin with **http://**, which stands for **Hypertext Transfer Protocol**, the communications protocol used to transfer pages on the Web. You access and view Web pages using a software program called a Web browser, or browser.

The Web pages that constitute a Web site are stored on a server, called a Web server. A **Web server** is a computer that delivers (serves) requested Web pages. For example, when you enter the URL *http://www.scsite.com/tdc4* in your browser, your browser sends a request to the server whose domain name is *scsite.com*. The server then fetches the page named tdc4 and sends it to your browser.

Web servers can store multiple Web sites. For example, many ISPs grant their subscribers storage space on a Web server for their personal, school, or company Web site.

HOW A WEB PAGE WORKS

A Web page (Figure 2-21 on the next page) is a hypertext or hypermedia document residing on an Internet computer. A Web page can contain text, graphics, video, and sound. A **hypertext** document contains text hyperlinks to other documents. A **hypermedia** document contains

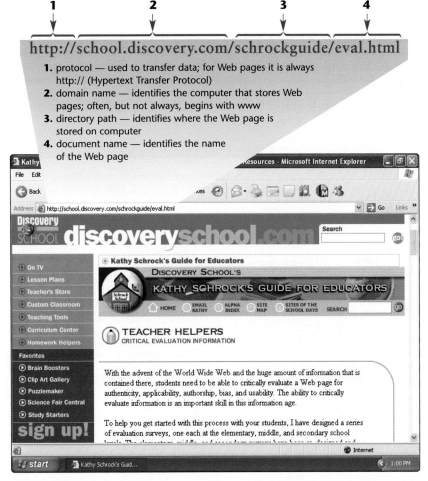

1. protocol — used to transfer data; for Web pages it is always http:// (Hypertext Transfer Protocol)
2. domain name — identifies the computer that stores Web pages; often, but not always, begins with www
3. directory path — identifies where the Web page is stored on computer
4. document name — identifies the name of the Web page

Figure 2-20 The components of a URL.

text, graphics, video, or sound hyperlinks that connect to other documents.

Three types of hyperlinks exist. **Target hyperlinks** link to another location in the same document. **Relative hyperlinks** link to another document on the same Internet computer. **Absolute hyperlinks** link to another document on a different Internet computer that could be across the country or across the world.

Hypertext and hypermedia allow students to learn in a nonlinear way. Reading a book from cover to cover is a linear way of learning. Branching off and investigating related topics as you encounter them is a nonlinear way of learning, also known as **discovery learning**. For example, as a student, you might learn about geology and want to learn more about mining. On the Web, you can click different links to access documents about mining, which then might stimulate your interest in old mining towns. You then could take a virtual tour and explore an old mining town, which might inspire you to read about a particular person who made

her fortune in mining. The discovery learning experience described in this example — in which students branch from one related topic to another in a nonlinear fashion — is powerful and effective.

The Web's capability to support such learning makes it an interesting place to explore and positions it as a valuable tool for teaching and learning. Exploration offers great opportunities for discovery learning. As students' interest inspires them to learn more, the Web allows them to continue to explore for additional sources of information on any given topic. **Web surfing** is displaying pages from one Web site after another and is like using a remote control to jump from one TV channel to another.

A **Webmaster** is the person responsible for developing Web pages and maintaining a Web site. Webmasters and other Web page developers create and format Web pages using **Hypertext Markup Language (HTML)**, which is a set of special codes, called **tags**, that define the placement and format of text, graphics, video, and sound on a Web page. Because HTML can be

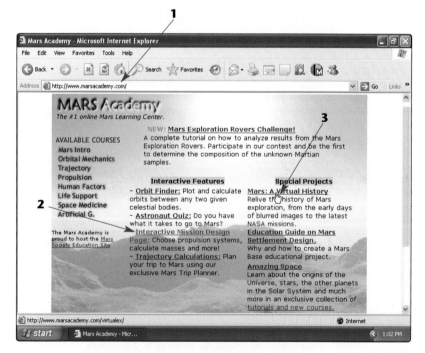

1. Web page address; also called location or URL
2. different color indicates document associated with this hypertext link has been viewed
3. pointer positioned over a hypertext link changes shape to a hand with a pointing finger

Figure 2-21 An example of a Web page.

difficult to learn and use, many other user-friendly tools exist for **Web publishing,** which is the development and maintenance of Web pages. Today, many teachers are utilizing user-friendly programs, such as Dreamweaver, FrontPage, Microsoft Word, Publisher, Netscape Composer, Apple-Works, and many other programs to publish and maintain their own classroom Web pages (Figure 2-22a). You will learn how to create your own Web page using Word in Chapter 3. You also will learn how to create and integrate curriculum pages into your lesson plans in Chapters 6 and 7.

WEB BROWSER SOFTWARE

As just discussed, you access and view Web pages using a software program called a Web browser. A **Web browser,** or **browser,** is a program that interprets HTML and displays Web pages and enables you to link to other Web pages and Web sites. Figure 2-22b shows the HTML source document, used to create the teacher's Web page shown in Figure 2-22a. Your Web browser translates the source document, which includes HTML tags, into a functional and beautiful Web page.

The first Web browsers used only text commands and displayed only text-based documents. In 1993, Marc Andreessen, a student at the University of Illinois, created a graphical Web browser called Mosaic. **Mosaic** displayed documents that included graphics and used a graphical interface. The graphical

interface made it easier and more enjoyable to view Web documents and contributed to the rapid growth of the Web. Andreessen later developed the Netscape Navigator Web browser.

Before you can use a Web browser to view pages on the World Wide Web, your computer or handheld device has to connect to the Internet through an ISP or online service. When the browser program opens, it retrieves and displays a home page (Figure 2-23 on the nest page). As discussed earlier, a home page often is used to describe the first page at a Web site. The

[a] A teacher's classroom Web page.

Figure 2-22 The HTML code (Figure 2-22b) for the top portion of the Web page shown in Figure 2-22a. Web browser software interprets the HTML tags and displays the text, graphics, and hyperlinks.

[b] HTML source document.

same term, home page, describes the Web page designated as the page to display each time you start your browser. Most browsers utilize its Web page as the default home page, but you may change your browser's home page at any time. Many teachers, for example, set their school's home page as their browser's home page so it is the first page they see when they start their browser.

After the browser retrieves a Web page using the page's URL, it can take anywhere from a few seconds to several minutes to display the page on your computer screen. The speed at which a Web page displays depends on the speed of the Internet connection and your computer and the amount of graphics on the Web page. To speed up the display of pages, Web browsers let you turn off the graphics and display text only.

Web-enabled mobile devices such as PDAs and smart phones use a special type of browser called a **microbrowser** (Figure 2-24), which is designed for small screens and has limited computing power. Many Web pages are designed specifically for display on mobile devices.

Browsers display hyperlinks to other documents either as underlined text of a different color or as a graphical image. When you position the mouse pointer over a

hyperlink, the mouse pointer changes to a small hand with a pointing finger. Some browsers also display the URL of the hyperlinked document at the bottom of the screen. You can display the document by clicking the hyperlink with a pointing device or by typing the URL in the location or Address text box of the Web browser. To remind you that you have seen a document, some browsers change the color of a text hyperlink after you click it.

Two ways to keep track of Web pages you have viewed are a history list and a favorites or bookmark list. A **history list** records the pages viewed during the time you are online, also known as a session. If you think you might want to return to a page in a future session, you can save its

WEB INFO

To access an interactive tutorial on using Internet Explorer, visit the Teachers Discovering Computers Web site (*scsite.com/tdc4*), click Chapter 2, click Web Info, and then click Explorer.

[a] microbrowser for a Web-enabled PDA

[b] microbrowser for a smart phone

Figure 2-23 Web page displayed in Internet Explorer.

Figure 2-24 Web pages displayed in microbrowsers on a PDA and a smart phone.

location as a favorite or bookmark. A **favorite** or **bookmark** consists of the title and URL of a page. Favorite lists, also called bookmarks, are stored on your computer, and may be used in future Web sessions. Favorites, bookmarks, and history lists allow you to display a Web page quickly by clicking the name in the list.

SEARCHING FOR INFORMATION ON THE WEB

Searching for information on the Web can be challenging due to the sheer volume of content on the Web. In addition, no central menu or catalog of Web site content and addresses exists. Many Web sites, however, do provide search tools and maintain organized directories of Web sites to help you locate specific information. **Search tools** enable users to locate information found at Web sites all over the world (Figure 2-25). Two basic types of search tools exist: search engines and subject directories.

A **search engine** is a specific type of search tool that finds Web sites, Web pages, and Internet files that match one or more keywords you enter. Some search engines look for simple word matches and others allow for more specific searches on a series of words or an entire phrase. Search engines do not actually search the entire Internet (such a search would take an extremely long time). Instead, they search an index or database of Internet sites and documents. Search tool companies continuously update their databases. Because of the explosive growth of the Internet and because search engines scan different parts of the Internet and in different ways, performing the same search using different search engines often yields different results.

Many search engines also provide subject directories. A **subject directory** is a type of search tool that allows users to navigate to areas of interest without having to enter keywords. Surfing subject directories is a simple matter of selecting topics and following the links for that topic. Subject directories are usually organized in categories such as education, sports, entertainment, or business. The special feature, Guide to World Wide Web Sites, Searching Techniques, and Search Tools, at the end of this chapter includes extensive information on using search tools. Also included is information on and links to a number of popular educational search tools.

MULTIMEDIA ON THE WEB

Most Web pages include more than just formatted text and hyperlinks. In fact, some of the more exciting Web developments involve **multimedia**, which is the combination of graphics, animation, audio, video, and virtual reality (VR). A Web page that incorporates color, sound, motion, and pictures with text has much more appeal than one with text on a plain background. Combining text, audio, video, animation, and sound brings a Web page to life; increases the types of information available on the Web; expands the Web's potential uses; and makes the Internet a more entertaining place to explore. Although multimedia Web pages often require more time to open because they contain large files such as video or audio clips, the pages usually are worth the wait.

Most browsers have the capability to display basic multimedia elements on a Web page. Sometimes, however, your browser needs an additional program called a plug-in. A **plug-in** is a program that extends the capability of the browser. You can download or copy plug-ins free from many Web sites (Figure 2-26 on the next page). In fact, Web pages that use multimedia elements often include links to

WEB INFO

To access an interactive tutorial on using favorites, visit the Teachers Discovering Computers Web site (*scsite.com/tdc4*), click Chapter 2, click Web Info, and then click Favorites.

WEB INFO

For links to many popular education-related search engines, visit the Teachers Discovering Computers Web site (*scsite.com/tdc4*), click Chapter 2, click Web Info, and then click Education Search Engines.

Figure 2-25 Google is a popular search engine.

Popular Plug-In Applications

Plug-In Application		Description	Web Address
Acrobat Reader	Get Adobe Reader	View, navigate, and print Portable Document Format (PDF) files — documents formatted to look on screen just as they look in print	adobe.com
Flash Player	Get macromedia FLASH PLAYER	View dazzling graphics and animation, hear outstanding sound and music, display Web pages across an entire screen	macromedia.com
QuickTime		View animation, music, audio, video, and VR panoramas and objects directly in a Web page	apple.com
RealOne Player	realPlayer	Listen to live and on-demand near-CD-quality audio and newscast-quality video; stream audio and video content for faster viewing; play MP3 files; create music CDs	real.com
Shockwave Player	macromedia SHOCKWAVE PLAYER	Experience dynamic interactive multimedia, 3-D graphics, and streaming audio	macromedia.com
Windows Media Player	WindowsMedia Player 9 Series FREE	Listen to live and on-demand audio; play or edit WMA and MP3 files; burn CDs; watch DVD movies	microsoft.com

Figure 2-26 Plug-ins can extend the multimedia capability of Web browsers. Users usually can download them free from the developers' Web sites.

Web sites containing the required plug-in. Most browsers include commonly used plug-ins, but users often have to update their browsers as new plug-ins become available. Some plug-ins run on mobile devices as well as computers. Others have special versions for mobile devices.

The following sections discuss Web developments in the multimedia areas of graphics, animation, audio, video, and virtual reality.

GRAPHICS A **graphic**, or **graphical image**, is a digital representation of nontext information such as a drawing, chart, or photograph. Graphics were the first medium used to enhance the text-based Internet. The introduction of graphical Web browsers allowed Web page developers to incorporate illustrations, logos, and other images into Web pages. Today, many Web pages use colorful graphical designs and images to convey messages (Figure 2-27).

Two common file formats for graphical images found on the Web are JPEG (pronounced JAY-peg) and GIF (pronounced jiff or giff). Figure 2-28 lists these and other file formats used on the Internet.

Figure 2-27 The use of colorful graphic designs and images enchances the visual appeal of the Web page and helps to convey the messages.

Common Graphics Formats Used on the Internet

Acronym	Name	File Extension
BMP	Bit map	.bmp
GIF	Graphics Interchange Format	.gif
JPEG	Joint Photographic Experts Group	.jpg
PCX	PC Paintbrush	.pcx
PNG	Portable Network Graphics	.png
TIFF	Tagged Image File Format	.tif

Figure 2-28 Graphics formats used on the Internet.

The Web contains thousands of image files on countless subjects that you can download at no cost and use for noncommercial purposes. Because some graphical files can be time-consuming to download, some Web sites use thumbnails on their pages. A **thumbnail** is a small version of a larger graphical image that usually you can click to display the full-sized image (Figure 2-29).

ANIMATION **Animation** is the appearance of motion created by displaying a series of still images in rapid sequence. Animated graphics make Web pages visually more interesting and draw attention to important information

or links. For example, text that is animated to scroll across the screen, called a **marquee** (pronounced mar-KEE), can serve as a ticker to display stock updates, news, school sports scores and events, or weather.

One popular type of animation, called an **animated GIF**, is a group of several images combined into a single GIF file. An abundance of education-related animations are available on the Web, many that you can download or copy at no cost.

AUDIO On the Web, you can listen to prerecorded audio clips and live audio. **Audio** is music, speech, or any other sound. Simple Web audio applications consist of individual

WEB INFO

To explore a site that provides free animated GIF files, visit the Teachers Discovering Computers Web site (*scsite.com/tdc4*), click Chapter 2, click Web Info, and then click Animated GIF.

Figure 2-29 After the visitor clicks the thumbnail of the George Washington painting in the top screen, a full-sized image of the painting appears in a separate window.

sound files that are available for downloading to a computer. After being downloaded, you can play or listen to the contents of these files. Audio files exist in a variety of formats, including MP3, WAV, WMA (Windows Media Audio), RealAudio, and QuickTime. Audio files are compressed to reduce their file sizes. For example, the MP3 format reduces an audio file to about one-tenth of its original size, while preserving the original quality of the sound.

Controversy concerning copyright infringement has surfaced due to the ease with which music can be transferred across the Internet. Users can download copyrighted music legally only if the copyright holder of the music has granted permission for users to download and play it. Many music publishers allow users to purchase and download an entire CD of music tracks to their hard disk.

Most current operating systems contain a program, called a **player**, that can play audio files on your computer. Windows Media Player, RealPlayer, and iTunes are popular players. If your player will not play a particular audio format, you can download the necessary player free from the Web.

More advanced Web audio applications use streaming audio. **Streaming** is the process of transferring data in a continuous and even flow. Streaming is important because most users do not have fast enough Internet connections to download large audio files quickly. **Streaming audio** enables you to listen to the sound file as it downloads to your computer.

Many radio and television stations use streaming audio to broadcast music, interviews, talk shows, sporting events, music videos, news, live concerts, and other segments (Figure 2-30).

Figure 2-30 Many radio and television stations use streaming audio to broadcast programs. This figure shows a National Public Radio news report playing in Windows Media Player.

VIDEO Video consists of full-motion images that are played back at various speeds. Many Web sites include real-time video to enhance your understanding of information or for entertainment (Figure 2-31).

Like audio, simple Web video applications consist of individual video files, such as movies or television clips, that a user must download completely before viewing. Because video segments usually are large and take a long time to download, they often are short.

Streaming video allows you to view longer or live video images as the video file downloads to your computer. Windows Media Player, RealPlayer, and Apple QuickTime can play downloaded or streaming video files.

Streaming video has the potential to create new possibilities for learning. As the speed of the Internet increases dramatically over the next few years, students from even the most remote schools will have access to thousands of full-motion videos from all over the world.

VIRTUAL REALITY Virtual reality (VR) is the simulation of a real or imagined environment that appears as a three-dimensional (3-D) space. On the Web, VR involves the display of 3-D images that you can explore and manipulate interactively. Using special VR software, a Web developer can create an entire 3-D site that contains infinite space and depth called a **VR world**. A VR world, for example, might show a room with furniture. You can walk through such a VR room by moving your pointing device forward, backward, or to the side. To view a VR world, you may need to update your Web browser by downloading a VR plug-in program.

Games are a popular use of virtual reality by K-12 digital students, but VR has many practical applications as well. Companies can use VR to showcase products or create advertisements. Architects create VR models of buildings and rooms to show their clients how a construction project will look before construction

WEB INFO

For more information on streaming video, visit the Teachers Discovering Computers Web site (*scsite.com/tdc4*), click Chapter 2, click Web Info, and then click Streaming Video.

Figure 2-31 A video broadcast from the Animal Planet television channel Web site playing in RealOne Player.

begins. Virtual reality also opens up a world of learning opportunities. Science educators, for example, can create VR models of molecules, organisms, and other structures for students to examine (Figure 2-32). Students also can take virtual tours of historic sites located all over the world. Several schools even use VR to allow parents to take a virtual tour of the school from their home.

Other Internet Services

Although the World Wide Web is the most talked about service on the Internet, many other Internet services are available. These services include e-mail and blogs, FTP, newsgroups, message boards, mailing lists, chat rooms, instant messaging, Role-Playing Games (RPGs), Massively Multiplayer Online Role-Playing Games (MMORGs), facebooks, and Internet telephony. Each of these services is discussed in the following sections.

E-MAIL

E-mail (**electronic mail**) is the transmission of messages and files via a computer network. E-mail was one of the original features of the Internet, enabling scientists and researchers working on government-sponsored projects to communicate with their colleagues at other locations. Today, e-mail enables administrators, teachers, and students to communicate with millions of Internet users all over the world. E-mail has become a primary communications method for both personal and business use.

Using an **e-mail program**, you can create, send, receive, forward, store, print, and delete messages. E-mail messages can be simple text or can include attachments such as word processing documents, graphics, audio or video clips, and even family pictures (Figure 2-33).

When you receive an e-mail message, your ISP's software stores the message in your personal mailbox. Your **mailbox** is a storage location usually residing on your computer that connects you to the Internet, such as the server operated by your ISP. A **mail server** is a server that contains users' mailboxes and

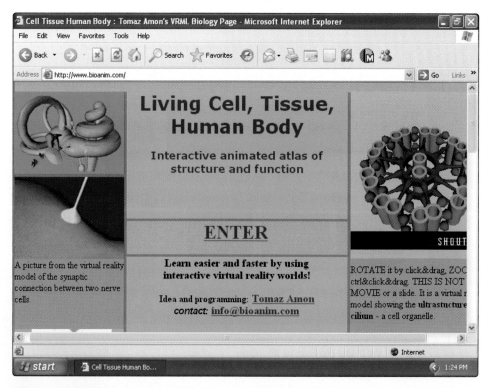

Figure 2-32 This instructional Web site uses VR to teach biology students about cells and body tissue.

associated e-mail messages. Most ISPs and online services provide an Internet e-mail program and a mailbox on a mail server as a standard part of their Internet access services. You also can use free e-mail services such as Hotmail or Yahoo! Mail.

An **e-mail address** is a combination of a username and a domain name that identifies the user so he can both send and receive messages (Figure 2-34). Your **username** is a unique combination of characters that identifies you, and it must differ from other usernames located on the same mail server. Your username sometimes is limited to eight characters and often is a combination of your first and last names, such as the initial of your first name plus your last name. You may choose a nickname or any combination of characters for your username, but unusual combinations might be harder to remember.

Although no complete listing of Internet e-mail addresses exists, several Internet sites list addresses collected from public sources. These sites also allow you to list your e-mail address voluntarily so others may find it. The site might prompt you for other information, such as the high school or college from which you graduated, so others can determine if you are the person they want to reach.

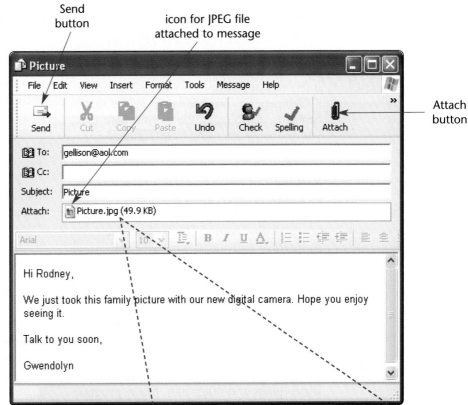

Send button

icon for JPEG file attached to message

Attach button

Figure 2-33 E-mail message with attached JPEG picture file.

user ID — often a combination of a person's first initial and last name

cbrown@ocps.k12.ca.us

domain name — location of a person's e-mail account

Figure 2-34 An example of an Internet e-mail address. Sometimes, the underscore character or a period separates sections of the user's name; for example, cindy_brown@ocps.k12.ca.us.

FTP

File Transfer Protocol (FTP) is an Internet standard that allows you to exchange files with other computers on the Internet. For example, if you click a link on a Web page in your browser window that begins to download a file to your hard disk, you probably are using FTP (Figure 2-35).

An **FTP server** is a computer that allows users to upload and download files using FTP. An FTP server contains one or more FTP sites. An **FTP site** is a collection of files, including text, graphics, audio, video, and program files. Some FTP sites limit file transfers to individuals who have authorized accounts (usernames and passwords) on the FTP server. Many corporations, for example, maintain FTP sites for their employees.

Other FTP sites allow **anonymous FTP**, whereby anyone can transfer some, if not all, available files. Many educational sites, for example, have FTP sites that use anonymous FTP to allow educators to download lesson plans and other files. Many program files located on anonymous FTP sites are freeware or shareware programs. Many FTP sites allow users to download educational and other application software for a free 30-day evaluation period. This allows teachers, administrators, and other users to evaluate software for content and appropriateness before purchasing.

To view or use an FTP file, first you must **download**, or copy, it to your computer.

In most cases, you click the filename to begin the download procedure. Large files on FTP sites often are compressed to reduce storage space and download transfer time. Before you use a compressed file, you must expand it with a decompression program, such as WinZip or Stuffit. Such programs usually are available at the FTP site or are packaged with the file you download.

In some cases, you may want to **upload**, or copy, a file to an FTP site. To upload files from your computer to an FTP site, you use an FTP program. Many ISPs include an FTP program when you subscribe to their service. Several FTP programs also are available on the Web. In addition, many operating systems such as Windows XP have built-in FTP capabilities.

NEWSGROUPS, MESSAGE BOARDS, AND BLOGS

A **newsgroup** is an online area in which users conduct written discussions about a particular subject. To participate in a discussion, a user sends a message to the newsgroup and other users in the newsgroup read and reply to the message. The entire collection of Internet newsgroups is called **Usenet**, which contains thousands of newsgroups on a multitude of topics. Some major topic areas include education, news, recreation, business, and computers.

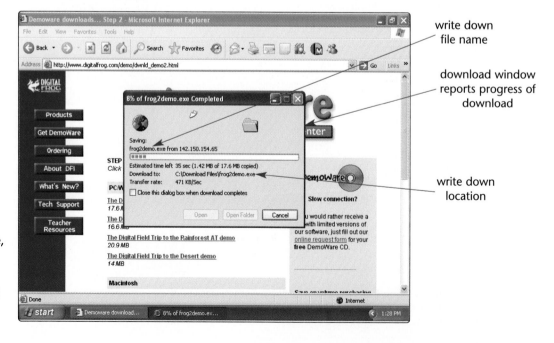

Figure 2-35
To ensure you can find the file when the download is complete, you should write down the file's name and the location in which the file is being saved.

A **news server** is a computer that stores and distributes newsgroup messages. Most universities, corporations, ISPs, online services, and other large organizations have a news server. Some newsgroups require you to enter your username and password to participate in the discussion. These types of newsgroups are used when the messages on the newsgroup are to be viewed only by authorized members, such as students taking a college course.

To participate in a newsgroup, you must use a program called a **newsreader**, which is included with most browsers. The newsreader enables you to access a newsgroup to read a previously entered message, called an **article**, and add an article of your own, called **posting**. A newsreader also keeps track of which articles you have and have not read.

Newsgroup members often post articles as a reply to another article — either to answer a question or to comment on material in the original article. These replies often cause the author of the original article, or others, to post additional articles related to the original article. The original article and all subsequent related replies are called a **thread** or **threaded discussion**. A thread can be short-lived or continue for some time, depending on the nature of the topic and the interest of the participants.

Using the newsreader, you can search for newsgroups discussing a particular subject, such as a type of musical instrument, brand of sports equipment, or educational topic. If you like the discussion in a particular newsgroup, you can **subscribe** to it, which means your newsreader saves the location so you can access it easily in the future.

A popular Web-based type of discussion group that does not require a newsreader is a message board. **Message boards** also are called discussion boards and typically are easier to use than newsgroups. Many Web sites provide message boards for their users (Figure 2-36).

A **blog**, short for Web log, is a Web site that uses a regularly updated journal format to reflect interests, opinions, and personalities of the author and sometimes site visitors. Blogs have an informal style that consists of a single individual's ideas or a collection of ideas and thoughts among visitors.

WEB INFO

For more information about message boards, visit the Teachers Discovering Computers Web site (*scsite.com/tdc4*), click Chapter 2, click Web Info, and then click Message Boards.

WEB INFO

For more information about blogs, visit the Teachers Discovering Computers Web site (*scsite.com/tdc4*), click Chapter 2, click Web Info, and then click Blogs.

Figure 2-36 Many education sites provide message boards for teachers and students.

MAILING LISTS

A **mailing list** is a group of e-mail names and addresses given a single name. When a user sends a message to a mailing list, every person on the list receives a copy of the message in her mailbox. To add your e-mail name and address to a mailing list, you subscribe to it; to remove your name, you **unsubscribe** from the mailing list. **LISTSERV** is a popular software program used to manage many educational mailing lists.

The basic difference between a newsgroup and a mailing list is that users on the mailing list discuss topics using e-mail, whereas newsgroup members use a newsreader for discussions. Thousands of mailing lists exist on a variety of topics in areas of entertainment, business, computers, society, culture, health, recreation, and education. To locate a mailing list dealing with a particular topic, you can use your Web browser to search for mailing lists or LISTSERV.

CHAT ROOMS

A **chat** is a real-time typed conversation that takes place on a computer. **Real time** means that something occurs immediately. With chat, when you enter a line of text on

your computer screen, your words immediately display on one or more participant's screens. To conduct a chat, you and the people with whom you are conversing must be online at the same time.

A **chat room** refers to the communications medium, or channel, that permits users to chat with each other. Anyone on the channel can participate in the conversation, which usually deals with a specific topic.

To start a chat session, you must connect to a chat server through a **chat client**, which is a program on your computer. Today's browsers usually include a chat client. If yours does not, you can download a chat client from the Web. Some chat clients are text-based only, whereas others support graphical and text-based chats. Some chat rooms support voice or video chats that allow users to hear and see each other.

After you install a chat client, you then can create or join a conversation on a chat server. The channel name should indicate the topic of discussion. The person who creates a channel acts as the channel operator and has responsibility for monitoring the conversation and disconnecting anyone who becomes disruptive. Users can share operator status or transfer operator status to someone else.

Numerous controlled and monitored chat rooms are available for K-12 students and teachers. Several Web sites also exist for the purpose of conducting chats. Some chat sites even allow participants to assume the role or appearance of a character.

INSTANT MESSAGING

Instant messaging (**IM**) is a real-time Internet communications service that notifies you when one or more people are online and then allows you to exchange messages or files, or join a private chat room with them (Figure 2-37). Many IM services can alert you to

WEB INFO

For more information on mailing lists, visit the Teachers Discovering Computers Web site (*scsite.com/tdc4*), click Chapter 2, click Web Info, and then click Mailing Lists.

message sent from Karen to Katy

Karen's message immediately displays on Katy's computer screen because she is online

Katy's response to Karen

Figure 2-37 Instant messaging is a very popular means of communication used by today's teenagers.

information, such as calendar appointments, stock quotes, weather, or sport scores.

People use IM on all types of computers, including handheld computers and Web-enabled devices. Although popular with all age groups, instant messaging services such as AOL Instant Messenger have become a staple of teenage life for tens of millions of middle and high school students from all around the world. IM has become the basic form of communications for the digital generation.

RPGS, MMORGS, FACEBOOKS, AND PODCASTING

Role-Playing Games (RPGs) are very popular with middle and high school students. RPGs are normally tied to themes or topics, such as Harry Potter RPGs and Star Wars RPGs. Many RPGs are created by a group of friends who have a common interest in a topic and you have to be invited to join. Others are created for people interested in specific topics. **Massively Multiplayer Online Role-Playing Games (MMORGs)** cover a wider range of topics and typically include people from all over the world.

Facebooks provide a new way for college students to meet and chat. After you register, you can upload your picture and set up your profile. Facebooks allow you to stay in touch with friends and make new friends based on your interests and your friends' interests.

Podcasting is a way of automatically publishing sound and more recently small picture or video files to the Internet. Users subscribe to a feed and receive new audio files automatically by using what is called a Really Simple Syndication (RSS) protocol that allows users to automatically receive the feeds. The original idea came from the desire for a way to create audio versions of blogs. A growing number of individuals use podcasting to create their own syndicated radio shows. In education, podcasting can be very useful for teachers who want to automatically send class content to their students, announcements, etc. A growing number of teachers and digital students who own iPods or other similar devices are using these digital communication tools to make it easier to keep up with current events and stay in touch with each other.

INTERNET TELEPHONY

Internet telephony, also called **Voice over IP** (Internet Protocol), enables users to speak to other users over the Internet using their desktop computer, mobile computer, or mobile device. That is, Internet telephony uses the Internet (instead of traditional telephone networks) to connect a calling party to one or more local or long-distance parties.

As you speak into a microphone or telephone connected to your computer, the Internet telephone software and the computer's sound card or the telephone adapter convert your spoken words (analog signals) to digital signals and then transmit the digitized audio over the Internet to the people you are calling. Software and equipment at the receiving end reverse the process so the receiving parties can hear what you said. Figure 2-38 illustrates a user's equipment configuration for Internet telephony.

WEB INFO

For more information about chat rooms, RPGs, MMORGs, facebooks, and podcasts, visit the Teachers Discovering Computers Web site (*scsite.com/tdc4*), click Chapter 2, click Web Info, and then click Chat Rooms, RPG, MMORG, Facebook, or Podcast.

FAQ

How popular is Internet telephony?

One study predicts that by 2007, more than five million people will subscribe to Internet telephony services.

cable/DSL modem

Internet

telephone adapter

personal computer

telephone

Figure 2-38 Equipment configuration for a user making a call via Internet telephony.

Netiquette

Netiquette, which is short for **Internet etiquette**, is the code of acceptable behaviors users should follow while on the Internet — that is, the conduct expected of individuals while online. Netiquette includes rules for all aspects of the Internet, including the Web, e-mail, FTP, newsgroups and message boards, chat rooms, and instant messaging. Figure 2-39 outlines the rules of netiquette.

Internet Security

Any time a school district or business connects its private network to a public network such as the Internet, it must consider security concerns such as unauthorized access to confidential information. To prevent unauthorized access, schools and businesses implement one or more layers of security. A **firewall** is a general term that refers to both hardware and software used to restrict access to data on a network. Firewalls deny network access to unauthorized personnel. For example, firewalls restrict students from access to inappropriate materials or sensitive information such as student grades and attendance records.

Even with netiquette guidelines, the Internet still opens up the possibility for inappropriate behaviors and content. For example, amidst the wealth of information and services on the Internet, some content may be inappropriate for certain people. Some Web sites, newsgroups, and chat rooms, for instance, contain content or discussions that are unsuitable for children. Schools need to ensure that students do not gain access to inappropriate or objectionable materials.

To assist schools and parents with these types of issues, many browsers include software that can screen out unacceptable content. You also can purchase stand-alone Internet **filtering software**, which allows parents, teachers, and others to block access to certain materials on the Internet.

Schools help protect students from the negative aspects of the Internet by using filtering software, firewalls, and teacher observation. Most schools also use an **Acceptable**

WEB INFO

For more information about filtering software, visit the Teachers Discovering Computers Web site (*scsite.com/tdc4*), click Chapter 2, click Web Info, and then click Filtering Software.

WEB INFO

For more information about Acceptable Use Policies (AUPs), visit the Teachers Discovering Computers Web site (*scsite.com/tdc4*), click Chapter 2, click Web Info, and then click AUP.

Netiquette

Golden Rule: *Treat others as you would like them to treat you.*

1. In e-mail, newsgroups, and chat rooms:
   - Keep messages brief using proper grammar and spelling.
   - Be careful when using sarcasm and humor, as it might be misinterpreted.
   - Be polite. Avoid offensive language.
   - Avoid sending or posting **flames**, which are abusive or insulting messages. Do not participate in **flame wars**, which are exchanges of flames.
   - Avoid sending spam, which is the Internet's version of junk mail. **Spam** is an unsolicited e-mail message or newsgroup posting sent to many recipients or newsgroups at once.
   - Do not use all capital letters, which is the equivalent of SHOUTING!
   - Use **emoticons** to express emotion. Popular emoticons include

:)	Smile	:\	Undecided
:(	Frown	:o	Surprised
:|	Indifference		

   - Use abbreviations and acronyms for phrases such as

BTW	by the way
FYI	for your information
FWIW	for what it's worth
IMHO	in my humble opinion
TTFN	ta ta for now
TYVM	thank you very much

   - Clearly identify a **spoiler**, which is a message that reveals a solution to a game or ending to a movie or program.

2. Read the **FAQ** (frequently asked questions) document, if one exists. Many newsgroups and Web pages have a FAQ.

3. Use your username for your personal use only.

4. Do not assume material is accurate or up to date. Be forgiving of others' mistakes.

5. Never read someone's private e-mail.

Figure 2-39 The rules of netiquette.

Use Policy (AUP), which is an outline of user standards that reminds teachers, students, and parents that they are guests on the Internet and that they need to use it appropriately. Most schools require students, teachers, and parents to sign AUPs. Chapter 8 discusses these and other security issues in greater detail.

The Impact of the Internet and the World Wide Web on Education

More than 500 years ago, Johannes Gutenberg developed a printing press that made the written word accessible to the public and revolutionized the way people shared information. The World Wide Web is the Gutenberg printing press of modern times — opening doors to new learning resources and opportunities and allowing the sharing of information and knowledge such as never before. Just a few years ago, most students were unable to visit the Grand Canyon, the White House, the Smithsonian Institution, the National Art Gallery, or the Louvre Museum. Today, students around the world can visit these historic places and thousands of others on the Web, exploring these locales on interactive and sometimes even virtual tours.

Not only does the Internet provide access to extensive text and multimedia resources, it also allows teachers and students to communicate with other teachers and students all over the world. For example, **ePALS** Classroom Exchange is a project designed to enable students to develop an understanding of different cultures through student e-mail exchanges (Figure 2-40). The mission of ePALS is to have students creatively write in primary and secondary languages, as well as do research and gather information about other cultures and individuals. Project ePALS is adaptable for any grade level in any country.

As the Internet expanded and evolved from a text-based communications system into the powerful multimedia communications system of today, educators quickly recognized the tremendous potential of the Internet — and especially the Web — to revolutionize the classroom. By providing a variety of learning tools, the Internet and the Web are transforming the way teachers instruct and the way students learn basic skills and core subjects. These changes have brought the Web to the forefront of instructional strategies in education in a very short period.

WEB INFO

For more information about ePALS, visit the Teachers Discovering Computers Web site (*scsite.com/tdc4*), click Chapter 2, click Web Info, and then click ePALS.

Figure 2-40 An online project, ePals, allows millions of students from all over the world to communicate with each other.

The potential of the Web for improving the way to teach K-12 students is enormous, is still growing, and will continue to expand for many years to come.

Throughout this textbook, hundreds of links and dozens of exercises will help you understand the incredible possibilities the Web offers for K-12 education in general and your classroom in particular.

The Future of the Internet and the World Wide Web

What is the future of the Internet and the World Wide Web? Without question, the Web will continue to evolve as a primary communications channel for people around the world. As the Web grows in size and operates at higher speeds, it will continue to have a major influence on restructuring K-12 education. Other predictions regarding the future of the Internet and the World Wide Web and its impact on education include the following:

- In the next few years, the Internet will connect most of the world's computers.

- By 2007, more than one billion wireless communication devices will be in use worldwide, and many of these products will have the ability to access the Web wirelessly.

- All K-12 teachers will have access to high-speed Internet in their classrooms.

- Wireless networks, wireless notebook computers, wireless mobile labs, wireless Tablet PCs, and other wireless devices will become commonplace in K-12 education.

- Everyday home and office appliances and other devices that use embedded computers, such as automobiles, will have built-in Internet access capabilities.

- Web search capabilities will be more intelligent and focused.

- Within a few years, the Web will operate at speeds 10,000 times faster than today.

- Businesses will continue to be the driving force behind the Web's expansion.

- Increased access speeds and greater availability will allow teachers and students to view thousands of full-motion videos over the Web.

- The Web will become an integral part of all education and will revolutionize the way students learn core subjects.

Finally, many experts believe that separate, proprietary networks used for telephone, television, and radio will merge with the Internet. Eventually, a single, integrated network will exist, made up of many different media that will carry all communications traffic.

Guide to World Wide Web Sites and Searching Techniques

At the end of this chapter is a special feature that contains links to and information about more than 200 popular up-to-date Web sites. This special feature also introduces you to using search tools and contains links and information on popular education-specific search tools.

The best way to learn how to use the Internet and the World Wide Web is to log on and explore. Choose a subject and use a search tool to see what is on the World Wide Web. To display this interactive special feature, use your browser to go to *scsite.com/tdc4* to open the textbook's Web site, then click Guide to WWW Sites on the left sidebar (Figure 2-41). Click the links to access the various Web sites and search tools.

FAQ

What is Wi-Fi?

Wi-Fi is wireless fidelity and outlines standards for wireless technology. To learn more about Wi-Fi and the wireless revolution, review the special feature, A World Without Wires, which follows Chapter 8.

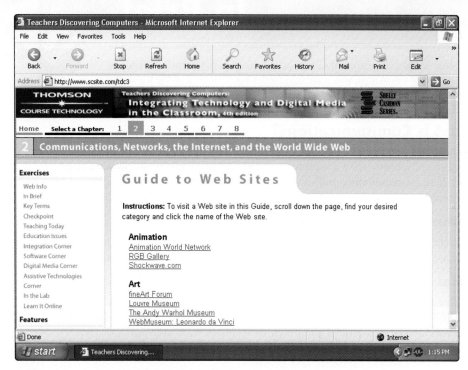

Figure 2-41 Guide to WWW Sites special feature displayed at this textbook's Web site.

Summary of Communications, Networks, the Internet, and the World Wide Web

Communications will continue to impact how you work, learn, teach, access information, and use computers. Because of communications technology, individuals, schools, and organizations no longer are limited to local data resources; they can obtain information instantly from anywhere in the world. Communications networks are just one way that school districts will use communications technology to meet current instructional and management challenges. In just a few years, the Internet and World Wide Web may redefine education, just as it has transformed modern businesses and today's society. As educators all over the world integrate the Internet and the World Wide Web into their classroom curriculum, their efforts are creating an educational revolution in today's schools — one that is having a significant positive impact on the quality of graduating students.

In Brief

INSTRUCTIONS: In Brief summarizes the concepts presented in this chapter. To listen to the audio version of this In Brief, visit scsite.com/tdc4. Click Chapter 2 at the top of the Web page and then click In Brief on the left sidebar.

1. What Is Communications?

Communications, sometimes called **telecommunications**, refers to the transmission of data between two or more computers using a communications channel. **Electronic mail (e-mail)**, **voice mail**, **facsimile (fax)**, **telecommuting**, **online services**, **videoconferencing**, the **Internet**, and the **World Wide Web** are examples of applications that rely on communications technology.

2. Communications Networks

A **communications network** is a collection of computers and other equipment organized to share, data, hardware, and software. Networks also require **communications software**.

3. Local and Wide Area Networks

A **local area network (LAN)** is a communications network that covers a limited geographical area, such as a school, an office, a building, or a group of buildings. A LAN consists of a number of computers connected to a central computer, or server. A wide area network (**WAN**) covers a large geographical region (such as a city or school district) and uses regular telephone cables, digital lines, microwaves, wireless systems, and satellites.

4. Benefits of Computer Networks

One benefit of networking is that administrators, teachers, and students can share computer hardware, software, and data resources. The most important benefit of networking school computers is that administrators, teachers, and students can access instantly the unlimited educational resources available on the Internet and communicate with other educators and students all over the world.

5. The Internet

The **Internet** is a worldwide collection of networks that link together millions of businesses, governments, educational institutions, and individuals via modems, telephone lines, and other communications devices and media. Each of these networks provides resources and data that add to the abundance of goods, services, and information accessible via the Internet.

6. How the Internet Works

The Internet operates by dividing data into separate parts, called **packets**, and sending the packets along the best route available to a destination computer. The software used to perform this technique, called **packet switching**, is a communications protocol named **Transmission Control Protocol/Internet Protocol (TCP/IP)**. People can connect to the Internet through an organization such as a school or company, an **online service provider** (**OSP**), or an **Internet service provider** (**ISP**).

7. The World Wide Web

The **World Wide Web**, or simply **Web**, consists of a worldwide collection of electronic documents that have built-in hyperlinks to other related documents. These **hyperlinks**, also called **links**, allow users to navigate quickly from one Web page to another, regardless of whether the Web pages are located on the same computer or on different computers in different countries.

8. How a Web Page Works

A **Web page** is an electronic document viewed on the Web. A Web page is a **hypertext** document (document with text hyperlinks) or **hypermedia** document (document with text, graphics, video, or sound hyperlinks) residing on an Internet computer. The three types of hyperlinks are **target hyperlinks** that move from one location in a document to another location in the same document; **relative hyperlinks** that move from one document to another document on the same Internet

In Brief

computer; and **absolute hyperlinks** that move from one document to
another document on a different Internet computer. Displaying pages one Web site after another is
called **Web surfing**. Web pages are created using **Hypertext Markup Language (HTML)**, which is a
set of special instructions that specifies links to other documents and how the page is displayed.

9. Web Browser Software

Web browser software is a program that interprets and displays Web pages and enables you to link
to other Web pages. Each time a browser is started, a **home page** appears. The browser retrieves
Web pages using a **Uniform Resource Locator (URL)**, which is an address that points to a specific
resource on the Internet. Browsers display hyperlinks either as underlined text of a different color
or as graphical images. A linked document can be displayed by clicking the hyperlink or by typing
its URL in the location bar or Address text box.

10. Web Search Tools

Search tools enable users to locate information found at Web sites all over the world. Two basic
types of search tools exist: search engines and subject directories. A **search engine** is a specific type
of search tool that finds Web sites, Web pages, and Internet files that match one or more keywords
you enter. A **subject directory** allows users to navigate to areas of interest without having to enter
keywords.

11. Multimedia on the Web

Some of the more exciting Web developments involve multimedia. Most browsers have the
capability of displaying basic multimedia elements on a Web page. Sometimes, however, the
browser needs an additional program called a **plug-in**, which extends the capability of the
browser. Web pages may include the following multimedia elements: **graphics**, **animation**, **audio**,
video, and **virtual reality (VR)**.

12. Other Internet Services

Although the Web is the most talked about service on the Internet, many other Internet services
are available. These services include e-mail, FTP, newsgroups, message boards, blogs, mailing lists,
chat rooms, instant messaging, and Internet telephony. **E-mail (electronic mail)** is the transmission
of messages and files via a computer network. **File Transfer Protocol (FTP)** is an Internet standard
that allows you to exchange files with other computers on the Internet. A **newsgroup** is an online
area in which users conduct written discussions about a particular subject. A **chat** is a real-time
typed conversation that takes place on a computer. **Instant messaging (IM)** is a real-time Internet
communications service that notifies you when one or more people are online, and then allows you
to exchange messages. **Internet telephony** enables users to speak to other users over the Internet
using their desktop computer, mobile computer, or mobile device.

13. Netiquette and Security

Netiquette is the code of acceptable behaviors users should follow while on the Internet. To
prevent unauthorized access, schools and businesses implement one or more layers of security.
A firewall is a general term that refers to both hardware and software used to restrict access to
data on a network. Internet **filtering software** allows parents, teachers, and others to block access
to certain materials on the Internet.

Key Terms

INSTRUCTIONS: Use the Key Terms list to help focus your study of the terms used in this chapter. To further enhance your understanding of the Key Terms in this chapter, visit scsite.com/tdc4. Click Chapter 2 at the top of the Web page and then click Key Terms on the left sidebar. Read the definition for each term and then access current and additional information about the term from the Web.

absolute hyperlink [84]
Acceptable Use Policy (AUP) [98]
Advanced Research Projects Agency (ARPA) [75]
analog signal [66]
animated GIF [89]
animation [89]
anonymous FTP [94]
ARPANET [76]
article [95]
audio [89]

backbone [76]
bandwidth [72]
blog [95]
bookmark [87]
broadband [72]
browser [85]

cable modem [79]
chat [96]
chat client [96]
chat room [96]
communications [65]
communications channel [66]
communications protocol [78]
communications software [66]

dial-up access [78]
digital signal [66]
digital subscriber line (DSL) [79]
discovery learning [84]
domain name [81]
download [94]

e-mail address [93]
e-mail program [92]
electronic mail (e-mail) [92]
emoticon [98]
ePALS [99]

facebook [97]
FAQ [98]
favorite [87]
File Transfer Protocol (FTP) [94]
filtering software [98]
firewall [98]
flame [98]
flame war [98]
FTP server [94]
FTP site [94]

graphical image [88]
graphics [88]

history list [86]
home network [68]
home page [83]

host [76]
http:// [83]
hyperlink [82]
hypermedia [83]
hypertext [83]
Hypertext Markup Language (HTML) [84]
Hypertext Transfer Protocol [83]

instant messaging (IM) [96]
internal modem [67]
Internet [73]
Internet2 (I2) [77]
Internet backbone [80]
Internet etiquette [98]
Internet service provider (ISP) [78]
Internet telephony [97]

link [82]
LISTSERV [96]
local area network (LAN) [68]

mailbox [92]
mailing list [96]
mail server [92]
marquee [89]
Massively Multiplayer Online Role-Playing Game (MMORG) [97]
message board [95]
microbrowser [86]
modem [66]
Mosaic [85]
multimedia [87]

national ISP [78]
National Science Foundation (NSF) [76]
Net [73]
netiquette [98]
network [66]
network interface card (NIC) [68]
newsgroup [94]
newsreader [95]
news server [95]
NSFnet [76]

online service provider (OSP) [78]

packet [77]
packet switching [78]
player [90]
plug-in [87]
podcasting [97]
posting [95]
power line communications (PLC) [80]
public Internet access point [80]

real time [96]
regional ISP [78]
relative hyperlink [84]
Role-Playing Game (RPG) [97]
routers [77]

satellite modem [80]
search engine [87]
search tool [87]
server [68]
spam [98]
spoiler [98]
streaming [90]
streaming audio [90]
streaming video [91]
subject directory [87]
subscribe [95]

tags [84]
target hyperlink [84]
telecommunications [65]
thread [95]
threaded discussion [95]
thumbnail [89]
traffic [76]
Transmission Control Protocol/Internet Protocol (TCP/IP) [78]
transmission media [66]
twisted-pair cable [66]

Uniform Resource Locator (URL) [83]
unsubscribe [96]
upload [94]
Usenet [94]
username [93]

video [91]
virtual reality (VR) [91]
Voice over IP (VoIP) [97]
VR world [91]

Web [82]
Web browser [85]
Webmaster [84]
Web log [95]
Web page [83]
Web publishing [85]
Web server [83]
Web site [83]
Web surfing [84]
wide area network (WAN) [68]
Wi-Fi [100]
wireless LAN (WLAN) [68]
wireless Internet service provider (WISP) [78]
World Wide Web [82]

Checkpoint

INSTRUCTIONS: Use the Checkpoint exercises to check your knowledge level of the chapter. To complete the Checkpoint exercises interactively, visit scsite.com/tdc4. Click Chapter 2 at the top of the Web page and then click Checkpoint on the left sidebar.

1. Label the Figure

Instructions: Identify the components of a communications system.

2. Matching

Instructions: Match each term from the column on the left with the best description from the column on the right.

____ 1. e-mail

____ 2. Webmaster

____ 3. network

____ 4. filtering software

____ 5. search tool

a. an individual responsible for developing Web pages and maintaining a Web site

b. a collection of computers and other equipment organized to share data, hardware, and software

c. the transmission of messages and files via a computer network

d. enables users to locate information found at Web sites all over the world

e. allows parents, teachers, and others to block access to certain materials on the Internet

3. Short Answer

Instructions: Write a brief answer to each of the following questions.

1. How are local area networks (LANs) different from wide area networks (WANs)? _____

2. What is a Web page? What purpose do hyperlinks have on a Web page? What is Hypertext Markup Language (HTML)? _____

3. Explain the process of streaming over the Web. How are streaming audio and streaming video similar? For what purposes is streaming used? _____

4. What is a firewall? What is filtering software? What is an Acceptable Use Policy (AUP)? Why is the use of firewalls, filtering software, and AUPs so important for K-12 networks? _____

5. What is a search tool? Name the two basic types of search tools and describe how each of these works. Which would you use to search for links in the category, Education? _____

Teaching Today

INSTRUCTIONS: Teaching Today provides an appreciation of the value that technology and the Web have for K-12 education. Each numbered segment contains one or more links that reinforce the information presented in the segment. To display this page from the Web, visit scsite.com/tdc4. Click Chapter 2 at the top of the Web page and then click Teaching Today on the left sidebar.

1. Lesson Plans

Using the Internet in the classroom has numerous benefits for teachers, who can use it to find current information, online resources for lesson plans and Web-based projects, and interactive content that engages all types of learners. What are some other benefits of using the Internet in the classroom? Are there disadvantages or problems you might encounter in using Internet resources? How might you avoid or solve these problems?

2. Search Engines

You have started using the computer lab to work on classroom projects with your students, which is a great opportunity for all students to get hands-on experiences with different technologies. Scanners, videos, CDs, DVDs, and many other technologies are available from which to choose. Students also can access the Internet. Managing your students in the lab while they explore these different technologies is a challenge. You decide to design a project so your students will work in groups to research a famous person in history. Do students need guidance on how to use a search engine to perform a proper search? Do they need help to avoid getting lost using the various technologies? Is asking the correct question or questions an important part of the solution for finding the correct answer? What about searching reference materials? Are students using primary and secondary resources? How could you design a plan in which the students collaborate to develop effective projects while you still manage a classroom of students working on different projects and technologies? How could you design research projects that go beyond the standard writing of a paper to engage students in using many different types of technologies in a collaborative way?

3. Electronic Mail

Electronic mail (e-mail) has become a preferred means of communications for many businesses, schools, and individuals. Whether using an internal network or the Internet for e-mail, you should be aware of netiquette guidelines to help

ensure that recipients understand the intent behind your e-mail messages. Some users, for example, add emoticons to an e-mail message to communicate intended emotions (by adding a smiley face to a funny comment, for example). How is using e-mail different from writing a letter? What are the similarities, if any? How might you use e-mail in your classroom with students? What benefits might your students experience from using e-mail?

4. Rules and Regulations

The Internet and the Web contain thousands of wonderful sites for educators and students of all ages. Unfortunately, the Web has sites that are inappropriate for children, and some that collect information that invade the privacy of adults and children. The Federal Trade Commission's Children's Online Privacy Protection Act (COPPA) was passed by Congress in October 1998 to protect children from those who would steal personal information. COPPA also provides information on how to locate sites that have been reviewed by experts and rated as safe for children. All teachers, students, and parents should become knowledgeable about the rules and regulations that exist to protect their identity. How can you ensure student privacy on the Internet? As a teacher, what can you do to teach your students about Internet safety, information privacy, and more?

Education Issues

INSTRUCTIONS: Education Issues provides several scenarios that allow you to explore controversial and current issues in education. Each numbered segment contains one or more links that reinforce the information presented in the segment. To display this page from the Web, visit scsite.com/tdc4. Click Chapter 2 at the top of the Web page and then click Education Issues on the left sidebar.

1. Digital Equity

More people are connected to the Internet than ever before, but a large population of users is still not connected. Students do not always have access to technology, the Internet, and the World Wide Web and this creates a division between the technology haves and have-nots, known as the digital divide. The National Telecommunications and Information Administration (NTIA) states that the gap between the haves and have-nots is increasing. You design a project that requires your students to work in groups and conduct research on a specific content area. Knowing that only a portion of your students have computers at home, how can you design meaningful homework assignments that take into account students who do not have access to computers or the Internet at home?

2. Diplomas Online

Attending a traditional college for an undergraduate, masters, or doctoral level degree can be a rewarding experience. However, many people do not have the opportunity or time to attend a traditional college. Many traditional colleges and universities address this problem with online classes and/or complete online degree programs. Recent research indicates that online classes are as good as or better than traditional classroom classes. Yet, many argue that even the best online classes lack some of the most important features of traditional classes, such as casual talks with professors and informal study groups in the dorm. Others argue that online classes can include these interactive components. What are some of the advantages and disadvantages of online classes? Does a degree earned online from a fully accredited online university have the same value as a traditional degree? What variables do you think would enhance or hinder the possibility of you receiving an online degree? What type of student do you think is best, and least, suited for online classes? Why?

3. Virtual High Schools

Today, many high schools, especially small rural high schools, have difficulty offering classes such as AP biology, Latin, AP calculus, and other similar classes due to budget constraints, classroom overcrowding, lack of qualified teachers, and other important issues. Currently, many school districts and states are addressing these problems by offering a variety of online classes. Most educators agree that the Internet has great potential for education and that online classes need to be part of the K-12 learning environment. Some districts have opened 100 percent online or virtual high schools, which has generated a heated debate among educators about the effectiveness

and even appropriateness of such schools. Do you think 100 percent online high schools are an effective solution? Why or why not? Substantiate your answer.

4. Net Censoring

Each day, schools, organizations, and individuals across the country continue in an ongoing debate about Internet censorship. A number of organizations, including the American Library Association (ALA), oppose the use of Internet filtering software programs. Some people feel that schools are censoring valuable information and that students would be better off with unlimited access, coupled with strict teacher observation and guidelines. Others, however, are very concerned about the use of the Internet in schools and do not want children using the Internet — even if filtering programs and Acceptable Use Policies (AUPs) are in place. Do you think schools should limit or ban Internet usage? How could you use the Internet effectively in your classroom without offending or angering parents?

Integration Corner

INSTRUCTIONS: Integration Corner provides extensive ideas and resources for integrating technology into your classroom-specific curriculum. To display this page from the Web and its links to approximately 100 educational Web sites, visit scsite.com/tdc4. Click Chapter 2 at the top of the Web page and then click Integration Corner on the left sidebar.

Integration Corner is designed for teachers and other educators who are looking for innovative ways to integrate technology into their content-specific curriculum. Integration Corner not only provides great Web sites with current information, but it also shows what other educators are doing in the field of educational technology. These Corners are designed for all educators regardless of their area of interest. Be sure to review information and sites outside of your teaching area because many great integration ideas in one area can be modified easily for use in other curricular areas.

Teachers and administrators will find other colleagues in their areas with whom to connect and share the successes and hurdles of integrating technology in a classroom or an entire school system. Consider this your one stop for integration ideas and resources. Links to educational Web sites are organized in the following 12 Corners, and different Web resources are available for each chapter. Figure 2-42 shows examples of the Web resources provided in the Chapter 2 Elementary Corner.

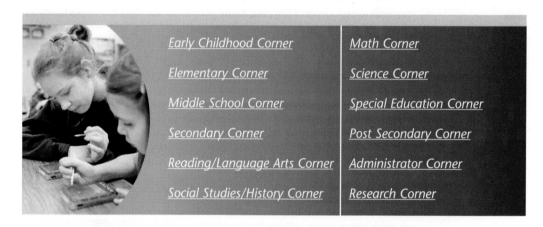

Early Childhood Corner   *Math Corner*

Elementary Corner   *Science Corner*

Middle School Corner   *Special Education Corner*

Secondary Corner   *Post Secondary Corner*

Reading/Language Arts Corner   *Administrator Corner*

Social Studies/History Corner   *Research Corner*

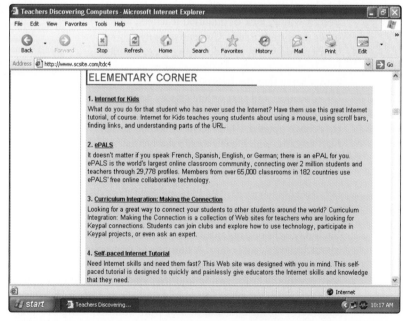

Figure 2-42 Examples of the Web resources provided in the Chapter 2 Elementary Corner.

Software Corner

INSTRUCTIONS: Software Corner provides information on popular software programs. Each numbered segment discusses specific software programs and contains a link to additional information about these programs. To display this page from the Web, visit scsite.com/tdc4. Click Chapter 2 at the top of the Web page and then click Software Corner on the left sidebar.

1. WebWhacker

If you have concerns about students accessing inappropriate Web sites while surfing the Internet, take a look at the software program, WebWhacker, which allows educators to *whack* Web sites and save them to a hard drive or a floppy disk. With WebWhacker, you simply determine how many levels of the Web site you need for your students to access and then save the necessary Web pages. Students will not even realize they are not on the Internet right away because the program saves the Web sites exactly as they look, complete with links, buttons, animations, and all other features intact and working. WebWhacker is a super way for you to download information, while keeping your students on task and protecting them from unsuitable Web information.

2. Bailey's Book House

Bailey's Book House, produced by EDMARK, provides seven activities for prekindergarten to second grade students to learn letters and their sounds, words, common adjectives, rhyming, storytelling, and more. Students can enjoy rhymes and give them zany endings just for fun. This software also allows students to create their own storybooks and greeting cards. Bailey's Book House is an excellent tool for teaching important beginning skills to preschoolers.

3. Math Companion

Math Companion is a powerful mathematical activity sheet generator developed for grades K-8 that has been aligned with 110 basic math objectives of the National Council for Teaching Mathematics (NCTM). Math Companion is a super tool for teachers and parents that provides students with many examples of mathematical problems. Math Companion, Volume 1, allows you to create custom activity sheets for word problems, basic math skills, and anagrams. You even can import line art graphics to create color-in activity sheets in minutes! Time, money, place value, fractions, and geometry are all covered in this program. Create games, flash cards, and worksheets using Math Companion, Volume 2. Both of these titles help students master important math skills.

4. Encarta Reference Library

Finding information for students to complete research papers and multimedia projects is made easy with the help of reference software; and it is easy to use. Simply type keywords and search. The Encarta Reference Library combines nine great resources that include Encarta Encyclopedia Deluxe, Encarta Interactive World Atlas, Learning Tools, and more. It also includes an almanac, a dictionary, and an authoritative resource on many topics that enhance reports and multimedia presentations in classrooms of all ages.

5. Digital Frog

High school science teachers will enjoy using Digital Frog; it explains a frog dissection without the disgusting smell of formaldehyde! Digital Frog uses full color video and detailed animations, including 3-D, to explain the dissection of a frog. Scientific definitions and human comparisons help clarify difficult concepts for students. The program uses narration, color photos, and graphics to explain the entire process.

Digital Media Corner

INSTRUCTIONS: Today's K-12 digital students need their learning to be meaningful and relevant to their lives. Digital Media Corner provides videos, ideas, and examples of how you can use digital media to enhance your teaching and your students' learning. To access the videos and links to additional information, visit scsite.com/tdc4. Click Chapter 2 at the top of the Web page and then click Digital Media on the left sidebar.

1. At the Movies — Choosing a Broadband Provider

Are you thinking about changing from dial-up Internet access to high-speed access? Do you want to be able to download larger files, including movies, streaming radio station shows, online games, entire photo albums, and much more? To learn more about Choosing a Broadband Provider, click the G4TechTV video link. Locate your video and click the corresponding High-Speed or Dial-up link, depending on your Internet connection.

2. At the Movies — Google Search Secrets

Using the Internet to gather information can seem daunting. Being able to properly utilize a search engine can benefit both you and your students. How might you and your students use Google to search for information for a research paper or a group project? To learn more, including seven secrets or search tricks, click the G4TechTV video link. Locate your video and click the corresponding High-Speed or Dial-up link, depending on your Internet connection.

3. At the Movies — Instant Message from Anywhere

Today's digital students use instant messaging (IM) as an essential tool to stay in touch with their friends, but until recently, it has been limited to use on a computer. New technology developments have cut the wires, and now you can take IM on the road. To learn more about wireless IM, click the G4TechTV video link. Locate your video and click the corresponding High-Speed or Dial-up link, depending on your Internet connection.

4. Two Way Interactive Connections in Education

As you learned in Chapter 1, the majority of U.S. public schools have implemented United Streaming's digital video library capabilities, but some schools are at the forefront of utilizing the speedy Internet for interactive education. TWICE, which stands for **Two Way Interactive Connections in Education**, promotes collaborative connections both nationally and regionally. On a national level, TWICE coordinates Read Across America Day: Connecting Classrooms for Literacy each March. TWICE provides Michigan schools the opportunity to conduct videoconference field trips, which provides Michigan students with interactive learning experiences all over the country. For example, students sheltered from snowy weather in Detroit can visit NASA for a launch in tropical Cape Canaveral, Florida. While on their virtual field trip, students have the full attention of a NASA employee who receives and answers their questions in real time!

5. Flash

Most people know the term Flash as a plug-in that allows users to view digital media enhancements on the Web. Flash is also a popular software application that is a dynamic digital media-creation program used to create interactive animations, Web sites, presentations, games, Flash movies, and much more. Math 6 is a Flash Web site designed for today's digital 6th graders that includes extensive lessons and other resources for teaching and learning sixth grade mathematics. These lessons are Flash-based games/animations in which text, graphics, and audio move and change as the lesson progresses as well as generate problems for students to solve. Math 6 also provides a glossary of math terms, an overview of the basic operations, and strategies.

Assistive Technologies Corner

INSTRUCTIONS: Assistive Technologies Corner provides information on current hardware, software, and peripherals that will assist you in delivering instruction to students with physical, cognitive, or sensory challenges. To access extensive additional information, visit scsite.com/tdc4. Click Chapter 2 at the top of the Web page and then click Assistive Technologies on the left sidebar.

1. How Does a Person Who is Deaf or Hard of Hearing Use the Telephone?

A student who is mildly hard of hearing may choose to use an amplified telephone, one that makes telephone communication louder and more understandable. Persons who are deaf or more severely hard of hearing have used teletypewriter (TTY) or Telecommunication Devices for the Deaf (TDD) for many years. A TTY has a keyboard, a text display, and a coupler. A regular phone connection is established between two users and both users must have a TTY. The phone handset is placed into the coupler fitted for both parts of the handset. One user begins typing. The words appear on the text display for both users and the conversation proceeds. At one time, these were large bulky machines; however, today's TTYs are portable and can connect to cell phones.

Another and newer tool allows high-quality video relay such as that provided by Sorenson Video Relay Service (VRS). The VRS uses a sign language interpreter to translate voice and sign communication. A user connects with the video relay service. The interpreter places the call, and all communication goes through the interpreter. One user with a video display and camera signs to the interpreter, who translates simultaneously to the voice telephone user. When the voice user speaks, the interpreter signs, and the message is viewed on the signer's video display. Wireless communication devices with QWERTY keyboards and the associated services have brought communication freedom to the deaf and hard of hearing. The wireless services of blackberry.com, for example, provide solutions, including instant messaging and wireless e-mail.

2. How Can a Blind or Visually Impaired Person Access the Graphical Web?

The graphical nature of today's Web provides the biggest obstacle to students with a visual disability. We can make accommodations through assistive technology. Visual impairments vary in severity and in type. A slight impairment may be accommodated by activating the built-in accessibility features of the browser. For most browsers, you can increase the size of the text that is viewed on the screen.

Blind users, however, require special software installed on their computers such as a screen reader that renders text to voice. Two popular screen readers are Freedom Scientific's JAWS and GW Micro's Window Eyes. Screen reader programs read all text that appears on the computer screen. Screen reader programs provide equal access for students. Because a blind user does not use a mouse, the screen reader requires keyboard skills. These programs are somewhat expensive. Somewhat less expensive is IBM's Homepage Reader, which is a talking browser. A blind user opens the browser and the Homepage Reader software reads the contents of the Web page aloud. A different voice indicates a link, and the user selects the link using the keyboard.

3. What About Web Page Accessibility?

A screen reader, a talking browser, or any assistive device can work well only with Web pages that are accessible, that is, they met the criteria for standards that allow smooth integration of technologies. However, many Web sites are not fully accessible because the code used to create them does not follow accessibility guidelines, or they use technologies that are simply not accessible. To determine if a Web page is accessible for the student, a teacher may visit Bobby Worldwide, which is a free site that allows users to test Web sites to verify that they are accessible.

Follow the instructions at the top of this page to display additional information and this chapter's links on assistive technologies.

In the Lab 2

INSTRUCTIONS: In the Lab provides word processing exercises that are divided into two areas, productivity and integration. To access the links to tutorials, productivity ideas, integration examples and ideas, and more, visit scsite.com/tdc4. Click Chapter 2 at the top of the Web page and then click In the Lab on the left sidebar.

PRODUCTIVITY IN THE CLASSROOM

Introduction: All students and teachers need to know how to write a professional cover letter as well as how to develop a résumé. Many of the popular word processing applications provide wizards and templates that take users through the steps of creating these special documents. Learning how to use these wizards and templates will save you time and provide useful guidance.

1. Using a Letter Wizard to Create a Cover Letter

Problem: As a recent graduate from a Master's program in Educational Technology, you are seeking a position as a technology coordinator at a local middle school. Open your word processing software and create a cover letter as described in the following set of steps. Use the letter shown in Figure 2-43 as an example. (*Hint:* if you do not have the suggested font, use any appropriate font.)

Instructions: Perform the following tasks.

1. Create a cover letter using a Letter Wizard. If possible, use a similar letterhead style as shown in Figure 2-43. Insert your own name and address when requested by the wizard.
2. Modify the cover letter so the font is 12-point Times or Times New Roman. Use today's date in the date line. Modify the inside address and message by personalizing the information to your specific situation.
3. Create a numbered list highlighting at least two of your qualifications.
4. Check the cover letter for spelling and grammar errors.
5. Save the cover letter on a floppy disk. Use an appropriate filename.
6. Print the cover letter.
7. Follow your instructor's directions for handing in the assignment.

2. Using a Résumé Wizard to Create a Résumé

Problem: You have prepared the cover letter in Figure 2-43 and now are ready to create a résumé similar to the one shown in Figure 2-44 on page 114 to send to the director of technology. You want your information to be clearly presented and to highlight your qualifications. Use a Résumé Wizard or template. (*Hint:* if you do not have the suggested font, use any appropriate font.)

Instructions: Perform the following tasks.

1. Use a Résumé Wizard to create a résumé. Use your name and address information.
2. Personalize the résumé using your specific information.
3. Check the résumé for spelling and grammar errors.
4. Save the résumé on a floppy disk using an appropriate filename.
5. Print a copy of the résumé.
6. Follow your instructor's directions for handing in the assignment.

In the Lab

JON MARC BOWERS

692 East First Street
Chapel Hill, NC 27516
(919) 555-4332

August 5, 2007

Ms. Roz Seguero
Director of Technology
Chapel Hill City School District
1452 Fort King Street
Chapel Hill, NC 27514

Dear Ms. Seguero,

I would like to be considered for the position of Technology Coordinator at Blue Ridge Middle School. I believe my training and experience will greatly assist the staff and students to effectively use and integrate technology.

I have been an educator for the past six years and I have organized and led numerous staff development workshops on a variety of software applications. I also have extensively integrated technology throughout my classroom curriculum.

I would like to mention my most important qualifications:

1. Recently completed a Master's degree in Educational Technology
2. Nationally Board Certified Educator 2002
3. Microsoft Office Specialist certified in Microsoft Word, Excel, and PowerPoint

I look forward to meeting with you to discuss this position further. Please contact me at (919) 555-4332 or e-mail me at jmbowers@spms.k12.nc.us.

Sincerely,

Jon Marc Bowers

Figure 2-43

In the Lab

Jon Marc Bowers
692 East First Street
Chapel Hill, NC 27516
(919) 555-4332
jmbowers@spms.k12.nc.us

OBJECTIVE: To obtain a position as Technology Coordinator to assist administrators and teachers in learning how to integrate technology effectively throughout their classroom curriculum that will positively impact student achievement.

QUALIFICATIONS
During my tenure at Orange Grove Middle School, I organized and led numerous technology staff development workshops on a variety of software applications including Word, PowerPoint, Excel, Access, HyperStudio, Inspiration, Photoshop, and Dreamweaver. I also created and maintained the school Web site and assisted other teachers in creating, posting, and maintaining their classroom Web pages. I assisted teachers with basic troubleshooting on both hardware and software. As part of my graduate program of study, I completed a 40-hour internship with the district technology coordinator and assisted with installing a new computer lab at a local elementary school.

EDUCATION
2002-2004 Master of Arts, Educational Technology, University of Central Florida, Orlando, FL
1995-1999 Bachelor of Arts, Middle Grades Education, University of North Carolina at Chapel Hill, Chapel Hill, NC

EMPLOYMENT
2004-Present
        Math Teacher, Blue Ridge Middle School
        Responsible for teaching all aspects of the 7th grade math curriculum for gifted students and regular education students. Develop and teach pre-algebra curriculum in a combination 7th/8th grade class.

1999-2004 Math Teacher, Orange Grove Middle School
        Responsible for teaching all aspects of the 7th grade math curriculum including pre-algebra and regular curriculum courses. Team leader for the 7th grade Math department. Organized meetings, reviewed curriculum and served on the textbook adoption committee. Technology committee member for three years and was teacher representative on the School Advisory Counsel. Organized and sponsored the Math Wizards after-school program that provided student tutoring, homework help, and mentoring.

AWARDS and PROFESSIONAL ACTIVITIES
        2004 - 1998 Member of the National Council of Teachers of Mathematics
        2003 - Teacher of the Year Orange Grove Middle School
        2002 - National Board Certification
        2000 - Rookie Teacher of the Year

Figure 2-44

INTEGRATION IN THE CLASSROOM

1. As a follow-up activity to career day at your school, you have your students locate job advertisements online. The students select a job they would be interested in and then use a wizard or template to write a cover letter. Use the cover letter shown in Figure 2-43 on the previous page as an example of the type of information the students should include in the first two paragraphs. The students also should include a numbered list highlighting two of their accomplishments or qualifications and then a closing paragraph with contact information. Create a cover letter to use as an example for your students. Include today's date, your name, and address.

2. Using the job they selected from the Internet, the students will create a résumé to go along with their cover letter. Create a résumé to use as an example for your students. Modify the résumé you created. Change the information in the résumé to match the cover letter in Integration in the Classroom number 1 above.

3. Your students have just finished reading a book of their choice and they are ready to begin working on their book reports. To make it more interesting, you want the students to select a character from their book, choose a job for the character, and write a cover letter and resume based on the character's life. Choose one of your favorite characters from a book and create a sample cover letter and resume for your students. Use today's date and your name and address as the potential employer.

Learn It Online

INSTRUCTIONS: Use the Learn It Online exercises to reinforce your understanding of the chapter concepts and increase your computer, information, and integration literacy. To access dozens of interactive student labs, practice tests, learning games, and more, visit scsite.com/tdc4. Click Chapter 2 at the top of the Web page and then click Learn It Online on the left sidebar.

1. Student Edition Labs — Connecting to the Internet, Getting the Most Out of Internet, E-Mail, and Network Basics

For the labs to work properly, you must have your screen resolution set to 1024x768 or higher. For a short tutorial on how to change your screen resolution, click here. You also will need Flash 7.0 or higher. To view these interactive labs, click the Student Edition Labs link. When the Student Edition Labs menu appears, click the desired or the assigned lab to begin. A new browser window opens. Follow the on-screen instructions to complete the lab. When finished, click the Exit button. If required, submit your results to your instructor.

2. Using Favorites

Click the Using Favorites link and complete the exercise that appears on the screen. Print just the first page of this Web site. On the back of the printout, write a brief summary explaining how to organize your favorites or bookmarks. If required, submit your results to your instructor.

3. Search Engine Tutorial

Click the Search Engine Tutorial link and complete the exercise that appears on the screen. Print just the first page of this Web site. On the back of the printout, write a brief summary of three new things that you learned about Web searching. If required, submit your results to your instructor.

4. Practice Test

Click the Practice Test link. Answer each question. When completed, enter your name and click the Grade Test button to submit the quiz for grading. Make a note of any missed questions. If required, submit your score to your instructor.

5. Who Wants to Be a Computer Genius?

Click the Computer Genius link to find out if you are a computer genius. Directions about how to play the game will be displayed. When you are ready to play, click the Play button. If required, submit your score to your instructor.

6. Wheel of Terms

Click the Wheel of Terms link to reinforce important terms you learned in this chapter by playing the Shelly Cashman Series version of this popular game. Directions about how to play the game will be displayed. When you are ready to play, click the Play button. If required, submit your score to your instructor.

7. Crossword Puzzle Challenge

Click the Crossword Puzzle link. Complete the puzzle to reinforce skills you learned in this chapter. Directions about how to play the game will be displayed. When you are ready to play, click the Play button. If required, submit the completed puzzle to your instructor.

Guide to World Wide Web Sites, Search Techniques, and Search Tools for Education

As you learned in Chapter 2, the World Wide Web is an exciting and highly dynamic medium that has revolutionized the way people access information. The riches of the World Wide Web are yours and your students if you can locate and utilize them effectively. You can display information on virtually any topic you can imagine, if you know the URL. Finding the information you and your students want can be a massive chore if you and your students do not know the URL or how to use Web search tools.

To help you locate information and useful Web sites, this special feature provides three resources:

1. **Guide to World Wide Web Sites:** This section provides specific information about a variety of Web pages organized in 15 different areas of interest. These are designed to provide you with an overview of what is available on the Web. Included are Web exercises at the end of each category to reinforce the material and help you and your students discover Web sites that may add a treasure trove of authentic and discovery learning. As you explore these sites, constantly ask yourself how you can integrate these sites and the information they provide to better prepare your digital students for lifelong learning and employment in the 21st century.

2. **Search Techniques:** This section provides an introduction to searching techniques, including how to use both subject directories and search engines to find educationally appropriate Web sites. Included is a list of portals with their search capabilities.

3. **Search Tools for Education:** This section provides an extensive list of popular education search tools with a brief description of each.

ON THE WEB: To gain access to links as well as additional and up-to-date information regarding the **Web sites** listed in this special feature, visit scsite.com/tdc4. Click any chapter at the top of the Web page and then click Guide to WWW Sites on the left sidebar. To gain access to the **Search Tools for Education**, visit scsite.com/tdc4. Click any chapter at the top of the Web page, scroll down, if necessary, and then click Search Tools on the left sidebar.

Fun and Entertainment
THAT'S ENTERTAINMENT

Rock 'n' Roll on the Web

Consumers place great significance on buying entertainment products for fun and recreation. Nearly 10 percent of the United States's economy is spent on attending concerts and buying DVDs, CDs, reading materials, sporting goods, and toys.

Many Web sites supplement our cravings for fun and entertainment. For example, you can see and hear the musicians inducted into the Rock and Roll Hall of Fame and Museum (Figure 1). If you need an update on your favorite reality-based television program or a preview of an upcoming movie, E! Online and Entertainment Tonight provides the latest features on television and movie stars. The Internet Movie Database contains credits and reviews of more than 400,000 titles.

Watch the surfers riding the waves in Hawaii and romp with pandas at the San Diego Zoo. Web cams, which are video cameras that display their output on Web pages, take armchair travelers across the world for views of natural attractions, historical monuments, colleges, and cities. Many Web sites featuring Web cams are listed in the table in Figure 2.

Fun and Entertainment Web Sites

Web Cams	URL
AfriCam Virtual Game Reserve	africam.com
Discovery Channel Cams	dsc.discovery.com/cams/cams.html
EarthCam — Webcam Network	earthcam.com
Iowa State Insect Zoo Live Camera	zoocam.ent.iastate.edu
Panda Cam San Diego Zoo	sandiegozoo.org/pandas/pandacam/index.html
The Automated Astrophysical Site-Testing Observatory (AASTO) (South Pole)	www.phys.unsw.edu.au/southpolediaries/webcam.html
Weather and Webcams from OnlineWeather.com and CamVista	onlineweather.com/v4/webcams/index.html
Wild Birds Unlimited Bird FeederCam	wbu.com/feedercam_home.htm
World Surf Cameras	surfrock.com.br/surfcam.htm
WorldLIVE	worldlive.cz/en/webcams

Entertainment	URL
AMG All Music Guide	allmusic.com
E! Online	eonline.com
Entertainment Tonight	etonline.com
Entertainment Weekly's EW.com	ew.com/ew
MSN Entertainment	entertainment.msn.com
Old Time Radio (OTR) — Radio Days: A Soundbite History	otr.com
Rock and Roll Hall of Fame and Museum	rockhall.com
The Internet Movie Database (IMDb)	imdb.com
World Radio Network (WRN)	wrn.org

For an updated list and Web links, click the special feature, Guide to WWW Sites, at the Teachers Discovering Computers Web site (scsite.com/tdc4).

FIGURE 1 Visitors exploring the Rock and Roll Hall of Fame and Museum Web site will find history, exhibitions, programs, and the names and particulars of the latest inductees.

FIGURE 2 When you visit Web sites offering fun and entertainment resources, you can be both amused and informed.

FUN AND ENTERTAINMENT WEB EXERCISES

1 Visit the WorldLIVE site listed in Figure 2. View two of the Web cams closest to your hometown, and describe the scenes. Then visit the Discovery Channel Cams Web site and view two of the animal cams in the Featured Cams. What do you observe? Visit another Web site listed in Figure 2 and describe the view. What are the benefits of having Web cams at these locations throughout the world?

2 What are your favorite movies? Use The Internet Movie Database Web site listed in Figure 2 to search for information about two of these films, and write a brief description of the biographies of the major stars and director for each movie. Then visit one of the entertainment Web sites and describe three of the featured stories. At the Rock and Roll Hall of Fame and Museum Web site, view the information on Elvis and one of your favorite musicians. Write a paragraph describing the information available about these rock stars.

Travel
GET PACKING!

Explore the World Without Leaving Home

When you are ready to arrange your next travel adventure or just want to explore destination possibilities, the Internet provides ample resources to set your plans in motion.

To discover exactly where your destination is on this planet, cartography Web sites, including MapQuest (Figure 3), Maps.com, and Rand McNally, allow you to pinpoint your destination. These Web pages generally are divided into geographical areas, such as North America and Europe.

Some good starting places are general travel Web sites such as Expedia Travel, Cheap Tickets, and Travelocity, which is owned by the electronic booking service travel agents use. These all-encompassing Web sites, including those in Figure 4, have tools to help you find the lowest prices and details on flights, car rentals, cruises, and hotels.

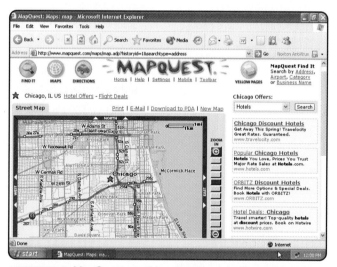

FIGURE 3 MapQuest provides directions, traffic reports, maps, and more.

Travel Web Sites

General Travel	URL
Cheap Tickets	cheaptickets.com
Expedia.com	expedia.com
Orbitz	orbitz.com
Travelocity.com	travelocity.com
Yahoo! Travel	travel.yahoo.com
Cartography	**URL**
Google Maps	maps.google.com
MapQuest	mapquest.com
Maps.com	maps.com
Rand McNally	randmcnally.com
Travel and City Guides	**URL**
All the Largest Cities of the World	greatestcities.com
Frommers.com	frommers.com
US-Parks.com — US National Parks Adventure Travel Guide	us-parks.com

For an updated list and Web links, click the special feature, Guide to WWW Sites, at the Teachers Discovering Computers Web site (scsite.com/tdc4).

FIGURE 4 These travel resources Web sites offer travel information to exciting destinations throughout the world.

TRAVEL WEB EXERCISES

1 As a classroom activity, have students visit one of the cartography Web sites listed in Figure 4 and obtain the directions from your school to one of these historical destinations: the White House in Washington, D.C.; the Grand Canyon near Flagstaff, Arizona; or the Mount Rushmore National Monument in Keystone, South Dakota. As an integration activity, students can compute how many miles is it to their destination as well as the estimated drive time. Then have students visit one of the general travel Web sites listed in the table and plan a flight from the nearest major airport to one of the three destinations mentioned previously for the week after school lets out and returning one week later. Lastly, have students generate a list of 20 questions to ask resident experts while they are on these trips.

2 Another classroom activity is to have students visit one of the travel and city guides Web sites listed in Figure 4, and choose a destination for a getaway this coming weekend. Students can write a one-page paper giving details about this location, such as popular hotels and lodging, expected weather, population, local universities, parks and recreation, ancient and modern history, and tours. Have students explain why they chose their particular destination, how they plan on getting there and back, as well as an expected total cost. Require students to provide a list of URLs used to complete this exercise.

Finance
MONEY MATTERS

Cashing In on Financial Advice

You can manage your money with advice from financial Web sites that offer online banking, tax help, personal finance, and small business and commercial services.

If you do not have a personal banker or a financial planner, consider a Web adviser to guide your investment decisions. The Motley Fool (Figure 5) provides commentary and education on investing strategies, financial news, and taxes.

If you are ready to ride the ups and downs of the NASDAQ and the Dow, an abundance of Web sites listed in Figure 6, including FreeEDGAR and Morningstar.com, can help you pick companies that fit your interests and financial needs.

Claiming to be the fastest, easiest tax publication on the planet, the Internal Revenue Service Web site contains procedures for filing tax appeals and contains IRS forms, publications, and legal regulations.

Finance Web Sites

Advice and Education	URL
Bankrate.com	bankrate.com
LendingTree	lendingtree.com
Loan.com	loan.com
MSN Money	money.msn.com
The Motley Fool	fool.com
Wells Fargo	wellsfargo.com
Yahoo! Finance	finance.yahoo.com
Stock Market	**URL**
E*TRADE Financial	us.etrade.com
Financial Engines	financialengines.com
FreeEDGAR®	www.freeedgar.com
Harris*direct*	harrisdirect.com
Merrill Lynch Direct	mldirect.ml.com
Morningstar.com	www.morningstar.com
The Vanguard Group	vanguard.com
Taxes	**URL**
H&R Block	hrblock.com
Internal Revenue Service	www.irs.gov

For an updated list and Web links, click the special feature, Guide to WWW Sites, at the Teachers Discovering Computers Web site (scsite.com/tdc4).

FIGURE 5 The Motley Fool Web site contains strategies and news stories related to personal financing and investing.

FIGURE 6 Financial resources Web sites offer general information, stock market analyses, and tax advice, as well as guidance and money-saving tips.

FINANCE WEB EXERCISES

1 Visit three advice and education Web sites listed in Figure 6 and read their top business world reports. Write a paragraph about each, summarizing these stories. Which stocks or mutual funds do these Web sites predict as being sound investments today? What are the current market indexes for the DJIA (Dow Jones Industrial Average), S&P 500, and NASDAQ, and how do these figures compare with the previous day's numbers?

2 To integrate this material, have students visit two of the stock market Web sites listed in Figure 6 and search for information about Microsoft, Adobe Systems, and one other software vendor. Students can write a paragraph about each of these stocks describing the revenues, net incomes, total assets for the previous year, current stock price per share, highest and lowest prices of each stock during the past year, and other relevant investment information.

Resources
LOOK IT UP

Web Resources Ease Computer Concerns

From dictionaries and encyclopedias to online technical support, the Web is filled with a plethora of resources to answer your computer questions.

Keep up with the latest developments by viewing online dictionaries and encyclopedias that add to their collections of computer and product terms on a regular basis. Shopping for a new computer can be a daunting experience, but many online guides, including PCWorld.com (Figure 7), can help you select the components that best fit your needs and budget.

If you are not confident in your ability to solve a problem alone, turn to online technical support. Web sites, such as those shown in Figure 8, often provide streaming how-to video lessons, tutorials, and real-time chats with experienced technicians. Hardware and software reviews, price comparisons, shareware, technical questions and answers, and breaking technology news are found on comprehensive portals.

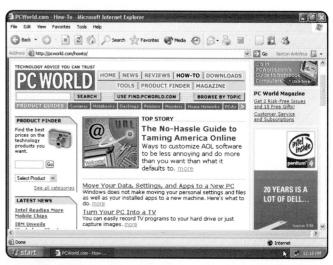

FIGURE 7 Buying and upgrading a computer is simplified with helpful Web sites such as PCWorld.com.

Resources Web Sites

Dictionaries and Encyclopedias	URL
CDT's Guide to Online Privacy	cdt.org/privacy/guide/terms
ComputerUser High-Tech Dictionary	computeruser.com/resources/dictionary
TechWeb: The Business Technology Network	www.techweb.com/encyclopedia
Webopedia: Online Computer Dictionary for Computer and Internet Terms	webopedia.com
whatis?com	whatis.com

Computer Shopping Guides	URL
A Computer Guide: Reviews on Software and Hardware	acomputerguide.com
The CPU Scorecard	cpuscorecard.com
The Online Computer Buying Guide™	grohol.com/computers
Viewz Desktop Computer Buying Guide	viewz.com/shoppingguide/compbuy.shtml
ZDNet	shopper-zdnet.com.com

FIGURE 8 A variety of Web resources can provide information about buying, repairing, and upgrading computers.

Upgrading Guides	URL
CNET Shopper.com	shopper.cnet.com
eHow™	ehow.com
Focus on Macs	macs.about.com
PCWorld.com	pcworld.com/howto
Upgrade Source	upgradesource.com

Online Technical Support	URL
Dux Computer Digest	duxcw.com
MSN Tech & Gadgets	computingcentral.msn.com
PC911	pcnineoneone.com
PC Pitstop	pcpitstop.com

Technical and Consumer Information	URL
CNET.com	cnet.com
CompInfo — The Computer Information Center	www.compinfo-center.com
NewsHub	newshub.com/tech
Wired News	wirednews.com
ZDNet	zdnet.com

For an updated list and Web links, click the special feature, Guide to WWW Sites, at the Teachers Discovering Computers Web site (scsite.com/tdc4).

RESOURCES WEB EXERCISES

1 As an integration activity with your class, brainstorm a list of 8 to 10 technology-related terms that they do not fully understand. Have students postulate what they think each term means and then look up its meaning at one of the dictionaries and encyclopedias Web sites in Figure 8. Have students compare the meaning to their guesses. Next, visit two of the listed computer shopping guide Web sites and choose the components needed to design a computer for your classroom. Have students create a list of parts needed and then comparison shop for those pieces from different Web sites.

2 As a class, visit three upgrading guides Web sites listed in Figure 8. Critically analyze each site and compose a review comparing the strengths and weaknesses of each focusing on criteria such as the clarity of instructions, thoroughness, and ease of navigation. Are these Web sites useful to classroom teachers as they troubleshoot their own technology problems?

Auctions
GOING ONCE, GOING TWICE

Rare, Common Items Flood Web Sites

Online auction Web sites can offer unusual items, including *Star Wars* props and memorabilia and a round of golf with Tiger Woods. eBay (Figure 9) is one of thousands of Internet auction Web sites and is the world's largest personal online trading community.

Traditional auction powerhouses, such as Christie's in London and Sotheby's on Manhattan's Upper East Side, are known for their big-ticket items, including a Tyrannosaurus rex fossil that sold for $8.4 million.

If those prices are a bit out of your league, you can turn to a wealth of other auction Web sites, including those listed in Figure 10, to find just the items you need, and maybe some you really do not need, for as little as $1. Categories include antiques and collectibles, automotive, computers, electronics, music, sports, sports cards and memorabilia, and toys.

Auction Web Sites

	URL
Christie's	christies.com
Dargate Auction Galleries	dargate.com
eBay®	ebay.com
musichotbid	musichotbid.com
Penbid.com	penbid.com
Sotheby's	sothebys.com
uBid™	ubid.com
Yahoo! Shopping Auctions	auctions.yahoo.com

For an updated list and Web links, click the special feature, Guide to WWW Sites, at the Teachers Discovering Computers Web site (scsite.com/tdc4).

FIGURE 10 These auction Web sites feature a wide variety of items.

AUCTIONS WEB EXERCISES

1 Visit the Christie's and Sotheby's Web sites and read about the items that have been sold recently. Find two unusual items that will be up for sale and have students rewrite the item description as if they were trying to convince one of their friends to purchase the item. Also, some people are very leery of bidding online so have your students come up with a short convincing argument explaining how safe the process has become.

2 Using one of the auction Web sites listed in Figure 10, search for two objects that pertain to your hobbies or interests. Describe why these items appeal to you as well as how to place a dollar value on them.

FIGURE 9 eBay is one of the world's more popular auction Web sites.

Government
STAMP OF APPROVAL

Making a Federal Case for Useful Information

When it is time to buy stamps to mail your correspondence, you no longer need to wait in long lines at your local post office. The U.S. Postal Service has authorized several corporations to sell stamps online.

You can recognize U.S. government Web sites on the Internet by their .gov top-level domain abbreviation. For example, The Library of Congress Web site is lcweb.loc.gov, as shown in Figure 11. Government and military Web sites offer a wide range of information, and some of the more popular sites are listed in Figure 12. The Time Service Department Web site will provide you with the correct time. If you are looking for a federal document, FedWorld lists thousands of documents distributed by the government on its Web site. For access to the names of your congressional representatives, visit the extensive Hieros Gamos Web site.

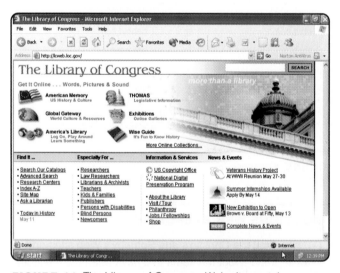

FIGURE 11 The Library of Congress Web site contains more than 119 million items written in 470 languages.

Government Resources Web Sites

Postage	URL
Endicia	endicia.com
Pitney Bowes	pb.com
Stamps.com	stamps.com

Government	URL
FedWorld	www.fedworld.gov
Hieros Gamos — Law and Legal Research Center	hg.org
NARA — United States National Archives and Records Administration	archives.gov
National Agricultural Library	www.nal.usda.gov
The Library of Congress	lcweb.loc.gov
THOMAS Legislative Information	thomas.loc.gov
Time Service Department	tycho.usno.navy.mil
United States Department of Education	ed.gov
United States Department of the Treasury	www.treas.gov
United States Government Printing Office	www.access.gpo.gov
United States National Library of Medicine	www.nlm.nih.gov
United States Patent and Trademark Office	www.uspto.gov
USAJOBS	www.usajobs.opm.gov
White House	whitehouse.gov

For an updated list and Web links, click the special feature, Guide to WWW Sites, at the Teachers Discovering Computers Web site (scsite.com/tdc4).

FIGURE 12 These Web sites offer information about buying U.S.-approved postage online and researching federal agencies.

GOVERNMENT WEB EXERCISES

1 View the three postage Web sites listed in Figure 12. Compare and contrast the available services on each one. Consider postage cost, necessary equipment, shipping services, security techniques, and tracking capability. Explain why you would or would not like to use this service.

2 Visit the Hieros Gamos Web sites listed in Figure 12. Locate the names and contact information of your two state senators as well as your local congressional representative. Find out what committees they serve upon and compile an informative flyer on this subject to distribute to interested parties on campus.

Shopping
CYBERMALL MANIA

Let Your Mouse Do Your Shopping

From groceries to clothing to computers, you can buy just about everything you need with just a few clicks of your mouse. Electronic retailers (e-tailers) are cashing in on cybershoppers' purchases. Books, computer software and hardware, and music are the hottest commodities.

Holiday sales account for a large portion of Internet purchases with more than nine million households doing some of their holiday shopping online. During this season, millions of shoppers visit Web sites such as BestBuy.com (Figure 13) daily. Macy's, Bloomingdale's and other e-tailers ship more than 300,000 boxes daily out of warehouses the size of 20 football fields and stocked with five million items.

FIGURE 13 Shopping for popular computer equipment online eliminates waiting in lines in stores.

The two categories of Internet shopping Web sites are those with physical counterparts, such as Eddie Bauer, Wal-Mart, and Tower Records, and those with only a Web presence, such as Amazon.com. Popular Web shopping sites are listed in Figure 14.

Shopping Web Sites

Apparel	URL
Eddie Bauer Since 1920	eddiebauer.com
J.Crew	jcrew.com
Lands' End	landsend.com
Books and Music	**URL**
Amazon.com	amazon.com
Barnes & Noble.com	bn.com
Tower Records	towerrecords.com
Computers and Electronics	**URL**
Crutchfield.com	crutchfield.com
BestBuy.com	bestbuy.com
buy.com	buy.com
Miscellaneous	**URL**
1-800-flowers.com	1800flowers.com
drugstore.com	drugstore.com
Froogle	froogle.com
The Sharper Image	sharperimage.com
Walmart.com	walmart.com

For an updated list and Web links, click the special feature, Guide to WWW Sites, at the Teachers Discovering Computers Web site (scsite.com/tdc4).

FIGURE 14 Making online purchases can help ease the strain of driving to and fighting the crowds in local malls.

SHOPPING WEB EXERCISES

1 Prepare for a night out on the town! Visit two of the three apparel Web sites listed in the table in Figure 14 and select a specific pair of jeans and shirt. Compare the prices of those items at the two stores including the cost of shipping to determine which Web site offers the better deal. Then visit two of the book and music Web sites and search for three CDs that you will listen to while you are out with your friends. Again, find the best deal. Create a chart to summarize your findings.

2 Visit two of the computers and electronics and two of the miscellaneous Web sites listed in Figure 14. Write a paragraph describing the features these Web sites offer compared with the same offerings from stores. In another paragraph, describe any disadvantages of shopping at these Web sites instead of actually seeing the merchandise. Then describe their policies for returning unwanted merchandise and for handling complaints.

Weather, Sports, and News
WHAT'S NEWS?

Weather, Sports, and News Web Sites Score Big Hits

Rain or sun? Hot or cold? Weather is the leading online news item, with at least 10,000 Web sites devoted to this field. The Weather Channel (Figure 15) receives more than 10 million hits each day.

Baseball may be the national pastime, but sports aficionados yearn for everything from auto racing to cricket. The Internet has more than one million pages of multimedia sports news, entertainment, and merchandise.

The Internet has emerged as a major source for news, with one-third of Americans going online at least once a week and 15 percent going online daily for reports of major news events. These viewers, who tend to be under the age of 50 and college graduates, are attracted to the Internet's flashy headline format, immediacy, and in-depth reports. Popular weather, sports, and news Web sites are listed in Figure 16.

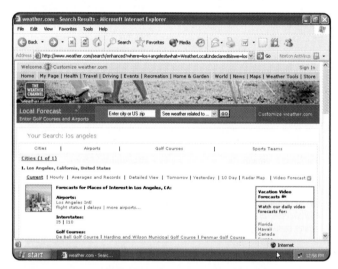

FIGURE 15 Local, national, and international weather conditions and details about breaking weather stories are available on The Weather Channel Web pages.

Weather, Sports, and News Web Sites

Weather	URL
Infoplease Weather	infoplease.com/weather.html
Intellicast.com	intellicast.com
STORMFAX®	stormfax.com
The Weather Channel	weather.com
WX.com	wx.com

Sports	URL
CBS SportsLine.com	cbs.sportsline.com
ESPN.com	espn.com
NCAAsports.com	ncaasports.com
OFFICIAL WEBSITE OF THE OLYMPIC MOVEMENT	olympic.org
SIRC — A World of Sport Information	sirc.ca
Sporting News Radio	radio.sportingnews.com

News	URL
MSNBC	msnbc.com
NYPOST.COM	nypost.com
onlinenewspapers.com	onlinenewspapers.com
Privacy.org	privacy.org
SiliconValley.com	siliconvalley.com
Starting Page Best News Sites	startingpage.com/html/news.html
USATODAY.com	usatoday.com
washingtonpost.com	washingtonpost.com

For an updated list and Web links, click the special feature, Guide to WWW Sites, at the Teachers Discovering Computers Web site (scsite.com/tdc4).

FIGURE 16 Keep informed about the latest weather, sports, and news events with these Web sites.

WEATHER, SPORTS, AND NEWS EXERCISES

1 Visit two of the weather Web sites listed in the table in Figure 16. How do they compare to the forecasts given by your local forecaster on the local news as well as in the local newspaper? Make a list of similarities and differences and be prepared to discuss with a classmate. Next, visit two of the sports Web sites in the table and critically review each on how they cover the content in your favorite sport.

2 Visit the onlinenewspapers.com and Starting Page Best News Sites Web sites in Figure 16 and select two newspapers from each site. Find a story that each site covers and critically review the similarities and differences in the writing style of each site for content as well as Web page design/readability for the user.

Learning
YEARN TO LEARN

Discover New Worlds Online

Although you may believe your education ends when you finally graduate from college, learning is a lifelong process. For example, enhancing your culinary skills can be a rewarding endeavor. No matter if you are a gourmet chef or a weekend cook, you will be cooking in style with the help of online resources, including those listed in Figure 17.

Learning Web Sites

Cooking	URL
Betty Crocker	bettycrocker.com
recipecenter.com	recipecenter.com
Internet	**URL**
Learn the Net	learnthenet.com
Search Engine Watch	searchenginewatch.com
Wiredguide™	wiredguide.com
Technology and Science	**URL**
HowStuffWorks	howstuffworks.com
ScienceMaster	sciencemaster.com
General Learning	**URL**
Bartleby.com: Great Books Online	bartleby.com
Blue Web'n	www.kn.pacbell.com/wired/bluewebn
MSN Encarta	encarta.msn.com

For an updated list and Web links, click the special feature, Guide to WWW Sites, at the Teachers Discovering Computers Web site (scsite.com/tdc4).

FIGURE 17 The information gleaned from these Web sites can help you learn about many aspects of our existence.

If you would rather sit in front of the computer than stand in front of the stove, you can increase your technological knowledge by visiting several Web sites with tutorials on building your own Web sites, the latest news about the Internet, and resources for visually impaired users.

Have you ever wondered how the Global Positioning System (GPS) works? Take a look at the ScienceMaster site to find details. You might be interested in finding out how your car's catalytic converter reduces pollution or how the Electoral College functions. Marshall Brain's HowStuffWorks Web site (Figure 18) is filled with articles and animations.

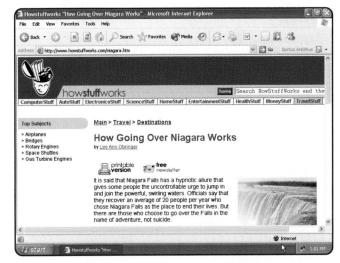

FIGURE 18 The HowStuffWorks Web site provides easy-to-understand information about technology and other facets of our lives.

LEARNING WEB EXERCISES

1. Visit one of the cooking Web sites listed in Figure 17 and find two recipes or cooking tips that you can use when preparing your next meal. Write a paragraph about each one, summarizing your discoveries. What are the advantages and disadvantages of accessing these Web sites on the new Web appliances that might someday be in your kitchen?

2. Using one of the technology and science Web sites and one of the other Web sites listed in Figure 17, search for information about communications and networks. Do these sites present information at a level most people can clearly understand? If not, how would you change the content so that it would reach a broader audience?

Science
$E = MC^2$

Rocket Science on the Web

For some people, space exploration is a hobby. Building and launching model rockets allow these scientists to participate in exploring the great frontier of space. For others, space exploration is their life. Numerous Web sites, including those in Figure 19, provide in-depth information about the universe.

Science Web Sites

Periodicals	URL
Archaeology Magazine	archaeology.org
Astronomy.com	astronomy.com
NewScientist.com	newscientist.com
OceanLink	oceanlink.island.net
Science Magazine	sciencemag.org
SCIENTIFIC AMERICAN.com	sciam.com
Resources	**URL**
National Science Foundation (NSF)	nsf.gov
Science.gov: FirstGov for Science	science.gov
SOFWeb	www.sofweb.vic.edu.au
Science Community	**URL**
American Scientist, The Magazine of Sigma Xi, The Scientific Research Society	amsci.org
Federation of American Scientists	fas.org
NASA	www.nasa.gov
Sigma Xi, The Scientific Research Society	sigmaxi.org

For an updated list and Web links, click the special feature, Guide to WWW Sites, at the Teachers Discovering Computers Web site (scsite.com/tdc4).

FIGURE 19 Resources available on the Internet offer a wide range of subjects for enthusiasts who want to delve into familiar and unknown territories in the world of science.

The NASA Liftoff Web site contains information about rockets, the space shuttle, the International Space Station, space transportation, and communications. Other science resources explore space-related questions about astronomy, physics, the earth sciences, microgravity, and robotics.

Rockets and space are not the only areas to explore in the world of science. Where can you find the latest pictures taken with the Hubble Space Telescope? Do you know which cities experienced an earthquake today? Have you ever wondered what a 3-D model of the amino acid glutamine looks like? You can find the answers to these questions and many others through the Librarians' Index to the Internet (lii.org) shown in Figure 20.

FIGURE 20 Numerous science resources are organized clearly in the Librarians' Index to the Internet.

SCIENCE WEB EXERCISES

1. Visit the NASA Web site listed in the table in Figure 19. View links about space-related topics, such as spacecrafts, the universe, or tracking satellites and spacecraft, and then write a summary of your findings. Think of ways to tie this into an astrology/astronomy unit as students plan a space journey to their favorite planet or lunar body and write about what they expect to find when they land.

2. Visit the Librarians' Index to the Internet at www.lii.org. Click Computers to view the page shown in Figure 20. Type Greatest Engineering Achievements in the Search LII Org text box and then press Enter. Pick two achievements, read their history, and write a paragraph summarizing each of these accomplishments. Then view two of the science Web sites listed in Figure 19 and write a paragraph about each of these Web sites describing the information each contains.

Environment
THE FATE OF THE ENVIRONMENT

Protecting the Planet's Ecosystem

From the rain forests of Africa to the marine life in the Pacific Ocean, the fragile ecosystem is under extreme stress. Many environmental groups have developed Internet sites, including those listed in Figure 21, in attempts to educate worldwide populations and to increase resource conservation.

Environment Web Sites

	URL
Central African Regional Program for the Environment (CARPE)	carpe.umd.edu
Earthjustice	www.earthjustice.org
EarthTrends: The Environmental Information Portal	earthtrends.wri.org
Environmental Defense	edf.org
Environmental Sites on the Internet	www.ima.kth.se/im/envsite/envsite.htm
EPA AirData — Access to Air Pollution Data	epa.gov/air/data
Green Solitaire.org	greensolitaire.bizland.com
GreenNet	www.gn.apc.org
The Center for a New American Dream	newdream.org
The Virtual Library of Ecology & Biodiversity	conbio.org/vl
USGS Acid rain data and reports	bqs.usgs.gov/acidrain
UWM Environmental Health, Safety & Risk Management	www.uwm.edu/Dept/EHSRM/EHSLINKS

For an updated list and Web links, click the special feature, Guide to WWW Sites, at the Teachers Discovering Computers Web site (scsite.com/tdc4).

FIGURE 21 Environment Web sites provide vast resources for ecological data and action groups.

On an international scale, the Environmental Sites on the Internet Web page developed by the Royal Institute of Technology in Stockholm, Sweden, has been rated as one of the better ecological Web sites. Its comprehensive listing of environmental concerns range from aquatic ecology to wetlands.

The U.S. federal government has a number of Web sites devoted to specific environmental concerns. For example, the U.S. Environmental Protection Agency (EPA) provides pollution data, including ozone levels and air pollutants, for specific areas. Its AirData Web site, shown in Figure 22, displays air pollution emissions and monitoring data from the entire United States and is the world's most extensive collection of air pollution data.

FIGURE 22 A visit to the EPA AirData Web site, with its extensive database, can assist you in checking your community's ozone and air pollutant levels.

ENVIRONMENT WEB EXERCISES

1 The Center for a New American Dream Web site encourages consumers to reduce the amount of junk mail sent to their homes. Using the table in Figure 21, visit the Web site and write a paragraph stating how many trees are leveled each year to provide paper for these mailings, how many garbage trucks are needed to haul this waste, and other statistics. Use this information to compose a letter that you can post online at environmentally friendly Web sites informing others about how they can help with this cause.

2 Visit the EPA AirData Web site. What is the highest ozone level recorded in your state this past year? Where are the nearest air pollution monitoring Web sites, and what are their levels? Where are the nearest sources of air pollution? Read two reports about two different topics, such as acid rain and air quality, and summarize their findings. Include information on who sponsored the research, who conducted the studies, when the data was collected, and the impact of this pollution on the atmosphere, water, forests, and human health. Whom would you contact for further information regarding the data and studies?

Health
NO PAIN, ALL GAIN

Store Personal Health Records Online

More than 70 million consumers use the Internet yearly to search for health information, so using the Web to store personal medical data is a natural extension of the Internet's capabilities. Internet health services and portals are available online to store your personal health history, including prescriptions, lab test results, doctor visits, allergies, and immunizations. Web sites such as WellMed (Figure 23) are free to consumers.

In minutes, you can register with a health Web site by choosing a username and password. Then, you create a record to enter your medical history. You also can store data for your emergency contacts, primary care physicians, specialists, blood type, cholesterol levels, blood pressure, and insurance plan. No matter where you are in the world, you and medical personnel can obtain records via the Internet or fax machine. Some popular online health database management systems are shown in Figure 24.

FIGURE 23 You can store health records for you and your family in the WellMed database.

Health Web Sites

	URL
AboutMyHealth	aboutmyhealth.com
Aetna InteliHealth	intelihealth.com
GlobalMedic	globalmedic.com
PersonalMD	personalmd.com
WebMD®	my.webmd.com/ my_health_record
WellMed	wellmed.com
For an updated list and Web links, click the special feature, Guide to WWW Sites, at the Teachers Discovering Computers Web site (scsite.com/tdc4).	

FIGURE 24 These Internet-based health database management systems Web sites allow you to organize your medical information and store it in an online database.

HEALTH WEB EXERCISES

1 Access one of the health Web sites listed in Figure 24. Register yourself or a family member, and then enter the full health history. Create an emergency medical card if the Web site provides the card option. Submit this record and emergency card to your instructor. Why do you think it would be helpful for teachers to have this information handy?

2 Visit three of the health Web sites listed in Figure 24. Describe the features of each. Which of the three is the most user-friendly? Why? How could you apply these sites to your classroom as well as your own personal life?

Research
SEARCH AND YE SHALL FIND

Info on the Web

A 2004 Web Usability survey conducted by the Nielsen Norman Group found that 88 percent of people log onto a computer and then use a search engine as their first action. Search engines require users to type words and phrases that characterize the information being sought. Yahoo! (Figure 25), Google, and AltaVista are some of the more popular search engines. The key to effective searching on the Web is composing search queries that narrow the search results and place the most relevant Web sites at the top of the results list.

Subject directories are collections of related Web sites. Yahoo! and LookSmart have two of the more comprehensive subject directories on the Web. Their organized lists often are called trees because a few main categories, such as Entertainment, Computing, Lifestyle, and Work, branch out to more specific subtopics. Popular search engines and subject directories are listed in Figure 26.

Research Web Sites

Search Engines	URL
AltaVista	altavista.com
Excite	excite.com
Fast Search & Transfer (FAST)	fastsearch.com
GO.com	go.com
Google	google.com
Northern Light®	northernlight.com
Yahoo!	yahoo.com

Subject Directories	URL
About	about.com
Librarians' Index to the Internet	lii.org
LookSmart	looksmart.com
The Internet Public Library	ipl.org
The WWW Virtual Library	vlib.org
Yahoo!	yahoo.com

For an updated list and Web links, click the special feature, Guide to WWW Sites, at the Teachers Discovering Computers Web site (scsite.com/tdc4).

FIGURE 25 The Yahoo! News search results for the word "technology" lists more than 83,000 stories.

FIGURE 26 Web users can find information by using search engines and subject directories.

RESEARCH WEB EXERCISES

1 Use two of the search engines listed in Figure 26 to find three Web sites that review the latest digital cameras from Sony and Kodak. Make a table listing the search engines, Web site names, and the cameras' model numbers, suggested retail price, megapixels, memory, and features.

2 If money were no object, virtually everyone would have an exquisite car. On the other hand, drivers need a practical vehicle to drive around town daily. Use one of the subject directories listed in Figure 26 to research your dream car and another directory to research your practical car. As an integration activity, have your students write a paragraph about each car describing the particular subject directory tree you used, the manufacturer's suggested retail price (MSRP) of the car, standard and optional equipment, engine size, miles per gallon, and safety features.

Careers
IN SEARCH OF THE PERFECT JOB

Web Helps Career Hunt

Although your teachers give you valuable training to prepare you for a career, they rarely teach you how to begin that career. You can broaden your horizons by searching the Internet for career information and job openings.

First, examine some of the job search Web sites. These resources list thousands of openings in hundreds of fields, companies, and locations. For example, the Monster Web site, shown in Figure 27, allows you to choose a broad job area, narrow your search to specific fields within that area, and then search for specific salary ranges, locations, and job functions.

When a company contacts you for an interview, learn as much about it and the industry as possible before the interview. Many of the Web sites listed in Figure 28 include detailed company profiles and links to their corporate Web sites.

Career Web Sites

Job Search	URL
BestJobsUSA.com	www.ultimatecareerfair.com
CareerBuilder	careerbuilder.com
CareerExchange.com	careerexchange.com
CareerNet	careernet.com
College Grad Job Hunter	collegegrad.com
EmploymentGuide.com	employmentguide.com
HotJobs.com	hotjobs.com
JobBankUSA.com	jobbankusa.com
JobWeb.com	www.jobweb.com
Monster	monster.com
MonsterTRAK	www.jobtrak.com
Spherion	spherion.com
USAJOBS	usajobs.opm.gov
VolunteerMatch	volunteermatch.org

Company/Industry Information	URL
Career ResourceCenter.com	www.resourcecenter.com
Forbes.com	www.forbes.com/2003/03/26/500sland.html
FORTUNE	fortune.com
Hoover's Online	hoovers.com
Occupational Outlook Handbook	stats.bls.gov/oco

For an updated list and Web links, click the special feature, Guide to WWW Sites, at the Teachers Discovering Computers Web site (scsite.com/tdc4).

FIGURE 28 Career Web sites provide a variety of job openings and information about major companies worldwide.

FIGURE 27 Monster's global online network connects companies with career-minded individuals.

CAREERS WEB EXERCISES

1 Use two of the job search Web sites listed in Figure 28 to find three companies with job openings in your field. Make a table listing the Web site name, position available, description, salary, location, desired education, and desired experience.

2 Explain to your students that it is a good idea to acquire information before graduation about the industry in which they would like to work. Are they interested in the automotive manufacturing industry, the restaurant service industry, or the financial industry? Students should use two of the company/industry information Web sites listed in Figure 28 to research a particular career related to their interests. Have students write a paragraph naming the Web sites and the specific information they found, such as the nature of the work, recommended training and qualifications, employment outlook, and earnings. Then, students should use two other Web sites to profile three companies with positions available in this field. Have the students write a paragraph about each of these companies, describing the headquarters' location, sales and earnings for the previous year, total number of employees, working conditions, perks, and competitors.

Arts and Literature
FIND SOME CULTURE

Get Ready to Read, Paint, and Dance

Brush up your knowledge of Shakespeare, grab a canvas, and put on your dancing shoes. Visual arts and literature Web sites, including those in Figure 29, are about to sweep you off your cyberfeet.

Arts and Literature Web Sites

Arts	URL
Access Place Arts	accessplace.com/arts.htm
Art News — absolutearts.com	absolutearts.com
GalleryGuide.org	galleryguide.org
Louvre Museum	www.louvre.fr
Montreal Museum of Fine Arts	www.mmfa.qc.ca
The Children's Museum of Indianapolis	childrensmuseum.org
The Getty	getty.edu
The New York Times: Arts	nytimes.com/pages/arts/index.html
Virtual Library museums pages (VLmp)	vlmp.museophile.com
Literature	**URL**
Bartleby.com	bartleby.com
Bibliomania	bibliomania.com
Electronic Literature Directory	directory.wordcircuits.com
Fantastic Fiction Bibliographies	fantasticfiction.co.uk
Project Gutenberg	promo.net/pg
shakespeare.com	shakespeare.com
The Modern Library eBook List	randomhouse.com/modernlibrary/ebookslist.html

For an updated list and Web links, click the special feature, Guide to WWW Sites, at the Teachers Discovering Computers Web site (scsite.com/tdc4).

FIGURE 29 Discover culture throughout the world by visiting these arts and literature Web sites.

The full text of hundreds of books is available online from the Bibliomania and Project Gutenberg Web sites. Shakespeare.com provides in-depth reviews and news of the world's most famous playwright and his works. The Bartleby.com Web site features biographies, definitions, quotations, dictionaries, and indexes.

When you are ready to absorb more culture, you can turn to various art Web sites. Many museums have images of their collections online. Among them are the Getty Museum in Los Angeles (Figure 30), the Montreal Museum of Fine Arts, and the Louvre Museum in Paris.

Access Place Arts and The New York Times Web sites focus on the arts and humanities and provide fascinating glimpses into the worlds of dance, music, performance, cinema, and other topics pertaining to creative expression.

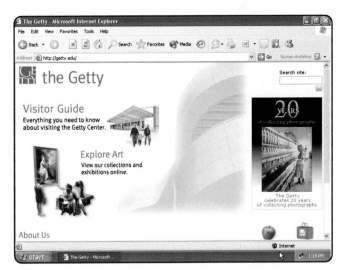

FIGURE 30 Permanent and temporary exhibitions, educational activities, and a bookstore are featured on the Getty Museum Web site.

ARTS AND LITERATURE WEB EXERCISES

1. Visit The Modern Library eBook List Web site listed in Figure 29 and view one book in the 20th CENTURY NOVELS, 19th CENTURY NOVELS, BRITISH LITERATURE, and HISTORY sections. Create a table with columns for the book name, author, cost, online store, local store, and description. Then read the excerpt from each of the four books and write a paragraph describing which of these four books is the most interesting to you. What are the advantages and disadvantages of reading classic literature electronically?

2. Using the arts Web sites listed in Figure 29, search for three temporary exhibitions in galleries throughout the world. Describe the venues, the artists, and the works. Then explore the sites to find out the permanent collections found in these same museums. Some people shop for gifts in the museums' stores. View and describe three items for sale.

Search Techniques

Successful Searching

Successful searching of the Web involves two key steps:

1. Briefly describe the information you are seeking. Start by identifying the main idea or concept in your topic and determine any synonyms, alternate spellings, or variant word forms for the concept.

2. Use the brief description with a search tool to display links to pages containing the desired information.

The two most common search tools are subject directories and search engines. You use a **subject directory** by clicking through its collection of categories and subcategories until you reach the information you want. You use a **search engine** to search for a keyword. The following sections describe how to use a subject directory and a search engine.

Some Web sites offer the functionality of both a subject directory and a search engine. Yahoo! and Google, for example, are widely used search engines that also provide a subject directory.

Using a Subject Directory

A subject directory provides categorized lists of links. These categorized lists are arranged by subject and then displayed in a series of menus. Using this type of search tool, you can locate a particular topic by starting from the top and clicking links through the different levels, going from the general to the specific. Each time you click a category link, the search tool displays a page of subcategory links from which you again choose. You continue in this fashion until the search tool displays a list of Web pages on the desired topic. Browsing a subject directory requires that you make assumptions about the topic's hierarchical placement within the categorized list.

For the following example, assume you have been assigned the task of conducting research on the Web to find out if there are any Web sites that will allow you and your students to ask questions about math issues. The assignment requires that you include at least one Web page citation. This example uses the Yahoo! (yahoo.com) search directory to locate information for your assignment.

Start your browser and then enter the URL www.yahoo.com in the Address text box. When the Yahoo! home page is displayed, scroll down and then point to the Education link, as shown in Figure 1.

Figure 1 Yahoo! home page.

Click Education. When the Education page is displayed, point to the K-12 link, as shown in Figure 2. Each time you click a category link, you move closer to the topic.

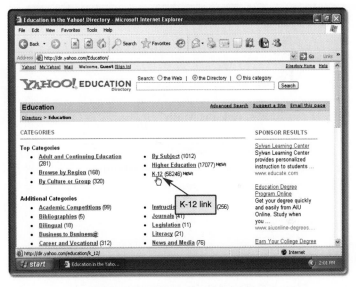

Figure 2 Education categories.

Click K-12. When the K-12 page is displayed, point to Mathematics, as shown in Figure 3.

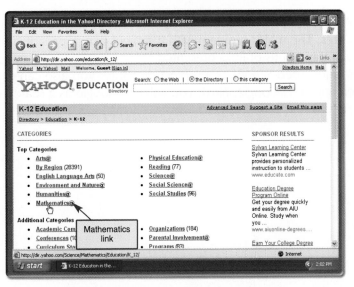

Figure 3 K-12 Education categories.

Figure 4 List of math sites.

Click Mathematics. The browser window displays a listing of sites dealing with K-12 mathematics. Scroll down and then point to Ask Dr. Math, as shown in Figure 4. Notice that the description after the link says that this is a question-and-answer service for K-12 math students and their teachers.

Figure 5 The Ask Dr. Math Web page.

Click Ask Dr. Math. When the page appears as shown in Figure 5, explore the site to see if this type of Web site can help you with your assignment.

With just a few clicks, the Yahoo! search directory displays information on a number of K-12 mathematics Web sites. The major problem with a subject directory is deciding which categories to choose as you work through the menus of links presented.

You just used Yahoo! as a subject directory; you also can use Yahoo! as a search directory. Another popular search engine is Google. Next, you will use Google as a search engine to locate information for your research assignment.

Using a Search Engine

Search engines require that you enter search text or keywords (single word, words, or phrase) that define what you are looking for, rather than clicking through menus of links. Search engines often respond with results that include thousands of links to Web pages, many of which have little or no bearing on the information you are seeking. You can eliminate the superfluous pages by carefully choosing a keyword (or words) that limits the search. The following example uses the Google search engine to search for the phrase "ask math questions."

1 Start your browser and then enter the URL www.google.com in the Address text box. When the Google home page is displayed, type ask math questions in the Search text box and then point to the Google Search button, as shown in Figure 6.

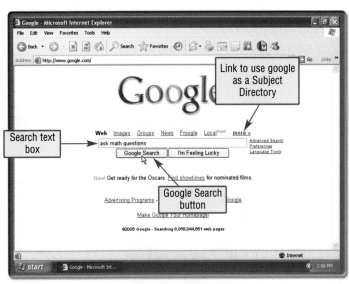

Figure 6 Google home page.

2 Click the Google Search button. When the results of the search are displayed, scroll through the links and read the descriptions. Point to The Math Forum - Ask Dr. Math link, as shown in Figure 7. The results in Figure 7 include more than 2.9 million links to Web pages concerning mathematics.

Most search engines sequence the results based on how close the keywords are to one another in the Web page titles and their descriptions.

Thus, the first few links probably contain more relevant information. To use Google as a subject directory, click the more link on the Google home page (see Figure 6).

Figure 7 Google search results.

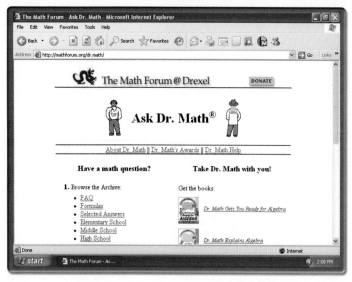

Figure 8 Ask Dr. Math home page.

Click the Math Forum - Ask Dr. Math link to display the Ask Dr. Math home page (Figure 8).

Figure 9 Google Scholar Web page

Google Scholar

Google launched Google Scholar, a new search engine (www.scholar.google.com) in early 2005 (Figure 9). Google Scholar allows users to search for scholarly literature, including peer-reviewed papers, thesis, books, preprints, abstracts, and technical reports from broad areas of research. Use Google Scholar to find articles from a wide variety of academic publishers, professional societies, preprint repositories and universities, as well as scholarly articles available across the Web.

Limiting the Search

If you enter a phrase with spaces between the keywords, most search engines return links to pages that include all of the words. Figure 10 lists some common operators, commands, and special characters you can use to refine your search.

Guidelines to Successful Searching

You can improve your Web searches by following these guidelines.

1. Use nouns as keywords, and put the most important terms first.

2. Use the asterisk (*) to find plurals of words. For example: retriev* returns retrieves, retrieval, retriever, and any other variation.

3. Type keywords in lowercase to find both lowercase and uppercase variations.

4. Use quotation marks to create phrases so the search engine finds the exact sequence of words.

5. Use a hyphen alternative. For example, use email OR e-mail.

6. Limit the search by language.

7. Use uppercase characters for Boolean operators in your search statements to differentiate between the words and operators.

8. Before you use a search engine, read its Help.

9. The Internet contains many search engines. If your search is unsuccessful with one search engine, try another.

Popular Search Sites

Most search sites include both a search engine and subject directory. Figure 11 contains a list of popular search sites and their URLs where you can access search engines and subject directories to search the Web. For additional information about search sites, visit www.searchenginewatch.com.

CATEGORY OF OPERATOR	OPERATOR	KEYWORD EXAMPLES	DESCRIPTION
Boolean	AND (+)	art AND music smoking health hazards fish +pollutants +runoff	Requires both words to be in the page. No operator between words or the plus sign (+) are shortcuts for the Boolean operator AND.
	OR	mental illness OR insane canine OR dog OR puppy flight attendant OR stewardess OR steward	Requires only one of the words to be in the page.
	AND NOT (–)	auto AND NOT SUV AND NOT convertible computers – programming shakespeare – hamlet – (romeo+juliet)	Excludes pages with the word following AND NOT. The minus sign (–) is a shortcut for the Boolean operator AND NOT.
Parentheses	( )	physics AND (relativity OR einstein)	Parentheses group portions of Boolean operators together.
Phrase Searching	" "	"harry potter" "19th century literature"	Requires the exact phrase within quotation marks to be in the page.
Wildcard	*	writ* clou*	The asterisk (*) at the end of words substitutes for any combination of characters.

Figure 10 Search engine keyword operators, commands, and special characters.

SEARCH SITE	URL
AllTheWeb	www.alltheweb.com
AltaVista	www.altavista.com
AOL Search	search.aol.com
Ask Jeeves	www.askjeeves.com
Google	www.google.com
HotBot	www.hotbot.com
InfoSpace	www.infospace.com
LookSmart	www.looksmart.com
Lycos	www.lycos.com
MSN Search	search.msn.com
Netscape Search	search.netscape.com
Overture	www.overture.com
Yahoo!	www.yahoo.com

Figure 11 Popular search sites.

Search Tools for Education

A number of outstanding search tools are tailored for use by K-12 educators. Figure 12 contains a list of the more popular education search tools. Many of these search tools contain both search engines and subject directories. In addition, a number of these search tools are reviewed by experienced educators to ensure the content and links are appropriate for K-12 students. To gain access to the **Search Tools for Education, visit scsite.com/tdc4. Click any chapter at the top of the Web page, scroll down, if necessary, and then click Search Tools on the left sidebar.**

Ask Jeeves for Kids

ajkids.com

Ask Jeeves for Kids is a Web site that makes it easy for kids to find answers to questions. When students visit this Web site, they can ask a question in plain English. After interacting with the student to confirm the question, Ask Jeeves for Kids displays a single Web site that answers their question.

Awesome Library

awesomelibrary.org

Awesome Library organizes 16,000 carefully reviewed links that are useful for teachers, students (kids or teens), parents, or librarians. This Web site also allows users to browse in 15 different languages.

Ben's Guide to U.S. Government for Kids

bensguide.gpo.gov

This government-sponsored site provides learning tools for K-12 students, parents, and teachers. It includes resources on how the United States government works and other related topics.

Blue Web'N

www.kn.pacbell.com/wired/bluewebn

Blue Web'N is a searchable database containing thousands of outstanding Internet learning Web sites categorized by subject area, audience, and type. It also includes lessons, activities, projects, resources, references, tools, and more.

Busy Teachers' WebSite K-12

www.ceismc.gatech.edu/busyt

This Web site is designed to offer teachers direct source materials, lesson plans, and classroom activities. Teachers learning how to use the Internet will have an enjoyable and rewarding experience navigating through this Web site.

Education World

www.education-world.com

Visit this complete, online resource guide where educators can access a search engine that identifies educational Web sites. You also will be able to connect to lesson plans, research materials, up-to-date news information from *USA TODAY*, monthly site reviews, employment listings, and articles written by education experts.

Figure 12

EduHound

www.eduhound.com

EduHound is a highly specialized educational directory with built-in resource links for educators, students, and parents. This wonderful Web site seeks to harness the vast informational resources on the World Wide Web, while enabling educators to use the Internet as a classroom tool.

emTech

www.emtech.net

This Web site contains more than 15,000 resources organized by topics for teachers, students, parents, and other education professionals.

FirstGov for Kids

kids.gov

This is the U.S. government interagency kids' portal and provides links to federal kids' Web sites along with some of the best kids' sites from other organizations, all grouped by subject. This is an outstanding site for kids to search for government resources.

Great Web Sites for Kids

www.ala.org/alsc/children_links.html

Looking for something fun and educational on the World Wide Web? You are likely to find it on this list of kids' Web sites compiled by the American Library Association.

Kathy Schrock's Guide for Educators

school.discovery.com/schrockguide

Kathy Schrock's Guide for Educators is a categorized list of Web sites that are useful for enhancing curriculum and professional growth. It is updated often to include the best Web sites for teaching and learning.

KidsClick!

sunsite.berkeley.edu/KidsClick!

This Web site for kids is compiled by librarians and contains a database of more than 5000 sites organized into more than 600 subjects.

Kid's Search Tools

www.rcls.org/ksearch.htm

This site allows kids to search using a variety of kid-safe search engines from a single page.

Learning Page

learningpage.com

This site contains a large collection of instructional materials that you can download and print, including lesson plans, books, worksheets, and many other materials.

Pedagonet

www.pedagonet.com

This Web site is a learning material and resource center where teachers can peruse a searchable database for sites related to their area plus teachers can submit requests to the site to publish needed resources.

Figure 12 *(continued)*

Sites for Teachers

www.sitesforteachers.com

Sites for Teachers includes links to Web sites that contain teacher resources and educational materials. Web sites are ranked according to popularity.

STEM-NET Theme Pages for Elementary Students and Teachers

www.stemnet.nf.ca/CITE/themes.html

This Web site contains a general listing of theme-related links on a broad range of educational topics, such as the solar system, bats, sea life, weather, inventions, and much, much more.

The Educator's Reference Desk

www.eduref.org

The Educator's Reference Desk presents many useful resources, such as 2000+ lesson plans, 3000+ links to online education information, and 200+ question archive responses.

The Gateway to Educational Materials (GEM)

www.thegateway.org

The Gateway to Educational Materials, sponsored by the U.S. Department of Education, is a consortium effort to provide educators with quick-and-easy access to thousands of educational resources, such as lesson plans and curriculum units found on various federal, state, university, nonprofit, and commercial Web sites.

Yahooligans!

www.yahooligans.com

Yahooligans is a browsable, searchable directory of Web sites for kids and teens. Each Web site has been carefully checked by experienced educators to ensure that the content and links are age-appropriate.

Figure 12 *(continued)*

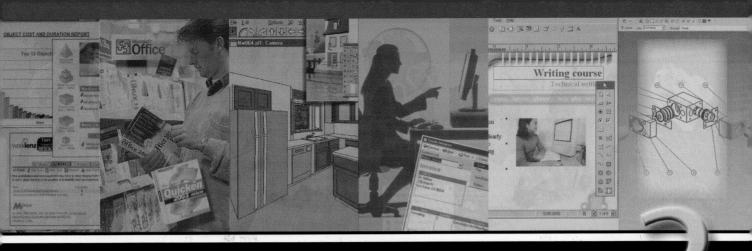

Application Software Productivity Tools for Educators

3

Objectives

After completing this chapter, you will be able to:
[ISTE NETS-T Standards I A-B, II A-E, III A-D, IV A-D, V B-D, VI B-E]

- Explain the role of an operating system and list the main operating systems used on today's computers

- Define and describe a user interface and a graphical user interface

- Identify the important features of widely used software applications

- Describe the advantages of software suites

- Explain how to create documents

- Discuss why the use of note taking software is important for K-12 schools

- List and describe learning aids and support tools that help you use and learn software applications

- Explain how to work with different versions of software applications

An essential aspect of building computer literacy is learning about software, which is the series of instructions that tell computer hardware how to perform tasks. Having a solid understanding of software — especially application software — will help you comprehend how administrators, teachers, students, and other individuals use personal computers in today's society. It also will help you use your computer to be more productive, organized, and well informed.

Application software such as word processing, spreadsheets, and e-mail programs can help you perform tasks such as creating documents, doing research, and managing projects. Before discussing various software applications used by teachers and students, however, this chapter provides a basic overview of the operating system and the user interface used on both Macintosh computers and PCs. As you learned in Chapter 1, the user interface controls how you work with any software, including application software.

Understanding application software can help advance your personal and professional goals by helping you manage student records, teach students with different academic needs, and work more productively. This chapter introduces you to the learning aids and tools available to help you and your students learn to use software applications. Finally, you will learn how to work with different versions of the same software on different computers. You can refer back to this chapter as you learn more about how computers are used today and how they can help you in your teaching career.

The Operating System

WEB INFO

For more information about Windows, visit the Teachers Discovering Computers Web site, (*scsite.com/tdc4*), click Chapter 3, click Web Info, and then click Windows.

As with most computer users, you are probably somewhat familiar with application software. To use any application software, however, your computer must be running another type of software — an operating system.

THE ROLE OF THE OPERATING SYSTEM

As described in Chapter 1, software can be categorized into two types: system software and application software. **System software** consists of programs that control the operations of the computer and its devices. As shown in Figure 3-1, system software serves as the interface between you (the user), your application software, and your computer's hardware. One type of system software, the **operating system,** contains instructions that coordinate all of the activities of the hardware devices in a computer. The operating system also contains instructions that allow you to run application software.

Before either a Macintosh computer or a PC can run any application software, the operating system must be loaded from the hard disk into the computer's memory. Each time you start your computer, the operating system is loaded, or copied, into memory from the computer's hard disk. After the operating system is loaded, it tells the computer how to perform functions, such as processing program instructions or transferring data between input and output devices and memory. The operating system, which remains in memory while the computer is running, allows you to communicate with the computer and other software, such as word processors, grade books, and other application programs. The operating system continues to run until the computer is turned off.

USING DIFFERENT OPERATING SYSTEMS

Each new release of an operating system contains new features that make computers more powerful and easy to use. In addition, the newest operating systems provide enhanced integration with the World Wide Web and increase the multimedia capabilities of computers. Due to budget constraints and other factors, however, schools and home users do not always upgrade their computers every time a new version of an operating system is released. As a result, a number of different versions of operating systems currently are running on school and home computers.

MICROSOFT WINDOWS Microsoft Windows, which often is referred to simply as Windows with a capital W, is the most used operating system in the world. A brief summary of the evolution of the various versions of Microsoft Windows that are in use today follows.

- Windows 98 — **Windows 98** was an upgrade to Windows 95 and is still a version of Windows found on some school and home computers.

- Windows 2000 — Microsoft marketed two versions of **Windows 2000:** Windows Millennium Edition, or

application software

↕

system software

Figure 3-1 System software is the interface between the user, the application software, and the computer's hardware. In this example, a user instructs the word processing software to print, the word processing software sends the print instructions to the system software, and the system software sends the print instructions to the printer.

Windows Me, for home users and Windows 2000 Professional, which is a network version for businesses and schools.

■ Windows XP — **Windows XP**, released in late 2001, is a significant upgrade to the Windows operating system and is available in four main editions: **Home Edition**, **Professional**, **Media Center Edition**, and **Tablet PC Edition**.

■ Windows XP Media Center Edition includes all the features of Windows XP Professional and is designed for Media Center PCs. A **Media Center PC** is a home entertainment personal computer that includes a mid- to high-end processor, large-capacity hard disk, CD and DVD drives, remote control, and advanced graphics and audio capabilities (Figure 3-2). These computers often use a television as their display device.

■ **Windows XP Tablet PC Edition** includes all of the Windows XP Professional features and the following additional features that are designed to make users more productive while working on their Tablet PCs: (1) Issue instructions to the Tablet PC using a digital pen on the write-on screen. (2) Save documents in handwritten form or convert them to typewritten text for use in other applications. (3) Add handwritten notes to documents created in other applications. (4) Enter text and instructions by speaking into the Tablet PC. The potential benefits of using note taking, speech recognition, and other Tablet-specific software programs to

improve teaching and learning in all areas of education are enormous. Some of these software programs are covered later in this chapter and in other chapters.

MACINTOSH OPERATING SYSTEM OR MAC OS Most users of Macintosh computers use one of two versions of Mac OS.

■ Mac OS, version 9.1 — Many Apple and Macintosh school computers use **Mac OS, version 9.1**.

■ Mac OS X — The **Mac OS X** version of the Macintosh operating system, released in 2001, is a significant upgrade to the Macintosh operating system in both appearance and use. Included with this version are enhanced speech recognition capabilities, multimedia capabilities, Web functionality, and improved CD-RW capabilities.

OTHER OPERATING SYSTEMS Two other common operating systems are UNIX and Linux.

■ UNIX — **UNIX** is a multitasking operating system developed for mainframe computers in the early 1970s by scientists at Bell Laboratories, a subsidiary of AT&T. Today, versions of UNIX are available for computers of all sizes.

■ Linux — **Linux** is a popular, multitasking UNIX-based operating system that is one of the faster growing operating systems in use today. Unlike Windows and Mac OS, both of which are proprietary systems, Linux is **open source software**, which means its code is available free to the public. Many application programs, utilities, and plug-ins have Linux versions, including OpenOffice.org, StarOffice, Mozilla, Netscape, Yahoo! Messenger, RealPlayer, QuickTime, and Acrobat Reader.

WEB INFO

For more information about Mac OS, visit the Teachers Discovering Computers Web site, (*scsite.com/tdc4*), click Chapter 3, click Web Info, and then click Mac OS.

Figure 3-2 With Windows XP Media Center Edition, users access recorded videos, pictures, music, television programs, radio stations, or movies via a remote control device.

THE ROLE OF THE USER INTERFACE

All software, including the operating system, is designed to communicate with the user in a certain way, through a user interface. A **user interface** controls how you enter data or instructions (input) and how information is presented on the screen (output).

One of the more common user interfaces is a graphical user interface. A **graphical user interface**, or **GUI** (pronounced gooey), combines text, graphics, and other visual cues to make software easier to use. In 1984, Apple introduced a new operating system based on a graphical user interface. Recognizing the value of this easy-to-use interface, many software companies followed suit, developing software that incorporates a graphical user interface.

Application Software

Recall that **application software** consists of programs designed to perform specific tasks for users. Application software, also called **application programs**, can be used for the following purposes:

- As a productivity/business tool

- Supporting school and professional activities

- Assisting with graphics and multimedia projects

- Helping with home and personal activities

- Facilitating communications

The table in Figure 3-3 categorizes popular types of application software by their general use. These five categories are not all-inclusive nor are they mutually exclusive; for example, e-mail can support productivity, a software suite can include Web page authoring tools, and tax preparation software can be used by a business. In the course of a day, week, or month, you are likely to find yourself using software from many of these categories, whether you are at school, home, or work. Even though you may not use all of the applications, you should at least be familiar with their capabilities.

Communications applications such as e-mail, Web browsers, and others were discussed in Chapter 2. This chapter gives a general overview of each of the other four categories and provides specific examples of applications in each category that are used on both PCs and Macintosh computers.

A wide variety of application software, such as word processing, is available as packaged software that can be purchased from software vendors in retail stores or on the Web. A particular software product, such as Microsoft Word, often is called a **software package**. Many application software packages also are available as shareware, freeware, and public-domain software; these packages, however, usually have fewer capabilities than retail software packages.

FAQ

Can I simply turn the computer off when I am finished?

No! You must use the operating system's shut-down procedure so various processes are closed in sequence and items in memory are released properly.

Figure 3-3 The five major categories of popular application software. You likely will use software from more than one of these categories.

Categories of Application Software

Productivity Business	Graphic Design/ Multimedia	School	Home/Personal	Communications
• Word Processing	• Desktop Publishing	• School/Student Management	• Personal Finance	• E-Mail
• Spreadsheet	• Paint/Image Editing	• Grade Book	• Tax Preparation	• Web Browser
• Presentation Graphics	• Multimedia Authoring	• Education/Reference	• Legal	• Chat Rooms
• Database	• Web Page Authoring	• Special Needs	• Entertainment	• Newsgroups
• Personal Information Management		• Note Taking		• Instant Messaging
• Software Suite				• Blogs

STARTING A SOFTWARE APPLICATION

To use application software, you must instruct the operating system to start the program. Figure 3-4 illustrates how to start and then interact with the Paint program on a PC using Microsoft Windows XP.

Both Mac OS and Microsoft Windows use the concept of a desktop to make the computer easier to use. The **desktop** is an on-screen work area that uses common graphical elements such as icons, buttons, windows, menus, and dialog boxes to make it easy and intuitive for users to interact with the computer. Step 1 of Figure 3-4 shows icons, buttons, and a pointer on the Windows XP desktop.

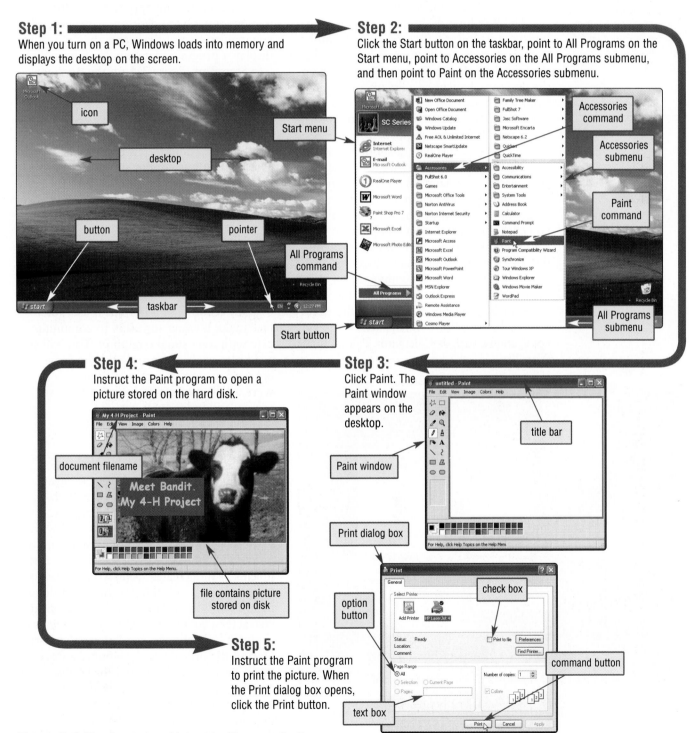

Step 1:
When you turn on a PC, Windows loads into memory and displays the desktop on the screen.

Step 2:
Click the Start button on the taskbar, point to All Programs on the Start menu, point to Accessories on the All Programs submenu, and then point to Paint on the Accessories submenu.

Step 4:
Instruct the Paint program to open a picture stored on the hard disk.

Step 3:
Click Paint. The Paint window appears on the desktop.

Step 5:
Instruct the Paint program to print the picture. When the Print dialog box opens, click the Print button.

Figure 3-4 How to start and interact with an application.

An **icon** is a small image that represents a program, an instruction, or some other object. A **button** is a graphical element (usually a rectangular or circular shape) that when selected, causes a specific action to take place. To select a button, typically you click it using a pointing device such as a mouse. You also can select a button using the keyboard. Icons, text, or a combination of both are used to identify buttons.

The Windows desktop contains a Start button in its lower-left corner, which can be used to start an application. When you click the Start button, the Start menu appears on the desktop. A **menu** is a list of commands from which you can make a selection. **Commands** are instructions that cause a computer program to perform a specific action. Some menus have a **submenu**, which is a list of commands that appears when you select a command on a previous menu. For example, as shown in Step 2 of Figure 3-4 on the previous page, when you click the Start button and point to the All Programs command on the Start menu, the All Programs submenu is displayed. Selecting the Accessories command on the All Programs submenu displays the Accessories submenu. As shown in the Accessories submenu, Windows includes several applications, such as Calculator, Paint, and WordPad.

You can start an application by clicking its program name on a menu or submenu. Doing so instructs the operating system to start the application by transferring the program's instructions from a storage medium into memory. For example, if you click Paint on the Accessories submenu, Windows transfers the program instructions from the computer's hard disk into memory.

Once started, an application is displayed in a window on the desktop. A **window** is a rectangular area of the screen that is used to display a program, data, and/or information (see Step 3 of Figure 3-4 on the previous page). The top of a window has a **title bar**, which is a horizontal space that contains the window's name.

One of the major advantages of a graphical user interface is that elements such as icons, buttons, and menus, usually are common across applications. After you learn the purpose and functionality of these elements, you can apply that knowledge to several software applications. Many of the features just described also are applicable to the desktop of the Macintosh operating system, which is arranged somewhat differently (Figure 3-5).

The features of a graphical user interface make it easier for users to communicate with a personal computer. You will see examples of these features and how they are used as you learn about various software applications used by schools, businesses, and individuals.

WORKING WITH SOFTWARE APPLICATIONS

While using many software applications, you have the ability to create, edit, format, print, and save documents. A **document** is a piece of work created with an application and saved on a disk with a unique filename. Many users think of documents as files created using word processing software. To a computer, however, a document is nothing more than a collection of characters, so a spreadsheet or graphic is as much a document as a letter or report. During the process of developing a document, you likely will switch back and forth among the following activities.

Creating involves developing the document by entering text or numbers, designing graphics, and performing other

Figure 3-5 The desktop of Mac OS X consists of an arrangement different from the Windows desktop; however, both operating systems contain similar features.

tasks using an input device, such as a keyboard or mouse. If you design a map using the graphics tools in Paint, for example, you are creating a document.

Editing is the process of making changes to the document's existing content. Common editing tasks include inserting, deleting, cutting, copying, and pasting items in a document. For example, using Paint, you can **insert**, or add, text to the map, such as the names of key landmarks. When you **delete**, you remove text or objects. To **cut** involves removing a portion of the document and electronically storing it in a temporary storage location called the **Clipboard**. When you **copy**, a portion of the document is duplicated and stored on the Clipboard. To place whatever is stored on the Clipboard into the document, you **paste** it into the document.

Formatting involves changing the appearance of a document. Formatting is important because the overall look of a document can significantly affect its ability to communicate effectively. For example, you might want to increase the size of the text to improve readability.

One often-used formatting task involves changing the font, font size, or font style of text. A **font** is a name assigned to a specific design of characters. Arial and Times New Roman are examples of fonts. The **font size** specifies the size of the characters in a particular font. Font size is gauged by a measurement system called **points**. A single point is about 1/72 of an inch in height. The text you are reading in this book is 10 point. Thus, each character is about 10/72 of an inch in height. A **font style** is used to add emphasis to a font. Examples of font styles are **bold**, *italic*, and <u>underline</u>. Examples of these and additional formatting features are shown in Figure 3-6.

While you are creating, editing, and formatting a document, it is held temporarily in memory. After you have completed these steps, you normally will save your document for future use. **Saving** is the process of copying a document from memory to a storage medium such as a 3.5-inch disk or hard disk. You should save the document frequently while working with it so your work will not be lost if the power fails or the computer crashes. Many applications

WEB INFO

For more information about fonts, visit the Teachers Discovering Computers Web site, (*scsite.com/tdc4*), click Chapter 3, click Web Info, and then click Font.

Figure 3-6
Examples of formatting features available with many productivity programs.

Header Example ◄—	*header appears at top of every page*		*date (and time) can appear in header or footer* —►	April 21, 2007

TYPEFACES & STYLES	Courier	Helvetica	Times New Roman
different typefaces and styles: bold, underline, and italic	**Courier Bold**	<u>Helvetica Underlined</u>	*Times New Roman Italic*

POINT SIZES — *different point sizes can be used to make type larger or smaller* — 6 point   8 point   10 point   **12 point**   **14 point**   20 point   **30 point**   **50 point**

COLUMNS & ALIGNMENT	This is an example of **left alignment**. Notice how the words at the beginning of each line are aligned with the left column margin.	This is an example of **justified alignment**. The spacing between words is adjusted so the words at the beginning and the end of the lines are aligned with the left and right column margins.	This is an example of **center alignment**. The words are centered in the column.	This is an example of **right alignment**. Notice how the words at the end of each line are aligned with the right column margin.
four columns with different alignments				

TABLES & GRAPHICS

three-column table can be moved as a single object

shading applied to every other row with border around table

Part Number	Description	Price
A101	widget	$ 9.95
B202	gizmo	$ 14.95
C303	thingee	$ 19.95
D404	doodad	$ 24.95

graphic can be placed anywhere on page

also have an optional **AutoSave** feature that automatically saves open documents at specified time periods.

Any document on which you are working or you have saved exists as a file. A **file** is a named collection of data, such as a document that you create, a program, or a set of data used by a program. To distinguish among various files, each file has a **filename**, which is a unique set of letters, numbers, and other characters that identifies the file.

After you have created a document, you can print it many times, with each copy looking just like the first. **Printing** is the process of sending a file to a printer to generate output on a medium such as paper. You also can send the document to others electronically, if your computer is connected to a network.

In some cases, when you instruct a program to perform an activity such as printing, a dialog box opens. A **dialog box** is a special window displayed by a program to provide information, present available options, or request a response using command buttons, option buttons, text boxes, and check boxes (Figure 3-7). A Print dialog box, for example, gives you many printing options, such as printing multiple copies or using different printers.

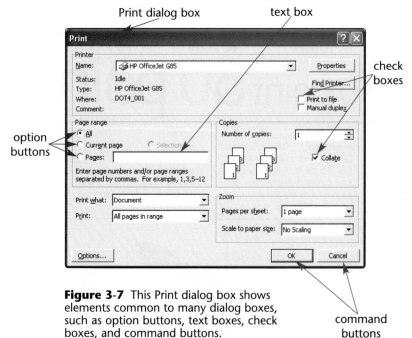

Print dialog box   text box

check boxes

option buttons

command buttons

Figure 3-7 This Print dialog box shows elements common to many dialog boxes, such as option buttons, text boxes, check boxes, and command buttons.

FAQ

Will a document print as it looks on the screen?

Yes, because most current application software is WYSIWYG (what you see is what you get). The application software embeds invisible codes around the text and graphics, which instruct the computer how to present the information.

VOICE RECOGNITION

Many software applications support voice recognition. **Voice recognition**, also called **speech recognition**, is the computer's capability of distinguishing spoken words. You speak into the computer's microphone and watch your words display on your screen as you talk. You also can edit and format a document by speaking or spelling instructions.

NOTE TAKING SOFTWARE

Note taking software is application software that enables users to enter typed text, handwritten comments, graphs, drawings, or sketches anywhere on a page and then save the page as part of an electronic notebook. The software can convert handwritten comments to typed text or store the notes in a handwritten form. Users also can include audio recordings as part of their notes.

After notes are captured (entered and saved), users can organize them, reuse them, and share them easily. The software allows the users to search through saved notes for specific text. Users can search through an entire notebook. Users can flag important notes with color, highlight, and shapes. On a desktop or notebook computer, users enter notes primarily via the keyboard or microphone. On a Tablet PC, however, the primary input device is a digital pen. Students may find note taking software more convenient and easier to use during class lectures, in libraries, and in other settings that previously required a pencil and tablet of paper for recording thoughts and discussions.

Note taking software incorporates many of the features found in word processing software, such as checking spelling, changing fonts and font sizes, adding colors, recognizing voice input, inserting audio and video clips, providing research capabilities, and so much more.

NOTE TAKING SOFTWARE AS A DIGITAL TOOL FOR DIGITAL KIDS

Did you ever experience the frustration of not being able to read your own written notes before a test? Have you searched through page after page of your written notes for the answer to specific questions? These problems, so typical of the experiences

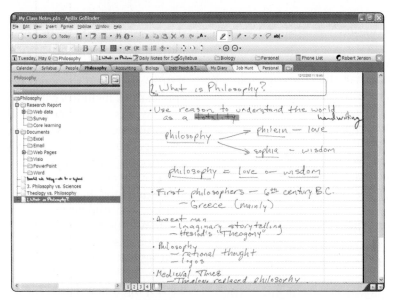

Figure 3-8 With note taking software, digital students and other mobile users can handwrite notes, draw sketches, type text, send handwritten e-mails, and more.

of digital immigrant teachers may be a thing of the past for today's digital kids. In fact, note taking software for this digital generation may be a perfect solution both inside and outside the classroom. By using note taking software, students can have digital documents that are legible, searchable, and editable; however, most students are still taking notes the traditional way, with paper and pencil (Figure 3-8). Although more and more K-12 students are bringing their laptops to class and typing their notes, many of these students cannot type as fast as they can write. With the power of note taking software, students can increase their

comprehension and capture more of the content.

Currently, several publishers are testing various ways of providing their content via the Web, Tablet PC, and traditional printed versions of their textbooks to determine which one is successful with students. Many experts are predicting that as Tablet PCs and other mobile note taking devices become mainstream, printed school and college textbooks will become obsolete. Instead, digital students will interact with digital versions of their textbooks (Figure 3-9).

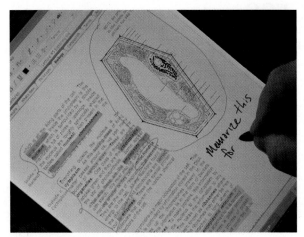

Figure 3-9 Education will reap many benefits as Tablet PCs and the multitude of software products being developed for them become mainstream.

WEB INFO

For more information about Microsoft Works, visit the Teachers Discovering Computers Web site, (*scsite.com/tdc4*), click Chapter 3, click Web Info, and then click Microsoft Works.

Productivity Software

Productivity software is designed to make people more effective and efficient while performing daily activities. Productivity software includes applications such as word processing, spreadsheet, database, presentation graphics, personal information management, and software suites. The features and functions of each of these applications are discussed in the following sections.

WORD PROCESSING SOFTWARE

One of the more widely used application software is **word processing software**, which is used to create, edit, and format documents that consist primarily of text (Figure 3-10). Millions of people use word processing software every day to create documents such as letters, memos, reports, fax cover sheets, mailing labels, and newsletters. The more popular word processing programs used in schools today are Microsoft Word, WordPerfect, and the word processing applications included with AppleWorks, ClarisWorks, and Microsoft Works. By acquiring solid word processing skills, teachers can increase their productivity significantly by using word processing software to create written documents, such as lesson plans, handouts, parent communications, and student tests.

In addition to supporting basic text, word processing software has many formatting features to make documents look professional and visually appealing. When developing a newsletter, for example, you can change the font and font size of headlines and headings, change the color of

document displays
in word processing
window

printed document

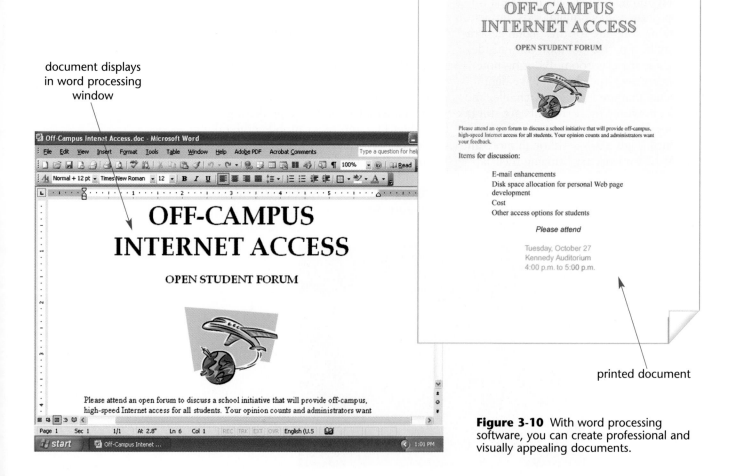

Figure 3-10 With word processing software, you can create professional and visually appealing documents.

characters, or organize text into newspaper-style columns. Any colors used for characters or other formatting will print as black or gray unless you have a color printer.

Most word processing software also can incorporate many types of graphics. For example, you can enhance a document by adding a **border,** which is a decorative line or pattern along one or more edges of a page or graphic. One type of graphic commonly included with word processing software is **clip art,** which is a collection of drawings, diagrams, and photographs that can be inserted in other documents. **Clip art collections,** which can contain several hundred to several thousand images, usually are grouped by type, such as buildings, people, or nature (Figure 3-11). If you want to use clip art not included in your word processing software package, you can create clip art and other graphics using Paint or other applications and **import** (bring into) the clip art into a word processing document. Paint and image editing software is discussed later in this chapter. After you insert, or import, a clip art image or other graphic into a document, you can move, resize, rotate, crop, and adjust its color.

All word processing software provides basic capabilities to help you create, edit, and format documents. For example, you can define the size of the paper on which to print, as well as the **margins** — that is, the portion of the page outside the main body of text, on the top, bottom, left, and right sides of the paper. The word processing

software automatically readjusts any text so it fits within the new definitions.

If you type text that extends beyond the page margin or window boundary, the word processor uses **wordwrap** to automatically position text at the beginning of the next line. Wordwrap allows you to type words in a paragraph continually without pressing the Enter key at the end of each line.

In some instances, for example if you create a multipage document, you can view only a portion of a document on the screen at a time. As you type more lines of text than can be displayed on the screen, the top portion of the document moves upward, or scrolls, off the screen. **Scrolling** is the process of moving different portions of the document into view on the screen.

A major advantage of using word processing software is that you can change easily what you have written. You can insert, delete, or rearrange words, sentences, or entire sections. You can use the **find** or **search** feature to locate all occurrences of a particular character, word, or phrase. This feature can be used in combination with the **replace** feature to substitute existing characters or words with new ones. Current word processing software packages even have a feature that automatically corrects errors and makes word substitutions as you type text.

To review the spelling of individual words, sections of a document, or the entire document, you can use a

WEB INFO

For samples of clip art available on the Internet, visit the Teachers Discovering Computers Web site, (*scsite.com/tdc4*), click Chapter 3, click Web Info, and then click Clip Art.

Lion 1

Iris

Puppy

Puffin

Conch 1

Trout

Mammoth

Figure 3-11 Clip art consists of previously created illustrations that can be added to documents. Clip art collections include graphic images that are grouped by type. These clip art examples are from an animals and nature collection.

WEB INFO

For details about spelling bees, visit the Teachers Discovering Computers Web site, (*scsite.com/tdc4*), click Chapter 3, click Web Info, and then click Spelling.

spelling checker, also called a **spell checker** (Figure 3-12). Spelling checker compares the words in the document with an electronic dictionary that is part of the word processing software. You can customize the electronic dictionary by adding words, such as names of companies, schools, streets, and cities, and personal names, so the software can spell check those words as well. Many word processing software packages allow you to check the spelling of a whole document at one time or check the spelling of single words as you type.

You also can insert headers and footers into a word processing document. A **header** is text you want at the top of each page; a **footer** is text you want at the bottom of each page. Page numbers, as well as company and school names, report titles, or dates are examples of items frequently included in headers and footers.

Many word processing programs make it quick and easy for teachers and students to create personalized documents using templates and special programs called wizards. A **template** is a document that contains the formatting necessary for a specific document type. A **wizard**, or **assistant,** is an automated tool that helps you complete a task by asking you questions and then automatically performing actions based on your answers. Many software applications include wizards. Word processing

software, for example, uses wizards to help you create memorandums, meeting agendas, letters, and other professional looking documents (Figure 3-13).

In addition to these basic features, most current word processing packages provide many other features, some of which are listed in the table in Figure 3-14 on the next page.

Figure 3-12
Spell checkers are included with most word processors. Shown is the spell checker included with AppleWorks.

[a] AppleWorks

Figure 3-13 A wizard, called an assistant in AppleWorks, allows teachers and students to create personalized flyers, newsletters, certificates, and more quickly. Figure 3-13a shows some of the assistants available in AppleWorks, and Figure 3-13b shows some of the templates available in Microsoft Word.

[b] Microsoft Word

Additional Word Processing Features

AutoCorrect	As you type words, the AutoCorrect feature corrects common spelling errors. AutoCorrect also corrects capitalization mistakes.
AutoFormat	As you type, the AutoFormat feature automatically applies formatting to the text. For example, it automatically numbers a list or converts a Web address to a hyperlink.
Collaboration	Collaboration includes discussions and online meetings. Discussions allow multiple users to enter comments in a document and read and reply to each other's comments. Through an online meeting, users share documents with others in real time and view changes as they are being made.
Columns	Most word processing software can arrange text in two or more columns to look like a newspaper or magazine. The text from the bottom of one column automatically flows to the top of the next column.
Grammar Checker	The grammar checker proofreads documents for grammar, writing style, sentence structure errors, and reading statistics.
Ink Input	Ink input supports input from a digital pen. Word processing software that supports ink input incorporates a user's handwritten text and drawings in a word processing document. Ink input is popular on Tablet PCs.
Macros	A *macro* is a sequence of keystrokes and instructions that a user records and saves. When you want to execute the same series of instructions, execute the macro instead.
Mail Merge	Mail merge creates form letters, mailing labels, and envelopes.
Reading Layout	For those users who prefer reading on the screen, reading layout increases the readability and legibility of an on-screen document by hiding unnecessary toolbars, increasing the size of displayed characters, and providing navigation tools.
Research	Some word processing software allows you to search through various forms of online and Internet reference information — based on selected text in a document. Research services available include a thesaurus, English and bilingual dictionaries, encyclopedias, and Web sites that provide information such as stock quotes, news articles, and company profiles.
Smart Tags	*Smart Tags* automatically appear on the screen when you perform a certain action. For example, typing an address causes a Smart Tag to appear. Clicking this Smart Tag provides options to display a map of the address or driving directions to or from the address.
Tables	Tables organize information into rows and columns. In addition to evenly spaced rows and columns, some word processing programs allow you to draw tables of any size or shape.
Templates	A *template* is a document that contains the formatting necessary for a specific document type. Templates usually exist for memos, fax cover sheets, and letters. In addition to templates provided with the software, users have access to many online templates through the software manufacturer's Web site.
Thesaurus	With a thesaurus, a user looks up a synonym (word with the same meaning) for a word in a document.
Tracking Changes	If multiple users work with a document, the word processing software highlights or color-codes changes made by various users.
Voice Recognition	With some word processing programs, users can speak into the computer's microphone and watch the spoken words appear on the screen as they speak. With these programs, users edit and format the document by speaking or spelling an instruction.
Web Page Development	Most word processing software allows users to create, edit, format, and convert documents to be displayed on the World Wide Web.

Figure 3-14 Some of the features included with word processing software.

SPREADSHEET SOFTWARE

Another widely used software application is **spreadsheet software**, which allows you to organize numeric data in rows and columns. These rows and columns collectively are called a **spreadsheet**, or **worksheet**. Manual spreadsheets created using pencil and paper have long been used to organize numeric data. The data in an electronic spreadsheet is organized in the same manner as it is in a manual spreadsheet (Figure 3-15 on the next page).

Individuals who frequently work with numbers, such as financial statements and payroll, use spreadsheets. Many teachers interact with spreadsheet programs on a daily basis. Every time teachers enter

cell C5   cell C9

Figure 3-15 With spreadsheet software, you create worksheets that contain numeric data arranged in rows and columns.

students' grade or attendance information into a computer, they are entering information into a special spreadsheet program, called an electronic grade book. K-12 grade book programs are discussed later in this chapter.

As with word processing software, most spreadsheet software has basic features to help you create, edit, and format electronic spreadsheets. These features, as included in several popular spreadsheet packages, are described below. Spreadsheet software included in Microsoft Works, AppleWorks, and ClarisWorks, as well as Microsoft Excel that is packaged with Microsoft Office are the programs typically used in schools.

Spreadsheet files normally have 256 columns and 65,536 rows. Each column is identified by a letter, and each row is identified by a number. The column letters begin with A and row numbers begin with 1. Only a small fraction of these columns and rows are displayed on the screen at one time. To view different parts of a worksheet, you can scroll to display it on your screen.

The intersection of a column and row is called a **cell**. Cells are identified by the column and row in which they are located. For example, the intersection of column C and row 5 is referred to as cell C5. In Figure 3-15, cell C5 contains the number 5,092.50, which represents Sophomore Tuition & Books expenses.

Cells may contain three types of data: labels (text), values (numbers), and formulas. The text, or **label**, entered in a cell is used to identify the data and help organize the spreadsheet. Using descriptive labels, such as Room & Board, Tuition & Books, and Clothes, helps make a spreadsheet more meaningful.

Many of the spreadsheet cells shown in Figure 3-15 contain a number, or a **value**. Other cells, however, contain formulas that are used to generate values. A **formula** performs calculations on the numeric data in the spreadsheet and displays the resulting value in the cell containing the formula. In Figure 3-15, for example, cell C9 contains the formula to calculate the projected total expenses for the student's sophomore year.

A **function** is a predefined formula that performs common calculations, such as adding the values in a group of cells. For example, instead of using the formula

=C4+C5+C6+C7+C8 to calculate the projected total expenses for the student's sophomore year, you should use the function =sum(C4:C8), which adds, or sums, the contents of cells C4, C5, C6, C7, and C8.

Another standard feature of spreadsheet software is the capability of turning numeric data into a **chart** that graphically illustrates the relationship of the numeric data. Visual representation of data in charts often makes it easier to analyze and interpret information. Most charts are variations of three basic chart types — line charts, pie charts, and column charts, as shown in Figure 3-16. To improve their appearance, most charts can be displayed or printed in a three-dimensional format.

As with word processing software, you can create professional looking spreadsheets quickly using wizards. Using the wizards in most popular spreadsheet packages is easy and allows you to create grade books, classroom and school schedules, charts, and more. Spreadsheet software also incorporates many of the features of word processing software, such as a spelling checker, font formatting, and the capability of converting an existing spreadsheet document into the standard document format for the World Wide Web. Because individual rows, columns, cells, or any combination of cells can be formatted, school districts and businesses often use spreadsheet programs to create their standardized forms.

DATABASE SOFTWARE

A **database** is a collection of data organized in a manner that allows access, retrieval, and use of that data. In a manual system, schools record information on paper and store it in a filing cabinet (Figure 3-17). In a computerized database, such as the one shown in Figure 3-20 on page 157, data is stored in an electronic format on a storage medium. **Database software** allows you to create a computerized database; add, change, and delete data; sort and retrieve data from the database; and create forms and reports using the data in the database.

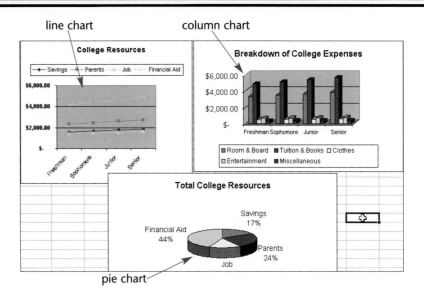

line chart column chart

pie chart

Figure 3-16 Three basic types of charts provided with spreadsheet software are line charts, column charts, and pie charts. The line chart, column chart, and pie chart shown were created from the data in the worksheet in Figure 3-15.

Figure 3-17 A database is similar to a manual system in which related data items are stored in files.

Database software is used extensively by businesses and other organizations to organize data and information about customers, employees, equipment, product inventory, sales information, and more. Schools use databases to organize data and information about students, staff members, school policies, equipment inventories, book inventories, purchases, and more. Database programs typically used in schools include Microsoft Access,

WEB INFO

For an example of how athletes use databases for training purposes, visit the Teachers Discovering Computers Web site, (*scsite.com/tdc4*), click Chapter 3, click Web Info, and then click Athlete.

FileMaker Pro, and the database software included in Microsoft Works, AppleWorks, and ClarisWorks.

When you use a database, you need to be familiar with the terms file, record, and field. Just as in a manual system, a **database file** is a collection of related data that is organized in records. Each **record** contains a collection of related facts called fields. A **field** is the smallest unit of information you can access in a database. For example, a student database file might consist of records containing names, address information, and parental or guardian information. All of the data that relates to one student is considered a record. Each fact in a record, such as the street address or telephone number, is called a field.

Figures 3-18 through 3-20 present the development of a database containing basic information about students enrolled in Ms. Eileen Tanner's second grade class at Martin Luther King Elementary School. This simple database contains the following information about each student: first name, last name, guardian's address, name, and telephone number.

Before you begin creating a database, make a list of the data items you want to organize (Figure 3-18). Each set of related information will become a record. Each item will become a field in the database. A field entry screen from Microsoft Works is shown in Figure 3-19. To identify the different fields, assign each field a unique name that is short, yet descriptive. For example, the field name for a student's last name could be Last Name, the field name for a student's first name could be First Name, and so on. Database programs differ slightly in how they require the user to enter or define fields.

After the database structure is created by defining the fields, data for individual database records can be entered. After data for all records is entered, the database can be used to produce information. Figure 3-20 shows the database after the information about the students has been entered.

As with word processing and spreadsheet software, database software includes wizards that allow teachers and students to create databases for use as address books, directories of parents and students, equipment and book inventories, and so on.

FAQ

How big is the largest database?

According to a recent survey, the world's largest database holds 29 trillion characters. In the next few years, the size of the largest database is expected to exceed 5 quadrillion characters.

**Ms. Tanner
Second Grade Class**

Angel Angelo
247 Powers West
Millie Angelo
555-6879

Jose Costa
3850 Grand Brook Lane
Maria Costa
555-6458

Elizabeth Belanoff
147 Indian Ridge Lane
Debbie Gayle
555-5656

Erinn Joiner
1320 Triple Lake Road
Billy Joiner
555-6231

Sara Beth Corbett
1094 Dunbar Avenue
Pauline Ford
555-3225

Cindy Morris
254 Oak Ridge Drive
Lee Morris
555-8999

one record

Figure 3-18 This figure shows a partial list of the student information Ms. Tanner will be entering in her student database.

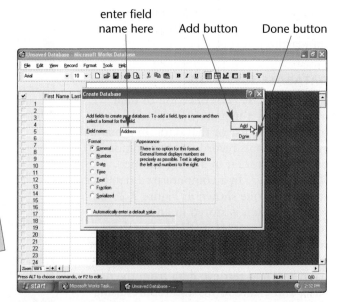

enter field name here   Add button   Done button

Figure 3-19 To create database fields in Microsoft Works, you simply type in each field name and then click the Add button. After entering all the fields you need and clicking the Done button in the Create Database dialog box, you are ready to enter the data in the new database.

fields

records

Figure 3-20 After data has been entered into a database, the records can be arranged in any order specified by users. In this example, the records have been organized alphabetically based on students' last names.

PRESENTATION GRAPHICS SOFTWARE

Using **presentation graphics software**, you can create documents called **presentations**, which you then use to communicate ideas, messages, and other information to a group, such as a class or auditorium of people. The presentations can be viewed as **slides** that are displayed on a large monitor or projected onto a screen. Slides also can be made into traditional overhead transparencies or printed and given to students as a handout (Figure 3-21 on the next page).

Presentation programs typically used in schools are the presentation software included in AppleWorks, ClarisWorks, and Microsoft PowerPoint packaged with Microsoft Office. As with all of the individual software programs in Microsoft Office, you can purchase and use PowerPoint separately.

Presentation graphics software typically provides an array of predefined presentation formats that define complementary colors for backgrounds, text, and other special effects. Presentation graphics software also provides a variety of layouts for each individual slide so you can create a title slide, a two-column slide, a slide with clip art, and others. Any text, charts, and graphics used in a slide can be enhanced with 3-D and other effects such as shading, shadows, and textures.

With presentation graphics software, you can incorporate objects from the clip art/image gallery into your slides to create multimedia presentations. A **clip art/image gallery** includes clip art images, pictures, video clips, and audio clips. A clip art/image gallery can be stored on a hard disk, a CD-ROM, or a DVD-ROM; you can also access clip art/image galleries on the Web. As with clip art collections, a clip art/image gallery typically is organized by categories, such as academic, business, entertainment, and transportation. For example, the transportation category may contain a clip art image of a bicycle, a photograph of a locomotive, a video clip of an airplane in flight, and an audio clip of a Model T car horn.

screen display

handout

Figure 3-21 Teachers and students use presentation graphics software to create electronic slides. The slides can be displayed on a computer, projected on a screen, printed and handed out, or made into transparencies.

When building a presentation, you can set the slide timing so the presentation automatically displays the next slide after a predetermined delay. You also can apply special effects to the transition between each slide. For example, one slide might slowly dissolve as the next slide comes into view.

To help organize the presentation, you can view small versions of all the slides in a slide sorter. A **slide sorter** presents a screen view similar to how 35mm slides would look on a photographer's light table

transparency

WEB INFO

For tips on using graphics effectively in a presentation, visit the Teachers Discovering Computers Web site, (*scsite.com/tdc4*), click Chapter 3, click Web Info, and then click Presentation.

(Figure 3-22 on the next page). The slide sorter allows you to arrange the slides in any order or display them one at a time by clicking the mouse or pressing a key on the keyboard.

Presentation graphics software also incorporates some of the features provided in word processing software, such as spell checking, formatting, and converting an existing slide show into a format that can be viewed on the World Wide Web.

Presentation graphics programs are important software programs for K-12 schools. Teachers can create and integrate electronic presentations into any classroom curriculum as an exciting alternative to the

Figure 3-22 This slide sorter screen shows a small version of each slide. Using a pointing device or the keyboard, users can rearrange the order of the slides.

traditional lecture-only teaching style (Figure 3-23). Students take great pride in creating their own presentations using presentation graphics software. Later chapters provide real-life examples of how teachers integrate presentation graphics software into their instruction and curriculum. A unique feature of presentation graphics software is that it allows you to create a presentation that presents information in a nonlinear format. When using overhead transparencies, teachers traditionally show one transparency after another in a predetermined order — that is, linear teaching and learning.

With presentation graphics software programs, teachers and students can create presentations easily with links to a variety of information sources. Teachers and students, for example, can create presentations

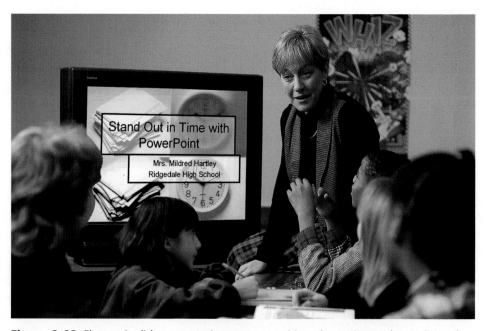

Figure 3-23 Electronic slide presentations are an exciting alternative to the traditional lecture-only teaching style.

with links to other slides, other presentations, other files and software programs, animations, audio and video clips, and even sites on the World Wide Web (Figure 3-24). Using these links, teachers and students can branch off in a nonlinear fashion at any point in a presentation, to display or access additional information.

The ability to modify presentation content according to student interest makes presentation graphics software a powerful teaching and learning tool. The In the Lab end-of-chapter section in Chapter 5 discusses using and integrating Microsoft PowerPoint in more depth.

PERSONAL INFORMATION MANAGERS

A **personal information manager (PIM)** is a software application installed on PDAs that includes an appointment calendar, address book, notepad, and other features to help you organize personal information such as appointments, task lists, and more, as shown in Figure 3-25 on the next page. A PIM allows you to take information that you tracked previously in a weekly or daily

hyperlinks to the Web

Figure 3-24 By clicking a hyperlink in a PowerPoint presentation, teachers and students can access another slide, slide presentation, sound clip, video clip, or a Web site instantly anywhere in the world.

FAQ

Are PDAs also called Pocket PCs?

Only some of them. A **Pocket PC** is a type of PDA that uses the Pocket PC operating system software developed by Microsoft; only a PDA that uses the Pocket PC software is called a Pocket PC.

calendar, and organize and store it on your computer. PIMs can manage many different types of information, such as telephone messages, project notes, reminders, task and address lists, and important dates and appointments.

An **appointment calendar** allows you to schedule activities for a particular day and time. With an **address book**, you can enter and maintain names, addresses, and telephone numbers of coworkers, family members, and friends. Instead of writing notes on a piece of paper, you can use a **notepad** to record ideas, reminders, and other important information.

Most PDAs contain many other features and built-in software programs in addition to those shown in Figure 3-25, including e-mail, Web browsing, instant messaging, and more. One of these features allows users to **synchronize**, or transfer, information and programs from the PDA to a personal computer and vice versa. Some PDAs transfer information wirelessly and others connect to the computer with a cable (Figure 3-26). Many PDAs allow you to transfer information to another PDA by a process called beaming. **Beaming** is a method of transferring data through an infrared port. As with personal computers, PDAs require an operating

Address Book/Contacts

To-Do List

Memos/Notepad

Calculator

Datebook/Calendar

Figure 3-25 Most PDAs come equipped with an address book, to-do list, notepad, calendar, and calculator.

Figure 3-26 Most PDAs allow the user to synchronize, or transfer, information and programs from a personal computer to the PDA and vice versa.

system. Common PDA operating systems include Palm OS, PocketPC, and Linux.

PDA SOFTWARE

In addition to PIMs or installed software, a large selection of software is available for PDAs for a variety of uses, including personal productivity, business, communications, medical, scientific, travel, global positioning, entertainment, games, multimedia, and education. You can download PDA applications from the Web (Figure 3-27) or purchase them at computer and electronic stores.

Downloading and installing programs is an easy process. First, you download the software program to your personal computer, and then you install the software on your PDA using your PDA's synchronization software.

Software purchased at stores usually is supplied on a CD-ROM. You use the CD-ROM to install the software on your personal computer and then use the PDA's synchronization software to install the software on your PDA. A significant number of PDA software programs are available as shareware, freeware, or trial editions and can be found at a number of Web sites (Figure 3-28).

Students and teachers can benefit from PDA software designed for educational uses. Figure 3-29 on the next page describes a few of the hundreds of PDA software programs that are designed for teachers and students both in K-12 schools and institutions of higher education.

Figure 3-27 PalmGear.com is a reseller of PDA software programs.

Figure 3-28 Download.com is a popular Web site for downloading shareware and freeware programs, including popular programs for PDAs.

Education Software for PDAs

Application	Description	Examples	Web Links
Teacher Management Tools	Tools that manage grading, attendance, rosters, curriculum standards, planning, assessment, reporting, contact information, and more.	• eStandards (Media-X) • Tracker and Seeker • Handango Teacher Suite	www.media-x.com/products/estandards/index.php www.schoolid.com/ www.handango.com/
Reference Materials and Other Teaching Applications	Different types of sources for information containing useful facts or information.	• Merriam-Webster® Dictionary • Dictionary ToGo • Formulas for Palm OS®	www.m-w.com www.learningtogo.com/sitemap.php www.standalone.com/palmos/formulas/
ERIC Reference List on PDAs	A bibliography presenting information on the educational uses of PDAs with Web links.	• Educational Resources Information Center (ERIC) search for CRIB on PDAs	www.eric.ed.gov/
Curriculum-Specific Applications	Applications designed to support specific curriculum needs and standards.	• ImagiMath • ImagiProbe • Quizzler • Mental Math • Scholastic Wireless	www.imagiworks.com/index5.html www.imagiworks.com/Pages/Products/ImagiProbe.html www.quizzlerpro.com/ www.aaamath.com/men.html teacher.scholastic.com/wireless/

Figure 3-29 Shown are just a few of the hundreds of ideas and software programs that can be used to benefit both students and teachers.

SOFTWARE SUITES AND INTEGRATED SOFTWARE

A **software suite** is a collection of individual application software packages sold as a single package (Figure 3-30). When you install the suite, you install the entire collection of applications at once, rather than installing each application individually. At a minimum, suites typically include word processing, spreadsheet, database, and presentation graphics.

Integrated software is software that combines applications such as word processing, spreadsheet, and database into a single, easy-to-use package. Unlike a software suite, however, you cannot purchase the applications in the integrated software package individually. Each application in an integrated software package is designed specifically to work as part of a larger set of applications (thus, the name integrated).

The applications within the integrated software package typically do not have all the capabilities of stand-alone productivity software applications. Integrated software thus is less expensive than a more powerful software suite. For many school, home, and personal users, however, the capabilities of an integrated software package more than meet their needs. Popular integrated software packages used in schools include **Microsoft Works** for PCs and **AppleWorks** for Macintosh computers (Figure 3-31).

Both integrated software and software suites offer two major advantages: lower cost and ease of use. Typically, buying a collection of software packages in a suite costs significantly less than purchasing the application packages separately. Software suites provide ease of use because

WEB INFO

For updated links to these and other PDA software sites, visit the Teachers Discovering Computers Web site, (*scsite.com/tdc4*), click Chapter 3, click Web Info, and then click PDA Software.

Figure 3-30 Microsoft Office is available in versions for both PC and Macintosh computers.

Figure 3-31 Two popular integrated software packages used on home and school computers. Microsoft Works often is found on PCs and contains word processing, spreadsheet, database, and communications software. AppleWorks is used on Macintosh computers and contains word processing, spreadsheet, database, paint, and presentation software.

the applications within a suite normally use a similar interface and have some common features. Thus, after you learn how to use one application in the suite, you are familiar with the other applications in the suite. For example, after you learn how to print using the suite's word processing package, you can apply the same skill to the spreadsheet, database, and presentation graphics software in the suite.

Graphics and Multimedia Software

In addition to productivity software, many individuals also work with software designed specifically for their fields of work. For example, engineers, architects, desktop publishers, and graphic artists often use powerful software that allows them to work with graphics and multimedia. Types of graphics and multimedia software include desktop publishing software, paint/image editing software, multimedia authoring tools, Web page authoring software, and many others. The features and functions of some of these applications are discussed in the following sections.

DESKTOP PUBLISHING SOFTWARE

Desktop publishing (DTP) software allows you to design, produce, and deliver sophisticated documents that contain text, graphics, and brilliant colors. Although many word processing packages have some of the capabilities of DTP software, professional designers and graphic artists use DTP software because it is designed specifically to support **page layout**, which is the process of arranging text and graphics in a document. DTP software is ideal for the production of high-quality color documents, such as newsletters, marketing literature, catalogs, and annual reports. In the past, documents of this type were created by slower, more expensive traditional publishing methods such as typesetting. Today's DTP software also allows you to convert a color document into a format for use on the World Wide Web.

Many home, school, and small business users use a much simpler, easy-to-understand DTP software designed for individual desktop publishing projects. Using this DTP software, you can create newsletters and brochures; postcards and greeting cards; letterhead and business cards; banners; calendars; logos; and other such documents (Figure 3-32). Personal DTP software guides you through the development of these documents by asking a series of

FAQ

Why can I not open some files on the Web, including brochures, applications, education articles, and reports?

Many companies and education journals save some documents using the Adobe PDF format. The PDF format allows readers to view a document without having the same program used to create the document. To view and print a PDF file, simply download the free Adobe Acrobat Reader software from the Adobe Web site (adobe.com).

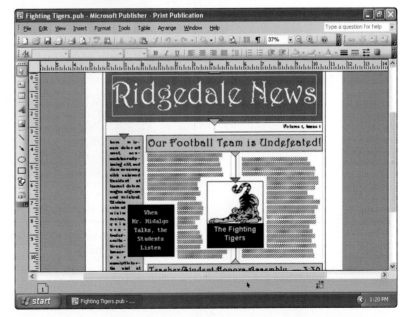

Figure 3-32 Teachers and students use desktop publishing software, such as Microsoft Publisher, to lay out school yearbooks and create flyers, certificates, newsletters, and other types of documents.

questions, offering numerous predefined layouts, and providing standard text you can add to documents. As you enter text, the personal DTP software checks your spelling. You can print your finished publications on a color printer or place them on the Web. Teachers and students use desktop publishing software such as Microsoft Publisher and Adobe PageMaker to lay out school yearbooks and create flyers, certificates, and newsletters.

PAINT/IMAGE EDITING SOFTWARE

Graphic artists, multimedia professionals, desktop publishers, and many others use paint software and image editing software to create and modify graphics, such as those used in DTP documents and Web pages (Figure 3-33). **Paint software** allows you to draw pictures, shapes, and other graphics using various tools on the screen, such as a pen, brush, eye dropper, and paint bucket. **Image editing software** provides the capabilities of paint software as well as the capability of modifying existing

graphics. For example, you can retouch photographs, adjust or enhance image colors, and add special effects such as shadows and glows.

Many home, school, and small business users opt for personal paint/image editing software. Personal paint/image editing software provides a much easier-to-use interface and usually has simplified capabilities, with functions tailored to the needs of the home and small business user. As with the professional versions, personal paint software includes various simplified tools that allow you to draw pictures, shapes, and other graphics.

Personal image editing software provides the capabilities of paint software, and the capability of modifying existing graphics. One popular type of image editing software, called **photo editing software**, allows you to edit digital photographs by removing red-eye, adding special effects, or creating electronic photo albums. When the photograph is complete, you can print it on labels, calendars, business cards, and banners; or place it on a Web page.

Figure 3-33 With image editing software, artists can create and modify a variety of graphic images.

VIDEO AND AUDIO EDITING SOFTWARE

Video consists of full-motion images played back at various speeds. With video editing software, you can modify a segment of a video, called a clip (Figure 3-34). For example, you can add and remove clips, or add special effects like sounds, banners, credits, and more. Video editing programs normally allow you to either edit or add audio components. Current PC and Macintosh operating systems include extensive audio and video editing capabilities; you and your students can even make your own movies.

CLIP ART/IMAGE GALLERY

Although many applications include clip art, you may find that you want a wider selection of graphics. One way to obtain them is to purchase a clip art/image gallery, which is a collection of clip art and photographs. In addition to clip art, many clip art/image galleries provide fonts, animations, sounds, video clips, and audio clips (Figure 3-35). You can use the images, fonts, and other items from the clip art/image gallery in all types of documents, such as letters, flyers, and class projects.

MULTIMEDIA AUTHORING SOFTWARE

Multimedia authoring software is used to create electronic presentations that can include text, graphics, video, audio, and animation. **HyperStudio** is an example of an easy-to-use multimedia authoring software program that allows the author to combine many multimedia elements into a series of interactive cards. The software helps you create presentations by allowing you to control the placement of text and graphics and the duration of sounds, video, and animation. After being created, such multimedia presentations often take the form of interactive computer-based presentations designed to facilitate learning and elicit direct student participation. Commercially produced multimedia presentations usually are stored and delivered via a CD-ROM or DVD-ROM, over a local area network, or via the Internet.

Figure 3-34 Users can use video editing software to modify video images.

Figure 3-35 Clip art/image galleries provide thousands of clip art images and photographs for use in documents such as letters, newsletters, greeting cards, class projects, and presentations.

WEB PAGE AUTHORING SOFTWARE

Web page authoring software is designed specifically to help you create Web pages, in addition to organizing, managing, and maintaining Web sites. As noted in previous sections, many application software packages include Web page authoring features that you can use to create Web pages and Web sites (Figure 3-36). Word processing programs, for example, contain enough features to satisfy the formatting and layout needs of teachers and students for building curriculum pages and other Web documents, as shown in Figure 3-37. A **curriculum page** is a teacher-created document that contains hyperlinks to teacher- selected Web sites that assist in teaching content-specific curriculum objectives.

Web page authoring software features allow you to create sophisticated multimedia Web pages that include graphics, video, audio, animation, and other special effects. Most word processors can be used to create Web pages. Other popular programs used by teachers and students to develop Web pages include **Microsoft Publisher, Microsoft FrontPage, Netscape Composer,** and **Macromedia Dreamweaver MX.** Many of these companies provide resources, tutorials, and more for teachers and students (Figure 3-38).

The special feature following this chapter provides you with step-by-step instructions for creating a teacher's Web page using Microsoft Word. In addition, the textbook Web site provides downloadable step-by-step instructions for creating a teacher's Web page in the latest version of Netscape Composer.

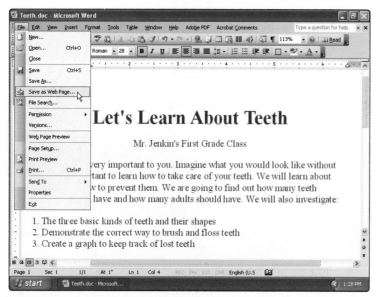

Figure 3-36 The figure shows you how to convert a word processing document automatically into the standard document format for the World Wide Web by saving it as a Web page. After being saved, the document can be published to the Web and viewed in any Web browser.

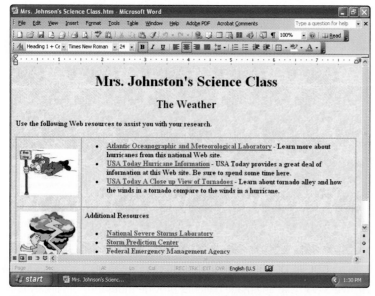

Figure 3-37 An example of a teacher-created curriculum page.

Software for School Use

Many school districts have undergone a period of transition in how they maintain student records and other pertinent information. An important factor driving this transition is the installation of networks.

Having networks in schools allows schools to manage and maintain information about students and teachers in a centralized way. At the lower end, some schools still maintain all student records manually or in software programs on individual computers. Teachers and other school personnel then periodically input student records manually into student management software

Figure 3-38 Most popular Web page authoring programs provide resources, tutorials, and more for teachers and students. In addition, many companies like Macromedia provide curriculum and integration ideas for teachers.

WEB INFO

For tips on using Macromedia Dreamweaver, visit the Teachers Discovering Computers Web site, (*scsite.com/tdc4*), click Chapter 3, click Web Info, and then click Macromedia Dreamweaver MX.

that stores grades and attendance records. Software for schools and professional use includes school management software, student management software, grade book software, educational and reference software, and software for students with special needs.

SCHOOL AND STUDENT MANAGEMENT SOFTWARE

Schools that have networked at least one computer in each classroom usually install school and student management software. When standardized throughout the school district, these programs can improve a school's ability to manage and analyze daily operations, budgets, and student information dramatically.

School management software is a centralized program that allows district and school personnel to manage the school district operations, such as budgeting, inventory, technology, and expenses. Most school management software packages allow a school district to keep a database of all district assets, salaries and benefits, and food services inventory; manage other school and department budgets; and track transportation vehicle maintenance and use. Some school management software also includes databases for attendance and other student information and has other functions similar to student management software. **Student management software** is a centralized program that allows administrators, teachers, and other staff to manage and track information about students, which includes attendance and academic records.

Recall from Chapter 2, Washington County Public Schools has networked all of its classroom computers (Figure 3-39). Teachers throughout the district enter attendance information into the district's student management software program shortly after classes begin. Within a few minutes, district and school administrators know exactly how many students are present. Teachers also enter student grades into the same grade book and attendance program installed on all district computers. Record keeping at Washington County Schools thus is fully automated.

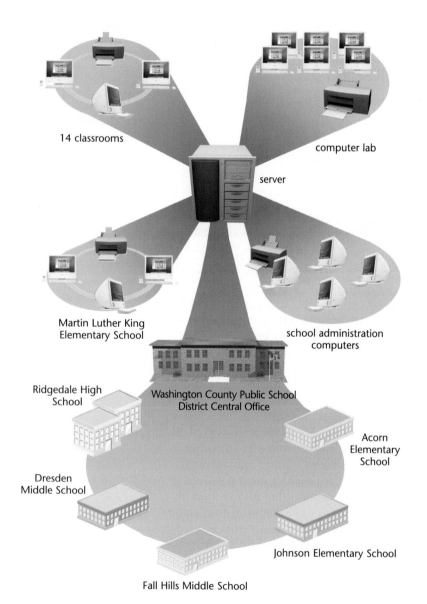

14 classrooms

computer lab

server

Martin Luther King Elementary School

school administration computers

Ridgedale High School

Washington County Public School District Central Office

Acorn Elementary School

Dresden Middle School

Johnson Elementary School

Fall Hills Middle School

Figure 3-39 Washington County Public Schools uses its wide area network that connects all district classrooms to track student attendance records, grades, and more.

GRADE BOOK SOFTWARE

Grade book software allows teachers to track and organize student tests, homework, lab work, and other scores. Most grade book software allows you to track thousands of students and hundreds of assignments within the same grade book and sort students by name, student number, or current average. Most programs allow teachers to weight various scores automatically, apply grading curves, adjust letter grade cutoffs, or use a customized grading scale, such as Fair, Good, Excellent, and so on. Grades can be displayed and entered as points, percentages, letter grades, or in a customized grading scale.

Grade book software also integrates with other software packages. Schools that use network-based or online testing programs, for example, can import student scores directly into the grade book. Teachers also can import and export grades and rosters to a word processing, spreadsheet, or database program.

At some schools, teachers enter attendance and student grades into the same grade book software, which is installed on all district computers. Not all schools have mandated standard grade book programs for teachers to use, however; so many teachers choose their own grade book programs. Numerous outstanding grade book and attendance programs are available for teachers. Some of these are shareware programs; others have trial versions that you can download from the Web for evaluation purposes. Popular grade book programs include Grade Machine, MicroGrade, GradeQuick, WebGrader, Easy Grade Pro, and Gradebook Plus. You also can create basic grade books using the wizards and templates in Microsoft Excel, AppleWorks, and other programs (Figure 3-40).

EDUCATIONAL AND REFERENCE SOFTWARE

Educational software supports learning objectives and goals. Educational software exists for just about any subject, from learning a foreign language to learning how to cook. Preschool to high school learners can use educational software to assist them with subjects such as reading and math or to prepare them for class or college entrance exams.

Figure 3-40 An example of a grade book that teachers can create using Microsoft Excel.

WEB INFO

For information about grade book programs, visit the Teachers Discovering Computers Web site, (*scsite.com/tdc4*), click Chapter 3, click Web Info, and then click Grade Books.

Educational software is covered in greater depth in later chapters. You also can find information about Web links to dozens of popular educational software programs in Software Corner at the end of each chapter.

Reference software provides valuable and thorough information for everyone in an educational setting and in the family. Popular reference software includes encyclopedias, dictionaries, health/medical guides, and travel directories (Figure 3-41). Chapter 5 covers many types of educational and reference software applications and discusses their features in detail.

FAQ

Are Microsoft Encarta, Britannica Reference Suite, and other popular reference software programs available on CD and DVD?

Yes, and the expanded storage capacity of CDs and DVDs allows manufacturers to add extensive, high-quality video segments, animations, graphics, and more.

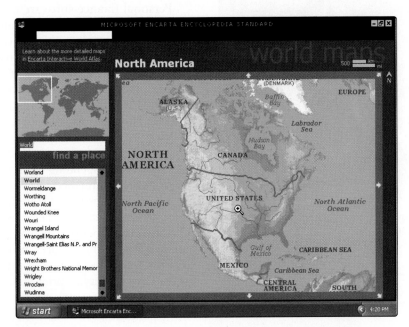

Figure 3-41 Reference software provides valuable and thorough information for all types of users. For example, Microsoft Encarta includes text, pictures, and videos on geography and thousands of other topics.

WEB INFO

For more information about a popular and free text-to-speech software program, visit the Teachers Discovering Computers Web site, (*scsite.com/tdc4*), click Chapter 3, click Web Info, and then click ReadPlease.

SPECIAL NEEDS SOFTWARE

Special needs software is designed specifically for students with physical impairments or learning disabilities, to assist them in completing school assignments and everyday tasks (Figure 3-42). Special needs software includes such programs as **speech synthesis software**, text enlargement programs, talking calculators, and more.

Today, teachers have many software options available to use as tools to enhance teaching and learning of students with special needs. Many software applications discussed in this chapter and educational multimedia applications discussed in Chapter 5 also can assist students with special needs. When students use these software programs in combination with assistive devices, such as touch screens and adaptive keyboards, their ability to succeed increases. These and other special input and output devices designed for use by students with special needs are discussed in Chapter 4. Examples of how teachers can integrate special needs software into their curriculum are covered in Chapters 5-7.

Figure 3-42 Using assistive technology software, teachers help students with disabilities learn subject-related content.

Recall that the textbook Web site includes an end-of-chapter section called Integration Corner. Included with Integration Corner for each chapter is Special Education Corner, where you will find dozens of links to special needs software programs and information on how other teachers are integrating technology with special needs students. Finally, the Assistive Technology Corner at the end of this chapter and on the Web provides extensive information and links to special needs software programs.

Software for Home and Personal Use

Many software applications are designed specifically for home or personal use. Personal software includes personal finance software, tax preparation software, legal software, entertainment software, and more. Most of the products in this category are relatively inexpensive, often priced at less than $50. The features and functions of some of these applications are discussed in the following sections.

PERSONAL FINANCE SOFTWARE

Personal finance software is a simplified accounting program that helps you pay bills; balance your checkbook; track your personal income and expenses, such as credit card bills; track investments; and evaluate financial plans (Figure 3-43). Popular personal finance software includes Quicken and Microsoft Money.

Using personal finance software can help you determine where, and for what purpose, you are spending money so you can manage your finances. Reports can summarize transactions by category (such as dining), by payee (such as the electric company), or by period (such as the last two months). Bill-paying features include the ability to print checks on your printer or have an outside service print your checks.

Figure 3-43 Many home users work with personal finance software to assist them with balancing their checkbook and paying bills.

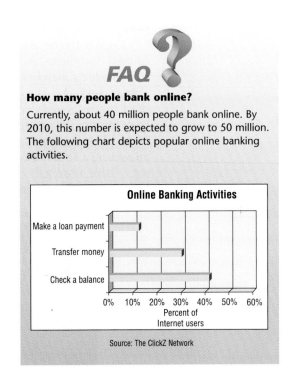

How many people bank online?

Currently, about 40 million people bank online. By 2010, this number is expected to grow to 50 million. The following chart depicts popular online banking activities.

Online Banking Activities

Source: The ClickZ Network

Personal finance software packages usually offer a variety of online services, which require access to the Web. For example, you can track your investments online, compare insurance rates from leading insurance companies, and even do your banking online. **Online banking** offers access to account balances, provides bill payment services, and allows you to download transactions and statements from the Web directly to your computer. In addition, with online banking, you can transfer money electronically from your checking to savings or vice versa. To obtain current credit card statements, bank statements, and account balances, you download transaction information from your bank using the Web.

Financial planning features include analyzing home and personal loans, preparing income taxes, and managing retirement savings. Other features in many personal finance packages include home inventory, budgeting, and tax-related transactions.

TAX PREPARATION SOFTWARE

Tax preparation software guides individuals, families, or small businesses through the process of filing federal taxes (Figure 3-44). Popular tax preparation software includes TurboTax and TaxCut. These software packages offer money-saving tax

tips, designed to lower your tax bill. After you answer a series of questions and complete basic forms, the tax preparation software creates and analyzes your tax forms to search for missed potential errors and deduction opportunities. After the forms are complete, you can print any necessary paperwork. Most tax preparation software packages even allow you to file your tax forms electronically.

Figure 3-44 Tax preparation software can assist you in preparing your federal and state tax returns efficiently and accurately. You even can file your return electronically using the Internet.

LEGAL SOFTWARE

Legal software assists in the preparation of legal documents and provides legal advice to individuals, families, and small businesses (Figure 3-45). Legal software provides standard contracts and documents associated with buying, selling, and renting property; estate planning; and preparing a will. By answering a series of questions or completing a form, the legal software tailors the legal document to your needs.

Figure 3-45 Legal software provides legal advice to individuals, families, and small businesses and assists in the preparation of legal documents.

After the legal document is created, you can file the paperwork with the appropriate agency, court, or office; or you can take the document to your attorney for her review and signature.

ENTERTAINMENT SOFTWARE

Entertainment software includes interactive games, videos, and other programs designed to support a hobby or just provide amusement and enjoyment. For example, you can use entertainment software to play games, make a family tree, compose music, or simulate flying an aircraft.

Learning Aids and Support Tools

Learning how to use an application software package effectively involves time and practice. To aid you in that learning process, your school may offer professional development classes or in-service workshops. In addition to these learning opportunities, many software applications and Web sites provide Help, tutorials, and FAQs. Thousands of books also are available to help you learn specific software packages. Many tutorials are packaged with software or are available free on the Web.

USING HELP

Help is the electronic equivalent of a user manual; it usually is integrated into an application software package (Figure 3-46). Help provides assistance that can increase your productivity and reduce your frustrations by minimizing the time you spend learning how to use an application software package.

In most packages, a function key or a button on the screen starts the Help feature. When you are using an application and have a question, you can use the Help feature to ask a question or access the Help topics by subject, keyword, or alphabetical order. Help displays a list of topics related to the keywords or questions you type.

Figure 3-46 Help provides assistance without having to leave your application.

Often Help is **context-sensitive**, meaning that the Help information is related to the current task being attempted. Most Help also points you to Web sites that provide updates and more comprehensive resources to answer your software questions. In many cases, Help has replaced the user manual altogether, and software developers no longer include user manuals along with the software.

OTHER LEARNING RESOURCES

If printed documentation is included with a software package, often it is organized as reference material rather than structured for learning. This makes it helpful after you know how to use a package, but difficult to use when you are first learning. For this reason, many **trade books** are available to help you learn to use the features of software application packages. These books are available where software is sold, in regular bookstores (Figure 3-47), or online. Web pages that contain an **FAQ (frequently asked questions)** section about application software abound on the Internet and help you find answers to common questions.

Tutorials are step-by-step instructions using real examples that show you how to use an application. Some tutorials are printed manuals; others are software-based or Internet-based, thus allowing you to use your computer to learn about an application software package.

Many colleges and K-12 school districts provide training on many of the applications discussed in this chapter. If you want more direction than is provided in Help, trade books, FAQs, and tutorials, contact your college or school district for a list of workshops and continuing education courses that they offer.

In addition to those discussed here, many other software programs are available for use in schools, homes, and businesses. In the following chapters, you will learn more about other types of educational software, including how-to guides, computer-assisted instructional software, educational games, tutorials, educational simulations, multimedia authoring software, and CD-ROM-based and Web-based multimedia applications.

Figure 3-47 Many bookstores sell trade books to help you learn to use the features of personal computer application packages.

Software Versions and Upgrades

Software programs, including operating systems, usually are designated by a **version** number. A new version of a software product designed to replace an older version of the same product is called an **upgrade**. As software manufacturers develop a newer version of a software package, the newer version usually is assigned higher numbers.

Most manufacturers designate major software releases by increasing the version number by a whole number, for example, version 4.0 to 5.0. To designate minor software improvements, manufacturers usually change the version number by less than a whole number change, such as version 4.0 to 4.2. Some manufacturers use calendar years to designate the latest version. For example, in 2000, Microsoft introduced Microsoft Windows 2000, which was an upgrade to Windows 98. Similar versions of software, however, can have different designations when used on Macintosh computers and PCs. Microsoft Office 2004 for Macintosh computers, for example, is basically the same as Microsoft Office 2003 for Windows.

USING DIFFERENT SOFTWARE VERSIONS

Because of the cost of software, most schools do not upgrade their software each time a manufacturer releases a new version. When schools purchase new computers, however, the latest versions of operating systems and application software often are preinstalled on the computers.

Teachers and students should know which versions of software applications are installed on their school, classroom, and home computers. Most software includes an About or Information command on the Help menu to indicate the software version (Figure 3-48). Often, teachers and students have different versions of the same software on their home and classroom computers; a teacher might have PowerPoint 2000 on a two-year old classroom computer and PowerPoint 2003 on a new home computer.

When working with different versions of the same software, two general rules can help make your work easier. First, an older version of a software package may not open a file created in a newer version of the software. Second, newer versions usually open files created in older versions.

To help alleviate this problem, most software programs allow you to save a document in a format compatible with earlier versions of the same software or in a different file format that can be read by another software program (Figure 3-49).

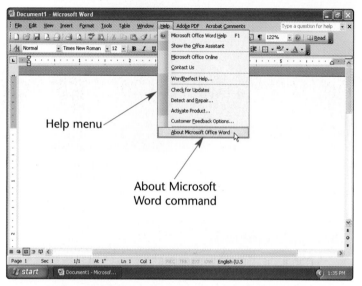

Help menu

About Microsoft Word command

Figure 3-48 To determine the version of a particular software program, on the Help menu click the last command, which normally opens a window that provides information about the software you are using.

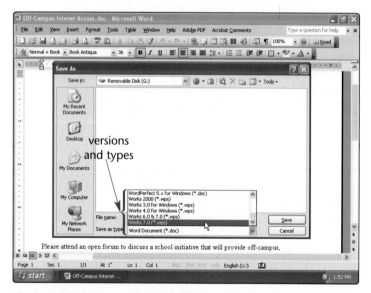

versions and types

Figure 3-49 Most software applications allow users to save their work in earlier versions of the same software or in a different file format that can be read by another software program.

WORKING WITH MACINTOSH COMPUTERS AND PCS

When teachers and students try to move between a Macintosh computer and a PC while working on a document or file, problems can occur. Even experienced users occasionally have problems working with the same document on both Macintosh and PC platforms. Some teachers and students, however, have a PC at home and Macintosh computers in their classrooms or vice versa — and thus have to use files on both platforms.

One source of the problem is that Macintosh computers and PCs format 3.5-inch disks differently. Although Macintosh computers can access a document or file saved on a PC-formatted disk, PCs normally cannot open files saved on a Macintosh-formatted disk. Working with both a Macintosh and a PC, however, is possible. One solution is to e-mail the file to yourself as an attachment, then you can open the file on the other computer, as long as you have e-mail access on both computers, without using a 3.5-inch disk. To be sure the document can be read on either computer, you can save it, if the file was created on a PC in a Macintosh format or a Rich Text format (Figure 3-50). After you have saved the file,

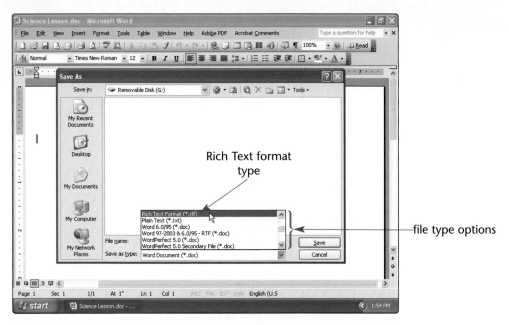

Figure 3-50 Many software programs allow files to be saved in various formats.

you can e-mail it and then open it on another computer. Another solution is to install and use a software program specifically designed to support PC to Mac and Mac to PC file conversions, such as MacLink Plus Deluxe or MacOpener.

If you have to work with files on both computer platforms, you should speak with experienced teachers and other users in similar circumstances; they can help you find a solution for your situation. You also can ask for assistance from your instructor or school technology coordinator.

Creating a Teacher's Web Page

At the end of this chapter is a step-by-step special feature that provides you with instructions on how to create a teacher's Web page using Microsoft Word. You also can download a similar step-by-step project that provides you with instructions on how to create a similar teacher's Web page in Netscape Composer. The special feature that follows Chapter 7 will provide you

with additional Web development skills, as you learn how to create and use curriculum pages.

Summary of Application Software Productivity Tools for Educators

In this chapter, you have learned about user interfaces and several software applications used in schools, businesses, and homes. You also have read about some of the learning aids and support tools that are available for application software. Understanding these software applications increases your computer literacy and helps you to understand how personal computers can help in your career as a teacher, in your classroom instruction, and at home. The next chapter introduces you to hardware applications for education; future chapters provide information on additional software applications used by educators and show you how to integrate various software applications into your classroom curriculum.

In Brief

INSTRUCTIONS: In brief summarizes the concepts presented in this chapter. To listen to the audio version of this In Brief, visit scsite.com/tdc4. Click Chapter 3 at the top of the Web page and then click In Brief on the left sidebar.

1. Application Software

Application software consists of programs designed to perform specific tasks for users. Packaged software can be purchased from software vendors in retail stores or on the Web. A particular software product such as Microsoft Word often is called a software package.

2. Role of the Operating System

System software consists of programs that control the operations of the computer and its devices. One type of system software, the operating system, contains instructions that coordinate all of the activities of the hardware devices in a computer. The operating system also contains instructions that allow the computer to run application software.

3. Role of the User Interface

All software, including the operating system, is designed to communicate with the user in a certain way, through a user interface. A user interface controls how users enter data or instructions (input) and how information is presented on the screen (output). One of the more common user interfaces is a graphical user interface. A graphical user interface, or GUI, combines text, graphics, and other visual cues to make software easier to use. Mac OS and Windows are popular graphical user interfaces.

4. Starting a Software Application

Mac OS and Windows use the concept of a desktop to make the computer easier to use. The desktop is an on-screen work area that uses common graphical elements such as icons, buttons, windows, menus, and dialog boxes. An icon is a small picture that represents a program, an instruction, or some other object. A button is a graphical element that when selected, causes a specific action to take place. A menu is a list of commands from which you can select. Commands are instructions that cause a computer program to perform a specific action.

5. Working with Software Applications

A document is a piece of work created with an application program and saved on a disk with a unique filename. Creating involves developing the document by entering text and performing other tasks using an input device such as a keyboard. Editing is the process of making changes to the document's existing content. Formatting involves changing the appearance of a document. Saving is the process of copying a document from memory to a storage medium. Printing is the process of sending a file to a printer to generate output.

6. Productivity Software

Productivity software is designed to help people work more effectively and efficiently while performing daily activities. Productivity software includes applications such as word processing, spreadsheet, database, presentation graphics, personal information management, and software suites.

7. Word Processing Software

The most widely used software is word processing software, which is used to create, edit, and format documents that consist primarily of text. The most popular word processing programs used in schools today are Microsoft Word and the word processing applications included with AppleWorks, ClarisWorks, and Microsoft Works.

In Brief

8. Spreadsheet Software

Another widely used software application is spreadsheet software, which allows you to organize numeric data in rows and columns. These rows and columns collectively are called a spreadsheet, or worksheet. Individuals who frequently work with numbers (for example, financial statements and payroll) use spreadsheets.

9. Database Software

A database is a collection of data organized in a manner that allows access, retrieval, and use of that data. In a computerized database, data is stored in an electronic format on a storage medium. Database software allows you to create a computerized database; add, change, and delete data; sort and retrieve data from the database; and create forms and reports using the data in the database.

10. Presentation Graphics Software

Presentation graphics software allows you to create documents called presentations, which are used to communicate ideas, messages, and other information to a group, such as a class or auditorium. The presentations can be viewed as slides that display on a large monitor or project onto a screen.

11. Software Suites and Integrated Software

A software suite is a collection of individual application software packages sold as a single package. Suites typically include word processing, spreadsheet, database, and presentation graphics software applications. Integrated software is software that combines applications such as word processing, spreadsheet, and database into a single, easy-to-use package. Unlike a software suite, however, you cannot purchase the applications in the integrated software package individually.

12. Graphics and Multimedia Software

Graphics and multimedia software include desktop publishing, paint/image editing, multimedia authoring, and Web page authoring software. Desktop publishing (DTP) software allows you to design, produce, and deliver sophisticated documents that contain text, graphics, and brilliant colors. Paint/image editing software allows you to create and modify graphics such as those used in DTP documents and Web pages. Multimedia authoring software is used to create electronic presentations that can include text, graphics, video, audio, and animation. Web page authoring software is software designed specifically for creating Web pages and organizing, managing, and maintaining Web sites.

13. Software for School and Professional Use

Software for schools and professional use includes school management software, student management software, grade book software, educational/reference software, and software for students with special needs. School management software is a centralized program that allows district and school personnel to manage the school district operations. Student management software allows administrators, teachers, and other staff to manage and track information on students. Grade book software is a program that allows teachers to track and organize student tests, homework, lab work, and other scores.

14. Educational and Reference Software

Educational software is designed for the learning environment. Educational software exists for just about any subject, from learning a foreign language to learning how to cook. Reference software provides valuable and thorough information for everyone in an educational setting and in the family. Popular reference software includes encyclopedias, dictionaries, health/medical guides, and travel directories.

15. Learning Aids and Support Tools

Help is the electronic equivalent of a user manual; it usually is integrated into an application software package. Trade books are available to help users learn to use the features of software application packages. These trade books are available where software is sold. Tutorials are step-by-step instructions using real examples that show users how to use an application.

Key Terms

3

INSTRUCTIONS: Use the Key Terms to help focus your study of the terms used in this chapter. To further enhance your understanding of the Key Terms in this chapter, visit scsite.com/tdc4. Click Chapter 3 at the top of the Web page and then click Key Terms on the left sidebar. Read the definition for each term and then access current and additional information about the term from the Web.

address book [162]
AppleWorks [164]
application program [144]
application software [144]
appointment calendar [162]
assistant [152]
AutoSave [148]

beaming [162]
border [151]
button [146]

cell [154]
chart [155]
clip art [151]
clip art collection [151]
clip art/image gallery [157]
Clipboard [147]
command [146]
context-sensitive [175]
copy [147]
creating [146]
curriculum page [168]
cut [147]

database [155]
database file [156]
database software [155]
delete [147]
desktop [145]
desktop publishing (DTP)
    software [165]
dialog box [148]
document [146]

editing [147]
educational software [170]
entertainment software [174]

FAQ (frequently asked
    questions) [175]
field [156]
file [148]
filename [148]
find [151]
font [147]
font size [147]
font style [147]
footer [152]
formatting [147]
formula [154]
function [154]

grade book software [170]
graphical user interface [144]
GUI [144]

header [152]
Help [174]
HyperStudio [167]

icon [146]
image editing software [166]
import [151]
insert [147]
integrated software [164]

label [154]
legal software [174]
Linux [143]

MAC OS, version 9.1 [143]
MAC OS X [143]
Macromedia Dreamweaver MX
    [168]
margins [151]
Media Center PC [143]
menu [146]
Microsoft FrontPage [168]
Microsoft Publisher [168]
Microsoft Windows [142]
Microsoft Works [164]
multimedia authoring software [167]

Netscape Composer [168]
note taking software [148]
notepad [162]

online banking [173]
open source software [143]
operating system [142]

page layout [165]
paint software [166]
paste [147]
personal finance software [172]
personal information manager
    (PIM) [161]
photo-editing software [166]
Pocket PC [162]
point [147]
presentation [157]
presentation graphics software
    [157]
printing [148]
productivity software [150]

record [156]
reference software [171]
replace [151]

saving [147]
school management software [169]
scrolling [151]
search [151]
slide sorter [158]
slides [157]
software package [144]
software suite [164]
special needs software [172]
speech recognition [148]
speech synthesis software [172]
spell checker [152]
spelling checker [152]
spreadsheet [153]
spreadsheet software [153]
student management software [169]
submenu [146]
synchronize [162]
system software [142]

tax preparation software [144]
template [152]
title bar [146]
trade book [175]
tutorial [175]

UNIX [143]
upgrade [175]
user interface [144]

value [154]
version [175]
video [167]
voice recognition [148]

Web page authoring software [168]
window [146]
Windows 98 [142]
Windows 2000 [142]
Windows XP [143]
Windows XP Home Edition [143]
Windows XP Media Center
    Edition [143]
Windows XP Professional [143]
Windows XP Tablet PC Edition
    [143]
wizard [152]
word processing software [150]
wordwrap [151]
worksheet [153]

Checkpoint

INSTRUCTIONS: Use the Checkpoint exercises to check your knowledge level of the chapter. To complete the Checkpoint exercises interactively, visit scsite.com/tdc4. Click Chapter 3 at the top of the Web page and then click Checkpoint on the left sidebar.

1. Label the Figure

Instructions: Identify each component of the Print dialog box.

2. Matching

Instructions: Match each term from the column on the left with the best description from the column on the right.

_____ 1. Clipboard

_____ 2. database

_____ 3. record

_____ 4. commands

_____ 5. cell

a. collection of related fields
b. instructions that cause software to perform specific actions
c. temporary storage location
d. intersection where a column and row meet
e. collection of data organized in a manner that allows access, retrieval, and use of that data

3. Short Answer

Instructions: Write a brief answer to each of the following questions.

1. What is a graphical user interface? Describe some common features of both the Windows and Macintosh graphical user interface. _____
2. Name and describe four different types of productivity software used by K-12 teachers. Which productivity software program do you use the most? Why? _____
3. What are the advantages of integrated software and software suites? Describe three popular integrated software or software suites used in K-12 schools. _____
4. What is a database? How are databases used in K-12 schools? _____
5. What are the advantages of using presentation graphics software programs? What are the disadvantages? How are teachers and students using presentation graphics programs? _____

Teaching Today

INSTRUCTIONS: Teaching Today provides an appreciation of the value that technology and the Web have for K-12 education. Each numbered segment contains one or more links that reinforce the information presented in the segment. To display this page from the Web, visit scsite.com/tdc4. Click Chapter 3 at the top of the Web page and then click Teaching Today on the left sidebar.

1. Software Suites

Your school uses Macintosh computers. Your principal is considering purchasing AppleWorks for all classroom and lab computers. You have never used AppleWorks; however, you are familiar with Microsoft Office for the Macintosh. He also is interested in open source software. Your principal has asked you to compare the different software packages and make a presentation to the school's teachers. How are the packages the same? How are the packages different? What type of support does each software package offer? Is one easier to use than the other? Why or why not? Is one easier to learn than the other? Why or why not?

2. Build Interdisciplinary Projects

As an elementary teacher, you must teach all subjects to your students. You have decided to teach a project that is interdisciplinary, combining language arts, social studies, math, and science. You also have decided to integrate technology throughout the lesson not only to do research but also to help students learn to become better researchers, writers, and presenters. The topic of your project is Ancient Egypt. You start by using the Media Center to gather books, CD-ROMs, reference materials, Web sites, and more. What kind of lesson plan can you develop to encourage your students to create a project using the Internet, reference software,

word processing, your curriculum-specific software, and presentation graphics software? Where could you locate sample lesson plans to help you get started? Explain your plan to integrate these software applications into an interdisciplinary lesson that includes two or more curriculum areas.

3. Software Products

Your principal just let you know that you will have students with special needs in your class this year. You are planning to purchase software for your classroom to integrate technology into the curriculum. What software can you purchase that will benefit both your regular students as well as your special-needs students? Explore software products for your grade level. Can you use these products in the classroom just described? What special features do these software packages include for special-needs learners? Will these features be useful with regular education students as well? Why or why not? What special technology tools are offered? Would these tools be useful with regular education students? Why or why not? How can you locate other software companies that sell educational software?

4. Software Vendors

Most state Departments of Education negotiate one-year or multiyear contracts with various vendors for educational software products. This enables schools to acquire software products at substantial discounts. Contact a school in your district or access your state's Department of Education Web site and find out about a few of the software products available through the state purchasing program. Compare these prices with purchasing the same software either online or at a local computer store. What kind of discounts are the schools receiving? How many titles are available through the state catalog? What procedures does a teacher have to go through to purchase software not in the catalog?

Education Issues

INSTRUCTIONS: Education Issues provides several scenarios that allow you to explore controversial and current issues in education. Each numbered segment contains one or more links that reinforce the information presented in the segment. To display this page from the Web, visit scsite.com/tdc4. Click Chapter 3 at the top of the Web page and then click Education Issues on the left sidebar.

1. Word Processing

Many teachers believe that word processing software improves the quality of written work by making it easier for students to create and edit documents. Students can use clip art, scanned images, or other computer graphics to enhance their work. Some people argue, however, that word processing software has become a crutch, eliminating the need to learn the rudiments of language. These people believe students are not forced to know basic grammar and spelling rules because word processing software alerts them to errors. How do you think word processing software has influenced written communication? Does it result in better student work or simply more correct yet mediocre work? What word processing features most enhance the quality of written material?

2. Reading Problems

You teach middle school, and this year you have the most challenging group of students you have ever had. Many of your students seem completely uninterested in learning or even in coming to school for that matter. As a result, you have continuous discipline problems and spend a lot of time sending students to the principal's office. After a few days, you become convinced that a deeper problem must exist, so you do a little research and find out that many of the students are below the 30th percentile in reading. You wonder how these students got this far without knowing how to read. Traditional reading programs obviously have not worked for these students. Using the Internet and other sources, do research to find out whether reading software programs and educational technology might be able to help them. Continue your research to investigate alternative techniques using technology that might motivate these students and help them to learn to read. Where could you locate software and innovative teaching strategies that could help you turn these students around?

3. Database Software

Increasingly sophisticated software applications have impacted not only business, entertainment, and recreation, but education as well. Database software can give students the opportunity to record, track, and analyze data on virtually any subject matter. Learning about database software also provides students with knowledge of an important software program that is used extensively in business and on the Web. Does learning and using database software help students develop higher-order thinking and problem-solving skills? What other advantages does using database software offer? What are some disadvantages to using database software in the classroom? How might another application described in this chapter be used to teach higher-order thinking skills or problem solving?

4. Computer Use in the Classroom

With the explosion of educational software, multimedia, digital media, and the Internet, educators still are learning the best use for computers in the classroom. Drill and practice? Problem solving? Games? A growing number of educators feel that students should be taught the software applications they will have to know to succeed in the workplace. From the applications presented in this chapter, make a list of five applications you think every student should learn, from more important to less important. Explain your ranking. At what level do you think each application should be taught? Why?

Integration Corner

INSTRUCTIONS: Integration Corner provides extensive ideas and resources for integrating technology into your classroom-specific curriculum. To display this page from the Web and its links to approximately 100 educational Web sites, visit scsite.com/tdc4. Click Chapter 3 at the top of the Web page and then click Integration Corner on the left sidebar.

Integration Corner is designed for teachers and other educators who are looking for innovative ways to integrate technology into their content-specific curriculum. Integration Corner not only provides great Web sites with current information but also shows what other educators are doing in the field of educational technology. Integration Corner is designed for all educators regardless of their interests. Expand your resources by reviewing information and Web sites outside of your teaching area because many great integration ideas in one area can be modified easily for use in other curricular areas.

Teachers and administrators will find other colleagues in their areas with whom to connect and share the successes and hurdles of integrating technology in a classroom or an entire school system. Consider Integration Corner your one stop for integration ideas and resources. Links to educational Web sites are organized in the following 12 Corners, and different Web resources are available for each chapter. Figure 3-51 shows examples of the Web resources provided in the Chapter 3 Middle School Corner.

Figure 3-51 Examples of the Web resources provided in the Chapter 3 Middle School Corner.

Software Corner

INSTRUCTIONS: Software Corner provides information on popular software programs. Each numbered segment discusses specific software programs and contains a link to additional information about these programs. To display this page from the Web, visit scsite.com/tdc4. Click Chapter 3 at the top of the Web page and then click Software Corner on the left sidebar.

1. PrimeTime Math

Teachers of exceptional students will find the PrimeTime Math series excellent support software for the math curriculum. PrimeTime Math engages students by providing stories about real-world professionals using math in real-life situations. This software meets the National Council of Teachers of Mathematics (NCTM) standards by building mathematical understanding through use of stories about crimes, medical emergencies, fires, and wilderness search and rescues, while at the same time assisting students in realizing the importance of math in the world in which they live.

2. Adobe Photoshop Elements

Adobe Photoshop Elements allows you and your students to edit pictures from resources such as those downloaded from digital cameras and the Internet. You can use these edited pictures to create multimedia digital projects, unique integration, and personalized calendars, student bulletin boards for classroom instruction, post to the Web, and much more. Using Adobe Photoshop Elements helps your classroom photos have a professionally finished look without a lot of hassle and the price is perfect for education!

3. Thinkology

Developing students' critical-thinking skills and creating learning opportunities that engage higher-order thinking skills always have been a struggle for teachers. Thinkology by Heartsoft helps K-3 students master essential critical thinking skills while having fun! Students are guided through a critical-thinking-skills journey with a cast of clever animated characters. Students learn to reason through concepts and are asked questions such as, does this make sense?

4. Kidspiration

Ever had trouble getting young learners to organize their thoughts and develop their great ideas into understandable concepts? Kidspiration is an excellent visual learning tool for teaching K-5 students to organize and express those great ideas through visual learning! Created for inexperienced readers and writers, Kidspiration helps students increase their confidence as they learn to understand concepts, organize information, write stories, and convey and share their thoughts. Brainstorming, visual mapping, thought webs, and other visual tools are used to enhance students' comprehension of concepts and information.

5. Tessellation Exploration

Do you want to make teaching tessellations to your middle and high school students fun and easy? One piece of software that makes the concept of tessellations easier to teach and allows students to practice is Tessellation Exploration by Tom Snyder Productions. The software includes an extensive tutorial on the concept of tessellations. Teachers can use the software as a tool to present the concept of tessellations. Next, students use Tessellation Exploration to construct their own tessellations, by selecting a base shape and moves, such as slides, flips, and turns; students watch their tessellation form before their eyes. Students can create slide shows with the tessellations or print them out.

Digital Media Corner

INSTRUCTIONS: Today's K-12 digital students need their learning to be meaningful and relevant to their lives. Digital Media Corner provides videos, ideas, and examples of how you can use digital media to enhance your teaching and your students' learning. To access the videos and links to additional information, visit scsite.com/tdc4. Click Chapter 3 at the top of the Web page and then click Digital Media on the left sidebar.

1. At the Movies — Black Viper's Windows XP Tips

Windows XP is a large and powerful program that often runs many applications that you will probably never use. These programs require a lot of resources that can be used by other programs. Which of these programs would you turn off to make your computer run more efficiently and faster? To view the Black Viper's Windows XP Tips movie, click the G4TechTV video link. Locate your video and click the corresponding High-Speed or Dial-up link, depending on your Internet connection.

2. At the Movies — Windows XP Media Center Edition

Windows XP Media Center Edition is software that easily can enable advanced multimedia interactivity on your computer. With one touch of the remote control, you can activate your music, photographs, videos, radio shows, or television programs. To view the Windows XP Media Center Edition movie, click the G4TechTV video link. Locate your video and click the corresponding High-Speed or Dial-up link, depending on your Internet connection.

3. At the Movies — History of Adobe

At the dawn of the computer age, computers were used mostly by scientists, and printers were large, cumbersome machines. The advent of desktop publishing gave average people access to the power of computing. Users were able to publish documents and images easily, and the computer became a tool for creative expression for everyone. How have desktop publishing and other software programs changed the way students research and write reports? To view the History of Adobe movie, click the G4TechTV video link. Locate your video and click the corresponding High-Speed or Dial-up link, depending on your Internet connection.

4. Adobe Software

A popular digital media production software application package is Adobe Creative Suite. The Adobe Creative Suite includes the widely used image editing program PhotoShop, the illustration creator Illustrator, the Web site development application GoLive, the page publisher InDesign, and Adobe Acrobat. Adobe's popularity is due in part to its high performance on both Windows and Macintosh platforms as well as its industry standard Portable Document Format or .PDF file format.

5. Microsoft Producer, Photo Story, and Movie Maker

Microsoft provides three free programs that can dramatically enhance digital projects. Microsoft Producer is an add-on for Microsoft PowerPoint and can help you easily capture, synchronize, and publish audio, video, slides, and images in your PowerPoint presentations. Photo Story for Windows brings your digital photos to life. You can add stunning special effects, soundtracks, and your own voice narration and much more to your photos and your digital storytelling projects. Using the free Movie Maker for Windows XP and the Creativity Fun Pack, you and your students can create and edit movies with a few simple drag-and-drops. You can delete bad shots and include only the best scenes. Introduce your classroom to Movie Maker.

Assistive Technologies Corner

INSTRUCTIONS: Assistive Technologies Corner provides information on current hardware, software, and peripherals that will assist you in delivering instruction to students with physical, cognitive, or sensory challenges. To access extensive additional information, visit scsite.com/tdc4. Click Chapter 3 at the top of the Web page and then click Assistive Technologies on the left sidebar.

1. Should Special Needs Software Be Available for All Teachers?

Yes! The educator's primary concern is to fit the software to the learner, and not the other way around. You can choose the appropriate assistive technology software when you consider the particular disability of the learner, the learner's strengths, and the learner's academic needs. A challenged student may need assistance with reading, or with communication, or with organizing and processing new information.

In the Chapter 1 Assistive Technologies Corner, you learned that operating systems have built-in accessibility features. Some of these features may be further enhanced with system software that affects the behavior of the computer across all other programs. You may choose to add new voices to the speech software built into the operating system of the computer or to add new large mouse pointers, for example, which will appear whether your students are using Microsoft Word or Internet Explorer. To change the size of the mouse pointer in Windows, click the Start button on the Windows taskbar and then click Control Panel. When the Control Panel window opens, double-click the Mouse icon. When the Mouse Properties dialog box opens, click the Pointer tab. Numerous mouse pointer options are available by clicking the Scheme list arrow.

2. What is Speech Synthesis Software?

Many strong application tools are available to enable student productivity. **Speech synthesis software** allows students with speech and vocal muscle disorders to participate in classroom discussions. Students assign shortcut keys to reproduce specific, frequently used phrases. Then, they use the shortcut keys to type in a response quickly; the word processing software reads the response in a computerized voice. Students with visual impairments may use software with text enlargement features. Other helpful software applications include an on-screen talking calculator that features big, colorful number buttons and high-quality speech synthesis.

3. What is Speech-to-Text Software?

Speech-to-text software is used by many nondisabled users to control computers and produce documents. In the classroom, this type of software assists learners with disabilities to produce a printed document. ScanSoft is speech-to-text dictation software for both Windows (Dragon Naturally Speaking) and Macintosh (IBM Via Voice) environments. As the student speaks, the software types. These software packages "learn" to respond to the voice of the user. iCommunicator puts the speech-to-text program in an enhanced environment that also provides sign language. Although not a substitute for a sign language interpreter, this software provides an alternative for students with unique communication challenges.

4. What is Text-to-Speech Software?

Software programs that read text aloud are called text-to-speech software. Kurzweil 3000 is a robust system available for struggling learners. With the Kurzweil system, any text from books or documents can be scanned and read aloud to the student. In addition to this enhanced text-to-speech feature, the Kurzweil system allows students to complete tests and worksheets. A built-in word processor displays the test, and the student types in responses. In addition, many freeware and shareware text-to-speech programs are available on the Internet.

Follow the instructions at the top of this page to display additional information and this chapter's links on assistive technologies.

In the Lab

INSTRUCTIONS: In the Lab provides spreadsheet exercises that are divided into two areas, productivity and integration. To access the links to tutorials, productivity ideas, integration examples and ideas, and more, visit scsite.com/tdc4. Click Chapter 3 at the top of the Web page and then click In the Lab on the left sidebar.

PRODUCTIVITY IN THE CLASSROOM

Introduction: Spreadsheets have many uses for both students and teachers in the classroom. Spreadsheets are a great teacher productivity tool. Grade books, lesson plans, rubrics, classroom inventory, textbook inventory, and many other time-saving documents can be created in a spreadsheet. Students can creatively display data using a spreadsheet's charting feature, in addition to sorting and manipulating data, thereby using higher-order thinking skills.

Many of the productivity software suites have spreadsheet programs. Excel is a part of the Microsoft Office suite. Microsoft Works and AppleWorks also have a spreadsheet program. Lotus 1-2-3 and Quattro Pro also are popular spreadsheet programs.

Spreadsheets are not just for math class. It is possible to integrate spreadsheets effectively into many different curriculum areas in ways that excite students and empower their learning.

1. Building a Grade Book Spreadsheet

Problem: Keeping a grade book by hand can be a tedious task. To save time, you have created your grade book in a spreadsheet program so you can calculate percentages and grades quickly, as shown in Figure 3-52. Open your spreadsheet software and create the grade book as described in the following steps. Use the grade book shown in Figure 3-52 as an example. (*Hint:* use Help to better understand the steps. If you do not have the suggested font, use any appropriate font.)

Instructions: Perform the following tasks.

1. Use the names and numbers displayed in Figure 3-52 to create a spreadsheet, then complete the remaining steps to format the spreadsheet.
2. Calculate the total and average for each student and for the entire class.
3. Personalize the spreadsheet title by inserting your name and curriculum area. Format the spreadsheet title in 16-point, Arial Black font and centered over columns A through H. Add a solid black border to cells A1:H1.
4. Use the AutoFormat option and select an appropriate table format for cells A2:H16. The numbers appear in the Number format with 0 decimal places.
5. Bold the Class Average label in cell A18 and then verify that the column headings in row 2 are bold. Calculate the class total and class average for each item. Add a solid black border to the bottom of cells A18:H18.

	A	B	C	D	E	F	G	H
1	\multicolumn{8}{c}{**Mr. Radcliff's 4th Period Language Arts Class**}							
2	*Student*		*Book Report*	*Vocab Quiz*	*Poem*	*Essay*	*Total*	*Average*
3	*First Name*	*Last Name*						
4	*Jenny*	*Carlson*	98	100	100	97	395	99
5	*Leah*	*Chambers*	80	70	85	90	325	81
6	*Brittany*	*Cook*	70	80	75	75	300	75
7	*Oliver*	*Flint*	78	80	90	95	343	86
8	*Maria*	*Gomez*	94	80	85	92	351	88
9	*Ema*	*Granger*	100	90	95	100	385	96
10	*Chelsea*	*Jackson*	85	100	75	90	350	88
11	*Cho*	*Ling*	92	90	85	95	362	91
12	*Devon*	*McBride*	75	90	85	90	340	85
13	*Justin*	*Pillman*	95	100	92	95	382	96
14	*Carlos*	*Ramirez*	93	90	95	95	373	93
15	*Harry*	*Rollins*	96	90	95	100	381	95
16	*Juan*	*Sanchez*	88	80	90	85	343	86
17								
18	Class Average		88	88	88	92	356	89
19								
20								

Figure 3-52

In the Lab

6. Create a custom header to show your name in the left section, course number or title in the middle section, and the current date in the right section.
7. Save the spreadsheet to the location of your choice using an appropriate filename.
8. Print the spreadsheet.
9. Follow directions from your instructor for turning in the assignment.

2. Building a Student Council Fund-Raiser Spreadsheet

Problem: You are the teacher sponsor of the student council at your high school. To raise money, student council members sell various items throughout the day and at special school functions. You want to see which items are the most profitable for the group and what time of day is the most successful, so you keep track of sales for four weeks. Using a spreadsheet program, prepare the spreadsheet and chart shown in **Figures 3-53** and **3-54**. (*Hint*: use Help to better understand the steps. If you do not have the suggested font or color, use any appropriate font or color.)

Instructions: Perform the following tasks.

1. Create the spreadsheet shown in Figure 3-53 using the numbers as displayed.
2. Calculate the total sales for each period, each item, and for the four weeks.
3. Personalize the spreadsheet title by inserting the name of your school. Add a gray, solid pattern to the foreground of cells A1:E1. Format the title as 16-point, Arial, bold, purple font and centered over columns A through E.
4. Format the subtitle, Student Council Fund-Raisers (Feb 1 - Feb 28), as 12-point, Arial, bold, black font and centered over columns A through E. Add a border around cells A2:E2.
5. Use AutoFormat and select an appropriate table format for the remaining portion of the spreadsheet. Display the numbers using the Currency format with two decimal places.

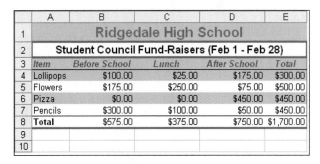

	A	B	C	D	E
1			Ridgedale High School		
2		Student Council Fund-Raisers (Feb 1 - Feb 28)			
3	*Item*	*Before School*	*Lunch*	*After School*	*Total*
4	Lollipops	$100.00	$25.00	$175.00	$300.00
5	Flowers	$175.00	$250.00	$75.00	$500.00
6	Pizza	$0.00	$0.00	$450.00	$450.00
7	Pencils	$300.00	$100.00	$50.00	$450.00
8	**Total**	$575.00	$375.00	$750.00	$1,700.00
9					
10					

Figure 3-53

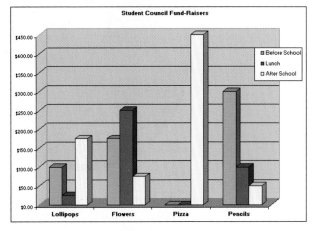

Figure 3-54

6. Create a custom header to show your name on the left, course number or title in the middle, and the current date on the right of the header.
7. Print the spreadsheet.
8. Create the 3-D Column chart from the spreadsheet data, as shown in **Figure 3-54**. Add the title, Student Council Fund-Raisers, to the chart. Include a border and gridlines for the chart.

In the Lab

3

9. Create a custom header to show your name at the left, course number or title in the middle section, and the current date in the right section. Print the 3-D Bar chart.

10. Save the spreadsheet and chart to the location of your choice using an appropriate filename.

11. Follow directions from your instructor for turning in the assignment.

INTEGRATION IN THE CLASSROOM

1. You are working on the concept of categorizing with your third-grade students. To meet state technology standards for students and to assist them with understanding this concept, you introduce spreadsheets and charts. Together with the class, you create a spreadsheet to show your students' favorite colors. You then create a 3-D Column chart to show their favorite colors graphically. Create a sample spreadsheet and 3-D Column chart to demonstrate the project for the students. Include a custom header to show your name in the left section, course number or title in the middle section, and the current date in the right section.

2. As a part of your Health Education class, you decide to have your students keep track of the total fat grams they consume daily during breakfast, lunch, dinner, and snacks for one week. You encourage students to examine the labels on products and nutrition tables for all foods consumed, including fast food. The students will create a spreadsheet including totals for each day of the week and each meal of the week to determine which days and meals are the healthiest. The students will also include a bar graph to illustrate their data. Create a sample spreadsheet and Bar chart to demonstrate the project for the students. Include a custom header to show your name on the left, course number or title in the middle, and the current date on the right of the header.

NUTRITIONAL TABLES

Burgers

Sandwiches and Side Orders

Breakfast

Drinks

Condiments/Components

3. Now that the students are aware of their total fat grams consumed, you want them to explore exercise options and burning calories. Students will select three types of aerobic exercise that they will participate in for 30 minutes, three times a week. They will need to determine how many calories each type of exercise will burn. (*Hint:* have the students search the World Wide Web.) The students will prepare a spreadsheet to record the total minutes spent exercising weekly and chart the number of calories each type of exercise burned over a one-week period. Create a sample spreadsheet and Pie chart to demonstrate the project for the students. Include a custom header to show your name on the left, course number or title in the middle, and the current date on the right of the header.

Learn It Online

INSTRUCTIONS: Use the Learn It Online exercises to reinforce your understanding of the chapter concepts and increase your computer, information, and integration literacy. To access dozens of interactive student labs, practice tests, learning games, and more, visit scsite.com/tdc4. Click Chapter 3 at the top of the Web page and then click Learn It Online on the left sidebar.

1. Student Edition Labs — Word Processing, Spreadsheets, Databases, Presentation Software, Creating Web Pages, and Web Design Principles

For the labs to work properly, you must have your screen resolution set to 1024x768 or higher. For a short tutorial on how to change your screen resolution, click here. You also will need Flash 7.0 or higher. To view these interactive labs, click the Students Edition Labs link. When the Student Edition Labs menu appears, click the desired or the assigned lab to begin. A new browser window will open. Follow the on-screen instructions to complete the lab. When finished, click the Exit button. If required, submit your results to your instructor.

2. Installing and Removing Software Programs

Click the Installing and Removing Software Programs link to learn how to install new software programs and how to uninstall previously installed software programs. Print just the first page of this Web page. On the back of the printout, write a brief summary explaining how to uninstall a program. If required, submit your results to your instructor.

3. Expanding Your Understanding

Click the Expand Your Understanding link to expand your understanding of Microsoft products and their use in K-12 classrooms. Microsoft seeks to help teachers and students use its products by maintaining an extensive array of user-friendly resources. Research this Web site and write a report summarizing your findings. If required, submit your report to your instructor.

4. Practice Test

Click the Practice Test link. Answer each question. When completed, enter your name and click the Grade Test button to submit the quiz for grading. Make a note of any missed questions. If required, submit your score to your instructor.

5. Who Wants to Be a Computer Genius?

Click the Computer Genius link to find out if you are a computer genius. Directions about how to play the game will be displayed. When you are ready to play, click the Play button. If required, submit your score to your instructor.

6. Wheel of Terms

Click the Wheel of Terms link to reinforce important terms you learned in this chapter by playing the Shelly Cashman Series version of this popular game. Directions about how to play the game will be displayed. When you are ready to play, click the Play button. If required, submit your score to your instructor.

7. Crossword Puzzle Challenge

Click the Crossword Puzzle link. Complete the puzzle to reinforce skills you learned in this chapter. Directions about how to play the game will be displayed. When you are ready to play, click the Play button. If required, submit the completed puzzle to your instructor.

Creating a Teacher's Web Page Using Microsoft Word

As you learned in Chapter 2, Web publishing is the development and maintenance of Web pages. Also, recall that Web pages are created using **Hypertext Markup Language (HTML)**, which is a set of special codes, called **tags**, that define the placement and format of text, graphics, video, and sound on a Web page.

Today, teachers and students do not have to learn HTML to create Web pages and Web sites. Instead, user-friendly programs allow teachers, students, and other users to create their own Web pages easily using basic word processing skills. Numerous software programs specifically designed for creating Web pages, called **HTML editors**, are available. Popular HTML editors used by educators include Adobe GoLive, Microsoft FrontPage, and Macromedia Dreamweaver.

Another popular and very easy-to-use program for creating Web pages is Netscape Composer, which is included with Netscape Communicator and, thus, is already installed on many home and school computers. If you do not have Netscape Communicator installed on your home or school computer, you can download a free copy from the Web. Complete step-by-step instructions for completing this project in the latest version of Netscape Composer are available either to download or print from the World Wide Web at *scsite.com/tdc4*, click the Chapter 3 link, and then click the link for the Special Feature.

As you have learned, Microsoft Word is a full-featured, word processing program that allows teachers and students to create and revise professional looking documents, such as letters, announcements, newsletters, flyers, brochures, reports, and much more. What you may not know is that Word also provides many tools that you and your students can use to create Web pages quickly and easily.

In this project, you will build a basic teacher's Web page called Mr. Handley's Home Page using Word (Figure 1). Mr. Handley is a history teacher at Ridgedale High School. You may find it helpful to refer back to Figure 1 to see the completed Web page as you work through this project. Included are step-by-step instructions using Word 2003 (part of Office 2003) installed on a PC. You also can create this project using Word 2002/2000 installed on a PC or Word installed on a Macintosh computer; however, you may encounter slight variations from the step-by-step instructions in this project.

FIGURE 1

Although Web pages can be as distinctive and different as the individuals who create them, a relatively small set of basic features are common to many Web pages. The **title** of a Web page is the text that appears on the title bar of the browser window when the page is being displayed; the title also can refer to the first line or main heading of a Web page. The **background** of a Web page is similar to the wallpaper in Windows or the image on the desktop of a Macintosh computer. It provides the backdrop against which other elements are shown. The background can be either a solid color or a small graphic image that is tiled, or repeated, across the entire page.

Normal text is the text that makes up the main information content of a Web page. Normal text also can be formatted so that it appears bold, italic, underlined, or in different colors. **Headings** are used to set off different paragraphs of text or different sections of a page. Headings usually are formatted in a larger font size than normal text and often are bold. **Horizontal lines**, also called **horizontal rules,** normally display across the page and are used to separate different sections of the page. **Images** are graphics and pictures that are contained on a Web page. Some images are animated and continuously change their appearance. **Links** are areas of the Web page, text or graphics, which when selected cause the browser to display another file or Web page, or play sounds or videos. Finally, many Web pages include an e-mail link to allow users to send an e-mail message from the Web page.

In this project, you will learn how to download graphics from the World Wide Web, open a new Word Web page, select a background image, create a title, insert and format text and headings, insert horizontal lines and graphics, create a linked list of favorite places, create an e-mail link, and save and view Mr. Handley's Home Page in your browser. Chapter 3 described the features of word processing software. This project assumes you possess basic word processing skills, such as entering, selecting, and formatting text.

Downloading Image Files

Clip art images are graphical images that are available for you to use on your Web and curriculum pages. Clip art images are either free or available for purchase. In addition, Microsoft provides more than 120,000 clip art images that are available free from its Design Gallery Live Web site. You also can download free images from hundreds of Web sites. This project requires that you download an e-mail image from the World Wide Web. The image will be used to identify the e-mail link. You can save the image to a USB flash drive, your computer's hard disk, or a 3.5-inch disk. You also will want to save the Web page to the same location as the e-mail image. Perform the following steps to download an image file from the World Wide Web.

Steps to Download Image Files

 Start your browser, type the URL scsite.com/tdc4 **in the Address text box, and then press the ENTER key. When the page opens, click the Chapter 3 link, and then click the link for the Special Feature.**

The browser displays the Teachers Discovering Computers Word project Web page.

 Right-click the e-mail image and then point to Save Picture As on the shortcut menu.

The shortcut menu is displayed (Figure 2). If you are using Netscape as your browser, point to the Save Image command. If you are using a Macintosh computer, press the mouse button for approximately two seconds to display the shortcut menu.

 When the Save As dialog box is displayed, click the Save in box arrow, select a location to save the image to, and then click the Save button in the Save As dialog box. Click the Close button in your browser window.

The e-mail image file is saved to the selected location.

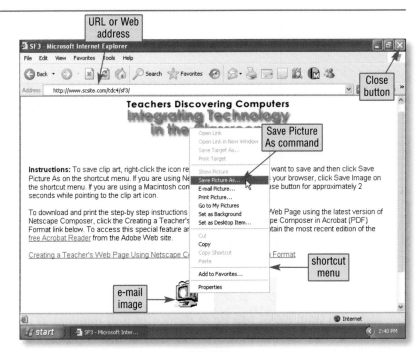

FIGURE 2

Starting Microsoft Word and Opening a New Web Page

The following steps show how to start Word and open a new Web page so you can begin developing Mr. Handley's Home Page. You start with a new Web page so you are working with the default settings.

Steps to Start Word and Open a New Web Page

1 **Start Microsoft Word.**

Word opens and displays a new, blank Word document (Figure 3).

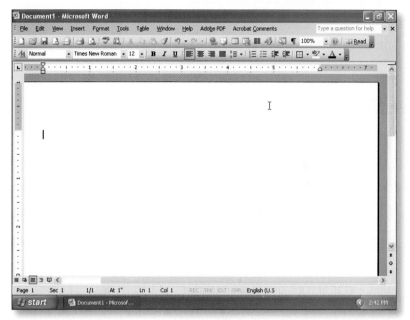

FIGURE 3

2 **Click File on the menu bar, and then click New. When the New Document task pane is displayed, point to Web page (Blank Web Page in Word 2002).**

Word displays the New Document task pane (Figure 4).

FIGURE 4

Click the Web page button. If the Word window is not maximized, double-click its title bar to maximize it. If necessary, click the Font Size box arrow on the Formatting toolbar and then click 12 in the Font Size list to change the font size to 12.

Word is opened and displays a new blank Web page (Figure 5). Depending on the computer you are working on, the default font size may display 10 or 12. Font size 12 is required for this Web page.

FIGURE 5

Selecting a Background Image

The background of a Web page is created by tiling, or repeating, a small graphic image many times across the page. Users can choose from thousands of graphic images to use for their Web page backgrounds. Background images can be downloaded from dozens of clip art Web sites, including the Microsoft Design Gallery Live Web site, or inserted from clip art CDs. For this project, you will use a textured background image that is available in Word.

Steps to Select a Background

Click Format on the menu bar, point to Background, and then point to Fill Effects (Figure 6).

FIGURE 6

Click Fill Effects. When Word displays the Fill Effects dialog box, click the Texture tab. Click the third texture, Parchment, and then point to the OK button.

Word displays the Fill Effects dialog box and the numerous textures that are available in the Texture area. The name and a sample of the selected texture are also displayed (Figure 7).

FIGURE 7

 Click the OK button.

Word tiles the Parchment texture across the Web page (Figure 8).

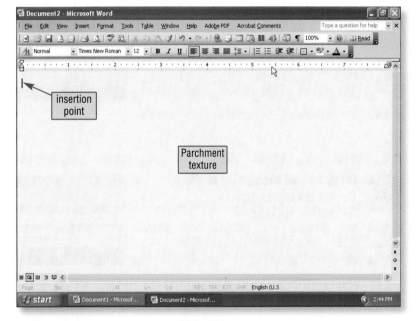

FIGURE 8

Entering and Formatting Text

Entering and formatting text on a Word Web page is the same as entering and formatting text in any other Word document. In the sequence of steps on the next pages, you will enter the title and other information for Mr. Handley's Home Page.

Steps to Enter and Format Text

Type Mr. Handley's Home Page **and then press the** ENTER **key. Drag through the text you just entered to select it, and then click the Font Size box arrow on the Formatting toolbar.**

Word inserts the title, moves the insertion point to the beginning of the next line, and selects the text (Figure 9). A list of available font sizes displays in the Font Size list.

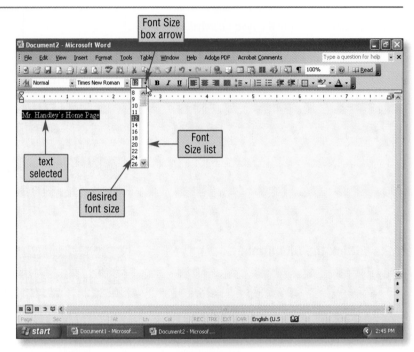

FIGURE 9

Click 24 and then point to the Center button on the Formatting toolbar.

Word increases the font size of the title to 24 (Figure 10).

FIGURE 10

3 Click the Center button, click the Font Color box arrow on the Formatting toolbar, and then point to the color Dark Red (row 2, column 1).

Word centers the title text and displays the Font Color palette (Figure 11).

FIGURE 11

4 Click Dark Red and then click below and to the left of the title to position the insertion point at the beginning of the next line.

The text appears in the color dark red and the insertion point is now positioned at the beginning of the next line (Figure 12).

5 Type Ridgedale High School and then press the ENTER key. Type 2400 Ridgedale Road and then press the ENTER key. Type Seattle, Washington 98104 and then press the ENTER key.

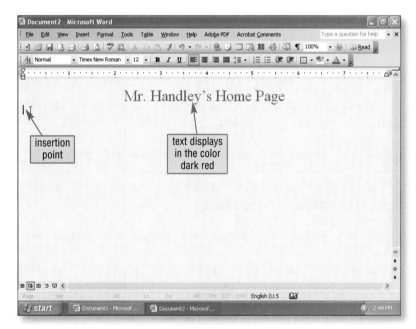

FIGURE 12

6 Drag through the three lines of text beginning with Ridgedale High School to select the school information. Click the Font Size box arrow on the Formatting toolbar, and then click 14. Click the Center button on the Formatting toolbar, and then click below and to the left of the entered text to position the insertion point at the beginning of the next line.

The text now appears in font size 14 and is centered below the title. The insertion point is positioned at the beginning of the next line (Figure 13).

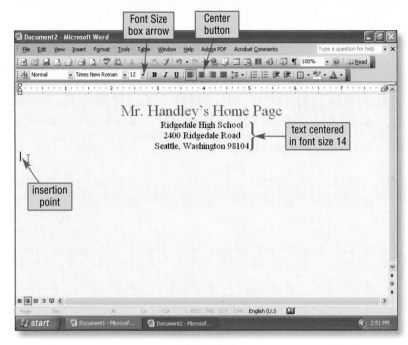

FIGURE 13

7 Press the ENTER key. Type Hi, my name is Mr. Matt Handley. I teach history at Ridgedale High School. I like teaching with technology, and my students are highly motivated when they can use computers and the Internet for history projects and assignments.

Word displays the text in the default color black and font size 12 (Figure 14).

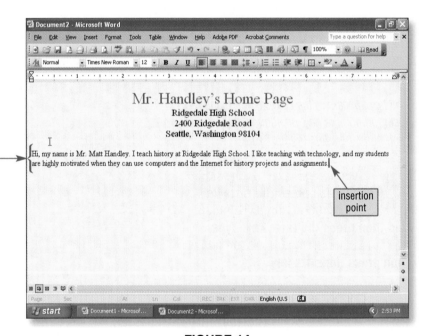

FIGURE 14

Inserting a Horizontal Line and a Heading

Horizontal lines, also called rules, are used to set apart different sections of a Web page. Perform the following steps to insert a horizontal line and then enter a heading.

Steps to Insert a Horizontal Line and a Heading

1 **Press the ENTER key twice. Click Format on the menu bar, and then click Borders and Shading. When Word displays the Borders and Shading dialog box, point to the Horizontal Line button at the bottom of the dialog box (Figure 15).**

FIGURE 15

2 **Click the Horizontal Line button. When Word displays the Horizontal Line dialog box, click the horizontal line as shown in Figure 16, and then point to the OK button.**

Word displays the selected horizontal line option with a blue border around it (Figure 16). A number of horizontal lines are available from which to choose. The options on your computer may be different from those shown in Figure 16.

FIGURE 16

Click the OK button.

Word inserts a horizontal line and the insertion point moves to the beginning of the next line (Figure 17). The horizontal line may display differently than shown depending on the computer you are working on and the version of Word you are using. The horizontal line will display normally when the Web page is viewed in your browser.

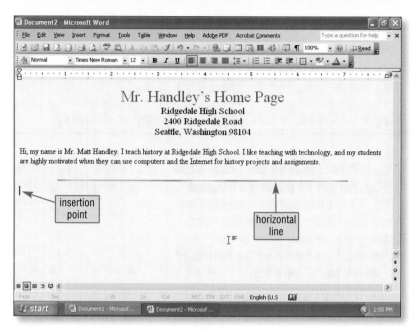

FIGURE 17

Press the ENTER key once. Type My Favorite History Links and then press the ENTER key. Select the text just entered, click the Font Size box arrow on the Formatting toolbar, click 18, and then click below and to the left of the entered text to position the insertion point at the beginning of the next line.

Word displays the heading in font size 18 and the insertion point is positioned at the beginning of the next line (Figure 18).

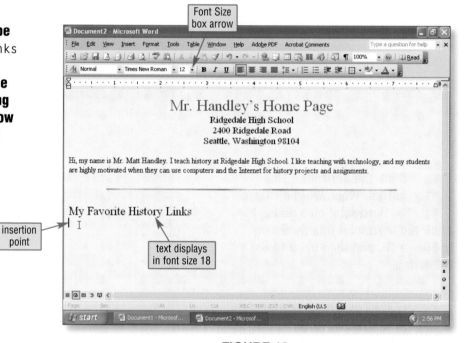

FIGURE 18

Creating Links to Web Sites

Using text and graphic links, you can create links for your students to Web sites on the World Wide Web. Perform the following steps to enter the names of three education-related Web sites and then link each name to its corresponding Web site by entering the Web site's Uniform Resource Locator (URL).

Steps to Create Links to Web Sites

1 **Press the ENTER key. Type** History Matters **and then press the ENTER key. Type** The History Channel **and then press the ENTER key. Type** On-This-Day **and then press the ENTER key.**

2 **Drag through the text, History Matters, and then click the Insert Hyperlink button on the Standard toolbar.**

The History Matters text is selected and Word displays the Insert Hyperlink dialog box (Figure 19).

FIGURE 19

3 **If necessary, click the Existing File or Web Page button in the Link to area, and then type** http://historymatters.gmu.edu **in the Address text box. Point to the OK button.**

The URL appears in the Address text box (Figure 20). In Word 2000, you need to type the URL in the Type the file or Web page name text box below the Text to display text box.

FIGURE 20

Click the OK button.

Word links the text to the entered Web site and the linked text appears underlined and in the default color blue (Figure 21).

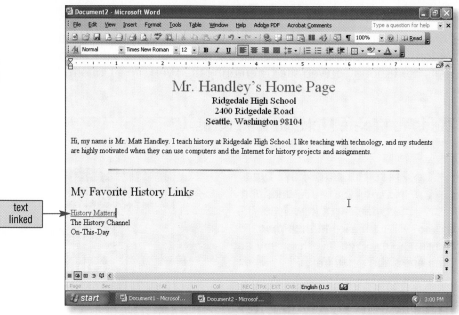

FIGURE 21

Repeat the procedures explained in Steps 2, 3, and 4 for the remaining two named Web sites, using the following URLs:

The History Channel
```
http://www.historychannel.com
```
On-This-Day
```
http://www.on-this-day.com
```

The Web page displays with the three links underlined and in the default color blue (Figure 22). The three Web sites are linked to their respective URLs.

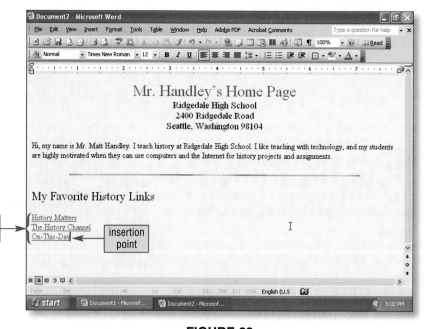

FIGURE 22

Inserting an Image, E-Mail Information, and an E-Mail Link

Adding graphics can enhance a Web page. Thousands of graphic images are available on the World Wide Web or in clip art galleries. Some graphics are animated and, thus, continuously change their appearance while the Web page is viewed in a browser. Many teachers and other users provide e-mail information and an e-mail link on their Web pages so students or others viewing the page can send e-mail messages directly from the page. Perform the following steps to add an image, e-mail information, and an e-mail link.

Steps to Insert an Image, E-Mail Information, and an E-Mail Link

1 **If necessary, position the insertion point at the end of the On-This-Day link, and then press the ENTER key twice. Click Insert on the menu bar. Point to Picture and then point to From File on the Picture submenu (Figure 23).**

FIGURE 23

2 **Click From File. If necessary, navigate to the location where you saved the e-mail image in the Look in list, and then double-click the e-mail image.**

The e-mail image appears and the insertion point is positioned to the right of the e-mail image (Figure 24). The image may not appear as shown or may appear only partially depending on the computer you are working with and the version of Word you are using. The image will display normally when the Web page is viewed in your browser.

FIGURE 24

3 Press the Spacebar twice and then type My class would like to hear from you. Please e-mail me! **Drag through the text to select it and then click the Insert Hyperlink button on the Standard toolbar.**

4 When Word displays the Insert Hyperlink dialog box, click the E-mail Address button in the Link to area, type mailto: matthandley@Ridgedale.k12.wa.us in the E-mail address text box, and then point to the OK button. If the E-mail address text box displays a previously entered e-mail address, drag through the text to select it before typing the new mailto address. If the mailto: entry appears, type the matthandley **e-mail address after the mailto: entry. Be sure there is no space after mailto:.**

The e-mail link text is selected on the Web page and the mailto: address appears in the E-mail address text box (Figure 25). The last e-mail address entered will be displayed automatically in the E-mail address text box or it may be blank. It is important that no spaces be typed between mailto: and the e-mail address and that the colon is included. The mailto: entry allows users to send e-mail messages from a Web page. Depending on the version of Word and the computer that you are using, Word may automatically enter the mailto: command in the E-mail address text box.

5 Click the OK button.

The text displays as an e-mail link. The text displays underlined and in default color blue (Figure 26).

FIGURE 25

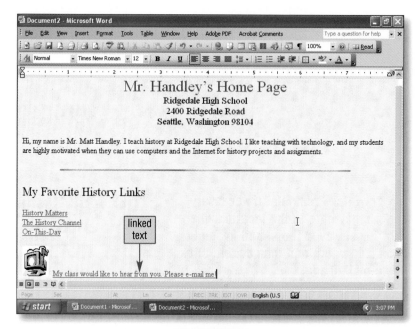

FIGURE 26

Saving and Previewing a Web Page

It is important to preview your Web page in your browser. This allows you to verify that the page appears as you want others to see it; sometimes, you may have to make minor adjustments to your page in Word so it is displayed correctly in your browser. If your school uses both Internet Explorer and Netscape, you might want to view your Web page in both browsers. Browser software sometimes displays Web pages differently.

Before you preview the Web page you have created, you should save it. Perform the following steps to save Mr. Handley's Home Page to a desired location and then view it in your browser.

Steps to Save and Preview a Web Page

1 Click the Save button on the Standard toolbar. When Word displays the Save As dialog box, click the Change Title button. When Word displays the Set Page Title dialog box, type `Mr. Handley's Home Page` in the Page title text box, and then point to the OK button.

The title of the Web page appears in the Page title text box. This is the title that will be displayed on the title bar when the Web page is viewed in a browser (Figure 27).

FIGURE 27

2 Click the OK button and then type `MrHandley` in the File name text box.

3 Click the Save as type box arrow and then click Web Page (*.htm; *html). If necessary, click the Save in box arrow, select the location you saved the e-mail image to in the Look in list, and then point to the Save button in the Save As dialog box (Figure 28).

FIGURE 28

4 Click the Save button in the Save As dialog box. Click File on the menu bar, and then point to Web Page Preview (Figure 29).

The MrHandley.htm file is saved to the desired location. The file is given an .htm extension, which indicates it is a Web page.

5 Click Web Page Preview.

Your default browser opens and displays Mr. Handley's Home Page (see Figure 1 on page 193).

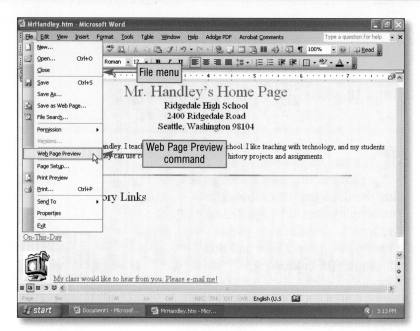

FIGURE 29

Printing and Opening a Web Page in Internet Explorer

Congratulations, you now have created a Web page using Microsoft Word. To print your Web page from your browser, click File on the menu bar and then click Print. After printing, close your browser and then close Word by clicking the Close buttons. If you saved your Web page on a USB flash drive, a 3.5-inch disk, or district server, you can display your Web page on another computer by opening the MrHandley.htm file in the new computer's browser.

Additional Web Page Authoring Features

Word has many other Web page authoring features. For example, you and your students can include tables, frames, sounds, videos, pictures, scrolling text, bullets, check boxes, option buttons, list boxes, text boxes, and much more on your Web pages. You also can upload your Web page to the World Wide Web. You will learn how to use additional Word Web page authoring features in the special feature that follows Chapter 7.

Hardware for Educators

4

Objectives

After completing this chapter, you will be able to:
[ISTE NETS-T Standards I A-B]

- Describe the system unit

- Define the term bit and describe how a series of bits are used to represent data

- Identify the major components of the system unit and explain their functions

- Explain how the CPU uses the four steps of a machine cycle to process data

- Describe the four types of input as well as input devices

- List the characteristics of a keyboard and identify various types of keyboards

- Identify various types of pointing devices

- Differentiate among the four types of output

- Identify the different types of output devices

- Explain differences among various types of printers

- Differentiate between storage and memory

- Identify types of storage media and devices

- Explain how data is stored on 3.5-inch disks, hard disks, CD-ROMs, and DVDs

- Differentiate between CD-ROMs and DVD-ROMs

During your teaching career or personal endeavors, you most likely will decide to purchase a new computer or upgrade an existing one. To be effective in this decision-making process and to be an informed teacher, you should possess a general knowledge of major computer components and how various computer components interact. In addition, the International Society for Technology in Education (ISTE) has developed a series of K-12 national technology standards and skills that K-12 students need to learn throughout their education. One of these technology standards recommends that graduating K-12 students demonstrate a sound understanding of the nature and operation of technology systems. To help you better understand these concepts, so that you in turn can help your students understand them, this chapter presents a brief look at some of the hardware components used for input, processing, output, and storage. Because Macintosh computers and PCs use similar, and in many cases identical, hardware components,

WEB INFO

For more information about the National Educational Technology Standards for Students (NETS-S), visit the Teachers Discovering Computers Web site (*scsite.com/tdc4*), click Chapter 4, click Web Info, and then click NETS-S.

the majority of information presented in this chapter applies to both computer platforms. In instances in which Macintosh computers and PCs use slightly different hardware, these differences are explained.

The System Unit

The **system unit** is a boxlike case that houses the electronic components a computer uses to process data (Figure 4-1). The system unit is made of metal or plastic and protects the electronic components from damage. On a personal computer, these components and most storage devices reside inside the system unit; other devices, such as a keyboard and monitor usually are located outside the system unit. Notebook computers, PDAs, and other mobile devices contain almost all of their components in

the system unit, including the keyboard and monitor or display. The following explanation of how data is represented in a computer will help you understand how the system unit processes data.

Data Representation

To understand fully how the various components of the system unit work together to process data, you need a basic understanding of how data is represented in a computer. Human speech is **analog**, meaning that it uses continuous signals to represent data and information. Most computers, by contrast, are **digital**, meaning that they understand only two discrete states: on and off. Computers are electronic devices powered by electricity, which has only two states: on or off. These two states

Figure 4-1 All sizes of computers have a system unit.

are represented by electronic circuits using two digits; 0 is used to represent the electronic state of off (absence of an electric charge) and 1 is used to represent the electronic state of on (presence of an electric charge) (Figure 4-2).

the smallest unit of data the computer can handle. By itself, a bit is not very informative. When eight bits are grouped together as a unit, they are called a **byte**. A byte is informative because it provides enough different combinations of 0s and 1s to represent 256 individual characters, including numbers, uppercase and lowercase letters of the alphabet, and punctuation marks (Figure 4-3).

The combinations of 0s and 1s used to represent characters are defined by patterns called a coding scheme. The most widely used coding scheme to represent data on many personal computers is the **American Standard Code for Information Interchange**, called **ASCII** (pronounced ASK-ee). Coding schemes such as ASCII make it possible for humans to interact with digital computers that recognize only bits. When you press a key on a keyboard, the keyboard converts that action into a binary form the computer understands. That is, every character is converted to its corresponding byte. The computer then processes that data in terms of bytes, which actually is a series of off/on electrical states. When processing is finished, the computer converts the bytes back into numbers, letters of the alphabet, or special characters to be displayed on a screen or printed (Figure 4-4 on the next page). All of these conversions take place so quickly that you do not even realize they are occurring.

BINARY DIGIT (BIT)	ELECTRONIC CHARGE	ELECTRONIC STATE
0		OFF
1		ON

Figure 4-2 A computer circuit represents the binary digits 0 or 1 electronically by the absence or presence of an electronic charge.

When people count, they use the digits 0 through 9, which are digits in the decimal system. Because a computer understands only two states, it uses a number system that has just two unique digits, 0 and 1. This numbering system is referred to as the **binary** system. Using just these two numbers, a computer can represent data electronically by turning circuits off or on.

Each off or on digital value is called a **bit** (short for **bi**nary digi**t**), and represents

WEB INFO

For more information about the American Standard Code for Information Interchange, visit the Teachers Discovering Computers Web site (*scsite.com/tdc4*), click Chapter 4, click Web Info, and then click ASCII.

Figure 4-3 Eight bits grouped together as a unit are called a byte. A byte is used to represent a single character in the computer.

Step 1:
The user presses the letter T key on the keyboard.

Step 2:
An electronic signal for the letter T is sent to the system unit.

Step 3:
The electronic signal that is sent when the key is pressed is the ASCII binary code (01010100) for the letter; the ASCII binary code is stored in memory for processing.

01010100

Step 4:
After processing, the ASCII binary code for the letter T is converted to an image and displayed on the output device.

Figure 4-4 Converting a letter to ASCII binary code form and back.

WEB INFO

For a more detailed description of motherboards, visit the Teachers Discovering Computers Web site (*scsite.com/tdc4*), click Chapter 4, click Web Info, and then click Motherboard.

The Components of the System Unit

The major components of the system unit discussed in the following sections include the motherboard, CPU, memory, expansion slots and expansion cards, and ports and connectors.

THE MOTHERBOARD

Many of the electronic components in the system unit reside on a circuit board called the **motherboard**. Figure 4-5 shows a photograph of a personal computer motherboard and identifies some of its components, including several different types of chips. A **chip** is a small piece of

adapter cards

processor

memory module
(RAM chips)

expansion slots
for adapter cards

memory slots

motherboard

Figure 4-5 The motherboard in a personal computer contains many chips and other electronic components.

semiconducting material usually no bigger than one-half-inch square and is made up of many layers of circuits and microscopic components that carry electronic signals. The motherboard in the system unit contains many different types of chips. Of these, one of the most important is the central processing unit (CPU).

THE CPU

The **central processing unit** (CPU) interprets and carries out the basic instructions that operate a computer. The CPU, also called the **processor** or **microprocessor**, manages most of a computer's operations. Most of the devices that connect to a computer communicate with the CPU to carry out tasks (Figure 4-6).

FAQ

What is the difference between a chip and an integrated circuit?

A computer chip is a small piece of material, usually silicon, on which integrated circuits are etched. An integrated circuit contains many microscopic pathways that carry electrical current, as well as millions of electronic components.

Figure 4-6 Most of the devices connected to a computer communicate with the CPU to carry out a task. The arrows in this figure represent the flow of data, instructions, and information.

In a personal computer, a single chip known as the processor contains the CPU (Figure 4-7). A processor contains a number of components, including a control unit, an arithmetic/logic unit, and a system clock. The following sections describe how these components work together to perform processing operations.

Pentium 4

Athlon

Centrino Mobile Technology

Celeron

G5

Figure 4-7 Most high-performance PCs use Pentium and Athlon processors. Basic PCs have a Celeron processor. High-performance Macintosh computers use the new G5 processor. Many high-performance notebook computers use Centrino mobile technology.

THE CONTROL UNIT   The **control unit,** one component of the CPU, directs and coordinates most of the operations in the computer. The control unit has a role much like a traffic cop. The control unit interprets each instruction issued by a program and then initiates the appropriate action to carry out the instruction. For every instruction, the control unit operates by repeating a set of four basic operations: (1) fetching an instruction, (2) decoding the instruction, (3) executing the instruction, and, if necessary, (4) storing the result.

Fetching is the process of obtaining a program instruction or data item from memory. **Decoding** is the process of translating the instruction into commands the computer understands. **Executing** is the process of carrying out the commands. **Storing** is the process of writing the result to memory. Together, these four instructions comprise the **machine cycle** or instruction cycle (Figure 4-8).

A student enters a math problem into the memory of the computer.

Step 1:
The control unit fetches the math problem's instructions and data from memory.

4700

The results in memory appear on the screen of the monitor.

STORE

FETCH

4

MEMORY

Step 4:
The results of the math problem are stored in memory.

3

1

PROCESSOR

Step 2:
The control unit decodes the math problem's instructions and sends the instructions and data to the ALU.

EXECUTE

DECODE

2

ALU

100 x 47 = 4700

CONTROL UNIT

Step 3:
The ALU performs calculations on the data.

100 x 47

Figure 4-8 This figure shows the steps involved in a machine cycle for a student wanting to solve a math problem on a computer. After the result is in memory, it can be displayed on a monitor, printed, or stored on a disk.

THE ARITHMETIC/LOGIC UNIT   The **arithmetic/logic unit (ALU)**, another component of the CPU, performs the execution part of the machine cycle. Specifically, the ALU performs arithmetic, comparison, and logical operations.

Arithmetic operations include addition, subtraction, multiplication, and division. **Comparison operations** involve comparing one data item with another to determine if the first item is greater than, equal to, or less than the other. Depending on the result of the comparison, different actions may occur. For example, to determine a student's letter grade, the student's numeric grade is compared with a set of numbers corresponding to various letter grades (for example, a numeric grade equal to or greater than 90 equates to a letter grade of A). If the student's numeric grade is equal to or greater than 90, then a letter grade of A is given; if the numeric grade is less than 90, a letter grade of A is not given and more comparisons are performed until a letter grade can be assigned. **Logical operations** work with conditions and logical operators such as AND, OR, and NOT. For example, if you wanted to search a job database for part-time work in the admissions office, you would search for any jobs classified as part-time AND listed under admissions.

THE SYSTEM CLOCK   The control unit relies on a small chip called the **system clock** to synchronize, or control the timing of, all computer operations. Just as your heart beats at a regular rate to keep your body functioning, the system clock generates regular electronic pulses, or ticks, that set the operating pace of components in the system unit. Think of the components of the CPU as members of a marching band that take their steps to the beat of the system clock drummer.

Clock speed is the speed at which a processor executes instructions and is measured in megahertz (MHz) and

gigahertz (GHz). One **megahertz** equates to one million ticks of the system clock in one second and one **gigahertz** equates to one billion ticks of the system clock in one second. Thus, a computer that operates at 4 GHz has 4 billion clock cycles, or ticks, in one second. The faster the clock speed, the more instructions the CPU can execute per second.

MEMORY

While performing a processing operation, a processor needs a place to store data and instructions temporarily. A computer uses **memory** to store data and information. The memory chips on the circuit boards in the system unit perform this function.

Memory stores three basic items: (1) the operating system and other system software that control the computer equipment; (2) the application software designed to carry out a specific task such as word processing; and (3) the data being processed by the application software. Recall that a computer stores a character as a series of 0s and 1s, called a byte. Thus, a byte is the basic storage unit in memory. When a computer transfers program instructions and data from a storage device into memory, the computer stores them as bytes. The computer stores each byte in a precise location in memory, called an address. An **address** is simply a unique number identifying the location of the byte in memory. The illustration in Figure 4-9

FAQ

Does the system clock also keep track of the current day and time?

No, a separate battery-backed chip, called the real-time clock, keeps track of the date and time in a computer. The battery continues to run the real-time clock even when the computer is off.

seat #A1   seat #A2   seat #A3   seat #A4   seat #A5   seat #A6

Figure 4-9 This figure shows how seats in a stadium are similar to addresses in memory: (1) a seat holds one person at a time and an address in memory holds a single byte, (2) both a seat and an address can be empty, and (3) a seat has a unique identifying number and so does an address.

shows how seats in a stadium are similar to addresses in memory: (1) a seat holds one person at a time and an address in memory holds a single byte, (2) both a seat and an address can be empty, and (3) a seat has a unique identifying number and so does an address. Thus, to access data or instructions in memory, the computer references the addresses that contain bytes of data.

Because a byte is such a small amount of storage, several terms have evolved to define storage size for memory and storage devices (Figure 4-10). A **kilobyte** of memory, abbreviated **KB** or **K**, is equal to 1024 bytes, but is usually rounded to 1000 bytes. A **megabyte**, abbreviated **MB**, is equal to approximately 1 million bytes. A **gigabyte**, abbreviated **GB**, is equal to approximately 1 billion bytes. A **terabyte** (**TB**) is equal to approximately 1 trillion bytes.

The system unit contains two types of memory: volatile and nonvolatile. The contents of **volatile memory** are lost (erased) when the computer's power is turned off. The contents of **nonvolatile memory**, on the other hand, are not lost when a computer is turned off or power to the computer is interrupted. RAM (random access memory) is an example of volatile memory. ROM (read-only memory) and flash memory are examples of nonvolatile memory. The following sections discuss each of these types of memory.

RANDOM ACCESS MEMORY (RAM) Some memory chips in the system unit are called **random access memory** (**RAM**). When the computer is powered on, certain operating system files, such as the files that determine how your desktop is displayed, are loaded from a storage device, such as a hard disk, into RAM. As long as the power remains on, these files remain in RAM. Because RAM is volatile, the programs and data stored in RAM are erased when the power to the computer is turned off. Any files or data created by a user that will be needed for future use must be copied from RAM to a storage device, such as a hard disk, before the power to the computer is turned off.

The most common form of RAM used in personal computers is **synchronous dynamic RAM**, or **SDRAM**. Today, most RAM is installed by using a **dual inline memory module (DIMM)**. A DIMM is a small circuit board that contains multiple RAM chips (Figure 4-11). Common DIMM sizes can hold 128, 256, and 512 megabytes of memory. DIMM chips are installed in special sockets on the motherboard and can be removed and replaced easily with higher-capacity RAM chips or with additional RAM chips. The amount of memory a computer can handle depends on the motherboard.

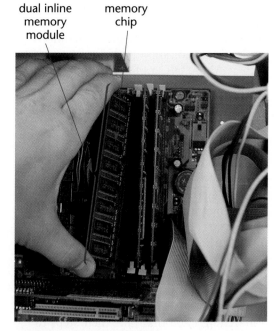

dual inline memory module   memory chip

Figure 4-11 This photo shows a dual inline memory module (DIMM).

Memory and Storage Sizes

	Term	Abbreviation	Approximate Memory Size	Exact Memory Amount	Approximate Pages of Text
	Kilobyte	KB or K	1 thousand bytes	1024 bytes	1/2
	Megabyte	MB	1 million bytes	1,048,576 bytes	500
	Gigabyte	GB	1 billion bytes	1,073,741,824 bytes	500,000
	Terabyte	TB	1 trillion bytes	1,099,511,627,776 bytes	500,000,000

Figure 4-10 This table outlines terms used to define storage size.

The amount of RAM a computer requires often depends on the types of applications to be used on the computer. Remember that a computer can manipulate only data that is in memory. RAM is something like the workspace you have on the top of your desk. Just as a desktop needs a certain amount of space to hold papers, pens, and your computer, a computer needs a certain amount of memory to store an application program and files.

The more RAM a computer has, the more programs and files it can work on at once. Having sufficient RAM (512 MB or higher) is important for manipulating graphics; downloading music, video clips, and movies; and creating and editing sound, digital images, and video.

A software package usually indicates the minimum amount of RAM and other system requirements. For an application to perform optimally, you usually need more than the minimum specifications on the software package.

READ-ONLY MEMORY (ROM)   Read-only memory (ROM) chips store information or instructions that do not change. For example, ROM chips contain the sequence of instructions the computer follows to load the operating system and other files when you first turn on the computer. Manufacturers permanently record instructions and data on ROM chips. Unlike RAM, ROM memory is nonvolatile because it retains its contents even when the power is turned off. In addition to personal computers, manufacturers install ROM chips in automobiles, home appliances, toys, educational games, and thousands of other items used by people everyday.

FLASH MEMORY   Flash memory is a type of nonvolatile memory that can be erased electronically and rewritten on. Most computers use flash memory to hold startup instructions because it allows the computer to update its contents easily. For example, when the computer changes from standard time to daylight saving time, the contents of a flash memory chip (and the real-time clock chip) change to reflect the new time. Flash memory chips are also used to store data and programs on many mobile computers and devices, such as PDAs, smart phones, printers, digital cameras, digital voice recorders, and pagers. When you enter names and addresses in a PDA or smart phone, a flash memory chip stores the data. Some MP3 players store music on flash memory chips (Figure 4-12); others store music on tiny hard disks or flash

Step 1:
Purchase and download MP3 music tracks from a Web site. With one end of a special cable connected to the system unit, connect the other end to the USB port in the MP3 player.

Step 2:
Instruct the computer to copy the MP3 music tracks to a flash memory chip in the MP3 player.

Step 3:
Plug the headphones in the MP3 player, push a button on the MP3 player, and listen to the music through the headphones.

Figure 4-12 How an MP3 player might store music on flash memory.

FAQ

How much music can I store on an MP3 player?

MP3 players that hold music on flash memory chips can hold up to 8 or 9 hours of music, which is about 120 songs in the WMA format or 60 songs in the MP3 format. MP3 players with tiny hard disks have a much greater storage capacity - from 1000 to 10,000 songs.

memory cards. A later section of this chapter discusses flash memory cards, which contain flash memory on a removable device instead of a chip.

EXPANSION SLOTS AND EXPANSION CARDS

An **expansion slot** is an opening, or socket, where a circuit board can be inserted into the motherboard. These circuit boards add new devices or capabilities to the computer such as more memory, higher-quality sound devices, a modem, or graphics capabilities. **Expansion card, adapter card,** and **expansion board** are terms used to describe these types of circuit boards. Sometimes a device, such as a modem, or feature, such as sound, is built in to the expansion card; other times a cable is used to connect the expansion card to a device outside the system unit, such as a scanner.

Some motherboards include all necessary capabilities and do not require adapter or expansion cards. Other motherboards require adapter cards to provide capabilities such as sound and video. A video adapter, also called a graphics adapter or card, converts computer output into a video signal that is sent through a cable to the monitor, which displays an image on the screen. A sound card is used to enhance the sound-generating capabilities of a personal computer by allowing sound to be input through a microphone and output through speakers.

Many of today's computers support **Plug and Play,** which refers to the computer's capability to configure expansion cards and other devices automatically as they are installed.

PC CARDS, FLASH MEMORY CARDS, AND USB FLASH DRIVES

Notebook and other mobile computers have a special type of expansion slot for installing PC cards. A **PC Card** is a thin credit card–sized device that adds memory, fax/modems, network cards, disk drives, and other capabilities to small computers (Figure 4-13). A **flash memory card** is a removable memory device that allows users to transfer data and information from a mobile device to a desktop computer. Another widely used type of removable

flash memory is the USB flash drive. Flash memory cards and USB flash drives are available in a variety of shapes and sizes (Figure 4-14) and are covered in more detail later in this chapter.

PC Card

Figure 4-13 This picture shows a PC Card in a PC Card slot on a notebook computer.

memory cards

USB flash drives

Figure 4-14 Removable flash memory devices are available in a range of sizes.

PORTS AND CONNECTORS

Cables are often used to attach external devices, such as a keyboard, monitor, printer, mouse, and microphone, to the system unit. A **port** is the point of attachment to the system unit. Most computers contain ports on the back as well as the front of the system unit (Figure 4-15).

Ports use different types of **connectors** that usually are either male or female and come in various sizes and shapes. Male connectors have one or more exposed pins, like the end of an electrical cord you plug into the wall. Female connectors have matching receptacles to accept the pins, like an electrical wall outlet.

WEB INFO

For an overview of how to troubleshoot a PC, visit the Teachers Discovering Computers Web site (*scsite.com/tdc4*), click Chapter 4, click Web Info, and then click Troubleshoot.

keyboard port

mouse port

printer port
(parallel port)

FireWire port

network port

speaker port

audio in port

S-video out port

parallel port

serial port

FM reception port

additional
audio
ports

FireWire
port

USB
ports

additional
speaker
ports

S-video in port

compostite video
in port

audio in ports

headphone port
(or jack)

microphone port

USB ports

microphone
port

monitor
port

audio in
ports

telephone
line in port

S-video
in port

cable TV port

Figure 4-15 Most computers have ports on the front and back of the system unit. Shown are the ports available on a media center PC. Macintosh computers have similar ports.

Two newer ports are USB and FireWire ports. The **Universal Serial Bus (USB) port** can connect up to 127 different peripheral devices with a single connector type. Newer personal computers typically contain six to eight USB ports either on the front or back of the system unit. The latest version, called the **USB 2.0 port,** is more advanced and faster, with speeds 40 times faster than the original USB port. The USB 2.0 port is used for devices that transfer a large amount of data, such as MP3 music players, DVDs, and removable hard disks.

Similar to a USB port, a **FireWire port** can connect multiple devices that require faster data transmission speeds, such as digital video cameras, digital VCRs, color printers, and DVD drives to a single connector. The FireWire port is found on newer PCs and Macintosh computers. Figure 4-16 shows how FireWire and USB ports are replacing other traditional ports.

Bluetooth technology uses radio waves to transmit data between two devices. Many computers, peripheral devices, PDAs, smart phones, cars, and other consumer

TRADITIONAL PORTS

SCSI   Parallel   Audio   Serial   Keyboard   Mouse

FireWire   USB 2.0   USB 2.0

NEW PORTS

Figure 4-16 FireWire and USB ports are replacing traditional ports.

FAQ

Can older USB devices plug into a USB 2.0 port?

Yes, USB 2.0 is backward compatible, which means that it supports older USB devices as well as new USB 2.0 devices.

electronics are Bluetooth-enabled, which means they contain a small chip that allows them to communicate with other Bluetooth-enabled computers and devices.

WEB INFO

To search for a solution to a specific hardware problem for a PC, visit the Teachers Discovering Computers Web site (*scsite.com/tdc4*), click Chapter 4, click Web Info, and then click Search.

What Is Input?

Input is what you enter into the memory of a computer. As soon as input is in memory, the CPU can access it and process the input into output. Input can be categorized into four types: data, programs, commands, and user responses (Figure 4-17).

- **Data** is a collection of unorganized facts. A computer manipulates and processes data into information that is useful, such as words, numbers, pictures, sounds, and so on. Although a single item of data should be called a datum, the term data commonly is used and accepted as both the singular and plural form of the word.

- A **program** is a series of instructions that tells a computer how to perform

the tasks necessary to process data into information. Programs are kept on storage media such as a hard disk, CD-ROM, or DVD-ROM. Programs respond to commands issued by a user.

- A **command** is an instruction given to a computer program. Commands can be issued by typing keywords or pressing special keys on the keyboard. A **keyword** is a special word, phrase, or code that a program understands as an instruction. Many programs also allow you to issue commands by selecting graphical objects. Today, most programs have a graphical user interface that uses icons, buttons, and other graphical objects to issue commands.

- Sometimes a program asks a question, such as Do you want to save the changes you made?, that requires a **user response**. Based on your response, the program performs specific actions. For example, if you answer Yes to this question, the program saves your changed file to a storage medium.

Figure 4-17
Input can be categorized as data, programs, commands, and user responses.

DATA

Mary Jones
Tests - 89, 93, 84
Absences - 4

PROGRAMS

GRADE BOOK
WORD PROCESSOR

YES NO CANCEL

USER RESPONSES

COMMANDS

What Are Input Devices?

An **input device** is any hardware component that allows you to enter data, programs, commands, and user responses into a computer. Input devices include keyboards, pointing devices, scanners and reading devices, digital cameras, audio and video input devices, and input devices for students with special needs. Many of these input devices are discussed in the following pages.

THE KEYBOARD

One of the primary input devices used with a computer is the keyboard. A **keyboard** is a group of switches resembling the keys on a typewriter that allow users to enter input. Most keyboards are similar to the ones shown in Figures 4-18a and 4-18b. You enter data, commands, and other input into a computer by pressing keys on the keyboard.

Personal computer keyboards usually contain from 101 to 105 keys; keyboards for smaller computers, such as notebook computers, contain fewer keys. A keyboard includes keys that allow you to type letters, numbers, spaces, punctuation marks, and other symbols such as the dollar sign ($) and the asterisk (*). A keyboard also contains special keys that allow you to enter data and instructions into the computer.

All computer keyboards have a typing area that includes the letters of the alphabet,

WEB INFO

To learn more about keyboards, visit the Teachers Discovering Computers Web site (*scsite.com/tdc4*), click Chapter 4, click Web Info, and then click Keyboard.

function keys   additional keys

[a] Apple Pro Keyboard

typing area   arrow keys   numeric keypad

function keys   CD/DVD controls

typing area

wrist rest

additional keys

NUM LOCK key

status lights

WINDOWS key

Internet and multimedia controls

WINDOWS key

APPLICATION key

arrow keys

numeric keypad

[b] PC keyboard

Figure 4-18
Macintosh and PC keyboards are similar. Figure 4-18a shows a typical Macintosh keyboard and Figure 4-18b shows a typical PC keyboard.

numbers, punctuation marks, and other basic keys. Because of the layout of its typing area, a standard computer keyboard sometimes is called a QWERTY keyboard. Pronounced KWER-tee, this keyboard layout is named after the first six letters on the top-left alphabetic line of the keyboard.

Many desktop computer keyboards also have a numeric keypad located on the right side of the keyboard. A **numeric keypad** is a calculator-style arrangement of keys representing numbers, a decimal point, and some basic mathematical operators. The numeric keypad is designed to make it easier to enter numbers.

Keyboards also contain keys that can be used to position the insertion point on the screen. The **insertion point**, or cursor, is a symbol that indicates where the next character you type will appear on the screen. Depending on the program, the symbol may be a vertical bar, a rectangle, or an underline. These keys, called arrow keys, allow you to move the insertion point right, left, up, or down. Most keyboards also contain keys such as HOME, END, PAGE UP, and PAGE DOWN that you can press to move the insertion point to the beginning or end of a line, page, or document.

Most keyboards also include toggle keys, which can be switched between two different states. The NUM LOCK key, for example, is a toggle key found on computer keyboards. When you press it once, it locks the numeric keypad so you can use it to type numbers. When you press the NUM LOCK key again, the numeric keypad is unlocked so the same keys serve as arrow keys that move the insertion point. The caps lock key is another example of a toggle key and is used on both PCs and Macintosh computers. Many keyboards have status lights in the upper-right corner that light up to indicate that a toggle key is activated.

Some keyboards include specialized buttons that allow you to access and use your CD/DVD drive, adjust speaker volume, open your e-mail program, start your Web browser, and more. Most keyboards attach to a serial port on the system unit via a cable. On notebook computers and handheld computers, the keyboard often is built onto the top of the system unit (Figure 4-19).

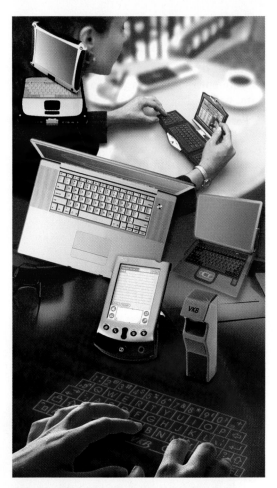

Figure 4-19 On notebook computers and mobile devices, the keyboard often is built onto the top of the system unit. Some keyboards can be detached or even virtual.

A popular keyboard used in K-12 classrooms is a **cordless keyboard**, also called a **wireless keyboard**. A cordless keyboard is a battery-operated device that transmits data using wireless technology, such as radio waves or infrared light waves (Figure 4-20). Cordless keyboards are available for use on both Macintosh computers and PCs. Some cordless keyboards include a pointing device.

Figure 4-20 Cordless keyboards can be passed easily from student to student while they work on group projects.

POINTING DEVICES

A **pointing device** is an input device that allows you to control a pointer on the screen. In a graphical user interface, a pointer, or mouse pointer, is a small symbol on the monitor's screen. A pointer often takes the shape of a block arrow (⬚), an I-beam (I), or a pointing hand (☝). Using a pointing device, you can position the pointer to move or select items on the screen. For example, you can use a pointing device to move the insertion point; select text, graphics, and other objects; and click buttons, icons, links, and menu commands. Common pointing devices include the mouse, touchpad and pointing stick, trackball, joystick, wheel, and touch screen.

MOUSE A mouse is the most widely used pointing device because it takes full advantage of a graphical user interface. Designed to fit comfortably under the palm of your hand, a **mouse** is an input device used to control the movement of the pointer on the screen and to make selections from the screen. The top of the mouse usually has one or two buttons; some have a small wheel. The mouse used with PCs usually is a two-button mouse (Figure 4-21); a one-button mouse is used with Macintosh computers (Figure 4-22). The most common type of mouse is a mechanical mouse. The bottom of a mechanical mouse is flat and contains a multidirectional mechanism, usually a small ball, which senses movement of the mouse.

The mouse often rests on a **mouse pad**, which usually is a rectangular rubber or foam pad that provides better traction for the mouse than the top of a desk. The mouse pad also protects the ball mechanism from a build up of dust and dirt, which could cause it to malfunction.

As you move the mouse across a flat surface such as a mouse pad, the pointer on the screen also moves. For example, when you move the mouse to the left, the pointer moves left on the screen. When you move the mouse to the right, the pointer moves right on the screen, and so on.

By using the mouse to move the pointer on the screen and then pressing, or **clicking**, the buttons on the mouse, you can perform actions such as pressing toolbar buttons, making menu selections, editing a document, and moving, or **dragging**, data from one location in a document to another. To press and release a mouse button twice without moving the mouse is called **double-clicking**. Double-clicking can be used to perform actions such as starting a program or opening a document. The function of the buttons on a two-button mouse can be changed to accommodate right- and left-handed individuals.

Other mouse types include an optical mouse and a cordless or wireless mouse. An **optical mouse** has no moving mechanical parts; instead, it uses devices that emit and sense light to detect the mouse's movement. A **cordless mouse** or **wireless mouse** is a battery-powered device that

mouse buttons   wheel button

ball mechanism

Figure 4-21 A mouse is used to control the movement of a pointer on the screen and make selections on the screen. Electronic circuits in a mouse translate the movement of the mouse into signals that are sent to the computer. Shown is a typical mouse used with PCs.

Figure 4-22 A Macintosh mouse usually has only one button.

transmits data using wireless technology, such as radio waves or infrared light waves. Many cordless keyboards also contain a wireless mouse.

TOUCHPAD AND POINTING STICK   A **touchpad** is a small, flat, rectangular pointing device that is sensitive to pressure and motion. Most touchpads have one or more buttons near the pad that work like mouse buttons. Touchpads often are found on notebook computers (Figure 4-23). To avoid using both a keyboard and a mouse with desktop computers, some schools purchase special keyboards that include a touchpad.

Figure 4-23 Many notebook computers have a touchpad that can be used to control the movement of the pointer.

touchpad

button

A **pointing stick** is a pressure-sensitive pointing device shaped like a pencil eraser that is positioned between keys on the keyboard (Figure 4-24). Some notebook computers contain both touchpads and pointing sticks.

pointing stick

buttons

Figure 4-24 Some notebook Educators use a pointing stick to control the movement of the pointer.

TRACKBALL   Some users opt for pointing devices other than a mouse, such as a trackball. Whereas a mouse has a ball mechanism on the bottom, a **trackball** is a stationary pointing device with a ball mechanism on its top (Figure 4-25).

The ball mechanism in a larger trackball is about the size of a Ping-Pong ball; notebook computers have small trackballs about the size of a marble. To move the pointer using a trackball, you rotate the ball mechanism with your thumb, fingers, or palm of your hand. Around the ball mechanism, a trackball usually has one or more buttons that work just like mouse buttons.

A trackball requires frequent cleaning because it picks up oils from fingers and dust from the environment. If you have limited desk space or use a notebook computer, however, a trackball is a good alternative to a mouse because you do not have to move the entire device.

Figure 4-25 A trackball is like an upside-down mouse. You rotate the ball with your thumb, fingers, or palm of your hand to move the pointer.

JOYSTICK AND WHEEL   Users running game software, such as a driving or flight simulation software, may prefer to use a joystick or wheel as their pointing device. A **joystick** is a vertical lever mounted on a base (Figure 4-26). You move the lever in different directions to control the actions of a vehicle or a player. The lever usually includes buttons, called triggers, that you can press to activate certain events. Some joysticks also have additional buttons that you can set to perform other actions.

joystick

wheel

pedal

Figure 4-26 Joysticks and wheels are used with game software to control the actions of a vehicle or player.

A **wheel** is a steering-wheel type input device. You turn the wheel to simulate driving a car or other vehicle. Most wheels also include foot pedals for acceleration and breaking action. A joystick and wheel typically attach via a cable to the game port on a sound card or game card, or to a USB port.

TOUCH SCREEN   A monitor that has a touch-sensitive panel on the screen is called a **touch screen**. You interact with the computer by touching areas of the screen with

your finger (Figure 4-27). In this case, the screen acts as an input device. To enter data, instructions, and information, you touch words, pictures, numbers, or locations identified on the screen. A touch screen often is used as the input device for a **kiosk**, which is a freestanding computer that provides information to the user. Visitors at museums, for example, can use a kiosk to access and print maps, facts on tours and exhibits, and other information.

Figure 4-27 A voter uses a kiosk touch screen to cast ballots in an election.

OPTICAL SCANNERS

An optical scanner, usually called simply a **scanner**, is an input device that captures an entire page of text or images such as photographs or artwork electronically. A scanner converts the text or image on the original document into digital data that can be stored on a disk and processed by the computer. The digitized data can be printed, displayed separately, or merged into another document for editing. Handheld devices that scan only a portion of a page at a time also are available.

PEN INPUT

Mobile users often enter data and instructions with a pen-type device. With pen input, users write, draw, and tap on a flat surface to enter input. The surface may be a monitor, a screen, or a special type of paper. Two devices used for pen input are the stylus and digital pen. A **stylus** is a small metal or plastic device that looks like a tiny ink pen but uses pressure instead of ink (Figure 4-28). A **digital pen**, which is slightly larger than a stylus, is available in two forms, some are pressure-sensitive, whereas others have a built-in digital camera.

Figure 4-29 Tablet PCs use a pressure-sensitive digital pen.

Digital pens that have built-in digital cameras work differently from pressure-sensitive digital pens. These pens look like ballpoint pens. In addition to a tiny digital camera, these pens contain a processor, memory, and an ink cartridge. As you write or draw on special digital paper with the pen, it captures every handwritten mark by taking more than 100 pictures per second and then stores the images in the pen's memory. You transfer the images from the pen to a computer (Figure 4-30) or mobile device, such as a smart phone. Some pens have a cradle for transferring images, whereas others communicate wirelessly using Bluetooth. Think of the potential of this new digital pen technology when used by today's digital students.

Figure 4-28 PDAs and smart phones use a stylus.

Some mobile computers and nearly all mobile devices have touch screens. Instead of using a finger to enter data and instructions, most of these devices include a pressure-sensitive digital pen or stylus. You write, draw, or make selections on the screen by touching the screen with the pen or stylus. For example, Tablet PCs use a pressure-sensitive digital pen (Figure 4-29) and PDAs use a stylus. Computers and mobile devices often use handwriting recognition software that transmits the handwritten letters and symbols into characters that the computer or device can process.

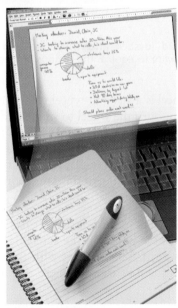

Figure 4-30 Some digital pens have a built-in digital camera that stores your handwritten marks and allows you to transfer your handwriting to a computer.

DIGITAL CAMERAS

A **digital camera** allows you to take pictures and store the photographed images digitally instead of on traditional film (Figure 4-31). After you have taken a picture or series of pictures, you download, or transfer a copy of, the pictures to your computer. As soon as the pictures are stored on your computer, they can be edited with photo editing software, printed, posted on a Web site, and more.

AUDIO AND VIDEO INPUT

Although characters (text and numbers) still are the primary forms of input into a computer, individuals increasingly are using other types of input, such as images, audio, and video. In the previous sections, you learned about a variety of ways to input image data. The next sections discuss methods used to input audio and video data into a computer. Audio and video data often are stored on a computer's hard disk.

Audio input is the process of recording music, speech, or sound effects. Most personal computers sold today are equipped with a sound card necessary to record high-quality sound. Recorded sound is input via a device such as a microphone, tape player, or audio CD player, which plugs into a port on the sound card.

With a microphone plugged into the microphone port on the sound card, you can record sounds using the computer. After you save the sound as a file, you can play it, add it to a document, or edit it using audio editing software.

Another use for a microphone is speech recognition. **Speech recognition**, also called **voice recognition**, is the capability of a computer to distinguish spoken words. Speech recognition programs do not understand speech; they only recognize a vocabulary of certain words. The vocabulary of speech recognition programs can range from two words (such as Yes and No) to more than two million words. Experts agree that voice recognition eventually will be added to all software programs.

Video input or video capture is the process of entering a full-motion recording into a computer. To capture video, you plug a video camera, VCR, or similar device into a video capture card, which converts the

Figure 4-31
A digital camera is used to take pictures so images can be stored on a computer.

analog video signal into a digital signal that a computer can understand. After the device is connected to the card, you can begin recording. After the video is saved, you can play the video, copy it onto a videotape, or edit it using video editing software.

Recent advances in audio and video technologies are allowing users to create and edit audio and video clips easily. The creation, use, and integration of audio and video in K-12 education is becoming popular. Creating and editing audio and video on both Macintosh computers and PCs is covered in greater detail in the special feature, Digital Imaging and Video Technology, which follows Chapter 5. Digital Media Corner at the end of each chapter addresses topics such as these, as well.

INPUTS FOR PDAs, SMART PHONES, AND TABLET PCs

Increasingly more people, including many teachers and students, are using a variety of mobile devices, such as PDAs, smart phones, and mobile computers such as the Tablet PC. A large variety of input alternatives are available for these devices and computers. Figure 4-32 on the next page provides examples of devices that can be used to input data into a PDA.

Voice is the traditional method of input for smart phones. Today, however, text messaging, instant messaging, and picture messaging have become popular methods of entering data and instructions into a smart phone.

WEB INFO

To learn more about digital cameras, visit the Teachers Discovering Computers Web site (*scsite.com/tdc4*), click Chapter 4, click Web Info, and then click Digital Cameras.

WEB INFO

For an explanation of speech recognition, visit the Teachers Discovering Computers Web site (*scsite.com/tdc4*), click Chapter 4, click Web Info, and then click Speech Recognition.

digital camera

pen input

pad of paper

pen/stylus

scanner

stylus

on-screen keyboard

Pocket PC

transfer data and instructions from desktop computer

cradle

Figure 4-32 Users have many options to input data into a PDA.

The primary input device for a Tablet PC is a digital pen, which allows users to write on the device's screen. To access other input devices, users can slide their Tablet PC in a docking station, which contains a power connection and provides connections to peripherals (Figure 4-33).

Additional input devices used in businesses, homes, and schools are described in Chapters 5 through 7, and in Digital Imaging and Video Technology (the special feature that follows Chapter 5), and A World Without Wires (the special feature that follows Chapter 8). Input devices for students with special needs are covered in this chapter's Assistive Technologies Corner.

Tablet PC

docking station

Figure 4-33 To use a slate Tablet PC while working at a desk, insert the Tablet PC in a docking station. Devices such as a keyboard and CD drive can be plugged in the docking station.

What Is Output?

Output is data that has been processed into a useful form called information. That is, a computer processes input into output. Computers generate several types of output, depending on the hardware and software being used and the requirements of the user. Four common types of output are text, graphics, audio, and video (Figure 4-34).

- **Text** consists of characters that are used to create words, sentences, and paragraphs. A character is a letter, number, punctuation mark, or any other symbol that requires one byte of computer storage space.

- **Graphics** are digital representations of nontext information, such as images, drawings, charts, pictures, and photographs. Displaying a series of still graphics creates an animation, a graphic that has the illusion of motion.

Many of today's software programs support graphics; others are designed specifically to create and edit graphics. Graphics programs, called image editors, allow you to alter graphics by including enhancements such as blended colors, animation, and other special effects.

- **Audio** is any music, speech, or other sound that is stored and produced by the computer. Recall that sound waves, such as the human voice or music, are analog. To store such sounds, a computer converts them from a continuous analog signal into a digital format.

- **Video** consists of photographic images that are played back at speeds that provide the appearance of full motion in real time. Video often is captured with a video input device such as a video camera or VCR.

Figure 4-34 Four common types of output are text, graphics, audio, and video.

What Are Output Devices?

An **output device** is any computer component capable of conveying information to a user. Commonly used output devices include monitors, printers, data projectors, facsimile machines, multifunction devices, speakers, and headsets. Each of these output devices is discussed in the following pages.

MONITORS AND DISPLAY DEVICES

A **display device** is an output device that displays text, graphics, and video information. A **monitor** is a display device that is housed in a plastic or metal case. Information shown on a display device often is called **soft copy** because the information exists electronically and is displayed for a temporary period.

Monitors for personal computers are available in a variety of sizes, with the more common being 15, 17, 19, and 21 inches. The size of a monitor is measured diagonally, from corner to corner. Most monitors are referred to by the diagonal measurement of the large glass tube inside the monitor, which is larger than the actual viewing area provided by the monitor (known as the viewable size). For example, a monitor listed as a 17-inch monitor may have a viewable size of only 15.7 inches.

Determining what size monitor to use depends on your intended use. A larger monitor allows you to view more information at once, but usually is more expensive. If you work on the Web or use multiple applications at one time, however, you may want to invest in at least a 17-inch monitor.

Like a television set, the core of most monitors is a large glass tube called a **cathode ray tube** (**CRT**) (Figure 4-35). The

cathode ray tube

screen   monitor

Figure 4-35 The core of most personal computer monitors is a cathode ray tube.

screen, which is the front of the tube, is coated with tiny dots of phosphor material that glow when electrically charged. The CRT moves an electron beam back and forth across the back of the screen, causing the dots to glow, which produces an image on the screen.

Each dot, called a **pixel** (short for picture element), is a single point in an electronic image (Figure 4-36). Monitors consist of hundreds, thousands, or millions of pixels arranged in rows and columns that can be used to create pictures. The pixels are so close together that they appear connected.

Many types of specialized monitors exist, including large display monitors and LCD monitors and displays.

WEB INFO

For more information about monitors, visit the Teachers Discovering Computers Web site (*scsite.com/tdc4*), click Chapter 4, click Web Info, and then click Monitor.

Figure 4-36 A pixel is a single dot of color, or point, in an electronic image.

LARGE DISPLAY MONITORS Large display **monitors** are large monitors that allow an audience or a group of students in a classroom to view images and multimedia displayed on a computer. These large display monitors are available in screen sizes from 27 inches to 36 inches. Although some teachers use large display monitors that are designed specifically for use with computers in schools (Figure 4-37), many teachers connect large screen televisions to their computers. Connecting a desktop computer to a standard large screen television requires an inexpensive converter. Some notebook computers now contain the necessary components to be connected directly to a large display monitor using a standard S-video cable.

Figure 4-37 Large display monitors are available in sizes up to 36 inches.

Some of the new large display monitors designed specifically for schools use high-definition television technology. **High-definition television (HDTV)** is a type of television set that works with digital broadcasting signals, supports a wider screen, and displays at a higher resolution than a standard television set.

For even larger displays, some businesses and a few schools are using gas plasma monitors, which can measure more than 60 inches wide. A **gas plasma monitor** is a flat-panel display that uses gas plasma technology, which substitutes a layer of gas for the liquid crystal material in an LCD monitor. Gas plasma monitors are very expensive (Figure 4-38).

Using large display monitors can significantly impact student learning by allowing teachers to integrate relevant content at the point of instruction. The benefits of using large display monitors in classrooms is detailed in Chapters 6 and 7.

Figure 4-38 Large gas plasma monitors can measure more than 60 inches wide.

FLAT PANEL MONITORS AND DISPLAYS
A **flat panel monitor**, also called an **LCD monitor**, is a desktop monitor that uses liquid crystal instead of a cathode-ray tube to present information on a screen (Figure 4-39). Flat panel monitors are available in 15, 17, 18, 20, 21, and 23 inches and consume less than one-third the power of CRT monitors. Even though they are more expensive than CRT monitors, flat panel monitors are very popular because they take up less space and produce crisp, bright images. Mobile computers, such as notebook computers and Tablet PCs, and mobile devices, such as PDAs and smart phones, use LCD monitors (Figure 4-40 on the next page). A flat panel monitor is not the same thing as a flat display. A flat display refers to a CRT monitor that has a flat screen.

Figure 4-39 An LCD monitor is much thinner and lighter than a CRT monitor.

Figure 4-40 Notebook computers and Tablet PCs have color LCD screens. Many PDAs and newer smart phones have color LCD displays too.

MONITOR QUALITY The quality of a monitor depends largely on its resolution, dot pitch, and refresh rate. The **resolution**, or sharpness and clarity, of a monitor is related directly to the number of pixels it can display. Resolution is expressed as two separate numbers: the number of columns of pixels and the number of rows of pixels a monitor can display. For example, a screen with an 800 × 600 (pronounced 800 by 600) resolution can display 800 columns and 600 rows of pixels (or a total of 480,000 pixels). Most newer monitors can display up to 1800 × 1440 pixels with 800 × 600 still typically the standard for many older school monitors. A monitor with a higher resolution displays a greater number of pixels, which provides a smoother but smaller image.

Another factor that determines monitor quality is **dot pitch**, which is the distance between each pixel on a monitor. The smaller the distance between the pixels, the sharper the displayed image.

Recall that an electron beam moving back and forth behind a CRT screen causes pixels on the screen to glow — thus creating an image. These pixels, however, only glow for a small fraction of a second before beginning to fade. The monitor thus redraws the picture many times per second so that the image does not fade. The speed at which the monitor redraws images on the screen is called the **refresh rate**. Some monitors display an **ENERGY STAR** label, which identifies the monitor as an energy-efficient product as defined by the Environmental Protection Agency (EPA). Monitors usually are equipped with controls to adjust the brightness, contrast, positioning, height, and width of images. Finally, many monitors sit on a tilt-and-swivel base so you can adjust the angle of the screen to minimize neck strain and reduce glare from overhead lighting.

PRINTERS

A **printer** is an output device that produces text and graphical information on a physical medium such as paper or transparency film. Printed information is called **hard copy** because it is a more permanent form of output than that presented on a monitor. Users can print a hard copy of a file in either portrait or landscape orientation. A page with **portrait orientation** is taller than it is wide, with information printed across the shorter width of the paper. A page with **landscape orientation** is wider than it is tall, with information printed across the widest part of the paper.

Because printing requirements vary greatly among users, manufacturers offer printers with varying speeds, capabilities, and printing methods. Until a few years ago, printing a document required connecting a computer to a printer with a cable via the USB or parallel port on the computer. Although many users today continue to print using this method, a variety of printing options are available, as shown in Figure 4-41.

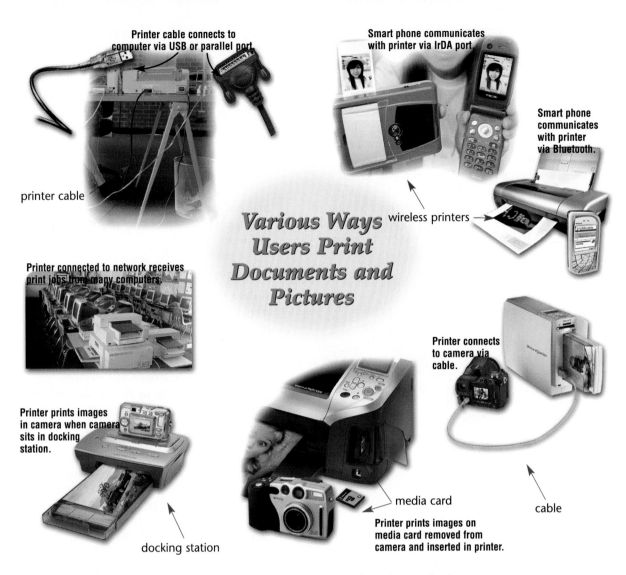

Printer cable connects to computer via USB or parallel port.

printer cable

Smart phone communicates with printer via IrDA port.

Smart phone communicates with printer via Bluetooth.

Various Ways Users Print Documents and Pictures

wireless printers

Printer connected to network receives print jobs from many computers.

Printer connects to camera via cable.

Printer prints images in camera when camera sits in docking station.

media card

cable

docking station

Printer prints images on media card removed from camera and inserted in printer.

Figure 4-41 Users print documents and pictures using a variety of printing methods.

NONIMPACT PRINTERS A nonimpact **printer** forms marks on a piece of paper without actually striking the paper. Two common types of nonimpact printers are ink-jet and laser printers.

Because of their reasonable cost and print quality, ink-jet printers often are used in homes and schools. An **ink-jet printer** is a type of nonimpact printer that forms marks by spraying tiny drops of liquid ink onto a piece of paper. Ink-jet printers can produce high-quality text and graphics in both black-and-white and color on a variety of media such as paper, envelopes, labels, or transparencies. Ink-jet printers use small ink cartridges that are replaced easily or may be refilled using inexpensive ink-jet refill kits. In addition, many ink-jet printers include software to help you create items such as announcements, banners, cards, and so on.

A **photo printer** is a color printer that produces photo lab quality pictures (Figure 4-42). Many photo printers use ink-jet technology and can print photos in various sizes.

Figure 4-42 Ink-jet photo printers are a popular type of color printer used at home.

A **laser printer** is a high-speed, high-quality nonimpact printer. Operating in a manner similar to a copy machine, a laser printer uses powdered ink, called toner, which is packaged in a cartridge. When electrically charged, the toner sticks to a special drum inside the printer and then is transferred to the paper through a combination of pressure and heat (Figure 4-43). When the toner runs out, you simply replace the cartridge.

Laser printers, in a manner similar to ink-jet printers, usually use individual sheets of letter and legal-size paper stored in a removable tray that slides into the printer case. Most printers also have a manual feed slot where you can insert individual sheets, transparencies, and envelopes.

Although laser printers cost more than ink-jet printers, laser printers quickly print very high-quality black-and-white text and graphics. Although color laser printers are available, they are expensive and rarely found in K-12 schools.

Other nonimpact printers include thermal printers, portable printers, label and postage printers, plotters, and large-format printers.

Figure 4-43 A laser printer operates similarly to a copy machine. Electrically charged toner sticks to a special drum inside the printer and then is transferred to the paper through a combination of pressure and heat.

DATA PROJECTORS

A **data projector** projects the image that displays on a computer screen onto a large screen, so that an audience, such as a classroom or school assembly, can see the image clearly (Figure 4-44). Data projectors range in size from large devices attached to a ceiling or wall in an auditorium to smaller, portable devices. Three types of smaller units are LCD projection panels, LCD projectors, and DLP (digital light processing) projectors. An LCD projection panel uses liquid crystal display technology and is designed to be placed on top of an overhead projector. An LCD projector, which also uses liquid crystal display technology, attaches directly to a computer and uses its own light source to display the information shown on the computer screen. A digital light processing (DLP) projector uses tiny mirrors to reflect

Figure 4-44 Data projectors produce sharp, bright images.

light, producing crisp, bright, colorful images that remain in focus and can be seen clearly even in a well-lit room.

FACSIMILE (FAX) MACHINE

A **facsimile (fax) machine** is a device that transmits and receives documents over telephone lines. The documents can contain text, graphics, or photos, or can be handwritten. When a document is sent or received via a fax machine, these documents are known as faxes. A fax machine scans the original document, converts the image into digitized data, and transmits the digitized image (Figure 4-45). A fax machine at the receiving end reads the incoming data, converts the digitized data into an image, and prints or stores a copy of the original image.

The fax machine just described is a stand-alone fax machine. You also can add fax capability to your computer via a fax modem. A fax modem is a communications device that allows you to send and receive electronic documents as faxes. A fax modem transmits electronic documents, such as a word processing letter or digital photo. A fax modem is like a regular modem except that it transmits documents to a fax machine or to another fax modem. When you receive a fax on your computer, you can view the document on the screen or print it using special fax software.

MULTIFUNCTION DEVICES

A **multifunction device (MFD)** is a single piece of equipment that provides the functionality of a printer, fax machine, copier, and scanner (Figure 4-46). The features of multifunction devices vary widely. For example, some use color ink-jet printer technology, whereas others include a black-and-white laser printer. Small businesses, home offices, and school administrative offices use multifunction devices because they take up less space and cost less than a separate printer, scanner, copy machine, and fax machine. Quality multifunction devices are available for less than $150.

Figure 4-46 This multifunctional device is a color printer, scanner, fax, and copy machine all in one device.

Figure 4-45 A stand-alone fax machine.

AUDIO OUTPUT

Audio output is any music, speech, or other sound produced by a computer. Sound is widely available on the Internet. You can listen to music on your computer by simply inserting an audio compact disc (CD) into the CD-ROM drive. You can hear sounds of video clips while viewing them on the monitor. Two commonly used devices for audio output are speakers and headsets.

Many computers have a small internal speaker, but it usually produces low-quality sound. For this reason, many personal computers are sold with stereo speakers. **Speakers** can be separate devices placed on either side of the monitor or they can be built in to the monitor or the system unit. Stereo speakers are connected to ports on the sound card. Most speakers have tone and volume controls.

When using speakers, anyone within listening distance can hear the output. Speakers are not always practical in classrooms and computer labs. Often, teachers and students use headsets that can be plugged into a port on the sound card (Figure 4-47). By using headsets, students will be able to concentrate better on the sound from their computers and they will not be disturbed by sounds on nearby computers.

What Is Storage?

Storage refers to the media on which data, instructions, and information are kept, as well as the devices that record and retrieve these items. To understand storage, you should understand the difference between how a computer uses memory and how it uses storage. As discussed earlier in this chapter, random access memory, called RAM, temporarily stores data and programs that are being processed. You also will recall that RAM is volatile because data and programs stored in memory are lost when the power is turned off or a power failure occurs.

Storage stores data, instructions, and information when they are not being processed. Think of storage as a filing cabinet used to hold file folders, and memory as the top of your desk (Figure 4-48). When you need to work with a file, you remove it from the filing cabinet (storage) and place it on your desk (memory). When you are finished with the file, you return it to the filing cabinet (storage). Storage is nonvolatile, which means that data, instructions, and information in storage are retained even when power is removed from the computer.

Figure 4-47 Headsets are used to help students focus on sounds coming from their computers and to prevent them from being disturbed by sounds coming from nearby computers.

Figure 4-48 Think of storage as a filing cabinet used to hold file folders and memory as the top of your desk. When you need to work with a file, you remove it from the filing cabinet (storage) and place it on your desk (memory). When you are finished with the file, you return it to the filing cabinet (storage).

Storage Media and Devices

A **storage medium** (media is the plural), also called **secondary storage**, is the physical material on which data, instructions, and information are kept. One commonly used storage medium is a **disk**, which is a round, flat piece of plastic or metal on which items such as data, instructions, and information can be encoded. A **storage device** is the mechanism used to record and retrieve these items to and from a storage medium.

Storage devices can function as sources of input and output. For example, each time the CPU transfers data, instructions, and information from a storage medium into memory — a process called reading — the storage device functions as an input source. When the CPU transfers these items from memory to a storage medium — a process called writing — the storage device functions as an output source.

The size, or capacity, of a storage device is measured by the amount of bytes (characters) it can hold. Storage capacity usually is measured in megabytes or gigabytes. Some devices can hold thousands of bytes, whereas others can store trillions of bytes. For example, a typical 3.5-inch disk can store 1.44 MB of data and a typical home computer's hard disk can store 80 GB of data.

Storage requirements among users vary greatly. A teacher, for example, might have a list of names, test scores, and average grades for 30 students that requires several hundred bytes of storage. Users of larger computers, such as banks or libraries, might need to store trillions of bytes worth of historical or catalog records. To meet the needs of a wide range of users, numerous types of storage media and storage devices exist, many of which are discussed in the following sections.

MAGNETIC DISKS

A **magnetic disk** uses magnetic patterns to store data, instructions, and information on the disk's surface. Depending on how the magnetic particles are aligned, they represent either a 0 bit or a 1 bit. Recall that a bit (binary digit) is the smallest unit of data a computer can process. Most magnetic disks are read/write storage media; that is, you can access (read) data from and place (write) data on a magnetic disk any number of times.

Before data can be read from or written to a magnetic disk, the disk must be formatted. **Formatting** is the process of preparing a disk for reading and writing by organizing the disk into storage locations called tracks and sectors (Figure 4-49). A **track** is a narrow storage ring around the disk — similar to the annual rings on a tree. A **sector** is a pie shaped section of the disk, which breaks the tracks into small arcs.

Three types of magnetic disks are 3.5-inch disks, Zip disks, and hard disks. Some of these disks are portable, which means you can remove the disk from one computer and use it in another.

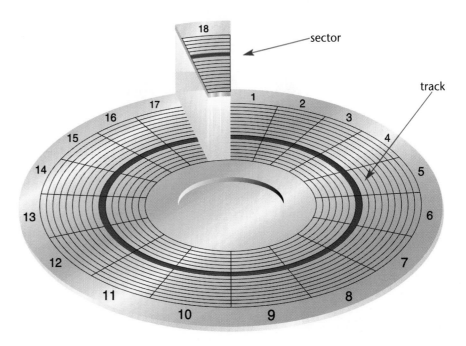

Figure 4-49 A track is a narrow recording band that forms a full circle on the surface of a disk. The disk's storage locations then are divided into pie-shaped sections, which break the tracks into small arcs called sectors.

FLOPPY DISKS

A **floppy disk** or **diskette** is a portable, inexpensive storage medium that consists of a thin, circular, flexible plastic disk with a magnetic coating enclosed in a square shaped plastic shell (Figure 4-50). In the early 1970s, IBM introduced a new type of storage medium, called the floppy disk. Because these early, 8-inch-wide disks had flexible plastic covers, many users referred to them as floppies or floppy diskettes. The next generation of floppies looked much the same but were only 5.25-inches wide. Today, the most widely used floppy disk is 3.5-inches wide. The flexible cover of the earlier floppy disks has been replaced with a rigid plastic outer cover. Thus, although today's 3.5-inch disks are not at all floppy, users still refer to them as floppy disks. Floppy disks, while still used by many teachers and students, are quickly being replaced with USB flash drives and other portable storage devices.

A **floppy disk drive** is a device that can read from and write to a floppy disk. Older personal computers usually have a floppy disk drive installed inside the system unit that is called drive A. Older Macintosh

computers also have one installed floppy disk drive and the drive is referred to simply as the floppy disk drive. Most new PCs and Macintosh computers do not come equipped with an internal floppy disk drive. External floppy disk drives can be attached to these newer computers using a USB port.

ZIP DISKS

A **Zip disk** is a type of portable magnetic media that can store from 100 MB to 750 MB of data (Figure 4-51). With these high-capacity disks, users can store large files containing graphics, audio, or video; transport a large number of files from one computer to another; or make a backup of the important files. A **backup** is a duplicate of a file, program, or disk that can be used if the original is lost, damaged, or destroyed. Like floppy disks, Zip disks are still used, but are quickly being replaced with USB flash drives and other portable storage devices.

HARD DISKS

When personal computers were introduced, software programs and their related files required small amounts of storage and files fit easily on floppy disks. As software became more complex and included graphical user interfaces and multimedia, file sizes and storage requirements increased. Today, hard disks, which provide for larger storage capacities, are the primary media for storing software programs and files. Current personal computer hard disks can store from 40 GB to 300 GB or more of data, instructions, and information.

A **hard disk** usually consists of several inflexible, circular disks, called platters, on which items such as data, instructions, and information are stored electronically. A **platter** in a hard disk is made of aluminum, glass, or ceramic and is coated with a material that allows data to be magnetically recorded on its surface. Although removable hard disks do exist, the hard disks in most personal computers are housed permanently inside

WEB INFO

For a discussion of backup procedures, visit the Teachers Discovering Computers Web site (*scsite.com/tdc4*), click Chapter 4, click Web Info, and then click Backup.

Disassembled 3.5-inch floppy disk

liners

shutter

flexible thin film

metal hub

magnetic coating

shell

Figure 4-50 In a 3.5-inch floppy disk, the thin circular flexible film is enclosed between two liners. A piece of metal called a shutter covers an opening to the recording surface in the rigid plastic shell.

built-in
Zip drive

Zip disk

Figure 4-51 Some older computers came equipped with a built-in Zip drive. You also can add an external Zip drive to a PC or Macintosh computer.

the system unit and are enclosed in an airtight, sealed case to protect the platters from contamination (Figure 4-52).

hard drive installed
in system unit

Figure 4-52 The hard disk in a personal computer normally is housed permanently inside the system unit.

Recall that a hard disk is a magnetic disk that stores data, instructions, and information using magnetic patterns. Hard disks also are read/write storage media; that is, you can both read from and write to a hard disk any number of times. Before you can write data, instructions, or information to a hard disk, the hard disk must be formatted. Usually, hard disk manufacturers format hard disks before they are

installed in computers. Typically, a hard disk is designated drive C on PCs and as the HD Disk on Macintosh computers.

MINIATURE HARD DISKS Many mobile devices and consumer electronics include miniature hard disks, which provide users with greater storage capacities than flash memory. These tiny hard disks are found in devices such as music players, digital cameras, smart phones, and PDAs. Miniature hard disks have storage capacities that range from 2 GB to 100 GB or more (Figure 4-53).

WEB INFO

For more information about hard disks, visit the Teachers Discovering Computers Web site (*scsite.com/tdc4*), click Chapter 4, click Web Info, and then click Hard Disk.

Figure 4-53 Miniature hard disks are used in a variety of electronic devices.

PORTABLE HARD DISKS Two types of portable hard disks are external hard disks and removable hard disks. An **external hard disk** is a separate hard disk that connects to a USB or FireWire port by a cable (Figure 4-54a). External hard disks can store 250 GB or higher. Removable external hard disks use cartridges that you insert and remove from an external hard disk drive (Figure 4-54b). Some external hard drives insert into a special bay in the system unit.

Sale prices for medium-capacity portable hard drives have dropped to $75 or less. Many teachers and other users have purchased a portable hard drive to supplement their home and school internal hard drives and to back up their home and school files.

programs. Just about every personal computer today includes some type of CD or DVD drive (Figure 4-55). Some CD and DVD drives are read only, meaning you cannot write (save) to the media. Others are read/write, which allows users to save to the disc just as they save to a hard disk.

On personal computers, the drive designation of a CD or DVD drive usually follows alphabetically after that of the hard disk. For example, if your hard disk is drive C, then the CD or DVD drive usually will be drive D. When you place a CD or DVD in a Macintosh computer, an icon that looks like a CD appears on the computer desktop.

[b] removable hard disk

[a] external hard disk

Figure 4-54 Examples of large-capacity portable hard disks.

OPTICAL DISCS

An **optical disc** is a type of storage medium that consists of a flat, round, portable disc made of metal, plastic, and lacquer that is written and read by a laser. Optical discs used in personal computers are 4.75 inches in diameter. Smaller computers and devices, however, use mini discs that have a diameter of 3 inches or less.

CDs AND DVDs

CDs and DVDs are a type of optical storage media that consists of a flat, round, portable, plastic disc with a protective metal coating. Recall from Chapter 1 that the term *disk* is used for magnetic media and *disc* is used for optical media.

CDs and DVDs primarily store music, movies, digital photographs, and software

WEB INFO

For more information about DVD-ROMs, visit the Teachers Discovering Computers Web site (*scsite.com/tdc4*), click Chapter 4, click Web Info, and then click DVD-ROM.

Push the button to slide the tray out.

Insert the disc, label side up.

Push the same button to close the tray.

Figure 4-55 To use CD and DVD drives, you push a button to open a tray, which causes the tray to slide out, insert the disc with the label side up, and then push the same button to close the tray.

CHARACTERISTICS OF CDs AND DVDs

CDs and DVDs are optical media that store data, information, music, and video in microscopic pits on the bottom portion of the disc. A high-powered laser light creates the pits. A lower-powered laser light reads items from the disc by reflecting light through the bottom of the disc, which usually is either gold or silver in color. The reflected light is converted into a series of bits the computer can process. Most manufacturers place a silk-screened label on the top of the disc.

CARE OF OPTICAL DISCS   Manufacturers guarantee that a properly cared for CD or DVD will last five years, but could last up to 100 years. Figure 4-56 outlines some guidelines for the proper care of CDs and DVDs. Never bend a disc. Exposing discs to extreme temperatures or humidity could cause them to warp. Stacking discs, touching the underside of discs, or exposing them to any type of contaminant may scratch a disc. If a disc becomes warped or if its

surface is scratched, data on the disc may be unreadable. Always place a CD or DVD in its protective case, called a jewel box or disc storage case, when you are finished using it.

CDs and DVDs are available in a variety of formats. The following sections discuss many of these formats.

TYPES OF OPTICAL DISCS

Many different formats of optical discs exist today. Two general categories are CDs and DVDs, with DVDs having a much greater storage capacity than CDs. Specific formats include CD-ROM, CD-R, CD-RW, DVD-ROM, DVD-R, DVD+R, DVD-RW, DVD+RW, and DVD+RAM. Figure 4-57 on the next page identifies each of these optical disc formats and specifies whether a user can read from the disc, write to the disc, and/or erase the disc. The following sections describe characteristics unique to each of these disc formats.

WEB INFO

For more information about CD-ROMs, visit the Teachers Discovering Computers Web site (*scsite.com/tdc4*), click Chapter 4, click Web Info, and then click CD-ROM.

Do not expose the disc to excessive heat or sunlight.

Do store the disc in a jewel box when not in use.

Do not eat, smoke, or drink near a disc.

Do not stack discs.

Do not touch the underside of the disc.

Do hold a disc by its edges.

Figure 4-56 Some guidelines for the proper care of CDs and DVDs.

Optical Disc Formats

Optical Disc	Read	Write	Erase	Optical Disc	Read	Write	Erase
CD-ROM	Y	N	N	DVD-R DVD+R	Y	Y	N
CD-R	Y	Y	N	DVD-RW DVD+RW DVD+RAM	Y	Y	Y
CD-RW	Y	Y	Y				
DVD-ROM	Y	N	N				

FIGURE 4-57   Manufacturers sell CD-ROM and DVD-ROM media prerecorded (written) with audio, video, and software. Users cannot change the contents of these discs. Users, however, can purchase the other formats of CDs and DVDs as blank media and record (write) their own data, videos, and information to these discs.

Figure 4-58 CD-ROMs are used to store and distribute multimedia software, including programs for children, education, games, and reference.

CD-ROM Compact disc read-only memory (CD-ROM; pronounced SEE-DEE-rom) is a type of optical disc that uses the same laser technology that audio CDs use for recording music. Unlike an audio CD, a CD-ROM can contain text, graphics, animation, and video, as well as sound. The contents of standard CD-ROMs are written, or **recorded**, by the manufacturer and only can be read and used; that is, they cannot be erased or modified — hence, the name read-only.

Because audio CDs and CD-ROMs use the same laser technology, you can use your CD-ROM drive to listen to an audio CD while working on your computer.

A CD-ROM can hold 650 MB of data, instructions, and information — about 450 times the capacity of a high-density 3.5-inch disk. Because CD-ROMs have such high storage capacities, they are used to store and distribute today's complex software, such as programs for children, education, games, and reference (Figure 4-58). Most of today's software programs are sold on CD; some programs even require that the disc be in the drive each time you use the program.

PICTURE CDs   A Kodak **Picture CD** is a type of compact disc that stores digital versions of a single roll of film using a .jpg file format. Many film developers offer Picture CD service when consumers drop off film to be developed. In addition to printed photographs and negatives, you also receive a Picture CD containing your pictures. The additional cost for a Picture CD varies, but often is only $1–2 per roll of film.

Standard CD-ROM drives can read a Picture CD. Using photo editing software and the photographs on the Picture CD, you can remove red eye, crop the photographs, enhance colors, and edit just about any aspect of the photograph. In addition, you can print photos from a Picture CD on glossy paper with an ink-jet printer. Many stores have kiosks at which you can print pictures from a Picture CD (Figure 4-59).

Step 1: Drop off the film to be developed. Mark the Picture CD box on the film-processing envelope.

Step 2: When you pick up prints and negatives, a Picture CD containing digital images of each photograph is included.

Step 3: At home, view images on your monitor and print images from the Picture CD on your ink-jet or photo printer. At a store, print images from the Picture CD at a kiosk.

Figure 4-59 How a Picture CD works.

CD-R AND CD-RW   Many computers today include either a CD-R or a CD-RW drive as standard equipment. Unlike standard CD-ROM drives, these new drives allow you to record your own data onto a CD-R or CD-RW disc.

A **compact disc-recordable (CD-R)** is a compact disc onto which you can record your own information, such as text, graphic, and audio. With a CD-R, you can write on part of the disc at one time and another part at a later time. You can write on each part only one time, and you cannot erase the disc's content. To write on a CD-R disc, you must have CD-R software and a CD-R drive.

A **compact disc-rewritable (CD-RW)** is an erasable disc you can write on multiple times. With CD-RW, the disc acts like a 3.5-inch or hard disk. You can easily

write and rewrite data multiple times. To write on a CD-RW disc, you must have CD-RW software and a CD-RW drive.

A popular use of CD-RW and CD-R discs is to create audio CDs. The steps in Figure 4-60 on the next page illustrate techniques for copying the song(s) from an existing CD or downloading the song(s) from the Web, in most cases for a fee.

DVDs: READ-ONLY AND REWRITABLE Although CDs have large storage capacities, even these are not large enough for many of today's complex programs. Some software, for example, is sold on five or more CDs. To meet the tremendous storage requirements of today's software, the digital video disc read-only memory (DVD-ROM) format was developed.

A **digital video disc read-only memory (DVD-ROM)** is an extremely high-capacity

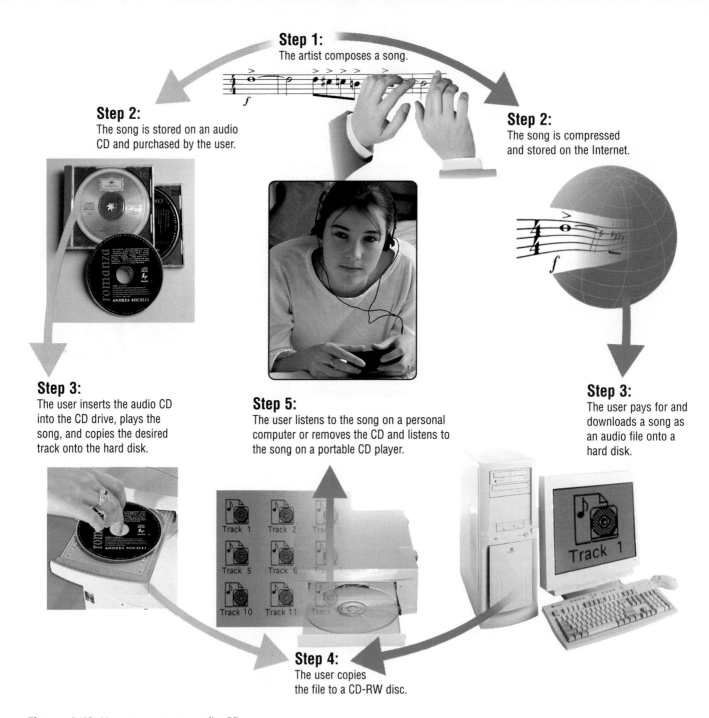

Step 1:
The artist composes a song.

Step 2:
The song is stored on an audio CD and purchased by the user.

Step 2:
The song is compressed and stored on the Internet.

Step 3:
The user inserts the audio CD into the CD drive, plays the song, and copies the desired track onto the hard disk.

Step 5:
The user listens to the song on a personal computer or removes the CD and listens to the song on a portable CD player.

Step 3:
The user pays for and downloads a song as an audio file onto a hard disk.

Step 4:
The user copies the file to a CD-RW disc.

Figure 4-60 How to create an audio CD.

CD capable of storing from 4.7 GB to 17 GB, more than enough to hold a telephone book containing every resident in the United States (Figure 4-61). Not only is the storage capacity greater than a CD, but the quality of a DVD far surpasses that of a CD. To read a DVD-ROM, you must have a **DVD-ROM drive**. Many computers now are sold with DVD-ROM drives that will read both CDs and DVDs.

As the cost of DVD technologies becomes more reasonable, many industry professionals believe that DVDs will eventually replace CDs, VCRs, and VHS tapes in our businesses, homes, and schools.

Many new computers come with a standard combination DVD-ROM/CD-RW drive or optional DVD-R/CD-RW. The DVD-R/CD-RW drive is called a Super-Drive on newer Macintosh computers.

Chapter 5 and the Digital Imaging and Video Technology special feature that follows Chapter 5 discuss in detail the processes of creating, editing, and using CD-R, CD-RW, and DVD+RW technology at home and in education.

MINIATURE MOBILE STORAGE MEDIA

Miniature mobile storage media allow mobile users to transport digital images, music, or documents to and from computers and other devices easily (Figure 4-62).

FAQ

Is it legal to copy songs onto a CD?

It is legal to copy songs from an audio CD that you purchase, as long as you use the copied music for your own personal use. It is not legal to download copyrighted music unless the song's copyright holder has granted permission; normally you must pay a fee to download songs legally.

DVD-ROM

DVD-ROM drive

Figure 4-61 A DVD-ROM is an extremely high-capacity compact disc capable of storing 4.7 GB to 17 GB.

DVDs are available in a variety of formats, including one which stores motion pictures. To view a DVD movie, you insert the DVD movie disc into a DVD player connected to your television or into a computer's DVD-ROM drive. Many computers that contain a DVD-ROM drive allow you to connect your computer directly to your television. Users also can purchase recordable (DVD-R) and rewritable (DVD+RW) versions of DVDs, which are similar to CD-R and CD-RW in the way they operate.

miniature mobile storage media

Figure 4-62 Many types of computers and devices use miniature mobile storage media.

Many computers, Tablet PCs, PDAs, smart phones, digital cameras, and music players have built-in slots or ports to read from and write to miniature mobile storage media. For computers or devices without built-in slots, users insert the media in separate peripherals, such as a card reader/writer or a device such as a digital photo viewer, which connects to a television port for on-screen picture viewing.

PDAs, digital cameras, music players, smart phones, and many other devices use miniature mobile storage media. The table in Figure 4-63 summarizes the storage capacities and uses of popular miniature storage media. The following sections briefly discuss the widely used miniature storage media: flash memory cards, USB flash drives, and smart cards.

Various Flash Memory Cards

Media Name	Storage Capacity	Use
CompactFlash	32 MB to 4 GB	Digital cameras, PDAs, smart phones, photo printers, music players, notebook computers, desktop computers
SmartMedia	32 MB to 128 MB	Digital cameras, PDAs, smart phones, photo printers, music players
Secure Digital	64 MB to 1 GB	Digital cameras, digital video cameras, PDAs, smart phones, photo printers, music players
xD Picture Card	64 MB to 512 MB	Digital cameras, photo printers
Memory Stick	256 MB to 2 GB	Digital cameras, digital video cameras, PDAs, photo printers, smart phones, notebook computers

FIGURE 4-63   A variety of flash memory cards.

FLASH MEMORY CARDS   A flash memory card is a type of solid-state media, which means it consists entirely of electronic components and contains no moving parts.

USB FLASH DRIVES   A USB flash drive, sometimes called a pen drive, is a flash memory storage device that plugs into a USB port on a computer or mobile device (Figure 4-64). Because these are Plug and Play devices, they are easy to use. These small and durable portable hard drives hold from 64 MB to 4 GB and higher and provide an inexpensively to moderately priced solution you can use to transfer files and programs between home and school computers. Experts predict that USB flash drives will eventually make 3.5-inch and Zip disks obsolete.

Figure 4-64 USB flash drives are popular with teachers and students and are small enough to be carried on a keychain.

SMART CARDS   A smart card, which is similar in size to a credit card or ATM card, stores data on a thin microprocessor embedded in the card. Smart cards contain a processor and have input, process, output, and storage capabilities. When you insert the smart card in a specialized card reader, the information on the smart card is read and, if necessary, updated.

Use of smart cards include storing medical records, vaccination data, and other healthcare and identification information; tracking information such as customer purchases or employee attendance, storing a prepaid amount of money; and authenticating users such as for Internet purchases.

Buyer's Guide

At the end of this chapter is a special feature that introduces you to purchasing, installing, maintaining, and troubleshooting a desktop or notebook computer.

A World Without Wires

A revolution in wireless technology and wireless devices is rapidly changing the way people work, play, and learn. To learn more about this wireless revolution and its potential impact on society and education, review the A World Without Wires special feature that follows Chapter 8.

Summary of Hardware for Educators

In this chapter, you learned about the various hardware components used in schools, businesses, and homes. First, you learned about some of the major components of the system unit. Next, you learned how to identify several types of input devices and how they operate. Third, you reviewed various output devices and learned how to identify and use them. Finally, you learned about storage devices. You should have a good understanding of the information processing cycle and how various hardware devices are used in education.

FAQ

Are some credit cards smart cards?

Yes. More than 60 million people around the world have a smart Visa card, which contains a microchip filled with their personal information. Credit card smart cards offer the consumer the convenience of using the card to make purchases in stores and online.

FAQ

Are mobile storage media also called smart cards?

No, a smart card, which is similar in size to a credit or ATM card, stores data on a thin microprocessor embedded in the card. Smart cards contain a processor and have input, process, output, and storage capabilities. Mobile storage media only have storage capabilities.

In Brief

INSTRUCTIONS: In Brief summarizes the concepts presented in this chapter. To listen to the audio version of this In Brief, visit scsite.com/tdc4. Click Chapter 4 at the top of the Web page and then click In Brief on the left sidebar.

1. The System Unit

The **system unit** is a boxlike case that houses the electronic components a computer uses to process data. The system unit is made of metal or plastic and protects the electronic components from damage. The major components in the system unit include the motherboard, the CPU and processor, memory, expansion slots and expansion cards, and ports and connectors.

2. Bits and Bytes

Most computers are **digital**, meaning that they understand only two discrete states: off and on. To store and process data, a computer must convert the data into a form it understands. Each off or on digital value is called a **bit** (short for **bi**nary dig**it**), and represents the smallest unit of data the computer can handle. When eight bits are grouped together as a unit, they are called a **byte**.

3. CPU and Processor

The **central processing unit** (**CPU**) interprets and carries out the basic instructions that operate a computer. The CPU manages most of a computer's operations. A chip known as the **processor** contains the CPU. A processor contains a number of components, including a control unit, an arithmetic/logic unit, and a system clock.

4. Memory

Computers use **memory** to store data and information temporarily. Several terms have evolved to define storage size as it relates to memory and storage devices. A **kilobyte** (**KB** or **K**) of memory is equal to 1000 bytes, a **megabyte** (**MB**) is equal to one million bytes, a **gigabyte** (**GB**) is equal to one billion bytes, and a **terabyte** is equal to one trillion bytes. Two common types of memory found in the system unit are RAM and ROM. **RAM** is an example of volatile memory and ROM is an example of nonvolatile memory. **Flash memory** is a type of nonvolatile memory that can be erased electronically and rewritten.

5. Types of Input

Input is entering data, programs, commands, and user responses into memory. **Data** is a collection of unorganized facts that, once processed, become information, such as words, numbers, pictures, and sounds. A **program** is a series of instructions that tells a computer how to perform tasks. A **command** is an instruction given to a computer program. **User response** is a user's input to a question from a program.

6. Keyboards

A **keyboard** is a group of switches resembling the keys on a typewriter that allows users to enter input. You enter data, commands, and other input into a computer by pressing keys on the keyboard. A keyboard contains keys that allow you to type letters, numbers, spaces, punctuation marks, and other symbols.

7. Pointing Devices

A **pointing device** is an input device that allows you to control the movement of the pointer on the screen and to make selections from the screen. Common pointing devices include the mouse, trackball, and joystick. A **mouse** is an input device that usually has one or two buttons and a ball mechanism on the bottom. A **trackball** is a stationary pointing device with a ball mechanism on its top. A **joystick** is a vertical lever mounted on a base.

8. Audio and Video Input

Audio input is the process of recording music, speech, or sound effects. Recorded sound is input via a device such as a microphone, tape player, or audio CD player. **Video input** is the process of entering

In Brief

a full-motion recording into a computer. To capture video, you plug a video camera, a VCR, or a similar device into a video capture card.

9. Types of Output

Output is data that has been processed into a useful form called information. Four common types of output are text, graphics, audio, and video. Text consists of characters that are used to create words, sentences, and paragraphs. Graphics are digital representations of nontext information, such as images and drawings. Audio is music, speech, or other sound that is stored and produced by the computer. Video consists of photographic images that are played back on a computer at speeds that provide the appearance of full motion in real time.

10. Output Devices

An **output device** is any computer component capable of conveying information to a user. Commonly used output devices include monitors, printers, data projectors, facsimile machines, multifunction devices, speakers, and headsets.

11. Monitors

A **monitor** is a display device that conveys text, graphics, and video information visually and is housed in a plastic or metal case. Monitors for personal computers are available in a variety of sizes, with the more common being 15, 17, 19, and 21 inches. Like a television set, the core of a monitor is a large glass tube called a **cathode ray tube** (CRT). The quality of a monitor depends largely on its resolution, dot pitch, and refresh rate.

12. Printers

A **printer** is an output device that produces text and graphical information on a physical medium such as paper or transparency film. Printers are grouped in two categories: impact and nonimpact. The more commonly used type of impact printer is a dot-matrix printer. A **nonimpact printer** forms marks on a piece of paper without actually striking the paper. Two common types of nonimpact printers are ink-jet and laser printers.

13. Storage

Storage refers to the media on which data, instructions, and information are kept, as well as the devices that record and retrieve these items. Storage is nonvolatile, which means that data and instructions in storage are retained even when power is removed from the computer. A **storage medium** is the physical material on which data, instructions, and information are kept. One commonly used storage medium is a **disk**, which is a round, flat piece of plastic or metal on which items such as data, instructions, and information can be encoded. A storage device is hardware used to read from and write to a storage medium.

14. Floppy and Hard Disks

A **floppy disk**, or **diskette**, is a portable, inexpensive storage medium that consists of a thin, circular, flexible plastic disk with a magnetic coating enclosed in a square-shaped plastic shell. Floppy disks are read/write magnetic storage media; that is, you can access (read) data from and place (write) data to a floppy disk any number of times. Hard disks provide for larger storage capacities and much faster access times than floppy disks and are the primary media for storing software programs and files. A **hard disk** usually consists of several inflexible, circular disks, called platters, on which items such as data, instructions, and information are stored electronically.

15. Optical and Other Storage Media

CDs and DVDs are a type of optical storage media that consists of a flat, round, portable, plastic disc with a protective metal coating. CDs and DVDs are available in a variety of formats. Popular mobile storage devices include Zip disks, flash memory cards, USB flash drives, and smart cards.

Key Terms

4

INSTRUCTIONS: Use the Key Terms to help focus your study of the terms used in this chapter. To further enhance your understanding of the Key Terms in this chapter, visit scsite.com/tdc4. Click Chapter 4 at the top of the Web page and then click Key Terms on the left sidebar. Read the definition for each term and then access current and additional information about the term from the Web.

adapter card [218]
address [215]
American Standard Code for Information Interchange (ASCII) [211]
analog [210]
arithmetic/logic unit (ALU) [215]
arithmetic operations [215]
audio [229]
audio input [227]
audio output [236]

backup [238]
binary [211]
bit [211]
byte [211]

cathode ray tube (CRT) [230]
central processing unit (CPU) [213]
chip [212]
clicking [223]
clock speed [215]
command [220]
compact disc read-only memory (CD-ROM) [242]
compact disc-recordable (CD-R) [243]
compact disc-rewritable (CD-RW) [243]
comparison operations [215]
connectors [218]
control unit [214]
cordless keyboard [222]
cordless mouse [223]

data [220]
data projector [234]
decoding [214]
digital [210]
digital camera [227]
digital pen [226]
digital video disc read-only memory (DVD-ROM) [243]
disk [237]
diskette [238]
display device [230]
dot pitch [232]
double-clicking [223]
dragging [223]
dual inline memory module (DIMM) [216]
DVD-ROM drive [244]

ENERGY STAR [232]
executing [214]
expansion board [218]
expansion card [218]
expansion slot [218]
external hard disk [240]

facsimile (fax) machine [235]
fetching [214]
FireWire port [219]
flash memory [217]
flash memory card [218]
flat panel monitor [231]
floppy disk [238]
floppy disk drive [238]
formatting [237]

gas plasma monitor [231]
gigabyte (GB) [216]
gigahertz (GHz) [215]
graphics [229]

hard copy [232]
hard disk [238]
high-definition television (HDTV) [231]

ink-jet printer [233]
input [220]
input device [221]
insertion point [222]

joystick [225]

keyboard [221]
keyword [220]
kilobyte (K or KB) [216]
kiosk [225]

landscape orientation [232]
large display monitors [231]
laser printer [234]
LCD monitor [231]
logical operations [215]

machine cycle [214]
magnetic disk [237]
megabyte (MB) [216]
megahertz (MHz) [215]
memory [215]
microprocessor [213]
monitor [230]
motherboard [212]
mouse [223]
mouse pad [223]
multifunction device (MFD) [235]

nonimpact printer [233]
nonvolatile memory [216]
numeric keypad [222]

optical disc [240]
optical mouse [223]
output [229]
output device [230]

PC Card [218]
photo printer [233]
Picture CD [243]
pixel [230]
platter [238]
Plug and Play [218]
pointing device [223]
pointing stick [224]
port [218]
portrait orientation [232]
printer [232]
processor [213]
program [220]

random access memory (RAM) [216]
read-only memory (ROM) [217]
recorded [242]
refresh rate [232]
resolution [232]

scanner [225]
secondary storage [237]
sector [237]
smart card [247]
soft copy [230]
speakers [236]
speech recognition [227]
storage [236]
storage device [237]
storage medium [237]
storing [214]
stylus [226]
synchronous dynamic RAM (SDRAM) [216]
system clock [215]
system unit [210]

terabyte (TB) [216]
text [229]
touchpad [224]
touch screen [225]
track [237]
trackball [224]

Universal Serial Bus (USB) port [219]
USB 2.0 port [219]
USB flash drive [247]
user response [220]

video [229]
video input [227]
voice recognition [227]
volatile memory [216]

wheel [225]
wireless keyboard [222]
wireless mouse [223]

Zip disk [238]

Checkpoint

INSTRUCTIONS: Use the Checkpoint exercises to check your knowledge level of the chapter. To complete the Checkpoint exercises interactively, visit scsite.com/tdc4. Click Chapter 4 at the top of the Web page and then click Checkpoint on the left sidebar.

1. Label the Figure

Instructions: Identify these areas or keys on a typical desktop computer keyboard.

1. _____
2. _____
3. _____
4. _____
5. _____
6. _____
7. _____
8. _____
9. _____
10. _____
11. _____
12. _____

2. Matching

Instructions: Match each term from the column on the left with the best description from the column on the right.

____ 1. byte
____ 2. scanner
____ 3. output
____ 4. smart card
____ 5. chip

a. small piece of semiconducting material usually no bigger than one-half-inch square
b. eight bits grouped together as a unit
c. data that has been processed into a useful form, called information
d. an input device that can capture an entire page of text electronically
e. stores data on a thin embedded processor

3. Short Answer

Instructions: Write a brief answer to each of the following questions.

1. What are the components of the system unit? What is the purpose of the central processing unit and system clock? _____
2. How are RAM and ROM similar? How are they different? What terminology is used to describe the storage capacity of RAM chips? _____
3. Which type of printer is used commonly in schools? What are some differences between ink-jet and laser printers? _____
4. What are two types of digital pens? What kind of digital pen does a Tablet PC use? What kind of digital pen does a PDA use? _____
5. What is an optical disc? What are the two general categories of optical discs? Which optical disc has the largest storage capacity? _____

Teaching Today

INSTRUCTIONS: Teaching Today provides an appreciation of the value that technology and the Web have for K-12 education. Each numbered segment contains one or more links that reinforce the information presented in the segment. To display this page from the Web, visit scsite.com/tdc4. Click Chapter 4 at the top of the Web page and then click Teaching Today on the left sidebar.

1. Graphing Calculators

Teachers are always looking for new technology tools to integrate in their classrooms. Math teachers have known for years that graphing calculators are excellent tools for teaching math. Students can use them not only to solve math problems, but also to see the solutions more graphically. Providing graphing calculators also can help students solve problems relating to other areas such as geometry, algebra, and art. Use the Internet to research other ways to integrate graphing calculators into other non-math teaching areas. Write a list of ideas that you discover in your research.

2. Portable Storage Media

Because of the need to move files from location to location, various portable storage media are used in schools and universities today. Older choices included 3.5-inch disks and Zip disks; some schools still are using this type of media. However, these are not the best storage media in all situations because they cannot hold enough information and they do not have the capacity to store large graphic and video files. If your students create digital media or multimedia projects, projects that contain a large number of graphics, or their own music scores, they will need portable storage devices that can provide sufficient storage space, such as flash media options. Some schools feel that disks pose a security risk because of viruses; when this is the case, these school do not allow students to use disks or other removable storage media and only let students save their work to the network. Do portable storage media have a role in the classroom? What are the advantages of using them? What other portable storage media could you and your students use in your classroom?

3. Podcasting

Podcasting is a method of publishing sound and small picture or video files to the Internet. Podcasting is also a method used to time-shift audio broadcasts to individual listeners who want to broadcast radio shows on their own schedule. The original idea came from the desire to find a way to create audio versions of blogs. The producer of the files simply publishes files to a Web site that allows users to subscribe to a download service or to use access software to receive new files as they are created. More recently, the concept has extended into the education realm. One major university feels so strongly abut the potential of podcasting that school officials have begun distributing iPods to all incoming freshmen. Professors will be using iPods to communicate with students, share their class notes, PowerPoint slides, and much more. Can you think of advantages and disadvantages of using iPods or similar devices in the classroom? What are the implications of podcasting on K-12 education and this digital generation?

4. Ink-Jet Printers

Last year, you received a color ink-jet printer — a Hewlett-Packard DeskJet — for your classroom. Until recently, the printer worked flawlessly. Lately, however, when you print a document, the ink is smearing and the print quality is poor. No one at your school can provide technical assistance or support. Where else might you find technical support? Which type of support would you prefer? Visit Hewlett-Packard's Web site and use its Web-based technical support to determine how to fix the printer problem described previously. How does Web-based support differ from face-to-face support or support via telephone? What are some advantages and disadvantages of Web-based support?

Education Issues

4

INSTRUCTIONS: Education Issues provides several scenarios that allow you to explore controversial and current issues in education. Each numbered segment contains one or more links that reinforce the information presented in the segment. To display this page from the Web, visit scsite.com/tdc4. Click Chapter 4 at the top of the Web page and then click Education Issues on the left sidebar.

1. Reading Comprehension

Over the last five years, reading scores have continued to drop in one of your local school districts. Knowing that reading is one of the more crucial life skills that all students must have to be successful, the district competed for and received a $1.3 million grant to help students become better readers. The grant focuses on integrating handheld devices, such as PDAs, in the classroom as a way to fuel students' enthusiasm for reading, which could improve reading literacy throughout the district. What do you think? Can PDAs be used to help teach students to be better readers? Should there be a mix? Are lesson plans available that support using PDAs? Defend your opinion.

2. Digital Age Learners

Research suggests that what many of us refer to as Attention Deficit Disorder (ADD) is really nothing more than a skill developed by some children that have been raised in the digital age. As a result, these research findings are revealing that the learning environment these students are placed in does not match their cognitive or digital learning style, which then affects motivation and achievement. Have some of these students rewired their brains to multitask? Can they can read e-mails, send instant messages and text messages over handheld devices, speak to one another in short sentences, and continue to watch movies and participate in multiple conversations, all while finishing their homework? The question is: when we try to place these students in the traditional learning environment, are we working against their cognitive or digital learning style? What are your thoughts about this theory for this new generation of digital kids? Do you see the differences in their learning? What suggestions to you have for reaching them? Do you think technology can add to the instructional possibilities? How? Give some suggestions and defend your answer.

3. Digital Data Lasts Forever

Up to 75 % of today's data never existed on paper. Historical data from thousands of years ago still exists because it was written down. Although written documents can be read hundreds of years after they were created, rapid changes in computer technology can make digital records almost inaccessible in just one decade. For most computer users, hardware changes have made data stored on once-popular 5.25-inch floppy disk or on the 8-inch floppy disk used in the early 1970s, unavailable today. Loss of data on aging CDs and DVDs threatens the stored photo and video memories. What about school data and software? A major state university recently admitted that almost 3000 students and school files could not be accessed due to lost or outdated software. Is the potential unavailability of digital data a problem? Why or why not? What can be done to keep today's digital information available for future generations?

4. Obsolete Equipment

Many businesses, government agencies, and parents donate obsolete technology to schools. Although fully operational, this equipment often is not capable of running multimedia software due to slow processors, lack of memory, lack of hard disk space, and the lack of a CD-ROM or DVD-ROM drive. Some teachers feel that any kind of technology, like older computers, digital cameras, video cameras, and so on is better than no technology. Do you agree or disagree? Does a use exist for these types of technologies in the classroom or in a school lab? How could you use them in your classroom? Should schools continue to accept older computers and other devices? Why or why not?

Integration Corner

4

INSTRUCTIONS: Integration Corner provides extensive ideas and resources for integrating technology into your classroom-specific curriculum. To display this page from the Web and its links to approximately 100 educational Web sites, visit scsite.com/tdc4. Click Chapter 4 at the top of the Web page and then click Integration Corner on the left sidebar.

Integration Corner is designed for teachers and other educators who are looking for innovative ways to integrate technology into their content-specific curriculum. Integration Corner not only provides great Web sites with current information but also shows what other educators are doing in the field of educational technology. Integration Corner is designed for all educators regardless of their interests. Expand your resources by reviewing information and Web sites outside of your teaching area because many great integration ideas in one area can be modified easily for use in other curricular areas.

Teachers and administrators will find other colleagues in their areas with whom to connect and share the successes and hurdles of integrating technology in a classroom or an entire school system. Consider Integration Corner your one stop for integration ideas and resources. Links to educational Web sites are organized in the following 12 Corners, and different Web resources are available for each chapter. Figure 4-65 shows examples of the Web resources provided in the Chapter 4 Secondary Corner.

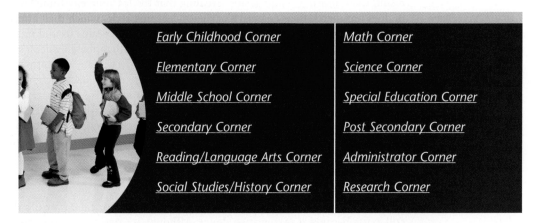

Early Childhood Corner

Elementary Corner

Middle School Corner

Secondary Corner

Reading/Language Arts Corner

Social Studies/History Corner

Math Corner

Science Corner

Special Education Corner

Post Secondary Corner

Administrator Corner

Research Corner

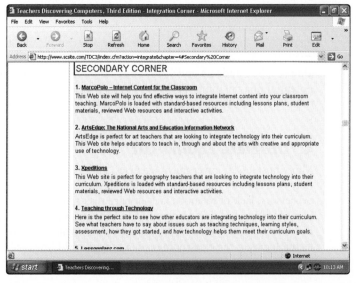

Figure 4-65 Examples of the Web resources provided in the Chapter 4 Secondary Corner.

Software Corner

INSTRUCTIONS: Software Corner provides information on popular software programs. Each numbered segment discusses specific software programs and contains a link to additional information about these programs. To display this page from the Web, visit scsite.com/tdc4. Click Chapter 4 at the top of the Web page and then click Software Corner on the left sidebar.

1. The Graph Club

The Graph Club, by Tom Snyder Productions, is an easy-to-use graphing tool every elementary classroom should have! You can create activities in which your students conduct research and graph their findings. The Graph Club allows students to construct and interpret pie, line, picture, and bar graphs. Students learn to use graphs to analyze data and solve problems, as well as write about graphs they create. Graphs can be printed by the page or even made in poster size for classroom use. The Graph Club is an innovative way to help your students understand and interpret graphs and is an excellent resource for standardized test preparation.

2. Millie's Math House

Millie's Math House is an excellent program for prekindergarten through second grade students. Seven activities provide students the opportunity to learn shapes, sizes, patterns, sequencing, and numbers. Students learn to count and practice addition and subtraction while making silly looking bugs and jelly bean cookies or even building mouse houses! This program is interactive and provides feedback, making Millie's Math House a great way to keep students interested while they learn.

3. Make-A-Story

Your students can learn to interact and write stories about Timmy & His Friends with Make-A-Story. Students choose different characters, settings, and actions, and then they can hear the stories read aloud in English or a foreign language. Students can work through 18 exciting activities to gain an appreciation of different cultures while comparing those cultures through number and word activities, stories, songs, games, and crafts. This is excellent software for developing cross-curricular activities for language arts, math, social studies, and creativity.

4. Grolier Multimedia Encyclopedia

Teachers and students need to work successfully on research reports and multimedia projects. Grolier Multimedia Encyclopedia can assist your students in creating awesome multimedia presentations with 15,500 images, full audio features, and more than 150 videos and panoramas of amazing sites. Research reports will be a snap for students with more than 60,000 articles and the Millennium feature, which chronicles important world events for the last 1000 years as well as Internet links. Grolier Multimedia Encyclopedia is an excellent resource for any classroom.

5. Geometer's Sketchpad

With Geometer's Sketchpad, by Key Curriculum Press, your students can explore and analyze geometric figures and concepts they are learning in the classroom. While preserving the geometric relationships of the shapes, students can manipulate the geometric figures created in Geometer's Sketchpad. Use Geometer's Sketchpad for presentations or allow your students to work alone or in groups. This software is extremely versatile and can be used from grades 5 through college. The software comes with an instructional video and documentation. The documentation includes tutorials and sample classroom activities. Extensive Internet resources also are available.

Digital Media Corner

INSTRUCTIONS: Today's K-12 digital students need their learning to be meaningful and relevant to their lives. Digital Media Corner provides videos, ideas, and examples of how you can use digital media to enhance your teaching and your students' learning. To access the videos and links to additional information, visit scsite.com/tdc4. Click Chapter 4 at the top of the Web page and then click Digital Media on the left sidebar.

1. At the Movies — Buying the Right Digital Camera

A single digital camera that is perfect for every user simply does not exist. When making the decision about which model of digital camera to purchase, you must consider how and where you will use the camera and what results you will expect. What options are important to consider? To learn more about buying the right digital camera, click the G4TechTV video link. Locate your video and click the corresponding High-Speed or Dial-up link, depending on your Internet connection.

2. At the Movies — Get the Best of Both Worlds with a Convertible Tablet PC

Taking classroom notes with pen and paper may be a thing of the past if the Tablet PC can offer you some options that are not available on a regular notebook or desktop computer. What are some of the drawbacks to using a Tablet PC? What are some of the benefits? To learn more about Tablet PCs, click the G4TechTV video link. Locate your video and click the corresponding High-Speed or Dial-up link, depending on your Internet connection.

3. At the Movies — USB Basics

A Universal Serial Bus (USB) is a peripheral bus standard developed by Intel that allows you to connect external equipment such as digital cameras, printers, and MP3 players. The USB standard enables communication between external plug-ins and your computer so that they can share information and power. How can you tell if your USB port is working? What are some ways you can troubleshoot your USB ports? To learn more about USB Basics, click the G4TechTV video link. Locate your video and click the corresponding High-Speed or Dial-up link, depending on your Internet connection.

4. At the Movies — Repair Your CD Scratches

Just because your favorite CD has a few scratches is no reason to discard it. A few options are available to help you keep those scratched CDs playing smoothly longer. How does resurfacing work to restore your scratched CD? What common household product can be used to repair a CD? To learn how to repair your CD scratches, click the G4TechTV video link. Locate your video and click the corresponding High-Speed or Dial-up link, depending on your Internet connection.

5. Reaching All Students

Look around your classroom, school, or mall, and you will see that most of today's digital kids have cell phones. Newer cell phones have photo, music, and video taking capabilities that could serve as a good digital technology alternative in the classroom by providing access to all students. This form of digital technology is a super way for all students to be able use their own cell phones to take photos for their digital media presentation. Third-party software vendors like Kodak and others provide a means to transfer the photos from the camera to the Web. These services also allow classroom teachers and students a location to store photo albums online for a small fee.

Assistive Technologies Corner

INSTRUCTIONS: Assistive Technologies Corner provides information on current hardware, software, and peripherals that will assist you in delivering instruction to students with physical, cognitive, or sensory challenges. To access extensive additional information, visit scsite.com/tdc4. Click Chapter 4 at the top of the Web page and then click Assistive Technologies on the left sidebar.

1. Why Have Specialized Hardware in the Classroom?

The growing presence of computers in everyone's lives has generated an awareness of the need to address computing requirements for those with physical limitations. Today, the Americans with Disabilities Act (ADA) requires that all schools ensure that students with all types of special needs are not excluded from participation in, or denied access to, educational programs or activities. In addition to speech recognition, which is ideal for students who are visually impaired or who have physical or cognitive limitations, other input devices are available.

2. Are There Alternatives to Keyboards?

Students with limited hand mobility who want to use a keyboard have several options. One option is to use a keyguard. A keyguard, when placed over the keyboard, prevents the student from inadvertently pressing keys and provides a guide so the student strikes only one key at a time. Another option is a screen-displayed keyboard, in which a graphic of a standard keyboard is displayed on the student's screen. Students then use a pointing device to press the keys on the screen-displayed keyboard.

Another type of input device is a touch window, or a touch screen. This is a device that attaches to the front of a monitor that allows students to select items by touching instead of using a keyboard. Yet another alternative input device is the Intellikeys keyboard. This powerful tool has a flexible design permitting teachers to customize the keyboard with special overlays or templates that fit over the keyboard. Using Intellikeys, students with mobility issues or with cognitive disabilities can participate independently in classroom learning activities.

3. What Other Input Devices Can Benefit Students With Special Needs?

A variety of input devices are available for students with motor disabilities. Joysticks and small trackballs that can be controlled with a thumb or one finger can be attached to a table, mounted to a wheelchair, or held in a student's hand. Students with limited hand mobility can use a head-mounted pointer to control the pointer or insertion point. A switch is used much as a mouse button is used. Switches are made in a vast array of colors, shapes, and sizes. They can be operated by a tap, a kick, a swipe, or a puff, and they integrate well with other devices such as Intellikeys.

Many of these input devices now are connected to computers by USB. The computer recognizes them instantly, which means setup time is minimal. Learning how to integrate software programs and hardware devices into your curriculum that allow students with special needs to use computers as tools for learning is covered in Chapters 6 and 7.

Follow the instructions at the top of this page to display additional information and this chapter's links on assistive technologies.

In the Lab

INSTRUCTIONS: In the Lab provides database exercises that are divided into two areas, productivity and integration. To access the links to tutorials, productivity ideas, integration examples and ideas, and more, visit scsite.com/tdc4. Click Chapter 4 at the top of the Web page and then click In the Lab on the left sidebar.

PRODUCTIVITY IN THE CLASSROOM

Introduction: Database software allows you to create, store, sort, and retrieve data. Databases enable computer users to manipulate large amounts of data to produce different results. A classic example of a database is your local telephone directory.

Many database programs have wizards that walk you through creating a database, often called a database table. When you first create a database, it may look very similar to a spreadsheet in layout and design. This often is referred to as Datasheet view or List view. In this view, you can see a number of the records in the database at one time. The rows in the database are called records. Records can contain information about a person, product, or event. The columns in the database are called fields. Fields contain a specific piece of information within a record. Most database applications have a Design view, also called Form view, where information is added one record at a time and only one record is displayed at a time. Be sure to use the Help feature of your database software to learn more about the different views and features.

To learn new skills, or to improve your current skills, click the following links: Microsoft Access, FileMaker Pro, Microsoft Works, and AppleWorks.

1. Creating and Formatting a Student Information Database

Problem: At the beginning of every school year, students are asked to fill out information cards. To save time and to begin teaching the students about databases, create a database that contains the fields shown in Figure 4-66. Then have the students enter their information into the database, keeping it updated throughout the year. This allows you always to have the most current information available.

Open your database software and create the Student Information Database. Use the field names shown in Figure 4-66. (*Hint:* use Help to better understand the steps.)

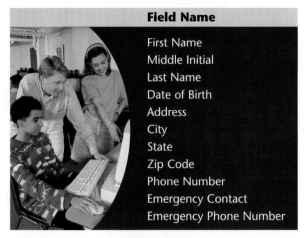

Field Name

First Name
Middle Initial
Last Name
Date of Birth
Address
City
State
Zip Code
Phone Number
Emergency Contact
Emergency Phone Number

Figure 4-66

Instructions: Perform the following tasks.

1. Create the database using the field names listed in Figure 4-66.
2. Determine the proper field widths and types so the information displays properly.
3. Enter student information to create 10 records. Enter your name for the first record.
4. Save the database to the location of your choice using an appropriate filename.
5. Print the database as a table or list.
6. Create a cover sheet using word processing software that includes your name, the current date, and the course title.
7. Follow the directions from your instructor for handing in this assignment.

In the Lab

4

2. Creating and Formatting a Hardware Inventory Database

Problem: At the end of every school year, you must turn in your classroom technology inventory. Creating the inventory by hand is time-consuming and tedious. Entering the information into a database will allow you to update the information quickly and generate the necessary reports. Create a database that contains information regarding the technology in your classroom. The contents of the database are shown in Figure 4-67. (*Hint*: use Help to understand the steps better.)

Technology Inventory Information

Manufacturer	Hardware	Serial Number	Year	Used By
Compaq	15" Monitor	023BA64WF389	2004	Students
Compaq	System Unit	CM29M-KY9KJ-TPBXJ-GRCCC-WVQRD	2005	Students
Compaq	17" Monitor	036ZV21LP912	2005	Students
Compaq	System Unit	CM21X-NY6NJ-PTAYK-BNUIU-MCWRD	2005	Students
Sony	15" Flat Screen Monitor	977AX56VR311	2006	Students
Dell	System Unit	00JKXW-KR2RR-JJ8870	2004	Students
Dell	Notebook Computer	6D3CJC58380WB	2006	Teacher
Compaq	Presario Notebook Computer	6D3CJC58380WB	2005	Students
Apple	iBook	CJ54404K39X	2006	Students
Apple	iMac	XA6352RG7Y7	2003	Students
Hewlett-Packard	Printer	SBG94AGWQK	2003	Teacher
Compaq	Printer	1M05DG2VXBP	2005	Students
Apple	Printer	CC552AAQ69O	2006	Students
Visioneer	Scanner	052C00900D1	2005	Students
Kodak	Digital Camera	144527D3	2006	Students

Figure 4-67

Instructions: Perform the following tasks.

1. Create the database using the five fields in Figure 4-67. Format the fields so the information is displayed properly.
2. Enter the data for the first 15 records from Figure 4-67 into the database.
3. Personalize the database by adding three additional records — the manufacturer, type of hardware, serial number (create a number if necessary), year purchased, and who uses the hardware item.
4. Save the database to the location of your choice using an appropriate filename.
5. Print the database as a table or list.
6. Create a cover sheet using word processing software that includes your name, the current date, and the course title.
7. Follow the directions from your instructor for handing in this assignment.

In the Lab

INTEGRATION IN THE CLASSROOM

1. Your science class is studying the <u>solar system</u>. The class is divided into groups and each group will gather the facts about their assigned planet. You have the students create a class database with the following fields: planet name, distance from the sun, number of moons, average temperature in Fahrenheit, length of year, size, atmosphere, and gravity at the surface. The students enter their findings and then compare and contrast the planets based on the different characteristics. Create a sample database selecting one planet and enter the appropriate information to demonstrate the project for the students. Include a header with your name and a footer with the current date.

2. Your third grade class is taking a field trip to the zoo. You want the students to have the opportunity to learn about animals in a creative way. Students will gather information about their <u>animals</u> from books, the Internet, and multimedia CD-ROMs. With the help of a parent volunteer, the students will enter their information into a simple database. You have selected the following fields for the database: animal name, country or origin, habitat, food, weight/size, and number of babies. Create a sample database selecting at least two zoo animals and enter the appropriate information to demonstrate the project for the students. Include a header with your name and a footer with the current date.

3. In math class, you have students work in groups to invest $5000 in a six-month certificate of deposit (CD). Students will use the Internet to gather information from local <u>banks and credit unions</u> and make a list of the current interest rates, minimum investment amounts, and total amounts earned in six months. The students then will create a database showing the name of the financial institution, its address and telephone number, the interest rate, the total value of the CD in six months, and the amount of interest earned. Create a sample database to demonstrate the project for the students. Include a header with your name and a footer with the current date.

Learn It Online

INSTRUCTIONS: Use the Learn It Online exercises to reinforce your understanding of the chapter concepts and increase your computer, information, and integration literacy. To access dozens of interactive student labs, practice tests, learning games, and more, visit scsite.com/tdc4. Click Chapter 4 at the top of the Web page and then click Learn It Online on the left sidebar.

1. Student Edition Labs — Binary Numbers, Input Devices, Maintaining a Hard Drive, and Understanding a Motherboard

For the labs to work properly, you must have your screen resolution set to 1024 × 768 or higher. For a short tutorial on how to change your screen resolution, click here. You also will need Flash 7.0 or higher. To view these interactive labs, click the Student Edition Labs link. When the Student Edition Labs menu appears, click the desired or the assigned lab to begin. A new browser window opens. Follow the on-screen instructions to complete the lab. When finished, click the Exit button. If required, submit your results to your instructor.

2. Purchasing and Installing Memory in a Computer

One of the less expensive and more effective ways to speed up a computer, that is make it capable of processing more programs at the same time and enable it to more effectively handle graphics, gaming, and other high-level programs, is to increase the amount of memory. Click the Purchasing and Installing Memory link to learn how to purchase and install new memory in your computer. Print just the first page of this Web page. On the back of the printout, write a brief summary explaining how to purchase and install memory in a computer. If required, submit your results to your instructor.

3. Expanding Your Understanding

Every computer today contains a sound card and associated hardware and software that allow you to play and record sound. Click the Expanding Your Understanding link to learn how to adjust the sound on your computer.

4. Practice Test

Click the Practice Test link. Answer each question. When completed, enter your name and click the Grade Test button to submit the quiz for grading. Make a note of any missed questions. If required, submit your score to your instructor.

5. Who Wants to Be a Computer Genius?

Click the Computer Genius link to find out if you are a computer genius. Directions about how to play the game will be displayed. When you are ready to play, click the Play button. If required, submit your score to your instructor.

6. Wheel of Terms

Click the Wheel of Terms link to reinforce important terms you learned in this chapter by playing the Shelly Cashman Series version of this popular game. Directions about how to play the game will be displayed. When you are ready to play, click the Play button. If required, submit your score to your instructor.

7. Crossword Puzzle Challenge

Click the Crossword Puzzle link. Complete the puzzle to reinforce skills you learned in this chapter. Directions about how to play the game will be displayed. When you are ready to play, click the Play button. If required, submit the completed puzzle to your instructor.

Buyer's Guide

How to Purchase a Personal Computer

At some point, perhaps while you are taking this course, you may decide to buy a personal computer or upgrade from your current computer. The decision is an important one and will require an investment of both time and money. Like many buyers, you may have little computer experience and find yourself unsure of how to proceed. You can get started by talking to your friends, coworkers, and instructors about their computers. What type of computers did they buy? Why? For what purposes do they use their computers? You also should answer the following four questions to help narrow your choices to a specific computer type, before reading this Buyer's Guide.

(a) desktop computer

(b) mobile computer (notebook computer or Tablet PC)

(c) personal mobile device (smart phone or PDA)

Should I buy a desktop or mobile computer or personal mobile device?

For what purposes will I use the computer?

Should I buy a Mac or PC?

Should the computer I buy be compatible with the computers at school or work?

FIGURE 1

1 **Do you want a desktop computer, mobile computer, or personal mobile device?** A desktop computer (Figure 1a) is designed as a stationary device that sits on or below a desk or table in a location such as a home, office, or dormitory room. A desktop computer must be plugged into an electrical outlet to operate. A mobile computer, such as a notebook computer or Tablet PC (Figure 1b), is smaller than a desktop computer, more portable, and has a battery that allows you to operate it for a period without an electrical outlet. A personal mobile device (Figure 1c) runs on a battery for a longer period of time than a notebook computer or Tablet PC and can fit in your pocket.

Desktop computers are a good option if you work mostly in one place and have plenty of space in your work area. Desktop computers generally give you more performance for your money.

Increasingly, more desktop computer users are buying mobile computers to take advantage of their portability to work in the library, at school, while traveling, and at home. The past disadvantages of mobile computers, such as lower processor speeds, poor-quality monitors, weight, short battery life, and significantly higher prices, have all but disappeared when compared with desktop computers.

If you are thinking of using a mobile computer to take notes in class or in business meetings, consider a Tablet PC with handwriting and drawing capabilities. Typically, note-taking involves writing text notes and drawing charts, schematics, and other illustrations. By allowing you to write and draw directly on the screen with a digital pen, a Tablet PC eliminates the distracting sound of the notebook keyboard tapping and allows you to capture drawings. Some notebook computers can convert to Tablet PCs.

A personal mobile device, such as a smart phone or a PDA, is ideal if you require a pocket-sized computing device as you move from place to place. Personal mobile devices provide personal organizer functions, such as a calendar, appointment book, address book, and many other applications. The small size of the processor, screen, and keyboard, however, limit a personal mobile device's capabilities when compared with a desktop or notebook computer or a Tablet PC. For this reason, most people who purchase personal mobile devices also have a desktop or notebook computer to handle heavy-duty applications.

Drawbacks of mobile computers and personal mobile devices are that they tend to have a shorter useful lifetime than desktop computers and lack the high-end capabilities. Their portability makes them susceptible to vibrations, heat or cold, and accidental drops, which can cause components such as hard disks or display devices to fail. Also, because of their size and portability, they are easy to lose and are the prime targets of thieves.

2 **For what purposes will you use the computer?** Having a general idea of the purposes for which you want to use your computer will help you decide on the type of computer to buy. At this point in your research, it is not necessary to know the exact application software titles or version numbers you might want to use. Knowing that you plan to use the computer primarily to create word processing, spreadsheet, database, and presentation documents, however, will point you in the direction of a desktop or notebook computer. If you want the portability of a smart phone or PDA, but you need more computing power, a Tablet PC may be the best alternative. You also must consider that some application software runs only on a Mac, whereas others run only on a PC with the Windows operating system. Still other software may run only on a PC running the UNIX or Linux operating system.

3 **Should the computer be compatible with the computers at school or work?** If you plan to bring work home, telecommute, or take distance education courses, you should purchase a computer that is compatible with those at school or work.

Compatibility is primarily a software issue. If your computer runs the same operating system version, such as Microsoft Windows XP, and the same application software, such as Microsoft Office, your computer will be able to read documents created at school or work and vice versa. Incompatible hardware can become an issue if you plan to connect directly to a school or office network using a cable or wireless technology. You usually can obtain the minimum system requirements from the Information Technology Department at your school or workplace.

4 **Should the computer be a Mac or PC?** If you ask a friend, coworker, or instructor, which is better — a Mac or a PC — you may be surprised by the strong opinion expressed in the response. No other topic in the computer industry causes more heated debate. The Mac has strengths, especially in the areas of graphics, movies, photos, and music. The PC, however, has become the industry standard with 95 percent of the market share. Figure 2 compares features of the Mac and PC in several different areas. Overall, the Mac and PC have more similarities than differences, and you should consider cost, compatibility, and other factors when choosing whether to purchase a Mac or a PC.

Area	Comparison
Cost and availability	A Mac is priced slightly higher than a PC. Mac peripherals also are more expensive. The PC offers more available models from a wide range of vendors. You can custom build, upgrade, and expand a PC for less money than a Mac.
Exterior design	The Mac has a more distinct and stylish appearance than most PCs.
Free software	Although free software for the Mac is available on the Internet, significantly more free software applications are available for the PC.
Market share	The PC dominates the personal computer market. Although the Mac sells well in education, publishing, Web design, graphics, and music, the PC is the overwhelming favorite of businesses.
Operating system	Users claim that Mac OS X provides a better all-around user experience than Microsoft Windows XP. Both the Mac and PC support other operating systems, such as Linux and UNIX.
Program control	Both have simple and intuitive graphical user interfaces. The Mac relies more on the mouse and less on keyboard shortcuts than the PC. The mouse on the Mac has one button, whereas the mouse on a PC has a minimum of two buttons.
Software availability	The basic application software most users require, such as Microsoft Office, is available for both the Mac and PC. More specialized software, however, often is available only for PCs. Many programs are released for PCs long before they are released for Macs.
Speed	The Mac provides faster processors than the PC.
Viruses	Dramatically fewer viruses attack Macs. Mac viruses also generally are less infectious than PC viruses.

FIGURE 2 Comparison of Mac and PC features.

After evaluating the answers to these four questions, you should have a general idea of how you plan to use your computer and the type of computer you want to buy. After you have decided on the type of computer you want, you can follow the guidelines presented in this Buyer's Guide to help you purchase a specific computer, along with software, peripherals, and other accessories.

Many of the desktop computer guidelines presented also apply to the purchase of a notebook computer, Tablet PC, and personal mobile device. Later in this Buyer's Guide, sections on purchasing a notebook computer or Tablet PC address additional considerations specific to those computer types.

This Buyer's Guide contains recommendations for purchasing a desktop computer, mobile computer, and a personal mobile device (PDA).

How to Purchase a Desktop Computer

After you have decided that a desktop computer is most suited to your computing needs, the next step is to determine specific software, hardware, peripheral devices, and services to purchase, as well as where to buy the computer.

1 **Determine the specific software you want to use on your computer.** Before deciding to purchase software, be sure it contains the features necessary for the tasks you want to perform. Rely on the computer users in whom you have confidence to help you decide on the software to use. The minimum requirements of the software you select may determine the operating system (Microsoft Windows XP, Linux, UNIX, Mac OS X) you need. If you have decided to use a particular operating system that does not support software you want to use, you may be able to purchase similar software from other manufacturers.

Many Web sites and trade magazines, such as those listed in Figure 3, provide reviews of software products. These Web sites frequently have articles that rate computers and software on cost, performance, and support.

Your hardware requirements depend on the minimum requirements of the software you will run on your computer. Some software requires more memory and disk space than others, as well as additional input, output, and storage devices. For example, suppose you want to run software that can copy the content of one CD or DVD directly to another CD or DVD, without first copying the data to your hard disk. To support that, you should consider a desktop computer or a high-end notebook computer because the computer will need two CD or DVD drives: one that reads from a CD or DVD, and one that reads from and writes to a CD or DVD. If you plan to run software

Type of Computer	Web Site	Web Address
PC	CNET Shopper	shopper.cnet.com
	PC World Magazine	pcworld.com
	BYTE Magazine	byte.com
	PC Magazine	zdnet.com/reviews
	Yahoo! Computers	computers.yahoo.com
	MSN Shopping	eshop.msn.com
	Dave's Guide to Buying a Home Computer	css.msu.edu/PC-Guide
Mac	Macworld Magazine	macworld.com
	Apple	apple.com
	Switch to Mac Campaign	apple.com/switch

For an updated list and Web links, click the special feature, Buyer's Guide, at the textbook Web site (scsite.com/tdc4).

FIGURE 3 Hardware and software reviews.

that allows your computer to work as an entertainment system, you will need a CD or DVD drive, quality speakers, and an upgraded sound card.

2 **Look for bundled software.** When you purchase a computer, it may come bundled with software. Some sellers even let you choose which software you want. Remember, however, that bundled software has value only if you would have purchased the software even if it had not come with the computer. At the very least, you probably will want word processing software and a browser to access the Internet. If you need additional applications, such as a spreadsheet, a database, or presentation graphics, consider purchasing Microsoft Works, Microsoft Office, OpenOffice.org, or Sun StarOffice, which include several programs at a reduced price.

3 **Avoid buying the least powerful computer available.** After you know the application software you want to use, you then can consider the following important criteria about the computer's components: (1) processor speed, (2) size and types of memory (RAM) and storage, (3) types of input/output devices, (4) types of ports and adapter cards, and (5) types of communications devices. The information in Figures 4 and 5 can help you determine which system components are best for you. Figure 4 outlines considerations for specific hardware components. Figure 5 (on page 267) provides a sample worksheet that lists PC recommendations for various categories of users: Home User, Small Office/Home Office User, and Mobile User. In the worksheet, the Home User category is divided into two groups: Application Home User and Game Home User. The Mobile User recommendations list criteria for a notebook computer, but do not include the PDA or Tablet PC options.

Computer technology changes rapidly, meaning a computer that seems powerful enough today may not serve your computing needs in a few years. In fact, studies show that many users regret not buying a more powerful computer. To avoid this, plan to buy a computer that will last you for a few years. You can help delay obsolescence by purchasing the fastest processor, the most memory, and the largest hard disk you can afford. If you must buy a less powerful computer, be sure you can upgrade it with additional memory, components, and peripheral devices as your computer requirements grow.

CD/DVD Drives: Most computers come with a 32X to 48X speed CD-ROM drive that can read CDs. If you plan to write music, audio files, and documents to a CD, you should consider upgrading to a CD-RW. An even better alternative is to upgrade to a DVD+RW combination drive. It allows you to read DVDs and CDs and to write data to (burn) a DVD or CD. A DVD has a capacity of at least 4.7 GB versus the 650 MB capacity of a CD.

Card Reader/Writer: A card reader/writer is useful for transferring data directly to and from a removable flash memory card, such as the ones used in your camera or music player. Make sure the card reader/writer can read from and write to the flash memory cards that you use.

Digital Camera: Consider an inexpensive point-and-shoot digital camera. They are small enough to carry around, usually operate automatically in terms of lighting and focus, and contain storage cards for storing photographs. A 2- to 4-megapixel camera with an 8-MB or 16-MB storage card is fine for creating images for use on the Web or to send via e-mail.

Digital Video Capture Device: A digital video capture device allows you to connect your computer to a camcorder or VCR and record, edit, manage, and then write video back on a VCR tape, a CD, or a DVD. The digital video capture device can be an external device or an adapter card. To create quality video (true 30 frames per second, full-sized TV), the digital video capture device should have a USB 2.0 or FireWire port. You will find that a standard USB port is too slow to maintain video quality. You also will need sufficient storage: an hour of data on a VCR tape takes up about 5 GB of disk storage.

Floppy Disk Drive: If you plan to use a floppy disk drive, make sure the computer you purchase has a standard 3.5-inch, 1.44 MB floppy disk drive. A floppy disk drive is useful for backing up and transferring files.

Hard Disk: It is recommended that you buy a computer with 40 to 60 GB if your primary interests are browsing the Web and using e-mail and Office suite-type applications; 60 to 80 GB if you also want to edit digital photographs; 80 to 100 GB if you plan to edit digital video or manipulate large audio files even occasionally; and 100 to 160 GB if you will edit digital video, movies, or photography often; store audio files and music; or consider yourself to be a power user.

Joystick/Wheel: If you use your computer to play games, you will want to purchase a joystick or a wheel. These devices, especially the more expensive ones, provide for realistic game play with force feedback, programmable buttons, and specialized levers and wheels.

Keyboard: The keyboard is one of the more important devices used to communicate with the computer. For this reason, make sure the keyboard you purchase has 101 to 105 keys, is comfortable and easy to use, and has a USB connection. A wireless keyboard should be considered.

Microphone: If you plan to record audio or use speech recognition to enter text and commands, purchase a close-talk headset with gain adjustment support.

Modem: Most computers come with a modem so that you can use your telephone line to dial out and access the Internet. Some modems also have fax capabilities. Your modem should be rated at 56 Kbps.

Monitor: The monitor is where you will view documents, read e-mail messages, and view pictures. A minimum of a 17-inch screen is recommended, but if you are planning to use your computer for graphic design or game playing, you may want to purchase a 19-inch or 21-inch monitor. The LCD flat panel monitor should be considered, especially if space is an issue.

FIGURE 4 Hardware guidelines.

(continued on next page)

Mouse: As you work with your computer, you use the mouse constantly. For this reason, spend a few extra dollars, if necessary, and purchase a mouse with an optical sensor and USB connection. The optical sensor replaces the need for a mouse ball, which means you do not need a mouse pad. For a PC, make sure your mouse has a wheel, which acts as a third button in addition to the top two buttons on the left and right. An ergonomic design is also important because your hand is on the mouse most of the time when you are using your computer. A wireless mouse should be considered to eliminate the cord and allow you to work at short distances from your computer.

Network Card: If you plan to connect to a network or use broadband (cable or DSL) to connect to the Internet, you will need to purchase a network card. Broadband connections require a 10/100 PCI Ethernet network card.

Printer: Your two basic printer choices are ink-jet and laser. Color ink-jet printers cost on average between $50 and $300. Laser printers cost from $200 to $2000. In general, the cheaper the printer, the lower the resolution and speed, and the more often you are required to change the ink cartridge or toner. Laser printers print faster and with a higher quality than an ink-jet printer prints, and their toner on average costs less. If you want color, go with a high-end ink-jet printer to ensure quality of print. Duty cycle (the number of pages you expect to print each month) also should be a determining factor. If your duty cycle is on the low end — hundreds of pages per month — stay with a high-end ink-jet printer, rather than purchasing a laser printer. If you plan to print photographs taken with a digital camera, you should purchase a photo printer. A photo printer is a dye-sublimation printer or an ink-jet printer with higher resolution and features that allow you to print quality photographs.

Processor: For a PC, a 2.8-GHz Intel or AMD processor is more than enough processor power for application home and small office/home office users. Game home, large business, and power users should upgrade to faster processors.

RAM: RAM plays a vital role in the speed of your computer. Make sure the computer you purchase has at least 512 MB of RAM. If you have extra money to invest in your computer, consider increasing the RAM to 1 GB or more. The extra money for RAM will be well spent.

Scanner: The most popular scanner purchased with a computer today is the flatbed scanner. When evaluating a flatbed scanner, check the color depth and resolution. Do not buy anything less than a color depth of 48 bits and a resolution of 1200 x 2400 dpi. The higher the color depth, the more accurate the color. A higher resolution picks up the more subtle gradations of color.

Sound Card: Most sound cards today support the Sound Blaster and General MIDI standards and should be capable of recording and playing digital audio. If you plan to turn your computer into an entertainment system or are a game home user, you will want to spend the extra money and upgrade from the standard sound card.

Speakers: After you have a good sound card, quality speakers and a separate subwoofer that amplifies the bass frequencies of the speakers can turn your computer into a premium stereo system.

PC Video Camera: A PC video camera is a small camera used to capture and display live video (in some cases with sound), primarily on a Web page. You also can capture, edit, and share video and still photos. The camera sits on your monitor or desk. Recommended minimum specifications include 640 x 480 resolution, a video with a rate of 30 frames per second, and a USB 2.0 or FireWire connection.

USB Flash Drive: If you work on different computers and need access to the same data and information, this portable miniature mobile storage device is ideal. USB flash drive capacity varies from 16 MB to 4 GB.

Video Graphics Card: Most standard video cards satisfy the monitor display needs of application home and small office users. If you are a game home user or a graphic designer, you will want to upgrade to a higher quality video card. The higher refresh rates will further enhance the display of games, graphics, and movies.

Wireless LAN Access Point: A Wireless LAN Access Point allows you to network several computers, so they can share files and access the Internet through a single cable modem or DSL connection. Each device that you connect requires a wireless card. A Wireless LAN Access Point can offer a range of operations up to several hundred feet, so be sure the device has a high-powered antenna.

External Hard Disk: Consider purchasing an external hard disk to back up important files. An alternative to purchasing an external hard disk is to purchase a CD-RW or DVD+RW and burn backups of key files on a CD or DVD.

FIGURE 4 Hardware guidelines (continued from previous page).

BASE COMPONENTS

HARDWARE	Application Home User	Game Home User	Small Office/Home Office User	Mobile User
Processor	Pentium 4 2.8 GHz	Pentium 4 2.8 GHz	Pentium 4 at 3.0 GHz	Pentium 4M at 2.4 GHz
RAM	512 MB	1 MB	512 MB	512 MB
Hard Disk	80 GB	120 GB	120 GB	60 GB
Monitor/LCS Flat Panel	17" or 19"	21"	19" or 21"	15.7" Wide Display
Video Graphics Card	256 MB	512 MB	256 MB	32 MB
CD/DVD Bay 1	48x CD-ROM	48x CD-ROM	48x CD-ROM	24x CD-RW/DVD
CD/DVD Bay 2	8x DVD+RW	12x DVD+RW	8x DVD+RW	4x DVD+RW
Floppy Disk Drive	3.5"	3.5"	3.5"	3.5"
Printer	Color Ink-jet	Color Ink-jet	18 ppm Laser	Portable Ink-jet
PC Video Camera	Yes	Yes	Yes	Yes
Fax/Modem	Yes	Yes	Yes	Yes
Microphone	Close-Talk Headset With Gain Adjustment	Close-Talk Headset With Gain Adjustment	Close-Talk Headset With Gain Adjustment	Close-Talk Headset With Gain Adjustment
Speakers	Stereo	Full-Dolby Surround	Stereo	Stereo
Pointing Device	IntelliMouse or Optical Mouse	Laser Mouse and Joystick	IntelliMouse or Optical Mouse	Touchpad or Pointing Stick and Laser Mouse
Keyboard	Yes	Yes	Yes	Built-In
Backup Disk/Tape Drive		External or Removable Hard Disk	External or Removable Hard Disk	External or Removable Hard Disk
USB Flash Drive	128 MB	256 MB	256 MB	256 MB
Sound Card	Sound Blaster Compatible	Sound Blaster Audigy 2	Sound Blaster Compatible	Built-In
Network Card	Yes	Yes	Yes	Yes
TV-Out Connector	Yes	Yes	Yes	Yes
USB Port	6	8	6	2
FireWire Port	2	2	2	1
SOFTWARE				
Operating System	Windows XP Home Edition with Service Pack 2	Windows XP Home Edition with Service Pack 2	Windows XP Proffesional with Service Pack 2	Windows XP Professional with Service Pack 2
Application Suite	Office 2003 Standard Edition	Office 2003 Standard Edition	Office 2003 Small Business Edition	Office 2003 Small Business Edition
Antivirus	Yes, 12-Mo. Subscription	Yes, 12-Mo. Subscription	Yes, 12-Mo. Subscription	Yes, 12-Mo. Subscription
Internet Access	Cable, DSL, or Dial-up	Cable or DSL	Cable, DSL, or Dial-up	Wireless or Dial-up
OTHER				
Surge Protector	Yes	Yes	Yes	Portible
Warranty	3-Year Limited, 1-Year Next Business Day On-site Service	3-Year Limited, 1-Year Next Business Day On-site Service	3-Year On-site Service	3-Year Limited, 1-Year Next Business Day On0site Service
Other		Wheel		Docking Station Carrying Case Fingerprint Scanner Portable Data Projector

Optional Components for All Categories					
802. 11g Wireless Card	Bluetooth Enabled	Biometric Input Device	Card Reader/Writer	Digital Camera	Digital Video Capture Card
Digital Video Camera	Dual-Monitor Support with Second Monitor	Ergonomic Keyboard	External Hard Disk Drive	Graphics Tablet	iPod Music Player
IrDa Port	Mouse Pad/Wrist Rest	Multifunctional Peripheral	Photo Printer	Portable Data Projector	Scanner
TV/FM Tuner	Uninterruptible Power Supply				

FIGURE 5 A summary sheet is an effective tool for summarizing and comparing the prices and components of different computer vendors.

4 Consider upgrades to the mouse, keyboard, monitor, printer, microphone, and speakers. You use these peripheral devices to interact with your computer, so you should make sure they are up to your standards. Review the peripheral devices listed in Figure 4 on pages 265 and 266 and then visit both local computer dealers and large retail stores to test the computers on display. Ask the salesperson what input and output devices would be best for you and whether you should upgrade beyond what comes standard. Consider purchasing a wireless keyboard and wireless mouse to eliminate bothersome wires on your desktop. A few extra dollars spent on these components when you initially purchase a computer can extend its usefulness by years.

5 Determine whether you want to use telephone lines or broadband (cable or DSL) to access the Internet. If your computer has a modem, you can access the Internet using a standard telephone line. Ordinarily, you call a local or toll-free 800 number to connect to an ISP (see Guideline 6 on the next page). Using a dial-up Internet connection is relatively inexpensive but slow.

DSL and cable connections provide much faster Internet connections, which are ideal if you want faster file download speeds for software, digital photos, and music. As you would expect, they also are more expensive. DSL, which is available through local telephone companies, also may require that you subscribe to an ISP. Cable Internet access is usually available through your local cable television provider and some online service providers (OSPs). If you use cable, you generally do not use a separate Internet service provider or online service provider.

6 **If you are using a dial-up or wireless connection to connect to the Internet, select an ISP or OSP.** You can access the Internet via telephone lines in one of two ways: an ISP or an OSP. Both provide Internet access for a monthly fee that ranges from $6 to $25. Local ISPs offer Internet access to users in a limited geographic region, through local telephone numbers. National ISPs provide access for users nationwide (including mobile users), through local and toll-free telephone numbers and cable. Because of their size, national ISPs generally offer more services and have a larger technical support staff than local ISPs. OSPs furnish Internet access as well as members-only features for users nationwide. Figure 6 lists several national ISPs and OSPs. Before you choose an ISP or OSP, compare such features as the number of access hours, monthly fees, available services (e-mail, Web page hosting, chat), and reliability.

Company	Service	Web Address
America Online	OSP	aol.com
AT&T Worldnet	ISP	www.att.net
Comcast	OSP	comcast.net
CompuServe	OSP	compuserve.com
EarthLink	ISP	earthlink.net
Juno	OSP	juno.com
NetZero	OSP	netzero.com
MSN	OSP	msn.com
SBC Prodigy	ISP/OSP	prodigy.net

For an updated list and Web links, click the special feature, Buyer's Guide, at the Teachers Discovering Computers Web site (scsite.com/tdc4).

FIGURE 6 National ISPs and OSPs.

7 **Use a worksheet to compare computers, services, and other considerations.** You can use a separate sheet of paper to take notes on each vendor's computer and then summarize the information on a worksheet, such as the one shown in Figure 7. You can use Figure 7 to compare prices for either a PC or a Mac. Most companies advertise a price for a base computer that includes components housed in the system unit (processor, RAM, sound card, video card), disk drives (floppy disk, hard disk, CD-ROM, CD-RW, DVD-ROM, and DVD+RW), keyboard, mouse, monitor, printer, speakers, and modem. Be aware, however, that some advertisements list prices for computers with only some of these components. Monitors and printers, for example, often are not included in a base computer's price. Depending on how you plan to use the computer, you may want to invest in additional or more powerful components. When you are comparing the prices of computers, make sure you are comparing identical or similar configurations.

PC or Mac Cost Comparison Worksheet

Dealers list prices for computers with most of these components (instead of listing individual component costs). Some dealers do not supply a monitor. Some dealers offer significant discounts, but you must subscribe to an Internet service for a specified period to receive the discounted price. To compare computers, enter overall system price at top and enter a 0 (zero) for components included in the system cost. For any additional components not covered in the system price, enter the cost in the appropriate cells.

Items to Purchase	Desired System (PC)	Desired System (Mac)	Local Dealer #1	Local Dealer #2	Online Dealer #1	Online Dealer #2	Comments
OVERALL SYSTEM							
Overall System Price	< $1,500	< $1,500					
HARDWARE							
Processor	Pentium 4 at 2.8 GHz	PowerPC G4 at 800 MHz					
RAM	512 MB	512 MB					
Hard Disk	80 GB	80 GB					
Monitor/LCD Flat Panel	17"	17"					
Video Graphics Card	128 MB	128 MB					
Floppy Disk Drive	3.5"	NA					
USB Flash Drive	128 MB	128 MB					
CD/DVD Bay 1	48x CD-ROM	4x DVD+RW					
CD/DVD Bay 2	8x DVD+RW	NA					
Speakers	Stereo	Stereo					
Sound Card	Sound Blaster Compatible	Sound Blaster Compatible					
USB Ports	6	6					
FireWire Port	2	2					
Network Card	Yes	Yes					
Fax/Modem	56 Kbps	56 Kbps					
Keyboard	Standard	Apple Pro Keyboard					
Pointing Device	IntelliMouse	IntelliMouse or Apple Pro Mouse					
Microphone	Close-Talk Headset with Gain Adjustment	Close-Talk Headset with Gain Adjustment					
Printer	Color Ink-Jet	Color Ink-Jet					
Backup	250 MB Zip	250 MB Zip					
SOFTWARE							
Operating System	Windows XP Home Edition	Mac OS X					
Application Software	Office 2003 Small Business Edition	Office 2004 for Mac					
Antivirus	Yes - 12 Mo. Subscription	Yes - 12 Mo. Subscription					
OTHER							
Card Reader							
Digital Camera	4-Megapixel	4-Megapixel					
Internet Connection	1-Year Subscription	1-Year Subscription					
Joystick	Yes	Yes					
PC Video Camera	With Microphone	With Microphone					
Scanner							
Surge Protector							
Warranty	3-Year On-Site Service	3-Year On-Site Service					
Wireless Card	Internal	Internal					
Wireless LAN Access Point	LinkSys	Apple AirPort					
Total Cost			$.	$.	$.	$.	

FIGURE 7 A worksheet is an effective tool for summarizing and comparing components and prices of different computer vendors.

8 **If you are buying a new computer, you have several purchasing options: buying from your school bookstore, a local computer dealer, a local large retail store, or ordering by mail via telephone or the Web.** Each purchasing option has certain advantages. Many college bookstores, for example, sign exclusive pricing agreements with computer manufacturers and, thus, can offer student discounts. Local dealers and local large retail stores, however, more easily can provide hands-on support. Mail-order companies that sell computers by telephone or online via the Web (Figure 8) often provide the lowest prices, but extend less personal service. Some major mail-order companies, however, have started to provide next-business-day, on-site services. A credit card usually is required to buy from a mail-order company. Figure 9 lists some of the more popular mail-order companies and their Web site addresses.

9 **If you are buying a used computer, stay with name brands such as Dell, Gateway, Hewlett-Packard, and Apple.** Although brand-name equipment can cost more, most brand-name computers have longer, more comprehensive warranties, are better supported, and have more authorized centers for repair services. As with new computers, you can purchase a used computer from local computer dealers, local large retail stores, or mail

order via the telephone or the Web. Classified ads and used computer sellers offer additional outlets for purchasing used computers. Figure 10 lists several major used computer brokers and their Web site addresses.

10 **If you have a computer and are upgrading to a new one, consider selling or trading in the old one.** If you are a replacement buyer, your older computer still may have value. If you cannot sell the computer through the classified ads, via a Web site, or to a friend, ask if the computer dealer will buy your old computer. An increasing number of companies are taking trade-ins, but do not expect too much money for your old computer. Other companies offer free disposal of your old PC.

11 **Be aware of hidden costs.** Before purchasing, be sure to consider any additional costs associated with buying a computer, such as an additional telephone line, a cable or DSL modem, an uninterruptible power supply (UPS), computer furniture, a USB flash drive, paper, and computer training classes you may want to take. Depending on where you buy your computer, the seller may be willing to include some or all of these in the computer purchase price.

FIGURE 8 Mail-order companies, such as Dell, sell computers online.

Type of Computer	Company	Web Address
PC	CNET Shopper	shopper.cnet.com
	Hewlett-Packard	hp.com
	CompUSA	compusa.com
	Dartek	dartek.com
	Dell	dell.com
	Gateway	gateway.com
Macintosh	Apple Computer	store.apple.com
	ClubMac	clubmac.com
	MacConnection	macconnection.com
	PC & MacExchange	macx.com

For an updated list and Web links, click the special feature, Buyer's Guide, at the Teachers Discovering Computers Web site (scsite.com/tdc4).

FIGURE 9 Computer mail-order companies.

Company	Web Address
Amazon.com	amazon.com
Off-Lease Computers	off-leasecomputers.com
American Computer Exchange	www.amcoex.com
U.S. Computer Exchange	usce.org
eBay	ebay.com

For an updated list and Web links, click the special feature, Buyer's Guide, at the Teachers Discovering Computers Web site (scsite.com/tdc4).

FIGURE 10 Used computer mail-order companies.

12 **Consider more than just price.** The lowest-cost computer may not be the best long-term buy. Consider such intangibles as the vendor's time in business, the vendor's regard for quality, and the vendor's reputation for support. If you need to upgrade your computer often, you may want to consider a leasing arrangement, in which you pay monthly lease fees, but can upgrade or add on to your computer as your equipment needs change. No matter what type of buyer you are, insist on a 30-day, no-questions-asked return policy on your computer.

13 **Avoid restocking fees.** Some companies charge a restocking fee of 10 to 20 percent as part of their money-back return policy. In some cases, no restocking fee for hardware is applied, but it is applied for software. Ask about the existence and terms of any restocking policies before you buy.

14 **Use a credit card to purchase your new computer.** Many credit cards offer purchase protection and extended warranty benefits that cover you in case of loss of or damage to purchased goods. Paying by credit card also gives you time to install and use the computer before you have to pay for it. Finally, if you are dissatisfied with the computer and are unable to reach an agreement with the seller, paying by credit card gives you certain rights regarding withholding payment until the dispute is resolved. Check your credit card terms for specific details.

15 **Consider purchasing an extended warranty or service plan.** If you use your computer for business or require fast resolution to major computer problems, consider purchasing an extended warranty or a service plan through a local dealer or third-party company. Most extended warranties cover the repair and replacement of computer components beyond the standard warranty. Most service plans ensure that your technical support calls receive priority response from technicians. You also can purchase an on-site service plan that states that a technician will come to your home, work, or school within 24 hours. If your computer includes a warranty and service agreement for a year or less, think about extending the service for two or three years when you buy the computer.

CENTURY COMPUTERS

Performance Guarantee
(See reverse for terms & conditions of this contract)

Invoice #: 1984409   Effective Date: 10/12/07
Invoice Date: 10/12/07   Expiration Date: 10/12/10

Customer Name: Leon, Richard   System & Serial Numbers
Date: 10/12/07   IMB computer
Address: 1123 Roxbury   S/N: US759290C
         Sycamore, IL 60178
Day phone: (815) 555-0303
Evening Phone: (728) 555-0203

John Smith   10/12/07
Print Name of Century's Authorized Signature   Date

How to Purchase a Notebook Computer

If you need computing capability when you travel or to use in lectures or meetings, you may find a notebook computer to be an appropriate choice. The guidelines mentioned in the previous section also apply to the purchase of a notebook computer. The following are additional considerations unique to notebook computers.

1 **Purchase a notebook computer with a sufficiently large active-matrix screen.** Active-matrix screens display high-quality color that is viewable from all angles. Less expensive, passive-matrix screens sometimes are difficult to see in low-light conditions and cannot be viewed from an angle. Notebook computers typically come with a 12.1-inch, 13.3-inch, 14.1-inch, or 15.7-inch display. For most users, a 14.1-inch display is satisfactory. If you intend to use your notebook computer as a desktop computer replacement, however, you may opt for a 15.7-inch display. Notebook computers with these larger displays weigh seven to ten pounds, however, so if you travel a lot and portability is essential, you might want a lighter computer with a smaller display. The lightest notebook computers, which weigh less than 3 pounds, are equipped with a 12.1-inch display. Regardless of size, the resolution of the display should be at least 1024 x 768 pixels. To compare the monitor size on various notebook computers, visit the company Web sites in Figure 11.

Type of Notebook	Company	Web Address
PC	Acer	global.acer.com
	Dell	dell.com
	Fujitsu	fujitsu.com
	Gateway	gateway.com
	Hewlett-Packard	hp.com
	IBM	ibm.com
	NEC	nec.com
	Sony	sony.com
	Toshiba	toshiba.com
Mac	Apple	apple.com

For an updated list and Web links, click the special feature, Buyer's Guide, at the Teachers Discovering Computers Web site (scsite.com/tdc4).

FIGURE 11 Companies that sell notebook computers.

2 **Experiment with different keyboards and pointing devices.** Notebook computer keyboards are far less standardized than those for desktop computers. Some notebook computers, for example, have wide wrist rests, whereas others have none. Notebook computers also use a range of pointing devices, including pointing sticks, touchpads, and trackballs. Before you purchase a notebook computer, try various types of keyboard and pointing devices to determine which is easiest for you to use. Regardless of the pointing device you select, you also may want to purchase a regular mouse to use when you are working at a desk or other large surface.

3 **Make sure the notebook computer you purchase has a CD and/or DVD drive.** Loading and installing software, especially large Office suites, is much faster if done from a CD-ROM, CD-RW, DVD-ROM, or DVD+RW. Today, most notebook computers come with an internal or external CD-ROM drive. Some notebook computers even come with a CD-ROM drive and a CD-RW drive or a DVD-ROM drive and a CD-RW or DVD+RW drive. Although DVD drives are slightly more expensive, they allow you to play CDs and DVD movies using your notebook computer and a headset.

4 **If necessary, upgrade the processor, memory, and disk storage at the time of purchase.** As with a desktop computer, upgrading your notebook computer's memory and disk storage usually is less expensive at the time of initial purchase. Some disk storage is custom designed for notebook computer manufacturers, meaning an upgrade might not be available in the future. If you are purchasing a lightweight notebook computer, it should include at least a 2.4-GHz processor, 512 MB of RAM, and 80 GB of storage.

5 **The availability of built-in ports on a notebook computer is important.** A notebook computer does not have a lot of room to add adapter cards. If you know the purpose for which you plan to use your notebook computer, you can determine the ports you will need. Most notebooks come with common ports, such as a mouse port, IrDA port, serial port, parallel port, video port, and USB port. If you plan to connect your notebook computer to a TV, however, you will need a PCtoTV port. If you want to connect to networks at school or in various offices, make sure the notebook computer you purchase has a built-in network card. If your notebook computer does not come with a built-in network wireless card, you will have to purchase an external network card that slides into an expansion slot in your notebook computer, as well as a network cable. If you expect to connect an iPod portable digital music player to your notebook computer, you will need a FireWire port.

6 **If you plan to use your notebook computer for note-taking at school or in meetings, consider a notebook computer that converts to a Tablet PC.** Some computer manufacturers have developed convertible notebook computers that allow the screen to rotate 180 degrees on a central hinge and then fold down to cover the keyboard and become a Tablet PC (Figure 12). You then can use a stylus to enter text or drawings into the computer by writing on the screen.

FIGURE 12 The Toshiba Protégé M200 notebook computer converts to a Tablet PC.

7 **Consider purchasing a notebook computer with a built-in wireless card to connect to your home network.** Many users today are setting up wireless home networks. With a wireless home network, the desktop computer functions as the server, and your notebook computer can access the desktop computer from any location in the house to share files and hardware, such as a printer, and browse the Web. If your notebook computer does not come with a built-in wireless card, you can purchase an external one that slides into your notebook computer. Most home wireless networks allow connections from distances of 150 to 800 feet.

8 **If you are going to use your notebook computer for long periods without access to an electrical outlet, purchase a second battery.** The trend among notebook computer users today is power and size over battery life, and notebook computer manufacturers have picked up on this. Many notebook computer users today are willing to give up longer battery life for a larger screen, faster processor, and more storage. In addition, some manufacturers typically sell the notebook with the lowest capacity battery. For this reason, you need to be careful in choosing a notebook computer if you plan to use it without access to electrical outlets for long periods, such as an airplane flight. You also might want to purchase a second battery as a backup. If you anticipate running your notebook computer on batteries frequently, choose a computer that uses lithium-ion batteries, which last longer than nickel cadmium or nickel hydride batteries.

9 **Purchase a well-padded and well-designed carrying case.** An amply padded carrying case will protect your notebook computer from the bumps it will receive while traveling. A well-designed carrying case will have room for accessories such as spare floppy disks, CDs and DVDs, a user manual, pens, and paperwork (Figure 13).

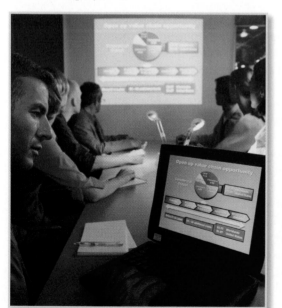

FIGURE 13 A well-designed notebook computer carrying case.

10 **If you travel overseas, obtain a set of electrical and telephone adapters.** Different countries use different outlets for electrical and telephone connections. Several manufacturers sell sets of adapters that will work in most countries.

11 **If you plan to connect your notebook computer to a video projector, make sure the notebook computer is compatible with the video projector.** You should check, for example, to be sure that your notebook computer will allow you to display an image on the computer screen and projection device at the same time (Figure 14). Also, ensure that your notebook computer has the ports required to connect to the video projector.

12 **For improved security, consider a fingerprint scanner.** More than a quarter of a million notebook computers are stolen or lost each year. If you have critical information stored on your notebook computer, consider purchasing one with a fingerprint scanner (Figure 15) to protect the data if your computer is stolen or lost. Fingerprint security offers a level of protection that extends well beyond the standard password protection.

FIGURE 15 Fingerprint scanner technology offers greater security than passwords.

FIGURE 14 A notebook computer connected to a video projector projects the image displayed on the screen.

How to Purchase a Tablet PC

The Tablet PC (Figure 16) combines the mobility features of a traditional notebook computer with the simplicity of pencil and paper, because you can create and save Office-type documents by writing and drawing directly on the screen with a digital pen. Tablet PCs use the Windows XP Tablet PC Edition operating system, which expands on Windows XP Professional by including digital pen and speech capabilities. A notebook computer and a Tablet PC have many similarities. For this reason, if you are considering purchasing a Tablet PC, review the guidelines for purchasing a notebook computer, as well as the following guidelines.

FIGURE 16 The lightweight Tablet PC, with its handwriting capabilities, is the latest addition to the family of mobile computers.

① **Make sure the Tablet PC fits your mobile computing needs.**   The Tablet PC is not for every mobile user. If you find yourself in need of a computer in class or you are spending more time in meetings than in your office, the Tablet PC may be the answer. Before you invest money in a Tablet PC, however, determine the programs you plan to use on it. You should not buy a Tablet PC simply because it is a new and interesting type of computer. For additional information on the Tablet PC, visit the Web sites listed in Figure 17. You may have to use the search capabilities on the home page of the companies listed to locate information about the Tablet PC.

Company	Web Address
Fujitsu	fujitsu.com
Hewlett-Packard	hp.com
Microsoft	microsoft.com/windowsxp/tabletpc
ViewSonic	viewsonic.com
For an updated list and Web links, click the special feature, Buyer's Guide, at the Teachers Discovering Computers Web site (scsite.com/tdc4).	

FIGURE 17   Companies involved with Tablet PCs and their Web sites.

② **Decide whether you want a convertible or pure Tablet PC.**   Convertible Tablet PCs have an attached keyboard and look like a notebook computer. You rotate the screen and lay it flat against the computer for note-taking. The pure Tablet PCs are slim and lightweight, weighing less than four pounds. They have the capability of easily docking at a desktop to gain access to a large monitor, keyboard, and mouse. If you spend a lot of time attending lectures or meetings, the pure Tablet PC is ideal. Acceptable specifications for a Tablet PC are shown in Figure 18.

Tablet PC Specifications	
Dimensions	12" × 9" × 1.2"
Weight	Less than 4 Pounds
Processor	Pentium III processor-M at 1.33 GHz
RAM	512 MB
Hard Disk	40 GB
Display	12.1" XGA TFT
Digitizer	Electromagnetic Digitizer
Battery	4-Cell (3-Hour)
USB	2
FireWire	1
Docking Station	Grab and Go with CD-ROM, Keyboard, and Mouse
Bluetooth Port	Yes
Wireless	802.11b/g Card
Network Card	10/100 Ethernet
Modem	56 Kbps
Speakers	Internal
Microphone	Internal
Operating System	Windows XP Tablet PC Edition
Application Software	Office Small Business Edition
Antivirus Software	Yes – 12 Month Subscription
Warranty	1-Year Limited Warranty Parts and Labor

FIGURE 18   Tablet PC specifications.

③ **Be sure the weight and dimensions are conducive to portability.**   The weight and dimensions of the Tablet PC are important because you carry it around like a notepad. The Tablet PC you buy should weigh four pounds or less. Its dimensions should be approximately 12 inches by 9 inches by 1.2 inches.

Port availability, battery life, and durability are even more important with a Tablet PC than they are with a notebook computer.
Make sure the Tablet PC you purchase has the ports required for the applications you plan to run. As with any mobile computer, battery life is important especially if you plan to use your Tablet PC for long periods without access to an electrical outlet. A Tablet PC must be durable because if you use it the way it was designed to be used, you will be handling it much like you handle a pad of paper.

 Experiment with different models of the Tablet PC to find the digital pen that works best for you. The key to making use of the Tablet PC is to be comfortable with its handwriting capabilities and on-screen keyboard. Not only is the digital pen used to write on the screen (Figure 19), you also use it to make gestures to complete tasks, in a manner similar to the way you use a mouse. Figure 20 compares the standard point-and-click of a mouse with the gestures made with a digital pen. Other gestures with the digital pen replicate some of the commonly used keys on a keyboard.

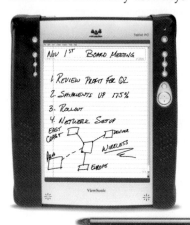

FIGURE 19 A Tablet PC lets you handwrite notes and draw on the screen using a digital pen.

Mouse	Digital Pen
Point	Point
Click	Tap
Double-click	Double-tap
Right-click	Tap and hold
Click and drag	Drag

FIGURE 20 Standard point-and-click of a mouse compared with the gestures made with a digital pen.

 Check out the comfort level of handwriting in different positions. You should be able to handwrite on a Tablet PC with your hand resting on the screen. You also should be able to handwrite holding the Tablet PC in one hand, as well as with it sitting in your lap.

Make sure the LCD display device has a resolution high enough to take advantage of Microsoft's ClearType technologies.
Tablet PCs use a digitizer under a standard 10.4-inch motion-sensitive LCD display to make the digital ink on the screen look like real ink on paper. To ensure you get the maximum benefits from the new ClearType technology, make sure the LCD display has a resolution of 800 × 600 in landscape mode and a 600 × 800 in portrait mode.

 Test the built-in Tablet PC microphone and speakers. With many application software packages recognizing human speech, such as Microsoft Office, it is important that the Tablet PC's built-in microphone operates at an acceptable level. If the microphone is not to your liking, you may want to purchase a close-talk headset with your Tablet PC. Increasingly more users are sending information as audio files, rather than relying solely on text. For this reason, you also should check the speakers on the Tablet PC to make sure they meet your standards.

Consider a Tablet PC with a built-in PC video camera. A PC video camera adds streaming video and still photography capabilities to your Tablet PC, while still allowing you to take notes in lectures or meetings.

 Review the docking capabilities of the Tablet PC.
The Microsoft Windows XP Tablet PC Edition operating system supports a grab-and-go form of docking, so you can pick up and take a docked Tablet PC with you, just as you would pick up a notepad on your way to a meeting (Figure 21).

FIGURE 21 A Tablet PC docked to create a desktop computer with the Tablet PC as the monitor.

Wireless access to the Internet and your e-mail is essential with a Tablet PC. Make sure the Tablet PC has wireless networking, so you can access the Internet and your e-mail anytime and anywhere. Your Tablet PC also should include standard network connections, such as dial-up and Ethernet connections.

 Review available accessories to purchase with your Tablet PC. Tablet PC accessories include docking stations, mouse units, keyboards, security cables, additional memory and storage, protective handgrips, screen protectors, and various types of digital pens.

How to Purchase a Personal Mobile Device

Whether you choose a PDA, smart phone, or smart pager depends on where, when, and how you will use the device. If you need to stay organized when you are on the go, a PDA may be the right choice. PDAs typically are categorized by the operating system they run. If you need to stay organized and in touch when on the go, a smart phone or smart pager may be the right choice. Just as with PDAs, smart phones and smart pagers are categorized by the operating system they run. The six primary operating systems for these devices are the Palm OS, Windows Mobile for Pocket PC, Windows Mobile for Smartphone, Symbian OS, Blackberry, and Embedded Linux.

This section lists guidelines you should consider when purchasing a PDA, smart phone, or smart pager. You also should visit the Web sites listed in Figure 22 to gather more information about the type of personal mobile device that best suits your computing needs.

1 **Determine the programs you plan to run on your device.** All PDAs and most smart phones and smart pagers can handle basic organizer-type software such as a calendar, address book, and notepad. The availability of other software depends on the operating system you choose. The depth and breadth of software for the Palm OS is significant, with more than 20,000 basic programs and over 600 wireless programs. Devices that run Windows-based operating systems, such as Windows Mobile or Windows Smartphone, may have fewer programs available, but the operating system and application software are similar to those with which you are familiar, such as Word and Excel. Some Symbian-based smart phones also include the capability to read and/or edit Microsoft Office documents.

2 **Consider how much you want to pay.** The price of a personal mobile device can range from $100 to $800, depending on its capabilities. Some Palm OS devices are at the lower end of the cost spectrum, and Windows-based devices often are at the higher end. For the latest prices, capabilities, and accessories, visit the Web sites listed in Figure 22.

3 **Determine whether you need wireless access to the Internet and e-mail or mobile telephone capabilities with your device.** Smart pagers give you access to e-mail and other data and Internet services. Smart phones typically include these features, but also include the ability to make and receive phone calls on cellular networks. Some PDAs and smart phones include wireless networking capability to allow you to connect to the Internet wirelessly. These wireless features and services allow personal mobile device users to access real-time information from anywhere to help make decisions while on the go.

4 **For wireless devices, determine how and where you will use the service.** When purchasing a wireless device, you must subscribe to a wireless service. Determine if the wireless network (carrier) you choose has service in the area where you plan to use the device. Some networks have high-speed data networks only in certain areas, such as large cities or business districts. Also, a few carriers allow you to use your device in other countries.

When purchasing a smart phone, determine if you plan to use the device more as a phone, PDA, or wireless data device. Some smart phones, such as those based on the Pocket PC Phone edition or the Palm OS, are geared more for use as a PDA and have a PDA form factor. Other smart phones, such as those based on Microsoft Smartphone or Symbian operating systems, mainly are phone devices that include robust PDA functionality. RIM Blackberry-based smart phones include robust data features that are oriented to accessing e-mail and wireless data services.

5 **Make sure your device has enough memory.** Memory (RAM) is not a major issue with low-end devices with monochrome displays and basic organizer functions. Memory is a major issue, however, for high-end devices that have color displays and wireless features. Without enough memory, the performance level of your device will drop dramatically. If you plan to purchase a high-end device running the Palm OS operating system, the device should have at least 16 MB of RAM. If you plan to purchase a high-end device running the Windows Mobile operating system, the PDA should have at least 48 MB of RAM.

6 **Practice with the touch screen, handwriting recognition, and built-in keyboard before deciding on a model.** To enter data into a PDA or smart phone, you use a pen like stylus to handwrite on the screen or to type on a keyboard. The keyboard either slides out or is mounted on the front of the device. With handwriting recognition, the device translates the handwriting into a computerized font. You also can use the stylus as a pointing device to select items on the screen and enter data by tapping on an on-screen keyboard. By practicing data entry before buying a device, you can learn if one device may be easier for you to use than another. You also can buy third-party software to improve a device's handwriting recognition.

7 **Decide whether you want a color display.** Pocket PC devices usually come with a color display that supports as many as 65,536 colors. Palm OS devices also have a color display, but the less expensive models display in 4 to 16 shades of gray. Symbian- and Blackberry-based devices also have the option for color displays. Having a color display does result in greater on-screen detail, but it also requires more memory and uses more power. Resolution also influences the quality of the display.

8 **Compare battery life.** Any mobile device is good only if it has the power required to run. For example, Palm OS devices with monochrome screens typically have a much longer battery life than Pocket PC devices with color screens. The use of wireless networking will shorten battery time considerably. To help alleviate this problem, most devices have incorporated rechargeable batteries that can be recharged by placing the device in a cradle or connecting it to a charger.

9 **Seriously consider the importance of ergonomics.** Will you put the device in your pocket, a carrying case, or wear it on your belt? How does it feel in your hand? Will you use it indoors or outdoors? Many screens are unreadable outdoors. Do you need extra ruggedness, such as would be required for use in construction, in a plant, or in a warehouse?

10 **Check out the accessories.** Determine which accessories you want for your personal mobile device. Accessories include carrying cases, portable mini- and full-sized keyboards, removable storage, modems, synchronization cradles and cables, car chargers, wireless communications, global positioning system modules, digital camera modules, expansion cards, dashboard mounts, replacement styli, hands-free headsets, and more.

11 **Decide whether you want additional functionality.** In general, off-the-shelf Microsoft operating system–based devices have broader functionality than devices with other operating systems. For example, voice-recording capability, e-book players, MP3 players, and video players are standard on most Pocket PC devices. If you are leaning towards a Palm OS device and want these additional functions, you may need to purchase additional software or expansion modules to add them later. Determine whether your employer permits devices with cameras on the premises, and if not, do not consider devices with cameras.

12 **Determine whether synchronization of data with other Devices or personal computers is important.** Most devices come with a cradle that connects to the USB or serial port on your computer so you can synchronize data on your device with your desktop or notebook computer. Increasingly more devices are Bluetooth and/or wireless networking enabled, which gives them the capability of synchronizing wirelessly. Many devices today also have an infrared port that allows you to synchronize data with any device that has a similar infrared port, including desktop and notebook computers or other personal mobile devices.

Web Site	Web Address
Hewlett-Packard	hp.com
CNET Shopper	shopper.cnet.com
palmOne	palmone.com
Microsoft	windowsmobile.com pocketpc.com microsoft.com/smartphone
PDA Buyers Guide	pdabuyersguide.com
Research in Motion	rim.com
Danger	danger.com
Symbian	symbian.com
Wireless Developer Network	wirelessdevnet.com
Sharp	myzaurus.com

For an updated list and Web links, click the special feature, Buyer's Guide, at the Teachers Discovering Computers Web site (scsite.com/tdc4).

FIGURE 22 Web site reviews and information about personal mobile devices.

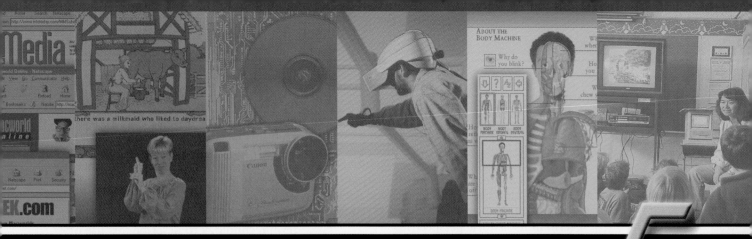

Integrating Digital Media and Educational Software Applications

5

Objectives

After completing this chapter, you will be able to:

[ISTE NETS-T Standards I A-B, II A-E, III A-D, V A-D, VI B]

- Explain the differences between digital media and multimedia

- Name and define the elements of multimedia and of digital media

- Explain different uses of digital media applications

- Discuss digital media applications on the Web

- Identify various K-12 software applications

- Specify what is meant by an interactive media

- Examine the uses of digital media authoring software programs

- Explain why digital media applications are important for education

Today, digital media and multimedia play an increasingly important role in education, business, and entertainment. Digital media is multimedia that has evolved into a discipline of its own. Digital media is the realization of the dream that computer engineers have had for years for the computer to evolve from being simply a device for computation into one that is a tool with which humans can communicate and learn. The concept of digital media is the next step in this evolution of the computer. **Interactivity**, which is one of the essential features of digital media applications, also allows for individualized instruction and exploration, both of which enrich the educational experience.

This chapter introduces you to many basic digital media and multimedia concepts, discusses educational applications of digital media, and describes various media elements of multimedia. First, you learn about the different types and uses of digital media applications. Next, the chapter provides examples of a few of the hundreds of outstanding digital media education software applications that are available for teaching and learning, many of which are inexpensive. You then learn how to create, design, and present digital media presentations. Finally, the chapter reinforces the potential of digital media software applications to change dramatically the way students learn.

What Is Digital Media?

The terms technology, multimedia, and digital media are not mutually exclusive. In fact, in common usage, these terms overlap and are often used interchangeably. A brief discussion of each term follows to put each term in its historic perspective.

Technology was the term first associated with computer use in the classroom. Computers found their way into schools to be used in specialized training programs, such as graphic arts and applied sciences, such as auto mechanics, used in vocational and production education, and used in the office for administrative tasks. Using the term technology to describe this use of computers was a logical step.

The term **multimedia** by definition means "more than one media." Multimedia incorporates a variety of elements, including text, graphics, audio, video, and animation. Originally, a multimedia presentation did not have to be digital. For example, multimedia might have incorporated a slide show for visuals, a tape recorder for audio, and an overhead projector for text. But as software and hardware became capable of and adept at handling more than one media, the term multimedia was coined to define computer software applications and presentations that utilized more than one media.

Recall from Chapter 1, that **digital media** is defined as those technologies that allow users to create new forms of interaction, expression, communication, and entertainment in a digital format. Digital media uses all the elements of multimedia but in a digital format (Figure 5-1). To be sure, digital media has not superseded or outdated the usefulness of the terms multimedia or technology. The term digital media simply underlines the pervasiveness of the use of digital formats for multimedia elements. Many applications previously defined as multimedia have seamlessly made the transition to digital media because they encompass all the elements of

Figure 5-1 Interactive digital media allows students to explore the world's knowledge in ways unheard of just a generation ago.

multimedia and digital media. The term digital media is evolving, and as a result, many digital media applications are still referred to as multimedia applications.

Have your students watched the space shuttle blast into orbit in person, viewed the Mona Lisa in the Louvre Museum, traveled to Egypt, or visited this nation's capital and explored its history? With digital media, your students can interact with and become part of these learning adventures and much more without ever physically setting foot outside of the classroom. Never before have students been able to explore the world in so many visual and interactive ways. Digital media is changing the way people work, learn, and play. Extensive research conducted over a period of more than 20 years confirms that the effective integration of multimedia applications, and now digital media, into the classroom curriculum can revolutionize the way today's digital students learn core and other subjects.

Digital media software refers to any computer-based presentation or application software that uses multimedia elements. By definition, digital media includes interaction, so some, but not all, digital media is also considered **interactive digital media**. Interactive digital media, by definition, allows users to move through information at their own pace. Interactive digital media also describes a digital media application that accepts input from the user by means of a keyboard, voice, simple movements, or a pointing device such as a mouse, and performs an action in response. Technology has evolved, for example, in video games where the player can indicate a response by simply making a gesture through an input device attached to his hand or foot. Well-designed applications provide feedback in the form of responses as the user progresses through the application or completes certain tasks.

The digital media application shown in Figure 5-2, for example, allows students to interact with and learn about the human body. The ability of users to interact with a digital media application is perhaps the most unique and important feature of digital media — a feature that has the potential to change dramatically the way digital students learn. Interactive digital media allows students to define their own learning paths, investigate topics in depth, and get immediate feedback from their exploration activities. Digital media applications also tend to engage and challenge students, thus encouraging them to think creatively and independently.

With many digital media applications, you navigate through the content by clicking links. Recall from Chapter 2 that Web pages use links to allow users to navigate quickly from one document to another. In a digital media application, links serve a similar function, allowing users to access information quickly and navigate from one topic to another in a nonlinear fashion. For example, while reading about Marco Polo, the user might click the keyword Travels to display a menu allowing the user to view a map of Marco Polo's journeys or listen to a reading from his travel journals.

Figure 5-2 The Ultimate Human Body by DK Multimedia is a popular educational program that allows students to interact with and learn about the human body. Clicking the heart, for example, allows students to see and hear a human heart in action.

In a digital media application, any clickable object — text, graphics, animation, and even videos — can function as a link. Figure 5-3 shows a menu of a digital media application that uses text, graphics, and animations as links to additional sources of information. The sections that follow provide an introduction to the different media elements contained originally in multimedia and now found in digital media applications.

barometer image link

Figure 5-3
The bottom screen shows a menu for one topic found in a popular nature encyclopedia. The menu provides text, buttons, and graphics that allow students or teachers to quickly choose a particular topic. Every object on the main menu is a link to discovery learning. The upper-right screen shows what happens when a user clicks the barometer. An enlarged barometer now provides numerous additional links to other digital media sources of information.

WEB INFO

For more information about digital media applications, visit the Teachers Discovering Computers Web site (*scsite.com/tdc4*), click Chapter 5, click Web Info, and then click Digital Media Applications.

Figure 5-4 The main menu from A Teacher's Guide to the HOLOCAUST Web site provides text and links that allow teachers and students to access the listed topic quickly.

TEXT

Text consists of characters that are used to create words, sentences, and paragraphs and is a fundamental element used in all multimedia applications. Multimedia applications not only use ordinary text to convey basic information, they also use a variety of textual effects to emphasize and clarify information. A different font size, color, or style, for example, often is used to emphasize certain words or phrases. Many multimedia and now digital media applications use text-based menus that allow you to select and display information on a certain topic (Figure 5-4).

GRAPHICS

Recall from Chapter 4 that a **graphic** is a digital representation of nontext information, such as a drawing, chart, or photograph. A graphic, also called a picture or image, contains no movement or animation.

In multimedia and digital media applications, graphics serve several functions. For one, graphics can illustrate certain concepts more vividly than text. A picture of Saturn, for example, clearly depicts the planet's rings in a way that text cannot. Graphics also play an important role in the learning process: many individuals — who are **visual learners** — may learn concepts faster or retain a higher percentage of material if they *see* the information presented graphically. Graphics also serve as navigational elements. Multimedia and digital media applications often use graphics as buttons that link to more information. The graphical user interfaces used on Macintosh computers, PCs, and graphical Web browsers also demonstrate the importance of graphics when using computers.

If you are creating a digital media presentation, you can obtain graphics in several ways. You can purchase a **clip art collection**, which is a set of previously created digital graphics that you can insert into a document. Many clip art collections are grouped by themes, such as Academic, Maps, and People. You also can create your own graphics using a paint or drawing program. Many presentation graphics and digital media authoring software packages, for example, include drawing tools for creating graphics, as shown in Figure 5-5. As you will learn later in the chapter, you can obtain photographs for use in digital media presentations by using a color scanner to digitize photos; taking photographs with a digital camera; or using a collection of photographs on a CD or DVD.

The lastest evolution of graphics technology is the move from two-dimensional (2D) to three-dimensional (3D) planes. Three-dimensional graphics provide the illusion of depth, creating a more realistic environment — which makes graphics more realistic and useful for simulation activities, such as flight simulators or video games.

Figure 5-5 Microsoft PowerPoint provides an AutoShapes palette on the Drawing toolbar that allows you to draw a 24-point star or other shapes to include in a digital media presentation. This type of graphic image is a resizeable, movable object that can be colored in many different ways or combined with other clip art, graphics, or text.

ANIMATION

Displaying a series of still graphics creates an **animation**, which is a graphic that has the illusion of motion if played back at the proper framing rate.. Animations range in scope from a basic graphic with a simple motion (for example, a blinking icon) to a detailed image with complex movements (such as a simulation of how an avalanche starts). As with graphics, animations can convey information more vividly than text alone. An animation showing the up-and-down movement of pistons and engine valves, as shown in Figures 5-6a through 5-6c for example, provides a better illustration of the workings of an internal combustion engine than a written explanation.

The use of animation has improved the quality of educational software dramatically and made Web sites more interesting for users. You can create your own detailed and highly dynamic animations using a graphics animation software package. In addition, you can obtain previously created animations from a CD, a DVD, or the Web.

AUDIO

Audio is any music, speech, or other sound. As with animation, audio allows digital media developers to provide information in a way that brings a concept or concepts to life. The vibration of a human heartbeat or the melodies of a symphony, for example, are concepts difficult to convey without the use of sound. Using audio in a digital media application to supplement text and graphics enhances understanding. An actor's narration added to the text of a Shakespearean play (Figure 5-7), for example, reinforces a student's grasp of the passage.

[b] piston down motion

[c] piston up motion

Figure 5-6 Microsoft's Encarta Encyclopedia contains numerous digital media animations, including a demonstration of how an internal combustion engine works. Figure 5-6a is a snapshot of the initial screen, Figure 5-6b shows that the piston has moved down during the intake stroke, and Figure 5-6c shows the piston moving up during the compression stroke.

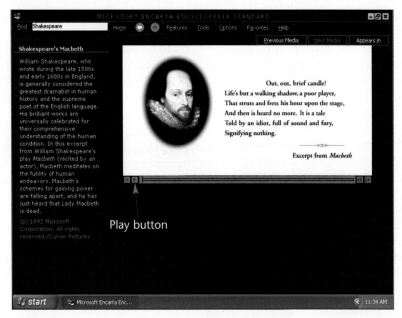

Figure 5-7 Interactive encyclopedias offer students many opportunities to hear the words and passages of great historical events and literary works, such as Shakespeare's *Macbeth*. By clicking the Play button, students hear passages from *Macbeth*.

You can obtain audio files for use in digital media applications in several different ways. One method is to capture sounds digitally using a microphone, tape or audio CD player, or any other audio input device that is plugged into a port on a sound card or a USB or FireWire port.

Musical Instrument Digital Interface (MIDI) is the electronic music industry's standard that defines how digital musical devices represent sounds electronically. Software programs that conform to the MIDI standard allow you to compose and edit music and other sounds. For example, you can change the speed, add notes, or rearrange the score to produce an entirely new sound. Most sound cards support the MIDI standard, so you can play and manipulate sounds on a computer that were created originally on another computer. As with graphics and animations, you also can purchase audio clips on a CD, DVD, or download them from thousands of Web sites.

VIDEO

Video consists of visual frames that are played back at speeds of 15 to 60 frames per second and provide full motion in real time. The integration of video into classroom curriculum has significantly influenced the way

that students learn core subjects. Videos can reinforce lectures and readings, provide a common base of knowledge, and show things that students would not otherwise experience. For example, after reading the text of one of Martin Luther King's speeches, students can watch a video of King delivering that same speech to an enthusiastic crowd.

To use video in a digital media application, you must capture, digitize, and edit the video using special video production hardware and software. As described in Chapter 4, video often is captured digitally with a video input device such as a digital video camera or VCR.

Due to the size of video files, incorporating video into a digital media application often is a challenge. Video files require tremendous amounts of storage space: a three-minute video segment, or **clip**, of high-quality video can take more than a gigabyte of storage. To decrease the size of the files, video is compressed.

Video compression is accomplished in many ways. One of them is by taking advantage of the fact that only a small portion of the image changes from frame to frame. A compressed video might store all the data in the first reference frame and then, assuming that the following frames

WEB INFO

For an overview of digital video software, visit the Teachers Discovering Computers Web site (*scsite.com/tdc4*), click Chapter 5, click Web Info, and then click Digital Video.

FAQ

Is there more than one MPEG standard?

Yes, as digital video has evolved, so have the standards. The latest standard is called MPEG 4.

are almost identical to it, store only the data in a reference frame that specifies the changes from the first frame to the next. The compression program continues to reduce the amount of stored data in this manner. Prior to viewing, the compressed video must be decompressed so that the video is restored to its original condition. The video compression software decompresses the video segment so it can be viewed. The **Motion Pictures Experts Group** has defined a set of standards for video compression and decompression called **MPEG** (pronounced em-peg). These standardized **CODEC** (**co**mpression and **dec**ompression) compression methods reduce the size of video files significantly.

Video compression and other improvements in video technology have allowed video to play a more important role in digital media applications. Technologies such as streaming video also have made video a viable part of digital media on the Web.

Digital Media Applications

A **digital media application** involves the use of digital media technology in education, business, and entertainment (Figure 5-8). Businesses use digital media, for example, in interactive advertisements and for job- and skill-training applications. Teachers use digital media applications to deliver

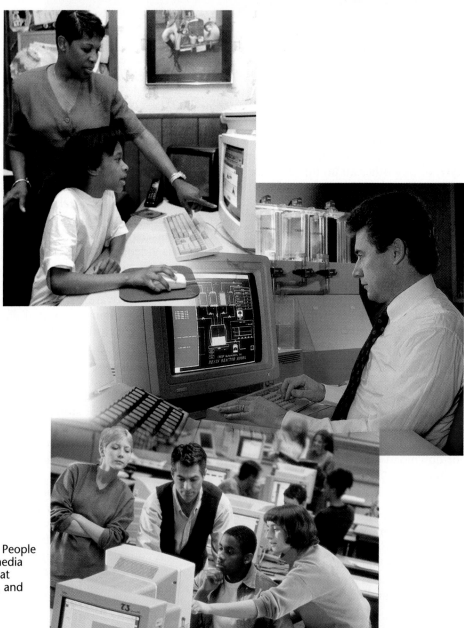

Figure 5-8 People use digital media applications at home, work, and school.

classroom presentations that enhance student learning. Students, in turn, use digital media applications to learn by reading, seeing, hearing, and interacting with the subject content. Digital media is used in a huge variety of computer games and other types of entertainment, as well.

Another important application of digital media is to create **simulations**, which are computer-based models of real-life situations. Digital media simulations often replace costly and sometimes hazardous demonstrations and training in areas such as chemistry, biology, medicine, and aviation.

The following sections provide a more detailed look at different types of well-known digital media applications, including computer-based training, electronic books and references, how-to guides, newspapers, and magazines. These sections also address the use of digital media in entertainment, virtual reality, information kiosks, and the importance of digital media on the World Wide Web. After learning about the various types of well-known digital media applications, you will learn about specific K-12 educational software applications used to improve teaching and learning by virtually all schools.

COMPUTER-BASED TRAINING (CBT)

Computer-based training (CBT) is a tool that allows individuals to learn by using and completing exercises using instructional software on computers. More recently, this type of training has been referred to as **individual lead training (ILT)** because the training focuses more on the learner than on the instructor. Computer-based training is popular in business, industry, and education to teach new skills or enhance the existing skills of employees. Athletes, for example, use digital media computer-based training programs to practice baseball, football, soccer, tennis, and golf skills, while airlines use digital CBT simulations to train employees. School districts and universities use face-to-face and online CBT to train teachers how to teach students math, reading, computer skills, and many other subjects. Interactive

CBT software called **courseware** usually is available on CD, DVD, or the Web.

One important advantage of computer-based training is that it allows for flexible, on-the-spot training. Businesses and schools, for example, can set up corporate training or teacher professional development labs so employees can update their skills without leaving the workplace (Figure 5-9). Installing CBT software on an employee's computer or on the company network provides even more flexibility — allowing employees to update their job skills right at their desks, at home, or while traveling.

Computer-based training provides a unique learning experience because learners receive instant feedback — in the form of positive response for correct answers or actions, additional information on incorrect answers, and immediate scoring and results. Testing and self-diagnostic features allow instructors to verify that an individual has mastered curriculum objectives and identify students who need additional instruction or practice. Computer-based training is especially effective for teaching software skills if the CBT is integrated with the software application because it allows students to practice using the software as they learn.

Figure 5-9 Teachers can learn innovative uses of technology, teaching strategies, and various subject-related software packages in a school district's professional development center.

ELECTRONIC BOOKS AND REFERENCES

WEB INFO

For more information about electronic books, visit the Teachers Discovering Computers Web site (*scsite.com/tdc4*), click Chapter 5, click Web Info, and then click Electronic Books.

Imagine a library in your hands and in the hands of your student. Read your favorite *Harry Potter* or *Star Wars* novel, delete it, and download the complete works of Hemingway. The electronic book became popular several years ago making reading a digital activity for digital kids. Many analysts predict that electronic books will revolutionize the publishing industry and impact education in many positive, imaginative, and yet-to-be determined ways.

An **electronic book**, or **e-book**, is a small, book-sized computer that allows users to read, save, highlight, bookmark, and add notes to online text. To obtain the same functionality of an e-book device for your personal computer, notebook computer, Tablet PC, or PDA, you can download and install free e-book reader software programs, such as Microsoft Reader and Adobe Acrobat eBook Reader, from the Web.

iPod Books are digital books that are accessed on an iPod using software that can be downloaded from the Apple iPod Web site (Figure 5-10). iPod Books are now available at various Web sites that provide books created by established authors as well as those created by students who author their own books and submit them for distribution.

Electronic books have many of the elements of a regular book, including pages of text and graphics. You generally turn the pages of an electronic book by clicking icons. A table of contents, glossary, and index also are available at the click of a button. To display a definition or a graphic, play a sound or video sequence, or connect to a Web site, you simply click a link (often a bold or underlined word).

E-book content is obtainable in a number of ways, from purchasing unlimited use or time-based permits, in which the e-book content disappears after the amount of time purchased has expired, to obtaining free e-book content.

Figure 5-10 Apple's iPod can store hundreds of digital books. Students can even load their own literary creations.

Figure 5-11 Geoffrey Chaucer's *The Canterbury Tales* is among the thousands of public domain reference and literacy works available from Project Gutenberg (*www.gutenberg.net*).

For example, **Project Gutenberg** makes thousands of literary and reference books and materials available free to everyone (Figure 5-11). The e-book revolution is just beginning to impact the way people live, teach, and learn; stay abreast of new and exciting ways to use and integrate e-book applications in teaching and learning.

Another popular type of electronic book is an electronic reference text, such as a digital media encyclopedia on CD or DVD. An **electronic reference text** is a digital version of a reference text, which uses text, graphics, sound, animation, and video to explain a topic or provide additional information. The multimedia encyclopedia, Microsoft Encarta, for example, includes the complete text of a multivolume encyclopedia. In addition to text-based information, Microsoft Encarta includes thousands of photos, animations, audio, and detailed illustrations. This array of digital media information is accessible via menus and links.

Electronic reference texts, such as digital media encyclopedias, also are available on the Web. Figure 5-12 lists a cross section of electronic reference texts that are available for home and school use.

Electronic Reference Texts

Name	Publisher	URL	Description
Encarta Encyclopedia Reference Library	Microsoft	www.microsoft.com	Combines nine great resources, including Encarta Encyclopedia Deluxe, Encarta Interactive World Atlas, Learning Tools, and more. Also includes translation dictionaries, homework tools, dynamic multimedia, streaming video, and updates.
Encarta Encyclopedia Deluxe	Microsoft	www.microsoft.com	Contains more than 60,000 articles, hundreds of photos, illustrations, maps, streaming video, a natural language search function, a dynamic timeline, virtual tours, 360-degree views, and text-to-speech capabilities.
Children's Encyclopedia	Dorling-Kindersley	www.dk.com	Delivers an interactive experience for younger students that combines fascinating and educational interactive reference materials that support learning by stimulating children's natural desire to explore.
Encyclopedia Britannica	Encyclopedia Britannica	www.britannica.com	Contains over 82,000 articles, more than 13,000 images, 1600 clickable maps and 4000 indexed timeline entries with Web links, videos, audio clips, and more.
American Sign Language Dictionary	Multimedia	www.m-2k.com	Uses text, QuickTime video, animations, and illustrations to teach 2600 signs; includes learning games and fingerspelling.

Figure 5-12 These electronic reference texts use digital media to clarify topics for students and supply additional information about thousands of subjects.

In addition to education, health and medicine are areas in which electronic references play an important role. For example, instead of using volumes of books, health professionals and students rely on electronic references for articles, photographs, illustrations, and animations that cover hundreds of health and first aid topics. Physical education, science, and medical students, for example, use the reference A.D.A.M. (Animated Dissection of Anatomy for Medicine) (Figure 5-13) to learn about the human body. Practicing physicians also use the software to communicate information to their patients.

Figure 5-13 Interactive CDs or DVDs such as A.D.A.M. can be used to study the respiratory system and other systems of the body.

HOW-TO GUIDES

Today, many interactive digital media applications are available to help individuals in their daily lives. These digital media applications fall into the broad category of how-to guides. **How-to guides** are digital media applications that include step-by-step instructions and interactive demonstrations to teach you practical new skills (Figure 5-14). Similar to computer-based training applications used by schools and businesses, how-to guides allow you to acquire new skills, become more productive, and try out your skills in a risk-free environment. The skills you learn with a how-to guide, however, usually apply to enhancing talents outside of your job.

How-to guides can help you buy a home or a car; design a garden; plan a vacation; repair your home, car, or computer; and more. Landscaping how-to guides, for example, allow you to design a landscape; place trees, shrubs, and flowers; and then add features such as pathways, fences, and retaining walls to complete the design (Figure 5-15). Many gardening how-to guides allow you to explore a database of plants with color photographs and the growth attributes of each one. Digital media how-to guides are available on CD, DVD, and the Web.

DIGITAL MEDIA NEWSPAPERS AND MAGAZINES (E-ZINES)

A **digital media newspaper** and a **digital media magazine** are digital versions of a newspaper or magazine distributed on CD, DVD, or via the World Wide Web. Many popular magazines and most newspapers have companion Web sites that provide digital media versions of some or all of their printed content (Figure 5-16). An **electronic magazine**, or **e-zine**, is a digital publication available on the Web.

How-to Guides on CD/DVD

Name	Publisher	URL	Description
3D Home Architect Home Design Deluxe 6	Broderbund	www.broderbund.com	Customize your current floor plans or plan a new home. Software has 2-D and 3-D editing tools.
The Complete Guide to Weddings	M2K	www.m-2k.com	Planning the ultimate wedding, but not sure where to start? This software will help you plan and organize every detail of your wedding from guest list, to seating arrangements, to negotiating prices for photographers and musicians.
Master Landscape & Home Design	Punch! Software	www.punchsoftware.com	Design a garden or entire yard by using scanned photos of your own property; choose trees, shrubs, flowers, and vines. You also can view sample gardens, and then view the plants as they grow and change with the seasons.
MasterCook Deluxe	ValuSoft	www.mastercook.com	Prepare more than 7000 dishes based on nutritional value and ingredients on hand. Watch instructional videos and adjust the portions to the number of servings needed.
Teach Yourself PC Maintenance	Learn2.com, Inc.	www.tutorials.com/	Learn computer concepts and terms and learn how to install drives and accessory hardware, such as memory, modems, maintenance tools, how to clean your keyboard, and more from interactive tutorials.

Figure 5-14 These how-to guides teach useful skills by using videos, interactive demonstrations, and animations.

Figure 5-15 This how-to landscaping guide shows a 3-D view of a house with plants, trees, patio, and garden area.

Digital Media Newspapers and Magazines

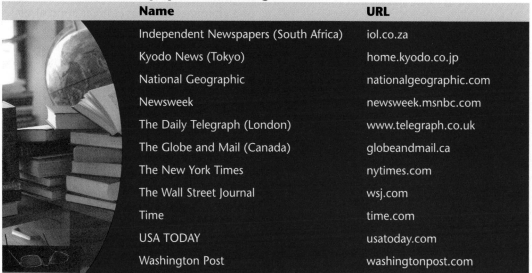

Name	URL
Independent Newspapers (South Africa)	iol.co.za
Kyodo News (Tokyo)	home.kyodo.co.jp
National Geographic	nationalgeographic.com
Newsweek	newsweek.msnbc.com
The Daily Telegraph (London)	www.telegraph.co.uk
The Globe and Mail (Canada)	globeandmail.ca
The New York Times	nytimes.com
The Wall Street Journal	wsj.com
Time	time.com
USA TODAY	usatoday.com
Washington Post	washingtonpost.com

Figure 5-16 This list contains only a few of the hundreds of digital media newspapers and magazines from dozens of countries that use video and audio clips, animations, and other interactive digital media tools to bring the world to homes and classrooms.

WEB INFO

To access an online educational magazine, visit the Teachers Discovering Computers Web site (*scsite.com/tdc4*), click Chapter 5, click Web Info, and then click Educational Magazine.

Digital media newspapers and magazines usually include the sections and articles found in print-based versions, such as departments, editorials, and more. Unlike printed publications, however, electronic magazines use many types of media to convey information. Audio and video clips can be included to showcase recent album releases or movies; animations can depict weather patterns or election results.

Figure 5-17 Many print-based journals and magazines have companion Web sites. *Technology & Learning* uses its Web site to provide the latest updates on educational technology and issues. Many online journals and magazines are searchable, allowing you to locate specific articles or information.

Some digital media magazines exist only in their digital format, whereas others are simply electronic versions of existing print magazines. Today, many print-based journals and magazines have companion Web sites that provide some or all of the magazine's printed content. Up-to-the-minute news, interactive polls, and digital media elements such as audio and video clips enhance the content found in the printed magazine (Figure 5-17).

ENTERTAINMENT AND EDUTAINMENT

As described, digital media combines text, graphics, audio, video, animation, and interactivity — thus making it ideal for entertainment. Digital media **computer games**, for example, use a combination of simulation, graphics, audio, and video to create a realistic and entertaining game situation. Often, the game simulates a real or fictitious world, in which you play the role of a character and have direct control of what happens in the game (Figure 5-18).

The music industry also sells interactive digital media applications on CDs and DVDs. Some interactive music CDs, for example, let you play musical instruments along with your favorite musician, read about the musician's life and interests, and even create your own version of popular songs. Like interactive games, these applications give you a character role and put you in control of the application. Many digital media applications are used for **edutainment**, which is an experience meant to be both educational and entertaining (Figure 5-19).

Figure 5-18
Entertainment applications, rich in digital media content, provide fun for both children and adults.

Entertainment Applications

Name	Publisher	URL	Description
Backyard Baseball	Infogames Entertainment	www.funkidsgames.com	Select players from 30 Major League Baseball teams or create your own team colors, ballpark, and strategy. Play online with other Windows users.
Dogz	Nintendo of America, Inc.	www.nintendo.com	Use voice recognition to train your Dogz to sit, fetch, or roll over; create custom scenes with the Play Scene Editor.
Motocross Madness	Microsoft	www.microsoft.com	Perform stunts on your motorbike while you race up to eight opponents online via the MSN Gaming Zone.
Empire in Arms	Matrix Games	www.matrixgames.com	Play this game of grand strategy alone or with up to six other players via e-mail or on the Internet.
The Sims	Electronic Arts	www.thesims.com	Develop characters in a neighborhood, build their homes, and display your creations on the World Wide Web with these open-ended games.

Edutainment Applications

Name	Publisher	URL	Description
ClueFinders	Broderbund	www.cluefinders.com	Go on amazing adventures through uncharted islands, rain forests, and other exotic locations with the ClueFinders gang. Your mission is to help the ClueFinders solve a mystery while mastering skills across the curriculum.
Harry Potter	Warner Brothers	www.harrypotter.com	Read extensive information on *Harry Potter* books at this official Harry Potter Web site where you can attend the Hogswarts School of Witchcraft and Wizardry, receive Quidditch training, and much more.
SimCity4	Electronic Arts	www.simcity.ea.com	Explore SimCity, one of the more widely used student edutainment games. With SimCity, you can create an entire city from the ground up.
Reader Rabbit	Broderbund	www.readerrabbit.com	Try out top-selling programs that teach young children problem solving, decision making, and logic skills. Offers help and prints reports.
The New Way Things Work	Global Software	www.learnatglobal.com	Discover how hundreds of machines work by viewing animations, illustrations, and videos.

Figure 5-19 Edutainment applications offer teachers and students both education and entertainment.

VIRTUAL REALITY

Virtual reality (VR) is the use of a computer to create an artificial environment that appears and feels like a real environment and allows you to explore space and manipulate the setting. In its simplest form, a virtual reality application displays a view that appears to be a three-dimensional view of a place or object, such as a landscape, a building, a molecule, or a red blood cell, which users can explore. The lastest evolution in VR is **converged media**, the interaction of virtual reality with live performance. Converged media is especially useful in things like police and military training where a totally live interaction might be dangerous.

Some forms of VR software require you to wear specialized headgear, body suits, and gloves to enhance the experience of the artificial environment (Figure 5-20). The headgear displays the artificial environment in front of your eyes. The body suit and gloves sense your motion and direction, allowing you to move through and pick up and hold items displayed in the virtual environment. Experts predict that body suits eventually will provide tactile feedback so you can experience the touch and feel of the virtual world.

Your first encounter with VR is likely to be a Web-based virtual reality game or virtual field trip. In such games, as you walk around the game's electronic landscape, the site notes your movements and changes your view of the landscape accordingly. Other VR Web sites allow you to take VR tours of a city, view hotel accommodations, or interact with local attractions.

Figure 5-20 A virtual reality body suit allows VR software to interpret the body movements of the wearer. The software then manipulates the image in the virtual environment and displays it in the headset.

The United States Senate Web site provides a virtual tour of the U.S. Capitol building. Students can take a guided tour or venture out on their own to tour the Capitol (Figure 5-21).

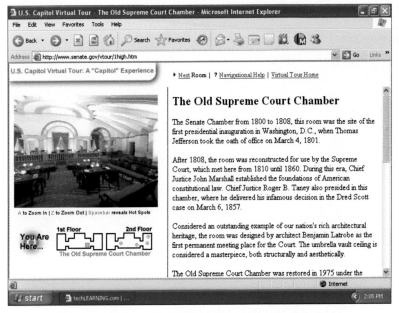

Figure 5-21 The Web allows students to take virtual tours of many historic locations all over the world. At this government Web site, students can take a guided tour of The Old Supreme Court Chamber.

Companies use VR for more practical, commercial applications as well. Office furniture companies have created virtual showrooms in which customers wander among and inspect available products. Automobile and airplane manufacturers are using virtual prototypes to test new models and shorten product design time. Telecommunications firms and others are using computer-based VR applications for employee training. As computing power and the use of the Web increase, practical applications of VR continue to emerge for education, business, and entertainment.

INFORMATION KIOSKS

An **information kiosk** is a computerized information or reference center that allows you to select various options to browse through or find specific information. A typical information kiosk is a self-service structure equipped with computer hardware and software. Kiosks often use touch screen monitors or keyboards for input devices and have all of the data and information needed for the application stored directly on the computer.

Information kiosks provide information in public places where visitors or customers have common questions. Locations such as shopping centers, hotels, airports, colleges, and universities, for example, use kiosks to provide information on available services, product locations, maps, and other information (Figure 5-22). Museums and libraries use kiosks to allow visitors to find the location of a specific exhibit. Kiosks providing Internet access also are expected to be popular in the near future.

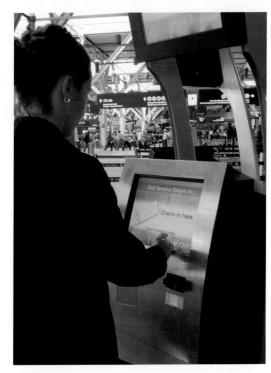

Figure 5-22 Airline travelers check in and print their boarding passes using a self-service kiosk.

DIGITAL MEDIA AND THE WORLD WIDE WEB

As you have learned while you have explored the multitude of Web sites provided at this textbook's Web site, digital media applications play an important role on the World Wide Web. In fact, much of the information on the Web today relies on digital media. Using digital media brings a Web page to life, increases the types of information available on the Web, expands the Web's potential uses, and makes the Internet a more entertaining and educational place to explore.

As described in Chapter 2, the Web uses many types of media to deliver information

WEB INFO

To take a virtual tour of a museum, visit the Teachers Discovering Computers Web site (*scsite.com/tdc4*), click Chapter 5, click Web Info, and then click Tour.

and enhance a user's Web experience (Figure 5-23). Graphics, animations, audio, and video reinforce text-based content and provide updated information. Many of the digital media applications described previously, including computer-based training, newspapers, e-zines, games, and virtual reality, are deliverable via the Web.

WEB-BASED TRAINING (WBT) AND DISTANCE LEARNING

Web-based training (WBT) is an approach to computer-based training that uses the technologies of the Internet and the World Wide Web. As with CBT, Web-based training typically consists of self-directed, self-paced instruction on a topic. Because it is delivered via the Web, however, WBT has the advantage of being able to offer up-to-date content on any type of computer platform. As a result, Web-based training already has replaced many traditional computer-based training applications.

Over the past few years, the number of organizations using Web-based training has exploded. Today, almost every major corporation in the United States provides employees with some type of Web-based training to teach new skills or upgrade their current skills.

Web-based training also is available for individuals at home or at work. Many school districts are using the Web to deliver all types of training to their teachers. This media offers anytime, anyplace training.

Today, anyone with access to the Web can take advantage of hundreds of digital media tutorials offered online. Such tutorials cover a range of topics, from how to change a flat tire to using and integrating Microsoft Office in the classroom (Figure 5-24). Many of these Web sites are free; others ask you to register and pay a fee to take the complete Web-based training course.

Distance learning, also called distance education, Web-based education, and distributed learning, is the delivery of education from one location to another; the learning takes place at a remote location. Most colleges and universities now offer numerous distance learning courses, usually in the form of Web-based or Web-enhanced

Figure 5-23 A NASA Web server offers textual and graphical information about the mission to Saturn.

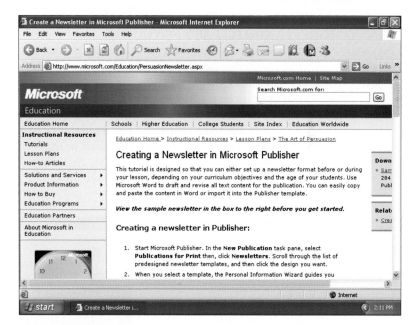

Figure 5-24 An example of the thousands of tutorials that are available on the Web.

courses (Figure 5-25 on the next page). A Web-based course, often called an **online course**, is a course that is taught mostly or completely on the Web, rather than in a traditional classroom. A **Web-enhanced course** is a traditional classroom course that uses the Web to enhance the content of the course.

Figure 5-25 Many colleges and universities provide their online courses using the WebCT e-learning system; other popular e-learning systems include Blackboard and eCollege.

COLLEGES AND UNIVERSITIES   Web-based courses offer many advantages for students who live far from a college or university campus, work full-time, or have scheduling conflicts; it allows them to attend class from home or other locations at any time that fits their schedule. The availability of Web-based courses has exploded in the past few years; experts estimate that more than 4 million students will take an online

course this year. Today, many university students will take one or more online classes during their college years. Many colleges and universities now offer advanced degrees, including doctorate degrees in which all required courses are offered online. Other colleges and universities offer advanced degrees in which the majority of required courses are offered online.

In addition, a number of fully accredited universities no longer provide traditional courses; 100 percent of their courses and degrees are provided online. For example, Walden University is one of the leading fully accredited 100% online universities in the world (Figure 5-26). Walden University provides online courses and graduate degrees in education, psychology, health and human services, management, engineering, computer science, business administration, and many other curriculum areas.

HIGH SCHOOLS   Most, if not all, states are now providing Web-based or online courses for their high school students (Figure 5-27). Web-based courses help prevent overcrowding and provide instruction for homebound students. Web-based courses also allow less-populated districts and schools in rural areas to share teachers.

By using the Web, these schools can offer specialized classes in French, Latin, calculus, and many other core and advanced subjects. By pooling resources and linking students from more than one school into a Web-based course, school districts can expand the number and type of classes they offer.

Many teachers now are Web-enhancing their classes (Figure 5-28). By **Web-enhancing** their classes, teachers provide their students with resources to enrich their learning experience. Parents also can access the Web sites to check on homework assignments, activities, student expectations, and more. Another benefit of using the Web in the classroom is having students interact with subject area experts. The Smithsonian Institute, for example, permits teachers and students to interact via the Web with the actual scientists who work for the Smithsonian. Many scientists want to increase educational opportunities for students, who someday may decide to become scientists.

Figure 5-26 Walden University is one of the leading online universities providing graduate degrees for teachers and administrators.

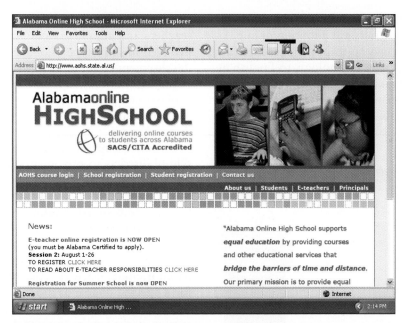

Figure 5-27 The Alabama Online High School enables principals to enroll students in online classes; for example, an individual student who needs a course that does not fit into her regular schedule or a group of students who need a course not offered in their school.

Figure 5-28 Many K-12 teachers provide extensive resources and more for their students by Web-enhancing their classes.

PROFESSIONAL DEVELOPMENT TRAINING

Until recently, in-service professional development training for teachers and administrators has remained basically unchanged for decades. Traditional in-service training involves teachers being trained in classrooms or labs and normally is conducted before or after school, on weekends, during in-service days, or during the summer.

Schools often have to provide costly substitutes when teachers are required to be out of the classroom to participate in extensive professional development training.

The traditional model of professional development training is undergoing a revolution — a Web-based or online revolution. Professional development training programs are being redefined in many school districts and state programs. States and school districts are adopting online training as a way to train their teachers in many areas, from technology, to English as a second language, to meeting recertification requirements, to a series of online courses leading to alternative certification. As a result of this professional development

revolution, hundreds of thousands of K-12 teachers and administrators now are involved in some type of online professional development training; and this is only the beginning. Currently, a great deal of in-service professional development training for teachers and administrators is being done online.

Many companies now work with school districts to provide graduate courses and online professional development training for teachers and administrators. Online professional development training can be self-paced or instructor-led. Most online professional development training available for teachers is self-paced. In **self-paced training**, teachers typically sign up for a specific course or module, and after completing all the requirements, they receive credit for the training. Some self-paced training courses provide access to a Help desk or instructors who can provide assistance. In contrast, **instructor-led training** involves continuous interaction with an instructor and the courses are more structured, often including schedules and assignment due dates. A number of school districts and even some states have developed online portals for their teachers to enroll in professional development courses, access resources, and receive assistance (Figure 5-29).

Figure 5-29 Many school districts provide extensive online professional development opportunities for their teachers and administrators.

K-12 Educational Software Applications

As described in previous sections, digital media is important not only for business and entertainment, but also for education. An **educational software application** refers to computer software products used to support teaching and learning of subject-related content. Interactive digital media applications enrich the learning process by providing individualized instruction and exploration; allowing students to examine their skills in a risk-free environment; and providing instant feedback, testing, and review. Many educational software applications now are correlated to state standards (Figure 5-30).

Figure 5-30 Destination Math is an example of an interactive digital media math problem that provides students with nontraditional ways to master math skills correlated to state standards.

up to 8 years old can learn and play with all of their favorite characters through games, music, stories, and more.

PBS also provides a Web site, PBS KIDS GO!, for digital kids ages 6–12, where they can share their opinions and stories, play games, solve puzzles, and much more (Figure 5-34). The *Ready to Learn* partnership also provides a Web site for parents (PBS Parents) and for teachers (PBS TeacherSource). To access all of these *Ready To Learn* Web sites, see the Web Info on the preceding page.

TUTORIALS

A **tutorial** is a teaching program designed to help individuals learn to use a product or concepts. Tutorials are designed to tutor, or instruct. Many software products contain built-in tutorials to teach the user how to use the software. Developers create educational tutorials that use the computer to provide an entire instructional area and are created so students can work their way through the tutorial to learn content without any help or other materials. The teaching solutions provided by tutorials range from a structured linear approach with specific content objectives to a nonlinear approach that offers alternative paths through the lesson based on students' responses, called **branching**. Branching reflects classroom learning theory by allowing students to excel at their own pace, providing feedback and remediation when needed. Figure 5-35 provides some of the features of effective educational tutorials.

EDUCATIONAL SIMULATIONS

An **educational computer simulation** or a **video game** is a computerized model of real life that represents a physical or simulated process. These programs are unique because the user can cause things to happen, change the conditions, and make decisions based on the criteria provided to simulate real-life situations. These interactive programs model some event, reality, real-life circumstances, or phenomenon. Simulations offer learners the opportunity to manipulate variables that affect the outcomes of the experience. Using simulation is not a new teaching strategy. As you learned earlier in this chapter, business

Figure 5-34 The PBS KIDS GO! Web site provides games, digital storytelling, and much more for digital kids ages 6–12.

Tutorial Features

- User-friendly
- Easy to navigate
- Available on both platforms
- Student-centered interactivity throughout software
- Learner control over delivery of content
- Active instructional techniques
- Innovative learning strategies
- Real-life learning experiences
- Motivational and appropriate for grade level
- Contains valid testing
- Appropriate sequence and scope of content
- Evaluated by educators

Figure 5-35 Features of effective educational tutorials.

and industry have been using simulation for many years.

Interest is growing in programs such as SimCity, Sim Theme Park, and Sim Coaster that let students design, interact, and provide more accurate explanations and

WEB INFO

To learn more about integrated learning systems, visit the Teachers Discovering Computers Web site (*scsite.com/tdc4*), click Chapter 5, click Web Info, and then click Integrated Learning System.

examples of real life. **SimCity** is a very popular simulation program for education (Figure 5-36). Students design cities, communities, neighborhoods, and businesses, including infrastructure, such as telephone lines, buildings, and more. As the cities grow in size and complexity, natural disasters and other realistic problems occur continuously requiring students to use all available city resources, including financial resources, to keep the cities running.

The availability of educational computer simulations on the Web is experiencing dramatic growth. A student can learn how a building is demolished, dissect a frog, see a real human heart in action, and more.

INTEGRATED LEARNING SYSTEMS

An **integrated learning system (ILS)** is a sophisticated software package usually developed by an established educational software corporation as a complete educational software solution in one package. These software solutions provide individual student diagnostic data through pretests, instruction based on the diagnostic data, continuous monitoring of student performance with automatic adjustments in instruction when needed, a variety of formats for teaching content, and multi-levels of content. Most integrated learning systems also offer a comprehensive management solution for maintaining the software and for tracking student use and progress. Although expensive, integrated learning systems are praised as a comprehensive software solution for low-achieving schools. Integrated learning systems are appealing to school administrators, school boards, and principals because they offer a full, flexible solution in one package.

A new type of software application has evolved that is similar to an ILS, called an open learning system or an advanced learning system (Figure 5-37). An **open learning system** or an **advanced learning system** is an integrated learning system that includes software titles from leading publishers. What makes this type of learning system different from a traditional ILS is the number of different software titles and activities these packages include. In addition, many ILS applications prescribe the solution for the student while the new open learning systems make the teacher the key player in determining and prescribing the appropriate assessment, choosing the ideal activities, matching the software to objectives and standards, and integrating the software into their curriculum.

Figure 5-36 SimCity, a popular simulation program, creates a real-life environment for development of problem-solving skills.

Figure 5-37 ClassWorks is a popular open learning system.

CURRICULUM-SPECIFIC EDUCATIONAL SOFTWARE

Today, hundreds of high-quality interactive and multimedia educational programs are available for use by K-12 educators. Most of these programs are available on CD and DVD, or are installed on school networks; others are available on the Web. Many of these educational software applications are designed for curriculum-specific teaching and learning and can be organized in categories as described in the following sections. These major categories are by no means all-inclusive, as many software programs are available for K-12 educators that can be used in dozens of curricular areas.

CREATIVITY   Creativity applications often have students start with a blank canvas, which allows them to use their imagination and ingenuity. Students can control the design of their projects completely, using the tools provided by the software application. Some applications provide students with ideas and premade backgrounds and images. Students typically have complete control over the design, graphics, and path they create. A number of popular software programs are available that fit in this category. Creativity software applications include Jump Start Artist (Figure 5-38), iLife, Inspiration, Kidspiration, Ultimate Writing and Creativity Center, Storybook Weaver, Studio MX, Microsoft Publisher, Paint Shop 15, Photoshop, Disney's Magic Artist, KidWorks, MovieWorks Deluxe, Kid Pix, Adobe Creative Suite Premium.

Figure 5-38 Jump Start Artist is an example of creativity software that helps young students express themselves artistically.

CRITICAL THINKING   Critical-thinking applications stimulate students to use critical-thinking skills (Figure 5-39). Students often are presented with a problem and a variety of ways to solve the problem. They must use critical-thinking skills to obtain the correct solution to the problem. Critical-thinking software applications include I SPY Harry Potter, GeoSarfari Series, TableTop Jr, The Way Things Work, Thinkin' Things collections, Zoombinis collection, BrainCogs, SimCity, and Thinkology.

[a] BrainCogs

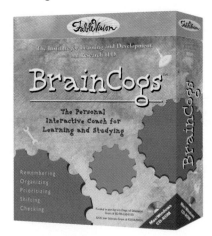

Figure 5-39
Dozens of critical-thinking applications are available for students of all ages. Figure 5-39a shows BrainCogs, which teaches higher-level thinking skills and encourages creativity. Figure 5-39b shows a popular program called The Way Things Work.

[b] The Way Things Work

EARLY LEARNING Early learning **applications** are designed to provide students in grades PreK-3 with a developmental head start in reading, language arts, math, science, and other curriculum areas (Figure 5-40). Students are presented with engaging graphics, a variety of paths, and a wide variety of activities. These fun and interactive programs include Kidspiration, Millie's Math House, Living Books Library, Sammy's Science House, the JumpStart series of software titles, Reader Rabbit's Reading series, and many more outstanding programs.

Figure 5-40 Early learning software applications are designed primarily for grades PreK-3, and provide students with a developmental head start. Displayed is a popular program called Kidspiration.

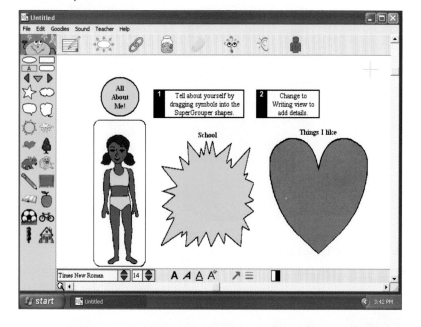

ESL/FOREIGN LANGUAGE ESL and foreign **language applications** provide K-12 students with assistance in learning English and other languages (Figure 5-41). These applications enable students to practice their skills in a nonthreatening environment. These language-specific programs include English Express Deluxe, The Heartsoft Best-Sellers ESL Version, EduOle, Instant Immersion English, Instant Immersion Spanish, Learn to Speak French, Learn to Speak Spanish, and dozens of other language programs designed for students in all grades. You also can download free translation software that lets your computer talk from the ReadPlease Web site. Other translation software allows you and your students to translate English to Spanish, French, German, and other languages.

LANGUAGE ARTS Language arts **applications**, available for all grade levels, support student learning throughout the reading and writing process (Figure 5-42). These applications try to engage students, encouraging them to learn critical skills in a fun and creative environment. Popular language arts programs include Ultimate Writing and Creativity Center, Student Writing Center, Clicker 4, the Reader Rabbit series, Vocabulary Development, the High School Reading Comprehension Series, Reading Blaster, and dozens more.

Figure 5-42 Language arts software is available for all grade levels. Shown is Reader Rabbit 1, a software designed for first graders.

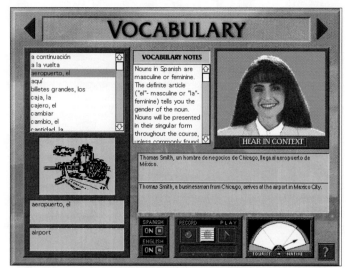

Figure 5-41 ESL and foreign language applications include software programs for Spanish, English, French, and many other languages. Shown is the popular Learn to Speak Spanish program.

MATH AND SCIENCE Math applications help students master basic and complex mathematics and are available for all grade levels (Figure 5-43). Many applications provide students with skill practice and problem-solving activities. **Science applications** are available for all grade levels and assist students in learning a wide variety of science concepts (Figure 5-44). Multimedia science applications can assist students in mastering difficult or abstract concepts by providing visual representations. Math programs include the Math Advantage series,

Destination Math, Mathosaurus, Geometer's Sketchpad, Math Blaster, Math WorkShop Deluxe, MathXpert, the Mighty Math series, Math Munchers, Math Companion, Tessellation Exploration, Wild West Math, and many more.

Science applications include Thinkin' Science, Virtual Labs, The Ultimate Human Body, I Love Science, Discovery Channel School series, Magic School Bus series, A.D.A.M. Essentials High School Suite, Pinball Science, GeoSafari, Earth Quest, Science Court, and numerous others.

[a] Math Advantage - Algebra

[b] MathXpert

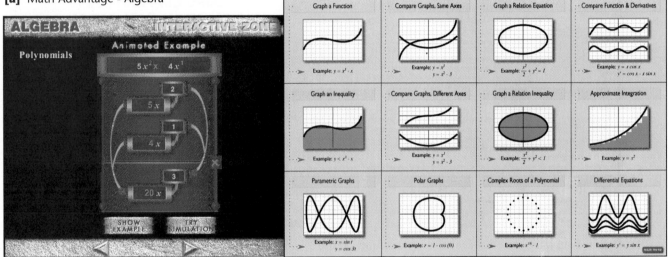

Figure 5-43 Math software engages and motivates students to learn basic and complex concepts. Figure 5-43a shows a Math Advantage Algebra 1 title, and Figure 5-43b displays MathXpert software. MathXpert is designed for high school students and covers hundreds of math concepts, including graphing.

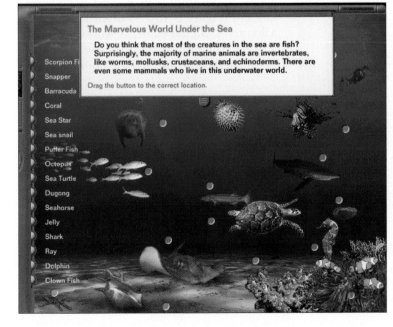

Figure 5-44 Science software allows all students to explore and interact with science concepts. Shown is the GeoSafari Knowledge Pad program on marine animals.

SOCIAL STUDIES   Social studies software applications encourage higher-order thinking skills, provide reinforcement of facts, and allow students to define their own path (Figure 5-45). Special-education teachers also can use these applications for teaching language skills. A few social studies programs include the Carmen Sandiego series, Oregon Trail, Amazon Trail, TimeLiner, Cradles of Civilization, Inspirer series, Chronicle Encyclopedia of History, and the Discovery Channel series.

Figure 5-45 Interactive digital media software, such as the Chronicle Encyclopedia of History, allows students to understand social studies concepts.

Figure 5-46 The basic software that comes with scanners allows users to edit scanned images and save the images in different file formats.

Creating and Presenting Digital Media Presentations

Creating or developing **digital media presentations** involves producing various digital media elements, defining the elements' relationships to each other, and then sequencing them in an appropriate order. Individuals often use digital media authoring software to help complete these tasks. Many options are available for you and your students to present digital media presentations.

OBTAINING GRAPHICS FOR A DIGITAL MEDIA APPLICATION

Graphics, including illustrations, photos, and animations, are essential elements in any digital media application. Teachers and students easily can add color images and photos to digital media applications using color scanners and digital cameras.

The basic software that comes with scanners (Figure 5-46) allows users to conduct basic editing of scanned images and also save scanned images in different file formats. A **color scanner** converts images into a digitized format for use in digital media applications (Figure 5-47). Sophisticated image editing programs are available for users who require a wider variety of image editing possibilities.

Another easy and effective way to obtain color photographs for a digital media application is by using a digital camera (Figure 5-48). As discussed in Chapter 4, **digital cameras** work much like regular cameras, except they use a small reusable disk or internal memory to store

Figure 5-47 A color scanner can convert images into digitized format for digital media applications and is easy to use.

digital photographs. You easily can transfer photographs taken with a digital camera to a computer's hard disk and then incorporate them into a digital media document or presentation. Many newer digital cameras have the capability to capture small amounts of moving images to be made into short video clips.

Figure 5-48 An easy and effective way to obtain digitized color photographs is by using a digital camera. After the photographs are input into a computer, they can be incorporated into a digital media application.

Digital images related to virtually any topic or area of interest can be downloaded from the Web, often without cost. For example, you can choose from thousands of clip art images and digital photos from the Microsoft Office Clip Art and Media Web site (Figure 5-49). In addition, you can purchase CDs or DVDs that contain thousands of digital images from retail stores or Web sites. After you have obtained the graphics you want, you can incorporate them into your digital media applications or presentations.

DIGITAL MEDIA AND WEB AUTHORING SOFTWARE

Digital media authoring software, also called an **authoring tool**, allows an individual to create an interactive digital media presentation or project that includes text, graphics, sound, animation, or video. A digital media presentation, however, is more than just a combination of these elements. Digital media authoring software lets you create the application or presentation by controlling the placement of text and graphics and the duration of sounds, video, and animations.

Recall that a digital media application also is interactive, meaning you can decide the amount and order of the material it contains. Digital media authoring software allows you to create interactivity by defining places in the program that respond to

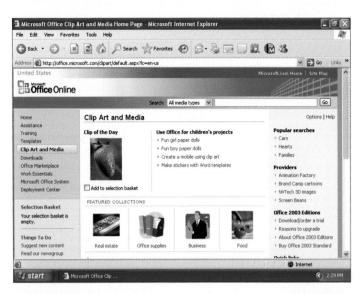

Figure 5-49 The Web comprises many sites from which teachers and students can download graphic images for use in multimedia applications.

user input. In a digital media application, for example, you might include a screen where users can click buttons to play a video or skip the video and move to the next screen.

Digital media developers in corporations and businesses use digital media authoring software programs, such as **Producer, Authorware, Flash,** and **Director.** Developers use these high-end programs to produce many of the hundreds of educational digital media applications used in schools today. Very few teachers use these high-end programs as they are expensive and more tailored to a commercial environment.

Many easy-to-use and less-expensive digital media authoring programs, however, are widely available and currently used by K-12 teachers and students in schools all over the world. As discussed throughout this textbook, today's youth are very well connected to all that is digital, as it makes up every aspect of their lives. Technology is a tool for them that they use without fear and they gravitate to it. Two of the more popular digital media authoring tools used in K-12 schools are Microsoft PowerPoint and Apple iLife.

Microsoft **PowerPoint** allows teachers and students to create multimedia presentations that can incorporate text, graphics, animation, audio, video, links, and most

WEB INFO

To access an interactive tutorial on using PowerPoint, visit the Teachers Discovering Computers Web site (*scsite.com/tdc4*), click Chapter 5, click Web Info, and then click PowerPoint.

importantly, interactivity. You can learn how to use and integrate PowerPoint in your classroom by completing the In the Lab activities at the end of this chapter and the step-by-step project on incorporating various digital elements into a PowerPoint presentation available for download at this chapter's Digital Media Corner. In addition, review Chapter 3's Digital Media Corner for more information on Producer and Photo Story, two free add-on programs for PowerPoint that can help you and your students easily capture, synchronize, and publish audio, video, and digital images in your PowerPoint presentations.

The **iLife** integrated suite, included on all new Apple computers, is designed for the digital media revolution (Figure 5-50). Included in iLife are photo editing and manipulation, music and voice-overs, video production, DVD creation, and much more. For more information on iLife, see this chapter's Digital Media Corner.

The digital media capabilities of both PowerPoint and iLife are integrated and seamless and so easy to use that even younger students can begin producing personalized digital media projects almost immediately. The integration makes organizing projects easier because all digital

assets (photos, music, and video clips, and so on) interlink. These tools help you, as the teacher, become a facilitator who guides the learning, rather than the lecturer who imparts knowledge.

These programs provides a wide range of opportunities for students to develop richly mediated stories, such as recording live scenes from plays as they perform; creating interactive electronic portfolios; designing and developing videos and/or slide shows of documentaries, political speeches, or historical moments; producing public service announcements that show their understanding of sensitive public policies; taking a stand by debating a topic; and/or demonstrating visually otherwise complex abstract concepts. The topics are endless, the possibilities without limits.

Other popular digital media authoring and Web development programs used by teachers and students include Macromedia Dreamweaver, Mediator 7, MovieWorks, Create Together, Netscape Composer, and Microsoft FrontPage. In addition, both Windows and Mac OS operating systems provide extensive resources that allow you and your students to create your own movies, burn CDs and DVDs, and create other digital media products.

PRESENTING DIGITAL MEDIA

Presenting your digital media presentations and having your students present their digital media projects may require a projection system so your students can see and hear the presentations and projects clearly. For most classroom presentations, a large monitor or large-screen television is a practical solution. Other solutions include using data projectors and electronic whiteboards.

LARGE MONITORS OR TELEVISIONS   The most practical and least expensive way for you and your students to present digital media in your classroom is to connect your classroom computer or a notebook computer to a large-screen monitor or a large-screen television. Many school districts provide their teachers with a large-screen monitor or a 27- or 32-inch television for classroom presentations. These large-screen monitors or televisions often are mounted

Figure 5-50   Apple's iLife was created for today's digital generation.

on rolling carts so teachers can use them in more than one classroom (Figure 5-51). Connecting most desktop computers to a television requires a special converter that converts the digital signal of a computer to the analog signal required by most televisions. AVerMedia sells an affordable PC/Mac-to-TV converter for less than $100 that allows you to project any computer application onto a big-screen TV. Some notebook computers now have the converter hardware and software built in and as a result can be connected directly to a television using a cable often supplied with the notebook computer.

Figure 5-51 Using a large-screen monitor or television connected to a computer is a common way to project computer images in a classroom so all students can view digital media presentations or interactive software programs. These systems also can be used to show videotapes using a VCR or DVDs using a DVD player.

DATA PROJECTORS   Recall that a **data projector** is a device that projects the image that appears on a computer screen onto a large screen so an audience, such as students in a classroom or school assembly, can see the image clearly (Figure 5-52). Data projectors are expensive and thus are not a practical option for every classroom. Most schools have at least one data projector that can be used by teachers; however, schools normally use data projectors when making presentations to a large group of students, teachers, or parents.

INTERACTIVE WHITEBOARDS   A teaching tool becoming increasingly popular with educators is the **interactive whiteboard**, also called an **electronic whiteboard**, which turns a computer and data projector into a powerful tool for teaching and learning. One

Figure 5-52 Data projectors are used to project a computer's image and other digital media capabilities onto a large screen.

interactive whiteboard, called a **SMART Board**, produced by Smart Technologies, is more than a presentation system (Figure 5-53). With a computer image projected onto the SMART Board, you can press on its large, touch-sensitive surface to access and control any computer application. In addition, you can write notes, draw diagrams, and highlight information. You then can save and print your notes and hand them out to students or make them available on your school's network. Another whiteboard option is the InterWrite SchoolBoard from the GTCO CalComp. InterWrite **SchoolPad** uses a Bluetooth wireless pad. SchoolPad can be used with InterWrite's interactive

WEB INFO

To learn more about interactive whiteboards, visit the Teachers Discovering Computers Web site (*scsite.com/tdc4*), click Chapter 5, click Web Info, and then click Interactive Whiteboards.

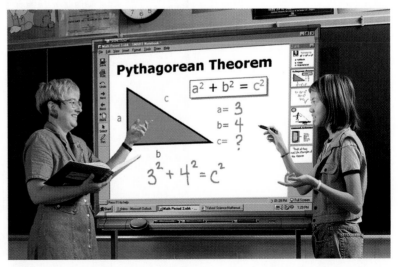

Figure 5-53 An electronic whiteboard is an interactive presentation system that turns a computer and data projector into a powerful tool for teaching and learning.

whiteboard or independently to create an electronic whiteboard on any wall surface. Using SchoolPad, you can control your computer from anywhere in the classroom.

Why Are Digital Media and Educational Software Applications Important for Education?

Digital media applications are changing the traditional dynamics of learning in classrooms. As previously noted, interactivity is one of the major features of digital media applications. The ability of users to interact with a digital media application is perhaps the single most critical feature of digital media and has enormous potential to improve learning in K-12 schools.

As mentioned earlier, extensive research conducted over a period of more than 20 years has shown that, when properly evaluated and integrated into teaching at the point of instruction, digital media applications are highly effective teaching tools. Studies indicate that students retain approximately 20 percent of what they see; 30 percent of what they hear; and 50 percent of what they see *and* hear. When a student has a chance to hear, see, *and*

interact with a learning environment, he can retain as much as 80 percent of the information. Digital media applications provide that interactive learning environment, which makes them powerful tools for teaching and learning (Figure 5-54).

One of the better reasons for teachers to utilize digital media software in the classroom is that it appeals to a variety of learning styles. Helping every student learn in her own, unique way ensures success for all students. Digital media software applications assist teachers in meeting this need by combining interactive software integrated with teaching strategies to enhance the learning process. Furthermore, digital media software is engaging and motivational for today's digital students.

Another important reason for students' increased retention is that they become active participants in the learning process instead of passive recipients of information. Interactive digital media applications engage students by asking them to define their own paths through an application, which often leads them to explore many related topics.

Many teachers have noted that students are motivated by and enjoy the process of creating their own interactive digital media presentation using digital media authoring software. Many students

WEB INFO

To learn more about learning styles, visit the Teachers Discovering Computers Web site (*scsite.com/tdc4*), click Chapter 5, click Web Info, and then click Learning Styles.

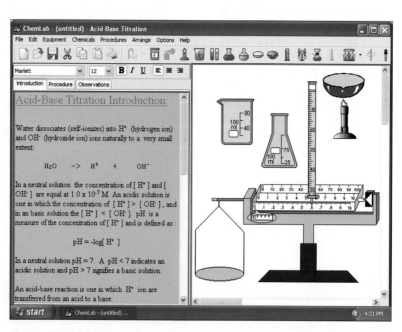

Figure 5-54 Digital media supports learning; interactive students become active learners.

enjoy conducting research and writing when their writing projects involve the creation of a digital media presentation — and they will more readily practice those skills. Further, the completion of a digital media project is a self-esteem and confidence booster for many students.

Teachers can use digital media software both as a productivity tool and as an integration tool. You can use a multimedia software application such as PowerPoint to introduce new concepts, present lectures, and demonstrate to students effective screen design and presentation techniques. In addition, teachers can create a digital media presentation to present a new concept and then provide students access to the presentation so they can easily review new information and interact directly with the software.

When teachers effectively use digital media software as a productivity tool, they are modeling for their students how to use this powerful software. This can be the first step in learning to integrate digital media software effectively into the curriculum. Teachers can have students demonstrate their learning by creating their own digital media presentations and presenting them to the class.

For digital media applications to reach their full potential in the classroom, teachers must evaluate digital media applications for content and appropriateness. Chapter 7 provides additional guidance on evaluating educational software and Web resources for the classroom.

Copyright is an important matter for you and your students to understand when using and creating digital media presentations. Copyright issues, including fair use guidelines, are covered in detail in Chapter 8. Finally, to reap the full benefits of digital media at home, you should consider investing in a high-speed DSL or cable connection to the Internet.

Digital Imaging and Video Technology

Using today's technologies, you and your digital students easily can learn how to create and edit digital graphics and video. Following this chapter is a special feature that introduces you to the world of digital imaging and video technology.

Summary of Integrating Digital Media and Educational Software Applications

This chapter examined how to use, and more important, integrate digital media and educational software applications in your classroom curriculum. First, you learned how the terms technology, multimedia, and digital media have evolved over the years. Next, you learned about the different elements used in digital media applications, the variety of digital media applications, and the growing popularity of distance learning. You then learned about educational software applications and how to create and present digital media presentations. Finally, the chapter reviewed the value of digital media in education. Effectively integrated digital media education software applications have the potential to impact education in many dramatic ways.

In Brief

INSTRUCTIONS: In Brief summarizes the concepts presented in this chapter. To listen to the audio version of this In Brief, visit scsite.com/tdc4. Click Chapter 5 at the top of the Web page and then click In Brief on the left sidebar.

1. What Is Digital Media?

Digital media is defined as those technologies that allow users to create new forms of interaction, expression, communication, and entertainment in a digital format. Multimedia is the combination of text, color, graphics, digital manipulation of photographs and music, presentation capabilities, and production. Digital media software refers to any computer-based presentation or application software that uses multimedia elements. Text consists of characters that are used to create words, sentences, and paragraphs and is a fundamental element used in all digital media applications. A graphic is a digital reprensentation of nontext information, such as a drawing, chart, or photograph. Displaying a series of still graphics creates an animation, which is a graphic that has the illusion of motion. Audio is any digitized music, speech, or other sound that is stored and produced by the computer. Video consists of visual frames that are played back at speeds of 15 to 60 frames per second and provides full motion in real time.

2. Digital Media Applications

A **digital media** or **multimedia application** involves the use of digital media technology for education, business, and entertainment. Businesses use digital media, for example, in interactive advertisements and for job- and skill-training applications. Another important application of interactive digital media is to create simulations, which are computer-based models of real-life situations. Digital media applications include computer-based training, electronic books and references, how-to guides, and magazines. Digital media also is used in entertainment, virtual reality, information kiosks, and on the Web.

3. Computer-Based Training

Computer-based training (CBT) is a tool by which individuals learn by using and completing exercises using instructional software on computers. Computer-based training is popular in business and industry to teach new skills or enhance the existing skills of employees. Computer-based training is effective especially for teaching software skills if the CBT is integrated with the software application because it allows students to practice as they learn.

4. Electronic Books and References

An **electronic book**, or **e-book**, is a small, book-sized computer that allows users to read, save, highlight, bookmark, and add notes to online text. Electronic books have many of the elements of a regular book, including pages of text and graphics. Generally, you turn the pages of an electronic book by clicking icons. **How-to guides** are digital media applications that include step-by-step instructions and interactive demonstrations to teach you practical new skills. A **digital media magazine** is a digital version of a magazine, which is distributed on CD or via the World Wide Web.

5. Entertainment and Edutainment

Digital media combines the media elements of television and interactivity, making it ideal for entertainment. Digital media computer games use graphics, sound, and video to create a realistic and entertaining game situation. Many digital media applications are used for edutainment, which is an experience meant to be both educational and entertaining. Virtual reality (VR) is the use of a computer to create an artificial environment that appears and feels like a real environment and allows a user to explore space and manipulate the setting. As computing power and the use of the Web increase, practical applications continue to emerge for education, business, and entertainment. An information kiosk is a computerized information or reference center that provides information in public locations.

In Brief

6. Digital Media and the World Wide Web

Digital media applications also play an important role on the World Wide Web, which is the part of the Internet that supports multimedia. The Web uses many types of digital media to deliver information and enhance a user's Web experience. **Web-based training (WBT)** is an approach to computer-based training that uses the technologies of the Internet and the World Wide Web.

7. Web-Based Training and Distance Learning

Many colleges and universities and some high schools offer Web-based or Web-enhanced courses. A **Web-based course** is a course that is taught mostly or completely on the Web, rather than in a traditional classroom. A **Web-enhanced course** is a course that uses the Web to enhance the content of a traditional classroom course. **Distance learning**, also called **distance education**, **Web-based education**, and **distributed learning**, is the delivery of education from one location to another.

8. K-12 Educational Software Applications

Digital media is important not only for business and entertainment, but also for education. An educational software application refers to computer software products used to support teaching and learning of subject-related content. **Educational software applications** are available in several different designs, forms, and curriculum levels. Educational applications include computer-assisted instruction, drill-and-practice software, educational games, tutorials, educational simulations, integrated learning systems, and Web-based education.

9. Drill-and-Practice, Games, and Tutorials

Drill-and-practice software first supplies factual information and then through repetitive exercises allows students to continue to work on the specific materials to remember the information. Educational games usually include a set of rules, and students can compete against other students or the game itself. **Computer games** can be an effective way to teach information through repetition and practice. A **tutorial** is a teaching program designed to help individuals learn to use a product or concepts.

10. Simulations and Integrated Learning Systems

An **educational computer simulation** is a computerized model of real life that represents a physical or simulated process. An **integrated learning system (ILS)** is a sophisticated software package usually developed by an established educational software corporation as a complete educational software solution in one package.

11. Curriculum-Specific Educational Software

Hundreds of high-quality, curriculum-specific, interactive and digital media educational programs are available for use by K-12 educators. Most of these programs are available on CD and DVD, or are installed on school networks; others are available on the Web.

12. Creating Digital Media Presentations

Creating or developing **digital media presentations** involves producing various digital media elements, defining the elements' relationships to each other, and then sequencing them in an appropriate order. **Digital media authoring software** allows an individual to create an interactive digital media presentation that includes text, graphics, sound, animation, or video. Two of the more popular digital media authoring tools used in K-12 schools are Microsoft PowerPoint and Apple iLife.

Key·Terms

INSTRUCTIONS: Use the Key Terms to help focus your study of the terms used in this chapter. To further enhance your understanding of the Key Terms in this chapter, visit scsite.com/tdc4. Click Chapter 5 at the top of the Web page and then click Key Terms on the left sidebar. Read the definition for each term and then access current and additional information about the term from the Web.

Exercises

Web Info

In Brief

Key Terms

Checkpoint

Teaching Today

Education Issues

Integration Corner

Software Corner

Digital Media Corner

Assistive Technologies Corner

In the Lab

Learn It Online

Features

Timeline

Guide to WWW Sites

Buyer's Guide

State/Federal Sites

Professional Sites

Search Tools

advanced learning system [300]
animation [282]
audio [282]
authoring tool [305]
Authorware [305]

branching [299]

clip [283]
clip art collection [281]
CODEC (compression and decompression) [284]
color scanner [304]
computer-assisted instruction (CAI) [297]
computer-based training (CBT) [285]
computer game [290]
converged media [291]
courseware [285]
creativity application [301]
critical-thinking application [301]

data projector [307]
digital camera [304]
digital media [310]
digital media application [284]
digital media authoring software [305]
digital media magazine [310]
digital media newspaper [288]
digital media presentation [304]
digital media software [279]
Director [305]
distance education [293]
distance learning [293]
distributed learning [293]
drill-and-practice software [298]

early learning application [302]
e-book [286]
educational computer simulation [299]
educational game [298]
educational software application [296]
edutainment [290]
electronic book [286]
electronic magazine [288]
electronic reference text [286]
electronic whiteboard [307]
ESL and foreign language application [302]
e-zine [288]

Flash [305]

graphics [304]

how-to guide [288]

iLife [306]
individual lead training (ILT) [285]
iPod Book [286]
information kiosk [292]
instructor-led training [296]
integrated learning system (ILS) [300]
interactive digital media [279]
interactive whiteboard [307]
interactivity [277]

language arts application [302]

math application [303]
Motion Pictures Experts Group (MPEG) [284]

multimedia [278]
Musical Instrument Digital Interface (MIDI) [283]

online course [293]
open learning system [300]

PowerPoint [305]
Project Gutenberg [286]

remediation [298]

science application [303]
self-paced training [296]
SimCity [300]
simulation [285]
skills-reinforcement software [298]
SchoolPad [307]
SMART Board [307]
social studies software application [304]

technology [278]
text [280]
ToolBook [309]
tutorial [299]

video [283]
video compression [283]
video games [299]
virtual reality (VR) [291]
visual learners [281]

Web-based course [311]
Web-based education [293]
Web-based training (WBT) [311]
Web-enhanced course [293]
Web-enhancing [294]

Checkpoint

INSTRUCTIONS: Use the Checkpoint excercises to check your knowledge level of the chapter. To complete the Checkpoint exercises interactively, visit scsite.com/tdc4. Click Chapter 5 at the top of the Web page and then click Checkpoint on the left sidebar.

1. Label the Figure

Instructions: Identify the multimedia devices.

2. Matching

Instructions: Match each term from the column on the left with the best description from the column on the right.

_____ 1. text
_____ 2. graphic
_____ 3. animation
_____ 4. audio
_____ 5. video

a. a graphic that has the illusion of motion
b. photographic images played back at speeds of 15 to 30 frames per second to provide the appearance of motion in real time
c. digitized music, speech, or other sounds stored and produced by a computer
d. characters used to create words, sentences, and paragraphs; a fundamental element in multimedia
e. digital representation of nontext information, such as a drawing, chart, or photograph

3. Short Answer

Instructions: Write a brief answer to each of the following questions.

1. Briefly describe why digital media and educational software applications are important for education. _____
2. Name four media components of digital media software? Briefly describe each. _____
3. What are the differences between electronic reference books and how-to guides? Which one is used more often in education? Why? _____
4. What is virtual reality? How do teachers, students, and others use virtual reality? Is virtual reality available on the Web? _____
5. What is meant by educational software applications? Briefly describe four different categories of educational software applications. _____

Teaching Today

INSTRUCTIONS: Teaching Today provides an appreciation of the value that technology and the Web have for K-12 education. Each numbered segment contains one or more links that reinforce the information presented in the segment. To display this page from the Web, visit scsite.com/tdc4. Click Chapter 5 at the top of the Web page and then click Teaching Today on the left sidebar.

1. Web Adventures

Many schools are using digital media applications and the Web to help students better understand the past or gain a greater appreciation of other cultures. For example, using a digital media application called Oregon Trail, students learn about westward expansion by experiencing the hardships and making decisions similar to those facing nineteenth-century settlers. At the Web site for Educational Web Adventures, students can participate in adventures such as Tracking The Tiger Trade, in which they go undercover to Asia to explore the illegal trade of tiger parts, or Amazon Interactive, a project focusing on the people and geography of the Ecuadorian Amazon. Are these kinds of digital media applications and Web adventures appropriate for all grade levels? How does their use compare with traditional approaches to instruction and learning? How do you think students feel about using these types of resources? How could you best use these types of resources in your classroom? What supplemental materials would you need?

2. Multimedia Software

You think your Physical Education students would learn more and be more motivated if you integrated digital media into your curriculum. You have heard from other teachers that a wide variety of Health, Nutrition, and Physical Education software is available. Where might you locate a list of such digital media software titles that meet the standards for the district and that can assist you in teaching your students? Where might you locate such a list on the Web? Do any of the lists you find provide other teachers' reviews of the software? Do any of these resources provide information about incorporating other technologies in the curriculum? In what other ways could you use digital media to motivate your students to learn? What other actions might you take to ensure that you make an informed decision when choosing digital media software that is most effective for you and your students?

3. Virtual Field Trip

You have been teaching your students about famous eighteenth- and nineteenth-century artists. As a final activity, you want to take your students on a field trip to an art museum. The nearest museum, however, is three hours away, so the trip requires bus transportation. Due to the cost of the proposed field trip, your principal has asked you to explore other possibilities. What other options do you have? Could you take your class on a virtual field trip to an art museum? How would you and your students feel about taking that type of field trip? What are some advantages of a virtual field trip? What are some disadvantages?

4. Geography

You are teaching geography to your class. For their final project, the students are to select an area they would like to visit and then prepare a digital media presentation describing the country or region, its culture, major landmarks, and famous sites. To gather information, the students will use digital media reference books and visit geography Web sites. Using the Web for your research, list five or six reference books and Web sites that you might suggest as resources. What other digital media resources could your students use? How do digital media resources support student learning?

Education Issues

INSTRUCTIONS: Education Issues provides several scenarios that allow you to explore controversial and current issues in education. Each numbered segment contains one or more links that reinforce the information presented in the segment. To display this page from the Web, visit scsite.com/tdc4. Click Chapter 5 at the top of the Web page and then click Education Issues on the left sidebar.

1. Virtual Dissection

Most people remember dissecting a frog in their high school biology class — the odor of formaldehyde, the nervous laughter, and the unsuspecting classmate who finds a webbed foot in his lunch bag. For many students, conventional dissections are being replaced by virtual dissections using digital media applications. Students use computers to view color graphics of a frog's anatomy and videos of biological systems, and to take interactive quizzes. Although these digital media programs on CD, DVD, and Web activities are supported by animal rights activists and squeamish students, many biology teachers believe there is no substitute for genuine dissection. Should digital media applications replace traditional dissection? Why or why not? Who should make the choice between virtual and traditional dissection? Why? On what basis should the choice be made?

2. Bringing the Past to the Present

A simulation on a popular digital media application lets students assume the role of a prominent Civil War general in an actual battle. Students direct and position their army. Confrontations are accompanied by video of battle reenactments. Critics argue that the use of these kinds of digital media applications lack the insight and detail of a traditional textbook. Supporters claim that, by being immersed in the battle, students gain a better understanding of the Civil War. What place do digital media applications have in learning history? Why? What are the advantages and disadvantages of digital media applications compared with traditional textbooks? In what historical studies, if any, would digital media applications be particularly appropriate? Why?

3. Information Overload

The amount of information available to people is growing every day — as scientists uncover new facts; physicians develop improved treatments; technology firms design unprecedented products; and journalists record history in the making. Technologies such as digital media CDs, DVDs, and digital media on the World Wide Web make this vast — some say overwhelming — amount of information easily available to teachers and students. As a result of this potential information overload, experts worry that students might be spending more time sifting through information than actually applying and utilizing information. What do you think? Can there ever be too much information? Why or why not? How could too much information adversely affect teachers and students? What can be done about information overload? How can teachers help students avoid this?

4. Digital Media Realism — Dealing with Tragedy

As a teacher, you are faced with helping your students deal with various types of issues. Most issues are easy to deal with and you know where to go to get advice and help. Helping students cope with tragedy, disaster, and loss is probably the most difficult. On September 11, 2001, the tragic events that unfolded in New York, Washington, D.C., and Pennsylvania affected parents, children, friends, fellow Americans, and people around the world. Many agencies and Web sites exist that can provide you with information to help your students deal with this and other types of tragedies. Should you talk to your students about these issues? Where do you locate resources? How do people learn from a tragedy such as this one? Do you turn this into a teachable moment? Or do you ignore the issue? What precautions should you take to ensure that the information you provide is age appropriate?

Integration Corner

5

INSTRUCTIONS: Integration Corner provides extensive ideas and resources for integrating technology into your classroom-specific curriculum. To display this page from the Web and its links to approximately 100 educational Web sites, visit scsite.com/tdc4. Click Chapter 5 at the top of the Web page and then click Integration Corner on the left sidebar.

Integration Corner is designed for teachers and other educators who are looking for innovative ways to integrate technology into their content-specific curriculum. Integration Corner not only provides great Web sites with current information, but also shows what other educators are doing in the field of educational technology. These Corners are designed for all educators regardless of their area of interest. Be sure to review information and Web sites outside of your teaching area because many great integration ideas in one area can be modified easily for use in other curricular areas.

Teachers and administrators will find other colleagues in their areas with whom to connect and share the successes and hurdles of integrating technology in a classroom or an entire school system. Consider Integration Corner your one stop for integration ideas and resources. Links to educational Web sites are organized in the following 12 Corners, and different Web resources are available for each chapter. Figure 5-55 shows examples of the Web resources provided in the Chapter 5 Special Education Corner.

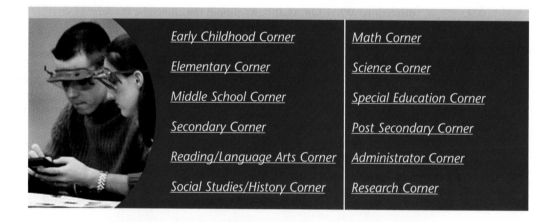

Early Childhood Corner   Math Corner

Elementary Corner   Science Corner

Middle School Corner   Special Education Corner

Secondary Corner   Post Secondary Corner

Reading/Language Arts Corner   Administrator Corner

Social Studies/History Corner   Research Corner

Figure 5-55 Examples of the Web resources provided in the Chapter 5 Special Education Corner.

Software Corner

INSTRUCTIONS: Software Corner provides information on popular software programs. Each numbered segment discusses specific software programs and contains a link to additional information about these programs. To display this page from the Web, visit scsite.com/tdc4. Click Chapter 5 at the top of the Web page and then click Software Corner on the left sidebar.

1. HyperStudio

HyperStudio is a K-12 hypermedia authoring software program still used in many schools that allows students to create digital media projects and presentations while providing an opportunity for curriculum integration. If you have wanted to use digital media with your students, HyperStudio is the perfect software for you and your students. HyperStudio incorporates the use of text, sound, graphics, animation, movies, and more to create interactive student projects. The Internet, digital cameras, CDs, DVDs, and other technologies also can be used with HyperStudio to create incredible projects. Teachers can use HyperStudio as an instructional tool through the presentation of lessons, as well as having students create their own presentations and small-group projects. Knowledge Adventure, the distributor of HyperStudio, provides an extensive Web site full of great resources!

2. ClassWorks

What if you could have 180 top software titles from leading software publishers such as Tom Snyder Productions, Knowledge Adventure, Davidson & Associates, and Scholastic Software at your fingertips with more than 8500 activities to support your curriculum? That might be an unbelievable undertaking, but what if you also had a customized system that could set the appropriate learning paths for your students? ClassWorks Gold is an open learning system that manages your favorite software titles and integrates them into the K-8 math and language arts curriculum with a cross-curricular approach. ClassWorks is a new approach to learning that lets teachers customize the individual student's learning paths. ClassWorks has an elaborate assessment system for reporting all student data. ClassWorks provides a great way to learn!

3. Math Blaster Series

Research confirms that the full integration of digital media math programs can improve retention of math concepts and thus math scores. Developed by educators, the Math Blaster Series from Knowledge Adventure offers interactive digital media programs for almost all age levels from pre-kindergarten to high school. Math Blaster helps students master math concepts and prepare for state and national testing. Key features include the SmartPoints reward system that motivates and helps students to achieve their personal best. Key skills covered include adding and subtracting, multiplying, understanding and using fractions, reading and understanding number patterns, reading and

Math Blaster Ages 7-9

analyzing charts, sorting complex sets, solving problems, and enhancing logic skills.

4. WebCT

WebCT, the world's leading provider of integrated e-learning systems for higher education, includes one of the world's top course management systems. WebCT is a powerful and comprehensive courseware tool used by colleges and K-12 institutions to offer online courses, professional development, and alternative types of training solutions. WebCT automates many tasks, including scoring true/false, multiple choice, and short answer exams and tracking student progress and activity. Teachers and students can interact and collaborate online using WebCT's bulletin board and internal e-mail system. Students also may upload their own Web pages into a special area within a course. WebCT provides teachers and school districts with a secure and efficient way of offering online courses to students.

Digital Media Corner

INSTRUCTIONS: Today's K-12 digital students need their learning to be meaningful and relevant to their lives. Digital Media Corner provides videos, ideas, and examples of how you can use digital media to enhance your teaching and your students' learning. To access the videos and links to additional information, visit scsite.com/tdc4. Click Chapter 5 at the top of the Web page and then click Digital Media on the left sidebar.

1. At the Movies — Conferencing with Video Phones

Interest in videoconferencing has surged since 9/11 as school districts and companies scramble to find a way to have face-to-face meetings without the hassle of flying. How could videoconferencing make communications in schools easier? To learn more about conferencing with video phones, click the G4TechTV video link. Locate your video and click the corresponding High-Speed or Dial-up link, depending on your Internet connection.

2. At the Movies — Finding a Job Online

It is easy to get discouraged while searching for employment. Today, more companies and many school districts are posting their job listings on the Internet, but less than half of all job seekers use the Internet to find work. How can you get the most out of your job hunting experience by using the Internet? What about locating job fairs? What do you feel is the most effective way to let potential employers know about you? To learn more about finding a job online, click the G4TechTV video link. Locate your video and click the corresponding High-Speed or Dial-up link, depending on your Internet connection.

3. At the Movies — Beam DVDs from Room to Room

With a device called Wavecom Sr., you can beam video from your VCR, DVD, satellite receiver, and other video devices to TVs all over your house wirelessly. You simply plug your various video devices into Wavecom Sr. and then using a remote control, you can beam your favorite videos to any TV in your house or apartment. To learn more about beaming video from room to room, click the G4TechTV video link. Locate your video and click the corresponding High-Speed or Dial-up link, depending on your Internet connection.

4. Digital Storytelling and iLife

One of the true values of digital media in education is its ability to empower teachers and students to develop stories using various forms of self expression. This is evident if you take a look at the iLife software suite that is loaded free on all Apple computers. iLife is an integration software application suite that includes support for telling stories using photographs (iPhoto), music (iTunes and Garage Band), and video (iMovie). Support for today's portable lifestyle is found on the iPod tools. Keynote, a presentation tool, can also be made to integrate with these storytelling products through its support for various forms of outputs, including QuickTime movies and Flash runtime files. What makes iLife products so powerful is their ability to integrate easily with one another and their ease of use. For example, you could start with a picture slide show set to music, then progress into full-motion video using the same contents, all the while keeping true to the storyline.

5. Creating Digital Projects with PowerPoint

Microsoft PowerPoint is usually considered a linear presentation software program; however, this program has all the features a student or teacher needs to create a digital story. Students can incorporate photos, graphics, personal drawings, video, interactivity, animation, and much more to create a digital project about any content. Because PowerPoint is so easy to use, students can began creating stories at the kindergarten level. A step-by-step project that teaches you how to incorporate various digital media elements into a PowerPoint presentation is available for download at this chapter's Digital Media Corner. In addition, a Do and Don'ts of PowerPoint presentations is provided to help you and your students create dynamic, but not overwhelming presentations.

Assistive Technologies Corner

INSTRUCTIONS: Assistive Technologies Corner provides information on current hardware, software, and peripherals that will assist you in delivering instruction to students with physical, cognitive, or sensory challenges. To access extensive additional information, visit scsite.com/tdc4. Click Chapter 5 at the top of the Web page and then click Assistive Technologies on the left sidebar.

1. How Can Multimedia Software Help Students with Special Needs?

Interactive digital media software provides special learning opportunities for students with physical or learning disabilities. Because these software products engage students with various digital media, students learn using their own learning styles. Because it is interactive, they can repeat lessons independently as necessary, and review or progress at their own pace.

Some digital media software is designed specifically for students with special needs. Virtual Reality Education for Assisted Learning (VREAL) places deaf or hard-of-hearing learners in a Virtual Reality scenario to learn math, reading, language arts, and science. The characters in the VR scenarios use speech, text, and sign language to direct and instruct students to solve real-life problems. For problem readers, or students with delayed language, Clicker by Crick Software presents words in grammatical groups. Students click on a word that then moves to a position in a modified word processor. After clicking on several words, the student hears the new sentence read aloud.

2. What Makes Software Accessible?

Teachers purchasing or using multimedia software should look for accessibility features. At the most basic level, an accessible program gives users alternative methods of receiving information. Audible output should be provided for all visual information. Because new information often is presented in video clips, students with visual impairments will need a voice-over describing what is happening in the video. Text captioning should be provided for all audible content. Software that includes video clips, for example, should have captions on the clips, or have captions that can be turned on and off. In this way, users have access to an alternative means of understanding the narration.

Captioned media improves comprehension not only for students with hearing disabilities, but also for students with reading disabilities, as well as ESL students. Motivation, confidence, and reading comprehension improve when media captions are visible.

3. How Can I Create Accessible Media?

Classroom teachers are creating their own learning videos for and with their students. The videos easily move to PowerPoint presentations, Web pages, or other interactive digital media projects. You can make these videos accessible for all students by using features in your video editing software.

Titles are words you type that are printed on the video you are editing. Video Edit Magic, a popular Windows program, lets you move titles to a subtitle position on the screen. You can type dialog from the clip directly onto your video for your own open captions. Apple's iMovie has a subtitle position built in to its titling feature. For longer clips, or extensive dialog, you may want to use a titling program. GeeThree's Slick Caption, for example, is an inexpensive and easy-to-use titling program available for the Macintosh platform.

You can also create captions that can be turned on and off. You will need the edited video clip, a script, and a media access program such as MAGpie, free from the National Center for Accessible Media. When you create media that all can use, everyone benefits!

Follow the instructions at the top of this page to display additional information and this chapter's links on assistive technologies.

In the Lab

INSTRUCTIONS: In the Lab provides Microsoft PowerPoint exercises that are divided into two areas, productivity and integration. To access the links to tutorials, productivity ideas, integration examples and ideas, and more, visit scsite.com/tdc4. Click Chapter 5 at the top of the Web page and then click In the Lab on the left sidebar.

PRODUCTIVITY IN THE CLASSROOM

Introduction: Chapter 5 introduces multimedia software applications and the positive impact they have on learning. Most schools today have a variety of multimedia applications, including Microsoft PowerPoint. Both teachers and students can use PowerPoint to create effective and interesting presentations. Students also can use PowerPoint as an authoring tool to create original stories and book reports. PowerPoint is an excellent tool for creating excitement, interest, and motivation in learning.

After working through these In the Lab activities, return to this section to learn new skills or to improve your current skills by clicking the following links: Learning Microsoft PowerPoint; PowerPoint FAQ; PowerPoint Tips for Windows and Mac OS.

1. Back to School Open House

Problem: To prepare for Parent Night at your school's Open House, your principal has asked all of the teachers at your school to create a short digital media presentation outlining classroom rules, homework policies, and necessary student supplies specific to your class. You decide to create your presentation in Microsoft PowerPoint. You create the presentation shown in Figure 5-56. (*Hint:* use Help to understand the steps better.) If you do not have a suggested template or font, use any appropriate template or font.

[a] Title Slide

[b] Slide 2

[c] Slide 3

[d] Slide 4

Figure 5-56

In the Lab

Instructions: Perform the following tasks.

1. Create a new presentation using the Profile design template. If you do not have the suggested design template, use any appropriate design.
2. Create the title slide shown in Figure 5-56a using your name in place of Mr. Aquilina and the subject you teach, or intend to teach, in place of Earth Science. Increase the font size of the paragraph, Class Policies, to 36 point.
3. Create the three bulleted list slides shown in Figures 5-56b through 5-56d, personalizing the lists to your specific subject area or grade level.
4. Click the Spelling button on the Standard toolbar. Correct any errors.
5. Save the presentation to a location of your choice using an appropriate filename.
6. Print the presentation.
7. Follow the directions from your instructor for handing in this assignment.

2. Adding Clip Art and Animation Effects to a Presentation

Problem: You decide to enhance your open house presentation from In the Lab 1 by adding clip art and slide transitions, as shown in Figure 5-57. You also decide to change to the Ocean design template. (*Hint:* use Help to understand the steps better.) Use any appropriate clip art image.

Instructions: Use the presentation created in In the Lab 1 for this assignment. Perform the following tasks.

1. Open the presentation you created for In the Lab 1.
2. Change the design template to the Ocean design template.
3. Insert appropriate clip art on three slides.
4. Resize the clip art as necessary. Resize and relocate the text boxes as needed.
5. Apply the Dissolve slide transition effect to Slides 2, 3, and 4.
6. Save the presentation with a different file name to a location of your choice.

[a] Title Slide

[b] Slide 2

[c] Slide 3

[d] Slide 4

Figure 5-57

In the Lab

7. Print the presentation as a handout with four slides per page.

8. Follow directions from your instructor for handing in the assignment.

3. Classroom Presentation

Problem: On the first day of school, you want to welcome your students to class and have them participate in an introduction activity. You decide to create a PowerPoint presentation to introduce yourself and provide examples of the type of information they might want to share in the activity.

Instructions: Create a PowerPoint presentation similar to the presentation illustrated in Figure 5-57 on the previous page. Use an appropriate template, attractive font style, size, and clip art images. Include the current date, your name, and e-mail address on the title slide. After you have created the presentation, save the presentation to a location of your choice using an appropriate filename. Print the presentation and then follow your instructor's directions for handing in the assignment.

INTEGRATION IN THE CLASSROOM

1. Your fourth grade students are learning about the life cycle of a butterfly. The students will work in groups to create a research project about one species of butterfly. They will start by gathering the following information: species scientific name; common name; range; four interesting facts; stages in the life cycle; eating habits and favorite flowers or plants; one predator; and one defense against predators. Students also will locate at least two images of the butterfly. Then, they will create a digital media presentation using PowerPoint that contains a title slide and at least four additional slides. Students will use bulleted lists to present their findings. They also will include at least two images of their butterfly in their presentation, as well as other suitable clip art. Select a species of butterfly and create a sample presentation. Enter the appropriate information to demonstrate the project for the students. Include the name of the butterfly you select, your name, and the current date on your title slide.

2. Your middle school geography class is studying different countries. For a culminating project, each student selects a country and researches its economy, land formations, temperature and climate, population, and places of interest or historic significance. The students then create Power-Point presentations to share their research with the class. The presentation should consist of a title slide and at least three other slides containing bulleted lists and images. Students need to include sound, transitions, graphic images, and Internet hypertext links in their presentations. The last slide of each presentation should list references. Prepare a PowerPoint presentation to present as an example for your students. Create a title slide and at least three additional slides with bulleted lists, graphic images, sounds, and transitions. Include your name, the current date, and the name of the country on the title slide. Include a list of references on the last slide.

3. William Shakespeare continues to influence modern theater. You want your high school drama students to understand the contributions of the past to theater and drama today. Students will be divided into four groups. Each group will research one of the following topics: the style and construction of the Globe Theater; forms of entertainment; customs of the theater; and costuming during the time of Shakespeare. Groups will create PowerPoint presentations to present their findings. The presentation should consist of a title slide, slides with bulleted lists, and images. Students also may include Internet hyperlinks. Remind students the hyperlink will only work if the computer they are using for their presentation has a live Internet connection. Prepare a presentation to present to the students as an example. Create a title slide and at least three additional slides with bulleted lists and graphic images. Include your name, the current date, and the topic on the title slide.

Learn It Online

INSTRUCTIONS: Use the Learn It Online exercises to reinforce your understanding of the chapter concepts and increase your computer, information, and integration literacy. To access dozens of interactive student labs, practice tests, learning games, and more, visit scsite.com/tdc4. Click Chapter 5 at the top of the Web page and then click Learn It Online on the left sidebar.

1. Student Edition Labs — Peripheral Devices, Working with Audio, Working with Graphics, and Working with Video.

For the labs to work properly, you must have your screen resolution set to 1024×768 or higher. For a short tutorial on how to change your screen resolution, click here. You also will need Flash 7.0 or higher. To view these interactive labs, click the Student Edition Labs link. When the Student Edition Labs menu appears, click the desired or the assigned lab to begin. A new browser window opens. Follow the on-screen instructions to complete the lab. When finished, click the Exit button. If required, submit your results to your instructor.

2. Bid on a Product at eBay

Online auctions have grown to be a favorite way to shop for many people. A leading online auction Web site is eBay. Have you wanted to bid on eBay but were worried that you might have difficulties? Click the eBay link to learn how to submit a bid for an item on eBay. If you submit a bid on eBay, you will see a warning message reminding you that when you bid on an item, you are entering into a contract to purchase the item if you are the successful bidder. Never make a bid unless you are prepared to make a purchase. Bidding on eBay is serious business.

3. Expanding Your Understanding

A PC video camera, sometimes called a Web cam, is a digital video camera that allows you to capture video and still images. You can use the videos in live instant messages or for live images over the Internet. You also can include the recordings of the videos on Web pages or in e-mail messages as attachments. Click the Expanding Your Understanding link to learn how to install and use a PC video camera.

4. Practice Test

Click the Practice Test link. Answer each question. When completed, enter your name and click the Grade Test button to submit the quiz for grading. Make a note of any missed questions. If required, submit your score to your instructor.

5. Who Wants to Be a Computer Genius?

Click the Computer Genius link to find out if you are a computer genius. Directions about how to play the game will be displayed. When you are ready to play, click the Play button. If required, submit your score to your instructor.

6. Wheel of Terms

Click the Wheel of Terms link to reinforce important terms you learned in this chapter by playing the Shelly Cashman Series version of this popular game. Directions about how to play the game will be displayed. When you are ready to play, click the Play button. If required, submit your score to your instructor.

7. Crossword Puzzle Challenge

Click the Crossword Puzzle link. Complete the puzzle to reinforce skills you learned in this chapter. Directions about how to play the game will be displayed. When you are ready to play, click the Play button. If required, submit the completed puzzle to your instructor.

Digital Imaging and Video Technology

Everywhere you look, people are capturing moments they want to remember. They take pictures or make movies of their vacations, birthday parties, activities, accomplishments, sporting events, weddings, and more. Because of the popularity of digital cameras and digital video cameras, increasingly more people desire to capture their memories digitally, instead of on film. With digital technology, teachers and students have the ability to modify and share the digital images and videos they create. When using special hardware and/or software, you and your students can copy, manipulate, print, and distribute digital images and videos using your personal or school computer and the Internet. The hardware and software covered in this special feature are, in reality, today's digital student's playground tools.

FIGURE 1   This figure shows a typical digital media PC system for the home.

Digital photography and recordings deliver significant benefits over film-based photography and movie making. With digital cameras, no developing is needed. Instead, the images reside on storage media, such as a hard disk, DVD disc, or flash memory card. Unlike film, storage media can be reused, which reduces costs, saves time, and provides immediate results. Digital technology allows greater control over the creative process, both while taking pictures and video and in the editing process. You can check results immediately after capturing a picture or video to determine whether it meets your expectations. If you are dissatisfied with a picture or video, you can erase it and recapture it, again and again.

As shown in Figure 1, a digital camera functions as an input device when it transmits pictures through a cable to a personal computer via a USB port or FireWire port. Using a digital camera in this way allows you to edit the pictures, save them on storage media, and print them using a photographic-quality printer via a parallel port or USB port.

Figure 1 illustrates how you might use a digital video camera with a personal computer. The process typically is the same for most digital video cameras. You capture the images or video with the video camera. Next, you connect the video camera to your personal computer using a FireWire or USB 2.0 port, or you place the storage media used in the digital camera in the computer. The video then is copied or downloaded to the computer's hard disk. Then, you can edit the video using video editing software. If desired, you can preview the video during the editing process on a television. Finally, you save the finished result to the desired media, such as a VHS tape or DVD+RW or, perhaps, e-mail the edited video. In this example, a VCR and a DVD player also can be used to input video from a VHS tape or a DVD.

USB

USB

photographic-quality printer (output)

personal computer

S-video-in

DVD recorder (input, output, storage)

S-video

S-video-out

VCR (input, output, storage)

DIGITAL IMAGING TECHNOLOGY

Digital imaging technology involves capturing and manipulating still photographic images in an electronic format. The following sections outline the steps involved in the process of using digital imaging technology.

1 Select a Digital Camera

A **digital camera** is a type of camera that stores photographed images electronically instead of on traditional film. Digital cameras are divided into three categories (Figure 2) based mainly on image resolution, features, and, of course, price. The image resolution is measured in pixels (short for picture element). The image quality increases with the number of pixels. The image resolution usually is measured in **megapixels** (million of pixels), often abbreviated as **MP**. Features of digital cameras include red-eye reduction, zoom, autofocus, flash, self-timer, and manual mode for fine-tuning settings. Figure 3 summarizes the three categories of digital cameras.

Types of Digital Cameras

Type	Resolution Range	Features	Price
Point-and-shoot cameras	Less than 6 MP	Fully automatic; fits in your pocket; easy to use; ideal for average consumer usage	Less than $600
Field cameras	Greater than 5 MP	Used by photojournalists; portable but flexible; provides ability to change lenses and use other attachments; great deal of control over exposure and other photo settings	$800 to $2000
Studio cameras	Greater than 5 MP	Stationary camera used for professional studio work; flexible; widest range of lenses and settings	$1500 and up

FIGURE 3 Digital cameras often are categorized by image resolution, features, and price.

(a) point-and-shoot

(b) field

(c) studio

FIGURE 2 The point-and-shoot digital camera (a) requires no adjustments before shooting. The field digital camera (b) offers improved quality and features that allow you to make manual adjustments before shooting and use a variety of lenses. The studio digital camera (c) offers better color and resolution and greater control over exposure and lenses.

2 Take Pictures

Digital cameras provide you with several options that are set before a picture is taken. Three of the more important options are the resolution, compression, and image file format in which the camera should save the picture. Although a camera might allow for a very high resolution, you can choose to take a picture at a lower resolution if the image does not require great detail or must be a small size. For example, you might want to use the image on a Web page where smaller image file sizes are beneficial.

Compression results in smaller image file sizes. Figure 4 illustrates the image file sizes for varying resolutions and compressions under standard photographic conditions using a 4-megapixel digital camera. Figure 4 also shows the average picture size for a given resolution. The camera may take more time to save an image at lower compression, resulting in a longer delay before the camera is ready to take another picture. A higher compression, however, may result in some loss of image quality. If a camera has a 16-MB flash memory card, you can determine the number of pictures the card can hold by dividing 16 MB by the file size. Flash memory cards are available in sizes from 16 MB to 8 GB.

Image File Size with a 4-megapixel Digital Camera

Resolution in Pixels	Compression			Picture Size in Inches
	Low	Medium	High	
	Resulting Image File Size			
2272 × 1704	2 MB	1.1 MB	556 KB	11 by 17
1600 × 1200	1 MB	558 KB	278 KB	8 by 10
1024 × 768	570 KB	320 KB	170 KB	4 by 6
640 × 480	249 KB	150 KB	84 KB	3 by 5

FIGURE 4 Image file sizes for varying resolutions and compressions under standard photographic conditions using a 4-megapixel digital camera.

Most digital cameras also allow you to choose an image file format. Two popular file formats are TIFF and JPEG. The **TIFF** file format saves the image uncompressed. All of the image detail is captured and stored, but the file sizes can be large. The **JPEG** file format is compressed. The resolution of the image may be the same as a TIFF file, but some detail may be lost in the image.

Finally, before you take the photograph, you should choose the type of media on which to store the resulting image file. Some cameras allow for a choice of media to which you can store the image, such as a CompactFlash card or Memory Stick, whereas others allow for only one type of storage media. One major advantage of a digital camera is that you can erase pictures from their media easily, freeing up space for new pictures.

3 Transfer and Manage Image Files

The method of transferring images from the camera to the personal computer differs greatly depending on the capabilities of both. Digital cameras use a variety of storage media (Figure 5). If your camera uses a flash memory card, such as a CompactFlash, Memory Stick, SmartMedia, or Secure Digital (SD), you can remove the media from the camera and place it in a slot on the personal computer or in a device, such as a card reader, connected to the personal computer. The Microdrive media shown in Figure 5 is a type of CompactFlash media. Your camera or card reader also may connect to the personal computer using a USB, USB 2.0, or FireWire (Figure 6) port. When you insert the memory card or connect the camera, software on the personal computer guides you through the process of transferring the images to the hard disk. Some operating systems and software recognize a memory card or camera as though it is another hard disk on the computer. This feature allows you to access the files, navigate them, and then copy, delete, or rename the files while the media still is in the camera.

After you transfer the files to the hard disk on your personal computer, you should organize the files by sorting them or renaming them so that information, such as the subject, date, time, and purpose, is saved along with the image. Finally, before altering the images digitally or using the images for other purposes, you should back up the images to another location, such as a CD or DVD, so the original image is recoverable.

FIGURE 5 Microdrives, CompactFlash, and Memory Sticks are popular storage devices for digital cameras.

FIGURE 6 Using a USB or FireWire connection, you can add a card reader to your personal computer.

④ Edit Images

Image editing software allows you to edit digital images. The following list summarizes the more common image enhancements or alterations:

- Adjust the contrast and brightness; correct lighting problems; or help give the photograph a particular feeling, such as warm or stark.
- Remove red-eye.
- Crop an image to remove unnecessary elements and resize it.
- Rotate the image to change its orientation.
- Add elements to the image, such as descriptive text, a date, a logo, or decorative items; create collages or add missing elements.
- Replace individual colors with a new color.
- Add special effects, such as texture or motion blurring to enhance the image.

Figure 7 shows some of the effects available in Jasc's Paint Shop Pro on the Artistic Effects submenu.

FIGURE 7   The capability of applying effects separates digital photography from film photography.

⑤ Print Images

After an image is digitally altered, it is ready to be printed. You can print images on a personal color printer or send them to a professional service that specializes in digital photo printing.

When printing the images yourself, make sure that the resolution used to create the image is high enough for the size of the print you want to create. For example, if the camera used a resolution of 640 × 480 pixels, the ideal print size is wallet size. If you print such an image at a size of 8-by-10 inches, the image will appear **pixelated**, or blurry. Use high-quality photo paper for the best results. A photo printer gives the best results when printing digital photography.

Many services print digital images, either over the Internet or through traditional photo developing locations and kiosks (Figure 8), such as those found in drug stores or shopping marts. Some services allow you to e-mail or upload the files to the service, specify the size, quality, and quantity of print; and then receive the finished prints via the postal service. Other services allow you to drop off flash memory cards, CD-ROMs, or 3.5-inch disks at a photo shop and later pick up the prints, just as you do with traditional photo developing shops.

FIGURE 8
A Pixel Magic Imaging Photo Ditto kiosk allows you to print digital images in high resolution on photo paper.

Distribute Images Electronically

6 Rather than printing images, you often need to use the images electronically. Depending on the electronic use of the image, the image may require additional processing. If you use the images on a Web site or want to e-mail a photo, you probably want to send a lower-resolution image. Image editing software allows you to lower the resolution of the image, resulting in a smaller file size. You also should use standard file formats when distributing an electronic photo. The JPEG format is viewable using most personal computers or Web browsers.

You can store very high-resolution photos on a DVD or a CD. **DVD and CD mastering software** (Figure 9) allows you to create slide show presentations on a recordable DVD or CD that can play in many home DVD players or personal computer DVD drives.

Finally, you should back up and store images that you distribute electronically with the same care as you store your traditional film negatives.

FIGURE 9 Nero PhotoShow Elite and similar software applications allow you to create your own photo slide show on DVD or CD.

DIGITAL VIDEO TECHNOLOGY

Digital video technology allows you to input, edit, manage, publish, and share your videos using a personal computer. With digital video technology, you can transform home videos into Hollywood-style movies by enhancing the videos with scrolling titles and transitions, cutting out or adding scenes, and adding background music and voice-over narration. The following sections outline the steps involved in the process of using digital video technology.

Select a Video Camera

1 Video cameras record in either analog or digital format. **Analog formats** include 8mm, Hi8, VHS, VHS-C, and Super VHS-C. The last three formats use the types of tapes similar to those used in a standard VCR. **Digital formats** include Mini-DV, MICROMV, Digital8, and DVD. Consumer digital video cameras are by far the most popular type among consumers. They fall into three general categories: high-end consumer, consumer, and webcasting and monitoring (Figure 10). Digital video cameras provide more features than analog video cameras, such as a higher level of zoom, better sound, or greater control over color and lighting.

(a) high-end consumer

(b) consumer

(c) webcasting and monitoring

FIGURE 10 The high-end consumer digital video camera (a) can produce professional-grade results. The consumer digital video camera (b) produces amateur-grade results. The webcasting and monitoring digital video camera (c) is appropriate for webcasting and security monitoring.

2 Record a Video

Most video cameras provide you with a choice of recording programs, which sometimes are called automatic settings. Each recording program includes a different combination of camera settings, so you can adjust the exposure and other functions to match the recording environment. Usually, several different programs are available, such as point and shoot, point and shoot with manual adjustment, sports, portrait, spotlit scenes, and low light. You also have the ability to select special digital effects, such as fade, wipe, and black and white. If you are shooting outside on a windy day, you can enable the wind screen to prevent wind noise. If you are shooting home videos, the point-and-shoot recording program is sufficient.

3 Transfer and Manage Videos

After recording the video, the next step is to transfer the video to your personal computer. Most video cameras connect directly to a USB 2.0 or FireWire port on your personal computer (Figure 11). Transferring video with a digital camera is easy because the video already is in a digital format that the computer can understand.

An analog camcorder or VCR requires additional hardware to convert the analog signals to a digital format before the video can be manipulated on a personal computer. The additional hardware includes a special video capture card using a standard RCA video cable or an S-video cable (Figure 12). *S-video* cables provide sharper images and greater overall quality. When you use video capture hardware with an analog video, be sure to close all open programs on your computer because capturing video requires a great deal of processing power.

FIGURE 11   A digital video camera is connected to the personal computer via a FireWire or USB 2.0 port. No additional hardware is needed.

FIGURE 12   An analog camcorder or VCR is connected to the personal computer via an S-video port on a video capture card.

When transferring video, plan to use approximately 15 to 30 gigabytes of hard disk storage space per hour of digital video. A typical video project requires about four times the amount of raw footage as the final product. Therefore, at the high end, a video that lasts an hour may require up to 120 gigabytes of storage for the raw footage, editing process, and final video. This storage requirement can vary depending on the software you use to copy the video from the video camera to the hard disk and the format you select to save the video. For example, Microsoft claims that the latest version of its Windows Movie Maker needs 10 gigabytes to save 15 hours of video when creating video for playback on a computer, but needs 10 gigabytes to save 1 hour of video when creating video for playback on a DVD or VCR.

The video transfer requires application software on the personal computer (Figure 13). Windows XP includes the Windows Movie Maker software that allows you to transfer the video from your video camera. Depending on the length of video and the type of connection used, the video may take a long time to download. Make certain that no other programs are running on your personal computer while transferring the video.

When transferring video, the software may allow you to choose a **file format** and a codec to store the video. A video file format holds the video information in a manner specified by a vendor, such as Apple or Microsoft. Three of the more popular file formats are listed in Figure 14.

File formats support codecs to encode the audio and video into the file formats. A particular file format may be able to store audio and video in a number of different codecs. A **codec** specifies how the audio and video is compressed and stored within the file. Figure 15 shows some options available for specifying a file format and codec in a video capture application. The dialog box in Figure 15 allows the user to determine whether the video is smoother in playback or if the video is more crisp, meaning that it includes more detail. The file format and codec you choose often is based on what you plan to do with the movie. For example, if you plan to stream video over the Web using RealNetworks software, the best choice for the file format is the RealMedia format, which uses the RealVideo codec.

After transferring the video to a personal computer, and before manipulating the video, you should store the video files in appropriate folders, named correctly, and backed up. Most video transfer application software helps manage these tasks.

Popular Video File Formats

File Format			File Extensions
Apple QuickTime			.MOV or .QT
Microsoft Windows Media Video			.WMV or .ASF
RealNetworks RealMedia			.RM or .RAM

FIGURE 14   Apple, Microsoft, and RealNetworks offer the more popular video file formats.

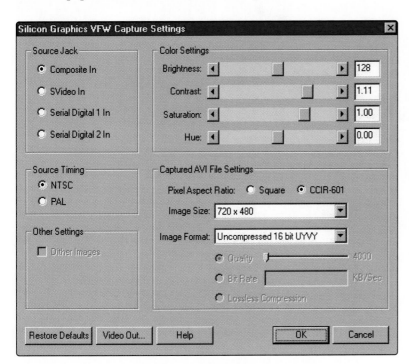

FIGURE 13   Some video editing software allows you to transfer your video from any video source to a hard disk. This dialog box allows the user to set various video parameters for capturing video from a camera or other device.

FIGURE 15   Video editing software applications allow you to specify a combination of file format and codec when saving a video.

④ Edit a Video

After the video is stored on your hard disk, the next step is to edit, or manipulate, the video. If you used a video capture card to transfer analog video to your computer (Figure 12 on page 330), the files may require extra initial processing. When you use a video capture card, some of the video frames may be lost in the transfer process. Some video editing programs allow you to fix this problem with **frame rate correction** tools.

The first step in the editing process is to split the video into smaller pieces, or *scenes*, that you can manipulate more easily. This process is called *splitting*. Most video software automatically splits the video into scenes, thus sparing you the task. After splitting, you should cut out unwanted scenes or portions of scenes. This process is called *pruning*.

After you create the scenes you want to use in your final production, you edit each individual scene. You can *crop*, or change the size of, scenes. That is, you may want to cut out the top or a side of a scene that is irrelevant. You also can resize the scene. For example, you may be creating a video that will be displayed in a Web browser. Making a smaller video, such as 320 × 200 pixels instead

of 640 × 480 pixels, results in a smaller file that transmits faster over the Internet.

If video has been recorded over a long period, using different cameras or under different lighting conditions, the video may need color correction. *Color correction* tools (Figure 16) analyze your video and match brightness, colors, and other attributes of video clips to ensure a smooth look to the video.

You can add logos, special effects, or titles to scenes. You can place a company logo or personal logo in a video to identify yourself or the company producing the video. Logos often are added on the lower-right corner of a video and remain for the duration of the video. Special effects include warping, changing from color to black and white, morphing, or zoom motion. *Morphing* is a special effect in which one video image is transformed into another image over the course of several frames of video, creating the illusion of metamorphosis. You usually add titles at the beginning and end of a video to give the video context. A training video may have titles throughout the video to label a particular scene, or each scene may begin with a title.

FIGURE 16   Color correction tools in video editing software allow a great deal of control over the mood of your video creation.

The next step in editing a video is to add audio effects, including voice-over narration and background music. Many video editing programs allow you to add additional tracks, or *layers*, of sound to a video in addition to the sound that was recorded on the video camera. You also can add special audio effects.

The final step in editing a video is to combine the scenes into a complete video (Figure 17). This process involves ordering scenes and adding transition effects between scenes (Figure 18). Video editing software allows you to combine scenes and separate each scene with a transition. *Transitions* include fading, wiping, blurry, bursts, ruptures, erosions, and more.

FIGURE 17   In Windows Movie Maker 2, scenes, shown on the top, are combined into a sequence on the bottom of the screen.

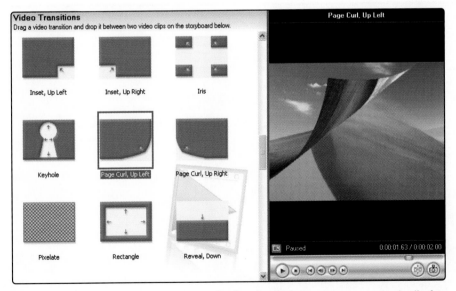

FIGURE 18   Smooth and dynamic transitions eliminate the hard cuts between scenes typically found in raw footage.

⑤ Distribute the Video

After editing the video, the final step is to distribute it or save it on an appropriate medium. You can save video in a variety of formats. Using special hardware, you can save the video on standard video tape. A *digital-to-analog converter* is necessary to allow your personal computer to transmit video to a VCR. A digital-to-analog converter may be an external device that connects to both the computer and input device, or may be a video capture card inside the computer.

Video also can be stored in digital formats in any of several DVD formats, on CD-R, or on video CD (VCD). *DVD* or *CD creation software*, which often is packaged with video editing software, allows you to create, or *master*, DVDs and CDs. You can add interactivity to your DVDs. For example, you can allow viewers to jump to certain scenes using a menu (Figure 19). A *video CD (VCD)* is a CD format that stores video on a CD-R that can be played in many DVD players.

You also can save your video creation in electronic format for distribution over the Web or via e-mail. Your video editing software must support the file format and codec you want to use. For example, RealNetworks's Helix media delivery system allows you to save media files in the RealVideo file formats.

Professionals use hardware and software that allow them to create a film version of digital video that can be played in movie theaters. This technology is becoming increasingly popular and has been used in such movies as the recent *Lord of the Rings* movies. Some Hollywood directors believe that eventually, all movies will be recorded and edited digitally.

After creating your final video for distribution or your personal video collection, you should back up the final video file. You can save your scenes for inclusion in other video creations or create new masters using different effects, transitions, and ordering of scenes.

FIGURE 19 DVD mastering software allows you to create interactive menus on your DVD.

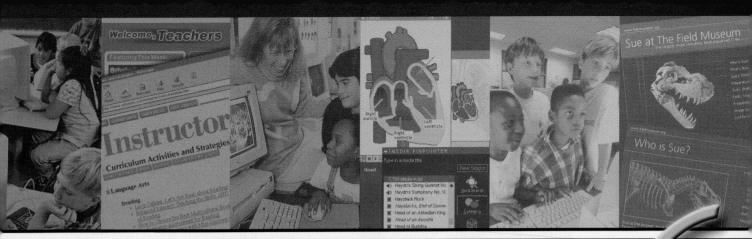

Technology, Digital Media, and Curriculum Integration

6

Objectives

After completing this chapter, you will be able to:
[ISTE NETS-T Standards I A-B, II A-E, III A-D, IV A-D, V A-D, VI A-E]

- Define curriculum and explain curriculum standards and learning benchmarks

- Explain technology integration, also called curriculum integration

- Describe the use of computers in computer labs versus classroom instruction

- Identify ways in which technology can positively influence learning

- Identify ways to plan for technology integration

- Explain various planning tools and instructional models

- Describe the steps of the ASSURE Model

- Identify ways to get started using technology at a new school

- Describe the use of learning centers

Throughout this textbook, you have learned about computers and other educational technologies, and you have seen the impact technology has on people's lives, schools, and classrooms. Every day, computers help many individuals accomplish job-related tasks more efficiently and effectively. For educators, computers and other technologies serve as the tools needed to implement new and evolving teaching strategies.

The first four chapters of this textbook focused on building computer and information literacy skills. Chapter 5 introduced you to integrating digital media and education software into your curriculum. This chapter provides you with a basic understanding of how to integrate technology across the curriculum. As you learned in Chapter 1, integration literacy is the ability to use computers and other technologies combined with a variety of teaching and learning strategies to enhance students' learning. Integration literacy means that teachers can determine how to match appropriate technologies to curriculum standards, benchmarks, and outcomes. Integration literacy relies on a solid foundation of computer and information literacy, both of which are essential for helping you integrate technology into your classroom curriculum.

What Is Curriculum?

Education can be defined as all the experiences, knowledge, and skills a learner gains from both school and society. Education literature defines the term "curriculum" in many ways. Often, curriculum is defined simply as that which is taught.

For the purposes of this textbook, **curriculum** is defined as the knowledge, skills, and performance standards students are expected to acquire in particular grade levels, or through sequences or clusters based on subject matter units of instruction, such as language arts, mathematics, science, English, history, physical education, and others (Figure 6-1). Curriculum often is designed at the state or school district level by a team of curriculum specialists, instructional leaders, and other experts. For curriculum to be implemented properly, teachers must not only understand the curriculum but also be empowered to personalize the curriculum in such a way as to meet the instructional needs of their students.

Many countries have Departments of Education or educational organizations that serve as the governing association for educational regulations and reform. Agencies in the United States include the federal Department of Education (DOE), and each state has its own Department of Education (Figures 6-2a and 6-2b).

The federal Department of Education is the governing body for public education in the United States. State Departments of Education provide their school districts with policies, directives, and updates to state public education issues. In addition, state DOEs provide access to up-to-date statistics, information about standards and accountability, teacher certification, scholarships, grants and funding sources, resources, and more.

State Departments of Education also provide their school districts with documents that describe curriculum standards and benchmarks for learning. These documents often are called **curriculum frameworks** or **curriculum guides**. Although curriculum frameworks usually include subject-specific standards, they often also include direction for specific content areas, benchmarks, activities, and forms of evaluation.

School curriculum frameworks include not only recommendations, but also examples that teachers can use to develop curriculum-based lesson plans. They usually are organized by subject and grade level. Curriculum frameworks can include specific curriculum standards, learning goals, and grade level expectations to assist teachers in meeting curriculum benchmarks.

WEB INFO

For more information about curriculum, visit the Teachers Discovering Computers Web site (*scsite.com/tdc4*), click Chapter 6, click Web Info, and then click Curriculum.

WEB INFO

For more information about mastery-level checklists, visit the Teachers Discovering Computer Web site (*scsite.com/tdc4*), click Chapter 6, click Web Info, and then click Mastery Checklist.

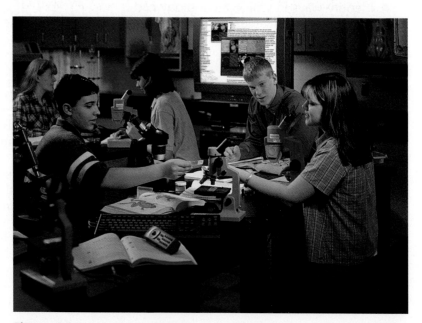

Figure 6-1 Integrating technology in the classroom helps teachers achieve the learning outcomes defined by the curriculum.

[a]

[b]

WEB INFO

To access the U.S. Department of Education Web site, visit the Teachers Discovering Computers Web site (*scsite.com/tdc4*), click Chapter 6, click Web Info, and then click Department of Education.

Figure 6-2 This figure shows the home page of [a] the U.S. Department of Education and [b] the Colorado Department of Education. The U.S. government and state education agencies provide parents, educators, and students with a multitude of resources and information.

FAQ

Does the No Child Left Behind Act (NCLB) require state curriculum standards?

Yes, NCLB requires each state to establish its own standards of what students should know and be able to do in the core content subjects.

Many school districts are drafting their own interpretations of state curriculum standards to improve learning and meet the needs of students. Many districts also are creating guides to help teachers teach curriculum standards by providing examples and mastery-level checklists with curriculum standards. Teachers usually have to include these documents with their lesson plans to show how students are mastering the skills necessary to be promoted to the next level. Some states and districts are incorporating **Grade Level Expectations (GLEs)** into their curriculum. The purpose of GLEs is to show the content and skills that students are expected to master for each subject area and to assist teachers in making sure students meet the content standards for a particular subject area. Many school districts have developed **Mastery Objective Checklists,** which are skills that must be mastered by a current grade level. These skills are usually listed on a grid or table for easy reference.

CURRICULUM STANDARDS AND BENCHMARKS

A **curriculum standard**, also called a **curriculum goal**, defines what a student is expected to know at certain stages of education. Curriculum standards for K-12 education are a collection of general concepts that school districts expect students to learn as they progress through grade levels. Curriculum standards vary from state to state and usually cover core subjects, such as language arts, mathematics, science, social studies, physical education, art, health, and foreign languages. A **benchmark**, or **learning objective**, is a specific, measurable outcome or indicator that usually is tied to a curriculum standard. Figure 6-3 lists a sample curriculum standard and appropriate, measurable benchmarks for language arts for different grade levels.

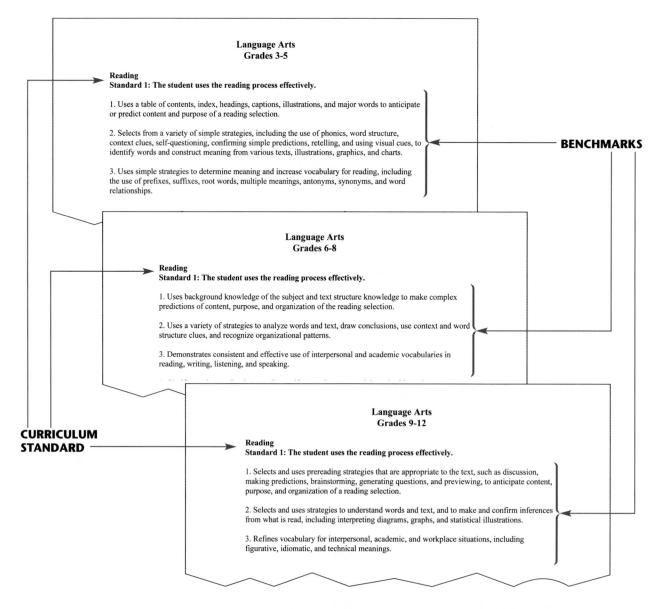

Figure 6-3 Each curriculum standard in the Florida Sunshine Standards has one or more measurable benchmarks. The first curriculum standard for reading in language arts, for example, is the same across grades, but the benchmarks increase in difficulty from grades 3 to 12.

What Is Technology Integration?

Defining curriculum is easy when compared with defining technology integration. First, **integration** by itself is defined as bringing different parts together to combine into a whole. Therefore, **technology integration,** also called **curriculum integration,** is the combination of all technology parts, such as hardware and software, together with each subject-related area of curriculum to enhance learning. Furthermore, technology integration is using technology to help meet the curriculum standards and learner outcomes of each lesson, unit, or activity.

Mastering the integration of technology into the curriculum is not easy. Extensive formal training and practical experiences are imperative for successful integration of technology at all levels of K-12 education. Technology cannot enhance learning unless teachers know how to use and integrate technology into curriculum-specific or discipline-specific areas.

First and foremost, teachers must remember that technology is only a tool to enhance or support instructional strategies. Educators should take steps to integrate technology throughout classroom experiences, activities, and projects — and find ways to use technology to teach curriculum-specific content while establishing connections between those subjects and the real world (Figure 6-4). This chapter assists you in learning the basics necessary to integrate technology into your classroom and provide the understanding needed to promote integration literacy.

A critical issue related to technology integration is that technology should not drive the curriculum. The curriculum, rather, should drive the technology; that is, teachers should use the appropriate technologies to enhance learning at the appropriate times (Figure 6-5). In the next section, you will learn the pros and cons of using computers located in a centralized computer lab or in individual classrooms.

CLASSROOM INTEGRATION VERSUS TRADITIONAL COMPUTER LABS

Educational technologists have become the advocates of integrating computers into

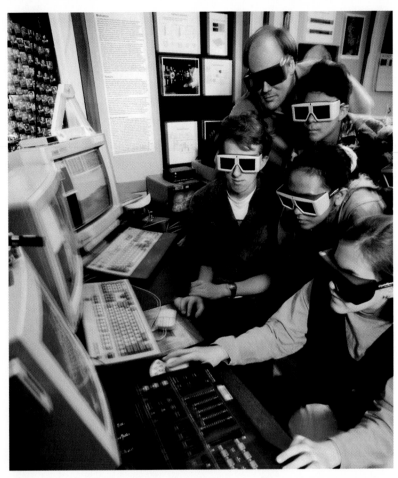

Figure 6-4 When a teacher integrates virtual reality technology in his classroom curriculum, students are introduced to many unique and positive learning experiences. For example, in this photo students are exploring the virtual world of 3-D modeling.

Figure 6-5 Many Web sites provide teachers with curriculum integration activities and strategies.

content areas. For years, teachers and administrators have focused their efforts on getting technology or computer labs into schools. A **computer lab**, or **technology lab**, usually is a designated classroom filled with computers and technology for groups of students to use (Figure 6-6). Lab computers usually are connected to the school's local area network (LAN) and provide many resources in a centralized area.

Figure 6-6 At many schools, computer labs give students access to computers and other technologies.

Teachers can schedule time in computer labs for an entire class period and use the labs for many purposes, such as whole-group instruction, small-group activities, or individual student-centered learning. In addition to computer labs, school media centers contain computers and also can be scheduled for use by classroom teachers. Computer labs are a popular approach to getting technology into K-12 schools. The primary reason administrators usually opt for computer labs first is due to cost and location. When computers are installed in the same location, they are easier to maintain and connect to a school network. Popular uses for networked school computer labs are for students to work through tutorial software and integrated learning systems software, which you learned about in Chapter 5.

Computer labs clearly provide solutions to some educational dilemmas and are an excellent addition to any school. Research shows that computers and related technologies, however, are more effective when integrated into subject content and

placed in the classroom — at the point of instruction. **Point of instruction** is having the technology in the classroom at the teachers' and students' fingertips (Figure 6-7).

If technology is readily available, teachers and students will use the technology more. An example is an elementary teacher teaching a lesson on frogs. Students want to see and learn more about frogs, so they start asking questions. Teachers can turn to the technologies in their classrooms, such as digital media software programs or the Web, to show how a frog jumps, where frogs live, and more.

Convenience is important and so is the availability of the technology at the time of instruction. Many educators refer to this as a teachable moment. When students are interested and ready to learn more about a topic, teachers have a **teachable moment**, which is an open window of opportunity for the information to be comprehended in greater detail by students (Figure 6-8). Computers, when placed in the hands of students and teachers, provide unique, effective, and powerful opportunities for many different types of teaching and learning by engaging the students in learning experiences. Research is revealing that students retain knowledge longer

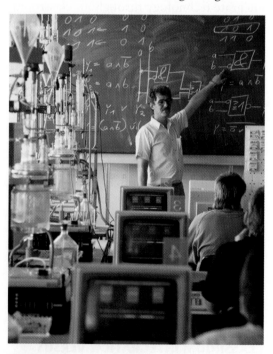

Figure 6-7 This teacher knows that by using computers at the point of instruction he can enhance the students' learning experiences.

Figure 6-8 A teacher often can identify a teachable moment just by looking in the faces of excited students who are motivated to learn!

when they are actively involved in using digital media to obtain curriculum standards and related benchmarks.

The Classroom in Action

To illustrate the benefits of having technology at the point of instruction, this section takes you into Mr. Balado's fifth-grade classroom at Martin Luther King Elementary School. Just as Mr. Balado finished reading his class a fictional story about a mouse that barely escaped being swallowed whole by a barn owl, several students raised their hands to ask questions. "How did the barn owl see the mouse in

the dark?" asked one student. Another student inquired, "Can an owl really scan the entire barn without moving off of its perch?" "What was the pellet that flew from the owl's mouth?" asked a third. Mr. Balado smiled because he expected these types of questions and knew they would open the door to a wonderful opportunity for learning. The questions clearly lead to a teachable moment, which he could maximize by using his classroom technologies.

Mr. Balado's classroom contains five student computers networked to the school's local area network and the World Wide Web. In addition, Mr. Balado has an instructional computer with access to the Web that is connected to a large screen television (similar to the classroom shown in Figure 6-9). Using a projector system to display the images or using a large screen television is an excellent way to allow all students to see what displays on the instructional computer's monitor, to see and hear interactive digital media applications, and to interact with the Web and educational software, while at the same time asking questions. These questions create enthusiasm and a desire for additional knowledge among the students.

Mr. Balado had planned and prepared for the integration of various technologies into his interdisciplinary lesson. First, he had searched the Web for sites that would

FAQ

Are projection systems still too expensive for the individual classroom?

No, they have come down significantly in price and some districts are making them standard equipment in all new classroom construction and adding them to existing classrooms.

Figure 6-9 Teachers easily can connect a computer to a television to display a computer monitor's image to the entire class.

be appropriate for the fifth-grade curriculum and would provide detailed information and research about different owl species and their environment, their food and hunting behaviors, their anatomy, and more. Locating the Web sites in advance allowed him to identify several excellent sites and eliminated the need to waste time searching for Web sites during class instruction time. In addition, Mr. Balado evaluated all of the Web sites in advance for their content and appropriateness for his fifth-grade students. Evaluation of technology resources is an important element in technology integration and is covered in detail in Chapter 7.

While interacting with the Web sites, students asked more questions, such as the following: Where do owls fall on the food chain? What specific foods do owls eat? How do owls gather food? What happens to the food after the owls swallow it whole? Why do owls hoot? Are owls mean animals that are always on the attack? What makes owls different from other birds? This was all part of Mr. Balado's instructional plan, and his students' questions continued as Mr. Balado actively engaged them in exploration and discovery learning at selected owl Web sites (Figure 6-10). The students were genuinely excited while exploring Web sites about these birds of prey; they were discovering new concepts while Mr. Balado guided their learning.

WEB INFO

To take a virtual tour of a museum, visit the Teachers Discovering Computers Web site (*scsite.com/tdc4*), click Chapter 6, click Web Info, and then click Virtual Tour.

With computers placed in his classroom for use at the point of instruction, Mr. Balado had his student' full attention. Together they explored interesting Web sites while traveling through interactive virtual field trips as wildlife biologists. **Virtual field trips** allow you to walk through doorways, down halls, and let you see everything in a three-dimensional world via a computer as if you were there. Mr. Balado's students were no longer only hearing a story about a fictional owl; they were now seeing, hearing, and interacting with a variety of owl species. After they looked at many owl facts, pictures, and video clips, Mr. Balado asked his students to outline narrative stories about owls, their prey, and the food chain. Later, he will take his students to a computer lab where they will use their outlines to write narratives.

Integrating Technology into the Curriculum

As this example illustrates, computers and other technologies can provide unique, effective, and powerful opportunities for many different types of teaching and learning. Educators recognize that technology can serve as an extremely powerful tool that can help alleviate some of the problems of today's schools. Motivating students to learn is one area that all educators constantly are trying to achieve. Technology has the potential to increase student motivation and class attendance. Using these technology tools with students with varying abilities has helped to address different learning styles and reach diverse learners. With the right approach, educators can integrate technologies such as computers, CDs, DVDs, application software, digital media applications and devices, e-books and electronic references, handheld computers, and the Web into almost any classroom situation. For technology to enhance student learning, however, it must be integrated into the curriculum.

The key to successful technology integration is identifying what you are trying to accomplish within your curriculum. First, you must consider what the standards

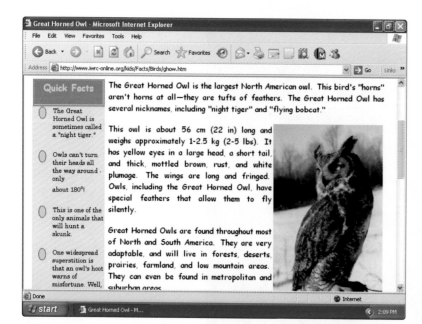

Figure 6-10 The Web provides vast amounts of information that allows students and teachers to discover innovative ways to enhance learning.

and related learning objectives are, and then you must identify an appropriate technology tool that will help you accomplish your instructional goals. Although this process sounds simple, complete integration of technology in all subject areas is complex and takes a great deal of planning. A later section of this chapter discusses how to plan for technology integration.

After you have determined specific standards and related learning objectives and you have identified technologies appropriate for areas of the curriculum, you then can begin to develop innovative ways to teach a diverse population of learners with different learning styles (Figure 6-11). A **learning style** refers to how individuals learn, including how they prefer to receive, process, and retain information. Learning styles vary among individuals. For example, some people learn better alone, while others learn better in groups. Many different types of learning styles exist and most individuals learn using a combination of several styles. The use of technologies such as digital media and the Web can help address learning styles and needs of today's digital generation.

By engaging students in different ways, technology encourages them to take a more active role in the learning process. To learn more about learning styles and theories, read the special feature that follows this chapter: Learning Theories and Educational Research.

Changing Instructional Strategies

When students play a more active role in the learning process, the teacher's role must change. Teachers are transitioning from the conventional lecture-practice-recall teaching methods — often called the sage on the stage — to a classroom in which teachers engage students in activities that allow them opportunities to construct knowledge — a new role called the guide on the side. That is, teachers are beginning to shift from being the dispenser of knowledge to being the facilitator of learning. Rather than dictating a learning process, a **facilitator of learning** motivates students to want to learn, guides the student learning process, and promotes a learning atmosphere and an appreciation for the subject.

Several assumptions must be considered as teachers become facilitators of learning. The first is that students can create their own learning and that the teachers' role is to assist their students in this process. A second assumption is that academic work extends beyond the mere

WEB INFO

To discover more about learning styles, visit the Teachers Discovering Computers Web site (*scsite.com/tdc4*), click Chapter 6, click Web Info, and then click Learning Styles.

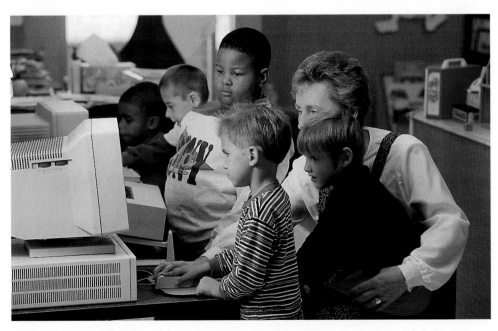

Figure 6-11 Technology is a tool that creates valuable learning experiences for many different types of learners.

storage of information. Instead, teachers want their students to be able to assimilate information and become problem solvers.

As teachers become facilitators of learning and incorporate technology into their instructional strategies, they will progress through several developmental stages. **Wellivers Instructional Transformation Model,** for example, describes five hierarchical stages of technology integration through which all teachers must progress to integrate technology effectively (Figure 6-12).

Barriers to Technology Integration

With all change comes barriers, and technology integration is no exception. Bill Gates stated in a speech, "In all areas of the curriculum, teachers must teach an information-based inquiry process to meet the demands of the information age. This is the challenge for the world's most important profession. Meeting this challenge will be impossible unless educators are willing to join the revolution and embrace the new technology tools available." Even after several years, these words still are true.

For more than two decades, several barriers have hindered technology integration in many schools. Such barriers include a lack of teacher training, lack of administration support, limited time for teacher planning, computer placement in remote locations making access difficult, budget constraints, and basic resistance to change by many educators.

WEB INFO

For more information about barriers to technology integration, visit the Teachers Discovering Computers Web site (*scsite.com/tdc4*), click Chapter 6, click Web Info, and then click Barriers.

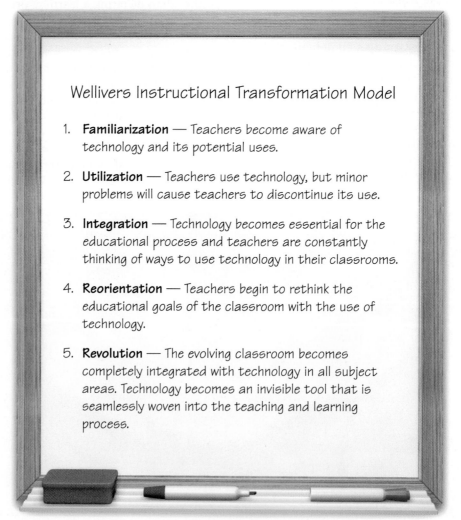

Wellivers Instructional Transformation Model

1. **Familiarization** — Teachers become aware of technology and its potential uses.

2. **Utilization** — Teachers use technology, but minor problems will cause teachers to discontinue its use.

3. **Integration** — Technology becomes essential for the educational process and teachers are constantly thinking of ways to use technology in their classrooms.

4. **Reorientation** — Teachers begin to rethink the educational goals of the classroom with the use of technology.

5. **Revolution** — The evolving classroom becomes completely integrated with technology in all subject areas. Technology becomes an invisible tool that is seamlessly woven into the teaching and learning process.

Figure 6-12 Wellivers Instructional Transformation Model describes five hierarchical stages for technology integration, through which all teachers must progress in order to integrate technology effectively.

Every educator looks at the integration of technology — and its challenges — from a different perspective. Technology coordinators view the problems of insufficient hardware, software, and training as major obstacles. Teachers consider the lack of time to develop technology-based lessons a concern. Administrators identify teachers' lack of experience using technology in instruction as yet another challenge. Teachers and administrators, however, can and are beginning to overcome these barriers with effective leadership, proper training, planning, and a commitment to enhancing teaching and learning using technology (Figure 6-13).

Technology Integration and the Learning Process

Before teachers can begin to develop integration skills, they must realize and understand how the integration of technology can enhance teaching and learning. Research shows that using technology in the classroom motivates students, encourages them to become problem solvers, and creates new avenues to explore information. Teachers also have found that using computers or computer-related technologies can capture and hold students' attention. Interactive technologies, such as software applications, digital media,

WEB INFO

For more information about technology training, visit the Teachers Discovering Computers Web site (*scsite.com/tdc4*), click Chapter 6, click Web Info, and then click Technology Training.

With Proper Technology Training, Teachers:

- Create relationships between active learning and active teaching.

- Develop an appreciation and an understanding of the potential of technology.

- Learn to be creators of digital media.

- Develop leadership skills and become role models for successful integration.

- Understand the power of technology integration.

- Design integrated curriculum activities.

- Learn the benefits of technology in the classroom.

- Develop ownership of the technology through authentic experiences.

- Learn to motivate students with technology.

- Achieve success by becoming informed and reflective decision makers.

- Become advocates for technology integration.

Figure 6-13 With proper training and planning, educators can overcome many of the barriers to effective technology integration.

reference guides, tutorials, animations, simulations, and the Web, are especially engaging as they allow students to determine the flow of information, review concepts, practice skills, do in-depth research, and more.

Technologies that provide interactivity, learner control, and student engagement are a natural choice for improving instruction. When used properly, technology is extremely beneficial in the learning process.

THE LEARNING PROCESS

For learning to take place, learners must be engaged in the process of education. One way to engage learners is to motivate them through authentic learning experiences. **Authentic learning** experiences are instructional activities that demonstrate real-life connections by associating the concept being taught with a real-life experience or event (Figure 6-14). For authentic learning to take place, teachers must involve students in the process of gathering, analyzing, and using information to make informed decisions that relate to real life.

When possible, teachers should promote **active learning**, which is a type of learning that occurs when students become engaged in inquiring, investigating, solving problems, and formulating and answering their own questions. Active learning also involves the process of students discussing, brainstorming, explaining, and debating issues with each other and with their teacher, both to determine solutions as well as to identify their own questions. Active learning promotes the retention of information, motivates students to extend their learning, and gives students a sense of ownership of the information they are presenting. Active learning is especially appropriate when teaching to a wide variety of learning styles.

A lesson on the human digestive system, for example, presents concepts that are difficult for students to understand. Students have never seen the digestive system, nor can they feel or touch it. For students to understand these new concepts, they must have background information, or a knowledge base on which to build. Providing a knowledge base on which students can build is called **anchored instruction**. Through anchored instruction, learning and teaching activities are designed around an anchor (or situation) that provides a scenario or problem enhanced with curriculum materials that allow exploration

WEB INFO

For more information about authentic learning experiences, visit the Teachers Discovering Computers Web site (*scsite.com/tdc4*), click Chapter 6, click Web Info, and then click Authentic Learning.

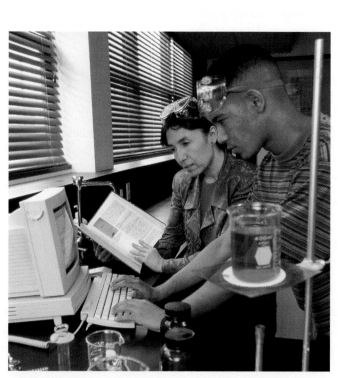

Figure 6-14 Learners are motivated to learn through authentic, real-life experiences.

by the learner. Anchored instruction also includes the component of **problem-based instruction,** in which students use the background (anchor) information to begin to solve and understand complex problems or concepts.

Providing students with opportunities to expand their knowledge base allows them to experience visionary exploration or discovery learning. Recall from Chapter 2 that **discovery learning** is a nonlinear learning process that occurs when you investigate related topics as you encounter them. Discovery learning also is an inquiry-based method of teaching and learning where students interact with their surroundings by exploring and manipulating objects, investigating and solving problems through inquiry, or performing hands-on exercises and experiments. When students discover and explore concepts on their own, they are more likely to understand and retain information. Discovery learning also helps students become better thinkers.

TECHNOLOGY AND THE LEARNING PROCESS

Technology can provide numerous tools to support many types of instruction and learning. To teach students about the human heart, for example, a teacher could integrate an educational software application such as Body Works or Microsoft Encarta into the lesson. **Body Works** is a digital media product for teaching related concepts about the human body. As you learned in the previous chapter, **Microsoft Encarta** is an interactive multimedia encyclopedia. These applications provide working visual models of how the various parts of the human heart interact (Figure 6-15). These applications thus allow students to see and experience clearly things they could never experience by reading a textbook. Applications such as these also allow students to build a **cognitive scaffold,** which is a mental bridge to build an understanding of complicated concepts.

Another benefit of integrating educational applications is that they encourage students to think not only in words and pictures, but also in colors, sounds, animations, and more. When people think, their

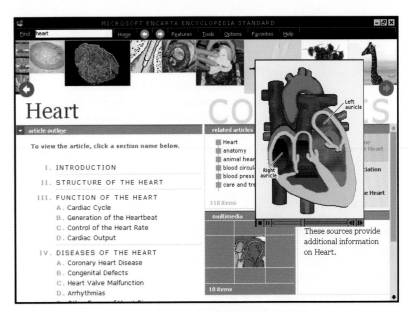

Figure 6-15 Microsoft Encarta is an educational software program that allows students to interact with a myriad of subjects. In this example, students see and hear how the human heart works.

thoughts are filled with sounds, images, colors, and movements. A young child, for example, will describe a fire engine by indicating its color and demonstrating the sounds and movements of fire engines going to a fire (Figure 6-16). Most traditional instruction, however, uses words and pictures only, often in two-color textbooks.

Figure 6-16 Everyone thinks in colors, images, sounds, and animations. A young child, for example, will describe a fire engine by imitating the sounds of a siren, indicating its color, and visualizing the sounds and movements of fire engines going to a fire.

Digital media tools allow students to have learning experiences in which concepts are brought to life with a variety of representations — video, audio, colors, pictures, simulations, and animations.

Technology helps teachers promote active learning and create authentic learning experiences by allowing students to conduct Web-based research, explore concepts in a digital media presentation, create a slide show for a history presentation, create a database of results from a group science project, and more. Technology also provides opportunities for anchored instruction. Students can watch a Web-based video clip of a Himalayan mountain-climbing expedition, for example, and then move on to examine the history of Tibet, the Sherpa culture, the physical effects of climbing in high altitudes, or how avalanches start.

Computers, digital media, and especially the Web create numerous opportunities for discovery learning. Many students may never be able to visit an extraordinary museum such as the Smithsonian Institution. The Web, however, can transport them to a world beyond their own, filled with infinite amounts of information — visually, audibly, and even virtually. Using discovery learning, you can break down classroom walls with technology, the Web, and most importantly

— imagination. Properly integrated technology allows students to understand concepts more clearly and learn no matter who or where they are.

The Internet and the World Wide Web have been called the **educational equalizer** — that is, they give students of all backgrounds, socioeconomic levels, learning styles, geographic locations, academic levels, and learning abilities access to the same information. Figure 6-17 illustrates how the Web brings these elements together to provide valuable learning experiences.

The Web allows students to experience educational opportunities previously not available. Students can publish their work, meet students with similar interests across the globe, and participate in shared learning experiences with classrooms worldwide. The Internet and Web also support projects in which students interact with authors, elected officials, or scientists conducting research. E-mail, blogs, and Web-based projects are ideal for teacher-monitored school projects that involve language arts, cultural learning, history, geography, social studies, science, or communications with friends around the world (Figure 6-18).

As illustrated by these examples, computers can provide many unique, effective, and powerful opportunities for

WEB INFO

For more ideas about how to use e-mail in the classroom, visit the Teachers Discovering Computers Web site (*scsite.com/tdc4*), click Chapter 6, click Web Info, and then click E-Mail Projects.

Figure 6-17 The Web, which provides access to a seemingly infinite amount of information, has the capability of addressing learner differences, and, thus, leveling the playing field for all students.

Figure 6-18 Using computers and the World Wide Web, students can join various projects to learn about other cultures and communicate with other students around the world.

WEB INFO

To learn more about cooperative learning, visit the Teachers Discovering Computers Web site (*scsite.com/tdc4*), click Chapter 6, click Web Info, and then click Cooperative Learning.

teaching and learning. Such opportunities include skill-building practice, interactive learning, and linking learners to instructional technology resources. In addition, computers support communications beyond classroom walls, thus enabling schools and communities to provide an environment for cooperative learning and the development of innovative opportunities for learning.

Cooperative learning refers to a method of instruction in which students work collaboratively in groups to achieve standards and related learning objectives. Instead of working alone on activities and projects, students share ideas, learn teamwork skills, and begin to help one another to accomplish tasks or achieve objectives. **Cooperative classroom activities** are student-centered, with the teacher serving as a facilitator and the students as information seekers. **Higher-order thinking skills** are the abilities to solve problems, engage in critical thinking, and interpret and solve complex issues. Teachers need to create activities for students to promote the use of higher-order thinking skills throughout their educational experiences (Figure 6-19).

By promoting new and enhanced learning experiences, properly integrated technology offers limitless possibilities for instruction and learning. Computers, digital media, the Web, and other technologies help students to understand concepts more clearly and help teachers develop unique

activities that maximize every teachable moment. Students become knowledge seekers and active learners who acquire knowledge and find different ways to interpret what they discover. Finally, technology can help improve students' abilities as independent thinkers and encourage them to become lifelong learners.

Figure 6-19 Computers support communications beyond classroom walls, thus providing an environment that allows for cooperative learning, development of higher-order thinking skills, and solving complex problems.

WEB INFO

For more information about technology strategies, visit the Teachers Discovering Computers Web site (*scsite.com/tdc4*), click Chapter 6, click Web Info, and then click Strategies.

WEB INFO

To view a school district's technology plan, visit the Teachers Discovering Computers Web site (*scsite.com/tdc4*), click Chapter 6, click Web Info, and then click Technology Plan.

Strategies for Integrating Technology into Teaching

The best strategy for curriculum integration is to put the technology into the hands of trained teachers, make it easily accessible, and let them decide how best to use it in their classrooms at the point of instruction. Teachers then can use an array of teaching strategies to develop a learning environment in which students are encouraged to be independent learners and take responsibility for their own learning.

The main goal of such teaching strategies is to provide a consistent application of technology tools to support instructional curriculum areas. Also, it is important to give every student the opportunity to work with computers and related technologies. When proper strategies are used for technology integration, students enjoy learning to use technology as well as the content in the subject-related curriculum areas.

Already, many experienced educators are integrating technology into subject-specific instruction — and have seen the benefits technology integration can bring to the learning experience. One critically important element in effective technology integration is continuous planning. For technology integration to be successful, careful planning is required at all levels, which involves district-level planning, school-level planning, and classroom-level planning. Each level must plan systematically so that technology is integrated effectively and seamlessly into all facets of education.

The Role of the School District

Effective curriculum integration cannot take place if support for technology integration does not come from several sources within the school district. School district administrators must plan carefully for every aspect of curriculum integration, from purchase to installation to teacher and staff training and technical support. Almost every school district has a detailed technology plan for technology integration. A **technology plan** is an outline that specifies the school district's procedures for purchasing equipment and software, and training teachers to use and then integrate technology into their classroom curriculum. Because of emerging and changing technologies, many school districts update their technology plans every one to three years. Many individual school technology committees review their technology plans every year to make sure they meet their district's plans.

To prepare educators to use the technology after it is implemented, administrators provide technology training with mentorship programs and follow-up staff development after training (Figure 6-20). A **mentorship program** teams new or novice teachers with experienced teachers to encourage new teachers to learn to integrate technology resources. Collaboration is promoted by sharing planning time and e-mail with other teaching professionals inside and outside the district. Experienced teachers guide new teachers by providing information and suggestions. In-house workshops

Figure 6-20 Mentorship programs allow teachers to learn computer and technology integration concepts from experienced teachers in a nonthreatening environment.

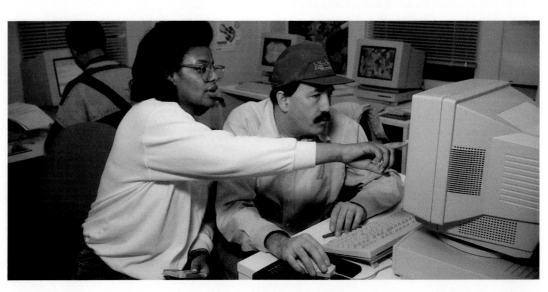

are provided so teachers learn to use and integrate the available technologies in their schools and classrooms.

Today, many federal, public, and state grant funding sources now are requiring that part of the funding be spent on teacher training. This funding has increased the number of teachers using and integrating technology.

In addition, numerous Web sites are dedicated to mentoring new and experienced teachers in everything from how to get started with technology to classroom management. These sites provide wonderful resources for teachers and offer an avenue for teachers to find ideas, advice, and support. Mentors can help new teachers become more effective in the classroom.

Planning for Technology Integration in the Classroom

Teachers must plan carefully for the use and integration of computers and technologies in the classroom. Just as planning is essential to effective instruction, it is required for effective use and integration of technology in the classroom. One important consideration is deciding on the most appropriate technology to achieve the desired learner outcomes. Teachers must plan how they will teach the curriculum, what areas they need to cover for content, and where they can use technology to meet curriculum standards and related learning objectives.

Another important consideration in the planning stage is preparing the classroom environment (Figure 6-21). The way in which you integrate technology into the curriculum will depend largely on how much technology is in your classroom or in your school. Whether you use one computer, two computers, or thirty computers, you must plan how and when you will use those computers and how you will enable your students to use those computers. The amount of planning will vary according to the arrangement of computers in your classroom and school and the scope of your lesson. Chapter 7 discusses these and other planning issues.

ONE-COMPUTER CLASSROOM

In classrooms with only one computer, teachers must plan to maximize the effectiveness of that one computer. In such classrooms, the computer most commonly is used for classroom presentations and demonstrations. To allow students to view the presentation or demonstration, teachers easily can project the monitor's content on a large screen television or a large display monitor. Using a television with a 27-inch or 32-inch screen usually is sufficient. If you do not have a large screen television in your classroom, the school's media center should be able to provide one. Televisions normally are available, as long as you plan ahead.

WEB INFO

For more information about curriculum planning with technology, visit the Teachers Discovering Computers Web site (*scsite.com/tdc4*), click Chapter 6, click Web Info, and then click Curriculum Planning.

WEB INFO

For additional strategies and applications for one-computer classrooms, visit the Teachers Discovering Computers Web site (*scsite.com/tdc4*), click Chapter 6, click Web Info, and then click One Computer.

Figure 6-21 Teachers must prepare their classrooms carefully for the integration of computers and other technologies.

Another option is to project the image onto a projection screen or classroom wall using a data projector or interactive whiteboard, described in Chapter 5. Schools normally have only a few of these devices, and you will have to plan ahead to schedule them for use in your classroom.

A good instructional strategy for the classroom computer is to introduce students to various types of software and create learning paths before taking the class to the computer lab. Using this instructional strategy optimizes the time students spend on computers while in the lab. Rather than spending time learning basic software skills, students can devote time to interacting with the computer to experience discovery learning.

In addition, teachers in a one-computer classroom can use the computer for the same purposes as described in the next sections on two or more computer classrooms. Many ways exist to enhance teaching and learning in the one-computer classroom. With only one computer available, however, additional planning might be required.

TWO-COMPUTER CLASSROOM

In classrooms with two computers, teachers must develop a strategy to manage their use. One computer could be used mainly for research on the Internet, presentations, Web-based projects, and e-mail. The other computer might be used as a writing center or for students to create digital media projects.

Regardless of how you use the computers, you should develop a strategy for how you will allocate computer use and how students' computer time will be managed. Questions that can assist with planning follow:

- Will both computers have the same hardware, software, and network access?

- Will one or both computers be connected to the Web?

- Will students rotate through using one or both computers on a daily basis?

- How much time will each student be allowed on each computer?

- Is it better to have the students work together on projects?

- How are you going to observe your students using the Internet?

- How will you evaluate student learning?

MORE THAN TWO COMPUTERS

Teachers who have several computers may find that arranging their classrooms in a single learning center or several learning centers, through which groups of students can rotate as they complete projects or activities, provides an environment for productive use of the computers (Figure 6-22). Other technologies also can be organized into learning centers, such as a video center in which students can use digital video cameras to record and watch themselves performing plays, creating and telling stories, or role-playing; a CD/DVD center where students can conduct research and learn new skills by interacting with instructional CDs and DVDs; a listening or reading center; a digital media production center where students can create their own digital media projects, and much more.

Figure 6-22 By using computers networked with Internet access, teachers can set up learning centers for students to work on projects.

Before setting up a computer center or centers, teachers should ask the planning questions previously cited, in addition to considering how many computers will be in each center and what other technologies, if any, might be included in the center. As indicated, the technologies a teacher utilizes will depend on the curriculum standards and learning objectives. Furthermore, part of preparing the classroom environment is being aware of the prerequisite skills necessary for students to be successful.

- Work with the computer lab teacher; you will need her help and expertise.

- Teach the lesson yourself or encourage the curriculum resource teacher to teach with you.

- Set up clear lab management rules.

- Provide well-thought-out lessons, with clear instructions.

- Make sure to use the available software, Internet, and other technologies to support your curriculum.

- Always, always have a backup plan for unexpected technology problems.

- Alternate between whole-group, small-group, and individual instruction and assignments.

Figure 6-23 Suggestions that will assist teachers in the computer lab to make the instructional lessons a successful learning experience for students.

USING A COMPUTER LAB

Because few classrooms include a computer for every student, using a computer lab allows teachers to provide learning opportunities that are not possible in a one-, two-, or even five-computer classroom. The most important advantage of using a computer lab is that all students are provided hands-on experience with using computer technology. Computer labs can be used successfully by teachers and students for tutorials, remediation, cooperative learning, computer skill instruction, digital production products, Internet research, whole class instruction, and integrated learning systems (ILS).

Computer labs have an added benefit of allowing students to interact with technology and software that is student centered. Taking your class to a computer lab, however, requires careful planning to use the allocated time efficiently and effectively. Managing instruction in a lab environment also requires that teachers carefully plan their learning strategies for this multi-computer environment.

The advantage of using a computer lab for instructional purposes is that all students have access to computers, the Internet, and software. Many times, other available technologies allow students to work on projects and develop additional technology skills, such as video production and much more. Figure 6-23 above lists some suggestions to help make your time in the computer lab a successful learning experience.

USING A WIRELESS MOBILE LAB

Today's wireless technology represents an evolution of products and services for businesses and education. Many innovative technologies have evolved and are being used in K-12 and higher education classrooms; these technologies provide teachers with new and exciting integration possibilities. One use of wireless technology is a **wireless mobile lab,** also called a **computer lab on wheels.** A wire-less mobile lab is a portable cart with wireless notebook computers that can be transported from one classroom to another (Figure 6-24). As you learned in previous chapters, wireless communications make technology more accessible and flexible. The wireless mobile lab uses all the advantages of wireless technology, bringing technology to the students without having to take them to a dedicated computer or technology lab. The computers can be moved almost anywhere and shared among classrooms. These mobile labs allow for expanded network capabilities and offer many instructional opportunities for teachers.

WEB INFO

For more information about wireless mobile labs, visit the Teachers Discovering Computers Web site (*scsite.com/tdc4*), click Chapter 6, click Web Info, and then click Wireless Labs.

Figure 6-24 A wireless mobile lab transports computers to the students instead of the students going to a computer lab.

Wireless mobile labs consist of wireless notebook computers that can be purchased in sets of 8, 10, 16, 24, and 36. The notebook computers are stored and transported on a special cart. The cart serves many purposes, such as moving the computers from classroom to classroom, storing the computers at night, charging the computers, and keeping them secure. The charging capabilities are very unique and each company that has developed mobile labs has its own unique configuration and ways you can charge the computers and external batteries.

Teachers and students both benefit from this access to technology. By bringing technology to the classroom at the point of instruction, wireless mobile labs effectively integrate technology into the classroom. Because of the many possibilities that wireless mobile labs can and are providing, many experts believe that wireless mobile labs eventually will replace many traditional, wired computer labs.

WEB INFO

For another example of how to use a KWL chart, visit the Teachers Discovering Computers Web site (*scsite.com/tdc4*), click Chapter 6, click Web Info, and then click KWL Chart.

Planning Lessons with Technology

One of the more important parts of technology planning is developing classroom lessons and activities that utilize technology. Students begin school having a varying degree of knowledge about computers and technology. Students should, at some point, be taught basic computer concepts and operations, but they will learn many basic computer skills just from everyday use. For the digital generation, technology has always been in every aspect of their lives. Educators need to realize that by integrating digital media and related technologies, students develop their own digital literacy, while at the same time, they are given new reasons to get excited and motivated about content and learning.

When planning lessons that use technology, teachers must consider the skills and knowledge level required for students to start and complete the lesson successfully. If technology is part of the lesson, teachers need to consider student technology skills. Many different tools are available to assess students' skill levels, such as a skill assessment survey. A **skill assessment survey** is designed to identify individual students' academic and technology skill levels and then create a starting point for developing instructional strategies.

KWL CHARTS

Another simple and effective tool to help in the planning process is a KWL chart. A **KWL chart** is an instructional planning chart to assist a teacher in identifying student understanding of curriculum standards and related objectives by having students state what they already Know, what they Want to Know, and then, based on that information recording what students Will Learn, as shown in Figure 6-25. A KWL chart is a very helpful planning tool in determining skill and knowledge levels of students before beginning almost any project. After a teacher has established the learning objectives, the KWL chart can be used as a survey tool to determine what students already know about a topic and what technology skills they will need for a project. The teacher and students then can determine what they will learn from the project and the technologies best suited to mastering the objectives.

As the project progresses, students are encouraged to list what they have learned on the KWL chart. Not only will students be learning subject-related matter, they will be learning new and different types of technology skills when using technology to accomplish tasks.

An alternative version of the KWL chart is a KWHL chart. A **KWHL chart** also is an instructional planning tool, but adds an additional component — How students will learn. This additional component creates an opportunity for students and teachers to plan for how the learning experiences will occur.

A great way to create active learning opportunities for your students is to let them create KWL and KWHL charts when you start a new topic or when they begin

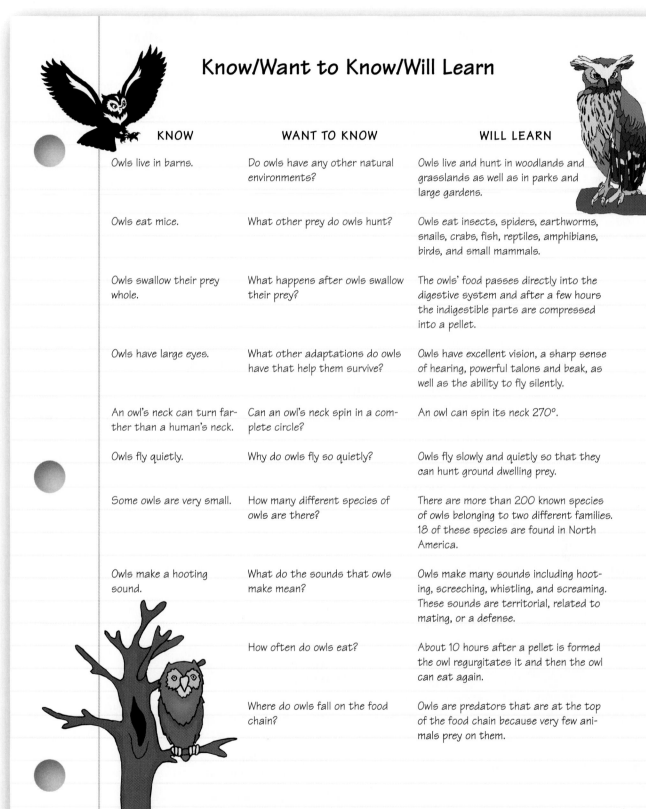

Know/Want to Know/Will Learn

KNOW	WANT TO KNOW	WILL LEARN
Owls live in barns.	Do owls have any other natural environments?	Owls live and hunt in woodlands and grasslands as well as in parks and large gardens.
Owls eat mice.	What other prey do owls hunt?	Owls eat insects, spiders, earthworms, snails, crabs, fish, reptiles, amphibians, birds, and small mammals.
Owls swallow their prey whole.	What happens after owls swallow their prey?	The owls' food passes directly into the digestive system and after a few hours the indigestible parts are compressed into a pellet.
Owls have large eyes.	What other adaptations do owls have that help them survive?	Owls have excellent vision, a sharp sense of hearing, powerful talons and beak, as well as the ability to fly silently.
An owl's neck can turn farther than a human's neck.	Can an owl's neck spin in a complete circle?	An owl can spin its neck 270°.
Owls fly quietly.	Why do owls fly so quietly?	Owls fly slowly and quietly so that they can hunt ground dwelling prey.
Some owls are very small.	How many different species of owls are there?	There are more than 200 known species of owls belonging to two different families. 18 of these species are found in North America.
Owls make a hooting sound.	What do the sounds that owls make mean?	Owls make many sounds including hooting, screeching, whistling, and screaming. These sounds are territorial, related to mating, or a defense.
	How often do owls eat?	About 10 hours after a pellet is formed the owl regurgitates it and then the owl can eat again.
	Where do owls fall on the food chain?	Owls are predators that are at the top of the food chain because very few animals prey on them.

Figure 6-25 A KWL chart is an instructional planning tool that assists teachers in creating curriculum-specific objectives based on the knowledge of their students.

to work on their own projects. You can conduct this exercise as a large group activity in which the whole class participates, or you can break up the class in small groups and then let the groups share their results. KWL and KWHL charts can be used in all subjects from kindergarten to university-level classes.

Instructional Models

Before you start a lesson, you plan the lesson, which is a process that involves using an instructional design or model. Effective teaching with technology also involves using an instructional model. An **instructional model** is a systematic guide for planning instruction or a lesson. When using and integrating technology, an instructional model and planning take on a more important role. Which technology you use is not the critical issue; what is important is that you integrate the technology effectively and the technology is appropriate to the learning objectives. Many instructional models are available from which you can choose. For the purpose of this textbook, the popular educational instructional model called the ASSURE Model is described.

THE ASSURE MODEL

The **ASSURE Model** developed by Heinich, Molenda, Russell, and Smaldina is a procedural guide for planning and delivering instruction that integrates technologies and media into the teaching process (Figure 6-26). The ASSURE Model is a well-known guide for developing any instructional lessons. The following is a description of the steps of the ASSURE Model and an explanation of how to use the model in your classroom.

ANALYZE THE LEARNER   Knowing your learner's skill level is important. Some students may come into your classroom with academic and technology skills that others do not possess. Teachers should plan for this situation. Know your audience and consider the diverse differences in the student population you are teaching.

STATE OBJECTIVES   **Student objectives** are statements of the type of skills and knowledge you expect students to be able to demonstrate at the end of instruction. When you have clear student objectives, you can select your materials and determine the focus and purpose of the lesson or project more wisely. Be sure to match student objectives to curriculum standards and learning objectives.

ASSURE Model

Analyze the Learner	• Who are the learners? • What are their skill levels? • What are their learning styles?
State Objectives	• What do you want the learners to gain knowledge of? • What are the specific learner outcomes?
Select Methods, Media, and Materials	• What methods of instruction do you plan to use? • What media are appropriate? • What materials will you need?
Utilize Methods, Media, and Materials	• How will you use the methods and media? • How will you use the materials? • What is your instructional strategy?
Require Learner Participation	• What will the learners be required to do? • Will the learners engage in active or passive learning?
Evaluate and Revise	• Did the lesson meet the objectives? • How will you evaluate content and technologies used? • How will you revise and improve?

Figure 6-26 The steps of the ASSURE Model, which is an instructional model used by educators to develop technology-enriched lessons.

SELECT METHODS, MEDIA, AND MATERIALS

Selection of methods, media, and materials includes three steps, which are (1) decide on the method of instruction, (2) choose the media format that is appropriate for the method, and (3) select, modify, update, or design materials for the instruction. Media and materials include all items you choose to meet the curriculum standard, such as print, technology, information resources, and related components. Media can take many forms, including CD, DVD, the Internet or the Web, a video, an overhead projector, a graphing calculator, special technology devices for learning, software, digital media, or any combination of these and other items (Figure 6-27). The first step is to decide which method best meets your needs, such as lecture, discovery, tutorials, demonstration, or creation of student projects. Next, you need to decide on the media, how you are going to use the media, and what you want the learners to do. Make sure the materials you identify are available and list what you are planning to use them for. Finally, determine if you need to modify any of the media or materials or design new media or materials.

UTILIZE METHODS, MEDIA, AND MATERIALS

Teachers should preview all media and materials they are planning to use, including videos, digital media applications, and Web sites. Although a software company may advertise that a particular software product contains the correct content for your objectives, you, as the teacher, must evaluate the content of all software. Again, refer to your learning objectives to assist you in determining this step. Next, you will need to prepare the classroom environment. Use these questions to guide you in making preparations:

- What equipment, software, or devices are required to use the media?

- Do you need to reserve extra equipment that you might not have in your classroom?

- How do you prepare your classroom to use the equipment?

- How do you prepare the students to use the media and materials?

Figure 6-27 Teachers must choose which media to use and when it is appropriate to use the technology.

REQUIRE LEARNER PARTICIPATION As previously discussed, the most effective learning situations are those that require active learning and ask learners to complete activities that build mastery toward the learning objectives. Classroom lessons should motivate students to be active learners who are involved in the process of learning, such as practicing, performing, solving, building, creating, and manipulating. As you develop these lessons, you must decide what information to include in the activities. If students are doing a research project using the Web, for example, they need guidelines of what to incorporate and how you will assess the outcome of the project. Chapter 7 discusses assessment tools in more detail.

EVALUATE AND REVISE At the end of a project or lesson, it is important to evaluate all aspects of the lesson, instruction, or learning experience. **Evaluation** is the method of appraising or determining the significance or worth of an item, action, or outcome. This **evaluation process** includes assessing learning objectives, reviewing, critiquing the learners' work or works based on specific standards, and evaluating reviews of the media and materials used. Teachers should conduct thoughtful reflection on all aspects of the instructional process. **Reflective evaluation** is thinking back on the components of the teaching and learning process and determining the effectiveness of the learner outcomes and the use of technology during the process (Figure 6-28). Students also should be asked to reflect on their learning experiences, their perceptions on the content learned, and their evaluation of the learning process.

WEB INFO

For assistance with creating lesson plans, visit the Teachers Discovering Computers Web site (*scsite.com/tdc4*), click Chapter 6, click Web Info, and then click Lesson Plans.

Critical Questions to Ask During the Evaluate and Revise Phase of the ASSURE Model

- Did students learn what you wanted them to learn?

- Can students demonstrate understanding of the content?

- Was the chosen technology effective in achieving the learning objectives?

- Were the learning objectives met using the technology?

- Should learning objectives be taught in a different format?

- Would these learning objectives be better taught without technology or with another technology?

- Can students work cooperatively with a partner on this lesson?

- Would parts of the content be better understood if students worked individually?

- What would you change?

- What would you keep the same?

- How will you revise this lesson?

Figure 6-28 Questions teachers should consider during the evaluation and revision phase.

The ASSURE Model is an example of one popular educational model that teachers can use to plan for technology integration into instruction. Emerging technologies will expand teachers' potential to communicate effectively, to convey ideas, and to amuse, encourage, and educate students. As you revise your lesson plans, you will need to evaluate and consider using new and emerging technologies.

As you can see, planning is important on all levels — from the district, to the classroom, to planning individual lessons. As a new teacher, planning for technology integration will present its challenges. The next section provides information on where to go for guidance and materials to help you plan for technology integration in your classroom.

Getting Started at a New School

Suppose you are a new teacher and it is the first day of preplanning week for teachers. You are excited to get that first glimpse of your new classroom. When you finally do, you discover you have two new networked computers and a color ink-jet printer in your classroom. Fortunately, you learned about Macintosh computers and PCs during your teacher education courses. Although you feel comfortable using computers, you immediately wonder how to get started and begin to consider ways to integrate these computers

into your classroom curriculum (Figure 6-29). As you start to plan for technology integration, you will need to consider many issues related to technology information and support, technology training, hardware, software, other technologies, and technology supplies.

INFORMATION ABOUT TECHNOLOGY

One of the first items to investigate is who else in the school is using technology in their classrooms. Individuals to consult are your principal, media specialist, curriculum resource teacher, technology committee members, or other teachers, especially those who teach the same grade level and subjects that you teach. These educators will know who else is integrating technology actively in their classrooms. Check to see if your school has a mentorship program.

Ascertain if your school has a technology committee and who the members are. You can get this information from your principal or assistant principal. Consult your teacher's manual for a list of various school committees and their members. A **technology committee** consists of teachers, administrators, and staff who consider, investigate, advise, and make recommendations to the principal and technology coordinator about technology-related issues. A **teacher's manual** is a booklet that contains information, rules and regulations, rights and responsibilities, and policies and procedures. It will provide answers to many of

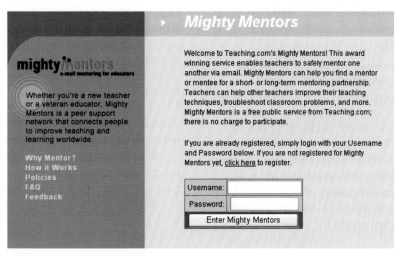

Figure 6-29 There are many Web sites dedicated to helping new teachers through online support and mentoring.

your questions. Most manuals are located on the school or school district Web site.

Finally, you should determine where you should go to get technology support. The principal, media specialist, school or district technology coordinator, and other teachers who use technology either can offer you support or guide you to where you can find support.

TECHNOLOGY TRAINING

Take time to find out if your school offers any professional development or in-service training for using and integrating technology. Most schools and school districts offer free training for teachers. **In-service** means training teachers after they have entered the profession of teaching. Your principal, curriculum resource teacher, technology coordinator, or district instructional technology coordinators are able to provide information on in-service training opportunities. Sometimes, school secretaries also will be up to date on this information.

For information about technology workshops, talk with your principal, curriculum resource teacher, other teachers, or district technology coordinator. Let these people know you are interested in any technology or other training that becomes available. If you have students with learning disabilities in your classroom, check with the district exceptional student education program specialist about training opportunities. Many school districts post the dates and times of in-service training and workshops on the district's Web site and other Web resources.

HARDWARE

Determining how you can obtain additional hardware or upgrade your classroom computers is another item to consider. As soon as you can, join your school's technology committee. Technology committees help make the decisions on what new technologies will be purchased, where these new technologies will be placed, and establishes how the technology plan for the school is implemented. You also may need to look into **educational grants** for additional funds. Your principal and curriculum coordinator usually receive notification of grant opportunities. Let them know you are interested in writing a grant and they will provide you with the information. If your district has a person

responsible for grant writing for the district or county, he can serve as a good source of information. In addition, you will find numerous grant opportunities on the Internet. Chapter 7 provides more information on locating and writing educational grants.

A question to consider is what type of equipment you can purchase if you receive grant funds. Before you write a grant, determine what kind of equipment you can purchase. Your principal, technology coordinator, curriculum coordinator, or members of the technology committee should be able to provide you with this information. If your school is networked, also check with the network administrator at the district level.

SOFTWARE

With hardware requirements decided, you will need to determine what kind of software is available to you and where you can find it. First, you should check your classroom computer for software that already is installed. To learn more about the software available at your school or on the school's network, ask the school media specialist, curriculum resource teacher, technology facilitator, or the district technology coordinator. If you are a special education teacher, you might check with your district exceptional student education coordinator, who should know what software is available for students with disabilities.

Next, determine the procedure for purchasing additional software. The school secretary or other teachers can direct you to the right person for this information. If your school is networked, it is important to check with the network coordinator before purchasing software so you can avoid buying software that already may be installed on the network or may conflict with the network. Many schools install computer-assisted instructional software programs on their network servers for use by all teachers.

Finally, you need to determine if your school district or state Department of Education has an adopted state bid list for purchasing software. Many states contract with companies to purchase specific software applications at reduced prices and these are included on a **state bid list**. Be sure to find out if your state has a special catalog of software titles that they have adopted (Figure 6-30). Curriculum

WEB INFO

For more information about grant opportunities, visit the Teachers Discovering Computers Web site (*scsite.com/tdc4*), click Chapter 6, click Web Info, and then click Grants.

Figure 6-30 Many states provide online access to state-approved electronic learning resources.

resource teachers, technology coordinators, or media specialists are good sources for this information. Your district office should maintain this information as well.

OTHER TECHNOLOGIES

Consider other technologies and where you can find them, such as a VCR, digital camera, digital video camera, scanner, projector, or a presentation television. Your media specialist usually handles scheduling and distribution of DVDs, VCRs, digital cameras, and other equipment (Figure 6-31). Reserve early because a sign-up sheet and allocation usually is based on a first-come, first-served basis. Ask about the length of time that you are allowed to keep checked-out equipment.

You also should ask where you can find a listing of educational software programs offered throughout the school or district for

Figure 6-31 A school's media center can be scheduled for teachers and students. The media specialist usually assists teachers with checking out all types of technologies.

use in the classroom. The media specialist usually has a list of software programs available on CDs, DVDs, and the school network for teachers to use in the classroom. A listing of instructional television programs and broadcast times, and any videotapes the school has or that are available to the school through interlibrary loan programs usually is maintained by the media specialist. She can inform you of the procedures for checking out CDs, DVDs, VCRs, and other equipment.

TECHNOLOGY SUPPLIES

A basic, but often overlooked, question to consider is how you can obtain additional supplies for use with computers and other technologies. If the bulb in your overhead projector burns out, for example, or you need paper or ink cartridges for your printer, how do you go about replacing these supplies? Generally, the media specialist can replace burned-out bulbs and solve other supply problems with projectors. In many schools, the school secretary usually handles orders for general supplies. A good starting point is to talk to the media specialists or technology coordinator and they will direct you to the appropriate person.

Now that you have some basic knowledge of where to go for guidance and materials to help you integrate technology into your classroom, consider how one teacher is putting it all together.

WEB INFO

To learn how to order technology and other school supplies online, visit the Teachers Discovering Computers Web site (*scsite.com/tdc4*), click Chapter 6, click Web Info, and then click Supplies.

Putting It All Together

As described earlier in this chapter, Mr. Balado is well aware that technology can make a difference in his fifth-grade students' learning — and he has been using technology to enhance his classroom lessons. After the students completed their narratives, Mr. Balado planned a highly integrated classroom strategy for teaching the science curriculum to his fifth graders. As part of the integrated learning environment, he provided carefully planned centers, which enabled him to divide his classroom for group activities and inquiry learning through these interdisciplinary lessons.

CREATING AN INTEGRATED LEARNING ENVIRONMENT

Centers, or **learning centers,** give you the opportunity to break your classroom into many different types of learning environments without ever leaving the room. Just as an office building has different offices in which work is accomplished, learning centers allow students to rotate around the classroom to complete projects or activities (Figure 6-32). Mr. Balado had an instructional plan for how the students would work through the centers in his classroom. In Mr. Balado's Owl Exploration, students took on the role of explorer and learned what it would be like to have a career as a wildlife biologist.

Figure 6-32 Learning centers are a great way to organize a classroom to optimize learning opportunities.

He had five computers in his classroom for student use and 22 students. He divided the students into groups of two and three; these students would work together throughout the levels of the project. Mr. Balado then assigned each group a North American species of owl to research.

Students were excited and surprised because most did not even know that there was more than one species of owl. Their assignment was twofold. First, they were to find out as much as possible about their owl species. Second, they would use their newly acquired knowledge to help inform the public on what needs to be done to ensure the safety of North American owls and to prevent them from becoming extinct. Instead of writing a report, students would create a research-based interactive digital media project, models, and more.

Mr. Balado gave each group the same guidance and questions to think about for their project, such as the following: What does a wildlife biologist really do? Where might a wildlife biologist have to travel? What kind of education would you need to be a wildlife biologist? Mr. Balado also instructed his students to conduct research on their species of owl, in a manner similar to the way wildlife biologists would conduct research, by answering questions such as the following: What does your owl look like? In what ecosystem would you find your owl? What does your owl eat? How large is your owl expected to grow and what is its average weight? He also asked each group to gather all the information the group felt was important for them and others in the class to understand their particular species of owl.

Mr. Balado knows that good questioning skills leads to concrete learning opportunities; so he asked the students to formulate their own questions and find answers to them. Many educators teach their students to use an **essential questioning technique**, which is looking for the most important or fundamental part of a topic. In this process, students develop their own questions, find their own answers, and develop their own meaning from the information they collect. By using this essential questioning technique, students discover insight and are motivated to learn more. When students have learned how to ask the appropriate questions, they have learned how to learn.

THE CLASSROOM CENTERS

For his lesson on North American owls, Mr. Balado sets up seven learning centers in his classroom. The centers include a discovery computer center, a Web search center with a computer connected to the Internet, a modeling center, the great explorers' library center, a scanning center with a computer set up for scanning pictures and other objects, a science center, and a digital media project center.

The discovery computer center includes two computers and a number of different CDs Mr. Balado checked out from the media center that cover predator and prey relationships, the food chain, and wildlife of North America. He purchased two CDs at his own expense. The Web search center has one computer that students can use to investigate various Web sites. Mr. Balado has provided links to these Web sites on his curriculum Web page. To locate these Web sites and other available media, Mr. Balado worked with the media specialist at his school. After he had collected and evaluated a list of sites for the students to conduct their research, Mr. Balado created a curriculum page so students would not be wasting time surfing the Web without supervision (Figure 6-33). Mr. Balado is quite aware of the dangers of inappropriate or inaccurate information available at some Web sites.

WEB INFO

For more information about creating learning centers, visit the Teachers Discovering Computers Web site (*scsite.com/tdc4*), click Chapter 6, click Web Info, and then click Learning Centers.

Figure 6-33 Teacher-created curriculum Web pages allow students to link directly to appropriate Web sites.

The modeling center has all types of modeling tools, modeling clay, paper, rocks, and many different-shaped items. This center is for students to create a three-dimensional model of their owls and other objects related to the project. At the next center, the great explorers library center, as shown in Figure 6-34, Mr. Balado has provided a collection of books, journals, and magazines for students to use to research owls and become great research scientists. The media specialist was instrumental in locating books and print materials through the state's interlibrary loan program, which was established by the state to assist teachers in obtaining resources from media centers throughout the state.

The scanning center had a computer set up with a flatbed scanner so students could scan pictures from books, magazines, and other sources for use in their projects. The science center had real owl pellets, owl pellet dissection data sheets, and bone sorting charts that Mr. Balado obtained from an Internet science company. This center also included two digital microscopes that the students could use to closely investigate their findings and take digital photographs of their discoveries. Mr. Balado set up this

center like a real science lab. He wanted to give his students authentic, hands-on experience to help them gain some understanding of what it takes to work as a scientist.

The last center was the digital media project center, which had one computer set up for students to create their digital media projects using either PowerPoint or iLife. Because the school had site licenses, PowerPoint and iLife were installed on all of the classroom computers so students could work on their projects as they progressed through the various centers. Students took the narratives they had written about owls and combined true facts they had now learned to create their own digital video story about an owl. Having students create the content makes the learning more memorable in two ways. First, they are learning by creating both text-based and visual content that addresses the dual coding theory as suggested by Paivio (you will learn more in the Learning Theories Special Feature at the end of this chapter). Second, because students are involved in discovery and constructivist learning, the content becomes personalized, and thus more relevant to them.

THE RESULTS OF TECHNOLOGY INTEGRATION

Students worked though the centers and created some of the most interesting and creative projects Mr. Balado had ever seen (Figure 6-35). One group had located a

WEB INFO

For more information about the benefits of technology integration, visit the Teachers Discovering Computers Web site (*scsite.com/tdc4*), click Chapter 6, click Web Info, and then click Benefits.

Figure 6-34 This learning center contains a variety of print resources for students to use to develop their research projects.

Figure 6-35 Using PowerPoint, students can create digital media projects.

picture of an owl soaring above its prey in a field, so for their model, they decided to create an owl flying above a field.

Most students could describe in detail all of the information they had learned about their species of owl — and, interestingly, each group had personalized its learning by giving its owl a nickname. The projects were outstanding; most of them contained many pictures and owl stories with actual research and details about North American owls and field wildlife biology.

Mr. Balado knew that his students were involved actively in their own learning and had interacted with numerous resources, Web sites, and software programs. By engaging in active learning at each center and using higher-order thinking skills, Mr. Balado's students, with his assistance, created their own questions, found their own answers, and created their own digital media projects. As a result of this process, Mr. Balado's students created new paths of knowledge for themselves that enhanced their learning, while achieving the unit learning objectives and benchmarks, and making sure to address curriculum standards.

As Mr. Balado and his students learned, technology can make a difference in the classroom if used appropriately and integrated into the curriculum. In addition, Mr. Balado noticed that his students' self-esteem, self-confidence, and writing skills improved as a result of creating their own projects (Figure 6-36). Students had prepared for the unit by reflecting on what they knew and what they wanted to know about owls (refer again to Figure 6-25 and the KWL chart). At the end of the unit, students reflected on their learning by

Figure 6-36 Students feel an amazing sense of pride and ownership when they complete their own projects.

articulating what they learned about owls. This reflection process helped Mr. Balado with his own reflective evaluation.

Learning Theories and Educational Research

At the end of this chapter is a special feature that provides information on educational learning theories and theorists. This special feature introduces you to educational terms, learning theories, educational research, and learning strategies that you should understand and apply to your own instructional strategies. All teaching strategies have learning theories and educational research embedded within the instructional framework. Learning theories help teachers form instructional strategies and technology integration techniques by providing a basic framework for teaching and learning. Teachers learn to combine the different strategies and integration methods that are most suitable and appropriate for teaching their students.

Summary of Technology and Curriculum Integration

As you have learned in this chapter, the best strategy for technology integration is to place technology into the hands of students and trained teachers, make it easily accessible, and let them decide how best to use it in their classrooms at the point of instruction. Teachers are the content experts who should evaluate all resources used in classrooms.

This chapter first discussed curriculum and technology issues as they apply to technology integration and then provided teachers with ideas, an instructional model, and effective planning strategies. The chapter then provided an introduction to the concept of technology integration that will help you build your integration literacy skills. Finally, this chapter showed you how one teacher, Mr. Balado, fully integrated technology into an interdisciplinary lesson. In Chapter 7, you will build upon the skills you have learned in this chapter and increase your integration literacy skills by learning implementation strategies and integration activities that are curriculum directed.

In Brief

INSTRUCTIONS: In Brief summarizes the concepts presented in this chapter. To listen to the audio version of this In Brief, visit scsite.com/tdc4. Click Chapter 6 at the top of the Web page and then click In Brief on the left sidebar.

1. Curriculum, Curriculum Standards, and Benchmarks

Curriculum is defined as all of the experiences a learner has under the supervision and guidance of teachers. A **curriculum standard**, also called a **curriculum goal**, defines what a student is expected to know at certain stages of education. A **benchmark**, or **learning objective**, is a specific, measurable outcome that usually is tied to a curriculum standard.

2. Technology Integration

Technology integration is the combination of all technology parts, such as hardware and software, together with each subject-related area of curriculum to enhance learning. Technology integration is using technology to help meet the curriculum standards and learner outcomes of each lesson, unit, or activity.

3. Technology Integration in the Curriculum

The key to successful technology integration is identifying what you are trying to accomplish within your curriculum. Teachers must consider what the curriculum standards and benchmarks are, identify an appropriate technology, and develop innovative ways to teach a diverse population of learners with different learning styles. A **learning style** refers to how individuals learn, including how they prefer to receive information, express themselves, and process information.

4. Changing Instructional Strategies

As students begin to play a more active role in the learning process, the teacher's role must change. Teachers are transitioning from the conventional lecture-practice-recall teaching methods to being the facilitator of learning. Rather than dictating a learning process, a **facilitator of learning** motivates students to want to learn, guides the student learning process, and promotes a learning atmosphere and an appreciation for the subject.

5. Barriers to Technology Integration

With all change comes barriers, and technology integration is no exception. Barriers include a lack of teacher training, lack of administration support, limited time for teacher planning, computer placement in remote locations making access difficult, budget constraints, and basic resistance to change by many educators.

6. Technology Integration and the Learning Process

For learning to take place, learners must be engaged in the process of education. **Authentic learning** experiences are instructional activities that demonstrate real-life connections by associating the concept being taught with a real-life activity or event. **Active learning** is a learning process in which students become engaged in inquiring, investigating, solving problems, and formulating and answering questions on their own.

7. Strategies for Integrating Technology into Teaching

The best strategy for curriculum integration is to put the technology into the hands of trained teachers, make it easily accessible, and let them decide how best to use it in their classrooms at the point of instruction. When proper strategies are used for technology integration, students enjoy learning to use technology as well as learning content in subject-related curriculum areas.

In Brief

6

8. The Role of the School District

School district administrators must plan carefully for every aspect of curriculum integration, from purchase, to installation, to teacher and staff training. Almost every school district has a detailed technology plan for curriculum integration. A **technology plan** is an outline that specifies the school district's procedures not only for purchasing equipment and software, but also for training teachers to use and then integrate technology into their classroom curriculum.

9. Technology Integration Plans for the Classroom

Teachers must plan carefully for the use and integration of computers and technologies in the classroom. They must plan how they will teach the curriculum, what areas they need to cover for content, and where they can use technology to meet learning objectives. Whether teachers use one computer, two computers, or thirty computers, however, they must plan how and when to use the computers and how they will enable students to use the computers.

10. Lesson Plans Based on Instructional Models

When planning lessons that use technology, teachers must consider the skills and knowledge level required for students to start and complete the lesson successfully. A **KWL chart** is a helpful planning tool in determining the skill and knowledge level of students prior to beginning almost any project. An **instructional model** is a systematic guide for planning instruction or a lesson. The ASSURE Model is a procedural guide for planning and delivering instruction that integrates technologies and media into the teaching process.

11. Technology Integration at a New School

Teachers need to consider many issues related to technology information and support, technology training, hardware, software, other technologies, and technology supplies. A **teacher's manual** is a booklet that contains information, rules and regulations, rights and responsibilities, and policies and procedures that will provide answers to many questions.

12. Learning Centers

Creating an integrated learning environment with centers is a great way to put it all together. **Centers,** or **learning centers,** give teachers the opportunity to break their classrooms into many different types of learning environments without ever leaving the room. Technology can make a difference in the classroom if used appropriately and integrated into the curriculum.

Key Terms

INSTRUCTIONS: Use the Key Terms to help focus your study of the terms used in this chapter. To further enhance your understanding of the Key Terms in this chapter, visit scsite.com/tdc4. Click Chapter 6 at the top of the Web page and then click Key Terms on the left sidebar. Read the definition for each term and then access current and additional information about the term from the Web.

active learning [346]
anchored instruction [346]
ASSURE Model [356]
authentic learning [346]

benchmark [338]
Body Works [347]

centers [362]
cognitive scaffold [347]
computer lab [340]
computer lab on wheels [353]
cooperative learning [349]
cooperative classroom activity [349]
curriculum [336]
curriculum framework [336]
curriculum goal [338]
curriculum guide [336]
curriculum integration [339]
curriculum standard [338]

discovery learning [347]

education [336]
educational equalizer [348]
educational grant [360]

essential questioning technique [360]
evaluation [358]
evaluation process [358]

facilitator of learning [343]

Grade Level Expectations (GLEs) [337]

higher-order thinking skills [349]

in-service [360]
instructional model [356]
integration [339]

KWHL chart [354]
KWL chart [354]

learning centers [362]
learning objective [338]
learning style [343]

Mastery Objective Checklist [337]
mentorship program [350]
Microsoft Encarta [347]

point of instruction [340]
problem-based instruction [347]

reflective evaluation [358]

skill assessment survey [354]
state bid list [360]
student objective [356]

teachable moment [340]
teacher's manual [359]
technology committee [359]
technology integration [339]
technology lab [340]
technology plan [350]

virtual field trip [342]

Wellivers Instructional Transformation Model [344]
wireless mobile lab [353]

Checkpoint

INSTRUCTIONS: Use the Checkpoint excercises to check your knowledge level of the chapter. To complete the Checkpoint exercises interactively, visit scsite.com/tdc4. Click Chapter 6 at the top of the Web page and then click Checkpoint on the left sidebar.

1. Label the Figure

Instructions: Identify the five hierarchy stages of the Wellivers Instructional Transformation Model.

Wellivers Instructional Transformation Model

1. _____ is when teachers become aware of technology and its potential uses.

2. _____ is when teachers use technology, but minor problems will cause teachers to discontinue its use.

3. _____ is when technology becomes essential for the educational process and teachers are constantly thinking of ways to use technology in their classrooms.

4. _____ is when teachers begin to rethink the educational goals of the classroom with the use of technology.

5. _____ is the evolving classroom that becomes completely integrated with technology in all subject areas. Technology becomes an invisible tool that is seamlessly woven into the teaching and learning process.

2. Matching

Instructions: Match each term from the column on the left with the best description from the column on the right.

____ 1. ASSURE Model

____ 2. authentic learning

____ 3. curriculum standards

____ 4. mentorship program

____ 5. KWL chart

a. lessons connected to real-life events

b. instructional planning tool to assist teachers in identifying curriculum objectives

c. procedural guide for planning and delivering instruction that integrates technology

d. collection of general concepts that school districts expect their students to learn

e. when new teachers team with experienced teachers

3. Short Answer

Instructions: Write a brief answer to each of the following questions.

1. What is the difference between a curriculum standard and a benchmark? Are both curriculum standards and benchmarks measurable? Why or why not? _____

2. What are learning styles? How can a teacher be a facilitator of learning and at the same time address various students' learning styles? _____

3. Name five barriers to technology integration. In your opinion, which barrier is the most important? Why? _____

4. Name three people who can help teachers find information on available technologies in their schools. Describe other sources that can assist teachers in locating technology resources. _____

5. Name three areas teachers must address when planning for technology integration in a one-computer classroom. Can these same planning strategies also work for a two-computer classroom? _____

Teaching Today

INSTRUCTIONS: Teaching Today provides an appreciation of the value that technology and the Web have for K-12 education. Each numbered segment contains one or more links that reinforce the information presented in the segment. To display this page from the Web, visit scsite.com/tdc4. Click Chapter 6 at the top of the Web page and then click Teaching Today on the left sidebar.

1. Lesson Plans

After using technology in your classroom, you are beginning to understand that using technology is different from integrating technology. You want to begin integrating technology into your social studies curriculum. Where do you begin? Are resources available on the Internet that can help you? Where can you locate examples of lesson plans that integrate technology but still support your curriculum? Can you modify these lessons to use in your classroom?

2. Grant Opportunities

Your school is located in a rural area, and technology funds are limited. You have used technology with students before and were encouraged by the results. You have one computer in your classroom and want to provide your students with greater access to technology. You have decided to explore possible grant opportunities. Your district is small, however, and does not have any grant programs. Very few businesses in your community offer grant opportunities. Where can you learn about other grant opportunities? Are there grants available specific to your circumstances? What are some other funding options? What other organizations in your community could you contact?

3. Mentoring

You want to integrate technology into your curriculum, but you do not know where to start. You want to provide the students with authentic learning activities and you need ideas. You consider talking to a teacher who integrates technology, but you do not know anyone. You have heard of a Web site where teachers can receive mentoring from other teachers as well as ask for advice and receive ideas. What are some advantages to finding assistance online? What are some disadvantages? Could you use this type of assistance for any subject? Why or why not? Could your students benefit from this type of interaction? Why or why not? How can you locate more resources such as this for yourself and for your students?

4. Storytelling

As a teacher, you know that by putting the technology in the hands of students you can create innovative learning experiences and increase motivation, all while teaching curriculum-specific content. You heard about an innovative project designed to get students writing stories about themselves called MeTV. The project is based on the principles of telling personal stories. Getting students to write is the crucial step in achieving many curriculum standards and is often one of the benchmarks associated with a standard. Getting students writing, especially about themselves, family, or community, is one way to encourage writing while strengthening writing skills. What kind of lesson plans can you develop using the project MeTV? What questions could you ask your students to get them thinking? What is a story circle? Could you find ways to weave a story throughout all curriculum areas? How?

![SchoolGrants - Find Grant Opportunities - Microsoft Internet Explorer window. Address: http://www.schoolgrants.org/grant_opps.htm. Image of children with text "For the kids ... www.schoolgrants.org". Left sidebar: Home, What's New, Services, Vendors, Newsletters, Let's Write a Grant CD. Main content heading: Grant Opportunities. Text: "Grant opportunities that will benefit K-12 schools, educators, and students are posted on the pages listed below. When you find an opportunity that appears to match your project goals, be sure to follow the links to the funder's site for more information."]

Education Issues 6

INSTRUCTIONS: Education Issues provides several scenarios that allow you to explore controversial and current issues in education. Each numbered segment contains one or more links that reinforce the information presented in the segment. To display this page from the Web, visit scsite.com/tdc4. Click Chapter 6 at the top of the Web page and then click Education Issues on the left sidebar.

1. Bilingual Education

A recent survey of state education agencies indicates that more than 4 million students with limited proficiency in English are enrolled in public schools and that this number is growing — dramatically, in many locations — every year. This trend poses unique challenges for educators who want to ensure that these students have the same opportunities as English-proficient students. In transitional bilingual education programs, instruction is provided for some subjects in the students' native language and part of the school day is spent on developing English skills. Bilingual education's critics argue that this approach keeps students in a cycle of native-language dependency that ultimately prevents them from making significant progress in English-language-acquisition and leads to lower test scores. These critics argue that these students must spend 100 percent of their time on task in English to master proficiency in English. What do you think? What Web site resources provide teachers with practical material for culturally diverse classrooms? What other technologies and teaching strategies can you use to enhance student learning?

2. Integrated Learning System

Your school district has spent a significant amount of money on a comprehensive integrated learning system that is available for all teachers to use throughout the district. This software generates tests and automatically tracks student progress. The software also includes thousands of interactive student assignments, data-driven decision-making capabilities, and the ability to create customized learning paths for your students so they can progress through the content at their own pace and path. What are some of the benefits of this type of software? What are some disadvantages? Does this type of software appeal to different learning styles? How could students with learning disabilities use this type of software?

3. Levels of Integration

It is the second month of the semester, and you are teaching seventh-grade science. The parents of one of your students contact you. They are upset because when their son was in elementary school, the majority of teachers were using technology in their classrooms. At your middle school, however, their son has not had the same opportunities. The parents are very concerned about the lack of technology. What can you do about this situation? To whom can you refer the parents? Do greater barriers to technology integration exist in middle schools than in elementary or high schools? Why or why not? How could you integrate technology into your seventh-grade science curriculum?

4. Integrating the Internet

In your school district, Internet access is available in all classrooms. Most teachers use the Internet for research. You want to integrate the Internet in a meaningful way; however, you need some ideas about how to start. Where can you find suggestions on how to integrate the Internet into your classroom? What kinds of projects are the best to start with? What are other appropriate uses for the Internet, besides conducting research? Does your district offer training on Internet technology integration issues or just on how to use technology? How can you integrate the Internet to stimulate authentic learning? Is it appropriate to integrate the Internet for every subject area? Why or why not?

Integration Corner

INSTRUCTIONS: Integration Corner provides extensive ideas and resources for integrating technology into your classroom-specific curriculum. To display this page from the Web and its links to approximately 100 educational Web sites, visit scsite.com/tdc4. Click Chapter 6 at the top of the Web page and then click Integration Corner on the left sidebar.

Integration Corner is designed for teachers and other educators who are looking for innovative ways to integrate technology into their content-specific curriculum. Integration Corner not only provides great Web sites with current information, but it also shows what other educators are doing in the field of educational technology. These Corners are designed for all educators regardless of their area of interest. Be sure to review information and sites outside of your teaching area because many great integration ideas in one area can be modified easily for use in other curricular areas.

Teachers and administrators will find other colleagues in their areas with whom to connect and share the successes and hurdles of integrating technology in a classroom or an entire school system. Consider Integration Corner your one stop for integration ideas and resources. Links to educational Web sites are organized in the following 12 Corners, and different Web resources are available for each chapter. Figure 6-37 shows examples of the Web resources provided in the Chapter 6 Post Secondary Corner.

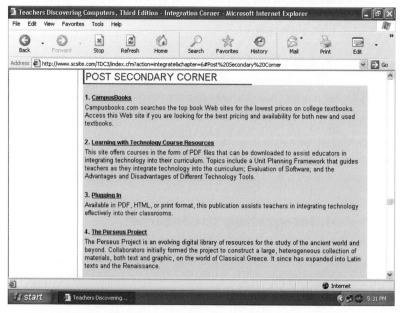

Figure 6-37 Examples of the Web resources provided in the Chapter 6 Post Secondary Corner.

Software Corner

INSTRUCTIONS: Software Corner provides information on popular software programs. Each numbered segment discusses specific software programs and contains a link to additional information about these programs. To display this page from the Web, visit scsite.com/tdc4. Click Chapter 6 at the top of the Web page and then click Software Corner on the left sidebar.

1. Mighty Math

Teaching students the concepts of pre-algebra and algebra can be a challenge. One software program that will help you meet this challenge is Mighty Math Astro Algebra from Riverdeep. Your students will be captains of a space ship and help the Algebra Alliance solve problems. Each new mission increases in complexity, and you can track student progress. The Grapher allows students to graph ordered pairs, equations, and inequalities. The VariaBlox feature allows students to use virtual manipulatives to solve mathematical problems. The AstroNet provides definitions, explanations, examples, and more. Mighty Math Astro Algebra is engaging and appeals to auditory, visual, and kinesthetic learners.

2. Science Plus

Let your students become scientists through interactive explorations with Science Plus Interactive Explorations. This software allows you and your students to have a virtual laboratory right in your own classroom, providing them with the resources to solve complex scientific problems in a real laboratory. Students investigate authentic, real-world problems, such as studying the temperatures of the volcanoes in Hawaii, researching soil chemistry and acid rain, designing the perfect toboggan ride, and much more. Dozens of explorations provide students with the opportunity to apply real-world solutions to scientific problems through the power of interactive laboratory simulations.

3. Reader Rabbit

Reader Rabbit's Reading Series from The Learning Company provides a playful and engaging way for elementary students to develop essential building blocks to learn to read. The program includes activities to help recognize words and phonics; learn to read, decode, and spell; and develop and enhance vocabulary skills, visual memory, and concentration. It contains four activities, each of which has four levels of difficulty. The activities in Reader Rabbit's Reading 2 for Grades 1-3 contain more than 1000 practice words and give students many opportunities to practice identifying consonant blends as well as short and long vowel sounds. A score chart tracks the number of correct responses and attempts, and displays the percentage of correct answers for each of the four levels. Included with the software is a teacher resource binder that includes a comprehensive user's guide, 17 detailed lesson plans, dozens of bonus ideas, Internet resources, a scope and sequence chart, and more.

4. Owl and Mouse Software

Help your students learn continents, countries, states, capitals, borders, physical features, historical facts, and cultural monuments with games, software (most of it free), and educational activities from Owl & Mouse Educational Software. Your students can learn geography with a free interactive map that teaches the locations of the major cultural monuments of the world. Use the world geography interactive map to teach the physical features of the world including rivers, mountains, lakes, deserts, and rainforests. Your students can learn the countries of different continents and their capitals with fun and educational map puzzle games, too.

Digital Media Corner

INSTRUCTIONS: Today's K-12 digital students need their learning to be meaningful and relevant to their lives. Digital Media Corner provides videos, ideas, and examples of how you can use digital media to enhance your teaching and your students' learning. To access the videos and links to additional information, visit scsite.com/tdc4. Click Chapter 6 at the top of the Web page and then click Digital Media on the left sidebar.

1. At the Movies — How to Tell When Your Hard Drive's About to Die

Thousands of people lose their photos, papers, tax returns, e-mail messages, addresses, and other data from their hard drives everyday – sometimes with serious personal, business, and financial consequences. Losing data is not a matter of if; it is a matter of when. Are there things you can do to drastically reduce the chances of losing your computer files? Is it possible to recover data from your hard drive if it crashes and if so, what does it cost to have a professional help you? To learn answers to these and other questions and to learn five things you can do to prevent losing data, click the G4TechTV video link. Locate your video and click the corresponding High-Speed or Dial-up link, depending on your Internet connection.

2. At the Movies — Plasma Versus LCD

Are you considering purchasing a new plasma or LCD-display TV? Basic differences exist between plasma and LCD-display TVs and by understanding these differences, you will be able to choose the display option that best suits your needs. You can compare and contrast the two technologies using simple criteria such as cost and size. To learn more about plasma versus LCD-display TVs, click the G4TechTV video link. Locate your video and click the corresponding High-Speed or Dial-up link, depending on your Internet connection.

3. At the Movies — Tracking Kids with GPS

Inventors using a new miniaturization process have merged cellular and Global Positioning System (GPS) tracking technology into a valuable instrument for parents who want an extra measure of security in protecting their children. One such system is called Digital Angel. Disguised as a simple wristwatch, this tracking device is able to track children who may become lost in a crowd or become a victim of kidnapping. What are the pros and cons of using technologies such as Digital Angel? To learn more about tracking your kids with GPS, click the G4TechTV video link. Locate your video and click the corresponding High-Speed or Dial-up link, depending on your Internet connection.

4. UB the Director

How do you encourage students to be interested in a book that does not relate directly to them? One technique is to use booktalking, which is a concept that means telling stories about the context and background in which the book is written. Booktalking allows students to read the content as if they were going to make a movie out of the book. Students are taught text-to-screen techniques and then learn how to pull important details from a book to create a book trailer. A book trailer is a short 2–3 minute video that encapsulates the essence of the book, main characters, metaphors, and so on. Using easy-to-use video editing software like Apple's iMovie, or Microsoft Movie Maker, students can easily build their own movies. Examples of trailers can be found at Digital Booktalk. In fact, this Web site accepts student-produced work.

5. Keynote

Keynote is a digital media presentation application that comes with Apple's iWork suite. Keynote includes features such as cinema-like transitions, pre-set animated text and titling effects, photo masking, and the ability to seamlessly add video clips. Keynote is easy to use allowing today's digital students to transition to learning the essence of digital storytelling. Keynote works seamlessly with iLife applications such as iPhoto.

Assistive Technologies Corner

INSTRUCTIONS: Assistive Technologies Corner provides information on current hardware, software, and peripherals that will assist you in delivering instruction to students with physical, cognitive, or sensory challenges. To access extensive additional information, visit scsite.com/tdc4. Click Chapter 6 at the top of the Web page and then click Assistive Technologies on the left sidebar.

1. Will Assistive Technology Help My Teaching? Yes!

Just as with students in a typical classroom, students with special needs must also attain curriculum standards. The teacher sets clear learning objectives based on the benchmarks, and plans for all students to attain those objectives, including those students with special needs. Technology helps engage all students in the learning process; however, technology can greatly enhance the learning process for students with special needs. Reminding educators that curriculum is central to instruction, the Center for Applied Special Technology (CAST) has developed the Universal Design for Learning, a theoretical curriculum design approach providing the fewest barriers to learning

In their book, _Teaching Every Student in the Digital Age: Universal Design for Learning_, Rose and Meyer remind teachers that access to information is not synonymous with access to learning, and that teachers must plan for learning, and not simply provide accessible information. Like all technology, assistive technologies need to be used at the right time, and with the appropriate curriculum goals in mind to provide access to learning.

2. What Are Some Ways to Use Assistive Technology to Help Students Learn?

Ms. Daniels at Fourth Street Elementary School has two students with dyslexia in her classroom. The class is beginning to read _Island of the Blue Dolphins_. Ms. Daniels uses the classroom Smart Board to present an Inspiration concept map, which will introduce students to the story's setting and provide them with background information. She will use the same program later to illustrate plot development as the story proceeds. Her dyslexic students depend on this organization to help them comprehend the whole story.

Strengthening of reading skills for many students is challenging, but especially for those students with dyslexia. Her students with dyslexia struggle through decoding and comprehension of the text during reading class, but with the graphical map they have a framework from which to proceed. In science class, these same students often use Kurzweil 3000, their text reader, to complete assigned classroom readings. Using a text reader helps them grasp science concepts quickly, and return to the printed text as needed.

Mr. Kamla's third grade class is studying energy. One of his students, Carla, who has cerebral palsy, finds it difficult to navigate the online tutorial with captioned video clips that Mr. Kamla created for the classroom learning center. Mr. Kamla used Intellitools' Overlay Maker to create a specialized template with large navigation keys that he places over the Intellikeys keyboard. Now, Carla is able to access the same tutorial as her classmates. Because the video clips he created are captioned, they provide all students with multisensory learning opportunities.

Mr. Kamla and Ms. Daniels often collaborate on their accessibility ideas. Last year, they adapted two WebQuests for a class with several students with emotional disturbances. They located a WebQuest on the Web that would meet their curriculum goals, but realized that the special needs students would not be able to participate fully. Following Bernie Dodge's suggestions for adapting existing WebQuests, they used more prompts and more details in the directions and in the accompanying printed materials. They structured the student interaction carefully and with tasks clearly focusing on the learning objectives. Making sure the WebQuest met accessibility standards, they published the WebQuest. Planning for learning by all students is simply good practice in any classroom. Choosing the right technology tool helps instructors explore a myriad of ways to engage all learners!

Follow the instructions at the top of this page to display additional information and this chapter's links on assistive technologies.

In the Lab

INSTRUCTIONS: In the Lab provides desktop publishing exercises that are divided into two areas, productivity and integration. To access the links to tutorials, productivity ideas, integration examples and ideas, and more, visit scsite.com/tdc4. Click Chapter 6 at the top of the Web page and then click In the Lab on the left sidebar.

PRODUCTIVITY IN THE CLASSROOM

Introduction: Desktop publishing provides teachers with effective and efficient ways to communicate with students, parents, faculty, and others in a professional manner. Many word processing applications, such as Microsoft Word, AppleWorks, and Microsoft Works, provide templates enabling users to create newsletters and many other documents with ease. Many excellent desktop publishing software applications also are available. Microsoft Publisher and Adobe Page-Maker are two popular programs used by educators. Exciting and innovative ways exist that allow teachers to integrate desktop publishing effectively into the curriculum. Students enjoy creating professional looking documents and finding creative ways to exhibit what they have learned.

1. Creating and Formatting a Parent Newsletter

Problem: As a kindergarten teacher, you believe it is important to send home monthly newsletters to keep parents informed of what is happening in the classroom. Open your word processing or desktop publishing software application and create a newsletter as described in the following list. Use the newsletter shown in Figure 6-38 as an example. If you are using a template, modify the newsletter design to accommodate the template. If you are using Microsoft Word, consider using tables, columns, section breaks, and text boxes to create the newsletter. (*Hint:* Use Help to understand the steps better.)

Instructions: Perform the following tasks.

1. Personalize the newsletter by inserting your name instead of Ms. Erhart's name and the grade level or subject you teach. Format the first and second heading lines in 16-point Times or Times New Roman font centered on the page.
2. Personalize the newsletter by using the current month and year. Enter the month and year (using the format Month, Year) right-aligned in 16-point Times or Times New Roman font.
3. Choose an appropriate picture, image, or clip art graphic, and then insert it on the page left-aligned.
4. Create an opening paragraph with a heading and at least three lines of text. Format the heading line in 14-point Times or Times New Roman font. Format the text in 12-point Times or Times New Roman font.
5. Create the body of the newsletter in two columns. Format section headings centered in uppercase 12-point Times or Times New Roman bold font. Format the text in 12-point Times or Times New Roman font.
6. Create a closing paragraph at the bottom of the newsletter. Format the text in 12-point Times or Times New Roman font.
7. Choose an appropriate picture, image, or clip art graphic and then insert it on the lower-right side of the newsletter.
8. Save the document to the location and with a filename of your choice. Print the document and then follow your instructor's directions for handing in the assignment.

In the Lab

Ms. Erhart's Kindergarten Class Newsletter

February, 2008

Winter Wonders

January passed quickly for our class! February holds many fun activities and lots of good learning. Please be sure to join us for our Valentine's Day party and mark February 23 on your calendar for our special Black History event!

COME OUT AND READ

Our class is hosting a Come Out and Read night! Students can wear pajamas and get comfy on big pillows as they enjoy a good book with a parent or sibling. We also will have a special storyteller coming in to share some exciting stories with the group. Be sure to join us for the fun!

WHAT'S HAPPENING IN CLASS

We continue to focus on letter recognition and letter sounds during February. We also are studying the seasons and reading stories about winter. These are the stories we will use in class. Check them out from the library to reinforce these concepts at home!

A Snowy Day, by Ezra Jack Keats
The Mitten, by Jan Brett
Little Polar Bear, by Hans de Beer
Mama, Do You Love Me?, by Barbara M. Joosse

BLACK HISTORY MONTH

February is Black History Month, and students will learn about the contributions of inspirational African-Americans. To continue our focus on reading during February, we will be using the following books:

The Story of Ruby Bridges, by Robert Coles
Under the Quilt of Night, by Deborah Hopkinson
Sweet Clara and the Freedom Quilt, by Deborah Hopkinson
Martin's Big Words: The Life of Dr. Martin Luther King, Jr., by Doreen Rappaport
Amazing Grace, by Mary Hoffman

The class will work together and create an exciting presentation for their families on February 23! Look for more information in our next newsletter.

Reading is such an important skill, and together we can prepare your children to be successful readers and lifelong learners. Please do not hesitate to contact me if you have any questions or comments. Remember, you are always welcome to come into our classroom and be a part of the learning experience!

Figure 6-38

In the Lab

2. Creating and Formatting a Department Newsletter

Problem: You are a member of your high school's Foreign Language Department. Your responsibility is to communicate information to the rest of the Foreign Language Department. You decide the easiest way to share new information is by creating a newsletter. Use the newsletter shown in Figure 6-39 as an example. (*Hint:* Use Help to understand the steps better.)

Instructions: Format the first and second heading lines in 14-point Arial bold font. Insert your name in place of Mr. Schatz in 12-point Times or Times New Roman bold font. Enter the current month and year (in the format Month, Year) in 14-point Arial bold font. Create the body of the newsletter in three columns. Personalize the information in the newsletter to reflect the grade level or subject that you teach. Format the section headings in 12-point Arial bold font. Format the text in 12-point Arial font. Format the country names in 11-point Arial bold font. Enter the Web site titles in 11-point Arial font. Format the Web site addresses in 10-point Arial font. Enter the quote in 12-point Times or Times New Roman italic font. Insert appropriate pictures, images, or clip art graphics.

After you have typed and formatted the newsletter, save the newsletter to a location and with a filename of your choice. Print the newsletter and then follow your instructor's directions for handing in the assignment.

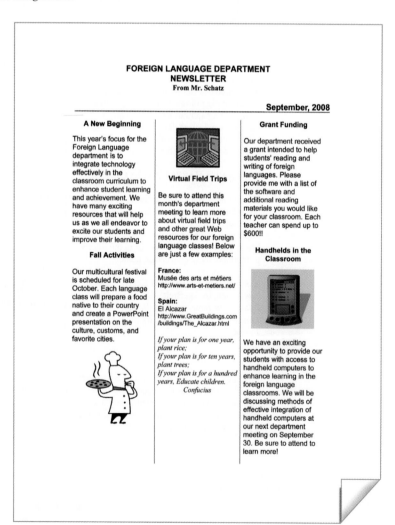

Figure 6-39

In the Lab

6

3. Creating and Formatting a Newsletter for a State Organization

Problem: You are the secretary for your subject area state organization. It is your responsibility to create a newsletter summarizing your state convention, providing information for the upcoming year's convention, and any other pertinent information.

Instructions: Create a newsletter similar to the newsletter illustrated in Figure 6-39. Use an appropriate layout, and then select font types and styles, font sizes, and clip art images for the newsletter. Include the current date, your name, and e-mail address. Save the newsletter to a location of your choice using an appropriate filename. Print the newsletter and then follow your instructor's directions for handing in the assignment.

INTEGRATION IN THE CLASSROOM

1. In honor of <u>Black History Month</u>, you have planned a cross-curricular project. You will divide students into groups and assign each group one of the following curricular areas: science, society and culture, math, art, music, or literature. Each group will choose one famous African-American to research who has made a significant contribution in the group's assigned field. Students then will create a newsletter outlining their findings. They will discuss the person's place of birth, family history, educational background, interests, and contributions to their particular field. Students will include at least one image in the newsletter. Select a famous African-American and create a sample newsletter for your students. Include your name and the current date in your sample newsletter.

2. Your high school Spanish class is studying cities in Spain. To reinforce reading and writing Spanish while learning about the country, students will create a newsletter written in Spanish. Students will work in groups and research three different cities in Spain. They will access and read <u>online newspapers</u> from the cities they select, gather <u>travel and tourist information</u>, obtain appropriate graphics that illustrate aspects of their chosen cities, and then create a newsletter in Spanish that presents the information they learned. Students will present their newsletter to the class and distribute a copy of it to each class member. Create a sample newsletter for your students. If you are not fluent in Spanish, select another foreign language. If you are not fluent in a foreign language, research three cities in Spain and create a newsletter presenting travel and tourist information written in English. Include your name, the current date, Web resources, and graphics in your sample newsletter.

3. While teaching the <u>American Revolution</u>, you team up with an English teacher to provide your students with a constructivist learning activity. Students will select one event that led up to the American Revolution and create a newsletter using information and images they locate from print resources and the Internet. Students will conduct their research in the history classroom and the English teacher will assist students with the layout, design, and writing techniques. Using the ideas and techniques you have learned in this In the Lab, create a sample newsletter for your students. Include your name, the current date, the course number, and course title in your newsletter.

Learn It Online

INSTRUCTIONS: Use the Learn It Online exercises to reinforce your understanding of the chapter concepts and increase your computer, information, and integration literacy. To access dozens of interactive student labs, practice tests, learning games, and more, visit scsite.com/tdc4. Click Chapter 6 at the top of the Web page and then click Learn It Online on the left sidebar.

1. Create and Use Your Own Web Log (BLOG)

A Web log, commonly referred to as a blog, can contain any information you want to place in it. Originally, blogs consisted of Web addresses, so that an individual or group with a specific interest could direct others to useful places on the Web. Today, blogs contain addresses, thoughts, diaries, and anything else a person or group wants to share. After you create a blog, you can update it. A variety of services are available on the Web to help you create and maintain your blog. Click the blog link to learn how to create and use your own blob.

2. Maintaining Your PC's Hard Disk

You computer's hard disk is used for the majority of your storage requirements. Maintaining your hard disk can help prevent the loss of data. In addition, it is important that your hard disk operates at peak efficiency. Click the Maintaining Your PC's Hard Disk link to learn how to maintain your PC's hard drive by detecting and repairing disk errors using the Check Disk utility, removing unused files and folders using the Disk Cleanup utility, and consolidating files and folders using the Disk Defragmenter utility.

3. Expanding Your Understanding

When you print using a computer, you control printing at two different points: first, before the printing actually begins, and second, after the document has been sent to the printer. Click the Expanding Your Understanding link to learn how to set the parameters for printing.

4. Practice Test

Click the Practice Test link. Answer each question. When completed, enter your name and click the Grade Test button to submit the quiz for grading. Make a note of any missed questions. If required, submit your score to your instructor.

5. Who Wants to Be a Computer Genius?

Click the Computer Genius link to find out if you are a computer genius. Directions about how to play the game will be displayed. When you are ready to play, click the Play button. If required, submit your score to your instructor.

6. Wheel of Terms

Click the Wheel of Terms link to reinforce important terms you learned in this chapter by playing the Shelly Cashman Series version of this popular game. Directions about how to play the game will be displayed. When you are ready to play, click the Play button. If required, submit your score to your instructor.

7. Crossword Puzzle Challenge

Click the Crossword Puzzle link. Complete the puzzle to reinforce skills you learned in this chapter. Directions about how to play the game will be displayed. When you are ready to play, click the Play button. If required, submit the completed puzzle to your instructor.

Learning Theories and Educational Research

A great deal of discussion has taken place about the definition of learning by educational theorists, researchers, and practitioners; yet, no universal definition of learning has been accepted. As a result, numerous definitions exist, and they vary greatly in describing the exact nature of learning. For this textbook, **learning** is defined as the process of gaining knowledge or skills acquired through instruction or study, or to modify behavior through exposure to a type of conditioning or form of gaining experience. A **theory** is a scientific set of principles presented to clarify or explain a phenomenon. **Learning theories** provide frameworks for interpreting the conditions and observations of teaching and learning and provide the bridge between education and research.

Educational research builds the foundation for the development of sound instructional strategies; however, it takes practice and moving the theory into practice to create the bridge that evolves into technology integration. Each new lesson you present to your students should be based on learning theory and educational research. These learning theories have been shown to enhance learning and increase motivation and student achievement. Which learning theory you use depends on what you want to teach, how you want to teach it, and who you are teaching. The latter is very important because as we have learned today's kids are totally different. The way they learn also is different.

Figure 1-5 in Chapter 1 listed the characteristics of today's digital generation. In addition to describing who these kids are and how they think, their traits have implications on teaching and learning. Today's students tend to process information at what Prensky refers to as a "twitch speed." Today's students often fail to spend time reflecting and processing information at what Craik and Lockhart refer to as **deep processing levels**. Research has found that deep processing levels are necessary for students to make sense of the information, to give meaning to the information, and to remember things for a longer period of time. Today's students' prefer graphics over text-based communications. This learning preference ties to Clark and Paivio's ideas on dual coding and how pictures interface with a person's abilities to recall information.

Today's students like to live, work, and play in digital social settings with others; this interaction is known as their **social network** (Figure 1). Even though today's digital students pride themselves on being individuals, they prefer instruction that involves interaction for themselves and with others. This learning preference ties directly to the work of Lev Vygotsky, Albert Bandura, and others. Recall the ARCS Motivational Model described in Chapter 1 and the ASSURE Model described early in this chapter and how both of these models are relevant to discussions about learning theories. Most models, including these, underline how important it is to know one's audience before developing class content and deciding how to mediate the instructional activities.

FIGURE 1 Today's digital students interact digitally in what is known as their social network, which is in total contrast to the way in which any previous generation interacted socially.

WEB INFO

For more information about Behaviorism, visit the Teachers Discovering Computers Web site (*scsite.com/tdc4*), click Chapter 6, click Web Info, and then click Behaviorism.

This special feature highlights some of the theories and theorists that will help you better integrate technology into your curriculum. For more information about specific learning theories and researchers, including reference materials, access the Web Info annotations located in the margins throughout this special feature. The first section discusses the behaviorism learning theory.

Behaviorism

Behaviorism is the prediction and control of human behavior in which introspection and/or independent thinking form no essential part of its methods. Behaviorism came into vogue during a period of time that coincided with the industrial revolution called **modernism** in which everything of value (including learning) was measured solely in terms of science. To a behaviorist, human learning is purely an objective and experimental branch of natural science. There is no internal cognitive processing of information.

The behaviorist recognizes no dividing line between man and animal: Both learn to behave solely through a system of positive and negative rewards. For some students, this type of conditioning works very well. Behaviorists such as Pavlov, Skinner, and Bandura have contributed a great deal to the understanding of human behavior, and an overview of their contributions are described in the following sections.

Ivan Pavlov

Ivan Pavlov (1849 – 1936) became famous for his behavioral experiments with dogs, and he won the Nobel Prize in Physiology in 1904 (Figure 2). Pavlov used conditioning to teach dogs to salivate when he rang a bell. When he provided the stimulus (food) and he achieved his desired reflex (salivation), he rang a bell. Eventually, the dogs associated the bell with food and they began to salivate when Pavlov rang the bell even if food was not present. This process was termed **classic conditioning** and refers to the natural reflex that occurs in response to a stimulus. Pavlov was a scientist, and he conducted these experiments to study digestion, but as a result, other behaviorists studied his work as an example of stimulus response. Some behaviorists felt this technique of stimulus response had human applications as well.

WEB INFO

For more information about Ivan Pavlov, visit the Teachers Discovering Computers Web site (*scsite.com/tdc4*), click Chapter 6, click Web Info, and then click Pavlov.

FIGURE 2 Ivan Pavlov's research into the physiology of digestion led him to create a science based on conditioned reflexes that won him the Nobel Prize in 1904.

B.F. Skinner

B.F. Skinner (1904 – 1990) describes another form of conditioning that is labeled as behavioral or operant conditioning (Figure 3). **Operant conditioning** describes learning that is controlled and results in shaping behavior through the reinforcement of stimulus response patterns. Skinner conducted experiments with pigeons and rewarded them when he saw them behaving in a desired manner. When a stimulus response pattern occurs, such as a pigeon turning (a stimulus), a reward is given (response). Eventually, Skinner was able to teach pigeons to dance using this technique. Ultimately, he taught pigeons to engage in complex tasks such as bowling in a specially constructed bowling alley.

WEB INFO

For more information about B.F. Skinner, visit the Teachers Discovering Computers Web site (*scsite.com/tdc4*), click Chapter 6, click Web Info, and then click Skinner.

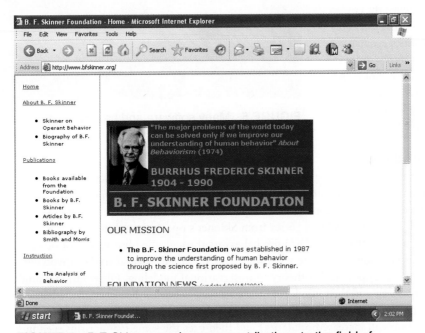

FIGURE 3 B.F. Skinner made many contributions to the field of psychology, including the theory of behavioral or operant conditioning.

Skinner believed that people shape their behavior based on the rewards or positive reinforcement they receive. Skinner believed human behavior, even the language development of children, is based on stimulus response theory. He observed that when children made attempts at sounds, parents smiled and reinforced that behavior. Eventually, the child learns to say the word correctly as parents and others reinforce her efforts.

In his experiments, Skinner found that reinforcement was a powerful motivator. He conducted experiments with people as well and he even used his own infant daughter. Skinner felt that when a child produces a desirable behavior and is rewarded for it, that behavior will be repeated. In contrast, if a response is negative, the behavior will be extinguished. Many classroom management techniques are based on these principles. Figure 4 compares classic and operant conditioning.

Classic Conditioning Pavlov	Operant Conditioning Skinner
Classic conditioning introduces the stimulus and then reinforces the reflex. A neutral stimulus (the bell) becomes analogous with a reflex (salivation).	Operant conditioning begins with a stimulus (behavior) and then is reinforced with a response (reward). A bond becomes established between the operant (stimulus/behavior) and the reward.

FIGURE 4 Classic versus operant conditioning.

Many forms of computer-based instruction and educational software are based on Skinner's operant conditioning. They provide positive reinforcement when a desired behavior occurs and negative reinforcement when the student does not provide the desired behavior. For instance, when the correct answer is given, the software program provides positive verbal and visual feedback for the student's correct response. As Figure 5 shows, even young children enjoy learning and getting positive feedback.

FIGURE 5 Many software and hardware developers are designing products to reinforce learning for younger students.

Albert Bandura

Albert Bandura (1925 –) has studied and is famous for his ideas on **social learning**, which he recently renamed, **Social Cognitive Theory**. Bandura focuses on those motivational factors and self-regulatory mechanisms that contribute to a person's behavior, rather than just environmental mechanisms, which differentiates his theories from Skinner's operant conditioning.

Bandura believes that people acquire behaviors through the observation of others and then by using those observations to imitate what they have observed. Several studies involving television commercials have supported this theory of observational modeling. **Observational modeling** is watching something and then mimicking the observed behavior. For example, when a person purchases a product advertised on TV based on claims made in the commercial (such as using a specific shampoo will increase popularity) and then uses the same mannerisms seen in the commercial (such as flipping one's hair while looking coyly over a shoulder), then that person is modeling the behavior shown in the commercial.

Social learning theory has been applied extensively in the context of behavior modification, which is widely used in training programs. In recent years, Bandura has focused his work on the concept of self-efficacy, which ties to motivation and cognition. **Self-efficacy** is a personal observation about one's self in regard to his perceived ability to learn things.

WEB INFO

For more information about Albert Bandera, visit the Teachers Discovering Computers Web site (*scsite.com/tdc4*), click Chapter 6, click Web info, and then click Bandera.

As he furthered his research, Bandura began to analyze a person's personality through the interaction of three things: the environment, the behavior, and the person's psychological processes. Bandura then started to consider a person's ability to retain information through images in the minds called **imagery**. It was at this time that he stopped being a strict behaviorist, and began to join the position of the cognitivists (Figure 6), a new movement that was just beginning to take root. So significant were his contributions to this movement, that he often has been called the father of the

FIGURE 6 Albert Bandura contributed many ideas to both behaviorist and cognitive learning theories.

cognitivist movement. In the next section, you will learn more about cognitive theory and cognitivists like Paivio, Gagne, Gardner, and Bloom.

Cognitivist

Cognitive theory is an offshoot of traditional psychological concepts of thinking, deciding, remembering, and so on. The cognitive psychologist views these activities in terms of how they underlie behavior. According to **cognitive theory**, activities like thinking and remembering seem like a behavior, thus, providing an avenue to use behavior analysis to measure their effect on learning. Because cognitivist theory came about as a reaction to behaviorist thinking that was in vogue at the time, there has always been a certain amount of tension between behaviorist and cognitivist approaches to learning.

Cognitivists objected to behaviorists because they felt that behaviorists thought learning was simply a reactionary phenomenon and ignored the idea that thinking plays a role. Paivio, Gagne, Gardner, and Bloom are just a few of the cognitivists who have contributed a great deal to the understanding of cognitive theory; their contributions are discussed in the sections that follow.

Allan Paivio

Paivio proposed that presenting information in both visual and verbal form enhances recall and recognition. He developed a considerable amount of research to support what has become referred to as the dual coding theory. **Dual coding** theory assumes that people process information in two distinctly different ways: (1) processing for images and (2) processing for language (Figure 7). This research supports the theory that today's visual learners learn in different ways depending on the medium. Dual coding theory identifies three subprocesses: (1) representational, in which verbal or nonverbal representations are directly influenced, (2) referential, in which the verbal system is activated by nonverbal communication forms or vice-versa, and (3) associative, in which both text-based systems and graphic representations can trigger mental associations. A given task may require any or all of the three kinds of processing and form the basis for the study of such things as learning a second language.

One of the shortcomings, according to some, is the fact that Paivio placed equal importance on verbal and non-verbal processing. Many theorists have since disputed these findings, in which they have shown that graphics tend to endure longer in one's memory but are not as economically processed. Even with its distracters, dual coding theory has long formed the basis of subsequent educational theories.

WEB INFO

For more information on dual coding theory, visit the Teachers Discovering Computers Web site (*scsite.com/tdc4*), click Chapter 6, click Web Info, and then click Dual Coding Theory.

FIGURE 7 Allan Paivio's dual coding theory helps explain how today's digital students process information.

WEB INFO

For more information about Robert Gagne, visit the Teachers Discovering Computers Web site (*scsite.com/tdc4*), click Chapter 6, click Web Info, and then click Gagne.

Robert Gagne

Robert Gagne (1916 – 2002), a psychologist and educator, developed his learning theories based partially on the behaviorist's and information-processing point of view. Gagne is known for his contributions in the area of cognitive learning hierarchies, which involves the development of skills based on a building-block principle. Gagne identified five major categories of learning: cognitive strategies, verbal information, intellectual skills, motor skills, and attitudes. He made an enormous contribution to learning theory and instructional systems design. While in the Air Force, he began to develop some of his ideas for his comprehensive learning theory. He incorporated characteristics of both behavior modification theory and performance education.

Gagne developed three principles that he viewed as integral for successful instruction: (1) providing instruction on the set of component tasks that build toward a final task, (2) ensuring that each component task is mastered, and (3) sequencing the component tasks to ensure optimal transfer to the final task. In other words, a teacher must teach alphabet recognition so that her students can read words. After students can read words, they can read a sentence, and then two sentences, and then a paragraph, and so on. This process reflects a hierarchy of components.

Careful planning must take place so that learning is optimal and instruction can be broken down into meticulously planned lessons. Gagne believed that a variety of internal and external conditions must be present for learning to occur and he also believed that learning results in observable behavior. The internal conditions can be described as states that include attention, motivation, and recall. The external conditions are the factors surrounding a person, such as timing and place. The observable behavior is the result of the internal process of learning. Further, Gagne discussed that learners must go through a hierarchy of skills from simple to complex and identified five areas of learning outcomes (Figure 8).

Categories of Learning Outcomes	Examples of Outcomes
1. Verbal information	Learner can state what has been learned.
2. Intellectual skills: composed of concrete and defined concepts	Learner can discriminate between facts, can identify colors, and can follow directions.
3. Cognitive strategies	Learner reads books.
4. Motor skills	Learner can use a mouse or joystick.
5. Attitudes	Learner prefers reading to watching TV.

FIGURE 8   Gagne's five areas of learning outcomes.

Gagne sought to understand what conditions were necessary for students to learn. Instruction is an external condition for learning that leads to the internal process of learning. To maximize the potential for the internal process of learning to occur, Gagne identified **nine events of instruction** (Figure 9).

Nine Events of Instruction

1. Gain attention of the learners
2. Inform learners of the objective
3. Stimulate recall of prior learning
4. Present the stimulus or lesson
5. Provide learning guidance and instruction
6. Elicit performance
7. Provide feedback
8. Assess performance
9. Enhance retention and transfer

FIGURE 9   Gagne's nine events of instruction can help teachers develop technology-enriched lesson plans.

Howard Gardner

Many researchers have focused on understanding and defining intelligence. They believe that intelligence is a key to understanding how students learn. **Intelligence** is the ability to gain knowledge, apply knowledge, manipulate one's environment, and think abstractly. Howard Gardner (1943 –) developed what he called the theory of multiple intelligences (Figure 10).

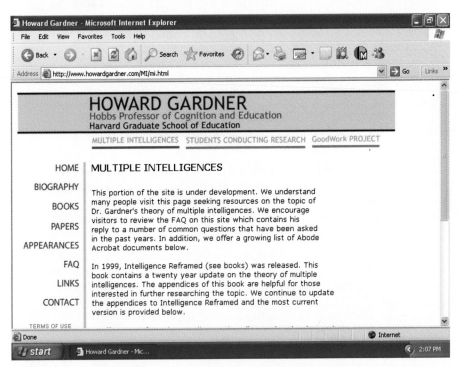

FIGURE 10 Howard Gardner is a professor at Harvard Graduate School of Education and is best known for his theory of multiple intelligences.

WEB INFO

For more information about Howard Gardner, visit the Teachers Discovering Computers Web site (*scsite.com/tdc4*), click Chapter 6, click Web Info, and then click Gardner.

Gardner, a professor at Harvard University, has conducted years of research on normal and gifted students and also studied adults with brain damage. In those who had been injured, he wanted to correlate what part of the brain had been injured and how the physical injury affected learning and other physical abilities. Through his original research, he concluded that individuals use eight different intelligences to perceive and understand the world. Gardner's eight intelligences and suggested integration strategies are described in Figure 11 (on the next page).

Gardner believes that individuals might have all of the intelligences, yet for each individual, one, two, or more intelligences may be more dominant than others. Gardner also believes that the intelligences are influenced by biological predispositions and learning opportunities in an individual's cultural context. The teacher-directed instructional method appeals strongly to the linguistic-verbal and logical-mathematical intelligences. Gardner suggests that instructional methods should include a variety of activities that support other intelligences, such as physical education, role-playing, arts, cooperative learning, reflections, and creative play.

A variety of assessment methods should be incorporated to accommodate the wide variety of student learning styles more accurately. An important observation Gardner made was identifying the need that educators take into account the differences in students' multiple intelligences and use them as a guide to personalize instruction and assessment, which results in the ability to design appropriate instructional strategies.

INTELLIGENCE	DESCRIPTION	TECHNOLOGY INTEGRATION
Linguistic–verbal	Ease in using language; think in words; sensitivity to rhythm and order; enjoy writing, reading, telling stories, and doing crossword puzzles	Word processing programs, prompted programs, label-making programs, word game programs, and programs that require the student to read and answer questions
Logical–mathematical	Ability to engage in inductive and deductive reasoning; use numbers effectively and to categorize, infer, make generalizations, and test hypotheses	Database programs, spreadsheet programs, problem-solving software, simulations that allow students to experiment with problems and observe results, and strategy game formats
Spatial–visual	Ability to visualize objects and special dimensions, think in images and pictures, like to draw and design, and enjoy puzzles	Draw and paint programs; graphic production software; reading programs that use visual clues such as color coding, desktop publishing, hyper-media, multimedia, concept mapping, and atlas programs
Body–kinesthetic	Ability to move the body with skill and control, expertise in using the body to express ideas and feelings	Software requiring alternate input such as joystick, mouse, touch window, or graphics tablet; keyboarding/word processing programs; graphics programs that produce blueprints for making 3-D models; and software that includes animated graphics
Musical	Ability to recognize patterns and sounds; sensitivity to pitch and rhythm; the capacity to perceive, express, transform or discern musical forms; think in tones, and learn through rhythm and melody	Programs that combine stories with songs; reading programs that associate letters/sounds with music; programs that use music as a reward; programs that allow students to create their own songs, hypermedia, and multimedia
Interpersonal	Ability to understand and communicate effectively with others, understand them, and interpret their behavior	Telecommunications programs, programs that address social issues, programs that include group participation or decision making, programs that turn learning into a social activity, and games that require two or more players
Intrapersonal	An awareness of oneself, goals, and emotions; the capacity for self-knowledge of one's own feelings; and the ability to use that knowledge for personal understanding	Tutorial software, programs that are self-paced, instructional games in which the opponent is the computer, programs that encourage self-awareness or build self-improvement skills, and programs that allow students to work independently
Naturalist	An awareness of the natural world around them; can identify people, plants, and other environmental features; can develop a sense of cause and effect in relation to natural occurrences such as weather; can formulate and test hypotheses	Problem-solving software, simulations that allow students to experiment with problems and observe results, strategy game formats, database software, concept mapping software, and weather probeware

FIGURE 11 Using Gardner's original eight multiple intelligences and technology integration, teachers can find ways to reach all students.

Benjamin Bloom

Benjamin Bloom (1913 – 1999), an educational psychologist, focused his research on students' cognitive learning domain (Figure 12). Bloom and a group of psychologists sought to classify learning behaviors to understand better how knowledge is absorbed. Bloom classified learning into three domains: cognitive, affective, and psychomotor. Bloom defined the **cognitive domain** as a student's intellectual level, in other words, what a student knows and how he organizes ideas and thoughts. He defined the **affective domain** as a student's emotions, interests, attitude, attention, and awareness. Finally, he categorized the **psychomotor domain**, which includes a student's motor skills and physical abilities. All of these domains can overlap in learning activities and are integrated throughout learning experiences.

WEB INFO

For more information about Benjamin Bloom, visit the Teachers Discovering Computers Web site (*scsite.com/tdc4*), click Chapter 6, click Web Info, and then click Bloom.

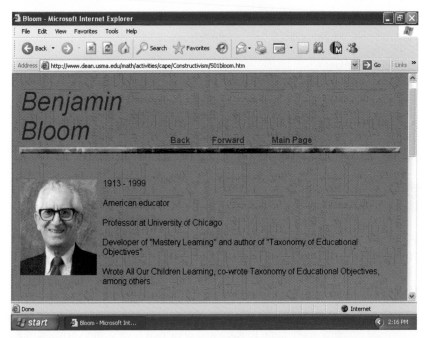

FIGURE 12   Benjamin Bloom's research focused on developing student problem-solving abilities and higher-order thinking skills. He was the creator of the concepts of Mastery Learning and Bloom's Taxonomy.

Bloom wanted to develop a practical means for classifying curriculum goals and objectives. Many educators today develop their curriculum goals and objectives with these three domains in mind. Educators are responsible for planning curriculum activities that support what students already should know and what they should learn. Teachers create their instructional plans based on state standards, learning objectives and learning theories. Teachers often arrange skills they want students to acquire using a scaffolding effect from simple to complex. Within the cognitive domain, Bloom identified six levels that can be used to acquire knowledge about a topic. The levels move from simple to complex and are designed to increase a student's comprehension. These levels commonly are referred to as **Bloom's Taxonomy** (Figure 13 on the next page).

Many teachers may not realize they are creating instructional plans that only challenge students within the first two levels. For instance, if students are learning about computers and then are asked to name only the parts and describe what they do, the activity has stayed in the Knowledge and Comprehension levels. If students are asked to propose how computers have changed their lives, the assignment has moved to the Analysis level.

Bloom's Taxonomy has been linked to mastery learning. **Mastery learning** is defined as a model for learning in which students continue to gain information and knowledge, working through modules or teacher instruction only after they have mastered the content of the previous modules. All students can learn given the correct conditions for learning and sufficient time. Bloom believed and demonstrated through his research that all children can learn. The critical ingredient is changing instructional methods so students can master the content.

WEB INFO

For more information about Bloom's Taxonomy, visit the Teachers Discovering Computers Web site (*scsite.com/tdc4*), click Chapter 6, click Web Info, and then click Bloom's Taxonomy.

COMPETENCIES	SKILLS
Knowledge: Learner can recall information.	Arrange, repeat, recall, define, list, match, name, order, write
Comprehension: Learner can explain and predict.	Discover, classify, explain, discuss, give examples, identify, explain, translate
Application: Learner can solve problems and use information.	Apply, demonstrate, solve, write, discover, experiment, interpret, show, present
Analysis: Learner can see patterns, organize parts, and recognize hidden meanings.	Analyze, experiment, examine, compare, contrast, associate, dissect, conclude, test
Synthesis: Learner can use previous ideas to create new ones, and relate ideas from several areas.	Collect, assemble, compose, develop, design, invent, create, plan, revise, write, theorize
Evaluation: Learner can compare and discriminate between ideas, judge, and value ideas.	Compare, assess, contrast, criticize, evaluate, judge, value, predict, estimate, appraise

FIGURE 13   The six levels of Bloom's Taxonomy move from simple to complex.

Constructivism

Extensive research has been conducted to assist educators in better understanding which instructional strategies will increase students' motivation to learn and determine their comprehension of a subject. Many researchers agree that traditional teacher-directed or lecture-based instruction often is limited in its effectiveness to reach today's learners. Teacher-directed instruction, however, still is used in many classrooms because of its ability to deliver information quickly; yet, students' understanding and comprehension can be low when this is the only teaching method used to address learning objectives and benchmarks.

Confucius once said, "I hear and I forget. I see and I remember. I do and I understand." Constructivists agree that students learn by doing. When students actively participate in the learning process by using critical-thinking skills to analyze a problem, they will create, or construct, their own understanding of a topic or problem. **Constructivist** theory, or **constructivism**, is based on a type of learning in which the learner forms, or constructs, much of what she learns or comprehends (Figure 14). The following sections describe four leading theorists of constructivism.

FIGURE 14   Leading theorists of constructivism include Jean Piaget, Seymour Papert, Jerome Bruner, Lev Vygotsky, and John Dewey.

Jerome Bruner

An American psychologist and educator, Jerome Bruner (1915 –) proposed that learning is an active process in which the learner constructs new ideas or concepts based on his current or past knowledge (Figure 15). Bruner believes that constructivist learners are active learners; they are actively engaged in the learning process. Constructivism emphasizes an integrated curriculum where students learn a subject in various ways or through many different activities.

WEB INFO

For more information about Constructivism, visit the Teachers Discovering Computers Web site (*scsite.com/tdc4*), click Chapter 6, click Web Info, and then click Constructivism.

FIGURE 15 Jerome Bruner's constructivist theory stresses that teachers actively should engage their students in their own learning.

Technology offers many strategies for the constructivist learning environment. When using the constructivist approach, students may complete a variety of activities while learning about a topic. For example, if students are studying endangered species, they may research this topic by using books, videos, and other digital media in the media center, as well as informational Web sites. They can then use an AlphaSmart to write up their findings in a word-processing document, study vocabulary words with electronic flash cards, create a drawing about endangered species in a paint program, create a spreadsheet to graph population changes over time, build a model with clay, and even learn songs about saving endangered animals or species.

WEB INFO

For more information about Jerome Bruner, visit the Teachers Discovering Computers Web site (*scsite.com/tdc4*), click Chapter 6, click Web Info, and then click Bruner.

Bruner's constructivist theory provides a framework for instruction based on the study of cognition. The theoretical concept of **cognition** suggests that an individual progresses through different intellectual stages. In constructivist theory, the learner selects and changes information to understand and make decisions, relying on higher-order thinking skills to solve a problem. An individual creates in her mind mental models that provide meaning and association to experiences that allow the individual to go beyond the given information. Bruner felt the teacher's role should be to encourage students through exploration and inquiry; in other words, learning should be discovery (Figure 16 on the next page).

As far as instruction is concerned, teachers should try to encourage students to discover concepts by themselves. Teachers should engage students by providing activities that guide students and create opportunities for discussion or for using the Socratic method of learning. The **Socratic method** is when students learn how to analyze problems, to think critically about one's own point of view and the opinions of others, as well as to articulate and defend their position. This method assists students in solving problems through questioning and answering techniques, which engages them in discussion. The task of the teacher is to take the materials to be learned and translate the information into a form appropriate for the learners' current level of understanding. Bruner felt that the curriculum should be organized in a spiral manner so that students continually build upon what they already have learned; this approach is called the **spiral curriculum**.

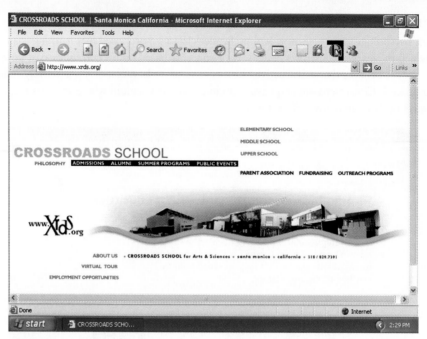

FIGURE 16   Many schools, such as CROSSROADS SCHOOL for Arts & Sciences, believe students should discover their own learning paths through active learning in areas such as intuition, imagination, artistic creativity, and physical expression.

Jean Piaget

The theories of Jean Piaget (1896 – 1980) profoundly influenced the constructivist movement (Figure 17). Piaget was a psychologist who developed the cognitive learning theory after he observed children for many years. Piaget perceived that children think very differently from adults. He felt children were active learners and did not need motivation from adults to learn. Piaget believed that children were constructing new knowledge as they moved through different cognitive stages, building on what they already knew. Furthermore, children interpret this knowledge differently as they progress through different stages.

WEB INFO

For more information about Jean Piaget, visit the Teachers Discovering Computers Web site (*scsite.com/tdc4*), click Chapter 6, click Web Info, and then click Piaget.

FIGURE 17   Jean Piaget was a psychologist who developed his learning theory after many years of observing children.

Piaget defined four cognitive stages (Figure 18). The first stage is called **sensorimotor**, when learning takes place primarily through the child's senses and motor actions. In the second stage, called **preoperational**, children begin to use symbols and images. Children use language symbols and play pretend games. An object such as a cardboard box can be a container, but it also can represent a house.

Next, children move from the two egocentric stages into the third stage called **concrete operational**. In this stage, beginning about age 7, children begin to think logically. This is the stage when children are beginning to learn many facts. They also can begin to understand other points of view besides their own. Piaget called his last cognitive stage **formal operational**. During this stage, which begins at about age 12, children transition from concrete thinking to more abstract. They can formulate a hypothesis and understand cause and effect. Children or adolescents begin to formulate their own beliefs and morals.

Cognitive Stages	Ages (Approximate)	Characteristics of Learning
Sensorimotor	Birth to 2 years	Imitation, learn through senses and motor activities, do not understand the world around them, and egocentric
Preoperational	2 to 6/7 years	Egocentric, pretend play, drawing ability, speech and communication development, concrete thinking, and intuitive reasoning
Concrete operational	6/7 to 11/12 years	Classification, logical reasoning, problem solving, and beginnings of abstract thinking
Formal operational	11/12 years through adulthood	Comparative reasoning, abstract thinking, deductive logic, and test hypotheses

FIGURE 18   Piaget's four cognitive stages.

Piaget felt that children are working cognitively toward equilibrium as they move through the four different cognitive stages. While they are learning, children create what Piaget called schema. **Schema** is their cognitive understanding or development at any given time. Piaget concluded that children assimilate new knowledge as they experience new things and learn new information, which Piaget called **assimilation**. Children fit this information or these experiences into their lives to change their knowledge base and to make sense of their environment and the world around them, this process Piaget called **accommodation**.

Through the insightful work of Piaget and others, researchers believe it is important to provide a rich learning environment for children to explore. Children learn by actively investigating a topic (Figure 19). Piaget's theories support the use and integration of technology because of the opportunities technology supplies to reach a diverse population of learners with different learning styles. Using Web Quests, scavenger and treasure hunts, curriculum pages, and many other educational technologies, teachers can create student-centered activities that actively engage students in the learning process.

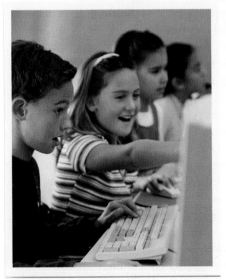

FIGURE 19   Student learning comes alive when teachers integrate the Internet and multimedia software into their classroom curriculum.

Lev Vygotsky

Lev Vygotsky (1896 – 1934), a Russian educational psychologist, also was interested in children's cognitive development (Figure 20). He developed what is known as **social cognition theory**. Although his ideas overlap in many ways with the traditional constructivists' point of view, Vygotsky believed that learning was influenced significantly by social development. He theorized that learning took place within the context of a child's social development and culture. For instance, when children vocalize, they learn that sounds have meanings and sounds become language. They learn that spoken language becomes the inner language that children use to think or develop cognitively. They also learn that gestures have meaning and are used to communicate and interact with others.

As stated earlier, Piaget believed children progressed through different stages of cognitive development and that achieving higher levels of thinking was not accomplished easily. Lev Vygotsky believed that a child's social environment could positively or negatively affect the child's cog-

WEB INFO

For more information about Lev Vygotsky, visit the Teachers Discovering Computers Web site (*scsite.com/tdc4*), click Chapter 6, click Web Info, and then click Vygotsky.

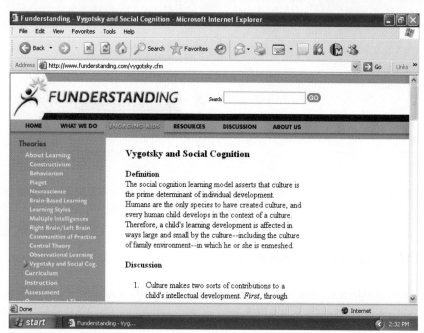

FIGURE 20   Lev Vygotsky was a Russian psychologist who believed that learning is influenced significantly by social development.

FIGURE 21   Vygotsky believed students should work collaboratively to share their different perspectives with each other. Here, students use handheld computers to work together to solve math problems.

nitive development. Vygotsky proposed that children have a **zone of proximal development**, which is the difference between the problem-solving ability that a child has learned and the potential that the child can achieve from collaboration with a more advanced peer or expert, such as a teacher.

If some form of expertise challenges a child, then greater cognitive development can occur. Vygotsky theorized that if a 9-year-old child worked on a problem with an adult or another child that was advanced, the 9-year-old would be able to learn the concept or ideas that were more complex than the 9-year-old could understand on his own; this is known as **collaborative learning**. With practice, the child then would be able to apply the new cognitive skills to other situations. Vygotsky felt students should work collaboratively to share their different perspectives with each other; then they could negotiate a solution and come to a much deeper understanding of a problem or tasks (Figure 21).

Furthermore, Vygotsky proposed that teachers should discover the level of each child's cognitive/social development, and build or construct their learning experiences from that point. He referred to this process as **scaffolding**. In education, a scaffold is altering of the **schemata**, which is an organized way of creating or providing a cognitive mental framework for understanding and remembering information. As teachers and other students provide information and different perspectives for each other, these sources can become a scaffold, a temporary source of knowledge. Then students assimilate this knowledge and build their own, thus removing the need for a scaffold.

Building on constructivism theory and Vygotsky's scaffolding, the Cognition and Technology Group at Vanderbilt (CTGV) developed **anchored instruction**. Anchored instruction is a model for technology-based learning and is a form of instruction where the student already has learned concepts and information, which form a basis for other information to connect to and build upon, and which is called the **anchor**. The CTGV wanted to create complex, realistic problems that students could explore and then develop potential solutions for those problems based on their exploration. When challenged with a problem, anchored instruction motivates students to build new ideas and anchor them to what they already have learned.

John Dewey

John Dewey (1859 – 1952) has influenced American education significantly (Figure 22). He was an educational psychologist, philosopher, and political activist who was an advocate for child-centered instruction. He believed that learning should engage and expand the experiences of the learners. He encouraged educators to reflect on their strategies and create activities that combine concrete and practical relevance to students' lives.

WEB INFO

For more information about John Dewey, visit the Teachers Discovering Computers Web site (*scsite.com/tdc4*), click Chapter 6, click Web Info, and then click Dewey.

Like Vygotsky, Dewey believed that education was a social process. He viewed school as a community that represented a larger picture. In 1896, Dewey began the University Elementary School, or Laboratory School. Many educators called this school the Dewey School. The school prospered and earned national attention. Dewey felt that school should be viewed as an extension of society and students should play an active role in it, working cooperatively with each other. Dewey viewed learning as student-directed with a teacher serving as a guide for resources. He believed students learn by doing and should be allowed to construct, create, and actively inquire. Dewey theorized that this type of learning truly prepared students to function well in society.

Dewey was part of a movement in the early 1900s that was called **progressive education**. Progressive education focused on educating the whole child, physically, mentally, and socially, and not on just the dispensation of facts and information. John Dewey's name also has been linked to other early movements, such as **pragmatism**. Pragmatists believed that the truth of a theory could be determined only if a theory worked. In other words, theory is valuable only for its practical application.

Dewey founded several schools in addition to his Laboratory School. He advocated educational reform, pursued philosophy, and supported many political issues, such as women's suffrage. Through his observations, he proposed that education begins with experience. He has been called, by some, the Father of American Education. His influence can be seen in American classrooms today — where children explore the curriculum, conduct science experiments, use manipulatives for math, and search the Internet for information.

FIGURE 22 John Dewey, an educational psychologist and philosopher, believed that learning should engage and expand the experiences of the learners.

Connecting with Today's Kids Through Game-Based Learning

Through the last few sections of this special feature, you have been exposed to some, but not all, of the theories and theorists for you to begin to develop a foundation and understanding of the principles of teaching and learning. As we have stated throughout this textbook, there is a new generation of learners — a digital generation.

Video games have been the center of considerable controversy and discussion in recent years. Many who believe that the excessive use of video games has led to a general decline in the academic achievement in schools by today's digital generation, especially those who are gamers. In some ways, they are correct. Peter Moore suggests that some students in today's digital generation are prone to actually powering down at school to conserve energy for that day's after school gaming activity in which the players are called upon to react and interact in a highly developed and fast-paced virtual world. Why are students willing to spend hours in front of a computer screen interacting with a game that requires using search and problem-based learning techniques to wind their way through the various encounters, but these same students are not interested in using those same skills in a more traditional learning environment? Does presentation matter? Does content matter? Several studies have reported a link between supposed antisocial behaviors and violent games; however, there have not been any results that can confirm cause and effect.

Further, stating or implying that playing games, regardless of their aggressiveness, actually promotes antisocial behaviors, has not been shown to be true. In fact, James Gee has identified thirty-six learning principles that can be found in all successful video games, regardless of content. The meta-learning principles are built in to the makeup of video games and are supported by current research on human learning and cognition. Figure 23 lists six of these principles.

WEB INFO

For more information about game-based learning, visit the Teachers Discovering Computers Web site (*scsite.com/tdc4*), click Chapter 6, click Web Info, and then click Game-Based Learning.

Learning Principles Found in Successful Video Games

1. How players form an identity to buy into the content

2. How players learn to connect different symbol systems (words, symbols, artifacts)

3. How players choose between various methods to solve a problem

4. How players identify, filter, and utilize different nonverbal cues

5. How players leverage their knowledge to reapply solutions learned from one situation to newly discovered ones

6. How players identify and develop a sense for story

FIGURE 23   This table lists just a few of the learning principles that James Gee suggests are based on human learning and cognitive science.

There are no manuals to teach players how to play the games. They do not seem to need them or want them. The construct of the games needs to be such that the process is self-revealing. As these learning principles are implied in the construct of the games, they actually provide better opportunities to teach things to students than most of what is being used to develop lesson activities in today's classroom — classrooms being occupied by digital, game-playing students. Perhaps educators should take a look at how games are constructed and utilize many of these same principles in their own school's curriculum. The results just may be surprising for educators and education.

Putting Theory into Practice

The next two Classroom in Action sections explore how actual teachers utilize learning theories in their classrooms to facilitate learning and achieve curriculum standards, while at the same time finding ways to reach today's digital students. The first story, *Teaching Kids to Think – The Thinking Ladder*, shows how an elementary teacher integrates technology and Bloom's Taxonomy to help her students develop higher-order thinking skills. The second, *Digital Kids – The Sam Schugg Story*, shows how the integration of technology with learning theory can inspire today's digital generation.

The Classroom in Action
Teaching Kids to Think – The Thinking Ladder

This section explores how one teacher puts learning theories into action. Nirsa Gautier, a fourth-grade teacher, was busy working on a simple spelling rule that her class was having difficulty remembering. Suddenly, she thought of a great idea using Bloom's Taxonomy that might enhance her lesson and assist her students' learning.

Mrs. Gautier stopped her spelling lesson and drew a ladder on the whiteboard (Figure 24). She listed the six thinking levels on the ladder and then explained each level in simple terms. She told her students that for them to be successful thinkers, they needed to progress to each level. The new class goal was to get to the highest level!

Mrs. Gautier then went back to the spelling lesson. She asked her students to identify what thinking level they were operating at on the thinking ladder. Some of the students were able to tell her immediately that they were at the Knowledge level. She explained that they could not move to higher levels of thinking success without mastering this basic knowledge. Now she had their attention! The class all agreed they had to remember the rule to move up the ladder.

Mrs. Gautier asked her students to work in groups collaboratively for five minutes to help each other remember the rule. She knew this was a great constructivist learning strategy. After five minutes, she randomly called on students to see if their group strategy had worked. To her amazement, every student she called on knew the rule! She congratulated the class on a job well done and then challenged them to move up to the next level of the thinking ladder.

After this experience, Mrs. Gautier created a large thinking ladder using a word processing program and placed it in the center of the classroom for her students to view. She wanted to make sure that she was integrating the thinking ladder learning strategy into every class lesson. Mrs. Gautier printed the thinking levels on cardstock, glued magnets on the back, and placed each thinking level on a rung of the ladder. This gave the students colorful visual cues as they moved along the thinking continuum to a higher thinking level. Mrs. Gautier also created a PowerPoint presentation using pictures that illustrated how the students move up the thinking ladder to thinking success (Figure 25 on the next page). In the presentation, she explained in more detail each thinking level and how to apply it when the students read, solve problems, and answer questions. Mrs. Gautier had her students discuss which questions were more difficult to answer. The students began to realize that higher-order thinking involves more time and thought. Consequently, Mrs. Gautier also realized that she must give her students more time to think before answering questions. She decided to call this *think time*.

To encourage higher-order thinking skills, Mrs. Gautier had her students develop questions based on a reading selection. The students responded in their journals and wrote three questions for the selection. Each question had to come from a different thinking level. She found that by asking students to write or construct their own thinking questions from different levels, they first must be able to think on that level. She then would have a student ask a question, another student answer the question, and a third student identify the thinking level. Mrs. Gautier found that often students created better

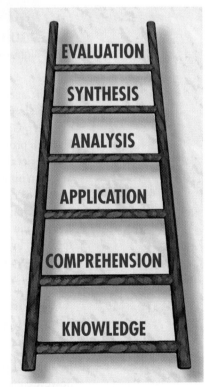

FIGURE 24 Mrs. Gautier's thinking ladder is based on Bloom's Taxonomy.

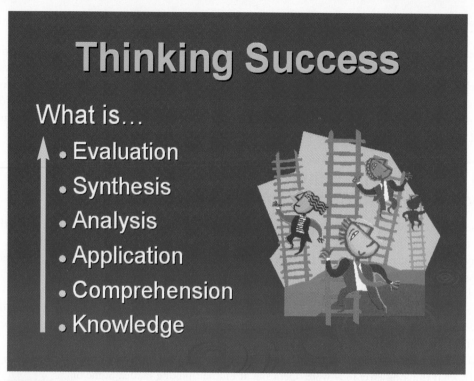

FIGURE 25 Mrs. Gautier uses PowerPoint to teach her students how to use higher-order thinking skills to move up the thinking ladder.

thinking questions than she did! In addition, many of the students were thrilled to know that they were able to answer questions that required higher-order thinking skills. They liked the challenge.

Mrs. Gautier works her thinking ladder into every subject. When the students create multimedia research projects, she makes sure to include an aspect of each thinking level in the assessment rubric used for evaluation. This guides the students to find information, analyze and evaluate what they read, and then apply it in a meaningful way. After introducing Bloom's Taxonomy in the class, Mrs. Gautier noticed a real excitement as students began to strive to move up the ladder of thinking success.

Teaching students thinking skills using Bloom's Taxonomy revolutionized the way Mrs. Gautier teaches and the way her students learn. Her students became more focused because not only were they thinking, but they were consciously developing the thinking process! They became more confident, taking more responsibility for their learning, and realizing that they must do the thinking to learn.

The Classroom in Action
Digital Kids – The Sam Schugg Story

Sam Schugg is your typical digital kid. He does not like going to high school and when he is there he does not pay attention for very long. It is almost like he is powering down in most of his classes; however, put him in front of a computer and he will pay attention for hours. He shines in his technology class in spite of the fact that he is very reserved and does not speak much. He goes to English class and cannot relate. He wants to be a game developer when he grows up and he feels that reading and writing will not be very important for him to enter that profession. He does okay in math and science but, once again, he does not see their relevance to his plans for the future. As a result, he struggles with his grades in all subjects except for his technology class. What makes matters worse is that all attempts to help remediate his weaknesses have yielded little results because previous efforts mostly centered on requiring him to read more books, to solve more word problems, and/or to conduct more experiments.

Things are about to change. His technology teacher, Bob Phelan, was just completing his studies in instructional design and felt that perhaps a new direction was needed. Banking on Sam's fondness for computers and gaming, Mr. Phelan decided to try a new way to reach Sam and many other students just like him in his technology class (Figure 26). Mr. Phelan met with Sam's English teacher, Rita Rivera, to discuss his plan. When discussing Sam's situation, Ms. Rivera said that Sam reacted like many of her students when she assigned books to be read, they always wanted to know why they had to read and not simply be allowed to watch the movie! This was frustrating to Ms. Rivera. Mr. Phelan suggested that the students produce a movie about a book. Not only would this activity utilize the students' strengths but it also could be based on many of the learning theories and ideas that Mr. Phelan wanted to put into practice. Mr. Phelan also knew that all students enjoyed stories and if he based the lessons on the premise of bringing out the concept of storytelling, this would be motivating to the students. They decided to combine their classes and teach together. Ms. Rivera could teach about storytelling and Mr. Phelan would teach them digital video editing. Mr. Phelan's students could mentor on the technical aspects of the project and learn about storytelling from the English teacher and her students.

WEB INFO

For more information on digital storytelling, visit the Teachers Discovering Computers Web site (*scsite.com/tdc4*), click Chapter 6, click Web Info, and then click Digital Storytelling.

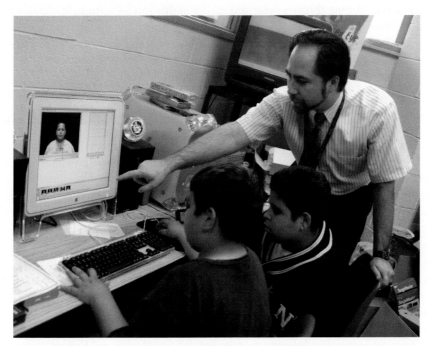

FIGURE 26   One technique to motivate today's students to read and write is for teachers to create lessons that integrate digital media.

First, they knew that most of the students in the school were visual learners. Both teachers agreed that, even though technology would be the entry point, the activity had to result in making students better readers and writers. After the videos were created, students would write about their experiences and include related vocabulary words. The idea seemed simple – use Robert Doman's ideas about teaching to students' strengths and then remediate the weaknesses. Student learning would be reinforced because they would be working with both images and texts, which was supported by Paivio's ideas about dual coding and Craik and Lockhart's and Bloom's ideas about levels of processing.

Producing their own videos fits the constructivists' ideas about students creating their own meaning while, at the same time, students would be encouraged to retain information because they would be learning by doing and that would also ensure deeper processing of their skills. The instructional plan also follows Gagne's building-block principles.

The teachers decided that everyone in the class would read the same book. They would start with the basic premise of story, then learn text-to-screen techniques of making movies, and move into visual storytelling techniques using a camera and/or photos and a video editor. Students would discuss how to

WEB INFO

For more information on creating movie trailers, visit the Teachers Discovering Computers Web site (*scsite.com/tdc4*), click Chapter 6, click Web Info, and then click Movie Trailers.

read the selected book as if they were going to make a movie out of it. The two teachers realized that making a full length movie would result in a very large project so they decided to ask that a trailer of the book be made. **Trailers** are short, 2–3 minute summaries of the book (similar to the movie previews shown for upcoming attractions in movie theaters). Using summarizing principles similar to what is done for book talks; the two teachers helped the students come up with their concepts. After the trailers were produced, the teachers would show all the projects, providing the students the opportunity to see how others view the content of the same books. The other students would review and evaluate each other's trailers using a rubric that the two teachers designed that focused on content. When they were done, students were asked to write out the essence of their trailer in narrative style using vocabulary words that the teachers required.

When the projects were presented, Sam Schugg's project was the best in the class. The students' evaluated his project with great feedback and he scored high on the rubric. He did not even complain during the writing portion of the assignment and on reflection said, "I was so surprised that I could do so well on this. I enjoyed this assignment!" The teachers could tell Sam had pride in his work.

This activity was successful because it was founded on sound instructional practices that incorporated many of the learning theories described earlier in this special feature. Students were motivated to read because they were focused on doing something with the information they obtained from the book. Now, instead of the reading being a passive activity, students are reading for a purpose and are involving themselves in the outcomes using a communication medium they are attracted to and one that is already a large part of their digital lives.

Summary of Learning Theories and Educational Research

Learning is a complex task. Understanding how students learn is an internal process that is difficult to observe. Educators can provide instruction and information, and assess how much information has been retained. Educational research and learning theories are important because they help educators to understand how students learn. From learning theories and research, teachers can improve their instruction and the way they provide information to learners, and they can improve teaching and learning environments.

Integrating technology into teaching is a very powerful way to weave these learning theories throughout the curriculum. Digital media technology appeals to a variety of learning styles and learning intelligences (Gardner). Students are more actively engaged in their learning when teachers effectively integrate technology (Bruner). Technology is effective with group projects, working in teams (Vygotsky and Dewey), and problem-solving activities requiring higher-order thinking skills that allow students to build new ideas from their current knowledge base (Bloom). Teachers even have used computer time effectively as part of a behavior management system (Pavlov and Skinner).

Learners are dynamic and no two will be the same. In this regard, theorists help teachers understand how to adapt instruction, information, and the environment for different learners. So, much is to be gained by understanding learning theories and what each theorist has contributed. Their ideas can help educators piece together the complex task of teaching all learners.

Integrating learning theories and technology into classroom instructional strategies can make a difference in student motivation and also can increase student achievement in your classroom!

For information on the references used in the creation of this special feature, see Appendix C or access this special feature's Web Info segments.

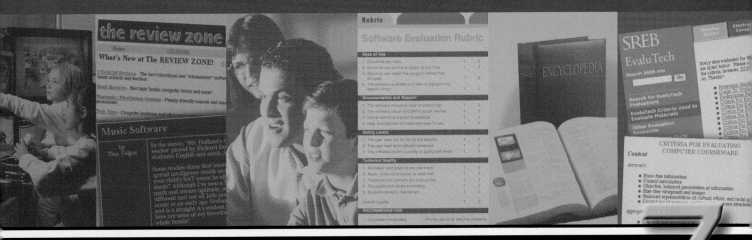

Evaluating Educational Technology and Integration Strategies

Objectives

After completing this chapter, you will be able to:

[ISTE NETS-T Standards I A-B, II A-E, III A-D, IV A-C, V A-D, VI A-C]

- Identify sources of information for evaluating technology and digital media

- Outline the considerations and tools used to evaluate software applications

- Describe and explain the key criteria used to evaluate Web resources

- Describe the tools for evaluating the effectiveness of technology

- Compare and analyze the methods used to evaluate student projects

- Identify different technology integration strategies by classroom layout

- Define and describe the value of a curriculum page

- Describe ways to integrate technology into specific curriculum subject areas

- Identify and compare possible sources of funding for classroom technology

As you learn about the various types of emerging technology and methods of integrating them into your classroom curriculum, undoubtedly, you will be called upon to evaluate the appropriateness of this technology and the effectiveness of its integration into the learning process. This chapter presents an overview of how to evaluate the many different types of technologies that are available today. It also offers specific strategies for how to integrate technology in your classroom based on the number of computers and other devices available to you and your students. Also provided are several subject-specific examples of curriculum integration activities, such as creating and using curriculum pages. Finally, this chapter suggests several ways you can raise funds to pay for state-of-the-art technology in your classroom to enhance the teaching and learning experience.

Evaluating Educational Technology

Evaluating the appropriateness and effectiveness of educational technology is an important aspect of integrating current technology into the classroom. To **evaluate** an item is to determine its value or judge its worth. Evaluating educational technology involves determining if the technology is appropriate and enhances the teaching and learning process. To be considered **appropriate**, educational technology must be suitable for the educational situation, must be motivational, and must promote learning at the correct levels of student ability and academic achievement. It also must address curriculum standards and related learning objectives.

Evaluating educational technology before instruction begins, during the instructional period, and after instruction has taken place is important (Figure 7-1). Before using software or sites on the World Wide Web, for example, teachers should determine if this technology meets their curriculum needs and if the product or content is developmentally and age appropriate for their classroom learning situation. Information from many sources helps teachers evaluate the appropriateness of educational technologies. Teachers should continue to evaluate the technology while it is being used and after the instruction using the technology is complete.

SOURCES OF INFORMATION

Finding the right educational technology can be difficult, especially for new users of technology, because each year, developers create hundreds of new educational software packages and Web sites for K-12 classroom use (Figure 7-2). To avoid confusion in this important task, teachers might rely on a variety of resources to help them identify and evaluate the appropriateness of educational technologies. These resources include material from school districts, state Departments of Education, professional educational organizations, hardware and software catalogs, recommendations of colleagues, published evaluations, technology conferences, and Web sites.

SCHOOL DISTRICTS AND STATE DEPARTMENTS OF EDUCATION

Many school districts compile software evaluations that provide guidance on subject-specific software. In addition, many state Departments of Education provide lists of software that are recommended and evaluated by educators. Teachers can access these lists and evaluations at state-sponsored Web sites or they can request them in printed form.

To assist you in locating these sources of information from your school district and state Department of Education, contact your technology coordinator, curriculum resource specialist, media specialist, technology committee, or other teachers.

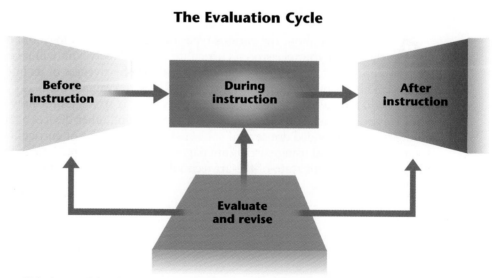

The Evaluation Cycle

Before instruction → **During instruction** → **After instruction**

Evaluate and revise

Figure 7-1 Successful technology integration requires evaluation during all phases of instruction.

Figure 7-2 Numerous high-quality educational software packages are available for classroom use.

PROFESSIONAL EDUCATIONAL ORGANIZATIONS Many local, state, regional, national, and international educational organizations provide extensive information on how to evaluate educational resources (Figure 7-3). Many of these groups provide Web sites with information and feedback on software program levels, content, and pricing.

CATALOGS Often, companies list hardware and software suited for educational use in their catalogs. These catalogs are a valuable resource to help identify technologies for your classroom. In addition to providing information about existing and new products, many software firms also provide information about how their products relate to curriculum and learning standards. You can order free catalogs from most companies by calling a toll-free number or completing an online form at the company's Web site. Many companies have online catalogs that also provide demos of their popular software titles.

RECOMMENDATIONS OF COLLEAGUES
A good way to identify software and other technology that has potential for your classroom is to talk to other educators. Colleagues can offer advice about outstanding products as well as about those products to avoid — advice that often is based on firsthand experience.

PUBLISHED EVALUATIONS Departments of Education, professional organizations, and other educational groups publish evaluations of new products. Numerous software developers include evaluations completed by educators on their Web sites. Many educational publications and journals also have sections dedicated to reviews of educational technologies. In addition, many online publications, journals, and other Web sites provide educators with comprehensive evaluations and reviews of educational software and hardware (Figure 7-4).

CONFERENCES Every year, dozens of national and state organizations host technology conferences (Figure 7-5). A **technology conference** is a meeting dedicated to providing a vast array of information and resources for teachers. This gathering might be large or small and includes workshops and presentations by educators and vendors on hundreds of technology topics. In addition, software and hardware vendors usually have booths staffed by representatives to provide teachers with demonstrations and information about their products.

WEB INFO

To preview Tom Synder software products, visit the Teachers Discovering Computers Web site (*scsite.com/tdc4*), click Chapter 7, click Web Info, and then click Tom Synder.

FAQ

How can teachers find out about technology conferences in their state or across the country?

Access T.H.E. Journal's conference calendar at: *www.theconferencecalendar.com* and search by month, year, state, and country.

Figure 7-3 Many local, state, regional, national, and international educational organizations maintain Web sites that provide teachers with evaluations of educational technologies.

WEB INFO

To learn more about EDTECH, visit the Teachers Discovering Computers Web site (*scsite.com/tdc4*), click Chapter 7, click Web Info, and then click EDTECH.

key word entered

search results

links to product reviews

Figure 7-4
Numerous online educational publications and journals have sections dedicated to reviews of educational technologies.

THE WEB By far, the Web is the most comprehensive source of tools and resources to help you evaluate educational technology. Teachers may visit thousands of Web sites dedicated to educational topics. Mailing lists, forums, newsgroups, discussion groups, and bulletin boards available on the Web also provide vast sources of information. One of the larger well-known mailing lists is EDTECH. The **EDTECH** mailing list allows educators from many different areas — teachers, administrators, technology coordinators, media specialists, and university faculty — to exchange information, comments, and ideas on educational issues.

Figure 7-5 Technology conferences provide teachers with valuable resources, information, and opportunities to discuss educational technology issues with other educators and vendors.

EVALUATING SOFTWARE APPLICATIONS

When you identify a software package as potentially suited to your curriculum needs, you should evaluate the software for appropriateness, review the accuracy of the content, and consider its relevance to the curriculum standards and related benchmarks. A cost-effective way to evaluate software is to download a free trial copy from some of the many software companies that offer these trial versions at their Web or FTP sites (Figure 7-6). Use it for the specified period to determine its suitability for your curriculum.

A rubric is a great tool for evaluating software. A **rubric** is a detailed scoring guide for assessment, based on subjective stated criteria. A software evaluation rubric typically provides a number of important evaluation criteria for specific areas, such as content, learning process, and ease of use, and then presents rating levels with specific standards for each.

Software evaluation rubrics help you and your students evaluate educational software. A **software evaluation rubric** is an assessment tool that provides a number of important evaluation criteria, including content, documentation and technical support, ability and academic levels, technical quality, and ease of use to help assess the quality of software or other items. A two-page Software Evaluation Rubric is shown in Figure 7-7 (on the next two pages).

Many schools develop their own software evaluation rubrics for teachers to use, while in other schools, teachers create their own software evaluation rubrics. The Web is a great resource for locating rubrics. Many different software evaluation rubrics are available on the Web for you to use or alter to fit your specific needs.

CONTENT When evaluating educational software, content is the most important area to consider. When examining software content, you need to determine if the software is valid. **Valid** means the software has well-grounded instructional properties, meets standards, provides appropriate content, and teaches what is intended.

Most software companies and distributors provide a description of the content and learning skills addressed by their software packages; most software companies match the skills the software teaches with specific curriculum standards and related benchmarks. When evaluating the content of a software application, always relate the content to your school's and state's specific curriculum standards and related benchmarks.

WEB INFO

To access software reviews, visit the Teachers Discovering Computers Web site (*scsite.com/tdc4*), click Chapter 7, click Web Info, and then click Software Reviews.

WEB INFO

For more examples of Web site evaluation rubrics for students, visit the Teachers Discovering Computers Web site (*scsite.com/tdc4*), click Chapter 7, click Web Info, and then click Rubrics.

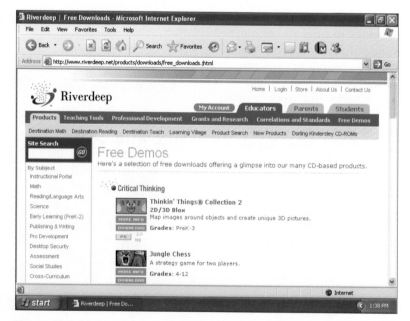

Figure 7-6 Many software companies allow you to download free evaluation copies of their software.

Rubric

Software Evaluation Rubric

Application Title:_____ Subject Area:_____

Version:_____ Producer/Publisher:_____

Purchased From: _____ Date Published: _____

Curriculum Standard(s): _____

Learning Objective(s):_____

Prerequisite Skills:_____

Configuration

Hardware/System Requirements: _____

_____

Type of Drive Required: DVD _____ CD_____ Network _____

Hard Disk Space Required: _____ Memory Required:_____

Program Categories: (Check all that apply)

☐ Presentation   ☐ Remediation   ☐ Educational Game

☐ Authoring   ☐ Simulation   ☐ ILS

☐ Problem Solving   ☐ Tutorial   ☐ Distance Learning

Other:_____

Skill/Ability/Grade Levels: _____

Content Standard(s):_____

_____

Technology Standard(s): _____

_____

Use the following system to rate the software

1 = Strongly disagree	2 = Disagree	NA = Not applicable
3 = Agree	4 = Strongly agree	

Content

	1	2	3	4	NA
1. The content is accurate and factual.	1	2	3	4	NA
2. The content is educationally appropriate.	1	2	3	4	NA
3. The content is free of errors.	1	2	3	4	NA
4. The content meets learning goals and objectives.	1	2	3	4	NA
5. The content is valid.	1	2	3	4	NA
6. The content is free of stereotypes and cultural bias.	1	2	3	4	NA
7. The content meets district and state standards.	1	2	3	4	NA

Figure 7-7 A software evaluation rubric helps teachers evaluate educational software packages.

Rubric

Software Evaluation Rubric

(1=Strongly disagree; 2=Disagree; 3=Agree; 4=Strongly agree; NA=Not applicable)

Ease of Use

1. Directions are clear.	1	2	3	4	NA
2. Students can exit the program at any time.	1	2	3	4	NA
3. Students can restart the program where they stopped.	1	2	3	4	NA
4. The software is reliable and free of disruption by system errors.	1	2	3	4	NA

Documentation and Support

1. The teacher/instructor manual is clear and thorough.	1	2	3	4	NA
2. The software has an 800/888 support number.	1	2	3	4	NA
3. Online technical support is available.	1	2	3	4	NA
4. Help and tutorials are clear and easy to use.	1	2	3	4	NA

Ability Levels

1. The user level can be set by the teacher.	1	2	3	4	NA
2. The user level automatically advances.	1	2	3	4	NA
3. The software covers a variety of ability/skill levels.	1	2	3	4	NA

Assessment

1. Software has built-in assessment and reporting tools.	1	2	3	4	NA
2. Assessment methods are appropriate and suited to learning objectives.	1	2	3	4	NA
3. Software documents and records student progress.	1	2	3	4	NA
4. Teachers easily can assess students' progress by evaluating progress reports.	1	2	3	4	NA

Technical Quality

1. Animation and graphics are used well.	1	2	3	4	NA
2. Audio (voice input/output) is used well.	1	2	3	4	NA
3. Feedback and prompts are appropriate.	1	2	3	4	NA
4. The application allows branching.	1	2	3	4	NA

Recommendation

☐ Purchase Immediately   ☐ Do Not Purchase

Comments:_____

_____

Evaluator:_____ Date:_____

Figure 7-7 *(continued)*

DOCUMENTATION AND TECHNICAL SUPPORT   When evaluating software, consider the technical support and documentation the software offers. **Documentation** is any printed or online information that provides assistance in installing, using, maintaining, and updating the software. You should review the documentation for readability and depth of coverage. **Technical support** is a service that hardware and software manufacturers and third-party service companies offer to customers to provide answers to questions, repairs, and other assistance. Companies usually provide technical support over the telephone or via the Web (Figure 7-8). Some firms even provide on-site support.

In addition to reviewing the available documentation and technical support, you also should determine if any other kinds of support are available, such as clear, easy-to-use aids and tutorials. Some software companies, for example, provide instructor resource guides and lesson plans to assist in integrating their software into curriculum areas.

ABILITY LEVELS AND ASSESSMENT   Educators need to evaluate whether the software can be used with more than one ability or academic level. An **ability level** refers to a student's current competency level or the skill level he can achieve for a specific learning objective. The **academic level** is based on the grade level with increments to determine if a student is performing at the appropriate level. Several software applications, such as math and reading software, adjust the academic level as students successfully move through specific skills. Numerous software applications allow you to set the academic, or ability levels at which you require students to work. Assessment is discussed starting on page 414.

TECHNICAL QUALITY AND EASE OF USE   **Technical quality** refers to how well the software presents itself and how well it works. Items to evaluate are the clarity of the screen design; appropriateness of feedback and student prompts; and use of graphics, animations, sound, and other media elements.

Ease of use, or user-friendliness, refers to anything that makes the software easy to use. Software should be easy for both teachers and students to use, while at

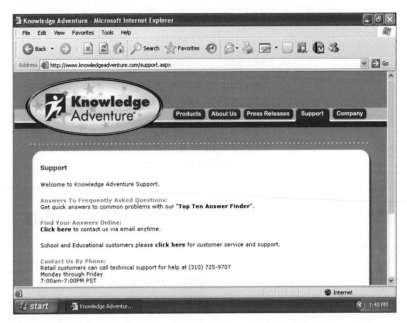

Figure 7-8 Many software manufacturers provide technical support for their products via the Web.

the same time maintaining the students' interest.

Student opinions also play an important role in successfully integrating new technology. Teachers need to be open and embrace the fact that today's digital students may be very technologically savvy. After you complete your evaluation, you might want to obtain feedback from students by allowing them to use and test the software. If students have a difficult time working through exercises, they might dislike the program and get frustrated. If students dislike the software, they will not enjoy using it even though they may learn. This dislike will limit the effectiveness of the software in classroom use. Make sure the software is easy to use and appropriate for your students' grade and ability levels.

EVALUATING WEB RESOURCES

The Web is an incredible resource for teachers. Not all of the information on the Web, however, is placed there by reliable sources. Web page authoring software has made it easy for anyone to create, or publish, a Web page or Web site that contains personal opinions, ideas, and philosophy. In contrast, before a book is published, the content is reviewed for accuracy and objectivity and the author's credentials are verified. After being published, the book's copyright date and table of contents allow

WEB INFO

For more details about evaluating Web sites, visit the Teachers Discovering Computers Web site (*scsite.com/tdc4*), click Chapter 7, click Web Info, and then click Web Site Evaluation.

users to determine the currency of the information and the book's depth of coverage. A Web site offers no such safeguards.

Because Web sites often contain inaccurate, incomplete, or biased information, evaluating Web resources presents a unique challenge. Teachers must know how to evaluate Web sites and teach their students how to do the same. When evaluating a Web site as an instructional source, you should consider criteria such as

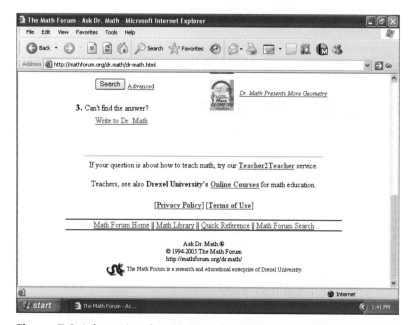

Figure 7-9 Information documenting the authority of a Web site often is found at the bottom of the Web site's home page.

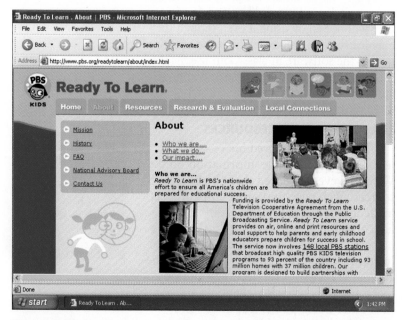

Figure 7-10 Teachers can consider this Web site authoritative because it was created by a number of public and private organizations.

authority, affiliation, content, audience, and Web design.

AUTHORITY When evaluating Web sites, **authority** refers to the credibility of the person or persons who author and create the site. Determining authority is the first place to start in the evaluation process (Figure 7-9). If the author is not a credible source for information, the information on the site might be unreliable. A Web site on asteroids by a distinguished astronomy professor, for example, has more authority than an astronomy Web site created by an amateur stargazer. When reviewing a Web site, answer the following questions:

- Is the author clearly identified? If you cannot identify the creator of the Web page, you might want to avoid this Web site.

- Examine the credentials of the author or organization of the Web site. What evidence indicates that the author qualifies to publish on this topic? The authority of the Web page shown in Figure 7-10, for example, is based on the credibility of several organizations and corporations.

- Has the author or organization listed experience, position, education, or other credentials? If you do not see this information immediately, refer to the bottom of the home page, which often provides additional information about the author's or organization's affiliation. Can the author be contacted for clarification? Listing an e-mail address and other pertinent information is important for establishing authority.

AFFILIATION **Affiliation** refers to the professional organization, school, school district, university, company, or government office with which a particular Web site is associated. A simple way to determine a site's affiliation is to examine the URL and domain name to identify what type of organization maintains the Web page. A site with a .com domain, for example, is operated by a commercial business; a .edu domain is controlled by an educational institution (Figure 7-11).

Well-known sources of information such as the U.S. government, universities, school districts, newspapers, and non-profit organizations usually have reliable facts on their Web sites. Also, it is good to examine the credentials and reputation of the organization or organizations affiliated with the Web site.

PURPOSE AND OBJECTIVITY   Purpose is the reason the Web site was created or the intent of the Web site. As you evaluate a Web site, you must ascertain if it is being provided as a public service, if it is free from bias, and why the author or creator is providing this information.

Objectivity is the process of determining or interpreting the intent or purpose of the Web page and if it is free of bias, such as advertising. If the purpose is not clearly stated, you must attempt to determine the purpose or intent of the Web page. Is the primary intent to provide information or sell a product? Does the author want to make a political point or have fun? Determining the purpose or intent of the Web site plays a critical role in the evaluation process.

CONTENT AND LEARNING PROCESS
Content is the information a Web page provides. Web pages use a variety of media to convey facts, opinions, and news. As you evaluate the content of a Web page, consider the following questions:

- Is the content valid and appropriate? Is the content popular or academic, satiric or serious?

- Does the information on the page relate to your curriculum and instructional standards?

- What topics are covered? Is the information clearly labeled and well organized?

- For what level is the information written? How thorough is the information?

- Do the links within the site add value and assist you in meeting your instructional goals?

As you evaluate the content of a Web page or Web site, keep the learning objectives and curriculum standards of the classroom in mind. Also, take the time to check the links to ensure they work and are appropriate for your intended audience.

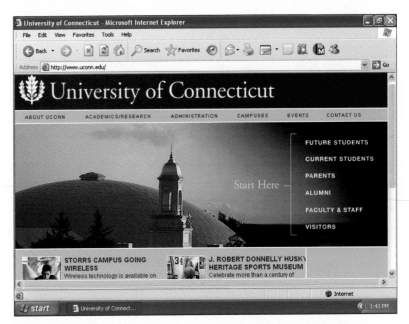

Figure 7-11 This Web site's affiliation is identifiable easily as the University of Connecticut.

Learning process is when the content engages students to use higher-order thinking skills to go beyond the simple acquisition of knowledge and become active learners. This is accomplished when the content challenges students to think, compare, reflect, hypothesize, and discuss.

AUDIENCE AND CURRENCY   The **audience** is the individual or group intended to view and use the Web page. You should review the Web page to determine if it is suitable for an audience such as your students. Is the content appropriate for your students? Can you use this Web page in your classroom? Again, keep your learning objectives in mind as you examine the Web page. **Currency** is the measure of how up to date, or timely, the Web page content is and how often it is updated. A good Web page states clearly when the page was last revised or updated.

DESIGN   The **design** of a Web site is the way it is arranged — that is, the way it uses instructional design principles to deliver content to the user. A well-designed Web site makes it easy and enjoyable for viewers to access the site's content and information. A poorly designed site where links or elements are organized in a confusing way can frustrate viewers because they cannot find the information they want.

An effective Web page loads in a reasonable amount of time, has a pleasing

WEB INFO

To learn the 10 Cs for evaluating Internet resources, visit the Teachers Discovering Computers Web site (*scsite.com/tdc4*), click Chapter 7, click Web Info, and then click 10 Cs.

visual appearance, is easy to navigate, and has links that are well organized, clearly marked, work properly, and lead to related materials.

Both in and out of the classroom, teachers and students should evaluate sites critically to maximize the value of the Web. To assist in the evaluation of Web sites, teachers often find rubrics useful.

A **Web evaluation rubric** is a detailed scoring guide for assessing the value and content of Web sites. As shown in the examples in Figure 7-12 and Figure 7-13, Web evaluation rubrics typically provide a number of important evaluation criteria for specific areas such as content, learning process, and authority of the author, and then present rating levels with specific standards for each. Students and teachers benefit from using rubrics. Figure 7-12 illustrates a user-friendly, engaging Student Web Site Evaluation Form. Figure 7-13 shows a more detailed Web evaluation rubric that might be used by a teacher. No matter which method you choose, the key is to have a predetermined way of effectively evaluating Web sites.

Evaluating the Effectiveness of Technology Integration

Integrating technology effectively into the curriculum requires planning, time, dedication, and resources. Because it is important to determine whether integration strategies

Student Web Site Evaluation Form

Student team members: _____

DESIGN			
Can move easily from page to page	☺	😐	☹
Good use of graphics (pictures and color)	☺	😐	☹
CONTENT			
Information is useful	☺	😐	☹
Content is as good or better than that of similar sites	☺	😐	☹
TECHNICAL ELEMENTS			
Pages load quickly (within 15 seconds)	☺	😐	☹
All links work	☺	😐	☹
CREDIBILITY			
Contact person is stated with his or her e-mail address	☺	😐	☹
The name of the host school or organization is given	☺	😐	☹
Date this site was last updated is provided	☺	😐	☹

page 1 of 1

Figure 7-12 Young students enjoy rubrics that are fun and user-friendly when evaluating Web sites.

Rubric

Web Evaluation Rubric

Title of Web Site: _____

Curriculum Area: _____

URL: _____

Learning Objectives that will be supported by this site: _____

_____

	Level 1	Level 2	Level 3	Level 4	Level
Authority	No author is listed and no e-mail contact is provided.	No author is listed but an e-mail contact is provided.	An author is listed with no credentials and you cannot tell if the author is the creator of the material.	An author is listed with appropriate credentials, and is the creator of the material.	
Affiliation	It is unclear what institution supports this information.	A commercial Internet provider supports the site, but it is unclear if the author has any connection with a larger institution.	The site is supported by a larger institution, but some bias is apparent in the information from the institution.	The site is supported by a reputable institution without bias in the information.	
Purpose	The purpose is unclear or cannot be determined.	The Web site has more than one purpose but meets only a few of my objectives.	The purpose is somewhat clear and meets most of my objectives.	The purpose of the Web site is clear and meets my objectives.	
Objectivity	The Web page is a virtual soapbox.	The Web site contains some bias and a great deal of advertising.	The Web site contains some advertising and minimal bias.	The Web site contains little advertising and is free of bias.	
Content	The information on the Web site does not relate to my objectives.	The information relates to my objectives, but many of the links do not work.	The information relates to my objectives, links work, but the site is not well organized.	The information relates to my objectives, the links work, and the site is well organized.	
Learning Process	The information will not challenge learners to think, reflect, discuss, compare, or classify.	The information will not challenge learners to think but does provide interesting facts for resource information.	The information at this Web site will provide some challenges for the learner to think but does not relate to my objectives.	The information challenges learners to use higher-order thinking skills, effectively engages the learner, and meets my learning objectives.	
Audience	The Web pages are not appropriate for my audience.	The Web pages are written above the level of my audience, but some of the information is useful.	The Web pages are written at an appropriate level for my audience and some of the information is useful.	The Web pages are written at an appropriate level and the information is suitable for my classroom.	
Currency	Information on the site has not been revised in the last 18 months, or no date can be located.	Information on the site has not been updated in the last year, but the information still is of good quality.	Information has been updated in the last six months and seems to reflect currency.	Information has been updated in the last three months and is accurate.	
Design	The Web site design is inappropriate for my audience.	The Web site loads slowly and the general appearance is poor.	The Web site loads well, but the site is not easy to navigate.	The Web site loads well, is easy to navigate, visually pleasing, and easy to read.	
				Total	

Figure 7-13 A rubric is helpful in evaluating the educational value of Web sites.

are working, teachers, schools, and school districts should take steps to evaluate the effectiveness of their technology integration.

Evaluating the effectiveness of technology can be challenging; no simple way exists to evaluate what works in all situations — all students, all technology, all schools, and all classrooms. Nor do any standard types of evaluation show the relationship between the technology and student achievement. Educators should not rely on the assumption that technology tools are having some impact. Instead, teachers and administrators must locate or develop techniques to measure the effectiveness of integrating technology.

The first step in evaluating educational technology's impact on student achievement is to develop indicators that measure a student's performance, skills acquired, and academic and ability levels obtained. Test scores are not the only, or even the best, indicators of the successful integration of technology. The types of learning best supported by technology are those not easily measured by traditional assessments such as standardized tests.

Due to the nature of technology and the way the learning environment is changing, educators must create and use different types of evaluation tools.

ASSESSMENT TOOLS FOR EVALUATING THE EFFECTIVENESS OF TECHNOLOGY INTEGRATION

Evaluating the effectiveness of educational technology can help you assess whether the technology is appropriate for the learner, meets learning objectives, and enhances the learning process. Traditionally, teachers use many different evaluation techniques in the final stage of instruction or when assessing **student performance**. To ensure that students meet the learning objectives, teachers must use many forms of assessment to evaluate student performance. **Assessment** is any method used to understand the current knowledge a student possesses; it can range from a teacher's subjective judgment based on a single observation of a student's performance to a state-mandated standardized test.

Reliable assessment information provides accurate estimates of student performance, permits appropriate generalizations about the students' skills and abilities, and

enables teachers or other decision makers to make appropriate decisions. **Traditional assessments** include testing in the form of multiple choice, fill-in-the blank, true/false, short answer, and essay questions.

Traditional forms of assessment also can be used to evaluate the effectiveness of technology. Just as technology opens many new and exciting doors for teaching and learning, technology also opens new doors for evaluating student performance. When integrating technology, some teachers and schools move toward a nontraditional approach of student assessment, known as alternative assessment. **Alternative assessment** uses nontraditional methods to determine whether students have mastered the appropriate content and skill level. Educators may adopt several approaches to alternative assessment, such as authentic, project-based, and portfolio assessment.

AUTHENTIC ASSESSMENT   Authentic assessment, project-based assessment, and portfolio assessment refer to alternative ways to evaluate students' performances to determine how well and in what ways they meet curriculum standards and related benchmarks.

Authentic assessment can be formal or informal and aims to present the student with tasks that mirror the objectives and challenges typical of their instructional activities. Students answer open-ended questions, create questions, conduct hands-on experiments, do research, write, revise and discuss papers, and create portfolios of their work over time. Authentic assessment is based on a method of learning called authentic learning. **Authentic learning** presents learning experiences that demonstrate real-life connections between students' lessons and the world in which they live.

Authentic assessment measures this learning by evaluating a student's ability to master practical benchmarks. Using authentic assessment, for example, a student may be asked to explain historical events, generate scientific hypotheses, solve math problems, create portfolios or presentations, or converse in a foreign language.

Authentic assessment helps students not only understand concepts and subject matter, but also helps them develop real-world skills, which they can apply outside the classroom and beyond the school environment. For example, teachers might look for evidence

WEB INFO

To explore technology assessment further, visit the Teachers Discovering Computers Web site (*scsite.com/tdc4*), click Chapter 7, click Web Info, and then click Assessing Technology.

of good collaboration skills, the ability to solve complex problems and make thoughtful decisions, and the ability to develop and make effective presentations. Authentic assessments reflect student learning over time and provide a better view of student performance, instead of performance based on just one item or one test. A teacher then has documentation of the student's progress throughout the entire project, which provides the teacher with evidence of growth and learning.

PROJECT-BASED ASSESSMENT Project-based assessment is an innovative approach to assessment that focuses on assessing student projects. It is based on a type of authentic learning called project-based learning. **Project-based learning** is a model for teaching and learning that focuses on creating learning opportunities for students by engaging them in real-world projects where they have an active role in completing meaningful tasks, constructing their own knowledge, solving problems, or creating realistic projects. Project-based learning transforms the teacher into the facilitator and the students into the doers or participants in the task at hand. When using any type of authentic learning technique, many teachers use a checklist, rating scale, or a rubric to evaluate the learning process.

PORTFOLIO ASSESSMENT Another popular form of alternative assessment is portfolio assessment. **Portfolio assessment** evaluates student assignments or projects over a period of time. Portfolios are an effective way to match assessment with learning goals. Some educators call this **embedded assessment** because assessment tasks are a part of the learning process. Through the process of creating their own assignments, students improve their abilities to assess their strengths and weaknesses and are able to apply these skills to other areas of study to become better learners. Because students work on long-term assignments, they usually have the opportunity to fix or learn from their mistakes and do a better job on future portfolio assignments.

For portfolio assessment to be successful, students must learn how to interact effectively with their teachers to ensure that they fully understand the teacher's assessment of each portfolio assignment. Only then will they be able to progress in creating better subsequent assignments.

When students receive guidance and support from their teachers and parents and gain an understanding of themselves as learners, they can experience amazing growth and powerful learning opportunities. The disadvantage of portfolio assessment is that creating and assessing portfolios takes longer to evaluate than a quick test and requires a great deal of work by both the student and the teacher. The results reveal, however, that portfolio assessment is well worth the investment.

In this digital age, electronic portfolios are starting to become more commonplace in K-12 and higher education. An **electronic portfolio**, or **e-folio**, is an electronically stored portfolio that contains student assignments or projects. Electronic portfolios offer a powerful way for students to create a variety of projects that contain digital media, reflective writings or narratives, drawings, audio, photos, and videos based on predetermined criteria that teachers can evaluate to assess learning.

CHECKLISTS, RATING SCALES, AND RUBRICS
A **checklist** is a predetermined list of performance criteria used in project-based and portfolio assessment. Figure 7-14 on the next page shows a Project Evaluation Checklist. After a student has met a criterion, the criterion is marked as complete. Checklists usually consist of yes and no questions used to determine if the item or items are present. Checklists allow you or your students to keep track of the items.

The benefit of a checklist for an assessment tool is that you can use this tool quickly and students understand very quickly if an item is or is not met. When creating your own checklist, you should include items that clearly show if benchmarks are being met. Another effective option is to have your students create their own checklists or add to yours.

A **rating scale** is a more complex form of a checklist that lists a numerical value, or rating, for each criterion. Assessment involves rating each student on her achievement for each criterion and specifying the total based on all criteria.

Another very popular form of alternative assessment is the rubric. As you recall, a rubric is a detailed assessment tool that makes it easy for teachers to assess the quality of an item, such as a learning project.

WEB INFO

To learn more about portfolio assessment, visit the Teachers Discovering Computers Web site (*scsite.com/tdc4*), click Chapter 7, click Web Info, and then click Portfolios.

FAQ

Are any schools using only electronic portfolios or e-folios to evaluate student work?

Yes, a few K-12 schools and many teacher education programs are using only electronic portfolios to evaluate student work.

Checklist

Project Evaluation Checklist

Date: _____

Student Name: _____

Project Title: _____

	YES	NO
CONTENT		
The project meets all learning objectives.	☐	☐
The project is original and creative.	☐	☐
Mastery of subject is evident.	☐	☐
Use of higher-order thinking skills is evident.	☐	☐
Information is accurate and the subject matter is appropriate.	☐	☐
Information is presented in a logical sequence.	☐	☐
A variety of reliable sources are used.	☐	☐
Sources are properly cited.	☐	☐
Words are spelled correctly and sentences are grammatically correct.	☐	☐
LAYOUT		
The project is visually appealing.	☐	☐
The project is easy to navigate.	☐	☐
The text is easy to read and follow.	☐	☐
Digital media features are used effectively.	☐	☐
Color and design scheme are appropriate.	☐	☐
ORGANIZATION		
Student completed a project storyboard.	☐	☐
Planning is demonstrated.	☐	☐
Project flows smoothly.	☐	☐
Project was completed.	☐	☐

Figure 7-14 Teachers often use alternative assessment tools such as checklists (shown here) and rating scales to evaluate student performance.

page 1 of 1

Rubrics help students understand how teachers will evaluate their projects by providing a range of criteria with information about how to meet each one. Rubrics describe specific and measurable criteria for several levels of quality against which teachers can evaluate completed projects.

Rubrics can help students and teachers define the value or quality of completed assignments. Rubrics also help students critique and revise their own assignments before handing them in. For example, rubrics help students make sure they have included all required elements and have met each criteria for grading. Although a rubric is similar to a checklist and a rating scale, it describes in greater detail the criteria and components that must be achieved.

TEACHER OBSERVATION   When evaluating technology integration or curriculum integration, one of the more widely used authentic assessment techniques is teacher observation. **Teacher observation,** as shown in Figure 7-15, is the result of teachers actively observing their students during the learning process.

Teachers notice whether students are highly motivated during the learning process when technology is used, observe how long the students work on a given objective, and observe the length of time students continue working on a task to master its content and skills. Teacher observation is a powerful assessment tool, and often it is used in combination with other assessment tools. All of these tools can be used to evaluate individual and group student projects.

EVALUATING TECHNOLOGY-BASED STUDENT PROJECTS

Today, skills in technology are essential for students to learn. Technology-based student projects help facilitate integrating technology and digital media into the curriculum. In the process, students learn how to use, manage, and understand technology and how it is used to synthesize and present information on a variety of subjects. Although it might seem like a good idea, you should avoid teaching technology as a separate subject. Instead, you should integrate it into a specific area of your curriculum.

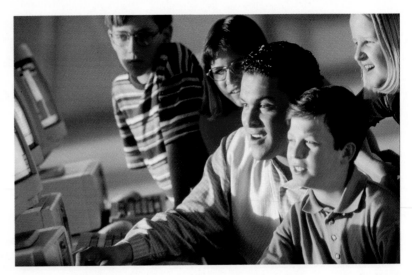

Figure 7-15 This teacher knows that teacher observation is critical when integrating technology.

Some software programs, such as those provided with integrated learning systems (ILS), for example ClassWorks, automatically track student progress. Others, such as Inspiration, iMovie, and PowerPoint, do not provide assessment components. These applications, however, are ideal for students to use to create projects that are innovative and motivational. Teachers who use these software programs for technology-based student projects need to develop effective assessment tools to measure their achievements.

Before a teacher presents a project's requirements to students, he should create an assessment rubric. Figure 7-16 on the next page illustrates a Student Project Evaluation Rubric that guides students on how they will be evaluated on projects. Rubrics are excellent for evaluating all types of student projects. They provide an authentic assessment of project-based learning activities. To determine the criteria to include in the rubric, ask yourself what the students should learn and how this learning will be evidenced in their projects. In the rubric, be sure to specify what students need to include in their projects and clearly inform the students how they will be evaluated.

Checklists, rating scales, and teacher observation also are valid assessment tools for technology-based student projects. Your curriculum standards and benchmarks should define and guide the selection and creation of your assessment tool.

FAQ

Is teacher observation really a powerful tool?

Yes! It is probably one of the most powerful tools that teachers use. A teacher needs to be aware of everything going on in the class room, regardless of whether it relates to technology.

Rubric

Student Project Evaluation Rubric

Student Name: _____

Group Members: _____

Project Title: _____

	Beginning	Developing	Accomplished	Exemplary
Development Process				
Student used quality reference materials and timely Web sites in gathering information.	0 1 2	3 4 5	6 7 8	9 10
Student completed project outline/storyboard.	0 1 2	3 4 5	6 7 8	9 10
Student obtained permission to use copyrighted materials.	0 1 2	3 4 5	6 7 8	9 10
Content				
Understanding of topic is evident.	0 1 2	3 4 5	6 7 8	9 10
Information is presented in a clear manner, is appropriate, and is accurate.	0 1 2	3 4 5	6 7 8	9 10
Content shows understanding of the learning objectives.	0 1 2	3 4 5	6 7 8	9 10
Student used higher-order thinking skills when analyzing and synthesizing content.	0 1 2	3 4 5	6 7 8	9 10
Important ideas related to topic are included and an understanding of important relationships is evident.	0 1 2	3 4 5	6 7 8	9 10
Includes properly cited sources.	0 1 2	3 4 5	6 7 8	9 10
Design				
The information is presented in a logical, interesting sequence.	0 1 2	3 4 5	6 7 8	9 10
Colors, images, animation, and sound enrich the content.	0 1 2	3 4 5	6 7 8	9 10
The project works and is technically sound.	0 1 2	3 4 5	6 7 8	9 10
Text is easy to read and students have followed rules of good screen design.	0 1 2	3 4 5	6 7 8	9 10
Accurate spelling and grammar are used throughout.	0 1 2	3 4 5	6 7 8	9 10
Presentation				
The student maintains eye contact with class.	0 1 2	3 4 5	6 7 8	9 10
The student speaks clearly and is easily heard.	0 1 2	3 4 5	6 7 8	9 10
The presentation is an appropriate length.	0 1 2	3 4 5	6 7 8	9 10

Total Possible _____   **Total** _____

Figure 7-16 A rubric guides students in determining how they will be evaluated on projects. This rubric, for example, is designed to evaluate students' digital media projects.

EVALUATING CONTENT   Your standards and benchmarks will help determine the content to include in student projects and how to assess this content. This should be the most important part of the project. For technology-based student projects, content may include factual information about a historical figure, key points included in a digital media math project, PE presentation, biology lab data in a spreadsheet, and other pertinent information. In addition, evaluation of the content should include a review of punctuation, grammar, spelling, coverage of material, presentation of the material in a logical order, and specific information such as a title, references, and information about the author.

EVALUATING PLANNING   Effective teaching involves planning. Students also must plan a project before creating it, if it is to be effective. When assigning technology-based projects, establish how you want students to plan and what tools they will use. A software planning tool such as **Inspiration** helps students and teachers quickly develop and communicate ideas using flowcharts, concept maps, and story webs through visual learning techniques (Figure 7-17). **Visual learning techniques** are methods that present ideas and information through graphical webs. Inspiration lets you build visual diagrams to work through the process of thinking, organizing thoughts, revealing patterns, and prioritizing information.

    Flowcharts are diagrams that show the step-by-step actions that must take place by plotting a sequence of events. Flowcharts are useful in helping students outline the individual tasks that must be performed to complete an action, a story, or an experiment and the sequence in which they must be performed. A **concept map** or **story web** helps students use flowcharting to understand the attributes and relationships of the main subject and provides a visual tool for brainstorming and planning (Figure 7-18). Another useful planning tool is a **storyboard**, which is a drawing that allows students to design and lay out a project or assignment before creating it on a computer.

EVALUATING CREATIVITY When evaluating student projects, teachers should consider

Figure 7-17 Inspiration is an excellent tool for teaching students how to organize their thoughts and ideas.

Figure 7-18 Using Inspiration software, students create a concept map to plan an undertaking such as this project on election campaigns.

students' originality, imaginative and innovative approach, and artistic abilities — all aspects of **creativity**. Creative student projects should be interesting and unique. Students should demonstrate an understanding of how to use the special effects offered by multimedia authoring software to enhance their projects, instead of distracting from its content. Color, clip art, and artwork should strengthen content, not distract from it.

PUTTING IT ALL TOGETHER — EVALUATING TECHNOLOGY INTEGRATION

Mrs. Vicki Osborne teaches social studies and other subjects at Fall Hills Middle School. She has one computer in her classroom and 26 students. Her middle school is on a **block schedule**, which is an alternative way of scheduling classes. This means the social studies class meets every other day for 90 minutes. Because it is a presidential election year, Mrs. Osborne would like her social studies students to research one of the presidential candidates and then prepare a digital media presentation to convey their findings to the class.

She has six goals for the lesson. The students will (1) work cooperatively in groups with three or four students in each group; (2) use reference materials and Web resources to research the candidate; (3) identify three major campaign issues for their candidate; (4) provide personal facts about the candidate, such as education, occupation prior to politics, and military service; (5) create a digital media project to present their research with either Power-Point or iMovie; and (6) use correct grammar, spelling, and punctuation in their presentation. She will use a rubric to evaluate the students' projects.

Mrs. Osborne began her social studies lesson by displaying her PowerPoint digital media presentation on a 32-inch television for easy viewing by all students. The first step was to brainstorm with her students about the lesson and create a concept map about the election process and the candidates (Figure 7-19). She also passed out a copy of her evaluation rubric, discussed the rubric with her students, and answered their questions. Students then were divided into groups to complete their first task.

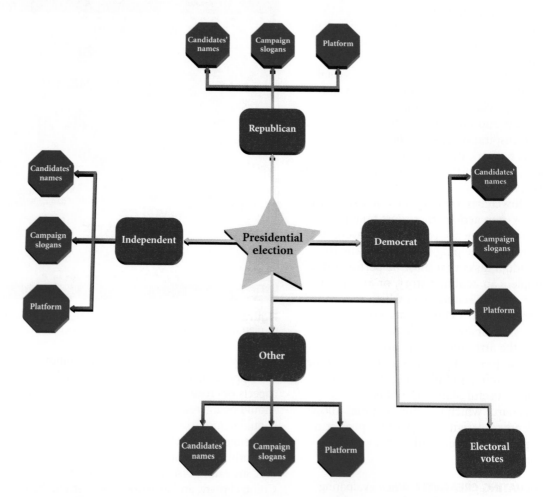

Figure 7-19 Mrs. Osborne and her students create a concept map showing their ideas on the election process and candidates.

Students were required to create a flow-chart or storyboard of their projects using concept mapping software such as Inspiration. Mrs. Osborne then approved their flow-chart drawings and storyboards. When the groups were ready to begin creating their projects, Mrs. Osborne borrowed an additional computer from another teacher and arranged for two groups to use computers in the media center. This allowed four groups to work on computers at the same time. Groups rotated through the four computers in 40-minute blocks (Figure 7-20).

When the groups finished their projects, Mrs. Osborne had each group present their project to the class in the media center. She also invited the principal, a local politician, the media specialist, and another social studies class to view the presentations. The students were very proud of their projects and enjoyed showing them to their peers, teachers, and school administrators. The school newspaper highlighted some of the projects. To make this an authentic learning experience, Mrs. Osborne's students created voting boxes and arranged for the students at Fall Hills Middle School to vote. Her students planned to compare the school election results with the results of the actual election after the presidential election three weeks later.

To integrate technology successfully, teachers must continuously evaluate educational technology before instruction begins, during the instructional period, and after instruction has taken place. Technology not only changes the learning process but also changes the teaching and evaluation processes. Teachers have the responsibility to evaluate and update assignments and activities continuously — on a daily, weekly, monthly, or semester basis — depending on the project or assignment.

To make learning more effective, often only minor changes and improvements are necessary. In other instances, however, teachers need to implement major revisions to reflect content, curriculum, or technology changes. The next few sections introduce you to other integration strategies, such as using technology in various classroom configurations and developing curriculum pages.

Integration Strategies

To help meet the constant challenge of motivating students to learn, teachers must change their traditional roles and become facilitators of learning. Technology plays a key role in easing this change because it allows teachers to use technology tools to enhance the learning environment,

FAQ

Are there other software programs that teachers and students can use to create concept maps or flowcharts?

Yes, concept maps, flowcharts, and diagrams can be created easily in most word processors, such as Microsoft Word, by using the drawing tools on the Drawing toolbar.

Figure 7-20 Centers allow students to work collaboratively in groups on student-centered projects.

motivate students, guide students in an active learning process, and encourage them to learn. The most effective way to integrate technology is to place the technology at the point of instruction — the classroom. Because of the ever-increasing need to motivate students to learn, teachers have a mandate to use the powerful tools of technology to enhance the learning environment.

Many different technologies, availability of computer labs, and different kinds and numbers of computers in the classroom are found in schools today (Figure 7-21). The following instructional strategies describe techniques to integrate technology into a one-computer classroom, a multi-computer classroom, and a computer lab.

ONE-COMPUTER CLASSROOM

Most classrooms are equipped with one digital media computer and are referred to as a **one-computer classroom**. Many ways exist in which to integrate educational technology with only one computer in the classroom. As you learned in Chapter 6, the most common practice is to use the computer for classroom presentations and demonstrations. By projecting the computer's image on a projection screen or large-screen television, you can use the computer to supplement and enhance your traditional lectures to accomplish whole-class instruction of learning objectives. You also can use the computer to introduce new concepts, prepare students for a lesson, describe background information for assignments, and explain evaluation criteria.

Figure 7-21 Technology can be integrated into many different classroom environments.

Another strategy permits students to work on the computer in small groups to foster collaboration and cooperative learning opportunities. Students also can use the computer to present their assignments, projects, and research activities to the entire class. In addition, you can use the computer to maintain records, create presentations and projects, do research, and communicate with other teachers (Figure 7-22).

To integrate technology in a one-computer classroom, follow these guidelines:

- Obtain Internet access. Use the Web's many educational resources, such as audio, video, and multimedia applications to enhance instruction and learning.

- Utilize educational application software. Both teachers and students can make use of the abundance of educational software available on CDs, DVDs, and school networks.

- Enhance lectures and presentations. Connect the computer to a television monitor, and then use the computer to enhance lectures, create and give presentations, and take students on virtual field trips.

- Use the computer as a teaching assistant. Tutor individual students by having them use drill and practice software, tutorials, simulations, and problem-solving software.

- Foster group and cooperative learning. Students can use the computer as an informational resource or a creation tool for group projects, such as digital media presentations.

- Write an ongoing story. Begin a story on the computer that serves as a creative writing center, and invite student authors to add to it daily. Before you begin, explain the rules for acceptable behavior, the types of content to be included in the story, and the types of entries that are satisfactory.

Figure 7-22 Teachers benefit from using a classroom computer to maintain grades and other important files.

- Start a class newsletter. Invite students to write articles and use word processing or desktop publishing software to create a class newsletter (Figure 7-23).

- Create a class blog. Ask your students to evaluate the way we receive information today by reading and comparing two to three different Web logs about a current event. Then, have them write a response in the class blog about the Web logs they thought were most accurate and compelling.

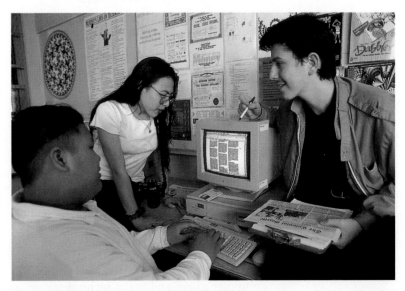

Figure 7-23 Students gain real-world skills by creating a class or school newsletter.

- Maintain a student database. Instead of having students fill out information forms, let them enter the information into a database on the computer. Students also can enter information on a variety of content-related subject areas, such as information on science projects, vocabulary words, historical places, and so on.

- Utilize the computer as a teacher productivity tool. The computer is an excellent medium for creating curriculum activities, lesson plans and tests, maintaining grades and attendance records, writing letters to parents, and creating achievement certificates. Purchasing gradebook or student information management software helps to streamline many daily management responsibilities.

- Use other low-cost input devices, such as AlphaSmarts and PDAs, for students to create first drafts, take notes in class, and enter data into their documents. Later, the data can be downloaded to the computer. This is a super time-saver and is ideal for student projects.

- Optimize computer lab time. Use the computer to introduce students to various types of software and thus create learning paths before taking students to the school's computer lab. This will optimize the time students spend on computers while in the computer lab.

- New emerging technologies allow you to create an exciting learning environment; for example, you can roll a complete computer lab into your classroom. If your school has a wireless mobile lab, schedule time to use the lab. This is a great way to move the technology you need into your one-computer classroom.

MULTICOMPUTER CLASSROOM

Having two or more computers in your classroom fosters additional learning opportunities that allow flexibility in computer usage and make technology integration an integral part of the curriculum. Remember, one-computer classroom strategies also apply to a classroom with two or more computers.

One way to use two or more computers is to set up the computers as separate learning centers for student use. Teachers can divide the centers by subject area and then create activities that continuously change to match the curriculum or lessons being taught. A math center, for example, might include CDs, DVDs, and network-based tutorials to reinforce math skills. A language arts center might include word processing software for creative writing projects; HyperStudio, PowerPoint, and Photoshop to create digital media presentations; as well as reading and spelling software skill programs.

A social studies center may allow students to use the Web as a research tool and correspond with other classrooms via the Internet to learn more about the culture, language, history, and geography of other regions. Software programs such as Oregon Trail and MapMaker Toolkit help reinforce mapping and geography skills in relation to other curriculum areas.

Learning centers are an effective way to create a flexible learning environment with many options for students. Teachers can integrate technologies into learning centers to create specialized centers such as a video center, a listening center, and a digital camera center.

To illustrate how one teacher is integrating technology into a science curriculum, consider the middle school classroom of Miss Julie Davis. At the beginning of class, she takes her students for a nature walk on school property to learn about trees, plants, changing seasons, and photosynthesis. During the nature walk, students notice a lot of trash on the school grounds. Students take their PDAs, smart phones, Neos, Pocket PCs, and Tablet PCs to enter data on a form Miss Davis created for them to fill out during their excursion. This way, the students enter their thoughts, explorations, and findings while they are in the environment, and not later, when they might have forgotten important information and findings.

She encourages her students to use digital cameras to take pictures of the trash, plants, trees, and other items of interest (Figure 7-24). In a follow-up discussion in class, the students decide the trash is a

WEB INFO

For more information about AlphaSmarts, visit the Teachers Discovering Computer Web site (*scsite.com/tdc4*), click Chapter 7, click Web Info, and then click AlphaSmarts.

form of pollution — and they should do something to make the school cleaner. Miss Davis recognizes this as a teachable moment and asks essential questions to start the students thinking. She asks, "Can we make a difference? How can we help prevent pollution, starting at school?" The students begin brainstorming. Following the discussion, Miss Davis shows the students a short CNN video on global warming.

The next day, Miss Davis continues the learning process by dividing the students into groups to begin their research projects on waste, environmentally hazardous materials, trees, plants, and air associated with the environment. Next, the students begin working on their KWLQS charts. A **KWLQS chart** is similar to the KWL chart discussed in Chapter 6, with the additions of *Q*, which stands for further questioning, and *S*, which stands for sharing (referring to the fact that students will share their projects with their fellow students). Miss Davis and the students decide to create a survey to examine all the environmental issues at the school. From the survey results, it is clear most students are aware that the school has to dispose of trash, but most of them have never focused on the hazardous products, such as cleaners, that need to be disposed. It is also clear that none of the students had thought about the school's various types of trash, or whether the school recycles, or whether the methods used for disposing of hazardous waste could harm the environment. Miss Davis places the students in groups and assigns each group different environmental issues to research.

Miss Davis is fortunate to have four digital media computers in her classroom. Two of the computers are used as Web research centers, while the other two are set up as creation centers. To complete group projects, students rotate through the Web centers and use her curriculum pages to locate resources from agriculture, environmental protection agencies, and other related Web sites (Figure 7-25). Then, they use the creation centers to develop presentations that suggest ways to protect the environment. The students incorporate their digital pictures into digital media projects.

While completing the projects, the students learn about citizenship and that

Figure 7-24 Students can import and edit images taken with a digital camera to enhance their projects.

Figure 7-25 Students easily can locate information dealing with pollution, global warming, and other environmental issues on the Web.

everyone is responsible for protecting the environment. They then decide to start a schoolwide cleanup project. The class creates flyers using Microsoft Publisher and posts them throughout the school so all the students and teachers will be aware of the environment. They also create a Web page, sharing what they have learned with the community.

As this example illustrates, using computers and other technologies in the classroom promotes active learning, involves the students, and provides a sense of ownership, or authentic learning, of the information being presented. Having two or more computers in the classroom — especially when they are used as learning centers — requires more planning and attention to detail than having just one computer. Before setting up a learning center or centers, teachers should consider how many computers will be in each center and what other technologies, if any, may be included in the center. After the centers are set up, teachers can work on managing and planning activities, scheduling rotation times through each center for the students as they complete projects and activities. Teachers can create a sign-up list or use a timing device so all students have a fair amount of time on the computers.

COMPUTER LABS

Computer labs offer teachers instructional opportunities that are not possible in a one-, two-, or even a five-computer classroom. The most important advantage of using a computer lab or a wireless mobile lab is that all students have hands-on experience using computer technology. Teachers may successfully use computer labs for drill and practice, remediation, collaborative learning, computer skill instruction (for example, word processing), Internet research, whole class instruction, and tutorials.

Students often learn technology skills or subject-specific skills in isolation from the rest of the curriculum while in school computer labs. The labs, however, can also support the technology integration that teaches curriculum standards and related benchmarks. They are not just a place to teach keyboarding, remedial math, and science drills. A lab with modern computers, scanners, Web access, and other technologies makes it possible to integrate computer-related skills into subject-directed curriculum areas. Teachers, for example, can integrate specific software applications into subject-area content.

WEB INFO

For a tutorial on creating Web scavenger hunts, visit the Teachers Discovering Computers Web site (scsite.com/tdc4), click Chapter 7, click Web Info, and then click Scavenger Hunt.

Teacher-created activities, such as Web scavenger hunts, also teach computer skills, while giving students direction. A **Web scavenger hunt** is an inquiry-oriented activity in which students explore the resources of the Web using discovery learning to find the answers to teacher-created questions (Figure 7-26). While searching for the answers, students use higher-order thinking skills. When teachers plan creative instructional activities in advance, the computer lab, along with other technologies and the Internet, can bring authentic excitement and enthusiasm to students who otherwise might be uninterested in their daily school work.

Curriculum Integration Activities

Many teachers already use computers and technology in their classrooms and computer labs to help meet curriculum standards. For curriculum integration to be effective, however, the curriculum should drive the technologies used in the classroom; that is, teachers should use the applicable technologies to enhance learning at the appropriate times.

As teachers use technology in the classroom, they are finding many different ways to integrate it into curriculum-specific learning objectives. Learning to integrate technology effectively, however, requires planning and practice. The more practice you have in teaching with and integrating technology, the more you will discover innovative ways to use technology to facilitate all types of instruction.

CURRICULUM PAGES

One of the bigger technology integration challenges that teachers face today is determining exactly how to use the Internet in their classrooms. Teachers who integrate the Internet successfully are using it in ways that engage students in problem solving, locating research information, and developing higher-order thinking skills. Supervising students and controlling Web activities with curriculum pages is crucial to the successful use of the Internet in classrooms. Recall from

Exercise

Roller Coaster Scavenger

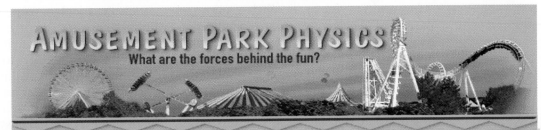

To learn more about the forces behind the fun, visit the Amusement Park Physics Web site at:

www.learner.org/exhibits/parkphysics

Part A: Visit the site and read about roller coasters to answer the questions that follow.

1. Do roller coasters have engines?_____

2. What drives a roller coaster? _____

3. What is the difference between running wheels and friction wheels? _____
_____

4. How do roller coasters stop? _____

5. What is centripetal force?_____

6. What is gravitational force? _____

7. Name and explain three physics terms that relate to roller coasters. _____

Part B: Follow the online instructions to design your own roller coaster and answer the questions that follow.

8. What hill height did you choose? Why? _____

9. What hill shape did you choose? Why? _____

10. Which exit path did you choose? Why? _____

11. What did you choose for the height of your second hill? Why?_____
_____

12. What type of loop did you add? Why? _____

13. Did your roller coaster design succeed or fail? Why?_____
_____
_____

On the back of this paper, list four additional facts that you have learned.

Good Luck!

Figure 7-26 A scavenger hunt is a great way to have students explore the resources of the Web while using their higher-order thinking skills at the same time.

Chapter 3 that a **curriculum page** is a teacher-created document that contains hyperlinks to teacher-selected Web sites that assist in teaching content-specific curriculum objectives. In addition, curriculum pages should support learning objectives by providing students with quality Web resources, links to additional information, and opportunities to learn more. Because your curriculum page contains links that you have already researched and evaluated, students waste no time needlessly surfing instead of learning. A curriculum page can be a useful tool to ensure students spend your precious class time linking quickly to Web sites that you know will provide valuable information that is relevant to your lesson. Curriculum pages are easy to create and are a valuable teaching tool for students to use when accessing the World Wide Web.

Simple curriculum pages contain hyperlinks to teacher-selected sites. More detailed curriculum pages provide hyperlinks to sites and instructions for constructive and purposeful activities that students complete when they get to the selected Web sites. Using curriculum pages with these types of activities helps students find answers to teacher-created questions and helps them create and answer their own questions. Figure 7-27 shows examples of teacher-created curriculum pages.

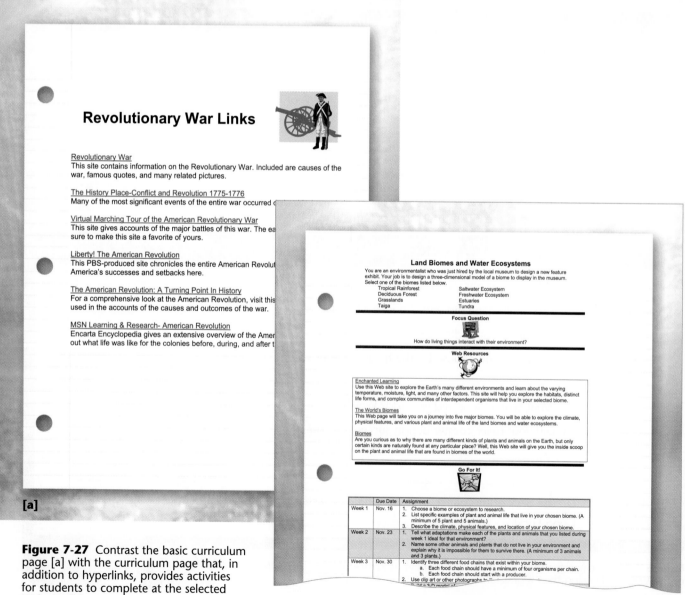

Figure 7-27 Contrast the basic curriculum page [a] with the curriculum page that, in addition to hyperlinks, provides activities for students to complete at the selected Web site [b].

CREATING LESSON PLANS

Planning is one of the most important variables for good instruction, and curriculum integration demands a great deal of planning. When first introducing technology into the classroom, many teachers try to incorporate technology into their existing lesson plans and activities. Because of the nature of the new technology tools, however, and because teaching and learning approaches must change, most teachers learn quickly this initial approach is only partially effective. To be successful in integrating technology, teachers must rethink and redesign activities and create new teaching and learning strategies as they progressively integrate technology across their curriculum. In other words, new technology tools require new instructional lessons.

Teachers do not have to rely solely on their own resourcefulness to create technology-enriched lesson plans and activities. Today, teachers may receive online advice from other educators by joining educational mailing lists, forums, newsgroups, discussion groups, bulletin boards, blogs, and **vlogs**, which are blogs that contain video. Teachers also may refer to the Educator's Reference Desk, which provides thousands of resources and services to the education community (Figure 7-28).

Numerous lesson plans and activities at thousands of educational Web sites are

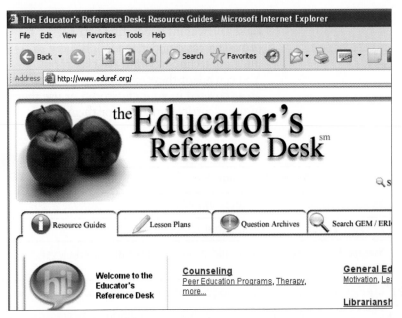

Figure 7-28 The Educator's Reference Desk provides thousands of high-quality resources for teachers.

available for teachers to use (Figure 7-29). Many such sites provide search engines to locate curriculum-specific lesson plans and activities for almost any K-12 area.

The following sections describe one interdisciplinary and seven subject-specific teacher-created curriculum integration activities. Each of these lesson plans are centered on a focus question and use a combination of learning processes and teaching strategies to assist in the delivery

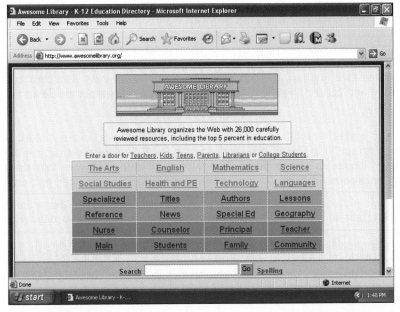

Figure 7-29 Teachers can locate an almost unlimited supply of lesson plans and activities at thousands of Web sites.

WEB INFO

For more information about using computers as tools for learning, visit the Teachers Discovering Computers Web site (*scsite.com/tdc4*), click Chapter 7, click Web Info, and then click Learning Tools.

of the instructional process. The purpose of these curriculum integration activities is to provide a basic understanding of how to integrate technology into the classroom. You can adapt these examples to subject areas covered in your classroom or use them in other curriculum areas for thematic instruction.

LANGUAGE ARTS INTEGRATION Language arts curriculum usually includes instruction in reading, writing, listening, viewing, speaking, and literature. Figure 7-30 shows a curriculum integration activity, called *Extra! Extra! Know All About It.*, that integrates technology into the subject areas of research and writing.

Language Arts

Curriculum Area:	Language Arts
Subject Area:	Research and Writing
Lesson Title:	Extra! Extra! Know All About It.
Suggested Grade Level:	4–6, could be adapted for any grade level
Equipment Needed:	Technology: Digital video camera, computer, microphones, TV, VCR Software: Digital video editing software Other: Teacher-created curriculum Web pages with Web resources about newscasting and news reporting; newspapers, prerecorded news stories that have been evaluated for age appropriateness, items students can use as props
Focus Question:	How can news stories help keep citizens informed?
Learning Objectives:	■ Students will be able to find the important parts of a news story. ■ Students will analyze the news story based on point of view. ■ Students will write a news story appropriate for a newspaper article. ■ Students will use digital media to create a news story appropriate for a newscast.
Instructions:	Introduce the task by asking students, "What is the purpose of newspaper articles and television news stories?" Allow several students to respond. Then ask, "What is the main difference between a newspaper article and a television newscast?" Give each student a who, what, when, where, why, and how graphic organizer. Tell students that they are going to fill out the graphic organizer as they watch several newscasts from different anchors. Discuss their findings. Watch the newscast again and have students determine what type of bias is presented as well as how the story would be different if it were told from a different point of view. Divide the class into groups of three or four students and give each group a newspaper. Have students choose a news article that they find interesting and fill out a graphic organizer for the article. Discuss their findings, the bias, and possible points of view. As a class, make a Venn Diagram comparing and contrasting the differences between a newspaper article and a television newscast. Give each group a photograph from a newspaper article that they have not read. Using the picture, have each group fill in the graphic organizer and write a newspaper article based on what they see. They will use Publisher or some other word processing software to make a final copy of their article. The groups will then use their photograph, graphic organizer, and completed news
Evaluation of Content:	Teacher observation along with a project rubric will be used to evaluate this activity. Students will be evaluated on their ability to present the same factual details using two different modes.
Evaluation of Curriculum Integration:	Using observation, teachers will evaluate the extent to which technology assisted students to master the objectives. Teachers also will determine if the selected technology met a variety of learning styles and whether students were able to acquire the needed technology skills while creating their digital media projects.

Figure 7-30 A sample lesson plan for *Extra! Extra! Know All About It.*

SOCIAL STUDIES INTEGRATION   Social studies curriculum usually encompasses instruction in history, geography, civics, and economics. Figure 7-31 shows a curriculum integration activity, called *What Wonderful Webs We Weave*, that integrates technology into the subject area of ancient Egypt.

Social Studies	
Curriculum Area:	Social Studies
Subject Area:	Ancient Egypt
Lesson Title:	What Wonderful Webs We Weave
Suggested Grade Level:	3-5
Equipment Needed:	Technology: Classroom computers or a computer lab, Internet access, and television monitor connected to a computer
	Software: Ancient civilizations CDs and DVDs, electronic encyclopedias, and Web editors such as Netscape Composer, Microsoft Word, or Macromedia Dreamweaver
	Other: Teacher-created curriculum Web pages related to ancient Egypt, books, magazines, and encyclopedias from the media center
Focus Question:	How are ancient Egyptian traditions reflected in our culture today?
Learning Objectives:	■ Students will describe what life was like in ancient Egypt; based on class discussions, and information found in books, CDs, DVDs, videotapes, and the Internet. ■ Students will work cooperatively in small groups and create Web pages using a Web editor to be published on the World Wide Web.

Figure 7-31   A sample lesson plan for *What Wonderful Webs We Weave*.   (continued)

Instructions:	Introduce the activity to students by asking the focus question, then use student responses to create a KWLQS chart about ancient Egypt. As a class, decide on five or six broad topics of study relating to ancient Egypt: mummies, pyramids, Pharaohs, and so on. Connect a classroom computer to a television monitor and view teacher-created curriculum Web pages about ancient Egypt. Discuss what makes a Web site interesting, attractive, and relevant. Distribute an evaluation rubric for the students' Web page project. Review the rubric with the students so they will understand how their Web page will be evaluated. Next, divide the class into small groups of three to four students. Have each group select one of the broad topics the class listed. Allow students to research their particular topic. They may use the CDs, DVDs, Web sites, books, magazines, and encyclopedias from the media center, the teacher-created curriculum Web pages, and the Internet. After students have finished their research, they will complete a planning worksheet. Students will plan their content, Web page layout, background, attention-getting titles, animated GIFs, pictures, and links to related Web sites. After students have created their Web pages on paper, they may create them using a Web editor. When the Web pages are complete, they can be posted on your school's server or on a free Web server site.
Evaluation of Content:	Teacher observation along with the project rubric will be used to evaluate this activity. In addition, students' planning worksheets will be used for assessment purposes. Quality of research, the information drawn from Web sites, and the extent to which the students answered the focus question also will be assessed.
Evaluation of Curriculum Integration:	Learning to access, analyze, and apply information from different resources is a necessary skill for students and will be observed. How well students locate information, determine what information is valuable, and apply that information will be examined. Student motivation and enthusiasm when creating a Web page also will assist with evaluating the technology.

Figure 7-31 *(continued)*

MATHEMATICS INTEGRATION **Mathematics curriculum** usually includes instruction in basic number concepts, measurements, geometry, algebra, calculus, and data analysis.

Figure 7-32 shows a curriculum integration activity, called *The Business of Professional Sports*, that integrates technology into the subject areas of measurement, problem solving, and geometry.

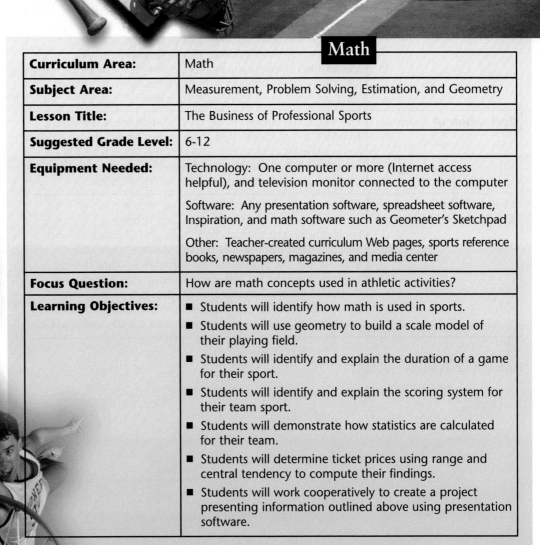

Math	
Curriculum Area:	Math
Subject Area:	Measurement, Problem Solving, Estimation, and Geometry
Lesson Title:	The Business of Professional Sports
Suggested Grade Level:	6-12
Equipment Needed:	Technology: One computer or more (Internet access helpful), and television monitor connected to the computer Software: Any presentation software, spreadsheet software, Inspiration, and math software such as Geometer's Sketchpad Other: Teacher-created curriculum Web pages, sports reference books, newspapers, magazines, and media center
Focus Question:	How are math concepts used in athletic activities?
Learning Objectives:	■ Students will identify how math is used in sports. ■ Students will use geometry to build a scale model of their playing field. ■ Students will identify and explain the duration of a game for their sport. ■ Students will identify and explain the scoring system for their team sport. ■ Students will demonstrate how statistics are calculated for their team. ■ Students will determine ticket prices using range and central tendency to compute their findings. ■ Students will work cooperatively to create a project presenting information outlined above using presentation software.

Figure 7-32 A sample lesson plan for *The Business of Professional Sports.*   *(continued)*

Instructions:	Have students list all the team sports they know. Create a concept map using Inspiration, projected to the class on the television monitor with Math as the center. Brainstorm with the class on how math is used in each of the sports they named, and then add these ideas to the concept map. Invite students to select their favorite team sport and then group students according to interest. Distribute an assessment rubric and discuss how it will be used to evaluate students' projects. Students will use the rubric and follow the learning objectives to determine what elements they will include in their project. Encourage them to use the Internet for research, as well as any resources from the media center including newspapers to calculate statistics. Provide each group with a designated time to use the computer. When groups are not using the computer, they may be using other resource materials to develop their projects. Coordinate with the media specialist students' access to other computers, or schedule time in the computer lab when the groups are working on their presentations. Have students use Geometer's Sketchpad to enter data and evaluate team statistics. Create graphs in Geometer's Sketchpad and compare. Have students create graphs using any spreadsheet software application, and these may be included in their projects. When groups have completed their projects, share them with the class.
Evaluation of Content:	The evaluation rubric will be used to determine the extent to which the students used the learning objectives to answer the focus question. Teachers will determine the extent of student learning by the level of student motivation and a demonstrated understanding of statistics.
Evaluation of Curriculum Integration:	Evaluate problem-solving skills based on the concept map students created to visualize their brainstorming responses. Furthermore, assess technology skills and problem-solving skills acquired through the use of software applications. Evaluate the use of spreadsheet software to learn how to organize information and see graphical representation of that information. Evaluate student presentations to determine if this process reinforces skills in communication, organization, problem-solving skills, and critical-thinking skills.

Figure 7-32 *(continued)*

SCIENCE INTEGRATION
Science curriculum usually contains instruction in physical sciences, earth and space sciences, and life sciences. Figure 7-33 shows a curriculum integration activity, called *Let's Think as a Scientist*, that integrates technology into the subject area of physical science.

Science	
Curriculum Area:	Science
Subject Area:	Physical Sciences
Lesson Title:	Let's Think as a Scientist
Suggested Grade Level:	K-12
Equipment Needed:	Technology: One computer and a television monitor connected to the computer Software: Thinkin' Science. This lesson can be adapted with other software-specific products. Other: Student computers if available
Focus Question:	Why is it necessary for scientists to have good observation skills?
Learning Objectives:	■ Students will practice observation and problem-solving skills. ■ Students will demonstrate understanding of content. ■ Students will interpret data. ■ Students will determine cause and effect between two events.
Instructions:	Begin this activity with a whole class discussion; use the focus question to guide the conversation. Thinkin' Science explores the earth, life, and physical sciences. Connect the computer to a television monitor or large screen. For this activity, go to Animal Tracking. Students will need to observe animals and then apply problem-solving skills. Students will explore animal behavior and then interpret data that is presented. Guide students by asking questions and drawing their attention to important events. To provide further practice of observation skills, and to increase problem-solving skills, use the activity, *What Did You See?* The students will be presented with a scene. The scene will disappear and students will have to re-create the scene. All students should tell you what needs to be placed in the scene. After you have used the software with the whole class, you can set it up in a learning center. *Note:* the software comes with a Teacher's Guide and reproducible activity sheets. You can place these in the learning center to support the students.
Evaluation of Content:	Students will be quizzed on content provided to determine if problem-solving skills and observation skills were mastered. The number of correctly answered questions from each student will determine attainment of content.
Evaluation of Curriculum Integration:	Teacher observation will be used to measure student attention and motivation. An additional evaluation will be identifying how many students utilize the software in the learning center.

Figure 7-33 A sample lesson plan for *Let's Think as a Scientist.*

TIGERGRAM

Please stand by, Mary!
Your zoo is about to receive its first-ever Siberian tiger, a six-year-old male called Stripes. He?s being moved to your zoo by the Siberian Tiger Species Survival Plan, a group of zookeepers trying to save the big cats by breeding them in zoos. There aren?t many of these special animals left in the wild?only about 400?and your mission is to make sure *this* one thrives

PHYSICAL EDUCATION AND HEALTH INTEGRATION Physical education and health curriculum usually includes instruction in basic health and physical education literacy. Figure 7-34 shows a curriculum integration activity, called *Eating Healthy!*, that integrates technology into the subject area of nutrition.

Physical Education and Health	
Curriculum Area:	Physical Education and Health
Subject Area:	Nutrition
Lesson Title:	Eating Healthy!
Suggested Grade Level:	2-4, could be adapted for any grade level
Equipment Needed:	Technology: Three computers, at least one with Internet access
	Software: PowerPoint or HyperStudio, database and drawing programs such as Microsoft Office, AppleWorks, Microsoft Works, Photoshop Elements, and Microsoft Paint
	Other: Teacher-created curriculum Web pages, books, nutrition brochures (from hospitals/health departments), and the Dole 5 A Day Web site (www.dole5aday.com)
Focus Question:	How do food choices affect your overall health?
Learning Objectives:	■ Students will be able to use the Internet to take the Dole 5 A Day Challenge.
	■ Students will create five recipes that include at least one serving of fruits/vegetables in each recipe.
	■ Students will enter one of their recipes into a class cookbook database.
	■ Students will work cooperatively to locate facts about their assigned fruit/vegetable using the Dole Fruit and Vegetable Encyclopedia and other resources.
	■ Students will be able to use PowerPoint or HyperStudio to create and present a multimedia project on their fruit/vegetable.
Instructions:	Individually, students will go to the Dole 5 A Day Web site to take the 5 A Day Challenge and to discover how food choices affect their health. Students will be given time to browse the Web page to learn more about why it is so important to eat at least five fruits/vegetables per day.
	Students will use the information from the Web site and nutrition brochures to create five recipes for their 5-day menu.
	Students will select their favorite recipe and add it to the class cookbook database. Students will create a creative cookbook cover using a desktop publishing or drawing program. They will print copies of the recipes to share with their families.
	Students will work in groups of two or three to create a digital media presentation on an assigned fruit/vegetable. Students will use books, nutrition brochures, and the Dole 5 A Day Web site to collect the information that they need to complete their projects.
Evaluation of Content:	Each student's menu item will be evaluated using a rubric (spelling and grammar included). Group projects also will be evaluated using a rubric (spelling and grammar included). Teachers will observe students as they work to determine whether students understand how food choices affect their overall health.
Evaluation of Curriculum Integration:	The effectiveness of the technology will be evaluated by testing students' content retention in a culminating quiz. Effectiveness will be apparent in student presentations. Students will gain valuable experience exploring Internet resources and learning how to use them to complete an assignment.

Figure 7-34 A sample lesson plan for *Eating Healthy!*

ARTS INTEGRATION Arts curriculum usually incorporates instruction in the visual and performing arts, including drawing, painting, dance, music, and theater. Figure 7-35 shows a curriculum integration activity, called *The Theory of Color*, that integrates technology into the subject area of color theory.

Art	
Curriculum Area:	Art (integrates Math)
Subject Area:	Color-Theory — Reinforcing Basic Reading, Writing, and Math Skills
Lesson Title:	The Theory of Color
Suggested Grade Level:	4-6, easily adapted to higher levels
Equipment Needed:	Technology: Requires access to a student computer lab. Requires computer connected to large monitor or TV. Software: PowerPoint and any paint program
Focus Question:	How does the world around you reflect colors?
Learning Objectives:	■ Students will increase understanding of color theory. ■ Students will increase use of reading, math, and writing in the art classroom. ■ Students will demonstrate abstract conceptualization of written materials. ■ Students will demonstrate skills in computer paint accessories.

Figure 7-35 A sample lesson plan for *The Theory of Color*. *(continued)*

Instructions:	Students are given a brief introduction explaining the goals of the lessons. They are told that an important part of the lesson is their own reading and writing skills. A simple pretest is given to allow students to demonstrate any preexisting knowledge of the content area.
	Color mixing: Using basic math skills and written directions, students prepare a series of diagrammatic color charts that teach basic color mixing and theory. The blank charts are prepared with the paint software. The color formulas will be written in a mathematical or fractional way (for example, Orange = fi Yellow + fi Red). Students will use eyedroppers to mix tempera paints to the proper proportion and paint samples as a permanent record in their portfolios.
	Relating reading and color theory: Based on the belief that children should be taught to visualize color as described in books or stories, children will read a series of excerpts from stories that include written descriptions of colors. Students will create color samples that show an understanding of the written excerpt and the colors described.
	Relating color to written descriptions: In contrast to the previous activity, students will be given blank lined pages for writing text. Each blank page will have a preprinted block of color. Students will be directed to create brief descriptive paragraphs that relate to each of the attached colors.
	Integrating technology: This lesson will be spread over time to allow adequate computer access time. Students will engage in a computer-oriented lesson that integrates what they have learned about colors with both reading and technology.
	Students will create a drawing with the paint program. The requirement for this piece of art will be that it clearly shows three primary colors, three secondary colors, one tint, and one shade.
Evaluation of Content:	A rubric will be used that the students easily can understand. Students will engage in critiques of each other's work. Critiques will be consolidated and students and instructors jointly will discuss the results of the exercises. The teacher also will assign individual student work. This will be based on the rubric to ensure consistency and reliability of results. Final results are compared with the pretest, where marked improvement in the students' understanding of color and color theory should be identified.
Evaluation of Curriculum Integration:	Teacher observation should be used to determine the quality of the projects. A teacher-created rubric should be used to determine the quality of the projects. Higher levels of complexity or variance in the final projects can be evaluated.

Figure 7-35 *(continued)*

COLOR MATTERS®

EXCEPTIONAL EDUCATION INTEGRATION

Exceptional education curriculum, or **special education curriculum**, usually contains instruction in all curriculum areas with adaptations made for students with unique characteristics or special needs. These students include those who are gifted, learning disabled, physically disabled, emotionally disabled, or mentally disabled. Instruction for regular-education students and exceptional-educational students is merging as teachers find that many of the technology resources and integration activities dramatically enhance the instruction of students with special needs. Teachers easily can modify many of the integration activities illustrated in Figure 7-30 through Figure 7-35 to meet the needs of exceptional educational students. Figure 7-36 shows a curriculum integration activity, called *Rain Forests Are in Trouble*, that integrates technology into the subject area of current events and can be used for all students, including students with special needs.

Special Education

Curriculum Area:	Science, Social Studies, Math, and Language Arts for special education students
Subject Area:	Current Events
Lesson Title:	Rain Forests Are in Trouble
Suggested Grade Level:	3-5 (This lesson has been developed for grade levels 3 to 5 special education students. This lesson can be used with 3rd to 12th grade with appropriate adaptations.)
Equipment Needed:	Technology: Computer and a television monitor or large screen, Internet access and use of the Welcome to the Amazon Web site
	Software: Microsoft Encarta or other electronic encyclopedias, and Internet sites on rain forests around the world.
	Other: Teacher-created curriculum Web pages on rain forests around the world, *The Lost Compound* video, 3×5 index cards, notebooks, pencils, pens
Focus Question:	Why are rain forests worth saving?
Learning Objectives:	■ Students will collect and analyze information about the rain forests.
	■ Students will describe a Web expedition to the Amazon using the Internet.
	■ Students will explain current research efforts on tropical rain forests.
	■ Students will demonstrate knowledge gained of tropical rain forest issues, and explore plant life cycles.
	■ Students will create a digital media research report.

Figure 7-36 A sample lesson plan for *Rain Forests Are in Trouble*.   *(continued)*

Instructions:	Start the activity by asking students what they know about rain forests. Use their responses to create a KWHL chart with the students. Students will work with partners and in groups of four. They will be given a list of Web sites about rain forests. They will access at least three different sites and take notes (3x5 index cards) about five different aspects of the rain forests. If an e-mail address is listed, students will write a short note asking a specific question they want to know about the rain forest. Students will work with their same team members and venture into the Amazon Web site. While there, they enter the options available at the Web site: Research, The Team, Map, About Netspedition, Equipment, and Venezuela and document a brief description of each. Next, they will give a brief description about one of the butterfly surveys, indicating date, location, and what types of butterflies were caught. The team then will access the log book and choose one specific day on the calendar. They will record the date, location, the temperature, a description of one of the photographs, a description of the author's feelings, and the name of the person entering the information. Students still work in their cooperative teams taking turns at the computer. If computer access for inputting data is difficult, use other input devices such as PDAs, AlphaSmarts, and Tablet PCs. Each student plays the role of a scientific expert, chemist, ecologist, botanist, or taxonomist using one of four unique student reference books. Teams watch the video on *The Lost Compound* and use on-screen instructions to guide them in analyzing information, collaborating, and making decisions. Students will create research projects on the computer with drawings, maps, and so on.
Evaluation of Content:	The projects the students complete will indicate whether the students grasped the concepts indicated by the preceding objectives. Students will be evaluated on their ability to analyze and present factual details This project could be used as an additional or follow-up assignment.
Evaluation of Curriculum Integration:	Teacher observation will help to verify if the technology assisted in meeting various learning styles and needs of special education students. Teacher observation will determine if technology assisted in student attention and motivation. Students will be evaluated on time on task and length of time students work to master content and technology skills. An additional evaluation will be looking at each student and his individual needs throughout the lesson.

Figure 7-36 *(continued)*

INTERDISCIPLINARY INTEGRATION   An **interdisciplinary curriculum** usually includes two or more academic disciplines or curriculum areas to form a cross-discipline or subject-integrated lesson. A **cross-discipline lesson** includes a combination of curriculum-specific areas, such as math or science, that are integrated with language arts. A **subject-integrated lesson** is a lesson that integrates multiple skills, such as speaking, reading, thinking, and writing with multiple subject areas such as math, science, and language arts to create a more holistic learning experience. An interdisciplinary curriculum can combine various skills or disciplines to make a lesson more fully integrated for authentic and inquiry-based learning. Figure 7-37 shows a curriculum-integration activity, called *Natural Disasters Occur Everywhere*, that integrates technology in the subject areas of writing, research, science, social studies, health, and art.

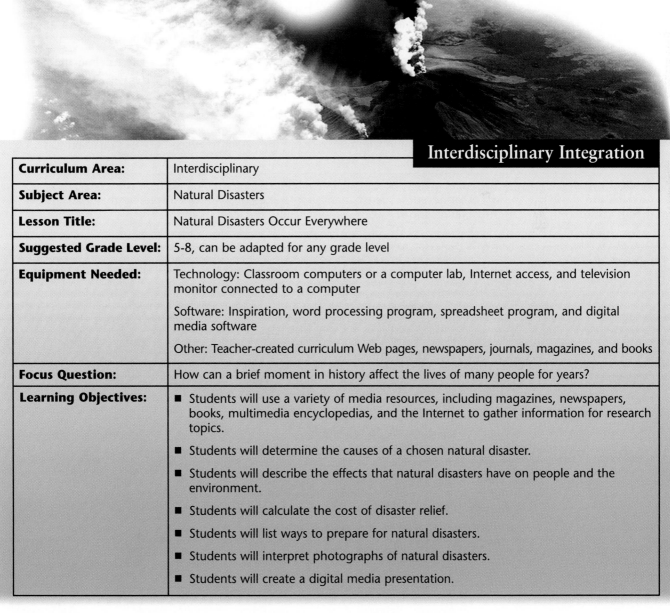

Interdisciplinary Integration

Curriculum Area:	Interdisciplinary
Subject Area:	Natural Disasters
Lesson Title:	Natural Disasters Occur Everywhere
Suggested Grade Level:	5-8, can be adapted for any grade level
Equipment Needed:	Technology: Classroom computers or a computer lab, Internet access, and television monitor connected to a computer
	Software: Inspiration, word processing program, spreadsheet program, and digital media software
	Other: Teacher-created curriculum Web pages, newspapers, journals, magazines, and books
Focus Question:	How can a brief moment in history affect the lives of many people for years?
Learning Objectives:	■ Students will use a variety of media resources, including magazines, newspapers, books, multimedia encyclopedias, and the Internet to gather information for research topics.
	■ Students will determine the causes of a chosen natural disaster.
	■ Students will describe the effects that natural disasters have on people and the environment.
	■ Students will calculate the cost of disaster relief.
	■ Students will list ways to prepare for natural disasters.
	■ Students will interpret photographs of natural disasters.
	■ Students will create a digital media presentation.

Figure 7-37 An interdisciplinary lesson plan for *Natural Disasters Occur Everywhere*.

(continued)

Instructions:	Introduce the task by asking the focus question. Allow several students to respond. Introduce the term natural disaster. Create a KWL chart to determine what students know about natural disasters and what they want to learn. Divide the class into groups of three or four students and have each group go to *ndrd.gsfc.nasa.gov* to select a natural disaster that they want to research. Distribute a predetermined assessment rubric and cover the evaluation procedures for the final project.
	Students will use the Internet and other resources to collect data on their chosen natural disaster. Students will use Inspiration to organize their data into a concept web; students should include information such as the type and cause of the natural disaster, where the disaster occurred, the effect on people and the environment, and the type of aid currently being sent.
	Students will find and save photographs that depict the effect the natural disaster had on people and the environment.
	Using the knowledge that they gained from their research, students will determine what type of aid they could put into a relief-care package for a family of four with a $100 budget. Students should also use the food pyramid as a guide to help choose healthy food items to include in their care package. Students will gather the prices of each item using newspaper ads, the Internet, and other available resources. They will use a spreadsheet program to calculate the cost of the care package with appropriate sales tax.
	Using the computer lab or classroom computers, students will create a culminating multimedia presentation to present their research findings and their plans for aiding the victims.
Evaluation of Content:	Teacher observation along with the project rubric will be used to evaluate this activity. Students will be evaluated on usage of the Web and other technology tools. The quality of research and information utilized and the extent to which the focus question was answered also will be assessed.
Evaluation of Curriculum Integration:	Students' ability to access, analyze, and apply information from different resources will be observed. Students' motivation and enthusiasm when creating the digital media presentation also will assist with evaluating the technology.

Figure 7-37 *(continued)*

Finding Funds to Support Classroom Technology Integration

One of the more difficult aspects of implementing technology in schools is finding and obtaining the funds for new technologies and the associated ongoing expenses. At present, many school districts do not have sufficient funding to incorporate technology at all levels throughout the district. For this reason, a classroom might not contain all the hardware and software to fully integrate technology and digital media into the curriculum.

Although the continued drop in computer and educational software prices lessens the problem, obtaining funding for classroom technology is still challenging. Many teachers, however, find that persistence often produces dramatic results. To increase the quantity and quality of technology in a classroom, a teacher first should ask the principal and other district administrators for additional classroom equipment and software. If you still need to obtain additional technology funding, you can turn to numerous other sources, including local school districts, public and private businesses, and government agencies.

FUND-RAISING DRIVES AND ACADEMIC CONTESTS

Class car washes, bake sales, and other activities can help raise money to purchase additional computers, hardware components, and software for classrooms. Local businesses such as banks, car dealerships, grocery stores, and department stores often respond to solicitations to improve the educational quality of the schools in their areas with donations. Corporations frequently are eager to become involved in active school technology programs — whether it is to contribute equipment, funds, or expertise. Teachers regularly write letters to local school business partners stating the school's needs to enlist their support. Even relatively small amounts of acquired funding can make a difference in the availability of technology in your classroom. Raising $100 will fund a new ink-jet printer, numerous educational CDs/DVDs, or a color scanner; $1000 will allow the purchase of a high-end multimedia computer with software, or several PDAs with software and accessories (Figure 7-38). Teachers should always get permission from the school's administration prior to raising funds.

WEB INFO

For more information about how to obtain equipment for your classroom, visit the Teachers Discovering Computers Web site (*scsite.com/tdc4*), click Chapter 7, click Web Info, and then click Free Equipment.

Figure 7-38
Teachers organize all kinds of class events, such as car washes and bake sales, to raise funds to purchase computers, printers, scanners, digital cameras, educational software, and other items for use in integrated classrooms.

Another way to obtain hardware and software for the classroom is to enter academic contests. Teachers can locate information about hundreds of academic contests on the Web and in educational journals and magazines.

Teachers should involve the community, especially parents, in fund-raising. The local school community holds its schools accountable for everything that goes on in the classroom, so enlisting the help of parents and business partners will broaden the base of support for the school's educational technology efforts. In addition, parents might have contacts or affiliations with local businesses or be able to provide further information on how to obtain funding. Another avenue for locating potential sources for technology funding is to showcase your classroom's use of technology for parents, business leaders, and school board members at your school's Parent Teacher Association (PTA), Parent Teacher Organization (PTO), or Parent Teacher Student Organization (PTSO) meetings.

Schools also should consider asking for volunteer services from the community in addition to or instead of asking for funds to pay for services. If funding for equipment maintenance is not available, for example, a local consultant might be willing to donate services. Many schools find that a combination of financial and volunteer support demonstrates the community's commitment to technology integration and strengthens the long-term community-school partnerships.

GRANTS

The majority of outside funding sources for technology fall under a general category called grants. **Grants** are funds provided by a funding source that transfers money, equipment, or services to the grantee. The **grantee** is the teacher, school, or organization to which the grant funds or equipment are transferred. Grants can be obtained from school districts, state Departments of Education, federal sources, foundations, and corporations. Grants range from a few hundred to millions of dollars. Many corporations maintain or support foundations that provide grants, both large and small, for creative projects.

To obtain a grant, a school district, school, or teacher must submit a grant proposal in response to a request for proposal (RFP). A **request for proposal (RFP)** is a document provided by the grant source that details the information teachers and schools need to provide to write a successful grant proposal. A **grant proposal** is the document the potential grantee sends to the funding source. Grant proposals can vary from a simple one-page application to an extensive multipage document.

When writing a grant, schools can take one of several approaches. A single person might write the grant proposal; teachers might write grant proposals with other teachers, media specialists, technology coordinators, curriculum resource specialist, and school district personnel; or if the proposal is extensive, the school districts might even employ a grant-writing specialist or consultant to write the proposal to increase the availability of technology in their classrooms.

The principal, curriculum resource specialist, and technology coordinator usually receive notification of grant opportunities. In addition, teachers can locate many grant opportunities on the Web (Figure 7-39). Teachers should always receive approval from school administration before applying for any grant.

WEB INFO

For more information about grant opportunities for educators, visit the Teachers Discovering Computers Web site (*scsite.com/tdc4*), click Chapter 7, click Web Info, and then click Grants.

Figure 7-39 Many Web sites provide teachers and administrators with current, extensive information on grants for education.

Creating a Curriculum Page

As you learned earlier in this chapter, curriculum pages are wonderful tools for enhancing your students' learning experience. The special feature at the end of Chapter 3 provided you with step-by-step instructions for creating a basic teacher's home page using Microsoft Word. The special feature that follows this chapter builds on your knowledge and enhances your Web page development skills by providing you with step-by-step instructions for creating a curriculum page using Word. In addition, you can download a similar step-by-step project that provides you with instructions on how to create a curriculum page in the latest version of Netscape Composer.

Summary of Evaluating Educational Technology and Integration Strategies

Technology will not make a difference in the quality of students graduating from K-12 schools unless teachers learn how to integrate the use of technology into their curriculum and use it as a tool to enhance learning. This chapter first introduced the various tools and resources teachers use to evaluate the appropriateness of educational technology and the effectiveness of technology integration. Next, a number of strategies were presented for integrating technology into one-computer classrooms and other K-12 instructional settings along with seven subject-specific curriculum integration activities. Finally, the chapter provided information on how to obtain funding to increase the availability of technology in your classroom.

In Brief

INSTRUCTIONS: In Brief summarizes the concepts presented in this chapter. To listen to the audio version of this In Brief, visit scsite.com/tdc4. Click Chapter 7 at the top of the Web page and then click In Brief on the left sidebar.

1. Evaluating Educational Technology

Evaluation of educational technology is important before instruction begins, during the instructional period, and after the instruction takes place. Educators can rely on a variety of resources to help them identify and evaluate the appropriateness of educational technologies, including resources available from school districts, state Departments of Education, professional educational organizations, catalogs, and Web sites.

2. Evaluating Software Applications

Teachers should evaluate software for appropriateness and accuracy of content and consider its relevance to curriculum learning objectives. Software evaluation rubrics help teachers evaluate educational software. A **rubric** is a detailed scoring guide for assessment, based on subjective stated criteria, that allows individuals to assess the quality of software or other items. A software evaluation rubric should list a number of important evaluation criteria, including content, documentation and technical support, ability and academic levels, technical quality, and ease of use.

3. Evaluating Web Resources

When evaluating a Web site as an instructional resource, teachers should consider characteristics such as authority, affiliation, audience, currency, and Web site design. **Authority** refers to the credibility of the author of the Web page or Web site. **Affiliation** refers to the professional organization, school, school district, university, company, or government office with which a particular Web site is connected. **Content** is the information provided on a Web page. The **audience** is the individual or group intended to view the Web page. **Currency** is a measure of how up to date, or timely, the Web page content is and how often it is updated.

4. Evaluating the Effectiveness of Technology Integration

When integrating technology, some teachers and schools are moving toward a nontraditional approach of student assessment, known as alternative assessment. **Alternative assessment** is using nontraditional methods to determine if students have mastered content and skill level. **Authentic assessment, project-based assessment,** and **portfolio assessment** refer to alternative ways to evaluate student performance to determine how well and in what way students are able to accomplish learning objectives and standards.

5. Evaluation Tools

When using authentic assessment, many teachers use checklists, rating scales, rubrics, and teacher observation. A **checklist** is a predetermined list of performance criteria. A **rating scale** is a more complex form of a checklist that lists a numerical value, or rating, for each criterion. A **rubric** is a detailed assessment tool that makes it easier for teachers to assess the quality of an item, such as a learning project. **Teacher observation** is when teachers actively observe their students during the learning process.

6. Evaluating Technology-Based Student Projects

Checklists, rating scales, and teacher observation are valid assessment tools for technology-based student projects. Curriculum goals and objectives should define and guide the selection and creation of the assessment tool. Student projects should be evaluated for content, planning, and creativity. Planning tools include flowcharts and concept maps. **Flowcharts** are diagrams that show the step-by-step actions that must take place through a sequence of events. A concept map or **story web** helps students use flowcharting to understand the attributes and relationships of the main subject and provides a visual tool for brainstorming and planning.

In Brief

7. Integration Strategies

To help meet the constant challenge of motivating students to learn, teachers must change their traditional roles to become facilitators of learning. Instructional strategies help teachers integrate technology into a one-computer classroom, a multicomputer classroom, and a computer lab. Most teachers will teach in a classroom with one multimedia computer, often referred to as the **one-computer classroom**. The most common usage of one computer is for classroom presentations and demonstrations. The most important advantage of using a computer lab is that all students are provided hands-on experience with using computer technology.

8. Curriculum Pages

Teachers who integrate the Internet successfully are utilizing it in ways to engage students in problem solving, finding research information, and developing higher-order thinking skills. Crucial to the successful use of the Internet in the classroom is supervising students and controlling Web activities by using curriculum pages. A **curriculum page** is a teacher-created document that contains hyperlinks to teacher-selected sites that have been evaluated for content and age appropriateness.

9. Creating Lesson Plans

To be successful when integrating technology, teachers must rethink and redesign activities and create new teaching and learning strategies. New technology tools require new instructional lessons. Teachers do not have to originate and create technology-enriched lesson plans and activities. They can find a multitude of lesson plans and activities at thousands of educational Web sites, which can be tailored to meet each teacher's needs. Many educational Web sites provide search engines that allow teachers to locate curriculum-specific lesson plans and activities for almost any K-12 curriculum area.

10. Finding Funds to Support Integration

Teachers can obtain funding for classroom technology from a number of sources, including people within their school district, businesses, private organizations, foundations, and the government. Class car washes, bake sales, and other activities raise money to purchase additional computers, other hardware components, and software for classrooms. Other ways to obtain these tools are to solicit corporate donations and enter academic contests.

11. Grants

The majority of outside funding sources for technology fall under a general category called grants. **Grants** are funds provided by a funding source that transfers money, equipment, or services to the grantee. The **grantee** is the teacher, school, or organization to which the grant funds or equipment are transferred. To obtain a grant, a school district, school, or teacher must submit a grant proposal in response to a request for proposal. A **request for proposal (RFP)** is a document provided by the grant source that details the information teachers and schools need to provide in order to write a successful grant proposal. A **grant proposal** is the document sent to the funding source.

Key Terms

INSTRUCTIONS: Use the Key Terms to help focus your study of the terms used in this chapter. To further enhance your understanding of the Key Terms in this chapter, visit scsite.com/tdc4. Click Chapter 7 at the top of the Web page and then click Key Terms on the left sidebar. Read the definition for each term and then access current and additional information about the term from the Web.

ability level [409]
academic level [409]
affiliation [410]
alternative assessment [414
appropriate [402]
arts curriculum [430]
assessment [414]
audience [411]
authentic assessment [414]
authentic learning [414]
authority [410]

block schedule [420]

checklist [415]
concept map [419]
content [411]
creativity [419]
cross-discipline lesson [441]
currency [411]
curriculum page [428]

design [411]
documentation [409]

e-folio [415]
ease of use [409]
EDTECH [405]
electronic portfolio [415]

embedded assessment [415]
evaluate [402]
exceptional education
    curriculum [439]

flowcharts [419]

grant proposal [444]
grantee [444]
grants [444]

Inspiration [419]
interdisciplinary curriculum [441]

KWLQS chart [425]

language arts curriculum [430]
learning process [411]

mathematics curriculum [433]

objectivity [411]
one-computer classroom [422]

physical education and health
    curriculum [436]
portfolio assessment [415]
project-based assessment [413]
project-based learning [415]
purpose [411]

rating scale [415]
reliable assessment [414J]
request for proposal (RFP) [444]
rubric [406]

science curriculum [435]
social studies curriculum [431]
software evaluation rubric [406]
special education curriculum [439]
storyboard [419]
story web [419]
student performance [414]
subject-integrated lesson [441]

teacher observation [417]
technical quality [409]
technical support [409]
technology conference [404]
traditional assessment [414]

valid [406]
visual learning technique [419]
vlog [429]

Web evaluation rubric [410]
Web scavenger hunt [426]

Checkpoint

INSTRUCTIONS: Use the Checkpoint exercises to check your knowledge level of the chapter. To complete the Checkpoint exercises interactively, visit scsite.com/tdc4. Click Chapter 7 at the top of the Web page and then click Checkpoint on the left sidebar.

1. Label the Figure

Instructions: Read each description in the grid that follows. Then identify the criteria category used to evaluate Web sites that the description describes.

1. _____ No author is listed and no e-mail contact is provided.	2. _____ It is unclear what institution supports this information.	3. _____ The purpose is unclear or cannot be determined.
4. _____ The Web page is a virtual soapbox.	5. _____ The information on the Web site does not relate to my objectives.	6. _____ The information will not challenge learners to think, reflect, discuss, compare, or classify.
7. _____ The Web pages are not appropriate for my audience.	8. _____ Information on the site has not been revised since 2003, or no date can be located.	9. _____ The Web site is not appropriate for my audience.

2. Matching

Instructions: Match each term from the column on the left with the best description from the column on the right.

_____ 1. curriculum page
_____ 2. request for proposal
_____ 3. checklist
_____ 4. evaluate
_____ 5. concept map

a. to determine the value or to judge the worth
b. provides a visual tool for brainstorming and planning
c. teacher-created document that contains hyperlinks to teacher-selected Web sites
d. predetermined list of performance criteria
e. a document provided by a grant source that details the information needed to write a grant

3. Short Answer

Instructions: Write a brief answer to each of the following questions.

1. Describe four resources where teachers can find information about how to evaluate educational software. Why is it important for teachers to evaluate software before using it in the classroom? _____

2. Should teachers evaluate Web resources for instructional value in the same way they evaluate print resources? Why or why not? _____

3. Describe three techniques for evaluating student technology projects. _____

4. Briefly describe three uses of technology in a one-computer classroom. Why does having more than one computer in a classroom allow for more flexibility and greater integration of technology? _____

5. Briefly describe grant funding for K-12 schools. Why are grants so important for many K-12 schools? Describe three ways in which teachers can obtain funding for classroom technology. _____

Teaching Today

INSTRUCTIONS: Teaching Today provides an appreciation of the value that technology and the Web have for K-12 education. Each numbered segment contains one or more links that reinforce the information presented in the segment. To display this page from the Web, visit scsite.com/tdc4. Click Chapter 7 at the top of the Web page and then click Teaching Today on the left sidebar.

1. Parent Teachers Organization

The Parent Teachers Organization (PTO) at your school has raised money to purchase software for all classes in your grade level. Your principal asks you to work with other teachers in your grade to make recommendations for software purchases to enhance the curriculum. Your principal asks you and the teachers to supply a wish list with seven to ten different titles, a detailed evaluation of each title, and pricing for each. Based on what you have learned in this chapter, what would be your next step in identifying appropriate software packages and then evaluating each? Where can you find software reviews? To what extent are these reviews helpful? What type of information can you gather about the software from these reviews? What kind of site-licensing and pricing are available for each package?

2. Classroom Computers

In your classroom, you may have one, two, or more computers. You may even have access to a wireless mobile lab. Although this is exciting, it presents new challenges for you as a teacher and for your students. No matter how many computers or technologies are available to you, effective class management is crucial and you have to plan and be well organized. One of the more difficult issues to manage is scheduling student use of various technologies. How would you set up your classroom to maximize the use of one, two, or more computers and how would you manage your class to ensure that all students get time on the computers? In what ways could you create learning communities in your classroom? Where could you locate ideas and suggestions to help you?

3. More Than One Curriculum Area

You teach students with special needs in a middle school. You want to integrate software applications into your curriculum to enhance your students' learning. You are looking for software applications that can be used in more than one curriculum area. You are familiar with programs such as PowerPoint and iLife and already are using them in different curriculum areas. Describe the ways in which two other applications described in this chapter can be used in more than one curriculum area. Test drive SimCity, a popular software program. Which curriculum areas can this type of software be used in? How would you integrate this type of software into your curriculum? What curriculum standards and related benchmarks could it help teach?

4. Evaluating Student Work

As you begin to integrate technology into your curriculum, you need alternative ways to assess student performance. In this chapter, you read about the rubrics that teachers use to assess performance. Itemize the key points to remember when evaluating student work. What alternative assessment tools can you use in your classroom? When is using alternative assessment tools most appropriate? When are other types of assessment tools most appropriate?

Education Issues

7

INSTRUCTIONS: Education Issues provides several scenarios that allow you to explore controversial and current issues in education. Each numbered segment contains one or more links that reinforce the information presented in the segment. To display this page from the Web, visit scsite.com/tdc4. Click Chapter 7 at the top of the Web page and then click Education Issues on the left sidebar.

1. Simulation Software

Increasingly sophisticated software applications not only have impacted business, entertainment, and recreation, but education as well. Simulation software gives students experience with designing a city, dissecting a frog, flying airplanes, saving a forest, or taking a virtual field trip. Many educators feel simulation software assists students in developing higher-order thinking skills and problem-solving skills. Opponents argue, however, that using these types of software merely leads students and does not help develop problem-solving skills. Eugene Thacker states that the use of simulation and the technologies that support simulation are a cultural trend, that they are more fashionable than educational, and that they are not a panacea that should replace good classroom instructional methodology. Do you agree with either side? Why or why not? Support your position with documentation. What advantages, if any, do simulation software applications offer? Do you think disadvantages might become evident when using the simulation software in the classroom? How might another application described in this chapter be used to teach higher-order thinking skills or problem-solving skills?

2. Video Games — Good or Bad?

There has been a lot of attention on whether video games are actually promoting aggressive behaviors in younger players. Studies have shown that many of today's youth spend up to 4–5 hours per day on computers. According to the Kaiser Family Foundation, 92% of American children play video games for 20 to 33 minutes per day. In his book, *What Video Games Have to Teach Us About Literacy and Learning*, James Gee is an outspoken advocate for the use of games to teach meta-learning principles. His research reveals even the so-called "shoot-em up" games can teach skills. On the other hand, there are those like Canadian psychology professor David Grossman who compares soldiers in training to children watching television. Grossman feels that both situations teach individuals to reject traditional values and create the illusion that the world is a dark and dangerous place. Grossman suggests that video games are increasingly desensitizing viewers — particularly children — to violence and has led a campaign in Canada to force media companies to become more accountable to this threat. Grossman is convinced that not only are media companies teaching violence but they are also teaching children to like it. What do you think? What implications might Grossman's campaign have on technology in education?

Education Issues

3. Evaluating Web Sites

A great deal of <u>information exists on the Internet</u> that is not what it appears to be. Sometimes, material seems authoritative and well written, but upon closer inspection, the material is biased, inaccurate, or out of date. Your school board feels it is a teacher's responsibility to teach students to recognize the quality and authority of information they find on the Internet. Do you agree or disagree? Why? How will you teach your students to do this? What criteria should students use when evaluating Web sites? Do students need to evaluate all Web sites? Support your answer with illustrations from existing Web sites.

4. Grants for Training

You locate a request for proposal (RFP) to fund a grant for notebook computers for all the teachers in your school. The grant will provide the notebook computers, but the school has to provide the teacher training. You want to develop the proposal with the help of the technology committee. You recognize this is a great opportunity to get technology into the hands of all teachers through the use of their own notebook computers. You think your school has an extremely good chance of being funded. The principal immediately says, "NO!" She feels the teachers should write grants only to obtain student computers. She also states that no funds are available for teacher training. Do you see a solution to this dilemma? What should you do? Where can you go to obtain more information and creative ideas for <u>writing the grant</u> and solving the <u>training issues</u>? How will you convince the principal that putting a notebook computer in each teacher's hands is an important initial step toward technology integration?

5. Alternative Assessment

Your first teaching job is at a very progressive new school that has technology in every classroom. During your college education, you learned a great deal about assessing student achievement through testing. You learned how to create appropriate traditional tests for subjects. This new school, however, has no traditional testing program. It has implemented an innovative approach to learning that uses only alternative assessment. No grades are assigned and all assessment is based on mastery learning. Do you think this is a good strategy? Support your position with reasons based on educational research. What <u>alternative assessment tools</u> can you use to meet the school's standards? Describe the advantages and disadvantages of this type of assessment.

Integration Corner

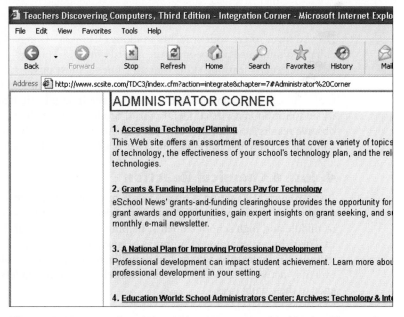

INSTRUCTIONS: Integration Corner provides extensive ideas and resources for integrating technology into your classroom-specific curriculum. To display this page from the Web and its links to approximately 100 educational Web sites, visit scsite.com/tdc4. Click Chapter 7 at the top of the Web page and then click Integration Corner on the left sidebar.

Integration Corner is designed for teachers and other educators who are looking for innovative ways to integrate technology into their content-specific curriculum. Integration Corner not only provides great Web sites with current information but also shows what other educators are doing in the field of educational technology. These Corners are designed for all educators regardless of their area of interest. Be sure to review information and Web sites outside of your teaching area because many great integration ideas in one area can be modified easily for use in other curricular areas.

Teachers and administrators will find other colleagues in their areas with whom to connect and share the successes and hurdles of integrating technology in a classroom or an entire school system. Consider Integration Corner your one stop for integration ideas and resources. Links to educational Web sites are organized in the following 12 Corners, and different Web resources are available for each chapter. Figure 7-40 shows examples of the Web resources provided in the Chapter 7 Administrator Corner.

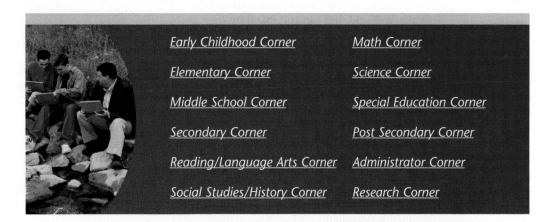

Early Childhood Corner   *Math Corner*

Elementary Corner   *Science Corner*

Middle School Corner   *Special Education Corner*

Secondary Corner   *Post Secondary Corner*

Reading/Language Arts Corner   *Administrator Corner*

Social Studies/History Corner   *Research Corner*

Figure 7-40 Examples of the Web resources provided in the Chapter 7 Administrator Corner.

Software Corner

INSTRUCTIONS: Software Corner provides information on popular software programs. Each numbered segment discusses specific software programs and contains a link to additional information about these programs. To display this page from the Web, visit scsite.com/tdc4. Click Chapter 7 at the top of the Web page and then click Software Corner on the left sidebar.

1. Inspiration

Inspiration is a powerful software product that allows students to think visually through webbing, concept mapping, and more. Inspiration provides students in grades 4-12 and beyond with the ability to organize and develop their thoughts before creating essays, reports, and presentations. Language arts teachers will find Inspiration an awesome writing and literature tool. History and science teachers can use Inspiration to create timelines and to plan research reports and projects. Inspiration can be integrated into all areas of the curriculum and will inspire your students to new heights!

2. Adobe Acrobat

Are you looking for a way to create professional documents that can be distributed electronically via various means including the Web and that can still maintain the integrity of images and formats that have been integrated using products like Adobe Photoshop, PageMaker, or other desktop publishing software? Adobe Acrobat is the perfect solution. Whether you are a novice just beginning to design formatted documents or a skilled designer, Adobe Acrobat helps you maintain control over how, when, and by whom your documents are accessed. Create and exchange documents, collect and compare comments, and tailor the security of a file in order to distribute your documents reliably and professionally.

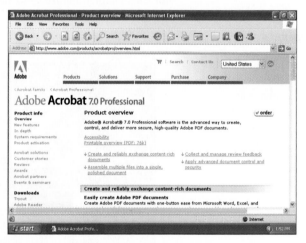

3. Thinkin' Things: Galactic Brain Benders

Do you want to get your students thinking? Thinkin' Things: Galactic Brain Benders is an enhanced multimedia version of the award-winning Thinkin' Things collection 3. Critical-thinking skills are crucial learning skills that all students must possess. Using higher-order thinking skills to solve problems and make decisions, your students organize and experiment with special-effects tools and can program a half-time show at the Intergalactic Rocket Bowl. Plus, they can alter gravity and motion in a virtual metal world! Students are challenged to imagine, test hypotheses, observe results, and develop conclusions. Additional Web-based challenges are provided to continue the fun and learning long after blast-off into the Galactic Brain Benders has started!

4. Just a Chemical Reaction

Just a Chemical Reaction is an awesome piece of software that lets you teach key facts and dates in the progress of chemistry. Because of its video game graphics, Just a Chemical Reaction will appeal to middle and high school students, helping them begin to understand chemistry before they realize it! The software contains 20 minutes of animated narration and 93 scientific concepts. It also includes 14 interactive activities and an illustrated periodic table. Just a Chemical Reaction uses everyday activities to which students can relate to better understand and explain chemistry's influence in their daily lives.

Digital Media Corner

INSTRUCTIONS: Today's K-12 digital students need their learning to be meaningful and relevant to their lives. Digital Media Corner provides videos, ideas, and examples of how you can use digital media to enhance your teaching and your students' learning. To access the videos and links to additional information, visit scsite.com/tdc4. Click Chapter 7 at the top of the Web page and then click Digital Media on the left sidebar.

1. At the Movies — LeapFrog

Ziff Davis Media's LeapFrog products are changing the way some children learn reading, writing, and arithmetic skills. LeapPads, a LeapFrog product, uses books embedded with NearTouch technology, which makes any part of a page touch-interactive. By using the special pen and touching it to words on the page, the voice program reads aloud the words. What are the pros and cons of using this technology to teach reading and math skills? To learn more about LeapFrog, click the G4TechTV video link. Locate your video and click the corresponding High-Speed or Dial-up link, depending on your Internet connection.

2. At the Movies — Internet Movie Database

You may have purchased and downloaded audio files, but have you considered buying and downloading a movie from the Internet? Two popular movie download sites are MovieLink and CinemaNow. What hardware and software do you need to download movies from the Internet? What kind of Internet connection will you need to download movies in a timely fashion? What impact might this service have for bringing educational movies to the classroom? To learn answers to these and other questions, click the G4TechTV video link. Locate your video and click the corresponding High-Speed or Dial-up link, depending on your Internet connection.

3. At the Movies — Stop Spam

You have set every possible mail control and blocked every unknown e-mail address, yet each day when you open your virtual mailbox, you find unwelcome advertisements. Besides setting your e-mail controls, what are some other steps you can take to stamp out spam? Why is this important in a classroom or lab environment? To learn more about stopping spam, click the G4TechTV video link. Locate your video and click the corresponding High-Speed or Dial-up link, depending on your Internet connection.

4. Digital Media in the Classroom

As you have learned throughout this textbook, digital media is everything from QuickTime movies to graphic design software applications. With so much information and technology out there, choosing the appropriate form of digital media to integrate in your curriculum can be intimidating. Evaluating digital media for appropriateness and usability is just like evaluating software, Web sites, and other technologies. The textbook presents guidelines for evaluating Web sites that include examining authority, affiliation, purpose and objectivity, content and learning process, audience and currency, and design of the digital media material encountered online, at a conference, or from peer educators. These guidelines are excellent for establishing the credibility of the digital media as well. The tools you use to conduct an evaluation of a Web site, a software application, or a digital media piece can be very similar; including the elements you evaluate!

5. Peer Evaluation of Student Projects

Many teachers believe that their main form of motivating students to participate in projects and activities is to use a project grade. An alternative assessment technique is to let student peers evaluate each other's projects. Digital media lends itself to the shared experience, in which all students can easily participate in the viewing of final projects. Teachers should develop a rubric for students to complete, including an area where peers can write constructive comments. After the students get the chance to review the peer evaluation, ask them to write a reflection about their project, discussing what they liked about it, what they might do differently, and what they learned from the peer evaluations.

Assistive Technologies Corner

INSTRUCTIONS: Assistive Technologies Corner provides information on current hardware, software, and peripherals that will assist you in delivering instruction to students with physical, cognitive, or sensory challenges. To access extensive additional information, visit scsite.com/tdc4. Click Chapter 7 at the top of the Web page and then click Assistive Technologies on the left sidebar.

1. How Can I Choose the Best Software for Students with Special Needs?

Many times, a student with significant physical or mental disabilities will come to the classroom with a technology plan as part of her IEP. When this is not the case, quality software will provide the best chance for success for a student with mild to moderate learning difficulties. To ensure a quality tool for a special needs user, the teacher might want to add some special considerations to the Software Evaluation Rubric (Figure 7-7) located in this chapter.

Technical Quality

1. Are captions available for video clips or audio files?
2. Will the software function using alternative input devices such as alternative keyboards?

Presentation of Information

1. Are directions presented using both visual and auditory means? Are directions intelligible with the sound turned off?
2. Is sufficient time given for the user to read and comprehend directions?
3. Are directions clear and are examples of user tasks provided?
4. Is text clear and easy to read? Does the user have control over size of text?

Content

1. Is content presented dependent on color, or only by a single mode (auditory or visual)?
2. Does content provide logical structures for information, and is the information presented using different structures?

2. How Can I Integrate Technology in the Special Needs Curriculum?

Integration activities for students with special needs enhance learning for all students. Exciting activities for learners with special needs may include some of the following.

Using **graphic organizing** tools (Inspiration, Kidspiration), students may
- Create a flowchart or timeline to plan their learning activities
- Create a similarities/differences chart for any new concept
- Create a concept map to demonstrate understanding

Using **digital video editing software** (iMovie, MovieMaker, and others), students may
- Create video clips to illustrate and share experiences
- Title or caption the video clips

Using **digital media tools** (KidPix, PowerPoint, and so on), students may
- Author and illustrate multimedia books to retell a story
- Prepare and illustrate researched information for presentation

Using **database tools** (AppleWorks, Microsoft Office), students may
- Collect and organize information such as a Zoo Animal database
- Create database reports or tables based on information for alternative presentation of information

3. Does Technology Enhance Learning for Students with Special Learning Needs?

Technology is a tool, not a cure for learning disabilities. Used with clearly planned learning goals and appropriate instructional strategies, almost all technology tools can help level the field for students with disabilities, providing equal access to the curriculum and opportunities for success.

Follow the instructions at the top of this page to display additional information and this chapter's links on assistive technologies.

In the Lab   7

INSTRUCTIONS: In the Lab provides curriculum page development exercises that are divided into two areas, productivity and integration. To access the links to tutorials, productivity ideas, integration examples and ideas, and more, visit scsite.com/tdc4. Click Chapter 7 at the top of the Web page and then click In the Lab on the left sidebar.

PRODUCTIVITY IN THE CLASSROOM

Introduction: As you have learned, many kinds of curriculum pages exist. For example, a curriculum page can serve as a guide, assisting students in locating quality information on the Internet. Teachers easily can create curriculum pages using a variety of software programs and Web editors. You already are familiar with using Microsoft Word to create Web pages, and Word is available on many home and school computers. In addition, Netscape, which includes the Web editor, Composer, can be downloaded free from the Web. Microsoft Publisher also can be used to create Web and curriculum pages. Some popular stand-alone Web editors used by educators include Adobe GoLive, Macromedia Dreamweaver, and Microsoft FrontPage.

Teachers can use curriculum pages in a variety of ways. One type of curriculum page is a list of annotated links focusing on one area of the curriculum or supporting one particular project. A curriculum page also can present students with a learning task, provide guidelines for how the task will be evaluated, and provide preselected Web sites that support the task.

Utilizing curriculum pages in the classroom provides many benefits. Students develop independent thinking and working skills, as well as higher-order thinking and problem-solving skills. Furthermore, preselecting Web sites maximizes the time students spend on the Internet and helps teachers to better supervise their students. Students also can create curriculum pages to provide evidence of their learning. This can be a powerful and exciting way for students to demonstrate their newly acquired knowledge and skills.

1. Creating and Formatting a Dental Health Curriculum Page

Problem: You are beginning a unit on dental health in your first-grade classroom. You want to create a curriculum page to use with the class to enhance the students' learning experience. Also, by using a curriculum page, the students will be able to go back and review Web sites after the unit is finished. The curriculum page is shown in Figure 7-41 on the next page. Open Microsoft Word, Netscape Composer, or any Web editing software and create the curriculum page as described in the following steps. Using the skills you learned by completing the special feature following Chapter 3, download the background and clip art image located on this chapter's special feature Web page (see page 463 for the Web page URL) or use any appropriate background and clip art image to personalize the page. (*Hint: use Help to understand the steps better.*)

Instructions: Perform the following tasks.

1. Insert the background image.
2. Display the first heading line, Let's Learn About Teeth, in 24-point Times or Times New Roman dark blue font.
3. Display the second heading line in 18-point Times or Times New Roman dark blue, bold font. Personalize the curriculum page by inserting your name instead of Ms. Yoshimura's name.
4. Insert a table with one row and two columns. Format the table to display as shown in Figure 7-41.
5. Insert an appropriate picture, image, or clip art graphic in the left column.
6. The two paragraphs and the bulleted list in the right column display in 14-point Times New Roman dark blue, bold font.
7. The line following the table and the bulleted list display in 14-point Times New Roman dark blue, bold font.

In the Lab

Figure 7-41

8. Link the words, About My Teeth, to http://www.ms-flossy.com/SmileysPlace. Link the words, The Tooth Fairy, to http://www.toothfairy.org/index.html. Link the words, Learning About Sealants, to http://www.ada.org/public/topics/sealants.asp. Link the words, 5 Steps to a Healthy Smile, to http://www.healthyteeth.org/prevention/5steps.html.

9. Save the curriculum page to the location and with a filename of your choice. Print the curriculum page and then follow your instructor's directions for handing in the assignment.

2. Creating and Formatting a Science Curriculum Page

Problem: Your eighth-grade science class has been studying the weather. As a final project, students must gather research and create a digital media presentation. You create a curriculum page to facilitate their research. The curriculum page is shown in Figure 7-42. Using the skills you learned by completing the special feature following Chapter 3, download the background and clip art image located on this chapter's special feature Web page (see page 463 for the Web page URL) or use any appropriate background and clip art image to personalize the page. (*Hint:* use Help to understand the steps better.)

Instructions: Insert the background image. Enter the first heading line in 24-point Times or Times New Roman font. Insert your name in place of Mr. Pawliger's name. Enter the subheading The Weather in 18-point Times or Times New Roman font. Insert a table with one row and two columns and format the table as shown in Figure 7-42. Insert a graphic in the left column of the table. The

In the Lab

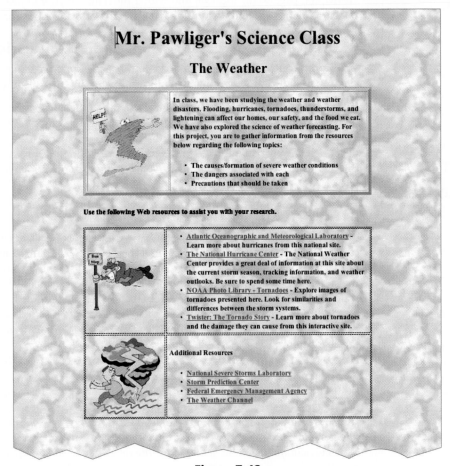

Figure 7-42

text and bulleted list in the right column display in 12-point Times New Roman bold font. The line immediately below the table displays in 12-point Times New Roman bold font.

Insert a table with two rows and two columns to help organize the links. Format the table to display as shown in Figure 7-42. (*Hint:* format the table to display without borders.) The text and bulleted lists display in 12-point Times New Roman bold font. Insert graphics and create the hypertext links using the Web site addresses (URLs) listed in the following table.

Internet Resources

Linked Text	Web Site
Atlantic Oceanographic and Meteorological Laboratory	www.aoml.noaa.gov
National Hurricane Center	www.nhc.noaa.gov
NOAA Photo Library - Tornadoes	www.photolib.noaa.gov/nssl/tornado1.html
Twister: The Tornado Story	whyfiles.org/013tornado/index.html
National Severe Storms Laboratory	www.nssl.noaa.gov
Storm Prediction Center	www.spc.noaa.gov
Federal Emergency Management Agency	www.fema.gov
The Weather Channel	www.weather.com

In the Lab

After you have typed and formatted the curriculum page, save the curriculum page to the location and with a file name of your choice. Print the curriculum page and then follow your instructor's directions for handing in the assignment.

3. Creating and Formatting a Subject-Specific Curriculum Page

Problem: You want to create a curriculum page to support a concept you are teaching in your classroom and to provide students with preselected Internet resources.

Instructions: Create a curriculum page similar to the curriculum page illustrated in Figure 7-42 on the previous page. Use appropriate layouts, font types, font styles, font sizes, and clip art images. Include your name and the subject area you teach. After you have created the curriculum page, save the curriculum page to the location of your choice using an appropriate filename. Print the curriculum page, and then follow your instructor's directions for handing in the assignment.

INTEGRATION IN THE CLASSROOM

1. While studying the fifty states, you have your elementary students work in pairs to design and create a curriculum page about the state of their choice. They are to include their names and the name of the state at the top of the curriculum page. They also will include a graphic of either the state or the state flag, a brief paragraph about the state, and a bulleted list that includes the state capital, state bird, and state flower. The students then will include three links to Internet resources that provide additional information about their state. Create a sample curriculum page for your students using the state of your birth or the state in which you currently live. Include your name on the curriculum page.

2. To help your middle school language arts students develop reading, vocabulary, and writing skills and increase their awareness of community and global issues, you begin a unit using newspapers in your classroom. You arrange for local newspapers to be donated to your classroom so each student has a copy. You also have students explore local newspapers and news sources online. You direct students to select an article from either a local newspaper or an online news source and create a curriculum page that summarizes the news item and contains at least three links to Internet resources that support or give further information on their selected topic. Students will present their curriculum pages to the class and you will have them posted on your school's server so all students can access the information. Create a sample curriculum page for your students. Include your name and school at the top of the curriculum page. Include your e-mail address and the current date at the bottom of the curriculum page.

3. Your music class has been studying famous composers. To prepare for the end-of-unit exam, you divide the students into five groups and have each group research one composer. The groups then create a curriculum page that other students use as they study. On their curriculum pages, students are required to include a graphic image, a brief paragraph about the composer, a bulleted list of the titles of at least five famous pieces, and at least four annotated links to Web resources. The curriculum pages will be placed on the computers in the classroom, media center, and computer lab. In addition, you will post the curriculum pages on the Web to assist the students in studying at home. Select a famous composer and create a sample curriculum page for your students. Include your name on your curriculum page. Include your e-mail address and the current date at the bottom of the curriculum page.

Learn It Online

INSTRUCTIONS: Use the Learn It Online exercises to reinforce your understanding of the chapter concepts and increase your computer, information, and integration literacy. To access dozens of interactive student labs, practice tests, learning games, and more, visit scsite.com/tdc4. Click Chapter 7 at the top of the Web page and then click Learn It Online on the left sidebar.

1. Evaluating Internet Resources

Evaluating information found on the World Wide Web is a critical skill that teachers and students must possess. Click the Evaluating Internet Resources link to complete an exercise and learn how to evaluate the quality of Internet resources.

2. Rubrics

Designing effective evaluation tools to assess student learning requires thought and preparation. One popular assessment tool is an assessment rubric. Click the Rubrics link to complete an exercise on how to create effective rubrics.

3. Expanding Your Understanding

Concept maps, flowcharts, story webs, storyboards, and other graphic organizers assist students with visualizing concepts and organizing information. Click the Expanding Your Understanding link to learn more about these concepts.

4. Practice Test

Click the Practice Test link. Answer each question. When completed, enter your name and click the Grade Test button to submit the quiz for grading. Make a note of any missed questions. If required, submit your score to your instructor.

5. Who Wants to Be a Computer Genius?

Click the Computer Genius link to find out if you are a computer genius. Directions about how to play the game will be displayed. When you are ready to play, click the Play button. If required, submit your score to your instructor.

6. Wheel of Terms

Click the Wheel of Terms link to reinforce important terms you learned in this chapter by playing the Shelly Cashman Series version of this popular game. Directions about how to play the game will be displayed. When you are ready to play, click the Play button. If required, submit your score to your instructor.

7. Crossword Puzzle Challenge

Click the Crossword Puzzle link. Complete the puzzle to reinforce skills you learned in this chapter. Directions about how to play the game will be displayed. When you are ready to play, click the Play button. If required, submit the completed puzzle to your instructor.

Creating a Curriculum Page Using Microsoft Word

As you have learned, many different kinds of curriculum pages exist, and you can use them many different ways. Curriculum pages should provide students with quality Internet resources that will enhance their learning of a particular concept. In addition, students should be able to gather information, learn more about a concept, and use Web resources to help prepare for a task. Instead of listing all information on one page, making it very long and intimidating, many teachers elect to create separate pages and link them to their home page. You link two pages together by creating a hyperlink between the two pages, also called a **relative link**. The result is that you create a **Web site**, which is a group of related HTML documents linked together.

This special feature provides you with step-by-step instructions on how to create a curriculum page that provides students with assignment information and Web links for a five-day period. The Web page, Mr. Handley's Home Page, which you created in the special feature that followed Chapter 3, will be used as the home page in this project. If you have not done so, you need to create the Web page detailed in the special feature following Chapter 3 before starting this project.

In this project, you will use many features of Microsoft Word to create a curriculum page, called Mr. Handley's American History Class, which is linked to Mr. Handley's Home Page that you created earlier (Figure 1). Recall that Mr. Handley is a history teacher at Ridgedale High School. You will find it helpful to refer to Figure 1 to see the completed Web page as you work through this project. Included in this special feature are step-by-step instructions for using Word 2003 (part of Office 2003) installed on a PC. You also can create this project using Word 2002/2000 installed on a PC or Word installed on a Macintosh computer; however, you might encounter slight variations from the step-by-step instructions in this project.

[b] Mr. Handley's American History Class curriculum page

FIGURE 1

[a] Mr. Handley's Home Page

As you learned, another popular and very easy-to-use program for creating Web and curriculum pages is Netscape Composer, which is included with Netscape Communicator. If you do not have Netscape Communicator installed on your home or school computer, you can download a free copy from the Web. Detailed step-by-step instructions for completing this project in the latest version of Netscape Composer are available to download and print from the World Wide Web at *scsite.com/tdc4*, click the Chapter 7 link, and then click the link for the Special Feature. (This is the same Web site that you will use later in this project to download graphics).

In this project, you will learn how to download graphics from the World Wide Web, open a new Web page to create your curriculum page, select a background image, create a title, insert and format text and headings, insert a horizontal line graphic and other graphics, use tables to organize assignment information, create numerous links to teacher-selected and evaluated history Web sites, and save your curriculum page. Next, you will open your previously created Web page, Mr. Handley's Home Page, and link the home page to your curriculum page. You will need to access the location on which you saved the Web page, Mr. Handley's Home Page. This project assumes that you possess basic word-processing skills and have completed the Mr. Handley's Home Page project. You might find it useful to review the step-by-step instructions that you used to create Mr. Handley's Home Page.

Downloading Image Files

Clip art images are graphical images you can use on Web and curriculum pages. This project requires you to download three graphics from the Web, including one you will use for the curriculum page background. Using procedures learned earlier, perform the following steps to download three image files.

Steps to Download Image Files

 Start your browser, type the URL `scsite.com/tdc4` in the Address text box, press the ENTER key, click Chapter 7, and then click the link for the Special Feature.

 When the textbook Web page for this special feature appears, right-click the flags background image, and then click Save Picture As on the shortcut menu.

 When the Save As dialog box opens, click the Save in box arrow, use the Look in box arrow to navigate to the location where you saved Mr. Handley's Home page. Select that file, and then click the Save button.

 Repeat Steps 2 and 3 to download two additional images: the yellow star and the horizontal line images.

 Close your browser.

Three additional image files are saved to the selected location.

Starting Microsoft Word and Opening a New Web Page

Perform the following steps to start Word and open a new Web page, so you can begin developing Mr. Handley's American History Class curriculum page.

Steps to Start Word and Open a New Web Page

 Start Word.

 Click File on the menu bar, and then click New When the New Document task pane is displayed, click the Web page button (Blank Web Page in Word 2002).

 If the Word Window is not maximized, double-click its title bar to maximize it. If necessary, click the Font Size box arrow on the Formatting toolbar and then click 12 in the Font Size listto change the font size to 12.

Word is opened and displays a new blank Web page (Figure 2). Depending on the computer you are working on, the default font size might display 10 or 12. Font size 12 is required for this Web page.

FIGURE 2

Inserting a Background Image and Entering and Formatting a Title

Recall that the background of a Web page is created by tiling a small graphic image many times across the page. For this project, you will use the flags background image that you downloaded as the background for this Web page. Perform the following steps to insert a background image.

Steps to Insert a Background Image

1 **Click Format on the menu bar, point to Background, and then click Fill Effects on the Background submenu. When the Fill Effects dialog box opens, click the Picture tab, and then point to the Select Picture button.**

Word displays the Picture sheet in the Fill Effects dialog box (Figure 3).

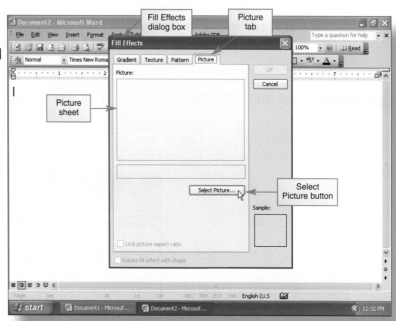

FIGURE 3

2 **Click the Select Picture button. When the Select Picture dialog box opens, if necessary, click the Look in box arrow and then select the location to which you saved the images. Double-click the flags background image, and then click the OK button in the Fill Effects dialog box.**

Word tiles the flags image across the Web page (Figure 4).

FIGURE 4

Entering and Formatting a Title

Perform the following steps to enter and format a title for the curriculum page.

Steps to Enter and Format a Title

 Type `Mr. Handley's American History Class` **and then press the** ENTER **key.**

 Select the text just entered, click the Font Size box arrow on the Formatting toolbar, and then click 26 in the Font Size list. With the text still selected, click the Bold button, and then click the Center button on the Formatting toolbar.

 Click below and to the left of the text to position the insertion point at the beginning of the next line.

The formatted title text appears as shown in Figure 5.

FIGURE 5

Inserting a Horizontal Line, a Heading, and Text

Next, you will enter a curriculum-appropriate and colorful horizontal line that you downloaded from the Web. You then will enter a curriculum-descriptive heading and text. Recall that horizontal lines are used to set apart different sections of a Web page. Perform the following steps to insert a horizontal line.

Steps to Insert a Horizontal Line

 Press the ENTER **key and then click the Center button on the Formatting toolbar.**

 Click Insert on the menu bar, point to Picture, and then click From File on the Picture submenu.

When the Insert Picture dialog box opens, if necessary, click the Look in box arrow and then navigate to the location where you saved the images. Double-click the horizontal line image.

Word inserts the horizontal line graphic centered at the insertion point (Figure 6). The horizontal line might display differently than shown depending on the computer you are working on and the version of Word you are using.

FIGURE 6

Entering a Heading

Next, you will enter a heading that describes the week's history topic.

Steps to Enter a Heading

 Press the ENTER key twice and make sure the insertion point still is centered.

 Type The Civil War **and then press the ENTER key.**

 Select the text just entered, click the Font Size box arrow on the Formatting toolbar, and then click 22 in the Font Size list. Click the Bold button on the Formatting toolbar.

 With the text still selected, click the Font Color box arrow on the Formatting toolbar, and then click the color Red (row 3, column 1) on the Font color palette.

 Click below the text you just entered to position the insertion point centered on the next line.

Word displays the heading centered, bold, in red, and in font size 22 (see Figure 7 on the next page). The insertion point appears centered on the next line.

Entering Text

Perform the following steps to enter the text that provides students with information concerning the dates of the assignments, group projects, and more.

Steps to Enter Text

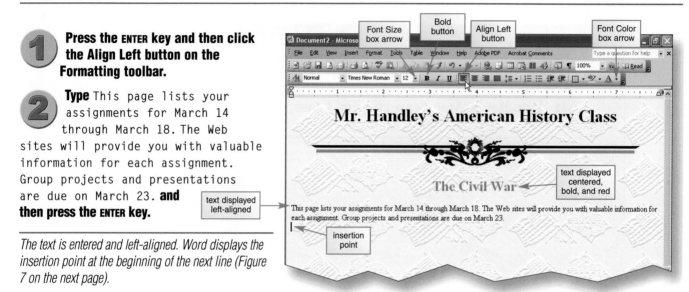

1 **Press the ENTER key and then click the Align Left button on the Formatting toolbar.**

2 **Type** This page lists your assignments for March 14 through March 18. The Web sites will provide you with valuable information for each assignment. Group projects and presentations are due on March 23. **and then press the ENTER key.**

The text is entered and left-aligned. Word displays the insertion point at the beginning of the next line (Figure 7 on the next page).

FIGURE 7

Inserting a Table

A Word **table** is a collection of rows and columns. The intersection of a row and column is called a **cell**. Using tables is a great way to organize and align information on a Web page. Word allows you to manipulate tables in many ways, including arranging rows and columns, changing column widths, typing text and inserting graphics in individual cells, and formating individual cells or the entire table with different colors and shadings. Sometimes, teachers completely remove the borders so all you see is the organized text and graphics. To learn more about using Word tables, use the Word Help system. Perform the following steps to insert a table.

Steps to Insert a Table

1 **Press the ENTER key. Click Table on the menu bar, point to Insert, and then click Table on the Insert submenu. When Word displays the Insert Table dialog box, type** 2 **in the Number of columns text box. Press the TAB key and then type** 4 **in the Number of rows text box. Point to the OK button.**

Word displays the Insert Table dialog box, 2 displays in the Number of columns text box, and 4 displays in the Number of rows text box (Figure 8).

FIGURE 8

Click the OK button.

Word inserts an empty table with 2 columns and 4 rows into the Web page. The insertion point displays in the first cell (row 1, column 1) of the table (Figure 9).

FIGURE 9

Formatting a Table

Word allows users to do many things with tables, including centering a table on a page, changing column widths, entering and formatting text and graphics, creating bulleted lists, inserting hyperlinks, formatting cells, and much, much more. The easiest way to move from cell to cell in a table is to use the Tab key.

Centering a Table and Changing Column Widths

Perform the following steps to center the table on the page and change the width of the columns.

Steps to Center a Table and Change Column Widths

1 **Position the mouse pointer over the Table Move handle just outside the upper-left corner of the table, and click to select the entire table. After the entire table is selected, click the Center button on the Formatting toolbar.**

2 **Click in the first cell of the first row to remove the selection.**

3 **Position the mouse pointer on the border between the two columns and then drag the border until it is positioned as shown in Figure 10 (at the 2" mark on the ruler).**

Word centers the table and changes the width of both columns (Figure 10). To center a table on the page, the entire table must be selected.

FIGURE 10

Entering and Formatting the Column Headings

Next, you will enter the column headings, center the column headings, and shade the cells containing the column headings.

Steps to Enter and Format the Column Headings

 Make sure the insertion point is in the first cell (row 1, column 1), type `Day`, and then press the TAB key. Type `Assignment` in the second cell in the heading row (row 1, column 2).

 Click in the margin to the left of the first row to select only row 1. Click the Bold button and then click the Center button on the Formatting toolbar.

 With the row still selected, click Format on the menu bar, and then click Borders and Shading.

 When the Borders and Shading dialog box opens, click the Shading tab, click Gray-15% on the Fill color palette (row 1, column 5), and then click the OK button.

 Click in the first cell in the second row to remove the selection.

The column headings appear bold, centered, and shaded gray (Figure 11).

FIGURE 11

Inserting a Graphic and Text

Next, you will enter a star graphic and a short description for Monday's assignment.

Steps to Insert a Graphic and Text

 With the insertion point in the first cell of the second row, click Insert on the menu bar, point to Picture, and then click From File on the Picture submenu.

2 When Word displays the Insert Picture dialog box opens, if necessary, click the **Look in** box arrow and then navigate to the location where you saved the images. Double-click the yellow star image.

3 Press the **SPACEBAR**, and then type `Monday: Events Leading To the Civil War` **as the daily topic in column 1.**

Word inserts the star graphic, and the text is entered (Figure 12).

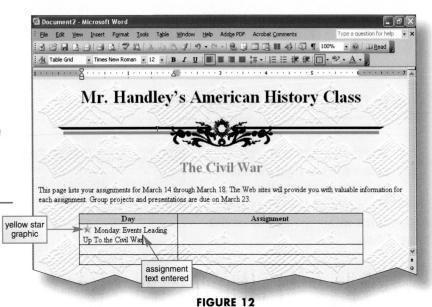

FIGURE 12

Entering Assignment Information

Next, you will enter the assignment information for Monday's assignment. You will create a bulleted list, indent bullets, and create hyperlinks to teacher-selected Web sites. Perform the following steps to enter the text.

Steps to Enter Assignment Information

1 Press the **TAB** key to position the insertion point in the second cell in row 2. Type `Read pp. 234-255 in your textbook. Be prepared to discuss the chapter readings and the following Web sites in class on Monday and Tuesday:` **and then press the ENTER key.**

2 Type `A Nation Divided` **and then press the ENTER key.** Type `President Lincoln's First Inaugural Address` **and then press the ENTER key.**

3 Type `Based upon classroom discussions and chapter readings, write a one-page reflection on slavery and the abolitionists during the time leading up to the Civil War. The reflection is due on Wednesday.` **as the final text entry.** **Do not press the ENTER key; doing so would insert a blank line.**

The text appears in the second cell of the second row (Figure 13).

FIGURE 13

Creating a Bulleted List in a Table

Perform the following steps to format the text you just entered as a bulleted list and then indent two of the text entries.

Steps to Create a Bulleted List in a Table

1 Select all of the text just entered in the right column of the second row and then click the Bullets button on the Formatting toolbar. Click within the cell to remove the selection.

Word formats the text as a bulleted list (Figure 14). The bullet style might be different depending on the computer you are working on and the version of Word you are using.

FIGURE 14

2 Select the second and third bullets. Click the Increase Indent button on the Formatting toolbar. Click within the cell to remove the selection.

Word increases the indent of the two lines of text and changes the bullet style (Figure 15). The bullet style might be different depending on the computer you are working on and the version of Word you are using.

FIGURE 15

If you want to change the bullet style, select the entire bulleted list, right-click the list, and then click Bullets and Numbering on the shortcut menu. When the Bullets and Numbering dialog box opens, if necessary, click the Bulleted tab. Click the desired bullet style and then click the OK button in the Bullets and Numbering dialog box.

Creating Links to Web Sites

Recall that curriculum pages contain links to Web sites that have been evaluated by the teacher to ensure they are appropriate and meet curriculum standards and related benchmarks. Perform the following steps to link text entries to Web sites by entering the Web site's Uniform Resource Locator (URL).

Steps to Create Links to Web Sites

 Select the first text entry to be linked, A Nation Divided, and then click the Insert Hyperlink button on the Standard toolbar.

 When the Insert Hyperlink dialog box opens, click the Existing File or Web Page button on the Link to bar if it is not selected, type `http://www.historyplace.com/civilwar` **in the Address text box, and then click the OK button. In Word 2000, type the URL in the Type the file or Web page name text box that is located below the Text to display text box.**

 Repeat the procedures in Steps 1 and 2 to link the text entry, President Lincoln's First Inaugural Address, using the following URL: `http://showcase.netins.net/web/creative/lincoln/speeches/linaug.htm`

Word links the text to the Web pages at the URLs you entered and displays the linked text as underlined and in the default color blue (Figure 16).

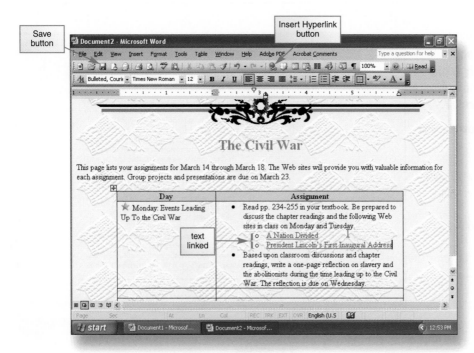

FIGURE 16

Saving a Web Page and Completing the Table

As you know, it is a good practice to save your documents regularly to eliminate retyping information in the event of a power or computer failure. To save the curriculum page to the selected location using the filename, Assignment, perform the following steps.

Steps to Save a Web Page

 Click the Save button on the Standard toolbar.

 When the Save As dialog box opens, click the Change Title button. Change the title to `March 14-18 Assignments` **in the Page title text box, and then click the OK button.**

 Type `Assignment` **in the File name text box.**

 Click the Save as type box arrow and then click Web Page (*.htm; *html). If necessary, click the Save in box arrow, navigate to the same location where you saved the images in the Look in list, and then click the Save button in the Save As dialog box.

Completing the Table

Using the procedures presented on pages 470 through 473, enter the yellow star graphic and the text for Wednesday's short description. Enter and format the text for Wednesday's assignment information.

Steps to Complete Wednesday's Assignment Information

 If necessary, click the scroll bar to see row 3 of the table and then add Wednesday's daily topic and assignment information in both cells of the third row, as shown in Figure 17.

Create links using the following text and URLs:

`Battle of Gettysburg: http: //www. americancivilwar.com/getty.html.` **and** `Battle of Fort Sumter: http: //www. civilwarhome.com/ ftsumter.htm`

Wednesday's daily topic and assignment information is entered and formatted (Figure 17).

FIGURE 17

Using the procedures presented on pages 470 through 473, enter the yellow star graphic and text for Friday's daily topic and then enter and format the text for Friday's assignment information.

Steps to Complete Friday's Assignment Information

 If necessary, click the scroll bar to see the final row of the table. Complete the table, as shown in Figure 18.

 Create links using the following text and URLs:

```
Gettysburg Address: http://lcweb.loc.gov/exhibits/gadd/
Gettysburg National Military Park: http://www.nps.gov/gett/index.htm
The American Civil War Homepage: http://www.sunsite.utk.edu/civil-war
The Valley of the Shadow: http://jefferson.village.virginia.edu/vshadow2
Civil War Medicine: http://www.civilwarhome.com/civilwarmedicineintro.htm
Rose O'Neal Greenhow Papers: http://scriptorium.lib.duke.edu/greenhow
```

Friday's daily topic and assignment information is entered and formatted (Figure 18).

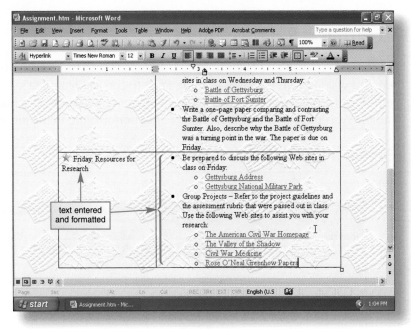

FIGURE 18

Checking Spelling and Saving the Web Page

Before you hyperlink the curriculum page you have created, you should check it for spelling and grammar errors and then save it. Perform the following steps to check spelling and correct any errors and then save your curriculum page.

Steps to Check Spelling and Save the Web Page

 Press CTRL+HOME to display the top of the curriculum page and then click the Spelling and Grammar button on the Standard toolbar. Correct any errors.

Click the Save button on the Standard toolbar.

Opening a Previously Created Web Page

After you have created and saved a Web page, you can open the Web page and revise it at any time, just like any other Word document. The following steps show how to open a previously created Web page so you can hyperlink Mr. Handley's Home Page to Mr. Handley's American History Class curriculum page.

Steps to Open a Previously Created Web Page

 Click File on the menu bar, and then click Open.

 When the Open dialog box opens, if necessary, click the Look in box arrow, navigate to and select the desired location, and then double-click the file, MrHandley.

Word displays the MrHandley Web page that you created previously in a Word window.

Editing a Web Page and Creating a Relative Link

The curriculum page that you created in this project will be linked to Mr. Handley's Home Page. First, you will edit Mr. Handley's Home Page and then you will link Mr. Handley's Home Page to the Mr. Handley's American History Class curriculum page using the Insert Hyperlink button. Recall that the hyperlink between two pages of a Web site is called a **relative link**. To edit a Web page and create a relative link, perform the following steps.

Steps to Edit a Web Page and Create a Relative Link

1 **Click to the right of the On-This-Day link and then press the ENTER key twice to position the insertion point.**

2 **Type** Weekly Assignments **and then press the ENTER key. Select the text just entered and then click the Font Size box arrow on the Formatting toolbar. Click 14 in the Font Size list. Click below the text entry to position the insertion point.**

The text is inserted and formatted. The insertion point appears below the Weekly Assignments text (Figure 19).

FIGURE 19

Press the ENTER key twice and then press the UP ARROW key once. Type March 14-18 **and then select the text just entered. Click the Insert Hyperlink button on the Standard toolbar.**

Word displays the Insert Hyperlink dialog box.

 If necessary, click the Existing File or Web Page button on the Link to bar. If necessary, click the Look in box arrow, navigate to and select the desired location, click Assignment, and then point to the OK button. In Word 2000, click the File button in the Browse for area. When the Link to File dialog box opens, if necessary, click the Look in box arrow, navigate to and select the desired location, and then double-click Assignment.

Word displays the files stored at the selected location and the Assignment Web page is selected (Figure 20).

 Click the OK button.

Word inserts a hyperlink for the selected text to the Assignment Web page and the selected text displays as underlined and in the default color blue (Figure 21).

FIGURE 20

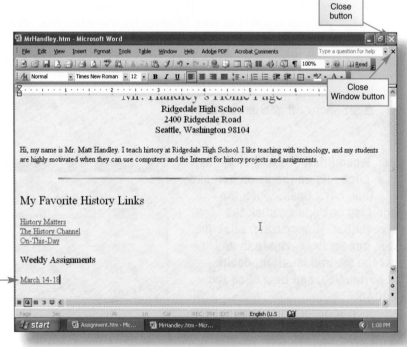

FIGURE 21

Saving and Quitting Word

Perform the following steps to save the changes you made to Mr. Handley's Home Page and then quit Word.

Steps to Save and Quit Word

 Click the Save button on the Standard toolbar.

 Click the Close Window button in the upper-right corner of the Word window to close Mr. Handley's Home Page (see Figure 21 on the previous page).

 Click the Close button in the upper-right corner of the title bar of the Word window to close the Assignment Web page and Word.

The additions you made to Mr. Handley's Home Page are saved. Word closes and the Windows desktop appears.

Checking Your Relative Link and Previewing Your Curriculum Page

Congratulations, you now have created a Web site using Word. You have linked Mr. Handley's Home Page to your newly created Assignment Web page using a relative link. Perform the following steps to preview the curriculum page you just created in your browser by using the link on Mr. Handley's Home Page.

Steps to Check Your Relative Link and Preview Your Curriculum Page

 Start Microsoft Internet Explorer.

 When Internet Explorer opens, click File on the menu bar, and then click Open. When the Open dialog box opens, click the Browse button. If necessary, click the Look in box arrow, navigate to and select the desired location, double-click MrHandley, and then click the OK button.

Internet Explorer displays Mr. Handley's Home Page (Figure 22).

Web page displays in browser window

link to Assignment Web page

FIGURE 22

Click the relative hyperlink March 14-18.

Note: If necessary click Yes to allow blocked content.

Internet Explorer displays Mr. Handley's American History Class Web page (Figure 23).

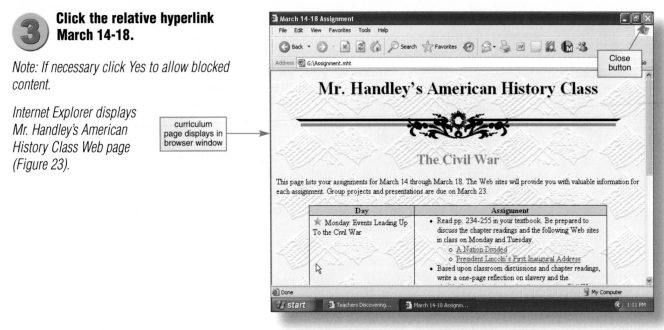

FIGURE 23

Quitting Internet Explorer

With your Web site created and previewed, your project is complete. To quit Internet Explorer, perform the following steps.

Steps to Quit Internet Explorer

1

Click the Close button in the upper-right corner of the Internet Explorer title bar (see Figure 23).

Both windows close and the Windows desktop is displayed.

As you have learned, you do not have to be a programmer to create Web and curriculum pages and link them together. Word provides a wealth of Web page creation tools. In addition, you will find that applying basic formatting options and using numerous other design techniques can help you easily create a variety of curriculum and Web pages. The following sections describe a few of the techniques and tools that you might find useful as you increase your Web development skills using Word.

Publishing Web Pages to a Web Server

You do not have to publish your Web and curriculum pages to a Web server to integrate effectively the multitude of resources available on the Internet in your classroom curriculum. You can have your students access your curriculum pages stored on the hard disks on the computers in your classroom, network drives, or removable drives. You also can create shortcuts to your Web and curriculum pages directly on the desktop of your PC or Macintosh classroom computers.

WEB INFO

To access a free Web site that allows teachers to publish their Web and curriculum pages, visit the Teachers Discovering Computers Web site (*scsite.com/tdc4*), click Chapter 7, click Web Info, and then click Web Publishing.

Publishing your Web and curriculum pages to a Web server, however, allows your students, their parents, and other teachers to access your curriculum materials, schedules, lessons, homework assignments, and more at anytime and from any Internet-enabled device. In Word, you can use the Save as Web Page command on the File menu to save your Web and curriculum pages on your school's Web server or on your Internet service provider's (ISP) Web server. Many schools and ISPs also provide tools and/or techniques that you can use to publish Web pages on their servers. Many free education Web sites also provide space for teachers to store their Web and curriculum pages. You can get help to publish your pages from many sources, including your instructor and your school's technology coordinator. Most universities and ISPs have Help desks that you can call to obtain information on how to publish your Web pages. In addition, most universities, ISPs, and free education Web sites provide tutorials at their Web sites that you can use to learn how to publish your Web and curriculum pages on their servers.

Saving Word Documents as Web Pages

In addition to creating curriculum and other Web pages starting with a blank Web page, Word also allows you to save any existing Word document as a Web page.

Saving a Word Document as a Web Page

Perform the following steps to save a Word document as a Web page.

Steps to Save a Word Document as a Web Page

 Start Word and open any Word document.

 Click File on the menu bar, and then click Save as Web Page.

 When the Save As dialog box opens, type the Web page name in the File name text box and then select the location where you want to save the Web page.

 Click the Save button in the Save As dialog box.

 Close Word.

Word saves the Word document as a Web page and displays it in Web Layout view after you perform Step 4.

Creating a Curriculum Page Without Typing URLs

Many URLs can be long and it is very easy to make mistakes when typing them into a Web browser. In Word, you can create a curriculum page without having to type URLs. Recall that curriculum pages can be simple or detailed. Often, teachers want to create a quick curriculum page, such as the one shown in Figure 7-27a on page 428. A basic curriculum page with teacher-evaluated links is valuable to both teachers and students. It allows students to access those pages in class without having to type lengthy URLs. Creating hyperlinks without having to type URLs is quick and easy to do; they can be created in a matter of minutes from your list of favorites or bookmarked sites. You and your students can use two techniques that will eliminate the need to type URLs: copying and pasting using the keyboard or having Word insert links automatically through the Insert Hyperlink dialog box.

Copying and Pasting Using Keyboard Shortcut Keys

The easiest way to prevent errors when entering URLs or e-mail addresses on curriculum or other Web pages is to copy and paste the Web or e-mail address using keyboard shortcut keys. Perform the following steps to copy and paste using keyboard shortcut keys.

Steps to Copy and Paste Using Keyboard Shortcut Keys

 Start your browser and then display the desired Web site.

 Select the URL in the Address box and then press CTRL+C to copy the address to the Windows Clipboard.

 Switch to a curriculum page, the Insert Hyperlink dialog box, or any Office document, and then press CTRL+V to paste or insert the address at the insertion point.

 Close Word and close your browser.

Having Word Enter Web Site Names and URLs Automatically

Word also allows you to add the name of a Web site and the corresponding URL without typing either. Word enters this information automatically in the Insert Hyperlink dialog box, utilizing the information in your browser. The following section details how to add the name of a Web site and link the text to its corresponding URL on a curriculum page automatically. Perform the following steps to see how easy it is to do.

Steps to Have Word Enter Web Site Names and URLs Automatically

 Start Internet Explorer.

 Start Word and open a new blank Web page or any other previously created curriculum page.

 Position the insertion point where you want to create a hyperlink. Click the Insert Hyperlink button on the Standard toolbar to display the Insert Hyperlink dialog box.

 Click the Internet Explorer button on the Windows taskbar to switch to Internet Explorer and then access the desired Web site.

Click the Word button on the Windows taskbar to switch back to the Word Web page.

Word automatically enters the name and URL of the Web page in the Text to display and Address text boxes in the Insert Hyperlink dialog box (Figure 24).

FIGURE 24

If desired, edit the Web site name in the Text to display text box and then click the OK button in the Insert Hyperlink dialog box.

Word enters the Web site name at the insertion point and hyperlinks the Web site name to its corresponding URL (Figure 25).

 Close Word and close your browser.

FIGURE 25

Editing a Web Page in Your Browser

One of the powerful features Office 2003 offers is the ability to edit a Web page directly in Internet Explorer. The following steps illustrate how to open and edit your Assignment Web page in Internet Explorer.

Steps to Edit a Web Page in Internet Explorer

 Start Internet Explorer. When Internet Explorer opens, click File on the menu bar and then click Open. When the Open dialog box opens, click the Browse button. If necessary, click the Look in box arrrow, navigate to and select the desired location, double-click the Assignment Web page, and then click the OK button. When the Web page opens, click File on the menu bar, and then point to Edit with Microsoft Office Word.

Internet Explorer displays the Assignment Web page (Figure 26). Internet Explorer determines which Office program you used to create the Web page and associates that program with the Edit button, Word in this case.

FIGURE 26

 Click Edit with Microsoft Office Word.

Internet Explorer starts Word and displays the Assignment Web page in the Word window in Web Layout view. You now can edit the Web page in Word as needed and then preview your changes in Internet Explorer (Figure 27).

FIGURE 27

Using the Web Tools Toolbar

Word has many other Web page authoring features. For example, you and your students can include sounds, videos, pictures, scrolling text, bullets, check boxes, option buttons, list boxes, text boxes, and much more on your Web pages. A floating Web Tools toolbar contains icons that provide access to a number of these authoring features (Figure 28). The Web Tools toolbar is floating because you can drag it anywhere on your desktop. The easiest way to see which of these tools can benefit you is to experiment with them. Open a blank Web page and the Web Tools toolbar and click the various buttons to use the Web authoring tools. To display the Web Tools toolbar, perform the following steps.

Steps to Display the Web Tools Toolbar

 Open a new Web page in Word using the steps on page 464.

 Click View on the menu bar, point to Toolbars, and then click Web Tools on the Toolbars submenu to display the Web Tools toolbar.

 After exploring the Web tools, close Word.

Word displays the Web Tools toolbar after you perform Step 2 (Figure 28).

FIGURE 28

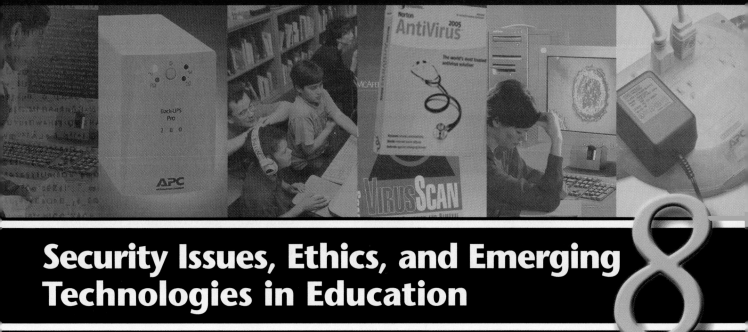

Security Issues, Ethics, and Emerging Technologies in Education

8

Objectives

After completing this chapter, you will be able to:
[ISTE NETS-T Standards I A-B, II A-E, V A-D, VI A-E]

- Identify security risks that threaten home and school computers

- Describe how computer viruses and malicious software programs work and the steps you can take to prevent viruses

- Describe different ways schools safeguard computers and networks

- Explain why computer backup is important and how it is accomplished

- Define what is meant by information privacy and its impact on schools

- Identify the components of copyright that impact education

- Describe the ethical issues related to Internet usage and steps schools are taking to address them

- Identify safe and healthy uses of technology resources

- Describe the emerging technologies that will transform traditional classrooms

E very day, businesses, schools, and individuals depend on computers to perform a variety of significant tasks, such as tracking sales, recording student grades, creating reports, searching the Web, and sending e-mail. People increasingly rely on computers to create, store, and manage critical information, so it is important to ensure that computers and software are protected from loss, damage, and misuse. School districts, for example, must take precautions to guarantee that student information, such as grades, attendance rates, personal and family data, and learning problems, is protected from loss and kept confidential.

This chapter identifies some potential risks to computers and software, and describes a number of safeguards that schools, businesses, and individuals can implement to minimize these risks. The chapter also discusses information privacy, including the current laws that keep certain data confidential. The chapter then reviews concerns about the ethical use of computers and which activities are right, wrong, or even criminal. Next, the chapter covers security, privacy, and the ethical issues that relate to how teachers and students use the information they find on the Internet. Finally, the chapter concludes with a discussion about health issues and emerging technologies in education.

Computer Security: Risks and Safeguards

Any event or action that has the potential of causing a loss of computer equipment, software, data and information, or processing capability is a **computer security risk**. Some of these risks, such as viruses, unauthorized access and use, and information theft, are a result of deliberate acts that are against the law. Any illegal act involving a computer generally is referred to as a **computer crime**. The following sections describe some of the more common computer security risks and the measures that you and your school can take to minimize or prevent their consequences.

COMPUTER VIRUSES

At 4:30 in the afternoon, Mrs. Vicki Reamy of Ridgedale High School is in her classroom making last-minute adjustments to the Excel spreadsheet she plans to use in tomorrow's third-period Business Education class. As she opens the spreadsheet file to make one last change, the top of the spreadsheet displays the message, "Something wonderful has happened, your PC is alive." Dismayed, she realizes that a computer virus has corrupted her spreadsheet and she has lost all her work.

A **virus** is a potentially damaging computer program designed to affect your computer negatively without your knowledge or permission by altering the way it works. More specifically, a virus is a segment of program code that implants itself in a computer file and spreads systematically from one file to another. Figure 8-1 answers frequently asked questions about computer viruses.

Computer viruses, however, do not generate by chance. Creators of virus programs write them for a specific purpose — usually either to spread from one file to another, to trigger a symptom, or to cause damage. Many viruses, for example, are designed to destroy or corrupt data stored on the infected computer. The symptom or damage caused by a virus, called the **virus payload**, can be harmless or it can cause

Figure 8-1 A virus spreads from one computer to another as illustrated in this figure.

A COMPUTER VIRUS: WHAT IT IS AND HOW IT SPREADS

How is a computer virus created?
A virus is illegal computer code that can do such things as alter programs or destroy data. Also, the virus can copy itself onto programs, thereby spreading its damaging effects.

How do viruses spread?
A piece of software that has a virus attached to it is called a host program. Usually, the virus is spread when the host program is shared. If the host program is copied, the virus is copied too, and it infects other software with which it comes into contact.

When does a virus attack?
Usually a virus attacks as soon as it comes in contact with other software or storage devices. Sometimes, a virus attacks at the time or date specified by the person who wrote the virus code. When the predetermined time or date registers on the computer's internal clock, the virus attacks. Sometimes, the virus code will display a message letting you know that the virus has done its damage.

Why are viruses not detected immediately?
People who copy and keep the host software are unaware that the virus exists because the virus is designed to hide from computer users for weeks or even months. Antivirus software can often, but not always, identify and quarantine viruses.

significant damage, as planned by the creator. Figure 8-2 outlines some common symptoms of virus infections.

Unfortunately, Vicki Reamy's experience is not unusual. Although viruses are a serious problem for both PC and Macintosh computer users, the majority of virus programs are intended to infect PCs. Currently, more than 85,000 known viruses or variants exist, and hundreds of new viruses or variants are identified every month. The increased use of networks and the Internet makes the spread of viruses easier than ever. Viruses commonly infect computers through e-mail attachments. Figure 8-3 on the next page shows how a virus can spread from one computer to another through an infected e-mail attachment. Before you open or execute any e-mail attachment, you should ensure that the e-mail message is from a trusted source and you should scan the attachment using antivirus software.

Although numerous variations are known, three main types of viruses exist: boot sector viruses, file viruses, and macro viruses. A **boot sector virus** replaces the boot program used to start the computer with a modified, infected version of the boot program. When the computer runs the infected boot program, it loads the virus into the computer's memory. Once a virus is in memory, it spreads to any storage media inserted into the computer. A **file virus** inserts virus code into program files; the virus then spreads to any program that accesses the infected file. A **macro virus** uses the macro language of an application, such as word processing or spreadsheet, to hide virus codes. When you open a document with an infected macro,

the macro virus loads into memory. Certain actions, such as saving the document, activate the virus. Macro viruses often are part of templates, which means they will infect any document created using one of the templates.

Two common variations of computer viruses, also known as **malicious software programs**, are worms and Trojan horses. A **worm** is a program that copies itself repeatedly in a computer's memory or on a network, using up resources and possibly shutting down the computer or network. Creators of worms often play on user psychology to entice people to download and run them. As a result, a number of well-known worms have hijacked e-mail systems and sent copies of themselves around the world in a matter of hours. The notorious Melissa worm quickly spread around the world causing serious harm to millions of computers. A **Trojan horse** (named after the Greek myth) is a malicious software program that hides within or is designed to look like a legitimate program.

Some viruses are relatively harmless pranks that temporarily freeze a computer or cause it to display sounds or messages. For example, when the Music Bug virus is triggered, the computer plays a few chords of music. Other viruses cause extensive damage to computer files and spread quickly throughout a network. For example, if a state administrator sends an e-mail message with an attached Excel spreadsheet infected with a macro virus to every school district in the state, the virus could quickly infect hundreds of computers.

FAQ

How long is an unprotected computer safe from intruders?

One security expert maintains that an unprotected computer could be compromised by an intruder within 20 minutes. Slammer and Nimda, two devastating worms, wreaked worldwide havoc in 10 and 30 minutes, respectively.

WEB INFO

For more information about computer viruses, visit the Teachers Discovering Computers Web site (*scsite.com/tdc4*), click Chapter 8, click Web Info, and then click Viruses.

Signs of Virus Infection

- An unusual message or graphical image appears on the computer screen
- An unusual sound or music plays randomly
- The available memory is less than what should be available
- A program or file suddenly is missing
- An unknown program or file mysteriously appears
- The size of a file changes without explanation
- A file becomes corrupted
- A program or file does not work properly

Figure 8-2 Viruses attack computers in a variety of ways. Listed here are some of the more common signs of virus infections.

Step 1:
Unscrupulous programmers create a
virus program. They hide the virus in a
Word document and attach the Word
document to an e-mail message.

Step 2:
They use the Internet to send the
e-mail message to thousands of users
around the world.

Step 3b:
Other users do not recognize the name of the
sender of the e-mail message. These users do not
open the attachment — instead they immediately delete the e-mail message. These users'
computers are not infected with the virus.

Step 3a:
Some users open the attachment
and their computers become
infected with the virus.

Figure 8-3 How a virus can spread through an e-mail attachment.

Some viruses are considered logic bombs or time bombs. A **logic bomb** is a program that activates when it detects a certain condition. One disgruntled worker, for example, planted a logic bomb that began destroying files when his name was added to a list of terminated employees. A **time bomb** is a type of logic bomb that activates on a particular date. A well-known time bomb is the **Michelangelo virus,** which destroys data on your hard disk on March 6, the date of Michelangelo's birthday. The World Wide Web is a great source for finding information about viruses and malicious software programs.

VIRUS DETECTION AND REMOVAL

Completely effective ways to keep a computer or network safe from computer viruses simply do not exist. You can, however, take precautions to protect your home and classroom computers from virus infections. Viruses normally are spread between computers by inserting an infected storage media (such as a CD or USB flash memory stick) in a computer or downloading an infected file from the Internet or via an e-mail attachment. Figure 8-4 lists a number of safe computing tips that can help you minimize the risk of viruses.

FAQ

Should I inform others if my computer gets a virus?

If you share data with other users, such as via e-mail attachments, instant messages, or removable storage media, you should inform these users of your virus infection. This courteous gesture allows fellow users to check their computers for viruses. In addition, you should inform your school's network specialists if you shared files or data with your school's computers.

Safe Computing Tips

A number of simple steps teachers can take will protect their home and classroom computers from viruses.

- **Purchase reliable antivirus software.** Most programs offer free virus definition updates. Upgrade antivirus software virus definitions every week.

- **Scan all removable media.** USB flash drives and other removable storage devices are common culprits for carrying viruses from one computer to another and spreading viruses throughout networks. If someone hands you a removable storage device that has been used in another system — scan it.

- **Scan all files downloaded from the Internet.** The number-one source for viruses is downloaded files. To be safe, download all files into a special folder on your hard drive and scan them for viruses immediately after downloading.

- **Scan all attached files before opening them.** It is possible to transfer a virus to your system by opening an attachment.

- **Turn off e-mail preview.** Although it is not likely that you will get a virus from reading your e-mail, many e-mail programs allow users to preview an e-mail message before or without opening it. Some sophisticated viruses and worms can deliver their payload when a user simply previews the message. Thus, users should turn off message preview in their e-mail programs.

- **Scan all software before using even if it is shrink-wrapped.** Viruses have been found in manufacturer-supplied software. Scan before installing software.

- **Avoid pirated, illegal copies of copyrighted software.** Not only is using them illegal, but they are a favorite source of viruses.

- **Never start your computer with removable media in the drives,** unless the media is uninfected.

- **Install antivirus programs on all of your school and home computers.** The cost of antivirus software is much less than the cost of rebuilding damaged files.

- **Install a personal firewall program.** See page 493 for more information on firewalls.

- **Back up your files often.** Even with the best antivirus software, realize that your computer's files can be infected. Be prepared to deal with the problem.

- **Set your antivirus program to scan automatically.** Most antivirus programs can be set up to scan the system automatically when booted and check it whenever removable media devices are accessed or files are opened.

Figure 8-4 Teachers can use a number of safe computing tips to minimize the risk of viruses.

WEB INFO

For details about antivirus programs, visit the Teachers Discovering Computers Web site (*scsite.com/tdc4*), click Chapter 8, click Web Info, and then click Vaccines.

Using an antivirus program is one of the more effective ways to protect against computer viruses. An **antivirus program** is designed to detect, disinfect, and protect computers and networks from viruses. Antivirus programs, also called **vaccines**, work by looking for programs that attempt to modify the boot program, the operating system, or other programs that normally are read from but not written to (Figure 8-5).

In addition to providing protection from viruses, most antivirus programs also have utilities to remove or repair infected

programs and files. If the virus has infected the boot program, however, the antivirus program may require you to restart the computer with a rescue disc. A **rescue disc** is normally a CD-ROM that contains an uninfected copy of key operating system commands and start-up information that enables the computer to restart correctly. After you have restarted the computer using a rescue disc, you can run repair and removal programs to remove infected files and repair damaged files. If the program cannot repair the damaged files, you might have to replace or restore them with uninfected backup copies of the files. Later sections in the chapter explain backup and restore procedures.

To help protect against viruses, most schools install antivirus programs on their networks and on individual computers throughout the school. Two popular antivirus programs used in schools and homes, shown in Figure 8-6, are Symantec Norton AntiVirus and McAfee VirusScan.

[a]

[b]

Figure 8-5 Antivirus programs check disk drives and memory for computer viruses. Figure 8-5a displays the Scan for Viruses screen that allows you to select the disk drives or files to be scanned. Figure 8-5b displays the status during the scan, and Figure 8-5c shows the results.

Figure 8-6 Symantec Norton AntiVirus and McAfee VirusScan are two popular antivirus programs used in schools, businesses, and homes.

[c]

When you install an antivirus program, you should set up the program to monitor a computer continuously for possible viruses, including continual scans of all removable storage media and files downloaded from the Internet (Figure 8-7). You also should set your antivirus program so it updates virus definitions automatically every week.

False warnings about viruses often spread via e-mail and over the Internet. Known as **virus hoaxes**, these warnings describe viruses that are not actually known to exist. Given the damage viruses cause, however, you should take the time to research the validity of any virus warnings you receive, in the event the warning is real. The Symantec Security Response – Hoax Web page regularly releases new virus hoax names. If you think you have received a message about a false virus, you can verify it at the Hoax Web page.

UNAUTHORIZED ACCESS AND USE

Unauthorized access is the use of a computer or network without permission. An individual who tries to access a computer or network illegally is called a **cracker** or hacker. The term, **hacker**, although originally a complimentary word for a computer enthusiast, now has a derogatory connotation because it refers to people who try to break into a computer, often intending to steal or corrupt its data. Crackers and hackers typically break into computers by connecting to the system via a modem and logging on as a user. Some intruders have no intent of causing damage to computer files; instead, they want to access data, information, or programs and use what they access for illegal purposes. Other intruders leave some evidence of their presence with a message or by deliberately altering data.

Unauthorized use is the use of a computer or data for unapproved or possibly illegal activities. Unauthorized use ranges from an employee using a company computer to send personal e-mail or to track his or her child's soccer league scores to someone gaining access to a bank system and completing an unauthorized transfer of funds.

One way to prevent unauthorized access to and use of computers is to implement **access controls**, which are security

measures that define who can access a computer, when they can access it, and what actions they can take while using the computer. To prevent unauthorized use and access to sensitive information, schools install different levels and types of access controls. Schools set up their networks so that users have access only to those programs, data, and information for which they are approved. Most schools and businesses provide authorized users with unique user identification (often called **user ID** or username) and a **password** that allows them to log on to the network to use e-mail, to transfer files, and to access other shared resources (Figure 8-8). When a user logs on to a computer or network by entering a

Figure 8-7 Using Norton AntiVirus Auto-Protect, users can opt for several different virus protection options.

Figure 8-8 Many schools require administrators, teachers, staff, and students to log on to the school's network with a unique user ID (or User name, as shown here) and password.

user ID and a password, the operating system checks to see if the user ID and password match the entries stored in an authorization file. If the entries match, the computer or network grants access.

Often, you are asked to select your own password by choosing a word or series of characters that will be easy to remember. If your password is too simple or obvious, such as your initials or birthday, however, others might guess it easily. Some suggestions to follow when you create a password are as follows:

- Use a combination of letters, digits, words, initials, and dates.

- Make the password at least eight characters (if supported by the software).

- Join two words together.

- Add one or more numbers at the beginning, middle, or end of a word.

- Choose words from other languages.

- Choose family names far back in your family tree.

- Choose a password you can type without looking at the keyboard.

Generally, the more creative your password, the harder it is for someone else to figure out. Even long and creative passwords, however, do not provide complete protection against unauthorized access. Some basic precautions to take include the following:

- Do not post passwords near your computer.

- Use a password that is easy to remember, so that you do not have to write it down.

- Change your password frequently.

- Do not share your password with anyone, especially telemarketers.

Following these guidelines helps to ensure that others will not use your password to access data, programs, or sensitive information stored on your computer or a school network.

At many schools, each user ID and password is associated with a specific level of computer and network access. A brief description of basic access levels schools use to prevent unauthorized access and use of sensitive information follows:

WEB INFO

For more information about unauthorized access, visit the Teachers Discovering Computers Web site (*scsite.com/tdc4*), click Chapter 8, click Web Info, and then click Unauthorized Access.

- Students usually can access only instructional materials and software. Although many schools also provide student access to the Internet and Web — many schools install filtering software on the networks to prevent students from viewing inappropriate Web sites. Students do not have network access to grades, attendance rates, and other sensitive and personal information.

- Teachers typically have access to all the programs, data, and information to which students have access; they usually have access to selected information about their students, such as grades and attendance. Teachers normally do not have access to information about other teachers, students, or any administrative files.

- Principals and assistant principals normally have access to all information that pertains to students enrolled at their schools; they may not access information about students attending other schools in the district.

- School district administrators and superintendents usually have access to all information stored on their districts' network servers.

POSSESSED OBJECTS AND BIOMETRIC DEVICES

A **possessed object** is any item that you must carry to gain access to a computer or computer facility. Examples are badges, cards, smart cards, and keys. The card you use in an automated teller machine (ATM) is a possessed object that allows access to your bank account. Possessed objects are often used in combination with a **personal identification number (PIN)** that is a numeric password that provides an additional level of security.

Biometric devices authenticate a person's identity by translating a personal characteristic, such as a fingerprint, into a digital code that then is compared with a digital code stored in the computer verifying the personal characteristic. If the digital code in the computer does not match the personal characteristic code, the computer denies access to the individual.

FIREWALLS

Despite efforts to protect the data on your computer's hard disk, it still is vulnerable to attacks from hackers. A **firewall** is a security system consisting of hardware and/or software that prevents unauthorized access to data and information on a network. Schools use firewalls to deny network access to outsiders and to restrict both student and teacher access to sensitive data (Figure 8-9). Many schools route all communications through a proxy server. A **proxy server** screens all incoming and outgoing messages.

If you are using Windows XP or Mac OS X, you already have a personal firewall that protects your computer from unauthorized access by monitoring all incoming network traffic. If you use a router, you also have a hardware firewall. Hardware firewalls stop many intrusions before they break into your computer.

For enhanced firewall protection and added features, some home and business users purchase stand-alone personal firewall software. A **personal firewall** is a software program that detects and protects your personal computer and its data from unauthorized intrusions. These products constantly monitor all transmissions to and from your computer and inform you of any attempted intrusions. These easy-to-use products are definitely worth their expense, which usually is less than $40. Figure 8-10 lists popular personal firewall products.

HARDWARE THEFT AND VANDALISM

For schools, hardware theft and vandalism present a difficult security challenge. To help minimize the theft of computers and associated equipment, schools can implement a variety of security precautions. In addition to installing security systems, many schools also install additional physical security devices such as cables that lock the equipment to a desk, cabinet, or floor (Figure 8-11). Schools also normally install deadbolt locks and alarm systems to protect the equipment in their computer labs.

Figure 8-9 A firewall restricts unauthorized intruders from accessing data, information, and programs on networks and individual computers.

Firewall Products

BlackICE PC Protection

McAfee Personal Firewall Plus

Norton Personal Firewall

Sygate Personal Firewall

ZoneAlarm

Figure 8-10 Popular personal firewall products.

Figure 8-11 Using cables to lock computers can help prevent the theft of desktop and mobile computer equipment.

WEB INFO

For more information about notebook computer security, visit the Teachers Discovering Computers Web site (*scsite.com/tdc4*), click Chapter 8, click Web Info, and then click Security.

With the increasing use of portable equipment such as notebook computers, iPods, smart phones, PDAs, and other handheld computers, hardware theft poses a more serious risk. Increasingly, K-12 schools and colleges are providing notebook computers for teachers and loaning them to students for short periods. Some universities and colleges even require that each entering student purchase a notebook computer. Users must take special care to protect their notebook computers. The size and weight of these smaller computers make them easy to steal, and their value makes them tempting targets for thieves (Figure 8-12).

Figure 8-12 The size and weight of notebook computers make them easy to steal, and their value makes them tempting targets for thieves. Schools and teachers need to take special precautions to prevent the theft of their notebook computers.

Common sense and a constant awareness of the risks are the best preventive measures against theft of notebook computers and other portable equipment. You should never, for example, leave a notebook computer unattended or out in the open in a public place, such as the cafeteria or on the seat of a car. Some schools install physical devices such as cables that temporarily lock notebook computers to a desk or table. As a precaution in case of theft, you also should back up the files stored on your notebook computer regularly.

Some schools purchase insurance policies to cover their notebook computers, desktop computers, and other computer equipment. In addition, schools can purchase a service that actually tracks down a stolen notebook computer. This unique

WEB INFO

For an overview of software and technology law, visit the Teachers Discovering Computers Web site (*scsite.com/tdc4*), click Chapter 8, click Web Info, and then click Software Law.

system often is called by its nickname, *the Lojack of the Computer World*. As soon as a person who has stolen a notebook computer uses the computer to access the Internet, the software on the computer sends a message regarding the location of the stolen computer to the school's system network administrator, who then notifies the police.

In addition to hardware theft, another area of concern for K-12 schools is vandalism. **Computer vandalism** takes many forms, from a student cutting a computer cable or deleting files to individuals breaking in a school and randomly smashing computers. Schools usually have written policies and procedures for handling various types of vandalism.

SOFTWARE THEFT

Like hardware theft and vandalism, software theft takes many forms — from a student physically stealing a CD to intentional piracy of software. **Software piracy** — the unauthorized and illegal duplication of copyrighted software — is by far the most common form of software theft.

When you purchase software, you actually do not *own* the software; instead, you have purchased the right to use the software, as outlined in the software license. A **software license** is an agreement that provides specific conditions for use of the software, which users must accept before using the software. Manufacturers usually print the terms of a software license on the software packaging, or in the case of software downloaded via the Web, a page at the manufacturer's site. The same agreement generally displays on a licensing acceptance screen during the software's setup program (Figure 8-13). Installation and use of the software constitutes the user's acceptance of the terms.

The most common type of license agreement included with software packages purchased by individual users is a **single-user license agreement**, or **end-user license agreement (EULA)**. An end-user license agreement typically includes numerous conditions, including the following:

■ Users may install the software on only one computer. Some license agreements allow users to install the software on one desktop computer and one notebook computer.

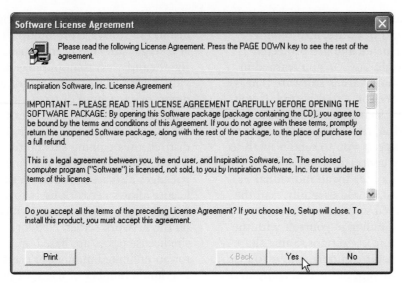

Figure 8-13 Purchasers of single-use software usually have to accept all the terms of the licensing agreement during installation of the software.

- Users may not install the software on a network, such as a school computer lab network.

- Users may make *one* copy for backup purposes.

- Users may not give copies to friends and colleagues.

Unless otherwise specified by a software license, you do not have the right to loan, rent, or in any way distribute software you purchase. This means you cannot install the software on both your home and classroom computer or on more than one classroom or home computer. Doing so is not only a violation of copyright law, but also a federal crime.

Software piracy introduces a number of risks into the software market: it increases the chance of viruses; reduces your ability to receive technical support; and significantly drives up the price of software for all users. Experts estimate that for every authorized copy of software in use, at least one unauthorized copy is made. One recent study reported that software piracy results in worldwide losses of more than billions of dollars per year.

Software piracy continues for several reasons. Some countries do not provide legal protection for software, while other countries rarely enforce laws. In addition, many buyers believe they have the right to copy the software for which they have paid

hundreds, even thousands of dollars — particularly when it is on an inexpensive CD or DVD.

Newer Microsoft Office and Windows products contain software-based product activation technology, which means you need to activate your Office and Windows products to use them. **Product activation** is an antipiracy technology designed to verify that software products have been licensed legitimately. Microsoft states that product activation is quick, simple, unobtrusive, and that it protects customer privacy.

Product activation works by verifying that a software program's product key, which you must use to install the product, has not been used on more personal computers than intended by the software's license. Software companies take illegal copying seriously and prosecute some offenders (including school districts, school administrators, and teachers) to the fullest extent of the law. Penalties include fines up to $250,000 and up to five years in jail.

Most schools have strict policies governing the installation and use of software and enforce their rules by periodically checking classroom and lab computers to ensure that all software is properly licensed. Teachers who are not completely familiar with their school's policies governing installation of software should check with the school's technology coordinator before installing any software on a classroom computer.

FAQ

How prevalent is software piracy?

Software piracy is rampant and costing U.S. corporations billions of dollars. A recent study showed that more than half of 86 countries polled had a piracy rate greater than 60 percent.

WEB INFO

For a list of freeware for the PC or Mac, visit the Teachers Discovering Computers Web site (*scsite.com/tdc4*), click Chapter 8, click Web Info, and then click PC Freeware or Mac Freeware.

Two additional types of software, shareware and freeware, also require license agreements and are protected under copyright law. As you learned in Chapter 1, **shareware** is software that is distributed free for a trial period. If you want to use a shareware program beyond the trial period, the developer (person or company) expects you to send a small fee. **Freeware,** by contrast, is software provided at no cost to a user by an individual or company. You should carefully read the license included with any shareware or freeware to familiarize yourself with the usage terms and conditions. Some shareware licenses, for example, allow you to install the software on several computers for the same fee, whereas others allow you to install the software on an unlimited number of computers in the same school for a minimal additional fee. Always scan shareware and freeware programs for viruses before installation and use.

To reduce software costs for schools and businesses with large numbers of users, software vendors often offer special discount pricing or site licensing. With discount pricing, the more copies of a program a school district purchases, the greater the discount. Purchasing a software

site license gives the buyer the right to install the software on multiple computers at a single site. Site licenses usually cost significantly less than purchasing an individual copy of the software for each computer; many school districts, in fact, purchase software site licenses that allow for use on computers throughout the district, thus gaining substantial savings.

Network site licenses for many software packages also are available. A **network site license** allows network users to share a single copy of the software, which resides on the network server. Network software site license prices are based on a fixed fee for an unlimited number of users, a maximum number of users, or per user.

A **community site license** gives an entire region or state the right to install an unlimited number of educational copies of a particular software program on individual computers or a network. As with other site licenses, a community site license provides substantial savings. Figure 8-14 summarizes the various types of software licenses used in education. A number of major software companies, such as Microsoft, provide site licenses for some of their software to K-12 schools at drastically reduced rates.

Type of License	Characteristics	Use in Schools
Single-user	Software can be installed on only one computer. Some license agreements allow users to install the software on one desktop computer and one notebook computer.	Used when a school needs only a few copies of a particular software. Commonly found in small schools and when purchasing specialized software programs.
Multiple-user	Software can be installed on a set number of computers, typically 5, 10, 50, or more. Cost varies based on number of computers.	Cost-effective method to install software on more than one computer. Most commonly used in schools.
Network License	Software is installed on the school's network. The license will specify and the software will control a specific number of simultaneous users, such as 50, 100, 250, or 500. Cost varies based on number of computers.	Cost-effective method of allowing students and teachers throughout the school to have access to an application software program. As schools continue to install networks, network licenses are becoming more common.
Community/State License	Frequently used with software distributed on CDs/DVDs. Any number of programs can be purchased for either Macintosh or PC platforms.	Very cost-effective method for school districts or states to purchase large quantities of software. Savings can be significant over individual CD or DVD pricing.

Figure 8-14 A summary of the various types of software licenses used in education.

INFORMATION THEFT

As you have learned, information is a valuable asset to an organization, such as a school district. The deliberate theft of information causes as much or more damage than the theft of hardware. Information theft typically occurs for a variety of reasons — organizations steal or buy stolen information to learn about competitors and individuals steal credit card and telephone charge card numbers to make purchases. Information theft often is linked to other types of computer crime. An individual, for example, may gain unauthorized access to a computer and then steal credit card numbers stored in a firm's accounting files.

Most organizations prevent information theft by implementing the user ID controls previously mentioned. Another way to protect sensitive data is to use encryption. **Encryption** is the process of converting readable data into unreadable characters by applying a formula that uses a code, called an **encryption key**. The person who receives the message uses the same encryption key to decrypt it (convert it back to readable data). Both the sender and receiver computers use the same encryption software. Any person illegally accessing the information sees only meaningless symbols (Figure 8-15).

School networks do contain a great deal of important and confidential information about students, teachers, and staff. Although information theft is not a major problem in schools, the potential is taken seriously. As a result, schools implement many of the security precautions described in this chapter.

SYSTEM FAILURE

Theft is not the only cause of hardware, software, data, or information loss. Any of these can occur during a **system failure**, which is a malfunction of a computer. System failures occur because of electrical power problems, hardware component failure, or software error.

One common cause of system failures in school and home computers is an abrupt variation in electrical power, which can cause data loss or damage computer components. In a school network, for example, a single power disturbance can damage multiple computers and their associated equipment. Two more common electrical power variations that

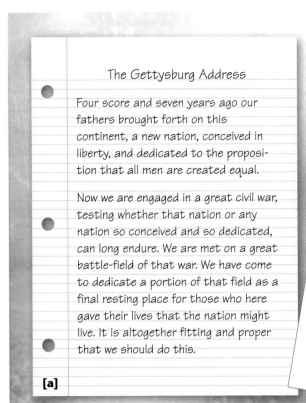

Figure 8-15 The first two paragraphs of the Gettysburg Address in plain text [a] and after the text is encrypted [b].

cause system failures are undervoltages and overvoltages.

An **undervoltage** occurs when the electrical power supply drops. In North America, electricity normally flows from the wall plug at approximately 120 volts. Any significant drop below 120 volts is considered an undervoltage. A **brownout** is a prolonged undervoltage; a **blackout** is a complete power failure. Undervoltages cause data loss and computer crashes but generally do not cause serious equipment damage.

An **overvoltage**, or **power surge**, occurs when the incoming electrical power increases significantly above the normal 120 volts. A momentary overvoltage, called a **spike**, occurs when the power increase lasts for less than one millisecond (one thousandth of a second). Spikes are caused by uncontrollable disturbances, such as lightning, or controllable disturbances, such as turning on a piece of equipment that uses the same electrical circuit. Overvoltages can cause immediate and permanent equipment damage.

To protect your computer equipment from overvoltages, you should use surge protectors. A **surge protector** is a device that uses special electrical components to smooth out minor voltage errors, provide a stable current flow, and keep an overvoltage from damaging computer equipment (Figure 8-16). Schools should use surge protectors for all classroom and lab computers and printers.

If your home computer connects to the Internet, you need to have surge protection not only for your computer, but also for your modem, telephone lines, DSL lines,

and other Internet cables. Many surge protectors include plug-ins for telephone lines and other cables (Figure 8-17). If your surge protector does not have these plug-ins, you can purchase separate devices to protect these lines. Overall, surge protectors provide an inexpensive way to protect computers and associated equipment. Basic surge protectors cost less than $15 and surge protectors that include protection from power surges over network cables cost less than $35.

in-out network connections

Figure 8-17 Home users should purchase a surge protector that includes an in-and-out connection for telephone lines and other network cables.

Although a surge protector absorbs a small overvoltage without damage, a large overvoltage, such as that caused by a lightning strike, will cause the surge protector to fail to protect the computer components. Surge protectors also are not completely effective; large power surges can bypass the surge protector and repeated small overvoltages can weaken a surge protector permanently.

For additional electrical protection, many home and school users connect their computers and printers to an uninterruptible power supply, instead of a surge protector. An **uninterruptible power supply (UPS)** is a device that contains surge protection circuits and one or more batteries that provide power during a temporary or permanent loss of power (Figure 8-18). The amount of time a UPS allows you to continue working depends on the electrical requirements of the computer and the size of the batteries in the UPS. A less expensive UPS provides enough

Figure 8-16 Circuits inside a surge protector safeguard equipment against overvoltages.

time for users to save their current work and properly shut down the computer after a power outage (about 10 minutes).

Figure 8-18 If power fails, an uninterruptible power supply (UPS) uses batteries to provide electricity for a limited time. A UPS also contains circuits that safeguard against overvoltages.

To ensure that their networks will continue to operate in the event of a power loss, most schools and businesses install UPSs to protect their network servers. Home users also should consider investing in a UPS, especially if they live in an area prone to power surges, power failures, and lightning strikes. For home users, the $30 to $175 investment in a UPS can prevent user frustration associated with most power-related computer problems, crashes, and loss of data. Some UPS manufacturers pay for any damage your computer sustains from power surges, including lightning strikes.

BACKING UP — THE ULTIMATE SAFEGUARD

To prevent data loss caused by a system failure or a computer virus, many schools, businesses, and home users back up their important files. A **backup** is a duplicate of a file, program, or disk that can be used if the original is lost, damaged, or destroyed. When a file is corrupted or destroyed, the backup copy is used to **restore**, or reload, the file on a computer or network file server. Schools and home users often overlook storing backup copies at another location, called an **off-site location**, as an additional precaution. This simple precaution prevents a single disaster, such as a fire, from

destroying both the primary and backup copies of important files.

Most schools have a **backup procedure** that outlines a regular plan of copying and backing up important data and program files. At many schools, the backup procedures cover only essential school programs, information, and data, such as student grades, attendance, and other personal information. Schools normally do not back up the files individual teachers or students create on their classroom computers. If your school does not provide backups for the files you create in your classroom, you should make backup copies of your school files periodically and store them on a portable hard drive or CDs. Likewise, you should back up the files you create on your home computer. Whether at school or home, backing up your important files prevents loss of lesson plans, curriculum pages, handouts, tests, and more — files that represent years of work. Teachers also should teach their students how to back up their homework, projects, and other files.

Creating backup copies of your files is not a difficult procedure. The easiest way is to copy your important files from your hard disk to a CD, USB flash drive, or portable hard drive. In addition, most personal computer operating systems include an easy-to-use backup utility program (Figure 8-19). Such utilities not only allow users to back up their important files, they also compress the backed up files so they require less storage space than the original files.

WEB INFO

To learn more about Microsoft Backup, visit the Teachers Discovering Computers Web site (*scsite.com/tdc4*), click Chapter 8, click Web Info, and then click Backup.

Figure 8-19 Microsoft Backup is a utility program that comes with Microsoft Windows and is an easy way to back up your important computer files.

WEB INFO

To explore Computer Ethics — Cyberethics, visit the Teachers Discovering Computers Web site (*scsite.com/tdc4*), click Chapter 8, click Web Info, and then click Cyberethics.

Ethics and the Information Age

As with any powerful technology, individuals can use computers for both good and bad actions. The standards that determine whether an action is good or bad are called **ethics**. **Computer ethics** are the moral guidelines that govern the use of computers, networks, and information systems (Figure 8-20). Five areas of computer ethics frequently discussed are (1) unauthorized use of computers, (2) hardware, software, and information theft, (3) information privacy, (4) copyright, and (5) the existence of objectionable materials on the Internet.

Unauthorized use of computers and hardware, copying software, and information theft were discussed earlier in this chapter. The following sections present the issues surrounding information privacy and copyright. The ethical issues related to objectionable materials on the Internet are discussed later in this chapter.

Computer Ethics for Educators

1. An educator will not use a computer to harm other people.

2. An educator will not interfere with others' computer work.

3. An educator will not look at others' computer files.

4. An educator will not use a computer to steal.

5. An educator will not use a computer to lie.

6. An educator will not copy or use software without paying for it.

7. An educator will not use others' computer resources without permission.

8. An educator will not use others' work.

9. An educator will think about the social impact of the programs he or she creates.

10. An educator always will use a computer in a way that shows respect and consideration for other people.

Modified from the *Ten Commandments for Computer Ethics* by the Computer Ethics Institute.

Figure 8-20 Computer ethics are the guidelines that govern the use of computers and information systems. This lists computer ethics for educators.

INFORMATION PRIVACY

Information privacy is the right of individuals and organizations to deny or restrict the collection and use of information about them. In the past, information privacy was easier to control because information was kept in separate locations, individual schools in a large school district maintained their own files, individual stores had their own credit files, government agencies had separate records, doctors had separate files, and so on.

Now it is feasible, both technically and economically, for schools, businesses, and other organizations to store large amounts of related data in a database or on one network server because of the widespread use of networks and increased storage capacity. These organizations also use computers to monitor student and employee activities. As a result, many people have concerns about how the unauthorized collection and use of data and monitoring affects their privacy. Figure 8-21 lists actions you can take to make your personal data more private.

UNAUTHORIZED COLLECTION AND USE OF INFORMATION Most individuals are surprised to learn that national marketing organizations often purchase the information individuals provide for magazine subscriptions, product warranty registration cards, contest entry forms, and other documents.

By combining this acquired data with other information obtained from public sources, such as driver's licenses and vehicle registration information, national marketing organizations create an **electronic profile** of an individual. The organizations then sell this electronic profile to organizations that distribute information on a product, service, or cause to a specific group of individuals (for example, all sports car owners over 40 years of age living in the southeastern United States).

Direct marketing supporters say that using information in this way lowers overall selling costs, which, in turn, lowers product prices. Critics contend that the information contained in these electronic profiles reveals more about individuals than anyone has a right to know. These same individuals believe that, at a minimum, companies should inform the individuals whose personal information they intend to sell or release and give the individuals the right to deny such use.

How to Safeguard Personal Information

1. Fill in only required information on forms, both in print and on the Web.

2. Do not preprint your telephone number or Social Security number on personal checks.

3. Have an unlisted or unpublished telephone number.

4. Find out how to block your telephone number from displaying on the receiver's system if Caller ID is available in your area.

5. Do not write your telephone number on charge or credit receipts.

6. Ask merchants not to write credit card numbers, telephone numbers, Social Security numbers, and driver's license numbers on the back of your personal checks.

7. Purchase goods with cash instead of credit or checks.

8. Avoid shopping clubs and buyers' cards.

9. If merchants ask personal questions, find out why they want to know before releasing the information.

10. Inform merchants that you do not want them to distribute your personal information.

11. Ask, in writing, to be removed from mailing lists.

12. Obtain your credit report once a year from each of the three major credit reporting agencies (Equifax, Experian, and TransUnion) and correct any errors.

13. Request a free copy of your medical records once a year from the Medical Information Bureau.

14. Install a cookie manager to filter cookies.

15. Clear your history file when you are finished browsing.

16. Set up a free e-mail account. Use this e-mail address for merchant forms.

17. Turn off File and Print Sharing on your Internet connection.

18. Install a personal firewall.

19. Sign-up for e-mail filtering through your Internet service provider or use an antispam program such as Brightmail.

20. Do not reply to spam for any reason. It might not be a good idea to unsubscribe to unsolicited spam; by sending back a message, you might only confirm that your e-mail account is active.

21. Surf the Web anonymously with programs such as Freedom Websecure or through an anonymous Web site such as Anonymizer.com.

Figure 8-21 Techniques to keep personal data private.

PHISHING Phishing is a scam in which a perpetrator sends an official-looking e-mail that attempts to obtain personal and financial information from the recipient. Some phishing e-mail messages ask the recipient to provide personal information in the reply; others direct the recipient to a phony Web site that collects the information. To help deter phishing scams and spam (discussed next), Microsoft and others are developing standards that will require e-mail messages to contain sender identification so recipients can verify the legitimacy of messages.

SPAM Spam is an unsolicited e-mail message or newsgroup posting sent to many recipients or newsgroups at once. The content of spam ranges from selling a product or service, to promoting a business opportunity, to advertising offensive materials. One study indicates the average user receives more than 1000 spam e-mail messages each year. Spam sent through an instant messaging system, instead of through e-mail, is called **spim**. Spam sent via Internet Telephony is called **split**.

You can reduce the amount of spam you receive using several techniques. Some e-mail programs have built-in settings that delete spam automatically. Other e-mail programs, such as Outlook Express, allow you to set up message rules that block all messages from a particular sender or subject. You also can sign up for e-mail filtering from your Internet service provider.

E-mail filtering is a service that blocks e-mail messages from designated sources. You can block unwanted e-mail messages by using an **antispam program** that attempts to remove spam before it reaches your inbox. The disadvantage of using e-mail filters and antispam programs is that sometimes they remove valid e-mail messages.

PRIVACY LAWS The concern about privacy has led to federal and state laws regarding storing and disclosing personal data and other computer-related issues (Figure 8-22). Common points in some of these laws include the following:

- A business or government agency collecting data about individuals should limit the information collected and only store what is necessary to carry out the organization's functions.

- After it has collected data about individuals, an organization must make provisions to restrict data access to only those employees who must use it to perform their job duties.

- An organization should release an individual's personal information outside the organization only after the individual has agreed to its disclosure.

- When an organization collects information about an individual, the organization must inform the individual that it is collecting data and give her the opportunity to determine the accuracy of the data.

Schools and school districts have a legal and moral responsibility to protect sensitive information, whether it is in printed form or stored electronically on school computers. Just like any other business, school districts must follow state and federal laws concerning storage and release of personal information about students, teachers, and staff personnel. For these reasons, school districts generally restrict access to sensitive information stored on their networks and in printed materials on a strict need-to-know basis.

Teachers also must follow federal and state laws concerning the storage and release of information about their students. Teachers should carefully read and make sure they understand all school district policies concerning the release of sensitive information as related to their students.

EMPLOYEE AND STUDENT MONITORING

Employee monitoring uses computers to observe, record, and review an individual's use of a computer, including communications such as e-mail, keyboard activity (used to measure productivity), and Internet sites visited. A frequently discussed issue is whether an employer has the right to read an employee's e-mail messages. Actual policies vary widely, with some organizations declaring they will review e-mail messages regularly, whereas others state they consider e-mail private and will protect it just like a letter sent through the postal service.

Most schools usually have very specific rules governing the use of e-mail and school networks by teachers, administrators, staff, and students. Some schools randomly monitor e-mail messages and the Internet sites visited by teachers, administrators, staff, and students, whereas other schools do not. Some schools also randomly monitor files stored on the school network.

Teachers should become familiar with all school policies concerning e-mail and computer and Internet usage. To ensure that individuals understand these policies, most schools require that teachers, students, staff, and parents sign an Acceptable Use Policy (AUP) that provides specific guidance for using school computers, networks, and the Internet. Teachers also should ensure that students fully understand that school personnel or their future employers might monitor their use of the organization's computer resources.

COPYRIGHT LAWS

As discussed earlier in this chapter, copyright laws cover software programs to protect them from piracy. Copyright law includes many other aspects, however, that teachers need to understand. The Copyright Act of 1976 and its numerous amendments apply to all creative works.

A **copyright** means the original author or creator of the work retains ownership of the work and has the exclusive right to reproduce and distribute the creative work.

WEB INFO

For a crash course on copyright basics, visit the Teachers Discovering Computers Web site (*scsite.com/tdc4*), click Chapter 8, click Web Info, and then click Crash Course.

DATE	LAW	PURPOSE
2003	**CAN-SPAM Act**	Gives law enforcement the right to impose penalties on people using the Internet to distribute spam.
2003	**Health Insurance Portability and Accountability Act (HIPAA)**	Describes how personal medical information can be used and disclosed. HIPAA became effective on April 14, 2003.
2002	**Dot Kids Implementation and Efficiency Act**	Establishes the Dot Kids domain that will list only Web sites that conform to policies to protect children under the age of 13. It will function similarly to the children's section of a library.
2001	**Provide Appropriate Tools Required to Intercept and Obstruct Terrorism (PATRIOT) Act**	Gives law enforcement the right to monitor people's activities, including Web and e-mail habits.
2000	**Children's Internet Protection Act (CIPA)**	Protects children from obscene and pornographic materials by requiring libraries to install filtering software on their computers. Upheld by the Supreme Court in July 2003.
1998	**Children's Online Privacy Protection Act (COPPA)**	Protects personal information for children under the age of 13.
1997	**No Electronic Theft (NET) Act**	Closes a narrow loophole in the law that allowed people to give away copyrighted material (such as software) on the Internet without legal repercussions.
1996	**National Information Infrastructure Protection Act**	Penalizes theft of information across state lines, threats against networks, and computer system trespassing.
1994	**Computer Abuse Amendments Act**	Amends 1984 act to outlaw transmission of harmful computer code such as viruses.
1992	**Cable Act**	Extends privacy of Cable Communications Policy Act of 1984 to include cellular and other wireless services.
1991	**Telephone Consumer Protection Act**	Restricts activities of telemarketers.
1988	**Computer Matching and Privacy Protection Act**	Regulates the use of government data to determine the eligibility of individuals for federal benefits.
1988	**Video Privacy Protection Act**	Forbids retailers from releasing or selling video-rental records without customer consent or a court order.
1986	**Electronic Communications Privacy Act (ECPA)**	Provides the same right of privacy protection for the postal delivery service and telephone companies to the new forms of electronic communications, such as voice mail, e-mail, and cellular telephones.
1984	**Cable Communications Policy Act**	Regulates disclosure of cable television subscriber records.
1984	**Computer Fraud and Abuse Act**	Outlaws unauthorized access of federal government computers.
1978	**Right to Financial Privacy Act**	Strictly outlines procedures federal agencies must follow when looking at customer records in banks.
1974	**Privacy Act**	Forbids federal agencies from allowing information to be used for a reason other than for which it was collected.
1974	**Family Educational Rights and Privacy Act**	Gives students and parents access to school records and limits disclosure of records to unauthorized parties.
1970	**Fair Credit Reporting Act**	Prohibits credit reporting agencies from releasing credit information to unauthorized people and allows consumers to review their own credit records.

Figure 8-22 Summary of the major U.S. government laws concerning privacy.

WEB INFO

To learn more about fair use, visit the Teachers Discovering Computers Web site (*scsite.com/tdc4*), click Chapter 8, click Web Info, and then click Fair Use.

All educators need to understand how copyright laws impact the manner in which they and their students use information created by others. Such an understanding is important because the building blocks of education use the creative works of others: books; videos; newspapers, magazines, and other reference materials; software; and information located on the World Wide Web.

Three areas of copyright directly impact today's classrooms: (1) illegal copying or using copyrighted software programs; (2) fair use laws and their application to the use of both printed copyrighted materials and copyrighted materials accessible on the Internet; and (3) use of copyrighted materials on teacher and student Web pages. The first area (illegal copying or using licensed and copyrighted software) was covered earlier in this chapter; the following sections cover the other two areas of copyright.

FAIR USE The Copyright Act of 1976 established **fair use,** or guidelines that allow educators to use and copy certain copyrighted materials for nonprofit educational purposes. Figure 8-23 shows Section 107 of U.S. Copyright Law, which deals with fair use. Copyright issues are complex and sometimes the laws are vague. School districts thus provide teachers with specific guidelines for using copyrighted materials in their classrooms. Schools can interpret copyright issues differently, so school policies concerning the use of copyrighted materials vary widely. Teachers need to read school policies concerning copyright carefully and understand them.

In addition to providing printed school policies on copyright issues, most schools provide teachers with information and answer questions about copyright issues. For information or answers to questions concerning software copyright issues, teachers should ask their school or district technology coordinator. For all other issues concerning copyright, fair use, and associated school district policies, teachers should speak with their media specialist. Media specialists receive training on copyright issues and deal with them on a daily basis. If in doubt, teachers should contact the creator of the work and ask for written permission to use his material.

Fair use guidelines apply to copyrighted materials on the Internet just as they apply to a copyrighted article published in a magazine. Basically, Web sites include two kinds of information: original copyrighted information and information without copyright restriction. Web pages that contain original information generally include a copyright statement on the page; the copyright statement normally contains the copyright symbol, the year, and the creator's name (Figure 8-24).

U.S. Copyright Law: Fair Use

(U.S. Code, Title 17, Chapter 1, Section 107)

§ 107. Limitations on exclusive rights: Fair use

Notwithstanding the provisions of sections 106 and 106A, the fair use of a copyrighted work, including such use by reproduction in copies or phonorecords or by any other means specified by that section, for purposes such as criticism, comment, news reporting, teaching (including multiple copies for classroom use), scholarship, or research, is not an infringement of copyright. In determining whether the use made of a work in any particular case is a fair use, the factors to be considered shall include:

(1) the purpose and character of the use, including whether such use is of a commercial nature or is for nonprofit educational purposes;

(2) the nature of the copyrighted work;

(3) the amount and substantiality of the portion used in relation to the copyrighted work as a whole; and

(4) the effect of the use upon the potential market for or value of the copyrighted work.

The fact that a work is unpublished shall not itself bar a finding of fair use if such finding is made upon consideration of all the above factors.

Figure 8-23 The Copyright Act of 1976 provides the structure for the copyright law. Section 107 of the U.S. Copyright Law defines Fair Use.

If a teacher uses copyrighted materials from the Internet, she must follow fair use guidelines, school policies, and any restrictions listed on the Web site. If the information located on the Web site does not include copyright restriction, it does not mean the creator is waiving his privileges under copyright. To be safe, you should assume everything on the Web is copyrighted. Always follow fair use guidelines and school policies when using Web materials for educational purposes. In addition, always give proper credit and use citations if appropriate.

These guidelines do not apply only to text-based materials on the Web. The Web also contains a multitude of graphics, animations, and audio and video files teachers can download and use for educational purposes or classroom presentations. When teachers download and use these materials, they must adhere to fair use guidelines, school policies, and any other restrictions noted on the Web site.

TEACHER AND STUDENT WEB PAGES

Teachers and students in school districts all over the country are creating and publishing their own Web pages (Figure 8-25). As previously discussed, **Web publishing** is the development and maintenance of Web pages. When developing these pages, teachers and students must take care to respect copyright laws and follow the guidelines outlined in the previous section.

Copyright laws do protect all original materials created by students and teachers and published on the Web. To ensure that this is clear, however, teachers and students may want to include a copyright statement at the bottom of their home page.

The use of copyrighted materials (text, graphics, animations, audio, and video) on teacher or student Web pages requires permission from the creator of the materials. Most Web pages include an e-mail link to use when asking for permission to use copyrighted materials. To use the materials on the Web, simply send a short e-mail message to the creator of the work and explain how you will use her work on your Web page. Many authors are more than willing to allow teachers to use their original text or artwork for educational purposes as long as they receive proper credit.

Figure 8-24 This educational Web page has a copyright statement. The copyright statement includes basic copyright information as well as other information.

Figure 8-25 Teachers and students in school districts all over the country are creating and publishing their own Web pages.

Many school districts have specific guidelines that teachers and students must follow when publishing Web pages on school servers. Teachers should carefully read all school rules before publishing any teacher or student Web pages. Some schools, for example, prohibit using any copyrighted materials on Web pages. In such instances, students and teachers must use only original material or material that is not copyrighted. Generally, teachers may use materials from government-sponsored Web sites, which are considered public domain (Figure 8-26). Anything considered **public domain** — including software or creative works — is free from copyright restrictions.

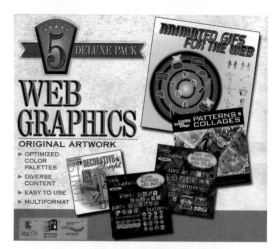

Figure 8-27 Web Graphics is a popular software package that provides teachers and students with thousands of graphics they can use on their published Web pages.

Figure 8-26 An example of a public domain government Web page. Government Web pages usually have a URL that contains or ends in .gov.

Most school districts purchase or have access to copyright-free CDs and DVDs or they subscribe to services that contain thousands of clip art images, photos, graphics, and audio and video clips. They make these copyright-free materials available for teachers and students to use on their Web pages and in class presentations and projects (Figure 8-27). In addition to respecting copyright law, teachers also must consider other issues related to Web page publishing. Teachers, for example, must protect their students from Internet users who might want to harm them by ensuring that no personal information about students is included on the Web pages. Figure 8-28 lists some basic guidelines that teachers should consider when creating Web pages.

Finally, a broadly interpreted issue known as intellectual property rights is beginning to play an important role in public education. The major intellectual property rights issue currently being discussed is who owns online content and

courses, both in higher education and K-12 education. A recent survey found that most institutions of higher education see content as the property of the instructor. More than half also believe that the instructor owns the actual course. Currently, most K-12 districts handle ownership of items such as tests, lesson plans, and other teaching materials and these districts see ownership as a nonissue. Some districts are beginning to clarify the ownership of online courses.

Internet Ethics and Objectionable Materials

As you already have learned in this chapter, the widespread use of the Internet — especially in today's schools and classrooms — raises many issues regarding security, privacy, and ethics. Of all of these, one issue is of particular concern for teachers and parents: the availability of **objectionable material** on the Internet, including racist literature, obscene pictures and videos, gambling, and age-restricted items such as cigarettes and alcohol.

Teachers and other school personnel must be concerned with three different types of Internet materials that fall under the general term, objectionable material. The first area includes all materials that most people consider pornographic, such

Web Page Guidelines

- Always protect the identity of your students.

- Never list student last names, telephone numbers, home addresses, or e-mail addresses.

- Use only first names of students on a Web site, but never in conjunction with other identifying information, such as a photograph.

- Use caution when including digital pictures of classrooms; avoid pictures that show close-ups of students.

- Never provide links to sites that are not appropriate for K-12 students or educational settings.

- List the function of all linked Web pages. Link only to pages that inform, explain, or teach a concept or curriculum area to students. Beware of linking to Web sites that persuade students.

- Avoid providing links to sites whose primary purpose is selling noneducational products and services, unless relevant to the subject under discussion.

- Avoid linking to Web pages that are not updated on a regular basis.

- Provide links to sites that help you achieve instructional and curriculum goals.

- Avoid discussing controversial issues on your Web site or linking to Web sites that discuss controversial issues, unless these issues are part of your curriculum.

- Carefully read and follow all guidelines and policies that your school district provides.

Figure 8-28 Guidelines that teachers should consider when creating teacher and student Web pages.

WEB INFO

For more information about Web page guidelines, visit the Teachers Discovering Computers Web site (*scsite.com/tdc4*), click Chapter 8, click Web Info, and then click Guidelines.

as obscene pictures, stories, graphics, articles, cartoons, and videos. The second area includes racist literature, controversial subjects such as gambling, and other similar materials. Teachers and parents usually easily identify Web sites that contain materials in these first two areas.

The third area includes Web sites that contain incorrect material and thus are inappropriate for K-12 students. Identifying this type of Web page is more difficult than identifying the first two. Because anyone can create and publish a Web page or Web site, some people deliberately create and publish materials on Web pages to fool unsuspecting people. Young students are

extremely vulnerable to being fooled by these sites. These Web sites appear perfectly appropriate for K-12 students but contain information that is historically and otherwise inaccurate. An elementary student might not know the difference between a site that is historically inaccurate about America's founding fathers and an educational site that is accurate.

Before the explosive growth of the Internet, it was difficult for most K-12 students to obtain and view objectionable materials, such as pornographic magazines. Today, anybody with Internet access can view a vast array of obscene and other inappropriate materials on the Web. Many people want to ban such materials from the Internet, whereas others would only restrict objectionable materials so they are not available to minors. Opponents argue that banning any material violates the constitutional right of free speech. Opponents state that instead of limiting Internet access and materials, schools should teach students right from wrong.

RECENT GOVERNMENT ACTIONS

Two recent government actions will help protect children from being exploited while on the Internet: the Dot Kids Implementation and Efficiency Act and the Children's Internet Protection Act.

DOT KIDS IMPLEMENTATION AND

EFFICIENCY ACT   President George W. Bush signed the Dot Kids Implementation and Efficiency Act on December 4, 2002. **Dot Kids** is part of the U.S. domain on the Internet and functions much like the children's section of a public library with content suitable for children under thirteen. As President Bush stated, "This bill is a wise and necessary step to safeguard our children while they use computers and discover the great possibilities of the Internet. Every site designated .kids will be a safe zone for children. The sites will be monitored for content, safety, and all objectionable materials will be removed. Online chat rooms and instant messaging will be prohibited, unless they can be certified as safe. The Web sites under this new domain will not connect a child to other online sites outside the child-friendly zone." In addition, the administrators of the domain will work with the U.S. Department of Justice and other federal agencies to prevent children using Dot Kids from being targeted by predators.

CHILDREN'S INTERNET PROTECTION ACT

Congress passed the **Children's Internet Protection Act (CIPA)** in 2000 to protect children from obscene, pornographic, and other information considered harmful to minors. CIPA requires that public libraries install filtering software to block Web sites that contain obscene images or content. As you learned in Chapter 2, filtering software programs prevent browsers from

WEB INFO

To access the Dot Kids Web site, visit the Teachers Discovering Computers Web site (*scsite.com/tdc4*), click Chapter 8, click Web Info, and then click Dot Kids.

displaying materials from targeted sites or sites that contain certain keywords or phrases. CIPA was challenged by opponents who argued that this law would obstruct appropriate, nonobscene material from being viewed. In July 2003, the U.S. Supreme Court upheld CIPA, arguing that it does not violate freedom of speech. As a result, all public libraries must install filters on their computers to block access to online pornography or lose federal funding.

Many K-12 schools and parents have proactively taken steps to protect their students and children from the negative aspects of the Internet. Although only a small percentage of the information available on the Internet is unsuitable for children at home or in K-12 schools, educators agree that such materials have no place in our classrooms. Teachers and parents need to ensure that children understand that inappropriate materials exist on the Internet. Children also need to understand that some individuals might try to exploit them via e-mail messages or in chat room conversations.

PARENTAL CONTROLS

Parents can take a number of steps to prevent children from accessing pornographic and other objectionable materials on the Internet. One approach to restricting access to certain material uses a rating system similar to the one used for videos, movies, and television shows. The rating system is understood by your Web browser, which allows you to set limits on the types of material available for viewing (Figure 8-29). If content at the Web site goes beyond the rating limitations you set in the Web browser, the site will not display. You prevent the rating limitations from being changed by using a password.

An effective approach to blocking objectionable materials is to install filtering software programs on any computer with Internet access. Many filtering software programs allow parents to filter harmful Web sites, restrict Internet access, monitor children's online activities, and prevent children from accidentally providing personal information in e-mail messages or in chat rooms (Figure 8-30).

Many Internet service providers provide software that allows users to control the content their Web browser will display. America Online, for example, allows home users to establish different accounts for adults and children. When a user logs on using a child's account, only appropriate pages will display. Parents can specify various settings, blocks, and access options for each child account; for example, parents can control who can send children instant messages. In addition, many Internet security programs that provide firewall and antivirus protection also include Web filtering capabilities (Figure 8-31).

Finally, the best way for parents to protect children is to monitor their children's activities while on the Internet both by direct and indirect observations. One technique is to keep the family computer in the family room or in an area where you can observe your children while they are working on the computer.

Figure 8-29 Many Web browsers use the ratings of the Internet Content Rating Association (ICRA), which indicate rating levels for material unsuitable for minors.

Figure 8-30 Net Nanny is a popular Internet filtering software program that provides parents with numerous options for protecting their kids as they surf the Web.

Figure 8-31 Many Internet security programs include content filtering capabilities, which parents can use to block Web sites and applications.

Because it is difficult to always monitor or observe children's Internet activities directly, you can check which Internet sites children are visiting by viewing the browser's history list (Figure 8-32). This simple but effective technique is useless, however, if children are allowed to clear the history list.

previously accessed   Web sites   History button
Web sites   accessed Today

Figure 8-32 A browser's history list records information about all the sites visited for a predetermined period.

EDUCATIONAL CONTROLS

As you have learned, businesses and parents have several available options to control access to inappropriate Internet sites. Most school districts also control student access to objectionable materials by implementing these controls and a few additional ones. For schools, attacking this problem requires a four-pronged approach: filtering software, Acceptable Use Policies, use of curriculum pages, and teacher observation. All four prongs of the approach are discussed in the following sections.

FILTERING SOFTWARE   As previously discussed, **filtering software programs** prevent the browser from accepting material from targeted sites or material that contains keywords or phrases. Schools install Internet filtering software on their networks and then constantly update the software programs to keep them as current

as possible. Although very effective, these filtering software programs do not prevent access to all objectionable and inappropriate materials. One drawback to using filtering software is that it also can block access to legitimate materials or research on controversial issues. A filtering software program is the first level of protection that many school districts use.

ACCEPTABLE USE POLICIES   Recognizing that teachers, students, administrators, and staff personnel need guidance, most schools develop specific standards for the ethical use of computers, school networks, and the Internet. These standards are called Acceptable Use Policies. As discussed in Chapter 1, an **Acceptable Use Policy (AUP)** is a set of rules that governs the use of school and school district computers, networks, and the Internet by teachers, administrators, staff, and students.

Acceptable Use Policies vary greatly from school district to school district. Many schools have separate AUPs for students, teachers, and staff personnel. Many school districts require both students and their parents to sign student AUPs. Some schools publish student AUPs on their Web sites, which allows new students and parents to print, review, sign, and then mail or deliver them to the school (Figure 8-33). Schools normally will not allow students or teachers to access the school's network or Internet unless a signed AUP is on file. Many AUPs contain the following guidelines:

- Notice that use of school computers, networks, and the Internet is a privilege, not a right

- Notice that students should behave as guests when on the Internet — that is, they should use good manners and be courteous

- List of rules and consequences concerning accessing objectionable Internet sites

- List of rules and consequences dealing with copyright issues

- Outline of proper use of all networks and computers

- List of rules covering online safety and release of personal information

- Notice that students who violate AUPs will face disciplinary action and possible permanent cancellation of school network and/or Internet access privileges

CURRICULUM PAGES As you learned in Chapter 7, a **curriculum page** is a teacher-created document or Web page that contains hyperlinks to teacher selected and evaluated Web sites that support learning objectives by providing students with quality Web resources, links to additional information, and opportunities to learn more. Using a curriculum page offers several advantages. Students quickly link to excellent sites, instead of the various locations they might find from searching the Internet for information. Because the teacher evaluates the linked sites for content and appropriateness before posting them, a curriculum page significantly reduces the chance students will view an inappropriate site. Furthermore, by providing links for students to click, a curriculum page eliminates the need for students to type URLs. Students often make mistakes typing URLs, which, in addition to wasting time, sometimes links them to inappropriate or incorrect sites.

TEACHER OBSERVATION Teacher **observation** or supervision permits teachers to monitor their students actively and continuously while they are on the Internet (Figure 8-34). Teacher observation is extremely important and, in most cases, a final measure to prevent students from accessing objectionable and inappropriate materials on the Internet. For teacher observation to be effective, teachers must constantly and actively watch what their students are doing in the classroom and viewing on the Internet. Teachers should direct students that, if they access an Internet site that contains objectionable material, they should immediately click their browser's Back button to return to the previous page and if this does not work simply close the browser. Either is a quick-and-easy way to prevent objectionable material from displaying in the browser. You also might want students to notify you if such a situation arises, so that you can add that site to the sites restricted by the filtering software. Some schools

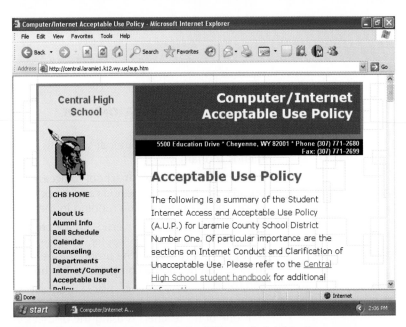

Figure 8-33 Many schools include AUPs on their Web sites so new teachers, students, and parents can print and review, sign, and then mail or deliver them to the school.

Figure 8-34 Teacher observations can prevent students from viewing objectionable or inappropriate material on the Internet.

have installed software programs on their lab computers, such as Apple's Remote Desktop for Macintosh computers, which enables teachers to keep an eye on all the computer screens in a classroom or lab.

As a final note, all educators should understand clearly the ethical issues covered in this chapter to model these concepts for their students and teach them to be ethical computer users. The questionnaire shown in Figure 8-35 on the next page will help you further understand these ethical concepts.

COMPUTER ETHICS QUESTIONNAIRE

	Ethical	Unethical	Crime
1. A teacher uses her computer at school to send e-mail to her friends and family.	☐	☐	☐
2. A teacher uses the Web at school to access stock market reports. So that he can periodically check the market, he leaves the Web connection running in the background all day.	☐	☐	☐
3. A principal installs a new version of a word processing program on her office computer. Because no one will be using the old version of the program, she takes it home and installs it on her home computer so her husband and children can use it.	☐	☐	☐
4. While checking teachers' e-mail messages, the principal finds that one of his teachers is using the district's e-mail system to bet on football games and does nothing about it.	☐	☐	☐
5. A school technology facilitator has her students develop PowerPoint tutorials. When the projects are completed, she offers to sell the tutorials to another school.	☐	☐	☐
6. A principal tells a teacher to install a piece of software on numerous computers on campus. The teacher knows the software has a single-user license, but because the principal said to install it, he does.	☐	☐	☐
7. Personnel in the district's computer center occasionally monitor computer use in the schools. They monitor how often and for what lengths of time particular teachers are connected to the Internet, as well as what sites have been visited.	☐	☐	☐
8. The media specialist uses photo retouching software to put her school name on another school's logo.	☐	☐	☐
9. A teacher downloads a piece of shareware software. He uses it for the allotted time and when asked to pay for the software, he simply closes the window and continues to use it.	☐	☐	☐
10. An educational learning company contacts a principal requesting information about students, including names and addresses. The company offers to provide students with free learning supplements. The principal sends the company her student database.	☐	☐	☐
11. Your students are creating Web pages of their own. They search the Internet for ideas. One of them finds a very cool home page and decides to copy the page, change the name, and use it.	☐	☐	☐
12. You are doing a unit on famous cartoon characters and go to the Disney Web site to get clip art for your curriculum page.	☐	☐	☐

Figure 8-35 Indicate whether you think each described situation is ethical, unethical, or a crime. Discuss your answers with other teachers; use this questionnaire as a springboard for a discussion about computer ethics with your students.

Health Issues

Users are a key component in any information system. Thus, protecting teachers and students is just as important as protecting hardware, software, and data. Many health-related issues concerning computer use can be minimized by teaching students at an early age how to use computers properly so they reduce their risk of injury. The following sections discuss health risks and preventions.

COMPUTERS AND HEALTH ISSUES

The Bureau of Labor Statistics reports that work-related musculoskeletal disorders account for one-third of all job-related injuries and illnesses. A **musculoskeletal disorder (MSD)**, also called a **repetitive strain injury (RSI)**, is an injury or disorder of the muscles, nerves, tendons, ligaments, and joints. Computer-related RSIs include tendonitis and carpal tunnel syndrome. The largest job-related injury and illness problems in the United States today are repetitive strain injuries. For this reason, the Occupational Safety and Health Administration (OSHA) has developed industry-specific and task-specific guidelines designed to prevent workplace injuries with respect to computer usage.

Tendonitis is inflammation of a tendon due to some repeated motion or stress on the tendon. **Carpal tunnel syndrome (CTS)** is inflammation of the nerve that connects the forearm to the palm of the wrist. Repeated or forceful bending of the wrist can cause CTS or tendonitis of the wrist. Symptoms of tendonitis of the wrist include extreme pain that extends from the forearm to the hand, along with tingling in the fingers. Symptoms of CTS include burning pain when the nerve is compressed, along with numbness and tingling in the thumb and first two fingers.

Long-term computer use can lead to tendonitis or CTS. Factors that cause these disorders include prolonged typing and mouse usage, or continual shifting between the mouse and the keyboard.

You can take many precautions to prevent these types of injuries both for yourself and your students. Take frequent breaks during computer sessions to exercise your hands and arms (Figure 8-36). To prevent injury due to typing, place a wrist rest between the keyboard and the edge of your desk. The wrist rest reduces strain on your wrist while typing. To prevent injury while using a mouse, place the mouse at least six inches from the edge of the desk. Finally, minimize the number of times you switch between the mouse and the keyboard, and avoid using the heel of your hand as a pivot point while typing or using the mouse.

HAND EXERCISES

- Spread fingers apart for several seconds while keeping wrists straight.
- Gently push back fingers and then thumb.
- Dangle arms loosely at sides and then shake arms and hands.

FIGURE 8-36 To reduce the chance of developing tendonitis or carpal tunnel syndrome, take frequent breaks during computer sessions to exercise your hands and arms.

Another type of health-related condition due to computer usage is **computer vision syndrome (CVS)**. You may have CVS if you have any of these conditions: sore, tired, burning, itching, or dry eyes; blurred or double vision; distance-blurred vision after prolonged staring at a display device; headache or sore neck; difficulty shifting focus between a display device and documents; difficulty focusing on the screen image; color fringes or after-images when you look away from the display device; and increasing sensitivity to light. Although eyestrain associated with CVS is not thought to have serious or long-term consequences, it is disruptive and unpleasant. Figure 8-37 outlines some techniques you can follow to ease eyestrain.

People who spend their workday using the computer sometimes complain of lower back pain, muscle fatigue, and emotional fatigue. Lower back pain sometimes is caused by poor posture. Always sit and have your students sit properly in the chair. Take a short break every 30 to 60 minutes — stand up, walk around, or stretch.

TECHNIQUES TO EASE EYESTRAIN

- Every 10 to 15 minutes, take an eye break.
  - Look into the distance and focus on an object for 20 to 30 seconds.
  - Roll your eyes in a complete circle.
  - Close your eyes and rest them for at least one minute.
- Blink your eyes every five seconds.
- Place your display device about an arm's length away from your eyes with the top of the screen at eye level or below.
- Use large fonts.
- If you wear glasses, ask your doctor about computer glasses.
- Adjust the lighting.

FIGURE 8-37 Following these tips can help reduce eyestrain while working on the computer.

ERGONOMICS

Ergonomics is an applied science devoted to incorporating comfort, efficiency, and safety into the design of items in the workplace. Ergonomic studies have shown that using the correct type and configuration of chair, keyboard, display device, and work surface helps users work comfortably and efficiently, and helps protect their health (Figure 8-38).

Many display devices and keyboards have features that help address ergonomic issues. Some keyboards have built-in wrist rests and can be purchased from any computer supply store. Other keyboards have an ergonomic design specifically to prevent RSI. Display devices usually have controls that allow you to adjust the brightness, contrast, positioning, height, and width of images. Most monitors have a tilt-and-swivel base, allowing you to adjust the angle of the screen to minimize neck strain and reduce glare from overhead lighting.

viewing angle: 20° to center of screen

viewing distance: 18 to 28 inches

arms: elbows at about 90° and arms and hands approximately parallel to **floor**

adjustable chair height: chair should have 4 or 5 legs for stability

keyboard height: 23 to 28 inches depending on height of user

feet: flat on floor

FIGURE 8-38 A well-designed work area should be flexible to allow adjustments to the height and build of different individuals. Good lighting and air quality also are important considerations.

Emerging Technologies

The classrooms and schools you attended throughout your 13 years of K-12 education probably were similar to the classrooms in which your parents sat — for some of you, the schools and furniture were exactly the same. More importantly, your educational experience and the educational experiences of your parents probably were very similar, too. Unlike society, which has dramatically changed, many schools and school curriculum have been slow to change during the past few decades.

Fortunately, the infusion of modern digital media computers, high-speed networks and Internet access, higher-quality educational software, and a realization by administrators that teachers must receive extensive and appropriate technology training is beginning to transform many classrooms. In some cases, the transformation is remarkable.

Due to the infusion of informational technologies and the World Wide Web, teachers no longer are bound by the four walls of traditional classrooms and the two covers of traditional textbooks (Figure 8-39). Furthermore, technology has helped a number of schools significantly improve the quality of their graduates.

Because of the strong commitment of federal, state, and local governments, thousands of organizations dedicated to improving education, and millions of concerned parents, the infusion of technologies into schools will continue — and continue explosively. Technology has only begun to influence the way teachers instruct and students learn. The following sections summarize seven emerging areas of educational technology that will continue to influence significantly the public education system: the digital media revolution, the World Wide Web, the next generation of software on DVDs, assistive technologies, Web- and video-enhanced digital textbooks, Web-based distance learning, and wireless technologies.

DIGITAL MEDIA REVOLUTION

As you have learned throughout this textbook, today's digital kids are different and they learn differently. You have

Figure 8-39 The Web has enormous potential to change the way teachers instruct and students learn due to the vast amount of current and education-related information available at thousands of Web sites.

learned a lot about all that is digital media. You have experienced many new and exciting software programs that thousands of students are using everyday to create digital media presentations and projects. An interactive digital media revolution is just beginning — a grass roots revolution being fueled by the needs and desires of today's digital students. This revolution will continue to profoundly impact the way teachers teach and the way today's digital students learn. To reach and motivate today's students, teachers must understand this digital media revolution and utilize current and future digital media technologies. This digital media revolution will shape a generation like never before in history, and teachers must eagerly adopt and integrate digital media technologies and create innovative teaching and learning opportunities for their students.

Another impact of this digital media revolution is a trend to move from using traditional textbooks and curriculum to an all digital curriculum. In the fall of 2005, Vail High School in Tucson became Arizona's first all wireless, all laptop, all digital public school. Vail's digital students will not be carrying around nor using traditional textbooks, instead, its curriculum will be completely digital, including extensive use of online resources.

THE WORLD WIDE WEB

The federal government is committed to ensuring that every K-12 classroom has high-speed Internet access and is investing billions of dollars to meet that goal. The following specific Internet improvements will directly influence the quality of the K-12 educational experience:

- The speed of the Internet will increase dramatically.

- The majority of PreK-12 students in most schools will be able to access thousands of full-motion videos on demand. Streaming video technology will allow teachers to bring live video footage of current and historical events into their classrooms, simply by clicking a video link. Teachers and students will have thousands of videos from which to choose. In addition, teachers and millions of students will be creating their own high-quality videos on a multitude of topics. More and more students will be reviewing their video productions on their iPods and other similar devices.

- Teachers and students will have instant access to tens of thousands of interactive Web-based educational software programs, including tutorials, exercises, virtual-reality tours, science experiments, games, and other subject-related activities.

Figure 8-40 Many educational Web sites are offering students and teachers opportunities to explore education topics interactively. This Web site, for example, allows young students to learn numbers, shapes, and number matching while having fun gaming.

Many of these online educational programs will be fully interactive, thus opening up incredible opportunities for discovery learning (Figure 8-40). Because of Bluetooth and other transfer technologies, many of these programs will be accessed by students on their iPods and other similar devices.

EDUCATIONAL SOFTWARE ON DVD

During the last 10 years, the influx of digital media computers with CD-ROM drives and the availability of hundreds of high-quality CD-based educational software programs impacted education significantly.

During the next five years, the availability of DVD-based education software programs will have an even greater impact on education. The huge storage capacity of DVDs will allow educational software developers to build programs that contain vast amounts of information, graphics, animations, video, and interactive links. These next-generation educational software programs on DVDs will include hours of high-quality full-motion video that teachers and students may access instantly.

ASSISTIVE TECHNOLOGIES

Dramatic improvements are being made in hardware, software, and Web-based tools that teachers will use to help instruct students with special needs. As you learned earlier, **assistive technologies** are innovative technologies that modify or adapt the classroom for special learning needs. Assistive technologies aid in teaching students who have physical, sensory, or cognitive disabilities. Emerging assistive technologies will provide teachers with innovative tools to help students with special needs overcome the disability that blocks or impedes their learning process.

Nationwide, funding for assistive technologies is increasing significantly. Teacher education programs and K-12 schools are placing more emphasis on assistive technologies, due to the number of students with disabilities who are mainstreamed into regular classrooms. According to the Individuals with Disabilities Education Act (IDEA) Amendments of 1997, regular classroom teachers must be part of the cross-curriculum and interdisciplinary team that teaches all students. Technology is the bridge that provides new strategies for all students to learn and succeed (Figure 8-41).

Guidelines. For example, for a Web site to be approved, it must (partial list):

- Provide text equivalents for all nontext elements (such as images, animations, video, and audio).

- Provide summaries of graphs and charts.

- Ensure that all information displayed in color also is available without color.

WebXACT is a free software program, created by the Watchfire Corporation that allows Web authors to identify changes they need to make to their pages so users with disabilities can more easily use their Web pages. Using WebXACT is simple; Web authors enter their URL and WebXACT will analyze the Web site for compliance (Figure 8-42). Additional information is provided at this chapter's Assistive Technologies Corner.

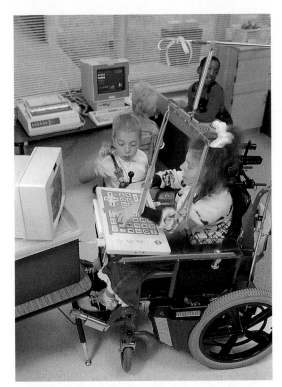

Figure 8-41 Technology can be the bridge that provides new strategies for all students to learn and succeed, including students with physical and other challenges.

In addition, many leaders express concern that current technologies are widening the gap between the economic haves and have-nots. Federal funding, private funding, and emerging technologies will help slow this crisis facing America. Schools will be provided funding and guidance to ensure that at-risk students have equal access to current and emerging technologies.

FEDERAL ACCESSIBILITY INITIATIVE
In 1998, Congress amended the Rehabilitation Act to require federal agencies to make their electronic and information technology accessible to people with disabilities. Under **Section 508**, agencies must give employees with disabilities and members of the public access to technology that is comparable to the access available to others. The law applies to all federal agencies when they develop, procure, maintain, or use electronic and information technology.

Education agencies can verify easily that their Web sites and pages meet Section 508 requirements by using a software program that analyzes Web sites and pages to see if they meet the World Wide Web Consortium's (W3C) Web content Accessibilities

Figure 8-42 This free site allows Web authors to check their Web sites to ensure that the Web sites meet accessibility guidelines.

WEB- AND VIDEO-ENHANCED DIGITAL TEXTBOOKS

For many years, K-12 textbooks remained basically unchanged. Recently, however, this began to change as the Web became an integral part of K-12 books. Traditional textbooks will fade into history as all areas of education create increasingly interactive and extensive Web- and video-enhanced digital textbooks. Many of these books will correlate to national and state curriculum standards and benchmarks.

Imagine teaching social studies, biology, or English literature using a Web- and video-enhanced digital textbook with an extensive Web site that continuously is updated and maintained by a team of experienced educators and provides students with discovery learning avenues and

WEB INFO

To see an example of a Web- and video-enhanced digital textbook, visit the Teachers Discovering Computers Web site (*scsite.com/tdc4*), click Chapter 8, click Web Info, and then click Textbook.

information about thousands of topics from thousands of sources all over the world.

Finally, a number of textbook publishers are predicting that traditional textbooks will become obsolete as more and more school districts adopt digital textbooks for their digital curriculum. These exciting and interactive Web- and video-enhanced digital textbooks will crumble the concrete and brick walls of traditional classrooms and remove the covers of traditional textbooks.

WEB-BASED DISTANCE LEARNING

Due to the increasingly diverse population of students, education is changing in an effort to meet the needs of this diverse and changing student body. These changes bring the Web to the forefront of instructional strategies in education — specifically, the use of Web-based distance learning.

Web-based distance learning already has experienced phenomenal growth in institutions of higher education and K-12 schools. The more common approach for schools to take, however, is to use the Web to enhance classes and instruction.

These Web-based teaching strategies are new and will continue to evolve for many years. Web-based strategies offer creative solutions for homebound students, home-schooled students, at-risk students, students who are physically challenged, and teacher shortages for specialized positions. Because many small or rural schools cannot offer

students courses such as Latin and French, or advanced-placement courses in math and science, states and school districts now offer students these specialized courses using the Web. Depending on the situation and school district policies, students take these Web-based courses at home, at a public library, or in a classroom — Internet access is the common agent for this remote instruction. For example, Florida Virtual School provides online classes and instruction to all public, private, and home-school students in Florida and other states (Figure 8-43).

A WORLD WITHOUT WIRES

The last decade of the twentieth century was dominated by the evolution of the World Wide Web. Although it seems certain that the Web will continue to evolve and mature, it is clear that the first decade of the twenty-first century is being dominated by the wireless revolution that is taking place globally. Today's wireless technology represents an evolution in products and services that quickly is transforming the way people live, work, learn, and teach. Wireless technology will continue to impact our K-12 education system dramatically in the following ways:

- Wireless communications will allow teachers and students to connect their smart phones, PDAs, notebook computers, Tablet PCs, iPods, and other wireless devices to a truly global high-speed network.

WEB INFO

To learn more about a Web-enhanced high-school class, visit the Teachers Discovering Computers Web site (*scsite.com/tdc4*), click Chapter 8, click Web Info, and then click Class.

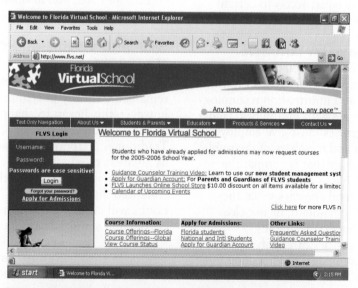

Figure 8-43 The Florida Virtual School opened in 1997 as a two-county initiative. Today, more than 35,000 high school students from all 67 Florida county school districts, charter and private schools, and other states enroll in more than 80 classes every year.

- Wireless desktop computers, Tablet PCs, mobile labs, and other devices will ensure that educational technology is used seamlessly at the point of instruction.

- Global wireless access will ensure that all children, regardless of their socioeconomic status, will have access to educational classroom materials and the world itself from their homes, their schools, and many other locations throughout their communities.

Wireless technologies already have changed the way you communicate with relatives, colleagues, and friends. Indeed, you are taking part in the wireless revolution that is sweeping the world and is just beginning to change and influence the way we teach and learn in our schools.

To learn more about the wireless revolution and how it will impact you, your students, and your family, review the special feature, A World Without Wires, that follows this chapter.

Summary of Security Issues, Ethics, and Emerging Technologies in Education

The livelihood of businesses, schools, and individuals depends on the computers and networks in use every day. This increased reliance on computers and information sent over networks makes it essential to take steps to protect the systems and information from known risks. At the same time, employees, teachers, and students also have an obligation to use computers responsibly and not abuse the power computers provide. This responsibility presents constant challenges, which sometimes weigh the rights of the individual against increased efficiency and productivity. Schools have the added responsibility and challenge of protecting their students from unethical practices and people.

Educational technologies are the tools whose effectiveness is determined by the knowledge, skill, experience, level of training, and ethics of the user. The educational technology knowledge you acquire should help you be better able to participate in decisions on how to use computers and other educational technologies, and using the Internet efficiently and ethically.

Summary of Teachers Discovering Computers

To be effective in using educational technology in their classrooms, teachers must be computer literate, information literate, and most importantly, integration literate. This textbook provided you with knowledge and skills in all three areas. What you have learned is only a beginning.

Teachers must continuously update their technology and technology integration skills. Teachers have an incredible responsibility — a far greater responsibility than any previous generation of teachers. The amount of knowledge that teachers must instill in their digital students is enormous and continues to expand at a phenomenal rate. To continue to prosper in the twenty-first century, educational institutions must provide today's digital students with a solid foundation of the basic skills and other core subjects. Used as instructional and productivity tools, current and emerging technologies help teachers make a difference in the quality of their students. Teachers can use and integrate technology to influence future generations in immensely positive ways. The possibilities really are limitless (Figure 8-44).

Figure 8-44 Teachers make a difference in the quality of their students' education when they integrate technology effectively.

In Brief

INSTRUCTIONS: In Brief summarizes the concepts presented in this chapter. To listen to the audio version of this In Brief, visit scsite.com/tdc4. Click Chapter 8 at the top of the Web page and then click In Brief on the left sidebar.

1. Computer Security Risks

A **computer security risk is** any event or action that can cause a loss of or damage to computer equipment, software, data and information, or processing capability. A **computer crime** is any illegal act involving a computer.

2. Computer Viruses

A **virus** is designed to affect computers negatively by altering the way they work. Many viruses are designed to destroy or corrupt data. A **boot sector virus** replaces the boot program used to start the computer with a modified, infected version of the boot program. A **file virus** inserts virus code into program files. A **macro virus** uses the macro language of an application to hide virus codes. Two common variations of computer viruses, often called **malicious software programs,** are worms and Trojan horses.

3. Virus Detection and Removal

Antivirus programs are designed to detect, disinfect, and protect computers and networks from viruses. Antivirus programs work by looking for programs that attempt to modify the boot program, the operating system, and other programs that normally are read from but not written to. Most antivirus programs also have utilities to remove or repair infected programs and files.

4. Unauthorized Access and Use

Unauthorized access is the use of a computer or network without permission. The term, **cracker** or hacker, refers to a person who tries to break into a computer often with the intent of stealing or corrupting its data. **Unauthorized use** is the use of a computer or data for unapproved or possibly illegal activities. Unauthorized access is prevented by establishing **access controls,** which are security measures that define who may access a computer or information.

5. Theft

Common sense and a constant awareness of the risks are the best preventive measures against theft of notebook computers and other portable equipment. **Software piracy** is the unauthorized and illegal duplication of copyrighted software. Software piracy is a violation of copyright law and is a federal crime. A **software license** is an agreement that provides specific conditions for use of the software, which users must accept before using the software.

6. System Failure

A **system failure** is a computer malfunction. System failures occur because of electrical power problems, hardware component failure, or a software error. An **undervoltage** occurs when the electrical power supply drops. An **overvoltage,** or **power surge,** occurs when the incoming electrical power increases significantly above the normal 120 volts. A **surge protector** keeps an overvoltage from damaging computer equipment.

7. Copyright Laws

The Copyright Act of 1976 applies to all creative works. A **copyright** means the original author or creator of the work retains exclusive ownership of the work. **Fair use** guidelines allow educators to use and copy certain copyrighted materials for nonprofit educational purposes.

In Brief

8. Internet Ethics

Objectionable materials on the Internet include racist literature and obscene pictures and videos. Computer ethics are the moral guidelines that govern the use of computers, networks, and information systems. **Filtering software programs** prevent browsers from displaying materials from targeted sites or materials that contain certain keywords or phrases.

9. Educational Controls

Controls to prevent student access to inappropriate Internet sites include filtering software, Acceptable Use Policies, use of curriculum pages, and teacher observation. An **Acceptable Use Policy (AUP)** is a set of rules that governs the use of school and school district computers, networks, and the Internet. A **curriculum page** is a teacher-created document or Web page that contains links to teacher chosen and evaluated Web sites that match curriculum goals. **Teacher observation** involves teachers monitoring their students actively and continuously while they are on the Internet.

10. Health Issues

A **repetitive strain injury (RSI)** is an injury or disorder of the muscles, nerves, tendons, ligaments, and joints. Common RSIs include tendonitis and carpal tunnel syndrome. **Tendonitis** is the inflammation of a tendon due to repeated motion or stress on the tendon. **Carpal tunnel syndrome (CTS)** is the inflammation of the nerve that connects the forearm to the palm of the hand. **Ergonomics** is an applied science devoted to incorporating comfort, efficiency, and safety into the design of items in the workplace.

11. Emerging Technologies

Emerging educational technologies that will influence public education significantly include the digital media revolution, the World Wide Web, the next generation of software on DVDs, assistive technologies, Web- and video-enhanced digital textbooks, Web-based training, and wireless technologies.

Key Terms

INSTRUCTIONS: Use the Key Terms to help focus your study of the terms used in this chapter. To further enhance your understanding of the Key Terms in this chapter, visit scsite.com/tdc4. Click Chapter 8 at the top of the Web page and then click Key Terms on the left sidebar. Read the definition for each term and then access current and additional information about the term from the Web.

Acceptable Use Policy (AUP) [510]
access control [491]
antispam program [502]
antivirus program [490]
assistive technologies [516]

backup [499]
backup procedure [499]
biometric device [492]
blackout [498]
boot sector virus [487]
brownout [498]

carpal tunnel syndrome (CTS) [513]
Children's Internet Protection Act (CIPA) [508]
community site license [496]
computer crime [486]
computer ethics [500]
computer security risk [486]
computer vandalism [494]
computer vision syndrome (CVS) [514]
copyright [502]
cracker [491]
curriculum page [511]

Dot Kids [508]

electronic profile [500]
e-mail filtering [502]
employee monitoring [502]
encryption [497]
encryption key [497]
end-user license agreement (EULA) [494]

ergonomics [514]
ethics [500]

fair use [504]
file virus [487]
filtering software programs [510]
firewall [493]
freeware [496]

hacker [491]

information privacy [500]

logic bomb [489]

macro virus [487]
malicious software programs [487]
Michelangelo virus [489]
musculoskeletal disorder (MSD) [513]

network site license [496]

objectionable material [506]
off-site location [499]
overvoltage [498]

password [491]
personal firewall [493]
personal identification number (PIN) [492]
phishing [501]
possessed object [492]
power surge [498]
product activation [495]
proxy server [493]
public domain [506]

repetitive strain injury (RSI) [513]
rescue disc [490]
restore [499]

Section 508 [517]
shareware [496]
single-user license agreement [494]
site license [496]
software license [494]
software piracy [494]
spam [501]
spike [498]
spim [501]
split [501]
surge protector [498]
system failure [497]

teacher observation [511]
tendonitis [513]
time bomb [489]
Trojan horse [487]

unauthorized access [491]
unauthorized use [491]
undervoltage [498]
uninterruptible power supply (UPS) [498]
user ID [491]

vaccine [490]
virus [486]
virus hoax [491]
virus payload [486]

Web publishing [505]
worm [487]

Checkpoint

INSTRUCTIONS: Use the Checkpoint exercises to check your knowledge level of the chapter. To complete the Checkpoint exercises interactively, visit scsite.com/tdc4. Click Chapter 8 at the top of the Web page and then click Checkpoint on the left sidebar.

1. Label the Figure

Instructions: Identify each type of software license.

Type of License	Characteristics	Use in Schools
1._____	Software can be installed on only one computer. Some license agreements allow users to install the software on one desktop computer and one notebook computer.	Used when a school needs only a few copies of a particular software. Commonly found in small schools and when purchasing specialized software programs.
2._____	Software can be installed on a set number of computers, typically 5, 10, 50, or more. Cost varies based on number of computers.	Cost-effective method to install software on more than one computer. Most commonly used in schools.
3._____	Software is installed on the school's network. The license will specify and the software will control a specific number of simultaneous users, such as 50, 100, 250, or 500. Cost varies based on number of computers.	Cost-effective method of allowing students and teachers throughout the school to have access to an application software program. As schools continue to install networks, network licenses are becoming more common.
4._____	Frequently used with software distributed on CDs/DVDs. Any number of programs can be purchased for either Macintosh or PC platforms.	Very cost-effective method for school districts or states to purchase large quantities of software. Savings can be significant over individual CD or DVD pricing.

2. Matching

Instructions: Match each term from the column on the left with the best description from the column on the right.

____ 1. filtering software

____ 2. curriculum page

____ 3. Trojan horse

____ 4. Web publishing

____ 5. computer ethics

a. teacher-created Web page that contains links to teacher chosen and evaluated Web sites

b. moral guidelines that govern the use of computers, networks, and information systems

c. prevents browser from displaying materials from certain Web sites

d. a virus designed to look like a legitimate program

e. the development and maintenance of Web pages

3. Short Answer

Instructions: Write a brief answer to each of the following questions.

1. What are computer security risks? What different types of security risks threaten school computers? What are some safeguards that minimize security risks? _____

2. What is a virus? Describe three types of viruses. Why are viruses commonly found in schools? What can teachers do to minimize the impact of viruses both at home and at school? _____

3. What are computer ethics? List and briefly explain five important areas of computer ethics. Describe two recent government actions that protect children while using the Internet. _____

4. What is an overvoltage? What precautions should teachers take to protect their computers and other electronic equipment from overvoltages, both at home and at school? _____

5. What is an Acceptable Use Policy (AUP)? Why are AUPs so important for K-12 schools? Describe two other ways to limit student access to inappropriate Internet sites. _____

Teaching Today

INSTRUCTIONS: Teaching Today provides an appreciation of the value that technology and the Web have for K-12 education. Each numbered segment contains one or more links that reinforce the information presented in the segment. To display this page from the Web, visit scsite.com/tdc4. Click Chapter 8 at the top of the Web page and then click Teaching Today on the left sidebar.

1. Filtering Software

Parents are concerned about objectionable materials found on the Internet and are looking for some kind of protection. Your district is considering installing filtering software. What are the benefits of filtering software? Is filtering software foolproof? Why or why not? What are the disadvantages of filtering software? What type of report would you make to your school board about installing filtering software? How could an Acceptable Use Policy address the issue of objectionable materials?

2. Acceptable Use Policy

You are an innovative teacher with three multi-media computers connected to the Internet in your classroom. You also have access to a wireless mobile lab and many other technologies. Your school has a schoolwide Acceptable Use Policy (AUP) for teachers, staff, students, and parents. You have been thinking, however, about having an additional AUP for your students and their parents, not only to protect the students, but also to have your students learn how to use different technologies responsibly and safely. What key components do you think your AUP should include? Do you think you should let your students help you create the AUP? Do you think this might be a good learning experience for the students? Why or why not? What are some consequences you think students should face for violating your classroom AUP? How will you enforce the AUP with students and parents?

3. Viruses

Recently, you have been hearing a lot about viruses. You have two computers in your classroom and they are connected to the Internet. In the past, you have not worried about viruses because your computers have never been infected. Other teachers, however, have been discussing a new virus affecting their computers. Where can you get reliable information about viruses? What kind of support is available on the Internet? Can you get a virus from the Internet? How can you protect your computers from getting a virus?

4. Fair Use

Based on Section 107 of the Copyright Act of 1976, also known as fair use, teachers are allowed to photocopy and use copyrighted materials in their classrooms for educational purposes. With the advent of digital media, the Internet, and the World Wide Web, legislators have had to reexamine fair use. How do you think fair use rules apply to digital media, the Internet, and the Web? Is using materials found on the Web different from using materials found in a copyrighted book? How can you determine if your use of copyrighted materials is governed by fair-use rules? Because it has become so easy to copy materials from so many different sources, how will you teach your students about copyright laws and fair use?

Education Issues

8

INSTRUCTIONS: Education Issues provides several scenarios that allow you to explore controversial and current issues in education. Each numbered segment contains one or more links that reinforce the information presented in the segment. To display this page from the Web, visit scsite.com/tdc4. Click Chapter 8 at the top of the Web page and then click Education Issues on the left sidebar.

1. Research and Term Papers

For years, the only way to write a term paper was to visit the library, walk through shelves of texts and journals to find what you needed — before you even started to write. Today, obtaining a paper is as easy as clicking a mouse button. Several sites on the Web now provide a searchable database of term papers gathered from college and high school students. Students can download a research or term paper, make any necessary changes, print a copy, and then turn it in as their own. How can instructors keep students from claiming the work of others as their own? Can you explain how using the Web for research differs from using it to copy someone's work? What should be the consequences for plagiarizing content from a Web site?

2. Teacher and Student Monitoring

Your school district maintains a policy that states classroom computers and Internet access are to be used for instructional purposes only. The district instructs teachers not to send or receive personal e-mail messages or instant messages (IMs), surf the Internet for fun, or play games on classroom computers. The district uses monitoring software to observe Internet activities. Some teachers feel they should be allowed to use the Internet or work on their personal projects during their lunch periods and after school. What limits, if any, should be placed on teachers' use of classroom computers? How closely should the school district be able to monitor teacher and student use? Why? Network specialists can see anything and everything on your computer. Should administrative personnel be allowed to monitor your e-mail messages and files on your school computer? Why or why not? Should you be allowed to monitor your students' e-mail messages? Why or why not?

3. Software Ethics

You recently purchased a DK Multimedia CD using your own funds for use on one computer in your classroom. Another teacher likes the software and borrows your CD so she can evaluate it for use in her classroom. A few weeks later, you find out that numerous other teachers in your school have a copy of the DK Multimedia CD. You ask the teacher about this and she says, "Oh, this is so cool. I have a CD-RW on my home computer and it is so easy to copy CDs. I am so proud of myself! I made one for everyone!" You know this breaks copyright laws, could get the school fined, and that it also is morally and ethically wrong. What to do? Should you tell the teacher, your principal, or technology facilitator? Could you be liable because you loaned her the original CD? How will you solve this dilemma?

4. Software Piracy

Software manufacturers are watching school districts closely for evidence of illegal use of software. Recently, a major school district was fined $300,000 for having multiple copies of nonlicensed software installed on classroom computers. Teachers often illegally install multiple copies of single-user programs on their classroom computers. What are some of the ethical issues regarding software piracy? Why is illegally installing software so prevalent in K-12 schools? How does the software industry deal with violators of software copyright law? Describe several ways in which school districts can prevent illegal software from being installed on school computers.

5. Students, School Buses and Lunches, and Biometrics

A Florida school district requires that students provide a biometric thumbprint both as they enter and as they leave their GPS-tracked school buses each day. The school system cites both safety and financial (the fact that more accurate counting and tracking of the bus usage will result in more state transportation funds) reasons for using GPS. An Ohio school system requires that students use a biometric thumbprint to pay for their school lunches. The school board cites the need to track the number of free and subsidized lunches that the schools provide better. Should children be required to provide biometric information to engage in common public school-related activities? Why or why not? What are the privacy issues involved and should parents be concerned?

Integration Corner

INSTRUCTIONS: Integration Corner provides extensive ideas and resources for integrating technology into your classroom-specific curriculum. To display this page from the Web and its links to approximately 100 educational Web sites, visit scsite.com/tdc4. Click Chapter 8 at the top of the Web page and then click Integration Corner on the left sidebar.

Integration Corner is designed for teachers and other educators who are looking for innovative ways to integrate technology into their content-specific curriculum. Integration Corner not only provides great Web sites with current information, but also shows what other educators are doing in the field of educational technology. These Corners are designed for all educators regardless of their area of interest. Be sure to review information and Web sites outside of your teaching area because many great integration ideas in one area can be modified easily for use in other curricular areas.

Teachers and administrators will find other colleagues in their areas with whom to connect and share the successes and hurdles of integrating technology into the classroom or an entire school system. Consider Integration Corner your one stop for integration ideas and resources. Links to educational Web sites are organized in the following 12 Corners, and different Web resources are available for each chapter. Figure 8-45 shows examples of the Web resources provided in the Chapter 8 Research Corner.

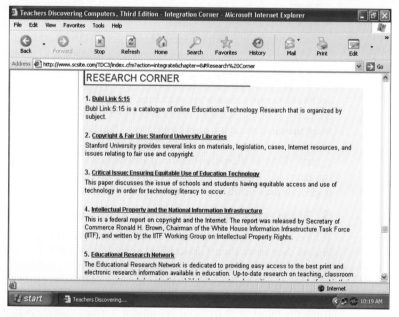

Figure 8-45 Examples of the Web resources provided in the Chapter 8 Research Corner.

Software Corner

INSTRUCTIONS: Software Corner provides information on popular software programs. Each numbered segment discusses specific software programs and contains a link to additional information about these programs. To display this page from the Web, visit scsite.com/tdc4. Click Chapter 8 at the top of the Web page and then click Software Corner on the left sidebar.

1. Antivirus Programs

Computer viruses spread faster than the common cold! When you and your students download files from the Internet, open e-mail attachments, or transport files between computers, you are at risk of getting a virus. Norton AntiVirus or McAfee's VirusScan will detect viruses in e-mail attachments, in files, on USB flash drives, and in your computer's system files. Both companies allow users to update their virus protection files online. These antivirus programs can be set up to scan your computer automatically on a regular basis. Their Web sites provide information about the latest viruses as well as news releases and virus tips to help consumers better protect themselves.

2. Ad-Aware SE Personal Edition

When using the Internet, problems are sometimes just one click away. Students are often lured by the "You have won!" pop-up ads that display on numerous Web sites. Unfortunately, many Web sites, including those with pop-up ads, install hidden files on computers that visit these sites. These hidden files cannot be removed by antivirus programs and, unfortunately, slow computers down significantly, sometimes even shutting down routers. One software program that can "sniff" out these files and quarantine or remove them from your computer is called Ad-Aware SE Personal Edition. This program allows you to scan and clean your computer's internal and external storage devices for annoying adware and spyware programs, allowing you to maintain a higher degree of privacy while you surf the Web.

3. Monitoring Software

Having an AUP is not always enough! Due to all the types of illegal activities that can take place using computers, many businesses, the military, and schools are purchasing software to monitor all activities on their computers. Spector Pro is one of the top-selling software programs for monitoring and recording every detail or keystroke of PC and Internet activity. Spector Pro provides the equivalent of a digital surveillance tape so that you can see everything students, teachers, or employees are doing on their computers. Spector Pro contains seven integrated tools that record the following: chats, instant messages, e-mails sent and received, Web sites visited, keystrokes typed, programs launched, and peer-to-peer file searching and swapping. In addition to monitoring and recording, Spector Pro has an advanced warning system that informs the system administrator when a PC being monitored has been used in an inappropriate manner.

4. Logal Science

Getting middle-school students interested in science is easiest when students can connect science with their everyday lives. Riverdeep strives to create this connection through real-life scenarios in its Logal Science series. The science curriculum spans from middle school to college level science concepts. Activities are designed with multimedia, streaming audio, animation, and a complete toolbox for student activities. Activities are packaged with lesson plans and printable screen shots for documentation. You can download science simulation activities and demos from Logal Middle School Science Gateways, Logal High School Science Gateways, or Logal High School Science Explorer at this Web site.

Digital Media Corner

INSTRUCTIONS: Today's K-12 digital students need their learning to be meaningful and relevant to their lives. Digital Media Corner provides videos, ideas, and examples of how you can use digital media to enhance your teaching and your students' learning. To access the videos and links to additional information, visit scsite.com/tdc4. Click Chapter 8 at the top of the Web page and then click Digital Media on the left sidebar.

1. At the Movies — Does Biometrics Violate Employee Privacy?

Many companies and some school districts are turning to high-tech methods of identifying and tracking employees and students. Biometric identification methods, which include fingerprint, iris, voice, hand, and facial scans, are gaining in popularity. These methods used to be associated with high-security facilities; but due to increased risk from terrorism, they are gaining popularity in other workplaces and school. Can biometric identification be used as a safety measure for teachers and students? To learn more about biometrics, click the G4TechTV video link. Locate your video and click the corresponding High-Speed or Dial-up link, depending on your Internet connection.

2. At the Movies — Detect Spyware on Your Computer

Some programs on your computer installed spyware along with the program when the program was installed. Different types of spyware exist, such as keystroke recorder spyware and advertising spyware. Spyware either collects information and sends it over the Internet to whoever installed it or stores it for later retrieval. To learn more about detecting spyware on your computer, click the G4TechTV video link. Locate your video and click the corresponding High-Speed or Dial-up link, depending on your Internet connection.

3. At the Movies — VeriChip

In 2001, Applied Digital Solutions introduced the VeriChip, which is similar to a MedicAlert bracelet. The chip is implanted under the skin instead of being worn externally. It is digitally inscribed with a number that, when read with a special scanner and entered into a database, gives doctors access to medial records. The company says the chip could be a lifesaver for people with illnesses that may inhibit their ability to communicate with doctors or life-squad personnel. Privacy rights experts say the chip could be used to track people remotely who are unaware they have been implanted with the chip. What are the pros and cons of making this technology widely available? To learn more VeriChips, click the G4TechTV video link. Locate your video and click the corresponding High-Speed or Dial-up link, depending on your Internet connection.

4. Visual Communicator

Today, students are creating digital media elements, and sharing them with classmates in project-based learning environments. Software has become so user-friendly that even young learners can include digital media in their projects by using products such as Visual Communicator. Visual Communicator is designed specifically for users who are novices at making videos. There are many ways educators can integrate the software into their discipline-specific curriculum through instruction, student projects, and assignments, such as multimedia video production projects, video booktalks, video science and math projects, video yearbooks, and more.

5. Video Yearbooks

Video yearbooks are not a new idea but some schools are trying a new idea this year. At the beginning of the school year, selected seniors are designated as journalists who are asked to record their daily lives and activities their senior year. Using smart phones or small handheld digital cameras, these journals are recorded and uploaded as video blogs or vlogs to a senior class Web site. These informal digital journals are then released to the students who can follow along. At the end of the year, the vlogs are consolidated using video postproduction editing techniques so they can be saved to a DVD for distribution as a video yearbook or combined with the traditional paper version of the yearbooks.

Assistive Technologies Corner

INSTRUCTIONS: Assistive Technologies Corner provides information on current hardware, software, and peripherals that will assist you in delivering instruction to students with physical, cognitive, or sensory challenges. To access extensive additional information, visit scsite.com/tdc4. Click Chapter 8 at the top of the Web page and then click Assistive Technologies on the left sidebar.

1. What Is the Federal Accessibility Initiative?

In 1998, Congress amended the Rehabilitation Act to require federal agencies to make their electronic and information technology accessible to people with disabilities. Under Section 508, agencies must give all persons with disabilities access to technology that is comparable to the access available to others. In addition, the World Wide Web Consortium (W3C) has developed accessibility guidelines encouraging Web authors worldwide to create accessible pages.

2. What Are Accessible Web Pages?

Accessible Web pages are constructed to be usable by anyone, even if the person is using assistive technology to access the Web page. Examples of assistive technologies are screen readers, screen magnifiers, voice recognition software, alternative keyboards, and Braille displays. We speak of accessible Web pages as being Section 508 compliant, or having AAA conformance to Web accessibility guidelines.

3. Do I Have to Make My Web Pages Accessible?

The Individuals with Disabilities Education Act (IDEA) of 1997 guarantees access to curriculum for all users. Many school districts have accessibility policies in place and compliance with those policies is a professional responsibility. After a teacher-created Web page is posted, all have access to it, including persons with disabilities.

4. So, How Can I Make My Pages Accessible?

An educator can begin an effort towards accessibility by considering the following issues when developing Web pages.

1. **Use valid code.** WYSIWYG (What You See Is What You Get) programs for Web authoring, such as Dreamweaver, have means for checking that the HTML code in the pages is valid (correct). Use the option to check code validity in your program of choice.
2. **Use CSS (Cascading Style Sheets) in styling pages.** In the preferences of your WYSIWYG program, choose anything that says, Use CSS.
3. **Provide text alternatives to images.** When you add an image to a page, write a descriptive phrase for the image, which a screen reader will voice.
4. **Make meaning independent of color.** "Click the red triangle" can be a difficult task for a color-blind person.
5. **Include visible text links** on a page for images that have hyperlinked hot spots.
6. **Use column-and-row tables for data only.** Put column and row headers in those data tables.
7. If you choose to use frames, be sure to **title each frame** you use.
8. **Do not depend on scripts** to make your Web site work. Some users (not only disabled users) may not be able to run the scripts.
9. **Caption video** before putting it on your site.
10. Provide users with an option to **skip repetitive links,** such as site navigation links.

Follow the instructions at the top of this page to display additional information and this chapter's links on assistive technologies.

In the Lab

INSTRUCTIONS: In the Lab provides rubric development exercises that are divided into two areas, productivity and integration. To access the links to tutorials, productivity ideas, integration examples and ideas, and more, visit scsite.com/tdc4. Click Chapter 8 at the top of the Web page and then click In the Lab on the left sidebar.

PRODUCTIVITY IN THE CLASSROOM

Introduction: Effectively integrating technology in the curriculum allows students to demonstrate their learning using creative, motivating, and nontraditional means. Digital media projects and presentations, as well as other technology-oriented presentations provide students with authentic learning activities and require a different form of assessment. Rubrics can provide teachers with a more authentic assessment tool.

Chapter 7 introduced the use of rubrics as a means of alternative assessment. Rubrics assist students in understanding teacher expectations and provide a clear outline when creating projects. Students also can use rubrics as a self-assessment tool. This encourages students to be more involved and responsible for their learning.

Teachers easily can create rubrics using numerous software applications, such as word processing, spreadsheet, Web editors, or other commercial products. Free online resources also are available that walk teachers through the process of creating a variety of rubrics and performance checklists.

1. Creating and Formatting a Problem-Solving Math Rubric

Problem: To encourage students in your sixth-grade math class to use higher-order thinking skills, you are beginning a unit on problem solving. Students will be given problems and have to write out how they solve the problem and their reasoning for selecting the approach they use. You design a rubric to guide your students through this process. The rubric is shown in Figure 8-46. Open your word processing, spreadsheet, or Web editing software and create the rubric as described in the following steps. (*Hint:* use any appropriate clip art image and font to personalize the rubric. Use Help to understand the steps better.)

Instructions: Perform the following tasks.

1. Insert the clip art image.
2. Format the first heading line, Mrs. Georgiev's, in 20-point Times or Times New Roman bold font. Personalize the rubric by inserting your name instead of Mrs. Georgiev's.
3. Format the second heading line, 6th Grade Math Class, in 20-point Times or Times New Roman bold font.
4. Format the third heading line, Math Problem-Solving Rubric, in 18-point Times or Times New Roman font.
5. Insert a table with six rows and five columns.
6. Center the row headings and format them in 12-point Times New Roman bold font.
7. Enter the table text as shown in Figure 8-46 and then format the text in 12-point Times New Roman font.
8. Personalize the school name and insert the current date. Format the school name and date in 12-point Times or Times New Roman bold font. Insert your e-mail address instead of Mrs. Georgiev's. Format the e-mail address in 12-point Times or Times New Roman, blue bold font.
9. Save the rubric to the location file of your choice using an appropriate filename. Print the rubric and then follow your instructor's directions for handing in the assignment.

In the Lab

8

Mrs. Georgiev's
6th Grade Math Class
Math Problem-Solving Rubric

Task	Beginning 1 - 2	Developing 3 - 4	Advancing 5	Score
Student uses math language to explain the problem.	Used a few math terms in the explanation of the solution and the explanation was brief.	Used some math terms in the explanation of the solution and the explanation was adequate.	Used math terms correctly throughout the explanation of the solution and the explanation was thorough and complete.	
Student explanation demonstrates understanding of the problem.	Misinterpreted parts of the problem.	Solved the problem with minor interpretation errors.	Answer demonstrates complete understanding of the problem.	
Student articulates plan for solving the problem.	The plan for solving the problem is partially correct.	The plan for solving the problem is correct but may lead to minor errors.	The plan for solving the problem is accurate and will lead to a correct solution.	
Student correctly solves the problem.	The answer is incorrect or not solved.	Part of the problem is solved correctly.	The answer is correct and the work supports the answer.	
			TOTAL POINTS	

Woodrow Wilson Middle School
April 12, 2007
b_georgiev@tricounty.k12.ia.us

Figure 8-46

In the Lab

2. Creating and Formatting a Multimedia Research Rubric

Problem: You want to introduce your high school students to a systematic approach to research. The students will access, evaluate, and use information from a variety of sources on an assigned topic. Then they will write a research paper and create a digital media presentation to present their findings to the class. At the beginning of the unit, you hand out the rubric shown in Figure 8-47. (*Hint:* use any appropriate clip art images and fonts to personalize the page. Use Help to understand the steps better.)

Mr. Hernandez
World History Class
Digital Media Research Project Rubric

Student Name: ——————————— Topic: —————— Date: ———

	Level 1	Level 2	Level 3	Level 4	Self–Score	Teacher Score
Research Process:						
Gathered information from journals, books, CD–ROMs, and the Internet	0 1 2	3 4 5	6 7 8	9 10		
Resources are current and reliable	0 1 2	3 4 5	6 7 8	9 10		
Extracted, synthesized, and applied appropriate information	0 1 2	3 4 5	6 7 8	9 10		
Writing Process:						
Organized information from resources to complete research paper	0 1 2	3 4 5	6 7 8	9 10		
Paper written following steps in writing process	0 1 2	3 4 5	6 7 8	9 10		
References documented using MLA citation style	0 1 2	3 4 5	6 7 8	9 10		
Multimedia Project:						
Presentation includes title slide, a minimum of seven content slides, and a bibliography slide	0 1 2	3 4 5	6 7 8	9 10		
Graphic images are used appropriately and gathered from a variety of resources	0 1 2	3 4 5	6 7 8	9 10		
Presentation is well organized, visually appealing, flows well	0 1 2	3 4 5	6 7 8	9 10		
Presentation:						
Demonstrates good speaking skills	0 1 2	3 4 5	6 7 8	9 10		
TOTAL POINTS:						

Figure 8-47

In the Lab

Instructions: Refer to Figure 8-47. Format the first and second heading lines in 16-point Lucinda Sans Unicode bold font. Insert your name in place of Mr. Hernandez. Format the third heading line in 14-point Lucinda Sans Unicode bold font. Insert clip art or graphic images. Format the Student Name, Topic, and Date headings in 10-point Lucinda Sans Unicode bold font. Format the section headings in 10-point Lucinda Sans Unicode bold underlined font. Format the the text in 10-point Lucinda Sans Unicode font.

After you have typed and formatted the rubric, save the rubric to the location of your choice using an appropriate filename. Print the rubric and then follow your instructor's directions for handing in the assignment.

3. Creating and Formatting a Subject-Specific Rubric

Problem: You want to create a rubric to evaluate student learning of a concept you are presenting. The rubric also will serve as a guide for students as they create their end-of-unit project that demonstrates their learning.

Instructions: Create a rubric similar to the rubrics illustrated in Figures 8-46 or 8-47. Use an appropriate layout; font types, styles, and sizes; and clip art images. Include your name and the subject area you teach. After you have created the rubric, save the rubric to the location of your choice using an appropriate filename. Print the rubric and then follow your instructor's directions for handing in the assignment.

INTEGRATION IN THE CLASSROOM

1. At the beginning of the school year, you want to establish classroom rules and criteria for positive behavior in your second-grade special education classroom. You decide to create a behavior rubric together with your students that will be used and sent home weekly to parents. You ask the students for their ideas about positive classroom behavior, and together, you and your students create a rubric on which you all agree. Create a sample behavior rubric for your students. Include your name, school name, and the current date on the rubric.

2. The students in your Earth Science class have been studying the environment and environmental hazards such as acid rain and oil spills. As a final project for the unit, students will work in groups and conduct a research activity. They will present their findings in either a PowerPoint presentation or a video. To encourage the students to take responsibility for their learning, you first assign each group to the task of developing a rubric that outlines the assessment criteria for their final project. You will assist the students as necessary; however, you believe they will have more ownership in their learning and be more motivated if they establish the majority of the criteria themselves. Create a sample rubric for your students to use as a guide. Include your name, subject area, project topic, and current date on the rubric.

3. Ask your students to research Web page evaluation rubrics on the Internet to prepare them to create Web pages. The students will work in groups to locate and print a minimum of five different Web page evaluation rubrics. They then will compare and contrast the different rubrics and determine what is important when creating a Web page. As a class, you will brainstorm, create a rubric, and then use this rubric to create Web pages. Include a column for self-evaluation. Locate at least three different Web page evaluation rubrics. From your research, create a rubric to use as an example for your students. Include your name and class at the top of the rubric. Include your e-mail address and the current date at the bottom of the rubric.

Learn It Online

INSTRUCTIONS: Use the Learn It Online exercises to reinforce your understanding of the chapter concepts and increase your computer, information, and integration literacy. To access dozens of interactive student labs, practice tests, learning games, and more, visit scsite.com/tdc4. Click Chapter 8 at the top of the Web page and then click Learn It Online on the left sidebar.

1. Student Edition Labs — Keeping Your Computer Virus Free, Protecting Your Privacy Online, and Wireless Networking

For the labs to work properly, you must have your screen resolution set to 1024x768 or higher. For a short tutorial on how to change your screen resolution, click here. You also will need Flash 7.0 or higher. To view these interactive labs, click the Student Edition Labs link. When the Student Edition Labs menu appears, click the desired or the assigned lab to begin. A new browser window will open. Follow the on-screen instructions to complete the lab. When finished, click the Exit button. If required, submit your results to your instructor.

2. Using the Windows XP Firewall

When you use the Internet, data is sent both from your computer to the Internet and from computers on the Internet to your computer. A firewall is a barrier that checks information coming from the Internet and either turns it away or allows it to pass through to your computer, based upon your firewall settings. It also checks data being sent from your computer to the Internet to ensure your computer is not sending unsolicited messages. Click the Windows XP Firewall link to learn how to control the firewall usage on your computer.

3. Expanding Your Understanding

All states have content specific accountability standards. To learn more about your state's content standards, click the State Standards link.

4. Practice Test

Click the Practice Test link. Answer each question. When completed, enter your name and click the Grade Test button to submit the quiz for grading. Make a note of any missed questions. If required, submit your score to your instructor.

5. Who Wants to Be a Computer Genius?

Click the Computer Genius link to find out if you are a computer genius. Directions about how to play the game will be displayed. When you are ready to play, click the Play button. If required, submit your score to your instructor.

6. Wheel of Terms

Click the Wheel of Terms link to reinforce important terms you learned in this chapter by playing the Shelly Cashman Series version of this popular game. Directions about how to play the game will be displayed. When you are ready to play, click the Play button. If required, submit your score to your instructor.

7. Crossword Puzzle Challenge

Click the Crossword Puzzle link. Complete the puzzle to reinforce skills you learned in this chapter. Directions about how to play the game will be displayed. When you are ready to play, click the Play button. If required, submit the completed puzzle to your instructor.

A World Without Wires

Each time you use your smart phone, tune your television to a soccer game being played on another continent, or listen to satellite radio in your car, you are enjoying the benefits of the world of wireless communications. New wireless devices, including smart phones and pagers, PDAs, Tablet PCs, and notebook computers with high-speed Internet access, simplify and expand your communications abilities. Wireless technology also is changing many other hardware devices that traditionally needed cords to transmit data, such as printers and video projectors.

Wireless communications technology is not new. More than 100 years ago, Guglielmo Marconi sent the first wireless teletype message by using radio waves. Today, Marconi's discoveries allow you to connect peripherals to your desktop computers without using wires and to build a wireless home network. You also can keep in touch with family and associates from anywhere in the world by telephone or e-mail using a variety of wireless products.

Wireless technology has transformed the way people work, communicate, and learn and has won popular acclaim worldwide in a very short period. Even the casual observer notices dramatic changes in the way computers are used in homes, schools, and businesses, as well as to send e-mail, communicate, access the Internet, display photos, and create and share files. Today's teachers and students are part of this wireless revolution — a revolution that is fundamentally changing the way students and teachers communicate and collaborate with each other.

Although Marconi laid the foundation for wireless technology more than a century ago, today's wireless products and standards represent an evolution of his original discoveries. Each day, the number of wireless devices increases as the price of connectivity decreases. As the world goes wireless, Asia and Western Europe have emerged as world leaders in wireless device use. Experts estimate that over 1 billion wireless devices are in use worldwide and hundreds of millions of wireless devices are sold every year.

This special feature looks at a wide variety of wireless products and illustrates how various segments of society, including K-12 education, use wireless technology. The following section provides a brief overview of wireless networks and some of the terms often associated with wireless technology.

WIRELESS NETWORKS AND TERMINOLOGY

Several years ago, Nicholas Negroponte, founder and director of MIT's Media Lab, predicted what has

come to be known as the Negroponte Flip. Negroponte predicted that communications media that formerly were wireless would become wired, and media that were formerly wired would become wireless. Evidence of the Negroponte Flip can be seen today in the emergence of cable television (wireless to wired) and the explosion in voice and data services over wireless networks (wired to wireless).

Wireless networks can be characterized generally by the area they cover. The following sections briefly describe wireless personal area networks, wireless local area networks, and wireless metropolitan and wide area networks.

Wireless Personal Area Network (WPAN)

A **wireless personal area network (WPAN)** is a short-range wireless network often based on Bluetooth technology. **Bluetooth** technology uses short-range radio waves to transmit data between two Bluetooth devices such as smart phones, headsets, microphones, digital cameras, fax machines, printers, desktop computers, Tablet PCs, notebook computers, and many other wireless devices (Figure 1). Bluetooth-equipped

Number of Wireless Devices

FIGURE 1 Bluetooth technology allows users to connect devices wirelessly in a multitude of ways.

devices *discover* each other and form *paired* connections. Examples of paired connections include a cellular telephone and a headset, a keyboard or printer and a PC, a notebook computer, and a PDA. To communicate with each other, Bluetooth devices should be within approximately 10 meters, or 33 feet, of each other. Some Bluetooth devices will work up to 100 feet or more from each other.

Many devices that traditionally have required wires, such as printers, keyboards, scanners, digital cameras, and notebook computers, are now manufactured with integrated Bluetooth technology. Both Mac OS X and Windows XP have built-in Bluetooth support that allows users easily to configure Bluetooth communications. For computers and devices not Bluetooth-enabled, you can purchase a Bluetooth wireless port adapter that will convert an existing USB port into a Bluetooth port (Figure 2). Using Bluetooth technology, your notebook or desktop computer can connect wirelessly to a variety of devices. Besides connecting Bluetooth-enabled devices, you also can easily transfer files from a PC to a Macintosh computer and vice versa using Bluetooth technology.

An emerging technology with greater bandwidth capabilities than Bluetooth is **Ultra-Wideband (UWB)**, which provides high-speed, wireless communications to devices throughout a digital home and office. Designed for WPANs, UWB enables wireless connection of multiple devices for transmission of video, audio, and other high-bandwidth data.

Today, most home computer and consumer electronic devices, from digital camcorders and DVD players to high-definition TVs, require wires, turning most home entertainment areas into a wired jungle. UWB could eliminate these wires and allow all electronic components for an entire home to be set up and connected to each other without a single wire, a true home without wires.

Wireless Local Area Networks (WLAN)

A **wireless local area network (WLAN)** is a network that uses wireless media, such as radio waves, to connect computers and devices in a limited space, such as a home, classroom, office building, or school. Wireless LANs are based on the Institute of Electrical and Electronics Engineers (IEEE) 802.11 standard. The term **802.11** refers to a family of specifications developed for wireless local area networks that allows computers and other devices to communicate via radio waves. The nonprofit organization, **Wi-Fi Alliance**, was established in 1999 and certifies the interoperability of 802.11 products (Figure 3). **Wi-Fi**, short for *wireless fidelity*, is a popular term used when referring to any type of 802.11 network. Currently, numerous standards for the 802.11 specification exist. The first and most common is 802.11b; 802.11a and 802.11g are more recent.

Wi-Fi networking hardware is becoming standard equipment on many notebook computers, PDAs, and other wireless devices. In many public locations, people connect their computers or devices to the Internet wirelessly using Wi-Fi standards through a **public Internet access point**. Users can connect to the Internet if their computers or devices have an appropriate network card and as long as they are in a hot spot. A **hot spot** is an area with the capabilities of wireless Internet connectivity. The area of most hot spots ranges from 100 to 300 feet when located inside a building and up to 1,000 feet when

FIGURE 2 Bluetooth USB adapters, like the one shown, can be purchased for less than $40.

FIGURE 3 The Wi-Fi Alliance certifies 802.11 products and provides extensive information and resources on wireless networks.

located in open or outdoor areas. Today, Wi-Fi public Internet access points are emerging everywhere, including bookstores, malls, airports, city parks, universities, downtown areas of major cities, and many other locations (Figure 4). In fact, some cities are set up as a Wi-Fi mesh network, in which each mesh node routes its data to the next available node until the data reaches its destination, usually an Internet connection.

Access to the Internet is now available via wireless devices in many places outside of your home, school, or office. A **cybercafé** is a coffeehouse or restaurant that provides computers with Internet access to its customers.

Many cybercafés today provide hot spots and Wi-Fi Internet access points for their customers. In addition, you can access the world wirelessly while traveling on airplanes,

trains, ferries, cruise ships, and even your car. Currently, tens of thousands of Wi-Fi hot spots exist worldwide and this number is expected to increase dramatically over the next few years. You can locate hot spots in your community and around the world by using the ZONE Finder search tool at the Wi-Fi Alliance Web site (Figure 5 on the next page).

Although some Wi-Fi distributors provide free Internet access, most charge a per-hour or per-minute fee. Users can easily identify hot spots by looking for the **Wi-Fi ZONE** logo (refer again to Figure 5). In addition, a grass roots movement called warchalking is helping users identify hot spots that provide free Wi-Fi access. **Warchalking** refers to the practice of using chalk to draw a series of symbols on sidewalks

FIGURE 4 Users can access the Web from many locations using Wi-Fi technology.

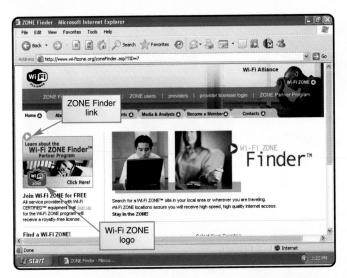

FIGURE 5 The ZONE Finder site lists service providers that meet industry standards.

to direct people to places that provide wireless access (Figure 6). The use of chalk to communicate messages to passerbys originated during the Great Depression to describe the practice of hobos who used chalk marks to indicate which homes would provide a meal.

FIGURE 6 This warchalking symbol indicates an open node, which is an area offering free wireless Internet access.

Wireless Metropolitan Area and Wide Area Networks

A **wireless metropolitan area network (WMAN)** is a wireless network designed to cover an urban area. WMANs are being installed in both large and small cities by organizations and for-profit companies dedicated to providing free or for-a-fee wireless access in public spaces.

For example, NYCwireless promotes wireless hot spots in public spaces such as parks, coffee shops, and building lobbies throughout the New York City region (Figure 7). NYCwireless also is working with public and other nonprofit organizations to provide broadband wireless Internet access to underserved communities.

A **wireless wide area network (WWAN)** is a wireless network that covers a wide geographic area and uses a variety of technologies including radio, satellite, and mobile telephone technologies. A number of major corporations such as Verizon, Sprint, AT&T, MCI, and others are creating wireless wide area networks to provide their customers access to the Internet from any location at any time.

FIGURE 7 The mission of NYCwireless is to provide free wireless Internet service in public spaces throughout the New York City area.

WIRELESS TECHNOLOGY AND EDUCATION

Wireless networking is becoming commonplace in institutions of higher education. According to a recent Campus Computing Survey of The Campus Computing Project, nearly 81 percent of surveyed institutions reported the use of WLANs, and 20 percent reported the use of full-campus wireless access.

For example, the University of Central Florida (UCF) has made wireless networking available over its entire campus—in classroom buildings, the library, administrative offices, the student union, residence halls, and even

FIGURE 8 The campus of the University of Central Florida and all new classroom buildings are designed to take advantage of the benefits of wireless networking, allowing students access to information, their classes, and each other from any campus location.

outdoor locations where students gather (Figure 8). In addition, students who visit the UCF library without their own notebook computers can check out wireless notebook computers for use throughout the library.

Today, schools and institutions of higher learning use wireless networks to access the same applications used on wired networks: electronic mail, Web access, and instant messaging. The main advantage that wireless brings is flexibility, which allows users to access e-mail and the Web at any time and from any location. Wireless networks also offer other unique benefits, such as the ability to easily set up temporary computing locations, network buildings that would be difficult or impossible to wire, or provide connections to every student in a classroom, auditorium, or outdoor setting.

Wireless networks also are becoming common in many K-12 schools and school districts (Figure 9). Every day, schools all over the world are discovering new benefits and advantages of using wireless networks. For example, teachers now can use interactive wireless

FIGURE 9 Students are actively engaged in taking a *wireless practice quiz*. Similar engagement, excitement, and competitiveness are difficult to create using traditional paper-and-pencil quizzes.

computers to determine how well students comprehend class material. They can ask students to respond to a multiple-choice or true-false question using a wireless keypad resembling a remote control. Within seconds, an infrared reader captures the students' responses, and a computer tabulates the results and tracks their scores. Students react exceedingly well to this type of interactivity in the assessment process.

The trend is clear, many K-12 schools and institutions of higher education are replacing their wired networks with high-speed or broadband wireless networks that use a variety of wireless devices, including the Tablet PC.

Wireless Tablet PC

The wireless Tablet PC is the ideal tool for today's classroom for many reasons. About the size of a spiral notebook, the Tablet PC combines all the power and speed of a desktop computer with Windows XP Tablet PC software, which enables pen- and voice-based computing (Figure 10). Just as the Internet is breaking down the traditional four walls of the classroom, the Tablet PC will break down traditional pencil-and-paper learning.

FIGURE 10 The Tablet PC has the potential to change paper-and-pencil learning forever.

WIRELESS TECHNOLOGY AND SOCIETY

Messaging is driving the wireless market explosion. Today, over 1 billion people send hundreds of billions of wireless messages monthly. In addition, over 80 percent of teenagers in the United States are sending wireless messages every day. Wireless nodes allow individuals to connect their cellular telephones and notebook computers to wireless Web modems and their handheld computers to school and corporate networks. People can access their e-mail, view photographs, run applications, and more.

The following sections describe just a few of the ways that the Wi-Fi revolution is impacting society.

Wireless Messaging

Users can send and receive wireless messages to and from smart phones, cellular telephones, or PDAs using text messaging, video messaging, wireless instant messaging, and picture messaging (Figure 11).

FIGURE 11 Options for wireless messaging.

TEXT MESSAGING A mobile device with **text messaging** capability allows users to receive short text messages on a smart phone or PDA. Most text messaging services limit messages to a specific number of characters, usually fewer than 300 characters.

VIDEO MESSAGING An emerging technology, **video messaging** allows users to take short video clips with a video phone complete with sound and text messaging and send them to another smart phone or computer (Figure 12).

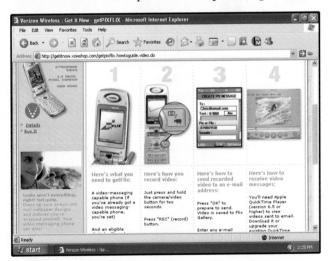

Figure 12 Verizon's wireless video phone allows users to record and send 15-second video clips complete with sound and up to 1000 characters of text to any e-mail address.

WIRELESS INSTANT MESSAGING Wireless instant messaging is a real-time Internet communications service that allows wireless mobile devices to exchange messages with one or more mobile devices or online users.

PICTURE MESSAGING Users can send digital graphics and pictures, as well as text messages with **picture messaging** to another smart phone, PDA, or computer. Smart phones and PDAs with picture messaging capability typically have a digital camera built in to the device.

Wireless Home Networking

A **wireless home network** connects your home computers and peripherals without the use of wires. Family members simultaneously can collaborate on projects, share digital files, print photos and documents, and

access the Internet. Notebook computer users can roam around the house and work as far as 500 feet from the wireless access point, which is the central network hub. Many home networking products are based on Wi-Fi standards and are becoming more affordable, plentiful, and easy to use; some manufacturers claim a buyer can link two computers together and to the Internet in less than one hour for less than $100. Figure 13 shows the steps to set up a wireless home network.

Service Industry

Health care professionals, police officers, package couriers, and retail sales personnel are using handheld computers to help them work more efficiently. Ambulance crews use PDAs to collect and transmit patient data while en route to hospitals. Doctors and nurses

Step 1:
Sign up for high-speed Internet service, such as through a cable or DSL modem.

Step 2:
Using a cable, connect the network card in a desktop computer to the combination router/wireless access point.

Step 3:
Using a cable, connect the combination router/wireless access point to the cable modem.

Step 4:
Install a wireless network card or network adapter in each desktop computer in the home network.

Step 5:
Insert a wireless PC Card into each notebook computer that will access the home network.

Step 6:
Insert a wireless flash card into each PDA that will access the home network.

Internet
wired desktop computer
wireless PDA
router/wireless access point
cable/DSL modem
wireless desktop computer
wireless notebook computer

FIGURE 13 This figure shows the steps necessary to set up a wireless home network.

access patients' records and then record treatments and prescribe medications.

Patrol officers conduct vehicle registration checks (Figure 14) and record crime scene details. Delivery personnel scan package bar codes to track pickup and delivery times and record signatures. Retail managers use PDAs to monitor, transfer, and reorder product inventory.

Global Positioning

Millions of hikers, boaters, pilots, drivers, and other navigators never feel lost with the aid of global positioning system (GPS) devices. These products rely on 24 satellites that circle the Earth twice a day in very precise orbits and transmit data back to Earth. The GPS products then use between 3 to 12 of these satellites to determine the receivers' precise geographic locations (Figure 15). Many GPS devices include color mapping capability that gives detail for any United States city. GPS modules also are available for handheld computers.

FIGURE 14 Instant wireless communications and wireless devices have changed the way police officers and other professionals do their jobs.

Step 1:
GPS satellites orbit Earth. Every thousandth of a second, each satellite sends a signal that indicates its current position to the GPS receiver.

Step 2:
A GPS receiver (such as in a car, a PDA, a watch, a handheld device, or a collar) determines its location on Earth by analyzing at least three separate satellite signals from the 24 satellites in orbit.

FIGURE 15 How GPS works.

Anyplace, Anytime Connectivity

Anyplace, anytime wireless connectivity makes it easy to synchronize files on your handheld computers and notebook computers. When you are on the road, you can connect your wireless devices to a school or office network and automatically transfer databases, appointments, to-do lists, and other files, just as if you were seated in front of your computer. Back at school or your office, you can update your notebook computer and handheld computer the instant you enter the room (Figure 16).

WIRELESS SUMMARY

Your pockets, purses, book bags, and backpacks may be overflowing with small electronic devices, but the wireless revolution is making headway to combine some of these products and simplify your life. Wireless networks are growing throughout the world, driven by convenience, cost, and access and are changing forever the ways people communicate and learn and how they work at home, school, or the office. At one time, computing abilities were limited by the length of wires; now communications and computing have no physical limitations. Wireless communication has removed the wires and opened the doors to anyplace, anytime communications and connectivity — creating a world without boundaries and a world without wires.

FIGURE 16 Wireless technology allows anyplace, anytime computing with the power of instant updating of information between devices.

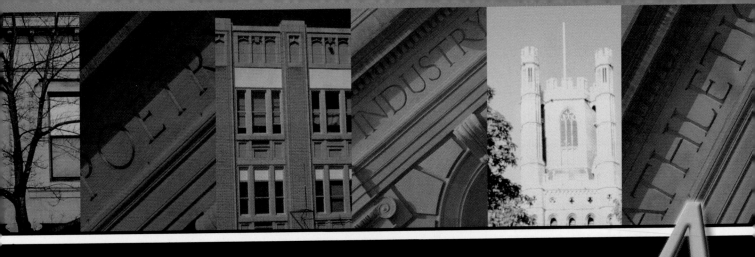

Appendix A

Guide to Professional Educational Organizations

INSTRUCTIONS: To gain World Wide Web access to additional and up-to-date information regarding this appendix and links to these organizations, start your browser and enter the URL, scsite.com/tdc4. When the Teachers Discovering Computers home page is displayed, click the Professional Sites link on the lower-left side of the home page.

Many public and private nonprofit professional organizations provide educators with a variety of Web resources, assistance with important issues that educators deal with on a daily basis, and much more. Professional educational organizations are dedicated to promoting and supporting improvement in student learning and educational practices and provide for professional growth in K-12 education and teacher education. These organizations also provide networking opportunities, information, and leadership in a variety of education areas, including information technology and other technologies integrated into the educational environment. A continually updated Guide to Professional Educational Organizations, which links the most current URLs for a representative cross section of professional organizations, can be found at the Teachers Discovering Computers Web site.

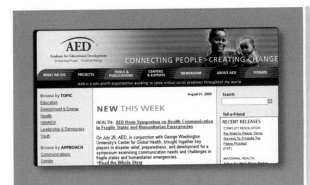

Academy for Educational Development (AED)
www.aed.org

This independent nonprofit organization is committed to solving critical social problems in the United States and abroad through education, social marketing, research, training, policy analysis, and innovative program design and management.

American Association of School Administrators (AASA)

www.aasa.org

The AASA, founded in 1865, is the professional organization for more than 13,000 educational leaders throughout the United States and abroad. The organization's focus is on supporting and developing effective school system leaders who are dedicated to the highest quality public education for all children.

American Federation of Teachers (AFT)

www.aft.org

Founded in 1916, the American Federation of Teachers is a national organization committed to teachers' professional interests. The AFT has more than 1.3 million public and professional members nationwide.

American School Counselor Association (ASCA)

www.schoolcounselor.org

ASCA is a professional organization for licensed school counselors that provides information and resources that support school counselors' efforts to help students focus on academic, personal/social, and career development.

Association for Career and Technical Education (ACTE)

www.acteonline.org

The Association for Career and Technical Education is the largest national education association in the United States that is dedicated to the advancement of career education for both youth and adults. ACTE offers a wide variety of valuable resources for teachers, counselors, and administrators. Start by reading About ACTE, where you will find a complete explanation of what it is and what it does. Do not miss the Member Services area with details on the many benefits offered through association membership.

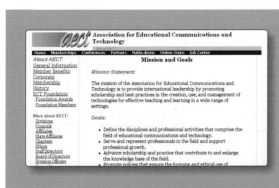

Association for Educational Communications and Technology
www.aect.org

The mission of the Association for Educational Communications and Technology, founded in 1923, is to provide leadership in educational communications and technology by linking professionals holding a common interest in the use of educational technology and its application to the learning process.

Association for Supervision and Curriculum Development (ASCD)
www.ascd.org

The ASCD, founded in 1943, is a unique international, nonprofit, nonpartisan association of professional educators of all grade levels and subject areas; it provides a forum for education issues and shares research, news, and information.

Association for the Advancement of Computing in Education (AACE)
www.aace.org

AACE, founded in 1981, is an international, educational, and professional not-for-profit organization dedicated to the advancement of the knowledge, the theory, and the improvement of the quality of learning and teaching at all levels with information technology.

Computer-Using Educators (CUE)
www.cue.org

Computer-Using Educators, Inc. was founded in 1978 with the goal to promote and develop instructional uses of technology in all disciplines and at all educational levels from preschool through college. CUE is the largest organization of this type in California and one of the largest in the country.

Consortium for School Networking (CoSN)
www.cosn.org

The Consortium for School Networking (CoSN) promotes the use of telecommunications to improve K-12 learning. Members represent state and local education agencies, nonprofits, companies, and individuals. CoSN is dedicated to promoting leadership development, advocacy, coalition building, and emerging technologies.

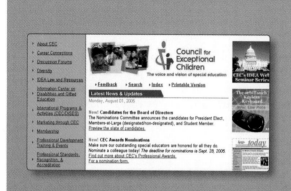

Council for Exceptional Children (CEC)
www.cec.sped.org

The Council for Exceptional Children (CEC) is the largest international professional organization dedicated to improving educational outcomes for individuals with exceptionalities, students with disabilities, and/or gifted students. Visit this Web site to find out how CEC campaigns for appropriate governmental policies, sets professional standards, provides continual professional development, advocates for newly and historically underserved individuals with exceptionalities, and helps professionals obtain conditions and resources necessary for effective professional practice.

Education Week on the Web
www.edweek.org

Education Week maintains a listing of dozens of education organizations with links to their home pages. You can review or search the list alphabetically or by subject.

International Society for Technology in Education (ISTE)
www.iste.org

ISTE consists of international leaders in educational technology. The organization promotes appropriate uses of information technology to support and improve learning, teaching, and administration in K-12 and teacher education.

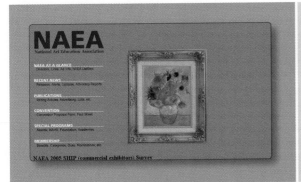

National Art Education Association (NAEA)
www.naea-reston.org

Founded in 1947, NAEA consists of more than 22,000 art educators from every level of instruction, from early childhood to university education. The NAEA is dedicated to quality art education in schools.

National Association for Multicultural Education (NAME)
www.nameorg.org

NAME is an active, growing organization that is working to bring together individuals and groups with an interest in multicultural education at all levels of education, different academic disciplines, and from diverse educational institutions and occupations. Membership includes educators from preschool through higher education and representatives from businesses and communities in 22 states.

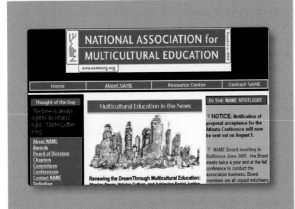

National Association for Music Education (MENC)
www.menc.org

MENC's mission is to advance music education as a profession, and to ensure that every child in America has access to a balanced, sequential, high-quality education that includes music as a core subject of study.

National Association for Sport and Physical Education (NASPE)
www.aahperd.org/naspe

The National Association for Sport and Physical Education enhances knowledge and professional practice in sport and physical activity through scientific study and dissemination of research-based and experiential knowledge to members and the public.

National Association for the Education of Young Children (NAEYC)

www.naeyc.org

Founded in 1926, NAEYC, the nation's largest and most influential organization of early childhood educators, constantly is striving to improve professional practice and working conditions in early childhood education and to build public support for high-quality early childhood programs for children from birth through third grade.

National Association of Elementary School Principals (NAESP)

www.naesp.org

The mission of NAESP is to lead in the advocacy and support of elementary school principals, middle school principals, and other education leaders in their commitment to all children.

National Association of Secondary School Principals (NASSP)

www.principals.org

This professional organization, founded in 1916, includes tens of thousands of middle level and high school principals, assistant principals, and aspiring principals from the United States and other countries around the world. Its mission is to promote excellence in school leadership by offering a wide variety of programs and services to assist members in administration, supervision, curriculum planning, and staff development.

National Business Education Association (NBEA)

www.nbea.org

The National Business Education Association (NBEA) is the nation's largest professional organization devoted exclusively to serving individuals and groups engaged in instruction, administration, research, and dissemination of information for and about business.

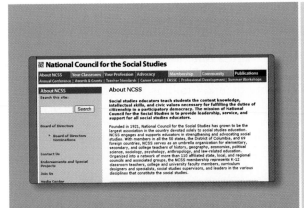

National Council for the Social Studies (NCSS)

www.ncss.org

NCSS engages and supports elementary, secondary, and college teachers of history, geography, economics, political science, sociology, psychology, anthropology, and law-related education. Check out this Web site and find out how to become an NCSS member and join the ranks of thousands of K-12 classroom teachers, college and university faculty members, curriculum designers and specialists, social studies supervisors, and leaders in the various disciplines.

National Council of Teachers of English (NCTE)

www.ncte.org

NCTE's mission is to improve the teaching and learning of English and the language arts at all levels of education. Since 1911, NCTE has provided opportunities for teachers to continue growing professionally. In addition, they founded a forum to deal with issues that affect the teaching of English.

National Council of Teachers of Mathematics (NCTM)

www.nctm.org

For more than 75 years, NCTM has been a recognized leader in efforts to ensure excellent mathematics education for all students, and an opportunity for every mathematics teacher to grow professionally. With about 100,000 members, NCTM is the largest association of mathematics educators in the world, providing professional development opportunities by holding annual regional leadership conferences, and publishing journals, books, videos, and software.

National Education Association (NEA)
www.nea.org

Founded in 1857, NEA is America's oldest and largest organization committed to advancing the cause of public education with more than 2.7 million members who work at every level of education, from preschool to university graduate programs. NEA has affiliates in every state and in more than 13,000 local communities across the United States dedicated to helping students.

National High School Association (NHSA)
www.nhsa.net

The National High School Association is a nonprofit membership association dedicated to improving the professional knowledge of high school educators so that all high school students may experience academic success. Members include administrators, teachers, parents, policymakers, and others interested in student achievement.

National Middle School Association (NMSA)
www.nmsa.org

The National Middle School Association is dedicated to improving the educational experiences of adolescents by providing vision, knowledge, and resources to all who serve them to develop healthy, productive, and ethical citizens. Learn how to become one of the 30,000 members that include principals, teachers, central office personnel, professors, college students, parents, community leaders, and educational consultants across the United States, Canada, and 46 other countries.

National PTA
www.pta.org

PTA is the largest volunteer child advocacy organization in the United States. It is an association of 6 million parents, educators, students, and other citizens who are active leaders in their schools and communities in facilitating parent education and involvement in schools.

National School Boards Association (NSBA)
www.nsba.org

The mission of the NSBA is to foster excellence and equity in public education through school board leadership. The NSBA believes local school boards are the nation's preeminent expression of grass roots democracy and that this form of governance of the public schools is fundamental to the continued success of public education.

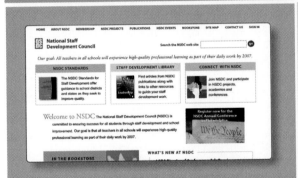

National Science Teachers Association (NSTA)
www.nsta.org

Founded in 1944, NSTA is the largest organization in the world committed to promoting excellence and innovation in science teaching and learning. NSTA's current membership of more than 55,000 includes science teachers, science supervisors, administrators, scientists, business and industry representatives, and others involved in science education.

National Staff Development Council (NSDC)
www.nsdc.org

NSDC is the largest nonprofit professional association committed to ensuring success for all students through staff development and school improvement.

Phi Delta Kappa (PDK)
www.pdkintl.org

Phi Delta Kappa (PDK) is an international association of professional educators. PDK's mission is to promote quality education, with particular emphasis on publicly supported education.

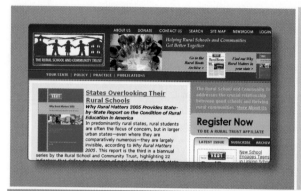

Rural School and Community Trust
www.ruraledu.org

Visit this Web site and you will learn more about this non-profit educational organization dedicated to enlarging student learning and improving community life by strengthening relationships between rural schools and communities and engaging students in community-based public work.

Teachers of English to Speakers of Other Languages, Inc. (TESOL)
www.tesol.org

TESOL's mission is to develop the expertise of its members and others involved in teaching English to speakers of other languages to help them foster effective communication in diverse settings while respecting individuals' language rights.

Guide to State and Federal Government Educational Web Sites

INSTRUCTIONS: To gain World Wide Web access to additional and up-to-date information regarding this appendix and links to these sites, start your browser and enter the URL, scsite.com/tdc4. When the Teachers Discovering Computers home page appears, click the State/Federal Sites link on the lower-left side of the home page.

The federal government, state governments, and state institutions and organizations provide a multitude of Web resources for K-12 teachers and students. Every day, hundreds of new and exciting education Web resources are added to these sites. A continually updated Guide to State and Federal Government Educational Web sites, which links to the most current URLs, can be found at the Teachers Discovering Computers Web site.

State Departments of Education

Site Name	Location (site locations begin with http://)
Alabama	www.alsde.edu/html
Alaska	www.educ.state.ak.us
Arizona	ade.state.az.us
Arkansas	arkedu.state.ar.us
California	www.cde.ca.gov
Colorado	www.cde.state.co.us
Connecticut	www.state.ct.us/sde
Delaware	www.doe.state.de.us
District of Columbia	www.k12.dc.us
Florida	www.fldoe.org
Georgia	www.doe.k12.ga.us
Hawaii	doe.k12.hi.us
Idaho	www.sde.state.id.us/Dept
Illinois	www.isbe.state.il.us
Indiana	www.doe.state.in.us
Iowa	www.state.ia.us/educate
Kansas	www.ksbe.state.ks.us
Kentucky	www.education.ky.gov
Louisiana	www.doe.state.la.us
Maine	www.state.me.us/education
Maryland	www.marylandpublicschools.org/MSDE
Massachusetts	www.doe.mass.edu
Michigan	www.michigan.gov/mde
Minnesota	www.education.state.mn.us
Mississippi	www.mde.k12.ms.us
Missouri	www.dese.state.mo.us
Montana	www.opi.state.mt.us
Nebraska	www.nde.state.ne.us

State Departments of Education (continued)

Site Name	Location (site locations begin with http://)
Nevada	www.doe.nv.gov
New Hampshire	www.ed.state.nh.us
New Jersey	www.state.nj.us/education
New Mexico	sde.state.nm.us
New York	www.nysed.gov
North Carolina	www.dpi.state.nc.us
North Dakota	www.dpi.state.nd.us
Ohio	www.ode.state.oh.us
Oklahoma	sde.state.ok.us
Oregon	www.ode.state.or.us
Pennsylvania	www.pde.state.pa.us
Rhode Island	www.ridoe.net
South Carolina	www.myscschools.com
South Dakota	www.doe.sd.gov
Tennessee	www.state.tn.us/education
Texas	www.tea.state.tx.us
Utah	www.usoe.k12.ut.us
Vermont	www.state.vt.us/educ
Virginia	www.pen.k12.va.us/go/VDOE
Washington	www.k12.wa.us
West Virginia	wvde.state.wv.us
Wisconsin	www.dpi.state.wi.us
Wyoming	www.k12.wy.us

Federal Government

Site Name	Location (site locations begin with http://)	Comment
The Educator's Reference Desk	www.eduref.org	The Educator's Reference Desk provides high-quality resources and services to the education community. Included are more than 2000 lesson plans, 3000 plus links to online education information, and more than 200 question archive responses.
Ben's Guide to U.S. Government for Kids	bensguide.gpo.gov/subject.html	Ben's Guide provides a comprehensive listing of government Web sites for kids.
Bureau of Land Management	www.blm.gov/education	This site, created by the U.S. Department of the Interior, presents learning opportunities associated with the 262 million acres of public lands that the Bureau of Land Management manages for all Americans. Included is extensive information for students, teachers, and adult learners to use in the classroom, informal outdoor settings, or virtual classrooms.
Comprehensive Regional Assistance Centers	www.ed.gov/programs/compcenters/index.html	The Department of Education funds these fifteen K-12 regional assistance centers to provide services to states, local education agencies, and schools.
Department of Defense (DoD)	web.lmi.org/edugate/	This Web site provides general information about educational programs sponsored in whole or in part by the Department of Defense. This gateway to education effort is sponsored by the DoD.
Department of Energy's KidZone	www.energy.gov/engine/content.do?BT_CODE=KIDS	This site, maintained by the Department of Energy Education, provides educational resources in science, technology, energy, math, and more. The site includes an Energy Glossary with more than 4000 energy definitions, as well as other energy-related terms for middle and secondary students.

Federal Government

Site Name	Location (site locations begin with http://)	Comment
Department of Justice Kids and Youth	www.usdoj.gov/kidspage/index.html	This informative Web site is designed for all students, teachers, and parents and provides great resources on Internet crimes, drug prevention, cyberethics for kids, justice for kids, and more.
EDSITEment	edsitement.neh.gov	This subject-based catalog from the National Endowment for the Humanities provides access to the top humanities sites on the Web. It includes online humanities resources from some of the world's great museums, libraries, cultural institutions, and universities for use directly in your classroom.
Educational Resources Information Center (ERIC)	www.eric.ed.gov	A nationwide information network funded by the U.S. Department of Education that acquires, catalogs, summarizes, and provides access to education information from many sources.
EPA — Kids, Students, and Teachers	www.epa.gov/epahome/students.htm	This U. S. Environmental Protection Agency (EPA) Web site provides fact sheets, interactive games, and more for kids, students, and teachers who want to learn about the environment or share what they know with others. The Web site can help you with all sorts of information about the EPA and the environment.
ERIC Clearinghouse for Science, Mathematics, and Environmental Education	www.ericse.org	This Web site, provided by ERIC, offers a variety of resources for teaching and learning about science, mathematics, and the environment.
Federal Communications Commission (FCC)	www.fcc.gov/learnnet	The FCC LearnNet Web site provides information about FCC programs that are working to bring every school in America into the information age.
Federal Resources for Educational Excellence (FREE)	www.ed.gov/free	FREE provides hundreds of Internet-based education resources supported by federal agencies available at one great Web site.
FedWorld	www.fedworld.gov	FedWorld is a comprehensive central access point for searching, locating, ordering, and acquiring government information.
FirstGov.gov	www.firstgov.gov	Visit the U.S. government's official Web portal that makes all of America's government services available worldwide.
FirstGov for Kids	www.kids.gov	This U.S. government interagency Kids' Portal provides links to federal kids' sites along with some of the best kids' sites from other organizations all grouped by subject.
Food and Drug Administration (FDA)	www.fda.gov	Learn about the latest FDA developments that will help keep you and your students informed about important health issues.
healthfinder®	www.healthfinder.gov	This Web site is an important source for educators to find reliable consumer, health, and human services information.
Institute of Education Sciences	www.ed.gov/offices/IES	The U. S. Department of Education provides educational research resources funded by Congress at this Web site.
Kidz Privacy	www.ftc.gov/bcp/conline/edcams/kidzprivacy/index.html	This site from the Federal Trade Commission covers the very important issue of children's privacy and how it affects kids, their parents, and teachers.
Library of Congress	www.loc.gov	The Library of Congress is an incredible library resource for students and teachers.
National Aeronautics and Space Administration (NASA)	www.nasa.gov	This awesome Web site covers NASA's extensive education program.
National Archives and Records Administration (NARA)	www.archives.gov/digital_classroom/index.html	The NARA site presents the Digital Classroom, which encourages teachers of students at all levels to use archival documents in the classroom.
National Endowment for the Humanities	www.neh.fed.us	Online projects at this Web site support learning in history, literature, philosophy, and other areas of the humanities.
National Gallery of Art	www.nga.gov	The National Gallery of Art (NGA) is home to the world's finest paintings and sculptures. This site offers a wealth of culture. It includes a link to NGA Kids for exciting animation and interactivity.
National Oceanic and Atmospheric Administration (NOAA)	www.noaa.gov	NOAA provides information about the weather, oceans, satellites, fisheries, climates, and more.

Federal Government

Site Name	Location (site locations begin with http://)	Comment
National Park Service (NPS)	www.nps.gov/learn	LearnNPS is your one stop for finding education materials about America's national parks; includes TeacherZONE and GoZONE for kids.
National Register of Historic Places: Teaching with Historic Places (TwHP)	www.cr.nps.gov/nr/twhp	TwHP offers great lesson plans and guidance on using historic places in teaching and learning.
National Science Foundation (NSF)	www.nsf.gov	The NSF Web site promotes the progress of science and health; it is a must stop for science teachers.
Peace Corps	www.peacecorps.gov/wws/index.html	The Peace Corps World Wise Schools education program is designed to help students gain a greater understanding of other cultures and countries.
Recreation.gov	www.recreation.gov/index.cfm	This is a fantastic Web site for anyone searching for information about recreational opportunities on federal lands.
Regional Educational Laboratories	www.relnetwork.org	This Web site provides information from research and practice to those involved in educational improvement at the local, state, and regional levels.
Regional Technology Consortia Program	bcol02.ed.gov/Programs/EROD/org_list.cfm?category_ID=RTC	This Web site gives information about the programs that are funded by the U. S. Department of Education to help K-12 schools integrate technology.
Smithsonian Center for Education and Museum Studies	smithsonianeducation.org	This essential source includes lesson plans, resource guides, field trips, and more for all educators.
students.gov	www.students.gov/STUGOVWebApp/index.jsp	This Web site contains great links to federal Web site resources for postsecondary students.
The Kennedy Center ARTSEDGE	artsedge.kennedy-center.org	The National Arts and Education Network links the arts and education through technology.
United States Department of Agriculture (USDA)	www.usda.gov/wps/portal/usdahome	The USDA provides extensive sources of research and education information about many important subjects for all ages.
United States Geological Survey (USGS)	www.education.usgs.gov	The USGS Learning Web site is dedicated to K-12 education, exploration, and lifelong learning.
U.S. Census Bureau	www.census.gov	Through this Web site, expose your students to timely, relevant, and quality data about the people and economy of the United States.
U.S. Department of Health and Human Services (HHS)	www.os.dhhs.gov	The HHS offers a wealth of information related to public health, privacy issues, grant programs, and more at this Web site.
U.S. Department of Education	www.ed.gov	All teachers should make this Web site a first stop as they embark on their teaching careers. The site provides information about student readiness, gives lesson ideas and materials, includes training and development sources, offers guidelines for applying for grants, and much more.
U.S. Department of Energy: Office of Science	www.science.doe.gov/index.htm	This Web site is dedicated to helping educate America's next generation of scientists.
U.S. Department of the Interior (DOI)	www.doi.gov	The DOI is dedicated to the internal development of the United States and the welfare of its people.
U.S. Fish and Wildlife Service	www.fws.gov	Learn how to protect the homes and lives of fish and wildlife at this interesting Web site.
USDA Forest Service	www.fs.fed.us	This Web site is a great resource for information about public lands in the United States; it includes a special section just for kids.
USDA for Kids	www.usda.gov/news/usdakids	This extraordinary Web site contains a treasure-trove of resources for children; adults will be intrigued too.
Welcome to the White House	www.whitehouse.gov	Welcome to the White House provides links to many collections, programs, and products of significant educational benefit; offers a wealth of information and news about the president, government, and history; and includes virtual tours and interactivity of value to all ages.

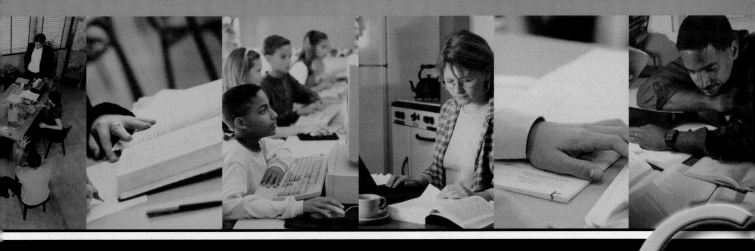

Appendix C

References

This Fourth Edition of *Teachers Discovering Computers* was created using information that was gathered, reviewed, and researched from various Web sites and other resources. You can review many of these resources by accessing the Teachers Discovering Computers, Fourth Edition Web site at *scsite.com/tdc4*. The textbook Web site contains links to hundreds of resources, including many research articles and Web sites dedicated to educational theory, education practice, instructional models, and research-based integration solutions. The following are additional references that were used in the preparation of this textbook.

Anderson, R., & Speck, B. (2001). *Using technology in k-8 literacy classrooms.* Columbus, OH: Prentice Hall.

Bandura, A. (1977). *Social learning theory.* New York: General Learning Press.

Bitter, G., & Pierson, M. (2005). *Using technology in the classroom* (6th ed.). Boston: Allyn & Bacon.

Bradt, K. M. (1997). Story as a way of knowing. Kansas City, MO: Sheed & Ward.

Branigan, C. (2003). *Schools urged to teach '21st-century' skills.* Retrieved August 2, 2005, from http://www.eschoolnews.com/news/showStoryalert.cfm?ArticleID=4506

Cermak, L. & Craik, F. (1979). *Levels of processing in human memory.* Hillsdale, NJ: Erlbaum.

Clark, J. M. & Paivio, A. (1991). Dual coding theory and education. *Educational Psychology Review*, 3(3), 149-170.

Craik, F. & Lockhart, R. (1972). Levels of processing: A framework for memory research. *Journal of Verbal Learning & Verbal Behavior*, 11, 671-684.

D'Agostino, P. R., O'Neill, B. J., & Paivio, A. (1977). Memory for pictures and words as a function of level of processing: Depth or dual coding? *Memory & Cognition*, 5, 252-256.

Dean, K. (2002). *PDAs good for education.* Retrieved May 25, 2005, from http://www.wired.com/news/school/0,1383,56297,00.html

Dexter, S., & Anderson, R. (1999). Teachers' views of computers as catalysts for changes in their teaching practice. *Journal of Research on Computing in Education*, 31(3), 221-239.

Doman, J. R. (1984). Learning problems and attention deficits. *Journal of the National Academy for Child Development*, 4(6).

eSchool News Online. (2005). *Textbooks give way to digital curriculum.* Retrieved July 12, 2005, from http://www.eschoolnews.com/news/showStoryts.cfm?ArticleID=5781&page=3

eSchool News Editors Report. (2005). *Multimedia creation tools in the classroom.* Retrieved July 6, 2005 from http://www.eschoolnews.com/resources/reports/multimediacreation/index.cfm

eSchool News Staff Report. (2003). *Quick! Tell me how to buy classroom & curriculum planning software.* Bethesda, MD: eSchool News.

Flores, A. (2002). *Learning and teaching mathematics with technology.* Retrieved May 4, 2005, from http://my.nctm.org/eresources/view_media.asp?article_id=1890

Forcier, R., & Descy, D. (2002). *The computer as an educational tool: productivity and problem solving* (3rd ed.). Columbus, OH: Prentice Hall.

Gee, J. P. (2005). What would a state of the art instructional video game look like? Innovate: *Journal of Online Education (1)*6, Retrieved August 2, 2005, http://www.innovateonline.info/index.php?view=article&id=80

Gee, J. P. (2003). *What video games have to teach us about learning and literacy.* New York: Palgrave MacMillan.

Grable, M., & Grable, C. (2004). I*ntegrating the Internet for meaningful learning* (4th ed.). Boston: Houghton Mifflin Company.

Gredler, M. (2004). *Learning and instruction: theory into practice* (5th ed.). Columbus, OH, Prentice Hall.

Gunter, G. (2001). Making a difference - using emerging technologies and teaching strategies to restructure an undergraduate technology course for preservice teachers. *Education Media International*, 38(1), 13-20.

Gunter, G.A. & Kenny, R. (2004). Video in the classroom: learning objects or objects of learning? *Association for Educational Communications and Technology International Conference (AECT) Annual*, Chicago, Illinois.

Gunter, G., & Murphy, D. (1997). Technology integration: The importance of administrative support. *Education Media International*, 34(3), 136-139.

Heinich, M., Molenda, M., Russell, J., & Smaldino, S. (2004). *Instructional media and technologies for learning* (8th ed.). Columbus, OH: Prentice Hall.

Intel Teach to the Future. (2003). *Intel innovation in education.* Retrieved May 25, 2005, from http://www97.intel.com/education/teach/index.htm

International Society for Technology in Education. (2003). *National educational technology standards (NETS) project.* Retrieved May 13, 2005, from http://cnets.iste.org

Kellough, R., & Kellough, N. (2003). *Teaching young adolescents: A guide to methods and resources* (4th ed.). Columbus, OH: Prentice Hall.

Kenny, R. F. (2004). *Teaching television in a digital world: Integrating media literacy* (2nd ed). Westport, CT: Libraries Unlimited.

Kenny, R. F. & Gunter, G. A. (2004). Digital booktalk: pairing books with potential readers. *Association for Educational Communications and Technology International Conference (AECT) Annual*, Chicago, Illinois.

Lauritzen, C. & Jaeger, M. (1997). *Integrating learning through story: The narrative curriculum.* Albany, NY: Delmar.

Lever-Duffy, J., McDonald, J., & Mizell, A. (2004). *Teaching and learning with technology* (2nd ed.). Boston: Allyn & Bacon.

Mathematica Policy Research, Inc. (2001). *Analysis of the 1999-2000 annual performance reports for preparing tomorrow's teachers to use technology final report.* Retrieved July 15, 2005, from http://www.ed.gov/offices/OUS/PES/higher.html#pt3

Meyer, K. (2003). The Web's impact on student learning. *T.H.E. Journal,* 30(10), 14-24.

Microsoft. (2002). *Microsoft computer dictionary* (5th ed.). Redmond, WA: Microsoft Press.

Morrison, G., Lowther, D., & DeMeulle, L. (1999). *Integrating computer technology into the classroom.* Columbus, OH: Merrill Education/Prentice Hall.

National Council for Accreditation of Teacher Education. (2002). *21st Century Learners: The Need for Tech-Savvy Teachers.* Retrieved July 7, 2005, from http://www.pt3.org/technology/ 21century_learners.html

National Center for Educational Statistics. (1999). Teachers' tools for the 21st century: A report on teachers' use of technology. *Publication # NCES 2000102.* Retrieved June 23, 2005, from http://nces.ed.gov/pubsearch/pubsinfo.asp?pubid=2000102

New Measure. (2003). *Helping you design rubrics.* Retrieved May 17, 2003, from http://www.rubrics.com

Newby, T., Stepich, D., Lehman, J., & Russell, J. (2005). *Instructional technology for teaching and learning: Designing instruction, integrating computers, and using media* (3rd ed.). Columbus, OH: Prentice Hall.

Ornstein, A., & Hunkins, F. (2004). *Curriculum foundations, principles, and theory* (4th ed.). Seattle, WA: Allyn & Bacon.

Paivio, A. (1986). *Mental Representations.* New York: Oxford University Press.

Policy Information Center. (2000, October). *How teaching matters.* Princeton, NJ: Education Testing Service.

Prensky, M. (2001). *Digital games-based learning.* New York: McGraw-Hill.

Preparing Tomorrow's Teachers to Use Technology. (2002). Retrieved July 30, 2005, from http://www.pt3.org

President's Committee of Advisors on Science and Technology. (1997). *Report to the president on the use of technology to strengthen k-12 education in the United States.* Retrieved June 19, 2005, from http://www.agiweb.org/hearings/pcastedu.html

Restak, R. M. (2003). *The new brain: How the modern age is rewiring your mind.* New York: Rodale St. Martins Press.

Robyler, M. (2005). *Integrating educational technology into teaching* (4th ed.). Columbus, OH: Prentice Hall.

Schunk, D. (2004). *Learning theories: An educational perspective* (4th ed.). Columbus, OH: Merrill Education/Prentice Hall.

Shelly, G., Cashman, T., Gunter, R., & Gunter, G. (2004). *Teachers discovering computers: Integrating technology in the classroom* (3rd ed.). Boston: Course Technology.

Shelly, G., Cashman, T., Gunter, R., & Gunter, G. (2005). *Teachers discovering and integrating Microsoft Office: Essential concepts and techniques* (2nd ed). Boston: Course Technology.

Shelly, G., Cashman, T., & Vermaat, M. (2005). *Microsoft Office xp: Introductory concepts and techniques.* Boston: Course Technology.

Shelly, G., Cashman, T., & Vermaat, M. (2006). *Discovering computers 2006: A gateway to information.* Boston: Course Technology.

Tapscott, D. (1998). *Growing up digital – The rise of the net generation.* New York: McGraw-Hill.

Tapscott, D. (1995). *The digital economy: Promise and peril in the age of networked intelligence.* New York: McGraw-Hill.

Taylor, R. & Gunter, G. A. (2005). *The k-12 literacy leadership fieldbook.* California: Corwin Press.

Thompson, A., Simonson, M.R., & Hargrave, C. (1996). *Educational technology: A review of the research* (2nd ed.). Ames, IO: Association for Educational Communications and Technology.

United States Department of Education. (2005). *No child left behind.* Retrieved August 3, 2005, from http://www.ed.gov/nclb/landing.jhtml

Universal Service Administrative Company. (2005). *E-rate.* Retrieved July 27, 2005, from http://www.sl.universalservice.org

Wikipedia. (2005). *Wikipedia: The free encyclopedia.* Retrieved June 11, 2005, http://en.wikipedia.org/wiki/Main_Page

Web-Based Education Commission (2000). *The power of the Internet for learning. The president and the congress of the United States.* Retrieved July 12, 2005, from http://interact.hpcnet.org/webcommission/index.htm

Welliver, P. (1990). *Instructional transformation: a module for change.* A report of the Pennsylvania regional computer resource center. University Park, PA: Pennsylvania State University.

Willis, J., Thompson, A., & Sadera, W. (1999). Research on technology and teacher education: Current status and future directions. *Educational Technology Research and Development,* 47(4), 29-45.

Index

* (asterisk), 137
" (double quotation marks), 137
(. . .) (parentheses), 137
+ (plus sign), 137

802.11 standard: family of specifications developed for wireless local area networks by the Institute of Electrical and Electronics Engineers (IEEE), 537

ability level: student's current competency level or the skill level they can achieve for a specific learning objective. 409

absolute hyperlink: a hyperlink to another document on a different Internet computer that could be across the country or across the world. 84

academic contests, 443–444

academic level: evaluation based on grade level with increments to determine if a student is performing at the appropriate level. 409

Acceptable Use Policy. See AUP (Acceptable Use Policy)

access controls: security measures that define who can access a computer, when they can access it, and what actions they can take while using the computer. 491–492

accessibility features, 40–41, 111
 accessibility initiatives and, 517
 hardware and, 257
 special needs software and, 172

Accessibility Wizard, 40

accommodation: process of a child learning by fitting information or experiences to his or her knowledge base, defined by Piaget. 393

Acrobat (Adobe), 88, 165, 454

Acrobat Reader (Adobe), 88

active learning: type of learning that provides students with the opportunity to be involved and interested in their own learning and gives them a sense of ownership of the information with which they are presented because they are actively involved in the learning process. 346–347

activity flyers, 41–43

ADA (Americans with Disabilities Act), 257

A.D.A.M. (Animated Dissection of Anatomy for Medicine), 287

adapter cards, 218

adaptive technology: refers to any equipment, modification, or accommodation that can improve a person's capacity to learn, to communicate, to solve a problem, or to complete a task through the use of a computer. Also called assistive technology. 40, 111, 187, 319, 375, 516–517

address: unique number identifying the location of a byte in memory. 215–216

address book: feature of personal information manager used to organize names, addresses, and telephone numbers. 162

administrators, school, standards for, 21–22

Adobe Acrobat, 88, 165, 454

Adobe PDF format, 165

advanced (open) learning systems, 300

affective domain: a student's emotions, interests, attitude, attention, and awareness, identified by Bloom. 389

affiliation: professional organization, school, school district, university, company, or government office with which a particular Web site is associated. 410–411, 446

age of convergence: the first decade of the twenty-first century. 5

alternative assessment: assessment that uses nontraditional methods to determine whether students have mastered appropriate content and skill level; approaches include authentic, project–based, and portfolio assessment. 414, 446, 452

ALU (arithmetic/logic unit): CPU component that performs the execution part of the machine cycle; includes performing arithmetic, comparison, and logical operations. 215

America Online, 268, 509

analog: representation of data using continuous signals. 210, 329

analog signal: A continuous electrical wave. 66

anchor: concepts and information that form a basis for other information upon which to connect and build. 395

anchored instruction: provision of a knowledge base on which students can build; learning and teaching activities are designed around an anchor (or situation) that provides a scenario or problem enhanced with curriculum materials that allow exploration by the learner. 346–347, 395

AND operator, 137, 215

Andreessen, Marc, 86

animated GIF: popular type of animation where a group of several images are combined into a single GIF file. 89

animation: multimedia element that creates the appearance of motion by displaying a series of still images in rapid sequence or a graphic that has the illusion of motion if played back at the proper framing rate.
 adding, 321
 described, 89, 282

anonymous FTP: ability for anyone accessing an FTP site to transfer some, if not all, available files. 94

anti-spam program: program used to block unwanted e-mail messages that works by attempting to remove spam before it reaches an e-mail inbox. Sometimes anti-spam programs remove valid e-mail messages. 502

antivirus program: program designed to detect, disinfect, and protect computers and networks from viruses; they work by looking for programs that attempt to modify the boot program, the operating system, or other programs that normally are read from but not written to. In addition to providing protection from viruses, most antivirus programs also have utilities to remove or repair infected programs and files. Also called a vaccine. 489, 490–491

Apple Computer. See Macintosh

AppleWorks: popular integrated software package for Macintosh computers. 152, 156, 157, 164–165

application software: programs designed to perform specific tasks for users; examples include educational, business, and scientific computer programs. Also called application, or software application. See also specific applications
 described, 16–18
 evaluating, 406–409
 productivity tools, 141–208

appointment calendar: feature of personal information manager used to schedule activities. 162

appropriate: describes educational technology that is suitable for the educational situation, must be motivational, and must promote learning at the correct levels of ability and academic achievement. 402

ARCS Motivational Model: was developed by John M. Keller in 1983 and is applicable to learning in the digital age. 8–9, 381

arithmetic operations: performed by the arithmetic/logic unit, include addition, subtraction, multiplication, and division operations. 215

ARPA (Advanced Research Projects Agency): Department of Defense agency that developed a networking project that the Internet has roots in, called ARPANET. 75–76

ARPANET: networking project that the Internet has roots in, developed by the Department of Defense, which effectively linked together scientific and academic researchers in the United States. 76

article: message on a newsgroup. 95

arts curriculum: curriculum that usually incorporates instruction in the visual and performing arts of drawing, painting, dance, music, and theater. 437–438

arts Web sites, 131

ASCII (American Standard Code for Information Interchange): most widely-used coding scheme to represent data on many personal computers. 211, 212

Ask Jeeves, 138

assessment: any method used to understand the current knowledge a student possesses; it can range from a teacher's subjective judgment based on a single observation of a student's performance to a state-mandated standardized test. 414–415, 417, 446

assimilation: new knowledge absorbed as a child experiences new things and learns new information, defined by Piaget. 393

assistant. *See* wizard

assistive technology: refers to any equipment, modification, or accommodation that can improve a person's capacity to learn, to communicate, to solve a problem, or to complete a task through the use of a computer. Also called adaptive technology. 40, 111, 187, 319, 375, 516–517

ASSURE Model: instructional model that is a procedural guide for planning and delivering instruction that integrates technologies and media into the teaching process. 356–359, 369, 381

asterisk (*), 137

AT&T Worldnet, 268

Athlon processors, 214

attention, capturing students', 8–9

auction Web sites, 121

audience: individual or group intended to view a Web page. 411, 446

audio: digitized music, speech, or any other sound that is stored and produced by a computer.
described, 89–90, 229, 282–283
editing software, 167
streaming, 90
players, 90

audio input: process of recording music, speech, or sound effects. 227

audio output: any music, speech, or other sound produced by a computer; widely available on the Internet. 236

AUP (Acceptable Use Policy): set of rules that governs the use of school and school district computers, networks, and the Internet by teachers, administrators, staff, and students. 98, 107–108, 510–511

authentic assessment: can be formal or informal and aims to present the student with tasks that mirror the objectives and challenges typical of their instructional activities. 414–415, 417, 446

authentic learning: learning experiences that demonstrate real-life connections between students' lessons and the world in which they live. 346–347, 414–415

authoring tools. *See* digital media authoring software; multimedia authoring software

authority: when evaluating Web sites, the credibility of the person or persons who author and create the site. 410, 412, 446

authorware: digital media authoring software program. 305

AutoSave: feature that automatically saves open documents as specified time periods. 148

AutoShapes palette, 281

auxiliary storage. *See* storage

Awesome Library, 138

backbone: main communication lines that have the heaviest amount of traffic (data packets) on the Internet. 76, 80–81

backgrounds, 193, 196–197, 465–466

backup: duplicate of a file, program, or disk that can be used if the original is lost, damaged, or destroyed. 238, 499

backup procedure: procedure that outlines a regular plan of copying and backing up important data and program files. 499

backward compatibility, 219

Bailey's Book House, 109

Bandura, Albert, 384, 559

bandwidth: measure of how fast data travels over transmission channels. 72

banking. *See* online banking

beaming: transfer of data from one PDA to another through an infrared port. 162

behaviorism: theory that centers on learning as it relates to behavior. 382–395

Ben's Guide to U.S. Government for Kids, 138

benchmark: specific, measurable learning objective or indicator that usually is tied to a curriculum standard. Also called learning objective. 338, 414

bilingual education, 371

binary: numbering system that uses just two unique digits: 0 and 1. 211

biometric device: a device that authenticates a person's identity by translating a personal characteristic, such as a fingerprint, into a digital code that then is compared with a digital code stored in the computer verifying a physical or behavioral characteristic. 492

bit: short for binary digit, representation of the smallest unit of data a computer can handle. 211

Black History Month, 379

blackout: complete power failure. 498

block schedule: alternative way of scheduling classes in which classes meet every other day instead of every day. 420–421

blog: short for Web log, is a Web site that uses a regularly updated journal format to reflect interests, opinions, and personalities

of the author and sometimes site visitors. 94–95, 380, 423, 429, 380

Bloom, Benjamin, 389–390

Bloom's Taxonomy: levels used to acquire knowledge about a topic, identified by Bloom. 389–390

Blue WEb'N, 138

Bluetooth: technology that uses short-range radio waves to transmit data between two Bluetooth devices. 536

BMP (bitmap) format, 88–89

Body Works: digital media educational software application for teaching all related concepts about the human body. 38, 347

boldface font, 147

bookmark: method of keeping track of Web pages that have been viewed; records the Web page title and URL, on a computer for use in future Web sessions. Also called favorites. 87

Boolean operators, 137

boot sector virus: virus that replaces the boot program used to start a computer with a modified, infected version of the boot program. When the computer runs the infected boot program, it loads the virus into the computer's memory. Once a virus is in memory, it spreads to any disk inserted into the computer. 487

border: decorative line or pattern along one or more edges of a page or graphic. 151

branching: nonlinear approach used by tutorials that offers alternative paths through a lesson based on students' responses. 84

broadband: technologies that transmit signals at much faster speeds than traditional network configurations. 72, 110

brownout: prolonged undervoltage. 498

browser: program that interprets HTML and displays Web pages and enables user to link to other Web pages and Web sites. Also called Web browser. *See also* Internet Explorer browser (Microsoft)
described, 20, 85–87
downloading images with, 463
filtering software and, 508–510
history of, 85
previewing Web pages with, 206–207
software, 85–87

Bruner, Jerome, 391

bulleted lists, 472–473

Busy Teachers' Web Site K–12, 138

button: graphical element (usually a rectangular or circular shape) that, when selected, causes a specific action to take place. 146

byte: eight bits grouped together as a unit. 211

NetZero, 268

news server: computer that stores and distributes newsgroup messages. 95

news Web sites, 124

newsgroup: online area in which users conduct written discussions about a particular subject. 94–95

newsletters, creating, 376–379

newspaper, digital media: digital version of a newspaper distributed on CD–ROM, DVDROM, or via the World Wide Web. 290

newsreader: program that enables access to a newsgroup to read previously entered messages, add articles, and keep tracks of which articles a user has and has not read. 95

NIC (network interface card): communications device that connects computers directly to a school or business network without using a modem. 68

nine events of instruction: events identified by Gagne to maximize the potential for the internal process of learning to occur. 386

No Child Left Behind Act (NCLB), 337

nonimpact printer: printer that forms marks on a piece of paper without actually striking the paper. 232

nonvolatile memory: type of memory in which contents are not lost when power is removed from a computer; example is ROM. 216

NOT operator, 215

note taking software: application software that enables users to enter typed text, handwritten comments, graphs, drawings, or sketches anywhere on a page and then save the page as part of an electronic notebook. 148–149

notebook computer: portable, personal computer small enough to fit on a user's lap. Also called laptop computer. 11, 270–272

Notepad: feature of personal information manager used to record ideas, reminders, and other important information. 162

NSF (National Science Foundation): organization that connected its huge network of five supercomputer centers, called NSFnet, to ARPANET. 76

NSFnet: national Science Foundation network of five supercomputer centers, connected to ARPANET, serving as the major backbone network of the Internet until 1995. 76

NTIA (National Telecommunications and Information Administration), 107, 553

numeric keypad: calculator-style arrangement of keys on a keyboard representing numbers, a decimal point, and some basic mathematical operators; used to facilitate entering numbers. 222

objectionable material: material that includes racist literature, obscene pictures and videos, and even gambling. Internet materials classified as objectionable material include (1) all materials that most people consider pornographic, such as obscene pictures, stories, graphics, articles, cartoons, and videos; (2) racist literature, controversial subjects such as gambling, and other similar materials; and (3) Web sites that contain incorrect material and thus are inappropriate for K-12 students. 506–512

objectivity: process of determining or interpreting the intent or purpose of a Web page and if it is free of bias, such as advertising. 411

observational modeling: watching something and then mimicking the observed behavior. 384

Office (Microsoft), 17, 59, 157

off-site location: location for storing backup copies. 499

one-computer classroom: classroom that is equipped with one multimedia computer. 351–352, 422–423, 447

online banking: offers access to account balances, provides bill payment services, and allows users to download transactions and statements from the Web. 173

online courses, 294–296

open learning system: integrated learning system that includes software titles from leading publishers. Also called advanced learning system. 300

open source software: software that has code available free to the public. 18, 143

operant conditioning: learning that is controlled and results in shaping behavior through the reinforcement of stimulus response patterns, described by Skinner. 381, 383

operating system: one of the more important programs on a computer that contains instructions that coordinate all of the activities of the hardware devices. 15–16, 142–144

operating system software (system software), described, 15–16, 142–144

optical disc: a type of storage medium that consists of a flat, round, portable disc made of metal, plastic, and lacquer that is written and read by a laser. 240–242

optical mouse: mouse that has no moving mechanical parts, instead it emits and senses light to detect the mouse's movement. 223

optical scanners, 225

OR operator, 137, 215

OSHA (Occupational Safety and Health Administration), 513

OSPs (online service providers): organization that provides access to the Internet, as well as members-only features that offer a variety of special content and services. 78, 267–268

output: data that has been processed into a useful form called information. Four common types of output are text, graphics, audio, and video. 4, 229

output device: Hardware used to convey the information generated by a computer to a user; includes a printer, a monitor, and speakers. 230–236

overvoltage: situation that occurs when incoming electrical power increases significantly above the normal 120 volts. Also called power surge. 498

Owl and Mouse Educational Software, 373

packaged software: application software designed to meet the needs of a variety of users. 18

packet: small piece of data sent over the Internet. 77

packet switching: technique of breaking a message into individual packets, sending the packets along the best route available, and reassembling the data. 78

page layout: process of arranging text and graphics in a document. 165–166

paint software: software used to draw pictures, shapes, and other graphics using various tools on the screen such as a pen, brush, eye dropper, and paint bucket. 166

Paivio, Allan, 385

Palm OS, 276

parental controls, 508–511

parentheses, 137

parents, use of computers by, 27

password: part of a unique user identification that allows users to log on to the network to use e-mail, transfer files, and access other shared resources. 491–492

paste: process of placing items stored on the Clipboard into a document. 147

PATRIOT Act, 503

Pavlov, Ivan, 381

PC Card: a thin credit card-sized device that adds memory, fax/modems, network cards, disk drives, and other capabilities to small computers. 218

PCs (personal computers): computer that performs all of its input, processing, output, and storage activities by itself.
buyer's guide, 262–274
described, 10–11
working with, 176–177

UNIX: multitasking operating system originally developed for mainframe computers but used today for computers of all sizes. 143

unsubscribe: process of removing name from mailing list. 96

upgrade: new version of software product designed to replace an older version of the same product. 96

upload: process of copying a file to an FTP site. 94

UPS (uninterruptible power supply): device that contains surge protection circuits and one or more batteries that provide power during a temporary or permanent loss of power, 498–499

URLs (Uniform Resource Locators): unique address for each Web page on a Web site; consists of a protocol, domain name, and sometimes the path to a specific Web page.
browsers and, 86
copying/pasting, 481
described, 83
entering, 473, 481–482
history lists and, 86–87

USB (universal serial bus) port: port that connects up to 127 different peripheral devices with a single connector type. 219

USB flash drive: a flash memory storage device that plugs into a USB port on a computer or mobile device. Also called pen drive. 218–219, 247

Usenet: entire collection of Internet newsgroups, containing thousands of newsgroups on a multitude of topics. 94–95

user ID: part of a unique user identification that allows users to log on to the network to use e-mail, transfer files, and access other shared resources. 491–492

user interface: part of all software with which a user interacts that controls how data and instructions are entered (input) and how the computer presents information on the screen (output). 15–16, 144–149

username: unique combination of characters that identifies a user. 93

user response: answer to a question asked by a program. 220

utility program: system software that performs a specific task, usually related to managing a computer, its devices, or its programs. 16

UWB (Ultra-Wideband): an emerging technology with greater bandwidth capabilities than Bluetooth that provides high speed, wireless communications to devices throughout a digital home and office. 16, 537

vaccines, 490. *See also* antivirus program

valid: software that has well-grounded instructional properties, provides

appropriate content, and teaches what is intended. 406

value: number in a spreadsheet cell. 154

vandalism, 493–494

version: number designation for software. 175–177

video: photographic images or visual frames that are played back at speeds of 15 to 60 frames per second and provide the appearance of full motion in real time.
cameras, 329–334
clips, 283
described, 91, 229
distributing, 334
editing, 167, 331–333
-enhanced digital textbooks, 517–518
recording, 330
streaming, 91
technology, 329–334
transferring/managing, 330–331

video compression: process of decreasing the size of video files. 283–284

video game. *See* games, computer

video input: process of entering a full-motion recording into a computer. Also called video capture. 227

video messaging: an emerging technology that allows users to take short video clips with a video phone complete with sound and text messaging and send them to another smart phone or computer. 541

violence, in schools, 36

virtual field trip: allow students to walk through doorways, down halls, and lets them see everything in a three-dimensional world via a computer as if they were there. 342

virtual high schools, 107

virtual reality (VR): use of a computer to create an artificial environment that appears and feels like a real environment and allows a user to explore space and manipulate the setting; appears as a three-dimensional (3-D) space. 87, 88, 91–92, 291–292

virus: potentially damaging computer program designed to effect a computer negatively without a user's knowledge or permission by altering the way it works. More specifically, a virus is a segment of program code that implants itself in a computer file and spreads systematically from one file to another.
described, 486–489
detecting/removing, 489–491

virus hoax: false warning about a virus often spread via e-mail and over the Internet. 491

virus payload: symptom or damage caused by a virus. 486, 489

visual learner: individual who learns concepts faster or retains a higher percentage of

material if information presented graphically. 281

visual learning technique: method that presents ideas and information through graphical webs, used in planning projects. 419

vlog: Blog that contains video. 431

voice recognition: computer's capability of distinguishing spoken words. Also called speech recognition. 148, 227

Voice over IP (VoIP), 97. *See also* Internet Telephony

volatile memory: type of memory in which contents are lost (erased) when a computer's power is turned off; example is RAM. 216

VR world: 3-D Web site that contains infinite space and depth. 91–92

Vygotsky, Lev, 394–395

W3C (World Wide Web Consortium), 517, 529

WANs (wide area network): network that covers a large geographical region (such as a city or school district) and uses regular telephone cables, digital lines, microwaves, wireless systems, satellites, or other combinations of communications channels. A WAN can consist of numerous local area networks organized into one larger network. 19–20, 68, 539

warchalking: the practice of using chalk to draw a series of symbols on sidewalks to direct people to places that provide wireless access. 538–539

WBT (Web–based training): approach to computer-based training that uses the technologies of the Internet and the World Wide Web and typically consists of self-directed, self-paced instruction on a topic. 293–294

weather Web sites, 124

Web (World Wide Web): the portion of the Internet consists of computer sites that contain billions of electronic documents called Web pages. *See also* browser; Web pages; Web sites
improved access to, 516
described, 20, 82–93
digital media and, 292–293
future of, 100
impact of, on education, 99–100
multimedia on, 87–92
searching, 87, 132–140

Web browser. *See* browser

Web-enhanced course: Course that uses the Web to enhance the content of the course. 293

Web-enhancing: Web classes that teachers provide their students with resources to enrich their learning experience. 294

Web evaluation rubric: detailed scoring guide for assessing the value and content of Web sites. 412–413

Photo Credits

Chapter 1: Page 1.01, Getty Images; Fig 1-1, Courtesy of EarthWalk Communications; Fig 1-2a, © Thomas Schweizer/CORBIS; Fig 1-2b Peter Beck/CORBIS; Fig 1-2c, Michael Newman/Photo Edit; Fig 1-2d, Hunter Freeman/Getty Images; Fig 1-2e, Bob Daemmrich/The Image Works; Figure 1-04a, Courtesy of Acer America Corp.; Figure 1-04b, Courtesy of Logitech, Inc.; Figure 1-04c, Courtesy of Logitech, Inc.; Figure 1-04d, Courtesy of Umax Systems GmbH; Figure 1-04e, Courtesy of SanDisk Corporation; Figure 1-04f, Courtesy of SanDisk Corporation; Figure 1-04g, Courtesy of Linksys, a Division of Cisco Systems Inc.; Figure 1-04h, Courtesy of Umax Systems GmbH; Figure 1-04i, Courtesy of Sony Electronics, Inc.; Figure1-04j , Courtesy of Epson America, Inc.; Fig 1-5, © Getty Images; Fig 1-7,© Getty Images; Fig 1-8, Courtesy of IBM Corporation; Fig 1-9, Courtesy of Apple Computer; Fig 1-10a, Courtesy of IBM Corporation; Fig 1-10b, Courtesy of Apple Computer; Fig 1-11, Courtesy of Apple Computer; Fig 1-12, Motion Computing Inc.; Fig 1-13, Courtesy of palmOne. palmOne, Zire, Tungsten, Treo, logos, stylizations and design marks associated with all the preceding, and trade dress associated with palmOne, Inc.'s products, are among the trademarks or registered trademarks owned by or exclusively licensed to palmOne, Inc; Fig 1-13b, Courtesy of Sony Electronics, Inc.; Fig 1-14, Courtesy of Fossil, Inc.; Fig 1-15, Toyota photo; Fig 1-15, © Patti McConville/Imagestate; Fig 1-15, Toyota photo; Fig 1-15, Toyota photo; Fig 1-15, © DiMaggio/Kalish/CORBIS; Fig 1-15, Toyota photo; Fig 1-17, Courtesy of Britannica, Inc.; Fig 1-18, Courtesy of Acer America Corp.; Fig 1-20, Courtesy of Microsoft Corporation; Fig 1-21, © Bonnie Kamin/Photo Edit; Fig 1-22, Courtesy of Sony Electronics, Inc., Courtesy of Motion Computing, Courtesy of Sony Electronics, Inc.; Fig 1-27, Jose L. Pelaez/CORBIS; Fig 1-28, © Comstock Images; Fig 1-29, David Young-Wolff/Photo Edit; Fig 1-30, Getty Images; Fig 1-31, © Jose Luis Pelaez/CORBIS; Fig 1-32, Tom McCarthy/Photo Edit; Fig 1-33, Courtesy of Consolidated High School District 230/Handheld Computers; Fig 1-34, Seth Resnick/ Getty Images; Fig 1-35, © ImageSource/Imagestate; Fig 1-35, Courtesy of Logitech; Fig 1-36, Gary Wagner/Stock Boston; Fig 1-37, © Getty Images; In Brief – 1, Springbrook HS and Apple Computer; Key Terms – 1, Getty Images; Courtesy of EarthWalk Communications; *Special Feature 1 Timeline*: 1937, Courtesy of Iowa State University; 1937, Courtesy of Iowa State University; 1937, Courtesy of Iowa State University; 1943, The Computer History Museum; 1943, The Computer History Museum; 1945, Courtesy of the Archives of the Institute for Advanced Study; 1946, From the Collections of the University of Pennsylvania Archives; 1947, © IBM Corporate Archives; 1947, © IBM Corporate Archives; 1951, Courtesy Unisys Corporation; 1952, Courtesy of Hagley Museum and Library; 1953, © IBM Corporate Archives; 1957, © IBM Corporate Archives; 1957, © IBM Corporate Archives; 1957, Courtesy of the Department of the Navy; 1958, Courtesy of M.I.T. Archives; 1959, © IBM Corporate Archives; 1960, Courtesy of Hagley Museum and Library; 1964, © IBM Corporate Archives; 1964, © IBM Corporate Archives; 1965, Courtesy of Dartmouth College; 1965, Courtesy of Digital Equipment Corporation; 1969, Courtesy of IBM Corporation. Unauthorized use not permitted; 1970, © IBM Corporate Archives; 1971, Courtesy of Intel Corporation; 1971, Courtesy of Intel Corporation; 1975, Courtesy of InfoWorld; 1975, The Computer History Museum; 1976, Courtesy of Apple Computer Corporation; 1976, © Bettmann/CORBIS; 1979, The Computer History Museum; 1980, © IBM Corporate Archives; 1980, Courtesy of Microsoft® Corporation; 1981, © IBM Corporate Archives; 1982, Courtesy of Zoom Telephonics, Inc.; 1983, © IBM Corporate Archives; 1983, Photo by Time Inc./Time Life Pictures/Getty Images; 1984, Courtesy of Hewlett-Packard Company; 1984, © IBM Corporate Archives; 1984, Courtesy of Apple Computer Corporation; 1987, © IBM Corporate Archives; 1989, © 1997-1998W3C (MIT, INRIA, Keio); 1992, Courtesy of Microsoft® Corporation; 1993, Courtesy of Intel Corporation; 1993, © AP/Wide World Photos; 1993, Courtesy of Netscape Communications Corporation; 1994, Courtesy of Netscape Communications Corporation; 1995, Box shot reprinted with permission from Microsoft® Corporation; 1995, Courtesy of Sun Microsystems, Inc.; 1996, © AP/Wide World Photos; 1996, Courtesy of Microsoft Corporation; 1997, Courtesy of Intel Corporation; 1997, Motion Picture & Television Archives; 1997, Courtesy of Denon Electronics; 1997, © AP/Wide World Photos; 1997, © IBM Corporate Archives; 1998, Box shot reprinted with permission from Microsoft® Corporation; 1998, Courtesy of Apple Computer Corporation; 1999, Box shot reprinted with permission from Microsoft® Corporation; 2000, Courtesy of Intel Corporation; 2001, Box shot reprinted with permission from Microsoft® Corporation; 2001, Courtesy of RCA; 2001, Courtesy of Apple Computer; 2002, © Scott Goodwin Photography; 2002, Courtesy of Sharp Electronics; 2002, Courtesy of palmOne,Inc.; 2002, Courtesy of RCA/Thomson Consumer Electronics; 2003, Courtesy of Hewlett-Packard Company; 2003, Courtesy of palmOne, Inc.; 2003, Courtesy of Intel Corporation; 2003, Courtesy of Microsoft Corporation; 2003, Courtesy of Microsoft Corporation; 2003, PhotoDisc/Getty Images; 2003, Box shot reprinted with permission from Microsoft® Corporation; 2003, Courtesy of Apple Computer; 2003, Courtesy of Sony Electronics Inc.; 2004, Courtesy of ViewSonic® Corporation. All rights reserved; 2004, © Transcend Information Inc. All rights reserved; 2004, Courtesy of SanDisk Corporation; 2004, Siemens AG Press Picture; 2004, Courtesy of Apple Computer; 2005, Courtesy of The Mozilla Foundation; 2005, Courtesy of palmOne, Inc. palmOne, Zire, Tungsten, Treo, logos, stylizations and design marks associated with all the preceding, and trade dress associated with palmOne, Inc.'s products, are among the trademarks or registered trademarks owned by or exclusively licensed to palmOne, Inc.; 2005, Courtesy of Apple Computer, Courtesy of IBM Corporation; *Chapter 2:* Figure 2-1a, Courtesy of Fujitsu Siemens Computers; Figure 2-1b, Courtesy of Acer America Corp.; Figure 2-1c, Courtesy of IBM Corporation; Figure 2-1d, Courtesy of Acer America Corp.; Figure 2-1e, Courtesy of Motion Computing; Figure 2-1f, Courtesy of Motorola; Figure 2-1g, Courtesy of Fujitsu Siemens Computers; Figure 2-1h, Toyota photo; Figure 2-3a1, Courtesy of Cnet USA, Inc.; Figure 2-3a2, Courtesy of Acer America Corp.; Figure 2-3a3, Courtesy of Sony Electronics Inc.; Figure 2-3b1, Courtesy of Sony Electronics Inc.; Figure 2-3b2, Courtesy of Acer America Corp.; Figure 2-3b3, Courtesy of Toshiba America Information Systems, Inc.; Figure 2-4a, Courtesy of Linksys, a Division of Cisco Systems Inc.; Figure 2-4b, Courtesy of Linksys, a Division of Cisco Systems Inc.; Figure 2-9, Courtesy of EarthWalk Communications; Figure 2-10, Copyright ©Amy Etra / Photo Edit. All rights reserved; Figure 2-12, Courtesy of Microsoft Corporation; Figure 2-13, Courtesy of the National Science Foundation; Figure 2-15a, Siemens press picture; Figure 2-15b, Courtesy of AT&T Wireless; Figure 2-15c, © Paul C. Chauncey/CORBIS; Figure 2-15d, ©LWA-Dann Tardif/CORBIS; Figure 2-1e, ©LWA-Dann Tardif/CORBIS; Figure 2-1f, © Paul C. Chauncey/CORBIS; Figure 2-15g, © Rob Lewine/CORBIS; Figure 2-16a, Courtesy of Saenix Technology Inc.; Figure 2-16b, Courtesy of Motorola, Inc.; Figure 2-16c, Courtesy of Panasonic; Figure 2-16d, © Erik S. Lesser/Bloomberg News /Landov; Figure 2-17a, Courtesy of Motorola, Inc.; Figure 2-17b, Courtesy of Terayon Communication Systems, Inc.; Figure 2-17c, © Stephen Chernin/Getty Images; Figure 2-17d, Courtesy of Fujitsu Siemens Computers; Figure 2-19a, Courtesy of Symbol Technologies, Inc.; Figure 2-19b, Courtesy of Ashland High School Horticulture Department; Figure 2-24a, © Nokia Corporation 2002; Figure 2-24b1, Courtesy of AT&T Wireless; Figure 2-24b2, © Siemens Photo; Figure 2-28, Courtesy of EarthWalk Communications; Figure 2-38a, Courtesy of D-Link Systems; Figure 2-38b, Courtesy of Vonage; Figure 2-38c, Courtesy of IBM Corporation; Figure in Checkpoint, #1, page 2.43, Courtesy of Cnet USA, Inc.; Figure in Checkpoint, #1, page 2.43, Courtesy of Acer America Corp.; Figure in Checkpoint, #1, page 2.43, Courtesy of Sony Electronics Inc.; Figure for Assistive Technologies Corner, page 2.47b, Courtesy of Clarity Products; *Chapter 2 Special Feature:* 2 SF Opener, © Photodisc Collection/Getty Images, © Manchan/Getty Images, © 2005 Masterfile Corporation, © David Oliver/Getty Images, © Via Productions/Brand X Pictures; Page 2.60, © Image Source / SuperStock ; Figure 11, © Getty Images; *Chapter 3*: Figure 3-1a, © Getty Images; Figure 3-1b, Courtesy of Xerox Corporation; Figure 3-2, © Getty Images; Figure 3-8, Courtesy of Agilix Labs, Inc.; Figure 3-9, Courtesy of

Agilix Labs, Inc.; Figure 3-17, © Scott Goodwin Photography; Figure 3-23, © James Schnepf/Getty Images; Figure 3-25, Courtesy of Dell Computer Corporation; Figure 3-25, © Getty Images; Figure 3-26, Courtesy of Sendo; Figure 3-30, Courtesy of Microsoft Corporation; Figure 3-31, Courtesy of Microsoft Corporation; Figure 3-33, Screen shot(s) are (c) Copyright 2003 Corel Corporation, reprinted by permission; Figure 3-34, Courtesy of Adobe; Figure 3-42, © Spencer C. Grant/Photo Edit; Figure 3-45, © 2003 Riverdeep Interactive Learning Limited, and its licensors; Figure 3-47, © Scott Goodwin Photography; *Special Feature 3*: SF Intro, © Getty Images; SF p 3.50, © Royalty-Free/Corbis; p 3.50, Stockbyte; p.3.56, © Getty Images; p 3.57, Stockbyte; p 3.60, © Getty Images; p.3.61, © Getty Images; p 3.63, © Getty Images; p 3.64, Stockbyte; p 3.65, BananaStock CD; p 3.66, Stockbyte; *Chapter 4*: Figure 4-1a, © Gateway, Inc.; Figure 4-1b, Courtesy of Apple Computer, Inc.; Figure 4-1c, Toshiba America Information Systems, Inc.; Figure 4-1d, Courtesy of Microsoft Corporation; Figure 4-1e, Toshiba America Information Systems, Inc.; Figure 4-1f, Courtesy of palmOne, Inc. palmOne, Zire, Tungsten, Treo, logos, stylizations and design marks associated with all the preceding, and trade dress associated with palmOne, Inc.'s products, are among the trademarks or registered trademarks owned by or exclusively licensed to palmOne, Inc.; Figure 4-5, © Scott Goodwin Photography; Figure 4-7a, Courtesy of Intel Corporation; Figure 4-7b, Courtesy of Advanced Micro Devices; Figure 4-7c, Courtesy of Intel Corporation; Figure 4-7d, Courtesy of Intel Corporation; Figure 4-7e, Courtesy of Motorola; Figure 4-8, © Image Source/ Imagestate; Figure 4-9, © AP/Wide World Photos; Figure 4-11, © Scott Goodwin Photography; Figure 4-12, MPIO FY200 (www.mpio.com); Figure 4-13, © Scott Goodwin Photography; Figure 4-14, Courtesy of Kingston Technology Company, Inc.; Figure 4-15, © Gary Herrington Photography; Figure 4-18, Courtesy of Logitech, Inc.; Figure 4-19a, Courtesy of © 1994-2003 Hewlett-Packard Company; Figure 4-19b, Courtesy of Intel Corporation; Figure 4-19c, Courtesy of Apple Computer, Inc.; Figure 4-19d, Courtesy of © 1994-2002 Telefonaktiebolaget LM Ericsson; Figure 4-19e, © Siemens Photo; Figure 4-20, Courtesy of EarthWalk Communication; Figure 4-22, Courtesy of Apple Computer, Inc.; Figure 4-23, Courtesy of Apple Computer, Inc.; Figure 4-24, Courtesy of IBM; Figure 4-25, © Comstock Images; Figure 4-26, Courtesy of Logitech, Inc.; Figure 4-27, © REUTERS/Jim Ruymen /Landov; Figure 4-28, Courtesy of Sony Ericsson Mobile Communications AB. All rights reserved; Figure 4-29, Courtesy of Wacom Technology Corp.; Figure 4-30, Courtesy of Logitech; Figure 4-31, © Olympus Optical Co., LTD. All Rights Reserved.; Figure 4-32a, Courtesy of ViewSonic® Corporation; Figure 4-32b, Courtesy of ViewSonic® Corporation; Figure 4-32c, Courtesy of Belkin Corporation; Figure 4-32d, Courtesy of LifeView, Inc.; Figure 4-32e, Courtesy of Seiko Instruments USA Inc.; Figure 4-32f, Courtesy of Socket Communications, Inc.; Figure 4-32g, Courtesy of IBM Corporation; Figure 4-32h, Courtesy of Handmark, Inc.; Figure 4-32i, Courtesy of ViewSonic® Corporation; Figure 4-33, Courtesy of Motion Computing, Inc.; Figure 4-35, Courtesy of ViewSonic® Corporation; Figure 4-37, Courtesy of EarthWalk Communications; Figure 4-38, Courtesy of ViewSonic® Corporation; Figure 4-39, Courtesy of Apple Computer, Inc.; Figure 4-40a, Courtesy of Dell Computer; Figure 4-40b, Courtesy of Acer America; Figure 4-40c, Courtesy of Sony Electronics, Inc.; Figure 4-40d, Courtesy of NEC Corporation; Figure 4-40e, Courtesy of Handspring; Figure 4-41a, © David Muir/Masterfile; Figure 4-41b, © Royalty-Free/ CORBIS; Figure 4-41c, © Chuck Savage/CORBIS; Figure 4-41d, Courtesy of Nokia; Figure 4-41e, © Oshikazu Tsuno/AFP/Getty Images; Figure 4-41f, ©David Young-Wolff / Photo Edit Inc.; Figure 4-41g, Courtesy of Sony Electronics Inc.; Figure 4-41h, Courtesy of Eastman Kodak Company; Figure 4-41i, Courtesy of Epson America, Inc.; Figure 4-41j, QV3000EX camera photo courtesy of Casio Inc.; Figure 4-41k, Courtesy of Epson America, Inc.; Figure 4-42, Courtesy of Epson America, Inc.; Figure 4-43, Courtesy of Xerox Corporation; Figure 4-44, Courtesy of InFocus Corp.; Figure 4-45, © Bob Daemmrich/The Image Works; Figure 4-46, Courtesy of © 1994-2003 Hewlett-Packard Company; Figure 4-47, © AP/Wide World Photos; Figure 4-51, Photo Courtesy of Iomega Corporation. Copyright (c) 2003 Iomega Corporation. All Rights Reserved. Zip is a registered trademark in the United States and/or other countries. Iomega, the stylized "i" logo and product images are property of Iomega Corporation in the United States and/or other countries.; Figure 4-52, Courtesy of Seagate Technologies; Figure 4-53, Courtesy of Toshiba America Information Systems, Inc.; Figure 4-54, Photo Courtesy of Iomega Corporation. Copyright (c) 2003 Iomega Corporation. All Rights Reserved. Zip is a registered trademark in the United States and/or other countries. Iomega, the stylized "i" logo and product images are property of Iomega Corporation in the United States and/or other countries. Figure 4-57, Courtesy of Merriam-Webster; Figure 4-57, Courtesy of Memorex Products, Inc.; Figure 4-57, Courtesy of Memorex Products, Inc.; Figure 4-57, © 2004 DeLorme (www.delorme.com); Figure 4-57, Courtesy of Memorex Products, Inc.; Figure 4-57, Courtesy of Memorex Products, Inc.; Figure 4-57, Courtesy of Memorex Products, Inc.; Figure 4-57, Courtesy of Memorex Products, Inc.; Figure 4-59, ©Michael Newman / Photo Edit — All rights reserved.; Figure 4-49c, Courtesy of Epson America, Inc.; Figure 4-62a, Courtesy of Fujitsu Siemens Computers; Figure 4-62b, Courtesy of SanDisk Corporation; Figure 4-62c, Courtesy of SanDisk Corporation; Figure 4-62d, Courtesy of palmOne, Inc. palmOne, Zire, Tungsten, Treo, logos, stylizations and design marks associated with all the preceeding, and trade dress associated with palmOne, Inc.'s products, are among the trademarks or registered trademarks owned by or exclusively licensed to palmOne, Inc.; Figure 4-62e, Siemens press picture; Figure 4-62f, Courtesy of Delkin Devices, Inc.; Figure 4-62g, Courtesy of JVC Company of America; Figure 4-63a, Courtesy of SanDisk Corporation; Figure 4-63b, Courtesy of SanDisk Corporation; Figure 4-63c, Courtesy of SanDisk Corporation; Figure 4-63d, Courtesy of Lexar Media, Inc.; Figure 4-63e, Courtesy of SanDisk Corporation; Figure on page 4.43, Checkpoint; Figure on Page 4.44, Teaching Today; Figure on Page 4.45, Education Issues; Figure on Assistive Technologies Corner page, Courtesy of Keytools Ltd.; Figure 4-66, for In the Lab, page 4.48, Nancy Sheehan/Photo Edit; Figure 4-67, for In the Lab, page 4.49, Seth Resnick/Getty Images; *Special Feature 4*: Figure 1a, Courtesy of IBM Corporation; Figure 1b1, Courtesy of Sony Electronics, Inc.; Figure 1b2, Courtesy of Motion Computing; Figure 1c1, Courtesy of palmOne, Inc.; Figure 1c2, Siemens press picture; Figure 1d, © Digital Vision/Getty Images; Figure 4a, Courtesy of JVC; Figure 4b, Courtesy of SanDisk Corporation; Figure 4c, Courtesy of UMAX; Figure 4d, Courtesy of Pinnacle Systems, Inc.; Figure 4f, Courtesy of Seagate; Figure 4g, Courtesy of Logitech; Figure 4h, Courtesy of Microsoft; Figure 4j, Courtesy of US Robotics; Figure 4k, Courtesy of ViewSonic Corporation; Figure 4l, Courtesy of Microsoft; Figure 4m, Courtesy of 3Com Corporation; Figure 4n, Courtesy of EPSON America, Inc.; Figure 4o, Courtesy of Intel Corporation; Figure 4p, Courtesy of Kingston Technology; Figure 4q, Courtesy of UMAX; Figure 4s, Courtesy of Logitech; Figure 4t, Courtesy of Logitech; Figure 4u, Courtesy of SanDisk Corporation; Figure 4v, Courtesy of 3Com Corporation; Figure 4x, Courtesy of Iomega; Figure 12, Courtesy of Toshiba America; Figure 13, Courtesy of Toshiba America; Figure 14, © Britt Erlanson/Getty Images; Figure 16, © Thomas Barwick/Getty Images; Figure 19, Courtesy of ViewSonic Corporation; Figure 21, Courtesy of Fujitsu Siemens Computers; *Chapter 5*: Figure 5-1, © Getty Images; Figure 5-8a, © Monica Graff/The Image Works; Figure 5-8b, Doug Martin/PhotoResearchers, Inc.; Figure 5-8c, Walter Hodges/Stone/Getty Images; Figure 5-9, Michael Newman/Photo Edit; Figure 5-10, Courtesy of Apple Computer; Figure 5-12, EyeWire/Getty Images; Figure 5-16, EyeWire/Getty Images; Figure 5-20, © CORBIS SYGMA; Figure 5-22, Courtesy of IBM Corporation; Figure 5-39a, Courtesy of FableVision; Figure 5-48, Courtesy of Sony Electronics Inc.; Figure 5-51, Courtesy of John M. Galloway, Photographer; Figure 5-52, Courtesy of InFocus; Figure 5-53, Courtesy of SMART Technologies, Inc.; Page 311, EyeWire/Getty Images; Page 315, Courtesy of Apple Computer, Courtesy of Sony Electronics Inc.; *Special Feature 5*: Intro, © Tim Kiusalaas/Masterfile; Intro, © J. Fisher/Zefa/Masterfile; Figure 01a, Courtesy of Nikon USA; Figure 01b, Courtesy of Sony Electronics Inc.; Figure 01c, Courtesy of BenQ America Corp.; Figure 01d,

Courtesy of Sony Electronics Inc.; Figure 01e, Courtesy of Canon USA Inc.; Figure 01f, Courtesy of Sony Electronics Inc.; Figure01f2, © Spike Mafford/Getty Images; Figure 01g, Courtesy of JVC Company of America; Page 326 & 327, © Getty Images; Figure 02a, Courtesy of Sony Electronics Inc.; Figure 02b, Courtesy of Canon U.S.A, Inc.; Figure 02c, Courtesy of Canon U.S.A, Inc.; Figure 05a, Courtesy of Hitachi Global Storage Technologies; Figure 05b, Courtesy of Lexar Media, Inc.; Figure 05c, Courtesy of Sony Electronics Inc.; Figure 06, Courtesy of SanDisk Corporation; Fgure 08, Courtesy of Pixel Magic Imaging™, Inc.; Figure 09, Courtesy of Ulead Systems, Inc.; Figure 10a, Courtesy of Sony Electronics Inc.; figure 10b, Courtesy of Sony Electronics Inc.; Figure 10c, Courtesy of Logitech; Figure 11a, Courtesy of Sony Electronics Inc.; Figure 11b, Courtesy of Sony Electronics Inc.; Figure 11, © Royalty-Free/CORBIS ; Figure 12a, Courtesy of Sony Electronics Inc.; Figure 12b, Courtesy of Pinnacle Systems, Inc.; Figure 12c, Courtesy of Matsushita Electric Corporation of America; Figure 12d, Courtesy of JVC Company of America; Figure 12, © Chase Jarvis/Getty Images; Figure 15, Courtesy of DivXNetworks, Inc.; Figure 16, Courtesy of Apple Computer Corporation; Figure 17, Courtesy of Microsoft Corporation; Figure 18a, Courtesy of Microsoft Corporation; Figure 19, Courtesy of Pinnacle Systems, Inc.; *Chapter 6*: Figure 6-1, Courtesy of Gateway;Figure 6-4, © Roger Ressmeyer/CORBIS; Figure 6-6, Courtesy of Springbrook High School and Apple Computer, Inc.; Figure 6-7, © Michael Rosenfeld/Getty Images; Figure 6-8, Copyright ©David Young-Wolff / Photo Edit — All rights reserved.; Figure 6-9, Copyright ©Mark Richards / Photo Edit — All rights reserved;. Figure 6-11, Will & Deni McIntyre/Photo Researchers, Inc.; Figure 6-14, © David Young-Wolff/Getty Images; Figure 6-16, © Getty Images; Figure 6-18, © Alan Levenson/Stone/Getty Images; Figure 6-19, Copyright ©Bill Aron / Photo Edit — All rights reserved.; Figure 6-20, K. Preuss/The Image Works; Figure 6-21, Ed Bock/CORBIS; Figure 6-22, Jim Pickerell/Getty Images; Figure 6-23, Courtesy of Earthwalk Communications; Figure 6-24, Courtesy of Earthwalk Communications; Figure 6-27, © Masterfile (Royalty-Free Div.) www.masterfile.com; Figure 6-27a, Courtesy of Sony Electronics Inc.; Figure 6-27b, Courtesy of IBM Corporation; Figure 6-27c, Courtesy of Sony Electronics Inc.; Figure 6-27d, Courtesy of Sony Electronics Inc.; Figure 6-27e, Courtesy of Logitech; Figure 6-27f, Courtesy of IBM Corporation; Figure 6-27g, Courtesy of Sony Electronics Inc.; Figure 6-27h, Courtesy of Sony Electronics Inc.; Figure 6-31, © Ryan McVay/Getty Images; Figure 6-32, © Ed Bock/CORBIS; Figure 6-34, © David Buffington/Getty Images; Figure 6-36, Copyright ©Mark Richards / Photo Edit — All rights reserved.; *Special Feature 6*: Figure 1, © Scott Tysick/Masterfile www.masterfile.com; Figure 5, Copyright ©Felicia Martinez / Photo Edit — All rights reserved; Figure 19, © Getty Images; Figure 21, © AP/Wide World Photos; Figure 26, © AP/Wide World Photos; *Chapter 7*: Figure 7-15, © Bruce Ayers/Getty Images; Figure 7-20, © Jim Craigmyle/Masterfile www.masterfile.com; Figure 7-21a, Seth Resnick/Stock Boston; Figure 7-21b, © AP/Wide World Photos; Figure 7-21c, Michael Newman/PhotoEdit; Figure 7-21c, Porter Gifford/Getty Images; Figure 7-22, Copyright ©David Young-Wolff / Photo Edit — All rights reserved.; Figure 7-23, Copyright ©Michael Newman / Photo Edit — All rights reserved; Figure 7-24, James Wilson/Woodfin Camp & Associates; Figure 7-30, Photodisc/Getty Images; Figure 7-31, Corel Corporation; Figure 7-32, Getty Images; KPT; Lexmark International; Getty Images; Figure 7-38, Courtesy of Microsoft Corporation; Courtesy of Britannica.com; Courtesy of Sony Electronics; Courtesy of Lexmark International; Courtesy of Dell; Courtesy of Hewlett-Packard; page447, © Getty Images; Page 453, © Getty Images; Page 455, Courtesy of EarthWalk Communications; Page 451, Courtesy of Symbol Technologies Inc.; *Special Feature 7*: Figure on page 7.61, © Getty Images; *Chapter 8:* Figure 8-6a, Courtesy of Symantec; Figure 8-06b, Courtesy of McAfee, Inc; Figure 8-10, Courtesy of Springbrook High School and Apple Computer, Inc; Figure 8-11, Courtesy of Innovative Security Products, Inc.; Figure 8-12, Courtesy of Apple Computer, Inc.; Figure 8-14, © Getty Images; Figure 8-16, Courtesy of American Power Conversion Corp; Figure 8-17, Courtesy of Belkin Corporation; Figure 8-18, Courtesy of American Power Conversion Corp; Figure 8-34, Michael Newman/PhotoEdit; Figure 8-38, © Getty Images; Figure 8-41, Will & Deni McIntyre/Photo Researchers; Figure 8-44, © A. Ramey/Woodfin Camp & AssocIates; Picture on page 8.37 (In Brief), © Getty Images; *Special Feature 8*: Opener 1a, © 2002 Dynamic Graphics Inc.; Opener 1b, Courtesy of Fujitsu-Siemens Computers; Opener 1c, Courtesy of Handspring; Opener 1d, Courtesy of Nokia; Figure 1a, Courtesy Sony Electronics Inc.; Figure 1b, Siemens press photo; Figure 1c, Courtesy of Sony Electronics Inc.; Figure 1d, Courtesy of Olympus; Figure 1e, Courtesy of Hewlett-Packard; Figure 1f, Courtesy of Epson American; Figure 2, Courtesy of Belkin Components; Figure 4a, © Getty Images; Figure 4b, © Getty Images; Figure 4c, © Stockbyte; Figure 4d, Siemens press photo; Figure 8a - e, Copyright © 2003 University of Central Florida Photos; Figure 13a, Courtesy of Dell Computer; Figure 13b, Courtesy of Linksys; Figure 13c, Courtesy of SMC; Figure 13d, Courtesy of Gateway; Figure 13e, Courtesy of Hewlett-Packard; Figure 13f, Courtesy of Dell Computer; Figure 13g, Courtesy of Handspring; Figure 14, Courtesy of Fujitsu-Siemens Computers; Figure 15a, Courtesy of Visteon; Figure 15b, © Harald Sund / The Image Bank; Figure 15c, © AP/Wide World Photos; Figure 15d, © Harald Sund / The Image Bank; Figure 15e, Magellan™ GPS Companion for the Handspring Visor. Used by Permission. Thales Navigation Inc. 2002; Figure 15f, © Getty Images; Figure 15g, Magellan™ SporTrak™ handheld GPS receiver. Used by permission. Thales Navigation Inc. 2003; Figure 15h, © Getty Images; Figure 15i, © Dante Burn-Forti/Getty Images; Figure 15j, Courtesy of GPS Tracks, Inc; Figure 16, Courtesy of Fujitsu-Siemens Computers.